Advances in Image Processing, Analysis and Recognition Technology

Advances in Image Processing, Analysis and Recognition Technology

Editor

Dariusz Frejlichowski

MDPI • Basel • Beijing • Wuhan • Barcelona • Belgrade • Manchester • Tokyo • Cluj • Tianjin

Editor
Dariusz Frejlichowski
West Pomeranian University of
Technology, Szczecin
Poland

Editorial Office
MDPI
St. Alban-Anlage 66
4052 Basel, Switzerland

This is a reprint of articles from the Special Issue published online in the open access journal *Applied Sciences* (ISSN 2076-3417) (available at: http://www.mdpi.com).

For citation purposes, cite each article independently as indicated on the article page online and as indicated below:

LastName, A.A.; LastName, B.B.; LastName, C.C. Article Title. *Journal Name* **Year**, *Volume Number*, Page Range.

ISBN 978-3-0365-3605-7 (Hbk)
ISBN 978-3-0365-3606-4 (PDF)

© 2022 by the authors. Articles in this book are Open Access and distributed under the Creative Commons Attribution (CC BY) license, which allows users to download, copy and build upon published articles, as long as the author and publisher are properly credited, which ensures maximum dissemination and a wider impact of our publications.
The book as a whole is distributed by MDPI under the terms and conditions of the Creative Commons license CC BY-NC-ND.

Contents

About the Editor vii

Dariusz Frejlichowski
Special Issue on "Advances in Image Processing, Analysis and Recognition Technology"
Reprinted from: *Appl. Sci.* **2020**, *10*, 7582, doi:10.3390/app10217582 1

María Prados-Privado, Javier García Villalón, Carlos Hugo Martínez-Martínez and Carlos Ivorra
Dental Images Recognition Technology and Applications: A Literature Review
Reprinted from: *Appl. Sci.* **2020**, *10*, 2856, doi:10.3390/app10082856 5

Alireza Rahimzadeganasl, Ugur Alganci and Cigdem Goksel
An Approach for the Pan Sharpening of Very High Resolution Satellite Images Using a CIELab Color Based Component Substitution Algorithm
Reprinted from: *Appl. Sci.* **2019**, *9*, 5234, doi:10.3390/app9235234 17

Man Liu, Peizhen Wang, Simin Chen and Dailin Zhang
The Classification of Inertinite Macerals in Coal Based on the Multifractal Spectrum Method
Reprinted from: *Appl. Sci.* **2019**, *9*, 5509, doi:10.3390/app9245509 47

Antoine Chauvet, Yoshihiro Sugaya, Tomo Miyazaki and Shinichiro Omachi
Optical Flow-Based Fast Motion Parameters Estimation for Affine Motion Compensation
Reprinted from: *Appl. Sci.* **2020**, *10*, 729, doi:10.3390/app10020729 63

Yuanwei Wang, Mei Yu, Gangyi Jiang, Zhiyong Pan and Jiqiang Lin
Image Registration Algorithm Based on Convolutional Neural Network and Local Homography Transformation
Reprinted from: *Appl. Sci.* **2020**, *10*, 732, doi:10.3390/app10030732 79

Jiali Tang, Chenrong Huang, Jian Liu and Hongjin Zhu
Image Super-Resolution Based on CNN Using Multilabel Gene Expression Programming
Reprinted from: *Appl. Sci.* **2020**, *10*, 854, doi:10.3390/app10030854 95

Kyung Joo Cheoi
Temporal Saliency-Based Suspicious Behavior Pattern Detection
Reprinted from: *Appl. Sci.* **2020**, *10*, 1020, doi:10.3390/app10031020 109

Yutaro Iwamoto, Naoaki Hashimoto and Yen-Wei Chen
Real-Time Haze Removal Using Normalised Pixel-Wise Dark-Channel Prior and Robust Atmospheric-Light Estimation
Reprinted from: *Appl. Sci.* **2020**, *10*, 1165, doi:10.3390/app10031165 127

Min Zhang, Yunhui Shi, Na Qi and Baocai Yin
Stable Sparse Model with Non-Tight Frame
Reprinted from: *Appl. Sci.* **2020**, *10*, 1771, doi:10.3390/app10051771 141

Tao Zhang, Wenli Du, Hao Wang, Qin Zeng and Long Fan
A Stronger Aadaptive Local Dimming Method with Details Preservation
Reprinted from: *Appl. Sci.* **2020**, *10*, 1820, doi:10.3390/app10051820 163

Paidamwoyo Mhangara, Willard Mapurisa and Naledzani Mudau
Comparison of Image Fusion Techniques Using *Satellite Pour l'Observation de la Terre* (SPOT) 6 Satellite Imagery
Reprinted from: *Appl. Sci.* **2020**, *10*, 1881, doi:10.3390/app10051881 179

Min Zhang, Yunhui Shi, Na Qi and Baocai Yin
Data-Driven Redundant Transform Based on Parseval Frames
Reprinted from: *Appl. Sci.* **2020**, *10*, 2891, doi:10.3390/app10082891 193

Direselign Addis Tadesse, Chuan-Ming Liu and Van-Dai Ta
Unconstrained Bilingual Scene Text Reading Using Octave as a Feature Extractor
Reprinted from: *Appl. Sci.* **2020**, *10*, 4474, doi:10.3390/app10134474 211

Giovanni Dimauro, Davide Di Pierro, Francesca Deperte, Lorenzo Simone and Pio Raffaele Fina
A Smartphone-Based Cell Segmentation to Support Nasal Cytology
Reprinted from: *Appl. Sci.* **2020**, *10*, 4567, doi:10.3390/app10134567 225

Yaonan Zhang, Jing Cui, Zhaobin Wang, Jianfang Kang and Yufang Min
Leaf Image Recognition Based on Bag of Features
Reprinted from: *Appl. Sci.* **2020**, *10*, 5177, doi:10.3390/app10155177 241

Yekta Said Can and M. Erdem Kabadayı
Automatic CNN-Based Arabic Numeral Spotting and Handwritten Digit Recognition by Using Deep Transfer Learning in Ottoman Population Registers
Reprinted from: *Appl. Sci.* **2020**, *10*, 5430, doi:10.3390/app10165430 259

Naoko Tsukamoto, Yoshihiro Sugaya and Shinichiro Omachi
Pansharpening by Complementing Compressed Sensing with Spectral Correction
Reprinted from: *Appl. Sci.* **2020**, *10*, 5789, doi:10.3390/app10175789 275

Biserka Petrovska, Tatjana Atanasova-Pacemska, Roberto Corizzo, Paolo Mignone, Petre Lameski and Eftim Zdravevski
Aerial Scene Classification through Fine-Tuning with Adaptive Learning Rates and Label Smoothing
Reprinted from: *Appl. Sci.* **2020**, *10*, 5792, doi:10.3390/app10175792 295

Yuzhen Chen and Wujie Zhou
Hybrid-Attention Network for RGB-D Salient Object Detection
Reprinted from: *Appl. Sci.* **2020**, *10*, 5806, doi:10.3390/app10175806 321

Hang Yu, Jiulu Gong and Derong Chen
Object Detection Using Multi-Scale Balanced Sampling
Reprinted from: *Appl. Sci.* **2020**, *10*, 6053, doi:10.3390/app10176053 331

Eugene Donskoi and Andrei Poliakov
Advances in Optical Image Analysis Textural Segmentation in Ironmaking
Reprinted from: *Appl. Sci.* **2020**, *10*, 6242, doi:10.3390/app10186242 347

Katarzyna Gościewska and Dariusz Frejlichowski
The Analysis of Shape Features for the Purpose of Exercise Types Classification Using Silhouette Sequences
Reprinted from: *Appl. Sci.* **2020**, *10*, 6728, doi:10.3390/app10196728 365

About the Editor

Dariusz Frejlichowski has been a Professor at the Faculty of Computer Science and Information Technology, West Pomeranian University of Technology, Szczecin (Poland) since 2019. He obtained his Master of Science degree in 2001, PhD degree in 2005, and his habilitation degree in 2012. His research activities are connected with image analysis, processing and recognition in many topics and applications, e.g., shape description and recognition, the fusion of various features representing an object of interest, content-based image retrieval, applications of image extraction and recognition methods in erythrocyte recognition, trademark recognition and retrieval, airplane silhouette recognition, ear biometrics, binary image compression, 3D shapes, the localisation of vehicles, license plate recognition, colour and shape fusion for CBIR, and many, many others.

Editorial

Special Issue on "Advances in Image Processing, Analysis and Recognition Technology"

Dariusz Frejlichowski

Faculty of Computer Science and Information Technology, West Pomeranian University of Technology, Szczecin, Zolnierska 52, 71-210 Szczecin, Poland; dfrejlichowski@wi.zut.edu.pl

Received: 21 October 2020; Accepted: 26 October 2020; Published: 28 October 2020

For many decades researchers have been trying to make computer analysis of images as effective as the human vision system is. For this purpose many algorithms and systems have been proposed so far. The whole process covers various stages including image processing, representation and recognition. The results of this work find many applications in computer-assisted areas of everyday life. They improve particular activities, give handy tools, sometimes only for entertainment, but quite often significantly increasing our safety. In fact, the practical implementation of image processing algorithms is particularly wide. Moreover, the rapid growth of computational complexity and computer efficiency has allowed for the development of more sophisticated and effective algorithms and tools. Although significant progress has been made so far, many issues still remain open, resulting in the need for the development of novel approaches.

The aim of this Special Issue on "Advances in Image Processing, Analysis and Recognition Technology" was to give the researchers the opportunity to provide new trends, latest achievements and research directions as well as present their current work on the important problem of image processing, analysis and recognition. The Special Issue includes 22 papers devoted to various aspects of digital image processing, analysis and recognition, of which there are 21 research articles and one review paper.

In [1] CIELab, a color-based component substitution pan sharpening algorithm is proposed for pan sharpening of the Pleiades Very High Resolution images. The proposed approach obtained promising results and improved the spectral and spatial information preservation. The pan sharpening was also the subject of [2]. In the latter, a method for pan sharpening by focusing on a compressed sensing technique was proposed.

The paper [3] provides a proposition of a texture description method with a set of multifractal descriptors for the identification of different macerals. The proposed method is based on the multifractal spectrum calculated from the method of multifractal detrended fluctuation analysis (MF-DFA).

A lightweight solution for the estimation of affine parameters in affine motion compensation is proposed in [4]. It tries to speed up the process by means of evaluating affine prediction when it is likely to bring no encoding efficiency benefit as well as estimating better initial values for the iteration process. The optical flow between the reference image and the current image is applied in order to estimate the best encoding mode and achieve a better initial estimation.

In paper [5] an image registration algorithm based on convolutional neural network (CNN) and local homography transformation is proposed. It applies firstly a novel sample and label generation method based on Moving Direct Linear Transformation (MDLT). Later, the local homography matrices between the two images are estimated by means of the MDLT and finally the image registration can be realized.

The Authors of [6] proposed a pre-classified deep-learning algorithm (MGEP-SRCNN) applying a Multi-label Gene Expression Programming (MGEP), which screens out a sample sub-bank with high relevance to the target image before image block extraction, pre-classifies samples in a multi-label framework, and then performs nonlinear mapping and image reconstruction.

The detection of suspicious behavior using video sequences in a CCTV video stream is the subject of [7]. The proposed method detected suspicious behavior with a temporal saliency map by combining the moving reactivity features of motion magnitude and gradient extracted by optical flow.

The paper [8] is devoted to the problem of haze removal from a single image in real-time. For this purpose, a normalized pixel-wise dark-channel prior is applied. In order to solve some problems with computational cost normalized pixel-wise haze estimation without losing the detailed structure of, the transmission map is used. The Authors additionally proposed robust atmospheric-light estimation using a coarse-to-fine search strategy and down-sampled haze estimation.

In [9] a stable sparse model with a non-tight frame (SSM-NTF) is proposed and a dictionary pair learning model to stably recover the signals is formulated. The approach is applied on various image restoration tasks such as denoising, super resolution and inpainting.

The paper [10] provides a proposition of a stronger adaptive local dimming method with details preservation. The approach, combining the advantages of some existing methods and introducing the combination of the subjective and objective evaluation, obtains a stronger adaptation. Additionally, in the paper the bi-histogram equalization algorithm is developed and a new pixel compensation method is proposed.

In [11] the Authors use image quality metrics to evaluate the performance of several image fusion techniques to assess the spectral and spatial quality of pan-sharpened images. They evaluated twelve pan-sharpening algorithms, and experimentally proved that the Local Mean and Variance Matching (IMVM) algorithm was the best in terms of spectral consistency and synthesis.

The Authors of [12] propose a data-driven redundant transform based on Parseval frames (DRTPF) by applying the frame and its dual frame as the backward and forward transform operators, respectively. The proposed model combines a synthesis and an analysis sparse systems.

In [13] the problem of bilingual scene text reading is considered. For this purpose, an octave convolution (OctConv) feature extractor and a time-restricted attention encoder–decoder module for end-to-end scene text reading are proposed and experimentally investigated.

The next contribution describes ideas of automatic cell segmentation and counting, which is an important problem in the analysis of microscopic images [14]. For this purpose fundamental yet effective image processing algorithms were applied.

In [15] the automatic recognition of leaf images is considered. The applied approach is based on a Dual-output pulse-coupled neural network and Bag of features. Additionally, Bag of contour fragments was applied for shape feature extraction. Finally, Linear Discriminant Analysis was used for feature dimensionality reduction, and a Linear Support Vector Machine for classification. The proposed approaches were experimentally investigated using several leaf image datasets.

The application of machine learning for the extraction of information from historical documents was the subject of works described in [16]. Because of the character of the data being investigated, (numerals were written in red) firstly a red color filter was applied in order to separate numerals from documents, and then a CNN-based segmentation method for spotting these numerals.

The Authors of [17] used a fine-tuning method for image classification of large-scale remote sensing datasets. The approach applies feature extraction from the fine-tuned neural networks, and remote sensing image classification with a Support Vector Machine model with linear and Radial Basis Function kernels.

In [18] a hybrid network based on an attention mechanism for stereoscopic salient object detection was proposed. It was combined with an encoder–decoder network. The described novel attention model is based on the fusion of RGB and depth attention maps.

The problem of small objects and objects with large scale variants detection was analyzed in [19]. For solving this problem, an approach based on multi-scale balanced sampling was proposed.

The submission [20] discusses the problems connected with the segmentation of similar phases in different ironmaking feedstock materials by means of automated optical image analysis and provides the description of the algorithms designed for textural identification.

In [21] the idea of applying simple shape features for action recognition based on binary silhouettes was proposed. It was shown that basic shape features can discriminate between short, primitive actions performed by a single person.

The last paper [22] provides a review of the approaches applied for dental images. The goal of the Authors was the description of the state of the art of artificial intelligence in dental applications, such as the detection of teeth, caries, filled teeth, crown, prosthesis, dental implants and endodontic treatment.

The above brief description of the contributions provides the conclusion that the possibilities of applying image processing, analysis and recognition techniques for various problems are wide. In the papers accepted for publication in the Special Issue the analysis of high resolution satellite [1,11], aerial [17], microscopic [3,14], optical [20] and dental [22] images was provided. Image registration [5], restoration [6,9], fusion [11], and denoising [12] were also taken into account as well as the haze removal from images [8], backlight extraction [10], pan sharpening [1,2] and object detection [18,19]. Some specific applications were also considered—text detection and recognition from natural images [13], leaf image recognition [15] and historical document analysis [16]. Finally, not only still images were processed. Video coding [4] and the analysis of video sequences for suspicious behavior detection [7] and action recognition [21] were analyzed as well.

Acknowledgments: The Guest Editor is thankful for the valuable contributions from the authors, and significant help of reviewers, the editor team of Applied Sciences, and especially Sharon Wang (Section Managing Editor).

Conflicts of Interest: The authors declare no conflict of interest.

References

1. Rahimzadeganasl, A.; Alganci, U.; Goksel, C. An Approach for the Pan Sharpening of Very High Resolution Satellite Images Using a CIELab Color Based Component Substitution Algorithm. *Appl. Sci.* **2019**, *9*, 5234. [CrossRef]
2. Tsukamoto, N.; Sugaya, Y.; Omachi, S. Pansharpening by Complementing Compressed Sensing with Spectral Correction. *Appl. Sci.* **2020**, *10*, 5789. [CrossRef]
3. Liu, M.; Wang, P.; Chen, S.; Zhang, D. The Classification of Inertinite Macerals in Coal Based on the Multifractal Spectrum Method. *Appl. Sci.* **2019**, *9*, 5509. [CrossRef]
4. Chauvet, A.; Sugaya, Y.; Miyazaki, T.; Omachi, S. Optical Flow-Based Fast Motion Parameters Estimation for Affine Motion Compensation. *Appl. Sci.* **2020**, *10*, 729. [CrossRef]
5. Wang, Y.; Yu, M.; Jiang, G.; Pan, Z.; Lin, J. Image Registration Algorithm Based on Convolutional Neural Network and Local Homography Transformation. *Appl. Sci.* **2020**, *10*, 732. [CrossRef]
6. Tang, J.; Huang, C.; Liu, J.; Zhu, H. Image Super-Resolution Based on CNN Using Multilabel Gene Expression Programming. *Appl. Sci.* **2020**, *10*, 854. [CrossRef]
7. Cheoi, K.J. Temporal Saliency-Based Suspicious Behavior Pattern Detection. *Appl. Sci.* **2020**, *10*, 1020. [CrossRef]
8. Iwamoto, Y.; Hashimoto, N.; Chen, Y.-W. Real-Time Haze Removal Using Normalised Pixel-Wise Dark-Channel Prior and Robust Atmospheric-Light Estimation. *Appl. Sci.* **2020**, *10*, 1165. [CrossRef]
9. Zhang, M.; Shi, Y.; Qi, N.; Yin, B. Stable Sparse Model with Non Tight Frame. *Appl. Sci.* **2020**, *10*, 1771. [CrossRef]
10. Zhang, T.; Du, W.; Wang, H.; Zeng, Q.; Fan, L. A Stronger Aadaptive Local Dimming Method with Details Preservation. *Appl. Sci.* **2020**, *10*, 1820. [CrossRef]
11. Mhangara, P.; Mapurisa, W.; Mudau, N. Comparison of Image Fusion Techniques Using *Satellite Pour l'Observation de la Terre* (SPOT) 6 Satellite Imagery. *Appl. Sci.* **2020**, *10*, 1881. [CrossRef]
12. Zhang, M.; Shi, Y.; Qi, N.; Yin, B. Data-Driven Redundant Transform Based on Parseval Frames. *Appl. Sci.* **2020**, *10*, 2891. [CrossRef]
13. Tadesse, D.A.; Liu, C.-M.; Ta, V.-D. Unconstrained Bilingual Scene Text Reading Using Octave as a Feature Extractor. *Appl. Sci.* **2020**, *10*, 4474. [CrossRef]
14. Dimauro, G.; Di Pierro, D.; Deperte, F.; Simone, L.; Fina, P.R. A Smartphone-Based Cell Segmentation to Support Nasal Cytology. *Appl. Sci.* **2020**, *10*, 4567. [CrossRef]

15. Zhang, Y.; Cui, J.; Wang, Z.; Kang, J.; Min, Y. Leaf Image Recognition Based on Bag of Features. *Appl. Sci.* **2020**, *10*, 5177. [CrossRef]
16. Can, Y.S.; Kabadayı, M.E. Automatic CNN-Based Arabic Numeral Spotting and Handwritten Digit Recognition by Using Deep Transfer Learning in Ottoman Population Registers. *Appl. Sci.* **2020**, *10*, 5430. [CrossRef]
17. Petrovska, B.; Atanasova-Pacemska, T.; Corizzo, R.; Mignone, P.; Lameski, P.; Zdravevski, E. Aerial Scene Classification through Fine-Tuning with Adaptive Learning Rates and Label Smoothing. *Appl. Sci.* **2020**, *10*, 5792. [CrossRef]
18. Chen, Y.; Zhou, W. Hybrid-Attention Network for RGB-D Salient Object Detection. *Appl. Sci.* **2020**, *10*, 5806. [CrossRef]
19. Yu, H.; Gong, J.; Chen, D. Object Detection Using Multi-Scale Balanced Sampling. *Appl. Sci.* **2020**, *10*, 6053. [CrossRef]
20. Donskoi, E.; Poliakov, A. Advances in Optical Image Analysis Textural Segmentation in Ironmaking. *Appl. Sci.* **2020**, *10*, 6242. [CrossRef]
21. Gościewska, K.; Frejlichowski, D. The Analysis of Shape Features for the Purpose of Exercise Types Classification Using Silhouette Sequences. *Appl. Sci.* **2020**, *10*, 6728. [CrossRef]
22. Prados-Privado, M.; Villalón, J.G.; Martínez-Martínez, C.H.; Ivorra, C. Dental Images Recognition Technology and Applications: A Literature Review. *Appl. Sci.* **2020**, *10*, 2856. [CrossRef]

Publisher's Note: MDPI stays neutral with regard to jurisdictional claims in published maps and institutional affiliations.

© 2020 by the author. Licensee MDPI, Basel, Switzerland. This article is an open access article distributed under the terms and conditions of the Creative Commons Attribution (CC BY) license (http://creativecommons.org/licenses/by/4.0/).

Review

Dental Images Recognition Technology and Applications: A Literature Review

María Prados-Privado [1,2,*], Javier García Villalón [1], Carlos Hugo Martínez-Martínez [1] and Carlos Ivorra [1]

1. Asisa Dental, Research Department, C/José Abascal, 32, 28003 Madrid, Spain; javier.villalon@asisadental.com (J.G.V.); carlos.martinez@asisa.es (C.H.M.-M.); carlos.ivorra@asisadental.com (C.I.)
2. Department of Signal Theory and Communications, Higher Polytechnic School, Universidad de Alcalá de Henares, Ctra. Madrid-Barcelona, Km. 33,600, 28805 Alcalá de Henares, Spain
* Correspondence: maria.prados@uah.es

Received: 25 March 2020; Accepted: 17 April 2020; Published: 20 April 2020

Abstract: Neural networks are increasingly being used in the field of dentistry. The aim of this literature review was to visualize the state of the art of artificial intelligence in dental applications, such as the detection of teeth, caries, filled teeth, crown, prosthesis, dental implants and endodontic treatment. A search was conducted in PubMed, the Institute of Electrical and Electronics Engineers (IEEE) Xplore and arXiv.org. Data extraction was performed independently by two reviewers. Eighteen studies were included. The variable teeth was the most analyzed ($n = 9$), followed by caries ($n = 7$). No studies detecting dental implants and filled teeth were found. Only two studies investigated endodontic applications. Panoramic radiographies were the most common image employed ($n = 5$), followed by periapical images ($n = 3$). Near-infrared light transillumination images were employed in two studies and bitewing and computed tomography (CT) were employed in one study. The included articles used a wide variety of neuronal networks to detect the described variables. In addition, the database used also had a great heterogeneity in the number of images. A standardized methodology should be used in order to increase the compatibility and robustness between studies because of the heterogeneity in the image database, type, neural architecture and results.

Keywords: artificial intelligence; dental application; images; detection

1. Introduction

Medical imaging techniques, such as computed tomography (CT) or X-ray among others, have been used in recent decades for the detection, diagnosis and treatment of different diseases [1].

A new and emerging field in dentistry is dental informatics, because of the possibility it offers to improve treatment and diagnosis [2], in addition to saving time and reducing stress and fatigue during daily practice [3]. Medical practice in general, and dentistry in particular, generates massive data from sources such as high-resolution medical imaging, biosensors with continuous output and electronic medical records [4]. The use of computer programs can help dental professionals in making decisions related to prevention, diagnosis or treatment planning, among others [5].

At present, one of the artificial intelligence methods employed in clinical fields is called deep learning [6]. Artificial intelligence is the term used to describe the algorithms designed for problem solving and reasoning [7]. The success of deep learning is mainly due to the progress in the computer capacity, the huge amount of data available and the development of algorithms [1]. This method has been proven and is used effectively in image-based diagnosis in several fields [8]. Convolutional neural networks (CNNs) are commonly used in applications relying on deep learning, which have been developed extremely quickly during the last decade [9], mainly as a choice for analyzing medical images. CNNs have been successfully employed in medicine, primarily in cancer, for the automated assessment of breast cancer in mammograms, skin cancer in clinical skin screenings, or diabetic retinopathy in eye examinations [10].

CNNs have been recently applied in dentistry to detect periodontal bone loss [11,12], caries on bitewing radiographs [13], apical lesions [14], or for medical image classification [12]. These kinds of neural networks can be used to detect structures, such as teeth or caries, to classify them and to segment them [15]. Neural networks need to be trained and optimized, and for that an image database is necessary.

There are several image techniques in the dentistry field depending on their use. Periapical images are employed to capture intact teeth, including front and posterior, as well as their surrounding bone; therefore, periapical images are very helpful to visualize the potential caries, periodontal bone loss and periapical diseases [16]. Bitewing images can only visualize the crowns of posterior teeth with simple layouts and considerably less overlaps [17]. Panoramic radiographies are very common in dentistry, because they allow for the screening of a broad anatomical region and at the same time, require a relatively low radiation dose [18].

The objective of this review of the literature was to visualize the state of the art of artificial intelligence in various dental applications, such as the detection of teeth, caries, filled teeth, or endodontic treatment, among others.

2. Materials and Methods

2.1. Review Questions

(1) What are the neural networks used to detect teeth, filled teeth, caries, dental implants and endodontic teeth?
(2) How is the database used in the construction of these networks?
(3) What are the outcome metrics and its values obtained by those neural networks?

2.2. Search Strategy

An electronic search was performed in MEDLINE/PubMed, the Institute of Electrical and Electronics Engineers (IEEE) Xplore and arXiv.org databases, up until 17 March, 2020. Most journal manuscripts in the medical field were published in MEDLINE/Pubmed. IEEE Xplore publishes articles related to computer science, electrical engineering and electronics (https://ieeexplore.ieee.org/Xplore/home.jsp). Among others, arXiv.org is an electronic archive for scientific manuscripts in the field of physics, computer science, and mathematics.

The search strategy used is detailed in Table 1.

Table 1. Search strategy.

Database	Search Strategy	Search Data
MEDLINE/PubMed	(deep learning OR artificial intelligence OR neural network *) AND (dentistry OR dental) AND (teeth OR tooth OR caries OR filling OR dental implant OR endodontic OR root treatment) AND detect NOT (review)	17 March, 2020
IEEE Xplore	(((((((((("Full Text Only": deep learning) OR "Full Text Only": artificial intelligence) OR "Full Text Only": neural network) AND "Full Text Only": teeth) OR "Full Text Only": endodontic) OR "Full Text Only": caries) OR "Full Text Only": filling) OR "Full Text Only": dental implant) AND "Document Title": detect)	17 March, 2020
arXiv.org	(deep learning OR artificial intelligence OR neural network *) AND (dentistry OR dental) AND (teeth OR tooth OR caries OR filling OR dental implant OR endodontic OR root treatment) AND detect	17 March, 2020

* This is a method to search in pubmed.

2.3. Study Selection

M.P.-P. and J.G.-V. performed the bibliography search and selected the articles that fulfilled the inclusion criteria. Both authors extracted independently the results. The references of the articles included in this study were manually reviewed.

2.4. Inclusion and Exclusion Criteria

The inclusion criteria were full manuscripts including conference proceedings that reported the use of neural network on detecting teeth, caries, filled teeth, dental implants and endodontic treatments. There were no restrictions on the language or the date of publication. Exclusion criteria were reviews, no dental application and no neural network employed.

3. Results

3.1. Study Selection

Figure 1 details a flowchart of the study selection. All of the electronic search strategies resulted in 387 potential manuscripts. A total of 378 studies were excluded because they did not meet the inclusion criteria. Additionally, a manual search was carried out to analyze the references cited in nine of the articles that were included in this work. Finally, nine more articles were incorporated from the manual search. At the end, a total of eighteen studies were analyzed.

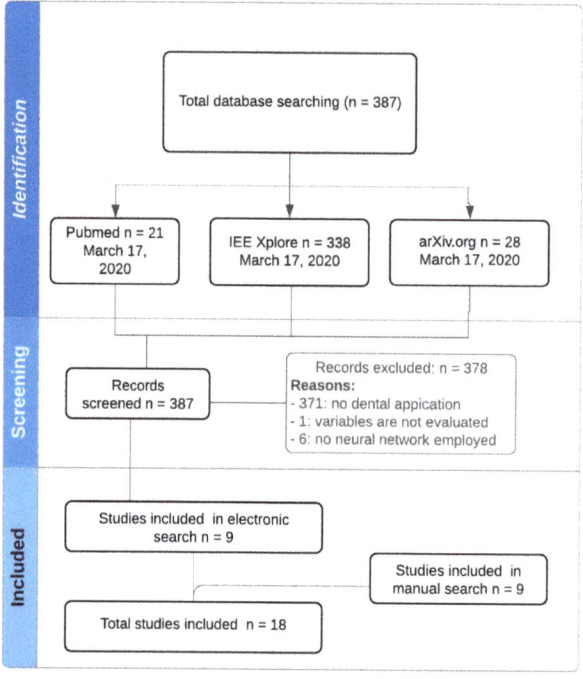

Figure 1. Flowchart.

3.2. Relevant Data of Included Studies

All of the included manuscripts were published between 2013 and 2020. Table 2 details the main characteristics of those included in the manuscript.

According to Table 2, the number of studies published increased each year and most of them were published in 2019. Selected works were published across seven countries, most of them in the United States ($n = 5$) and England ($n = 5$).

Regarding the variables detected by the included studies, the variable of teeth was the most analyzed ($n = 9$) followed by variable caries ($n = 7$). No studies detecting variables of dental implants and filled teeth were found. Only two studies investigated endodontic applications.

The total image database varied from 52 to 9812 images, with a mean of 1379 images. Panoramic radiographies were the most common image employed ($n = 7$) followed by periapical images ($n = 3$). Near-infrared light transillumination images were employed in two studies and bitewing and CT and radiovisiography were each employed in one study. No image type was detailed in two of the studies.

Table 2. Main characteristics of included studies.

Authors	Journal	Country, Year	Variable Detected	Image	Total Image Database	Neural Network	Outcome Metrics	Outcome Metrics Values
Schwendicke et al. [10]	Journal of Dentistry	England, 2019	Caries	Near-infrared light transillumination	226	Resnet18 Resnext50	AUC/Sensitivity/Specificity	0.74/0.59/0.76
Fukuda et al. [19]	Oral Radiology	Japan, 2019	Vertical root fracture (endodontic)	Panoramic radiography	300	DetectNet	Recall/Precision/F measure	0.75/0.93/0.83.
Ekert et al. [14]	Journal of Endodontics	USA, 2019	Endodontic	Panoramic radiography	85	CNN	AUC/Sensitivity	Molar: 0.89/0.74 Other teeth: 0.85/0.65
Chen et al. [16]	Scientific Reports	England, 2019	Teeth	Periapical images	1250	Faster R-CNN	Recall/Precision	0.728/0.771
Tuzoff [3]	Dentomaxillofacial Radiology	England, 2019	Teeth	Panoramic radiography	1352	Faster R-CNN	Sensitivity/Precision	0.9941/0.9945
Zhang et al. [20]	Computerized Medical Imaging and Graphics	USA, 2018	Teeth	Periapical images	700	Faster-RCNN/ region-based fully convolutional networks (R-FCN).	Precision/Recall	0.958/0.961
Raith et al. [21]	Computers in Biology and Medicine	England, 2017	Teeth	-	-	ANN	Performance	0.93
Srivastava et al. [22]	NIPS 2047 workshop on Machine Learning for Health (NIPS 2017 ML4H)	USA, 2017	Caries	Bitewing	3000	FCNN (deep fully convolutional neural network)	Recall/Precision/F1-Score	0.805/0.615/0.7
Jader et al. [23]	IEEE	Brazil, 2018	Teeth	Panoramic radiography	1500	Mask R-CNN	Accuracy/F1-score/Precision/Recall/Specificity	0.98/0.88/0.94/0.84/0.99
Miki et al. [24]	Computers in Biology and Medicine	USA, 2017	Teeth	Cone-beam computed tomography (CT)	52	AlexNet	Accuracy	0.88
Veleminská et al. [25]	Anthropologischer Anzeiger	Germany, 2013	Teeth	Panoramic radiography	1393	RBFNN GAME	Accuracy	-
Casalengo et al. [26]	Journal of Dental Research	USA, 2019	Caries	Near-infrared transillumination	217	CNNs for semantic segmentation	AUC	0.836 and 0.856 for occlusal and proximal lesions, respectively

Table 2. Cont.

Authors	Journal	Country, Year	Variable Detected	Image	Total Image Database	Neural Network	Outcome Metrics	Outcome Metrics Values
Lee et al. [13]	Journal of Dentistry	England, 2018	Caries	Periapical	3000	Deep CNN algorithm weight factors	Accuracy/AUC	premolar, molar, and both premolar and molar: 0.89, 0.88, and 0.82/0.917, 0.89, 0.845
Zanella-Calzada et al. [27]	Bioengineering	Switzerland, 2018	Caries	-	9812	ANN	Accuracy/AUC	0.69/0.75
Muramatsu et al. [28]	Oral Radiology	Japan, 2020	Teeth	Panoramic radiographs	100	Object detection network using fourfold cross-validation method	Sensitivity/Accuracy	0.964/0.932
Prajapati et al. [29]	5th International Symposium on Computational and Business Intelligence	United Arab Emirates, 2017	Caries	Radiovisiography images	251	CNN	Accuracy	0.875
Oktay, A. [30]	IEEE	Turkey, 2017	Teeth	Panoramic radiographs	100	AlexNet	Accuracy	>0.92
Geetha et al. [31]	Health Information Science and Systems	Switzerland, 2020	Caries	Intraoral radiographs	105	Back-propagation neural network	Accuracy/ Precision recall	0.971/0.987

3.3. Tooth Detection

A deep convolutional neural network (DCNN) with an AlexNet architecture was employed by Miki et al. for classifying tooth types on dental cone-beam computed tomography (CT) images. In that study, the authors employed forty-two images to train the network and ten images to test it and obtained a relatively high accuracy (above 80%) [24].

A mask region-based convolutional neural network (Mask R-CNN) was employed by Jader et al. to obtain the profile of each tool, employing 1500 panoramic X-ray radiographies. The outcome metrics employed in this study were accuracy, F1-score, precision, recall and specificity, with values of 0.98, 0.88, 0.94, 0.84, and 0.99, respectively [23].

Faster regions with convolutional neural network features (faster R-CNN) in the TensorFlow tool package were used by Chen et al. to detect and number the teeth in dental periapical films [16]. Here, 800 images were employed as the training dataset, 200 as the test dataset and 250 as the validation dataset. The outcome metrics were recall and precision, which obtained 0.728 and 0.771, respectively. Chen et al. also employed a neural network to predict the missing teeth number.

Periapical images with faster-RCNN and region-based fully convolutional networks (R-FCN) were employed by Zhang et al. Here, 700 images were employed to train the network, 200 were employed to test and 100 to validate the network. The method proposed by Zhang et al. achieved a high precision close to 95.8% and a recall of 0.961 [20].

The efficiencies of a radial basis function neural network (RBFNN) and of a GAME neural network in predicting the age of the Czech population between three and 17 years were compared by Velemínská et al. This study employed a panoramic X-ray of 1393 individuals aged from three to 17 years. In this case, standard deviation was measured [25].

A total of 1352 panoramic images were employed by Tuzoff et al. to detect teeth using a Faster R-CNN architecture [3]. This study obtained a sensitivity of 0.9941 and a precision of 0.9945.

By employing a CNN architecture and the PyBrain library, Raith et al. classified teeth and obtained a performance of 0.93 [21].

One hundred dental panoramic radiographs were employed by Muramatsu et al. for an object detection network using a four-fold cross-validation method. The tooth detection sensitivity was 96.4% and the accuracy was 93.2% [28].

A database of 100 panoramic radiographs with an AlexNet architecture was employed by Oktay to detect teeth with an accuracy of over 0.92, depending on the type of tooth (molar, incisor, and premolars) [30].

3.4. Caries Detection

Two deep convolutional neural networks (CNNs), Resnet18 and Restext50, were applied by Schwendicke et al. to detect caries lesions in near-infrared light transillumination (NILT) images [10]. In this study, 226 extracted permanent human teeth (113 premolars and 113 molars) were employed. According to their results, the two models performed similarly in predicting the caries on tooth segments of the NILT images. The area under the curve (AUC), sensitivity and the specificity were evaluated with results of 0.74, 0.59, and 0.76, respectively.

A deep learning model was employed by Casalengo et al. for the automated detection and localization of dental lesions in 217 near-infrared transillumination images of upper and lower molars and premolars. Here, 185 images were used to train the network and 32 images were used to validate it. The results concluded an area under curve (AUC) of 85.6% for proximal lesions and an AUC of 83.6% for occlusal lesions [26].

A total of 3000 periapical radiographies were employed by Lee et al. to detect dental caries [13]. From the total dataset, 25.9% of the images were maxillary premolars, 25.6% were maxillary molars, 24.1% were mandibular premolars and 24.4% were mandibular molars. The authors implemented deep CNN algorithm weight factors. A pre-trained GoogleNet Inception v3 CNN network was used for preprocessing and the datasets were trained using transfer learning. For detecting caries, this study obtained an accuracy of 89%, 88% and 82% in premolar, molar and premolar-molar, respectively, and for AUC, values of 0.917, 0.89, and 0.845 were obtained for premolar, molar and premolar-molar, respectively.

Caries from given socioeconomic and dietary factors were analyzed by Zanella-Calzada et al. employing an ANN to determine the state of health [27]. An ANN designed with seven layers, four dense layers and three dropout layers, was used in this study. A total of 9812 subjects were employed, 70% of them were used for training and the remaining 30% for testing. The results obtained an accuracy of approximately 0.69 and an AUC of 0.75.

A total of 3000 bitewings images were employed by Srivasta et al. to detect dental caries with a deep fully convolutional neural network. The results of this study were a recall of 0.805, a precision of 0.615 and a F1-score of 0.7 [22].

A total of 251 radiovisiography images were employed by Prajapati et al. to detect caries with a convolutional neural network, which achieved an accuracy of 0.875 [29].

A back-propagation neural network with a database of 105 intra-oral images was employed by Geetha et al. to detect caries. This architecture achieved an accuracy of 0.971 and a precision recall curve (PRC) area of 0.987 [31].

3.5. Dental Implant and Filled Teeth Detection

Implant treatment is a common practice in different clinical situations for replacing teeth. However, no studies were found that used artificial intelligence and neural networks to detect implants on radiographs. The same is true for filled teeth detection.

3.6. Endodontic Treatment Detection

A convolutional neural network (CNN) system was employed by Fukuda et al. for detecting vertical root fractures (VRFs) in panoramic radiographies [19]. Three hundred images were used as an image dataset, of which 240 images were assigned to a training set and 60 images were assigned to a test set. This study constructed a CNN-based deep learning model using DetectNet with DIGITS version 5.0 (city and country), and obtained a recall of 0.75, a mean precision of 0.93 and a F measure of 0.83.

Deep convolutional neural networks (CNNs) based in Keras were applied by Ekert et al. to detect apical lesions on panoramic dental radiographs [14]. A total of 85 images were employed, which obtained an AUC of 0.89 in molars and 0.85 in other teeth and a sensitivity of 0.74 and 0.65 in molars and other teeth.

4. Discussion

The goal of this literature review was to visualize the state of the art of artificial intelligence in detecting different dental situations, such as the detection of teeth, caries, filled teeth, endodontic treatments and dental implants.

Neural networks can have single or multiple layers, with nodes or neurons interconnected that allows signals to travel through the network. ANNs are typically divided into three layers of neurons, namely: input (receives the information), hidden (extracts patterns and performs the internal processing), and output (presents the final network output) [32,33]. Training is the process to optimize parameters [34]. Figure 2 details the architecture for teeth detection.

More and more industries are using artificial intelligence to make increasingly complex decisions, and many alternatives are available to them [32]. However, in view of our results, there is a paucity of guidance on selecting the appropriate methods tailored to the health-care industry.

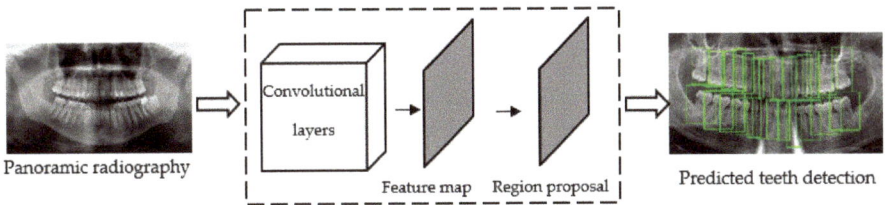

Figure 2. System architecture for teeth detection.

The benefit of neural networks in medicine and dentistry is related to their ability to process large amounts of data for analyzing, diagnosing and disease monitoring. Deep learning has become a great ally in the field of medicine in general and is beginning to be one in dentistry. According to the year of publication of the studies included in this review, 2019 was the year in which the most articles were published.

The results provided by artificial intelligence have a great dependence on the data with which they learn and are trained, that is, on the input data and the image employed to detect each variable. All of the studies included in this review employed radiographs, mainly panoramic radiographies. In this sense, it would be interesting to apply neural networks and artificial intelligence in other types of radiological studies such as cone beam computed tomography (CBCT) or cephalometry, which allow clinicians to make a complete anatomical examination. Lee et al. evaluated the detection and diagnosis of different lesions employing CBCT and a deep convolutional neural network [35]. Before being possible to detect the variables analyzed in this review, teeth must be detected. Panoramic radiography is the most common technique in general dentistry, which captures the entire mouth in a single 2D image [36,37], and it is common to use artificial intelligence to detect the presence or absence of a tooth. The main advantages of these types of images are: the patient comfort compared with other techniques, such as intraoral images (bitewing and periapical); the low radiation exposure; and the ability to evaluate a larger area of the maxilla and mandible [37].

Panoramic radiographies are useful to evaluate endodontic treatments, periapical lesions and disorders in bones, among others [38]. This type of image has obtained the best results in tooth detection if we compare it with the study that used periapical images to detect this variable. In addition, the results obtained by the studies that detected teeth were superior to the rest of the variables analyzed, regardless of the network or type of image used.

Caries is one of the most common chronic diseases in the oral field, with a great impact on a patient's health [39]. Clinical examination is the main method for caries detection, with radiographic examination being a complementary diagnostic tool [40]. According to experience and scientific literature, intraoral bitewing images are the most effective in detecting caries lesions [41]. However, only one study included in this review employed bitewings to detect caries. Two studies used near-infrared transillumination images and one employed periapical images. The best results were obtained in the study where periapical images were used to detect caries.

A variety of CNN architectures were found in the studies included in this literature review. Convolutional networks are designed to process data that come in the form of multiple arrays and that are structured in a series of stages [42]. In recent decades, CNNs have been applied with success for the detection, segmentation and recognition of objects in images. In this review, convolutional networks applied to the detection of dental variables were used.

Faster regions with convolutional neural network features (Faster R-CNN) are composed of two modules. The first module is a deep fully convolutional network that suggests regions and the second module is the Fast R-CNN detector [43]. ResNets are residual networks, which is a CNN designed to allow for thousands of convolutional layers. Deep Neural Network for Object Detection (DetectNet) outputs the XY coordinates of a detected object. This kind of neural network has been applied in different medical fields [19,44]. Keras is a library of open source neural networks written in Python. PyBrain is a machine-learning library for Python, whose objective is to provide flexible, easy-to-use and powerful algorithms for machine-learning tasks [45]. Mask R-CNN is an extension of Faster R-CNN, by adding a branch for predicting segmentation masks on each region of interest (ROI) [46]. AlexNet was introduced in 2012 and employs an eight-layer convolutional neural network as follows: five convolutional layers, two fully connected hidden layers, and one fully connected output layer [47].

In addition to the wide variety of neural network architectures, the studies included in this work also presented a great variety in terms of the number of images used. The manuscripts included in this review published in 2017 and 2018 are those that show a larger database compared with the articles published in 2019 and 2020. However, there is no relationship between the database used and the results obtained, nor between the database and the variables detected.

The possible and future clinical applications of artificial intelligence and neural networks is the prediction of a phenomenon. Probabilistic neural networks can be used in dentistry to predict fractures, as Johari et al. indicated, where a probabilistic neural network was designed to diagnose a fracture in endodontically treated teeth [48].

In view of the results shown in this review and the included studies, the authors suggest the use of neural networks that are capable of predicting possible diseases or possible treatment failures for future clinical applications in the field of dentistry.

5. Conclusions

Because of the great heterogeneity in terms of the image database and the type, results and architectures of neural networks, a standardized methodology is needed in order to increase the compatibility and robustness between studies.

Author Contributions: All of the authors have read and agreed to the published version of the manuscript. Conceptualization, M.P.-P.; methodology, M.P.-P. and J.G.V.; data curation, M.P.-P. and J.G.V.; writing—original draft preparation, M.P.-P.; writing—review and editing, C.H.M.-M.; visualization, M.P.-P., J.G.V., C.H.M.-M. and C.I.; supervision, C.I.; funding acquisition, C.H.M.-M. and C.I. All authors have read and agreed to the published version of the manuscript.

Funding: This research was funded by Asisa Dental S.A.U.

Conflicts of Interest: The authors declare no conflict of interest.

References

1. Shen, D.; Wu, G.; Suk, H.-I. Deep Learning in Medical Image Analysis. *Annu. Rev. Biomed. Eng.* **2017**, *19*, 221–248. [CrossRef] [PubMed]
2. Ehtesham, H.; Safdari, R.; Mansourian, A.; Tahmasebian, S.; Mohammadzadeh, N.; Pourshahidi, S. Developing a new intelligent system for the diagnosis of oral medicine with case-based reasoning approach. *Oral Dis.* **2019**, *25*, 1555–1563. [CrossRef] [PubMed]
3. Tuzoff, D.V.; Tuzova, L.N.; Bornstein, M.M.; Krasnov, A.S.; Kharchenko, M.A.; Nikolenko, S.I.; Sveshnikov, M.M.; Bednenko, G.B. Tooth detection and numbering in panoramic radiographs using convolutional neural networks. *Dentomaxillofacial Radiol.* **2019**, *48*, 20180051. [CrossRef] [PubMed]
4. Topol, E.J. High-performance medicine: The convergence of human and artificial intelligence. *Nat. Med.* **2019**, *25*, 44–56. [CrossRef]
5. Mendonça, E.A. Clinical decision support systems: Perspectives in dentistry. *J. Dent. Educ.* **2004**, *68*, 589–597.
6. Hiraiwa, T.; Ariji, Y.; Fukuda, M.; Kise, Y.; Nakata, K.; Katsumata, A.; Fujita, H.; Ariji, E. A deep-learning artificial intelligence system for assessment of root morphology of the mandibular first molar on panoramic radiography. *Dentomaxillofacial Radiol.* **2019**, *48*, 20180218. [CrossRef]
7. Currie, G. Intelligent Imaging: Anatomy of Machine Learning and Deep Learning. *J. Nucl. Med. Technol.* **2019**, *47*, 273–281. [CrossRef]
8. Xue, Y.; Zhang, R.; Deng, Y.; Chen, K.; Jiang, T. A preliminary examination of the diagnostic value of deep learning in hip osteoarthritis. *PLoS ONE* **2017**, *12*, e0178992. [CrossRef]

9. Sklan, J.E.S.; Plassard, A.J.; Fabbri, D.; Landman, B.A. Toward content-based image retrieval with deep convolutional neural networks. In *Medical Imaging 2015: Biomedical Applications in Molecular, Structural, and Functional Imaging*; International Society for Optics and Photonics: Bellingham, WA, USA, 2015; Volume 9417.
10. Schwendicke, F.; Elhennawy, K.; Paris, S.; Friebertshäuser, P.; Krois, J. Deep Learning for Caries Lesion Detection in Near-Infrared Light Transillumination Images: A Pilot Study. *J. Dent.* **2019**, 103260. [CrossRef]
11. Krois, J.; Ekert, T.; Meinhold, L.; Golla, T.; Kharbot, B.; Wittemeier, A.; Dörfer, C.; Schwendicke, F. Deep Learning for the Radiographic Detection of Periodontal Bone Loss. *Sci. Rep.* **2019**, *9*, 8495. [CrossRef]
12. Lee, J.-H.; Kim, D.; Jeong, S.-N.; Choi, S.-H. Diagnosis and prediction of periodontally compromised teeth using a deep learning-based convolutional neural network algorithm. *J. Periodontal Implant Sci.* **2018**, *48*, 114. [CrossRef] [PubMed]
13. Lee, J.-H.; Kim, D.-H.; Jeong, S.-N.; Choi, S.-H. Detection and diagnosis of dental caries using a deep learning-based convolutional neural network algorithm. *J. Dent.* **2018**, *77*, 106–111. [CrossRef] [PubMed]
14. Ekert, T.; Krois, J.; Meinhold, L.; Elhennawy, K.; Emara, R.; Golla, T.; Schwendicke, F. Deep Learning for the Radiographic Detection of Apical Lesions. *J. Endod.* **2019**, *45*, 917–922.e5. [CrossRef] [PubMed]
15. Schwendicke, F.; Golla, T.; Dreher, M.; Krois, J. Convolutional neural networks for dental image diagnostics: A scoping review. *J. Dent.* **2019**, *91*, 103226. [CrossRef] [PubMed]
16. Chen, H.; Zhang, K.; Lyu, P.; Li, H.; Zhang, L.; Wu, J.; Lee, C.-H. A deep learning approach to automatic teeth detection and numbering based on object detection in dental periapical films. *Sci. Rep.* **2019**, *9*, 3840. [CrossRef]
17. Mahoor, M.H.; Abdel-Mottaleb, M. Classification and numbering of teeth in dental bitewing images. *Pattern Recognit.* **2005**, *38*, 577–586. [CrossRef]
18. Nardi, C.; Calistri, L.; Grazzini, G.; Desideri, I.; Lorini, C.; Occhipinti, M.; Mungai, F.; Colagrande, S. Is Panoramic Radiography an Accurate Imaging Technique for the Detection of Endodontically Treated Asymptomatic Apical Periodontitis? *J. Endod.* **2018**, *44*, 1500–1508. [CrossRef]
19. Fukuda, M.; Inamoto, K.; Shibata, N.; Ariji, Y.; Yanashita, Y.; Kutsuna, S.; Nakata, K.; Katsumata, A.; Fujita, H.; Ariji, E. Evaluation of an artificial intelligence system for detecting vertical root fracture on panoramic radiography. *Oral Radiol.* **2019**. [CrossRef]
20. Zhang, K.; Wu, J.; Chen, H.; Lyu, P. An effective teeth recognition method using label tree with cascade network structure. *Comput. Med. Imaging Graph.* **2018**, *68*, 61–70. [CrossRef]
21. Raith, S.; Vogel, E.P.; Anees, N.; Keul, C.; Güth, J.-F.; Edelhoff, D.; Fischer, H. Artificial Neural Networks as a powerful numerical tool to classify specific features of a tooth based on 3D scan data. *Comput. Biol. Med.* **2017**, *80*, 65–76. [CrossRef]
22. Srivastava, M.M.; Kumar, P.; Pradhan, L.; Varadarajan, S. Detection of Tooth caries in Bitewing Radiographs using Deep Learning. In Proceedings of the Thirty-first Annual Conference on Neural Information Processing Systems (NIPS 2017), Long Beach, CA, USA, 4–9 December 2017; p. 4.
23. Jader, G.; Fontineli, J.; Ruiz, M.; Abdalla, K.; Pithon, M.; Oliveira, L. Deep Instance Segmentation of Teeth in Panoramic X-Ray Images. In Proceedings of the 2018 31st SIBGRAPI Conference on Graphics, Patterns and Images (SIBGRAPI), Parana, Brazil, 29 October–1 November 2018; pp. 400–407.
24. Miki, Y.; Muramatsu, C.; Hayashi, T.; Zhou, X.; Hara, T.; Katsumata, A.; Fujita, H. Classification of teeth in cone-beam CT using deep convolutional neural network. *Comput. Biol. Med.* **2017**, *80*, 24–29. [CrossRef] [PubMed]
25. Velemínská, J.; Pílný, A.; Čepek, M.; Koťová, M.; Kubelková, R. Dental age estimation and different predictive ability of various tooth types in the Czech population: Data mining methods. *Anthropol. Anzeiger* **2013**, *70*, 331–345. [CrossRef]
26. Casalegno, F.; Newton, T.; Daher, R.; Abdelaziz, M.; Lodi-Rizzini, A.; Schürmann, F.; Krejci, I.; Markram, H. Caries Detection with Near-Infrared Transillumination Using Deep Learning. *J. Dent. Res.* **2019**, *98*, 1227–1233. [CrossRef] [PubMed]
27. Zanella-Calzada, L.; Galván-Tejada, C.; Chávez-Lamas, N.; Rivas-Gutierrez, J.; Magallanes-Quintanar, R.; Celaya-Padilla, J.; Galván-Tejada, J.; Gamboa-Rosales, H. Deep Artificial Neural Networks for the Diagnostic of Caries Using Socioeconomic and Nutritional Features as Determinants: Data from NHANES 2013–2014. *Bioengineering* **2018**, *5*, 47. [CrossRef] [PubMed]

28. Muramatsu, C.; Morishita, T.; Takahashi, R.; Hayashi, T.; Nishiyama, W.; Ariji, Y.; Zhou, X.; Hara, T.; Katsumata, A.; Ariji, E.; et al. Tooth detection and classification on panoramic radiographs for automatic dental chart filing: Improved classification by multi-sized input data. *Oral Radiol.* **2020**. [CrossRef] [PubMed]
29. Prajapati, S.A.; Nagaraj, R.; Mitra, S. Classification of dental diseases using CNN and transfer learning. In Proceedings of the 2017 5th International Symposium on Computational and Business Intelligence (ISCBI), Dubai, United Arab Emirates, 11–14 August 2017; pp. 70–74.
30. Betul Oktay, A. Tooth detection with Convolutional Neural Networks. In Proceedings of the 2017 Medical Technologies National Congress (TIPTEKNO), Trabzon, Turkey, 12–14 October 2017; pp. 1–4.
31. Geetha, V.; Aprameya, K.S.; Hinduja, D.M. Dental caries diagnosis in digital radiographs using back-propagation neural network. *Heal. Inf. Sci. Syst.* **2020**, *8*, 8. [CrossRef] [PubMed]
32. Shahid, N.; Rappon, T.; Berta, W. Applications of artificial neural networks in health care organizational decision-making: A scoping review. *PLoS ONE* **2019**, *14*, e0212356. [CrossRef]
33. Da Silva, I.; Hernane Spatti, S.; Andrade Flauzino, R. Artificial Neural Network Architectures and Training Processes. In *Artificial Neural Networks: A Practical Course*; Springer International Publishing: Berlin, Germany, 2017; pp. 21–28.
34. Yamashita, R.; Nishio, M.; Do, R.K.G.; Togashi, K. Convolutional neural networks: An overview and application in radiology. *Insights Imaging* **2018**, *9*, 611–629. [CrossRef]
35. Lee, J.-H.; Kim, D.-H.; Jeong, S.-N. Diagnosis of Cystic Lesions Using Panoramic and Cone Beam Computed Tomographic Images Based on Deep Learning Neural Network. *Oral Dis.* **2020**, *26*, 152–158. [CrossRef]
36. Farman, A.G. There are good reasons for selecting panoramic radiography to replace the intraoral full-mouth series. *Oral Surgery, Oral Med. Oral Pathol. Oral Radiol. Endodontology* **2002**, *94*, 653–654. [CrossRef]
37. Kim, J.; Lee, H.-S.; Song, I.-S.; Jung, K.-H. DeNTNet: Deep Neural Transfer Network for the detection of periodontal bone loss using panoramic dental radiographs. *Sci. Rep.* **2019**, *9*, 17615. [CrossRef]
38. Moll, M.A.; Seuthe, M.; von See, C.; Zapf, A.; Hornecker, E.; Mausberg, R.F.; Ziebolz, D. Comparison of clinical and dental panoramic findings: A practice-based crossover study. *BMC Oral Health* **2013**, *13*, 48. [CrossRef] [PubMed]
39. Chen, K.J.; Gao, S.S.; Duangthip, D.; Lo, E.C.M.; Chu, C.H. Prevalence of early childhood caries among 5-year-old children: A systematic review. *J. Investig. Clin. Dent.* **2019**, *10*, e12376. [CrossRef] [PubMed]
40. Wenzel, A. Dental caries. In *Oral radiology. Principles and Interpretation.*; Elsevier Mosby: St. Louis, MO, USA, 2014; pp. 285–298.
41. Pakbaznejad Esmaeili, E.; Pakkala, T.; Haukka, J.; Siukosaari, P. Low reproducibility between oral radiologists and general dentists with regards to radiographic diagnosis of caries. *Acta Odontol. Scand.* **2018**, *76*, 346–350. [CrossRef] [PubMed]
42. LeCun, Y.; Bengio, Y.; Hinton, G. Deep learning. *Nature* **2015**, *521*, 436–444. [CrossRef] [PubMed]
43. Ren, S.; He, K.; Girshick, R.; Sun, J. Faster R-CNN: Towards Real-Time Object Detection with Region Proposal Networks. *Comput. Vis. Pattern Recognit.* **2015**, *39*, 91–99. [CrossRef] [PubMed]
44. Zhao, Z.-Q.; Zheng, P.; Xu, S.-T.; Wu, X. Object Detection With Deep Learning: A Review. *IEEE Trans. Neural Networks Learn. Syst.* **2019**, *30*, 3212–3232. [CrossRef]
45. Schaul, T.; Bayer, J.; Wierstra, D.; Sun, Y.; Felder, M.; Sehnke, F.; Rückstieß, T.; Schmidhuber, J. PyBrain. *J. Mach. Learn. Res.* **2010**, *11*, 743–746.
46. He, K.; Gkioxari, G.; Dollar, P.; Girshick, R. Mask R-CNN. *IEEE Trans. Pattern Anal. Mach. Intell.* **2020**, *42*, 386–397. [CrossRef]
47. Krizhevsky, A.; Sutskever, I.; Hinton, G. Imagenet classification with deep convolutional neural networks. *Adv. Neural Inf. Process. Syst.* **2012**, 1097–1105. [CrossRef]
48. Johari, M.; Esmaeili, F.; Andalib, A.; Garjani, S.; Saberkari, H. Detection of vertical root fractures in intact and endodontically treated premolar teeth by designing a probabilistic neural network: An ex vivo study. *Dentomaxillofacial Radiol.* **2017**, *46*, 20160107. [CrossRef] [PubMed]

© 2020 by the authors. Licensee MDPI, Basel, Switzerland. This article is an open access article distributed under the terms and conditions of the Creative Commons Attribution (CC BY) license (http://creativecommons.org/licenses/by/4.0/).

Article

An Approach for the Pan Sharpening of Very High Resolution Satellite Images Using a CIELab Color Based Component Substitution Algorithm

Alireza Rahimzadeganasl [1], Ugur Alganci [2] and Cigdem Goksel [2,*]

[1] Science and Technology Institute, Istanbul Technical University, Maslak, Istanbul 34469, Turkey; rahimzadegan16@itu.edu.tr
[2] Department of Geomatics Engineering, Faculty of Civil Engineering, Istanbul Technical University, Maslak, Istanbul 34469, Turkey; alganci@itu.edu.tr
* Correspondence: goksel@itu.edu.tr; Tel.: +90-212-285-3806

Received: 2 October 2019; Accepted: 29 November 2019; Published: 1 December 2019

Abstract: Recent very high spatial resolution (VHR) remote sensing satellites provide high spatial resolution panchromatic (Pan) images in addition to multispectral (MS) images. The pan sharpening process has a critical role in image processing tasks and geospatial information extraction from satellite images. In this research, CIELab color based component substitution Pan sharpening algorithm was proposed for Pan sharpening of the Pleiades VHR images. The proposed method was compared with the state-of-the-art Pan sharpening methods, such as IHS, EHLERS, NNDiffuse and GIHS. The selected study region included ten test sites, each of them representing complex landscapes with various land categories, to evaluate the performance of Pan sharpening methods in varying land surface characteristics. The spatial and spectral performance of the Pan sharpening methods were evaluated by eleven accuracy metrics and visual interpretation. The results of the evaluation indicated that proposed CIELab color-based method reached promising results and improved the spectral and spatial information preservation.

Keywords: CIELab; component Substitution; Pan sharpening; Pléiades VHR Image

1. Introduction

The earth observation satellites with very high resolution (VHR) optical sensors provide a multispectral (MS) image and a panchromatic (Pan) image that are acquired simultaneously in order to provide essential accommodation between spectral and spatial resolution, which is an important consideration for optical satellite sensors due to their physical limitations [1,2]. Spectral diversity is important for modeling the spectral characteristics of different land cover/use classes and identifying them; on the other hand, spatial information is very crucial for identifying spatial details and geometric characteristics. The Pan image provides high spatial resolution with a single, wide range spectral band, whereas the MS image provides several spectral bands in different sections of the electromagnetic spectrum with low spatial resolution in order to meet the abovementioned requirements.

The fusion of Pan and MS images that are acquired over the same area from the single or multiple satellite system is referred to as Pan sharpening. The main aim of Pan sharpening is to create a high-resolution MS image, having the spatial resolution of Pan but preserving the spectral characteristics of MS [3]. Unlike the challenging problem of multi-sensor data fusion, single sensor Pan sharpening does not need image-to-image registration, as the Pan and MS sensors are mounted on the same platform and the images are acquired simultaneously with well-matching viewing geometry [4]. Several earth observation satellites, such as Geo-Eye, OrbView, QuickBird, WorldView, Pléiades and

Spot, have this capability, and bundle (PAN+MS) products from these systems can be used directly as the input for Pan sharpening.

An ideal Pan sharpening algorithm leads to the best performance in spatial and spectral domains by keeping the spatial resolution of a Pan image and preserving the spectral characteristics of an MS image. Launching of VHR sensors led to the appearance of diverse Pan sharpening methods in recent decades [5–7]. In addition, Pan sharpening is a primary image enhancement step for many remote sensing applications, such as object detection [8], change detection [9], image segmentation and clustering [10,11], scene interpretation and visual image analysis [12]. Commonly, image fusion can be classified into three levels—pixel level, feature level and decision or knowledge level—while the Pan sharpening is categorized as a sub-pixel level process [13,14].

Pan sharpening algorithms can be divided into four groups: (1) rationing methods; (2) injection-based methods; (3) model-based methods; and (4) component substitution (CS) methods. Of these methods, CS algorithms are more practical because of their calculation speed and performance compatibility. The CS methods can be categorized into four classes according to the transform matrix used in the algorithm; which are principle component analysis (PCA) [15,16], intensity-hue-saturation (IHS) [7,17], Gram–Schmidt (GS) [18,19] and generalized component substitution (GCS) [5,20]. The common and general limitation of all CS-based methods is the distortion in spectral characteristics when compared to original MS image [21,22].

This research proposes a robust CS method for Pan sharpening the Pleiades VHR satellite images with the aim of enhanced spatial resolution and reduced spectral distortion. The principle of the proposed method is similar to the IHS method, where a uniform CIELab color space based on human eye spectral response is used instead of IHS color space [23]. The CIELab color space has been used for different image processing tasks. Wirth and Nikitenko, 2010 [24], investigated the performance of CIELab color space on the application of unsharp masking and fuzzy morphological sharpening algorithms. In the study of [25], the experiments of the content-based image retrieval (CBIR) were used to evaluate the performance of CIELab and the other three color spaces (RGB, CIELuv and HSV) on an image retrieval process. In addition, CIELab color space was used to help different image segmentation tasks [26,27]. In a previous Pan sharpening research, color normalization-based on CIELab color space aided the image fusion algorithm with sharpening a Hyperion hyperspectral image with an Ikonos Pan image using the spectral mixing-based color preservation model [28]. In another study, a remote sensing image fusion technique using CIELab color space was proposed by Jin et al. [29]. In that study, the authors improved the performance of image fusion techniques by combining non-subsampled shearlet transform and pulse coupled neural network. However, this approach is computationally complicated and there is lack of a specific satellite dataset.

Although the CIELab method is used in different image processing tasks applied on natural and satellite images, evaluation of its performance on the Pan sharpening process is limited and there is no detailed evaluation of this method on VHR image Pan sharpening by considering the different landscape characteristics and with use of spatial and spectral metrics in addition to visual interpretation yet, to our knowledge. This research focused on proposing a robust, CIELab-based Pan sharpening approach and aimed to fill the abovementioned gap in detailed investigation and accuracy assessment of CIELab-based Pan sharpening in the literature. In this research, results from the proposed method were compared with the results from the six well-known methods, which are Ehlers, Generalized IHS, IHS, Gram-Schmitt, HCS and NNDiffuse methods. Pleiades satellite images of ten different test sites having different landscape characteristics were comparatively evaluated to check the spatial and spectral performance of the proposed method with quantitative accuracy metrics. In addition, visual interpretation-based analyses were performed on the results in order to discuss the performances of methods. The results illustrated advantages of using uniform color space for the aim of the Pan sharpening application.

2. State of Art

A brief review of the state of the art methods that used for comparative analysis with respect to the proposed method are presented in Table 1.

Table 1. The brief review of state of the art Pan sharpening methods.

Method	Description	References
IHS Method	In this system, the total amount of the brightness in one color is represented through intensity channel. The wavelength property of the color and the purity of the color are represented by hue and saturation respectively.	[30,31]
EHLERS (FFT-Enhanced IHS Transform) Method	The fundamental idea of this method is modifying the Pan image in the way that it looks more similar to the intensity component of MS image. This method uses FFT (fast fourier transform) filtering for partial replacement instead of entire replacement of the intensity component.	[32]
NNDiffuse (Nearest-neighbor diffusion-based) Method	This method, considers each pixel spectrum as a weighted linear combination of spectra of its sideward neighboring super pixels in the Pan sharpened image. Algorithm uses various factors like intensity smoothness (σ), spatial smoothness (σ_s) and pixel size ratio for conducting the Pan sharpening	[33,34]
GIHS (Generalized IHS) Method	Directly applying of IHS method needs many multiplication and addition operations, which makes the Pan sharpening operation computationally inefficient. GIHS method develops a computationally efficient Pan sharpening method, which does not require coordinate transformation	[35]
Gram-Schmidt Method	This method uses the Gram-Schmidt orthogonalization for converting the original low-resolution MS bands, which are linearly independent vectors, into a set of orthogonal vectors. The first vector in the orthogonal space is considered as simulated Pan image, which produced by weighted aggregation of the consecutive original MS bands.	[21,22]
Hyperspherical Color Sharpening Method	The Hyperspherical Color Sharpening method (HCS) is a Pan sharpening method designed for WorldView-2 sensor imagery and can be applied to any MS data containing 3bands or more. HCS approach is based on transforming original color space to hyperspherical color space.	[36,37]

3. Methodology and Accuracy Assessment

This research proposes a new Pan sharpening method that relies on the CIELab transform, which modifies the color components of images to be used for Pan sharpening of VHR satellite images. The flowchart of the proposed method is given in Figure 1, and the details of the proposed method are described in the sub sections.

3.1. Multispectral Image Transform to CIELab Color System

The RGB color system was designed in such a way that it includes nearly all primary colors and can be comprehended by human vision. Nevertheless, it is a tough task to deal with RGB color due to strong correlation between its components [29]. In this study, a uniform and complete color model, the CIELab color system, was used. In this uniform color system, a variation in the coordinates of the color component provides the same amount of variation in the luminance and saturation components [10]. Besides, this color space is projected to draw human vision, unlike the RGB and CMYK (cyan, magenta, yellow, black) color spaces [38]. The CIELab color system was used in the proposed Pan sharpening approach in order to reduce the spectral distortion, while maintaining the color perception of human vision [39].

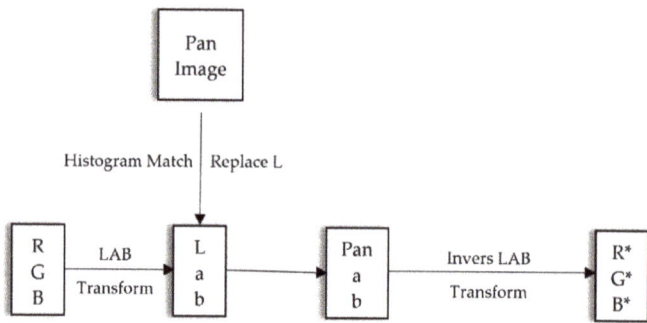

Figure 1. CIELab image Pan sharpening flowchart.

The design of the CIELab color system is based on Hering's theory, which indicates that only red (R), green (G), blue (B) and yellow (Y) are unique among the thousands of colors that are used to characterize the hue component [40]. Although, other colors can be produced using these unique colors (for example it is possible to obtain orange by mixing red and yellow), they (R, G, B and Y) can be described only with their own name. R, G, B and Y, with black (B) and white (W), constitutes a color system with six basic color properties and three opponent pairs: R/G, Y/B and B/W. The opponency idea rises from observation upon colors attributes, which proves no color could be characterized using both blue and yellow or red and green together [41]. A blue shade of yellow does not exist. These three opponent pairs are represented in the form of a three-dimensional color space, as illustrated in Figure 2. In this figure, the vertical axis L* represents the luminance, in which perfect black is represented by 0 and perfect white is represented by 100. The a* and the b* are the axes that are perpendicular to luminance indicated chromaticity, and stand for redness/greenness and yellowness/blueness, respectively. Positive values represent redness (for a* component) and yellowness (for b* component), whereas greenness and blueness are denoted with negative values.

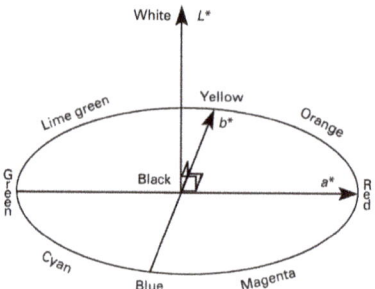

Figure 2. CIELab color space [41].

The L*, a* and b* values are computed using XYZ values. The XYZ system that was based on the RGB color space was presented by the International Commission on Illumination, CIE (Commission international de l'éclairage), in the 1920s and patented in 1931. The difference of RGB and XYZ lies in the light sources. The R, G and B elements are real light sources of known characteristics, whereas the X, Y and Z elements are three theoretical sources, which are selected in a way that all visible colors can be defined as a density of just-positive units of the three primary sources [10].

Occasionally, the colorimetric calculations with the use of color matching functions produce negative lobs. This problem can be solved by transforming the real light sources to these theoretical sources. In this color space, red, green and blue colors are more saturated than any spectral RGB. X, Y and Z components, represent red, green and blue colors respectively. RGB to XYZ and its reverse transformations can be performed by following equations:

$$\begin{bmatrix} X \\ Y \\ Z \end{bmatrix} = \begin{bmatrix} 0.4124564 & 0.3575761 & 0.1804375 \\ 0.2126729 & 0.7151522 & 0.0721750 \\ 0.0193339 & 0.1191920 & 0.9503041 \end{bmatrix} \bullet \begin{bmatrix} R \\ G \\ B \end{bmatrix} \qquad (1)$$

$$\begin{bmatrix} R \\ G \\ B \end{bmatrix} = \begin{bmatrix} 3.2404542 & -1.5371385 & -0.4985314 \\ -0.9692660 & 1.8760108 & 0.0415560 \\ 0.0556434 & -0.2040259 & 1.0572252 \end{bmatrix} \bullet \begin{bmatrix} X \\ Y \\ Z \end{bmatrix} \qquad (2)$$

Lab system is calculated by the following equations [23]:

$$L = 116 \; F_Y - 16 \qquad (3)$$

$$a = 500 \; [F_X - F_Y] \qquad (4)$$

$$b = 200[F_Y - F_Z] \qquad (5)$$

$$\text{Where } F_X = (\frac{X}{X_n})^{\frac{1}{3}} \text{ if } (\frac{X}{X_n}) > (\frac{24}{116})^3 \qquad (6)$$

$$\text{And } F_X = (\frac{841}{108})(\frac{X}{X_n}) + \frac{16}{116} \text{ if } (\frac{X}{X_n}) \le (\frac{24}{116})^3, \qquad (7)$$

where X_n is the tristimulus value of a perfect white object color stimulus, which the light reflected from a perfect diffuser under the chosen illuminant. F_Y and F_Z values are calculated in the same way as F_X.

3.2. Pan-Sharpening

In the Pan sharpening procedure, the MS image should be resampled to the same pixel size of the Pan image before converting it to CIELab color space. In this research, the bicubic interpolation method was used to resample 2 m resolution Pleiades MS images into 50 cm resolution to match the pixel size of Pleiades Pan image. This resampled dataset is used in all Pan sharpening methods used in this research, including the proposed one. After converting the MS image from RGB to CIELab space, the Pan sharpening process continues with replacing the Pan image with the L* component. Unlike the proposed method in [29] study, there is no need for color space conversion of Pan image in the proposed method, which leads to low computation and less data distortion. Before replacing the L* band of MS with the Pan image, there is a histogram matching step that could be considered as preprocessing step. After resampling the MS image to the same size of Pan image and converting the MS image color space, the histogram of Pan image has to be matched with the histogram of L* component in order to minimize the spectral differences [42]. For performing histogram matching task, mean and standard deviation normalizations were used [43]:

$$Pan^{HM} = (Pan - \mu_{Pan}) \frac{\sigma_l}{\sigma_{Pan}} + \mu_l, \qquad (8)$$

where Pan^{HM} stands for histogram matched Pan image, μ stands for mean and σ represents standad deviation. After these preprocessing steps, the L* component is replaced with a Pan image. The Pan sharpened image is then produced by implementing inverse conversion of CIELab color system on the Pan*a*b* image and results in a new MS image with high spatial resolution.

3.3. Accuracy Assessment

Several metrics were proposed to assess the accuracy of Pan-sharpened images that use the precise, high-resolution MS image as a reference image. In this research, the first seven metrics provided in Table 2 were used for the spectral quality assessment, while the later four metrics were used for spatial quality assessment of the results. Although metrics provide important quantitative insights about the algorithm performance, qualitative assessment of the color preservation quality and spatial improvements in object representation is required. Thus, results obtained from the Pan sharpening algorithms were also evaluated with visual inspection.

Table 2. The description of all accuracy indices (definition of terms provided in List A1).

Quality Metric	Description	Formula	What Value to Look for (Higher/Lower)	Reference
RMSE	Root Mean Square Error (RMSE) is used to calculate the variation in DN values for checking the difference between the Pan sharpened and reference image.	$RMSE = \sqrt{\frac{1}{MN}\sum_{i=1}^{M}\sum_{j=1}^{N}(MS(i,j)-PS(i,j))^2}$	Lower (near to zero)	[45]
ERGAS	Relative dimensionless global error synthesis (ERGAS) is used to calculate the accuracy of Pan sharpened image considering normalized average error of each band of the result image.	$ERGAS = 100\frac{dh}{dl}\sqrt{\frac{1}{n}\sum_{i=1}^{n}\left(\frac{RMSE(i)}{Mean(i)}\right)^2}$	Lower (near to zero)	[45]
SAM	Spectral Angle Mapper (SAM) represents the spectral similarity between the Pan sharpened and reference MS image using the average spectral angle		Lower (near to zero)	[36]
RASE	Relative average spectral error (RASE) is an error index to calculate average performance of Pan sharpening algorithm into spectral bands.	$RASE = \frac{100}{\mu}\sqrt{\frac{1}{b}\sum_{i=1}^{b}RMSE}$	Lower (near to zero)	[46]
PSNR	Peak signal-to-noise ratio is widely used metric for comparison of distorted (Pan sharpened) and original (reference) image.	$PSNR = 20\log_{10}\left[\frac{L^2}{\frac{1}{MN}\sum_{i=1}^{M}\sum_{j=1}^{N}(I_r(i,j)-I_p(i,j))^2}\right]$	Higher Value	[47]
QAVG	The Average Quality index based on quality index is used to model the difference between reference and Pan sharpened images as a combination of three different factors: loss of correlation, luminance distortions and contrast distortion. As QI can only be applied to one band, the average value of three or more bands (QAVG) is used for calculating a global spectral quality index for multiband images.	$QI = \frac{4\sigma_{xy}\overline{x}\overline{y}}{(\sigma_x^2+\sigma_y^2)[(\overline{x})^2+(\overline{y})^2]}$	Higher Value (Close to 1)	[48]
SSIM	Structural Similarity index (SSIM) is a method for measuring the structural similarity between reference and Pan sharpened images. This method compares the local patterns (luminance, contrast and structure) using means and standard deviations of two images.	$SSIM = \frac{(2\mu_{I_r}\mu_{I_p}+C_1)(2\sigma_{I_rI_p}+C_2)}{(\mu^2_{I_r}+\mu^2_{I_p}+C_1)(\sigma^2_{I_r}+\sigma^2_{I_p}+C_2)}$	Higher Value	[2]
CC	To assess the spatial quality of Pan sharpened images, the correlation coefficient between the Pan image and the intensity component of the Pan sharpened image is used.	$CC = \frac{2C_{rf}}{C_r+C_f}$	Higher Value (Close to 1)	[49]
ZHOU index	Zhou's spatial index uses a high frequency Laplacian filter for extracting high frequency information from both Pan and Pan sharpened images. Correlation coefficient is then calculated between filtered Pan image and each band of Pan sharpened image. The average of calculated cc is considered as spatial quality index.	$\text{Laplacian Kernel} = \begin{bmatrix} -1 & -1 & -1 \\ -1 & 8 & -1 \\ -1 & -1 & -1 \end{bmatrix}$	Higher Value (Close to 1)	[50]
SRMSE	Sobel based RMSE (SRMSE) is an index for spatial accuracy assessment that uses absolute edge magnitude difference of Pan and Pan sharpened image. This index utilizes 3 × 3 vertical and horizontal Sobel filter kernels for calculating the gradient of edge intensities. RMSE then calculated between Pan and Pan sharpened edge magnitude images.	$M = \sqrt{M_x^2 + M_y^2}$ $\text{Where } M_x = \begin{bmatrix} -1 & 0 & 1 \\ -2 & 0 & 2 \\ -1 & 0 & 1 \end{bmatrix} \times \text{image}$ $\text{And } M_y = \begin{bmatrix} -1 & -2 & -1 \\ 0 & 0 & 0 \\ 1 & 2 & 1 \end{bmatrix} \times \text{image}$	Lower (near to zero)	[51]
Sp-ERGAS	Spatial ERGAS (Sp-ERGAS) is an index for spatial quality assessment of Pan sharpened image, which uses spatial RMSE for assessment procedure	$\text{Spatial ERGAS} = 100\frac{dh}{dl}\sqrt{\frac{1}{n}\sum_{i=1}^{n}\left(\frac{Spatial\_RMSE(i)}{Pan(i)}\right)^2}$	Lower (near to zero)	[52]

4. Experimental Results

4.1. Dataset

The primary product of Pléiades satellite images were used for performing experimental analysis of the proposed method. The Pléiades program, which was launched by CNES (the French space agency), is the optical Earth imaging component of French–Italian ORFEO (Optical and Radar Federated Earth Observation). The Pléiades constellation consists of two satellites with VHR optical sensors. The Pléiades 1A launched on 17.12.2011 and Pléiades 1B launched on 2.12.2012. Both of the satellites provide 0.5 m spatial resolution for the Pan sensor and 2 m for MS sensor with 20 km swath width and 12 bit radiometric resolution [44].

The dataset used in this research consists of three Pleiades image scenes, which cover different landscape characteristics (Table 3). The locations of scenes are provided in Figure 3. Ten different sub frames were selected from these image scenes, in order to evaluate the performance of Pan sharpening methods for varying landscape characteristics and seasonal conditions (Table 4).

Figure 3. The locations of the Pléiades image scenes overlaid on Google Earth©.

Table 3. The description of three datasets.

No	Location	Acquisition Data	Platform
D1	Istanbul	2017-04-09	PHR 1A
D2	Izmir	2015-12-04	PHR 1B
D3	Aydin	2018-04-10	PHR 1B

Table 4. The description of ten selected data frames.

Image	Location	Type	Objects
F1	Istanbul	Rural	Trees, Vegetation, Bare roads, Bare soil
F2	Istanbul	Urban	Buildings, Roads, Squares, Trees, Bare soil
F3	Istanbul	Suburban	Vegetation, Roads and highways, Buildings, Bare soil, Industry buildings, Green fields
F4	Izmir	Urban	Buildings, Roads, Vegetation, Bare soil
F5	Izmir	Rural	Agricultural fields, Bare roads
F6	Izmir	Rural	Trees, Mountain, Bare roads
F7	Izmir	Suburban	Industry buildings, Agricultural fields, Roads, Bare soil
F8	Aydin	Suburban	Agricultural fields, Roads, Bare roads, Trees, Buildings, Bare soil
F9	Aydin	Urban	Buildings, Roads, Trees, Bare soil, Green fields
F10	Aydin	Rural	Trees, vegetation, agricultural fields, buildings, roads, Bare roads

Four sub frames cover rural areas that contain forests with different types of trees with varying heights and barren roads between them, and mountains and agricultural fields. Three sub frames cover urban areas that include complex buildings, roads and highways. Finally, three sub frames cover sub-urban areas that include all the complex buildings, factories, vegetation, roads, trees and bare soil parts to perform a precise survey on effects of the proposed method in Pan sharpening of vegetation, impervious and soil surfaces simultaneously.

4.2. Performing the Algorithm and Accuracy Assessment

To measure the performance of Pan sharpening results using the metrics that were presented in Section 3.3, the Wald protocol was used, due to lack of reference a high-resolution MS image [53]. According to Wald protocol, all Pan sharpening experiments were done using degraded datasets, which are produced by decreasing spatial resolution of the original dataset (reduce MS and Pan, respectively, to 8 m and 2 m). The Pan sharpening results obtained that way, can be compared with the original MS images for an accuracy assessment procedure. In this paper, six Pan sharpening methods and eleven accuracy indexes are evaluated to perform a comparative accuracy assessment of the proposed method. The numerical results of the accuracy indexes are presented in Tables A1–A6. The visuals belonging to Pan sharpening results of ten frames are presented in Figures A1–A10. In each figure, parts a and b are the original Pléiades MS and Pan images, respectively. Parts c, d and e are the Pan sharpened results from the CIElab, GIHS and GS methods, respectively. The Pan sharpened images from the HCS, IHS, NNDiffuse and Ehlers methods are shown in parts f–i, respectively.

4.3. Experimental Results from Rural Areas

Figures A1–A4 belongs the Pan sharpening results of the rural test sites (frame F1 from D1 dataset, frames F5 and F6 from D2 and Frame F10 from D3 datasets). Each figure belongs to a representative part from the whole image focusing on rural areas and presents visual comparison different Pan sharpening techniques.

The visual comparison of the Pan sharpening methods reveals that spatial resolution of MS images improved significantly in all methods. As for spectral information, parts c, e and h show that the CIELab GS and NNDiffuse methods protect the spectral characteristics better; specifically, for the bands belonging to the visible region. The color-based visual interpretation in vegetated and forest areas in Figures A2–A4 inform us that the Pan-sharpened and original MS images are very similar to each other for GS and CIELab methods. Similar comments can be made on NNDiffuse and CIELab methods in Figure A1. On the other hand, visual comparison of part a with parts d, f, g and i reveals that the remaining four methods were not able to preserve the spectral characteristics of vegetated and forest areas. Particularly, IHS, Ehlers and HCS methods inherited the high frequency impact over vegetated area and could not preserve original spectral/color information for the first test site. In addition, the result of the HCS method is more blurred than the others. The GIHS and—in some cases—the NNDiffuse methods, preserved the color information better than the IHS, Ehlers and HCS; nevertheless, observable spectral distortion is apparent in their resulting products. The GS method has good performance in the case of vegetation except Figure A1 part e, while results are not satisfactory in pathways and their surroundings. In addition, obvious distortions are apparent in the shadowed areas. Detailed investigation on Figure A3 (e) reveals that there is an obvious distortion in snowy parts of the frame almost in all methods except the proposed CIELab, which resulted in a nearly blue color instead of white snow color. However, CIELab method could be able to preserve the texture and keep the small variances in the color when compared to original MS image. Besides, visual interpretation of the CIELab Pan sharpening results (part c in all figures) demonstrated that use of this color space for Pan sharpening could help to distinguish different tree types and vegetation from each other in the absence of NIR band.

The seven quality metrics, which were presented in Table 2, were used for spectral quality assessment of the Pan sharpening results. Numerical results from these metrics for the rural frames (F1, F5, F6 and F10) are presented in Table A1. The metric values were calculated band by band, and the average values of three bands were used for the accuracy assessment procedure. Numerical results of ERGAS, RASE, RMSE and SAM metrics indicated that the proposed CIELab method produced better results than the remaining methods and was followed by the GS method for most of the metrics. Metric-based results were in line with the visual interpretation. The CIELab method also provided the highest accuracies according to the QAVG and PSNR metrics. In addition, the proposed method provides the value 1 for the SSIM metric, which is the best possible value. Moreover, the IHS method provides worst results for all quality indexes, with respect to Table A1. Lastly, Ehlers, GIHS and HCS methods provide lower accuracies in some cases. This unstable manner of these methods across different scenes is another problem that should be considered.

To assess the spatial quality of Pan sharpened images, the CC, the Zhou index, Sobel RMSE and spatial ERGAS indexes that are presented in Section 3.3, were calculated by comparing the Pan image and the intensity component of the Pan sharpened images. Numerical results of these metrics are presented in Table A2. According to comparative evaluation, the Pan sharpened image from the proposed CIELab method provided the highest spatial CC and Zhou values and lowest SRMSE and SP ERGAS values. These results indicate that the proposed method has the best spatial performance among all methods tested. Ehlers, HIS and HCS methods provided the lowest spatial performances according to the values presented in Table A2.

As a result, the proposed CIELab method provided the best performance for the rural scenes based on the visual interpretation and spectral and spatial quality metrics results.

4.4. Experimental Results from Urban Areas

Figure A5 through Figure A7 belongs to the Pan sharpening results of the urban test sites (frames F2, F4 and F9 from D1, D2 and D3 datasets respectively). Each figure belongs to a representative part from the whole image focusing on the buildings and roads, and presents visual comparison between different Pan sharpening techniques on the differently sized and oriented buildings and roads in the urban areas.

Visual comparison results of urban areas revealed that all the Pan sharpened images inherited the high spatial information from the Pan image, and likewise, the results of rural areas. Roads and buildings could be better identified in all Pan sharpened images compared to original MS image. As for spectral information, Figure A5 c,e,h, informed us that CIELab, GS and NNDiffuse methods preserved the spectral characteristics and color information in urban areas. In particular, the color information from the buildings with brick rooves are similar to the original MS image. Visual comparison of Figure A5 part a with parts d, f, g and i illustrated that of IHS, HCS, GIHS and Ehlers methods are not able to preserve the original spectral characteristics of buildings as well as the other three approaches did. In particular, Ehlers, HCS and IHS methods provided blurred and smoggy results with faded and paled colors. Parts g and I from Figures A6 and A7 support that HIS and Ehlers methods provide worst visual results among all methods tested. Part e in Figures A6 and A7 reveals the weakest side of GS method; that is, the poor performance in the Pan sharpening of white tones. White colors tend to seem blueish in results of this method. It is obvious from part f in Figures A6 and A7 that the HCS method provided the most blurred result. GIHS and NNDiffuse methods have acceptable results in comparison with the results from other methods (except CIELab method). Detailed investigation of Figures A6 and A7, parts d and h, prove that NNDiffuse method produces distortion in the shadowed areas and GIHS method has poor performance in vegetated areas and trees. Visual interpretation of Figure A5(c), Figure A6(c) and Figure A7(c) reveal the fact that the proposed CIELab method protected spectral properties of original MS image more than the other methods.

Numerical results of spectral quality assessment of Pan sharpened images belonging to the urban test sites (F2, F4 and F9) are presented in Table A3. Metric values demonstrated that the CIELab method provided the most promising results among all Pan sharpening methods used in this research. This method presented the lowest values for the ERGAS, RASE, RMSE and SAM metrics and highest values for QAVG, PSNR and SSIM metrics (again, the highest possible value obtained for SSIM). HCS and IHS methods provided the worst results for most of the metrics. Once again, the second performance rank for spectral quality was obtained by GS method in most of the metrics.

Table A4 presents the spatial quality metrics results that were calculated from Pan image and the intensity component of Pan sharpened images for the urban test sites. Similar to the rural test sites, the proposed CIELab method provided the highest CC and Zhou values alongside of lowest SRMSE and SP ERGAS values for urban images, which demonstrated the high spatial quality. In particular, there is great gap between the numeric results of SRMSE and SP ERGAS indexes presented with CIELab method and other methods. Ehlers, IHS and HCS methods acted as the worst methods in the case of spatial indexes, which is consistent with the visual results. Consequently, the proposed CIELab method provided the best performance for the urban test sites (frames F2, F4 and F9) as well, based on the visual interpretation and spectral/spatial quality metrics.

4.5. Experimental Results from Suburban Areas

Figures A8–A10 present the representative portions of the original images and Pan sharpening results of the suburban test sites from F3, F7 and F8 frames respectively.

Similar to the urban and rural areas, visual comparison of original MS and Pan sharpened images of this category revealed that all the Pan sharpened images produced higher spatial information than original MS image and benefited from Pan image detail level. However, the visual performance of suburban areas was variable, unlike the urban and rural areas. Results from frame F3 (Figure A8) show that all methods had acceptable performance except Ehlers and HIS. Nevertheless, small amount of distortion in vegetation and shadowed areas is apparent in the results of NNDiffuse and HCS methods.

Figure A9 illustrates the effectiveness of the CIELab method in Pan sharpening process. There is an obvious color distortion in all methods except proposed Lab method's result. Parts e, g and i demonstrate similar distortion in the results of Ehlers, GS and HIS methods with a green dominant color distortion, while other three methods, which are presented in parts d, f and h, have purple dominant color distortion. These color distortions are apparent for all surface types including roads, rooves and other objects. The CIELab was the only method that provided acceptable performance for this test frame. Ehlers and IHS methods could not provide good performance for the last test frame, as is observable in parts c and g of the Figure A10. Parts d and f prove that the results of the GIHS and HCS are blurred and not acceptable. Green and white tones distortion is obvious in the result of GS (Part e from Figure A10). The CIELab method illustrates the best performance again in this frame. Regardless of the distortion in shadowed areas, NNDiffuse provided most similar results to original MS image after the CIELab results.

Numerical results of spectral quality assessment of Pan sharpened images belonging to suburban areas (frames F3, F7 and F8) are presented in Table A5. Once again, CIELab method provides the highest values for the QAVG, PSNR and SSIM metrics, while it achieves the lowest values for the ERGAS, RASE, RMSE and SAM metrics. The GS method has the second place again, similar to the urban and rural test sites by achieving better numeric values for most of the metrics. Similar to previous test site results, the Ehlers and IHS methods have the worst performance between all tested methods.

Spatial quality assessment of Pan sharpening results for the frames F3, F7 and F8 are presented in Table A6. The proposed CIELab method illustrated an unrivaled performance in the case of the spatial quality metrics. For the CC and Zhou index, the highest correlation values that indicate high spatial quality are provided by the CIELab method. Moreover, the lowest SRMSE and SP ERGAS values achieved by the proposed method are another proof of high spatial quality of this method. Ehlers, HCS and IHS methods present the lowest CC and Zhou values with the highest SRMSE and SP ERGAS values, which indicate the poor spatial performances of these methods, like their spectral performances.

4.6. Thematic Accuracy Evaluation with Spectral Index

The performance of the conventional and proposed Pan sharpening methods were evaluated with several quality indices and visual interpretation in this research. However, the effects of Pan sharpening on the information extraction, process such as image classification, segmentation and index-based analysis is another important concern that requires conservation of spectral properties of the MS image after Pan sharpening. One of the indirect methods frequently used to evaluate the abovementioned situation is to apply the spectral index on the MS and Pan sharpened images, and investigate their consistency. As only visible bands of the images were used in this research, the visible atmospherically resistant index (VARI) proposed by Gitelson et al., 2002 [54] was used for the evaluation as it uses the all visible bands for calculation.

$$VARI = \frac{Green - Red}{Green + Red - Blue}. \qquad (9)$$

The test site F3 was selected for this evaluation, as it is one of the most challenging sites in the dataset due to complex and heterogeneous land cover characteristics. The VARI index was applied on both the MS and CIELab Pan sharpened images, and a binary classification was performed with the use of the same threshold to map the manmade and natural lands in the region. According to results presented in Figure 4, same level of information extraction could be achieved with CIELab Pan sharpened image and it even provided better thematic representation by providing better geometric representations of the objects and less of the salt and pepper effect observed in the vegetated areas located in the north and south parts of the image.

4.7. Overall Comments

When the numerical values from the seven spectral metrics for three different test sites (Tables A1, A3 and A5) were evaluated, the proposed CIELab had a consistent behavior for different metrics and for different land categories, and ranked as the first among all methods. On the other hand, for the other Pan sharpening methods, different metrics provided various accuracies and did not show a consistent manner for different metrics and even, for different images, the same metric. As an example, the GS method generally had the second ranking for the ERGAS metric for different test sites. However, in the case of the RASE metric, the GS method had second ranking just for some images, while the GIHS method took the second rank for the remaining images. This phenomenon is similar for the worse results; there is no one method that can be mentioned as the worst for all test sites and all metrics. All facts about the consistent manner of the proposed method can also be asserted for the spatial metrics. The CIELab method had the best spatial performance for the all ten test sites, while second through seventh rankings were variable across different metrics and different images. As an outcome, it is evident that the proposed method presents the best results considering spectral and spatial quality metrics and visual interpretation for ten different sites having different landscape characteristics. Moreover, it provided efficient spectral conservation performance according to comparative evaluation performed with binary classification of VARI index. An overall ranking is provided in Table 5, according to expert judgement by considering the quantitative, metric-based results and visual interpretation results together for different landscapes across spectral and spatial domains. Lastly, in order to check the consistency of spectral quality indices through each band of the images, these indices were calculated band-by-band for the test site F3 (Table A7). According to this evaluation, the averaged values for each index are in accordance with the band-based calculations and indices, providing consistent characteristics across image bands in most of the cases.

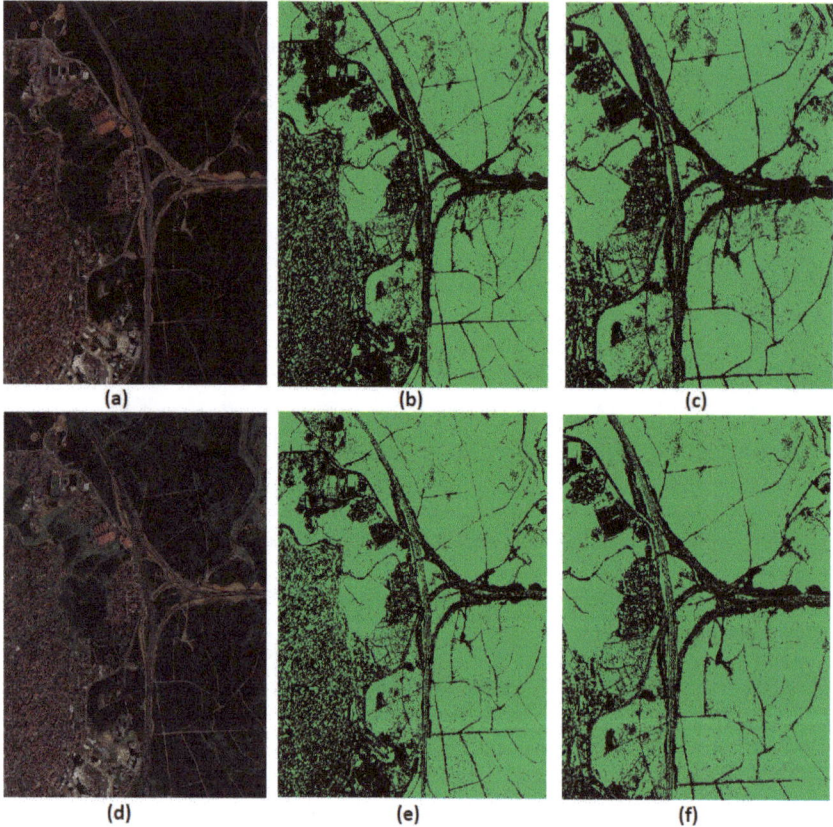

Figure 4. Comparison of visible atmospherically resistant index (VARI) index results extracted from multispectral (MS) and CIELab pansharpened images of test site F3. (**a**) Original MS, (**b**) threshold applied VARI of MS, (**c**) zoomed region from VARI of MS, (**d**) original CIELab, (**e**) threshold applied VARI of CIELab and (**f**) zoomed region from VARI of CIELab.

Table 5. The overall relative ranking of the methods evaluated.

Method	Rural		Urban		Suburban	
	Spectral	Spatial	Spectral	Spatial	Spectral	Spatial
CIELab	Good	Good	Good	Good	Good	Moderate
GIHS	Moderate	Moderate	Moderate	Moderate	Poor	Poor
GS	Good	Good	Moderate	Moderate	Poor	Moderate
HCS	Poor	Moderate	Poor	Poor	Poor	Poor
HIS	Poor	Poor	Poor	Poor	Moderate	Poor
NNDiffuse	Moderate	Moderate	Moderate	Poor	Poor	Moderate
Ehlers	Poor	Poor	Poor	Poor	Moderate	Poor

5. Conclusions

This research proposed an effective, component substitution-based image Pan sharpening method that uses CIELab color space for Pan sharpening of the VHR Pléiades satellite images. Ten test sites with different landscape characteristics were selected to evaluate the performance of the proposed method in conjunction with six common Pan sharpening algorithms; namely, GS, HCS, IHS, EHLERS, NNDiffuse and GIHS. The comparative evaluation results from Pléiades VHR images supports that the proposed CS algorithm is powerful and ensures better performance compared to the other Pan sharpening methods according to the spectral and spatial accuracy assessment procedures and the visual interpretation. In addition, results indicated that proposed method provided comparatively consistent results, while the performance of other methods varyied with respect to land surface characteristics of the region. As an example for RMSE metric, the best values among the all ten sites were obtained for forest and vegetated areas. Pan sharpening in urban areas resulted in coarser metric values, which illustrate the impact of different land characteristics on the performance of Pan sharpening algorithms. Characteristics of unique CIELab color space, led to producing similar brightness characteristics in Pan sharpened images compared to original MS image. The nature of L* component of MS image helps to preserve spectral and spatial information of original MS and Pan images, respectively. Further improvement of the CIELab-based method could be the implementation of this approach for Pan sharpening of satellite images with more than three bands. In addition, further studies are planned to evaluate the performance of CIELab in fusions of satellite images from different sources. Lastly, other accuracy assessment approaches, such as comparisons of classification and segmentation results of Pan sharpened images, could also help future investigations.

Author Contributions: conceptualization, A.R., U.A. and C.G.; methodology, A.R., U.A. and C.G.; formal analysis, A.R.; investigation, A.R.; data curation, A.R.; writing—original draft preparation, A.R., U.A. and C.G.; writing—review and editing, A.R. and U.A.; visualization, A.R.; supervision, U.A. and C.G.; project administration, C.G.

Funding: This research received no external funding.

Acknowledgments: Great appreciation to ITU CSCRS for providing VHR "Pléiades" images. The authors would also like to acknowledge the many useful contributions of Elif Sertel.

Conflicts of Interest: The authors declare no conflict of interest.

Appendix A

Figure A1. Result and comparison of the proposed Pan sharpening method for the F1 (zoomed) area, which is represented in a true color (RGB) combination. (**a**) MS; (**b**) Pan; (**c**) Lab; (**d**) GIHS; (**e**) GS; (**f**) HCS; (**g**) IHS; (**h**) NNDiffuse; (**i**) Ehlers.

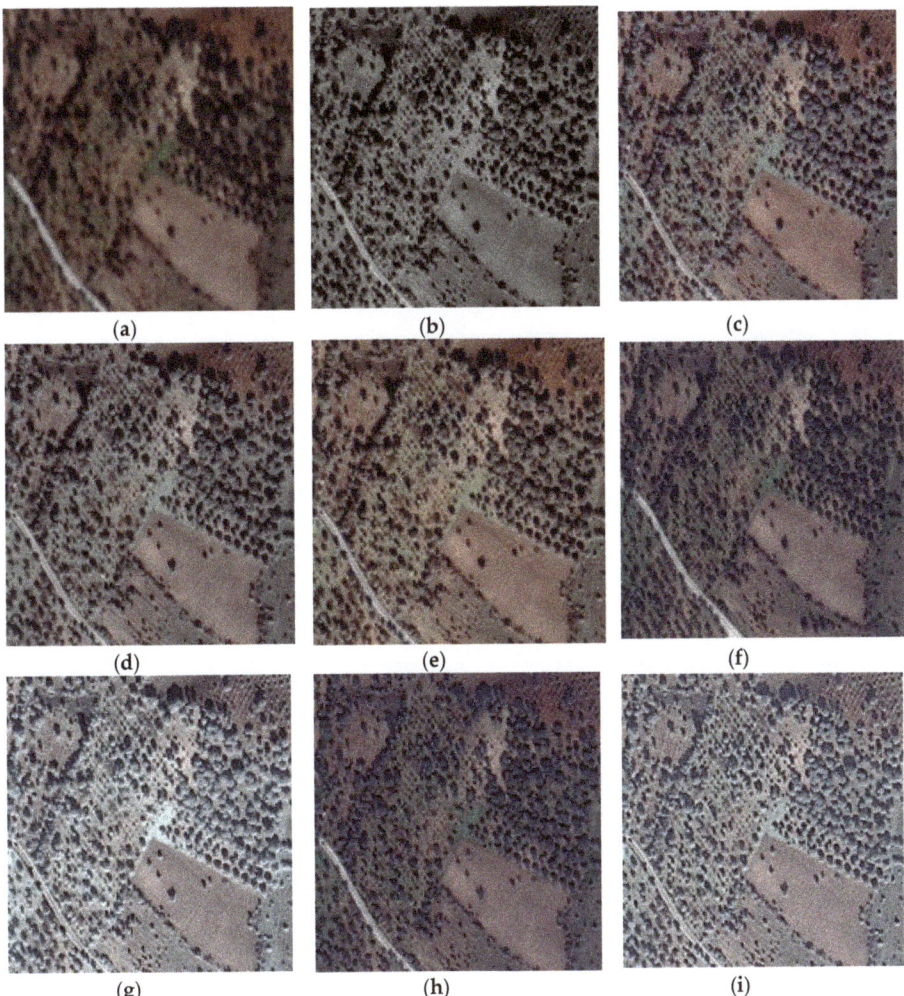

Figure A2. Result and comparison of the proposed Pan sharpening method for the F5 area (zoomed), which is represented in a true color (RGB) combination. (**a**) MS; (**b**) Pan; (**c**) Lab; (**d**) GIHS; (**e**) GS; (**f**) HCS; (**g**) IHS; (**h**) NNDiffuse; (**i**) Ehlers.

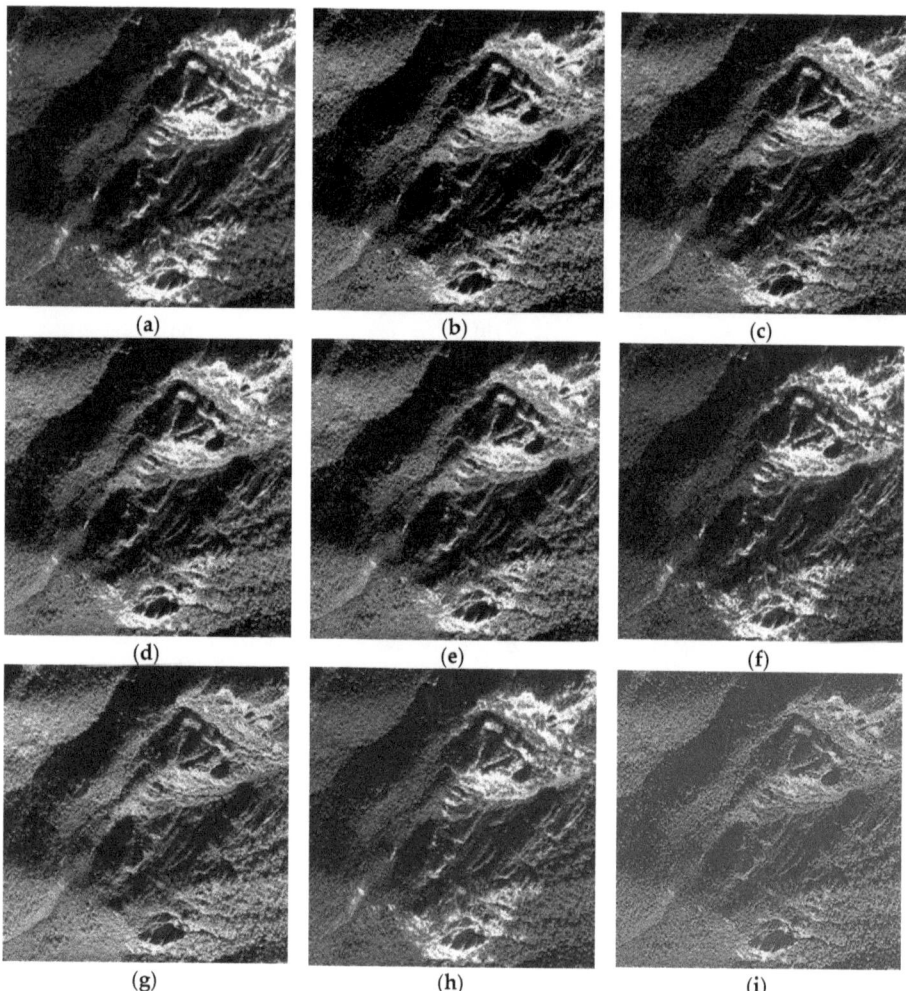

Figure A3. Result and comparison of the proposed Pan sharpening method for the F6 area (zoomed), which is represented in a true color (RGB) combination. (**a**) MS; (**b**) Pan; (**c**) Lab; (**d**) GIHS; (**e**) GS; (**f**) HCS; (**g**) IHS; (**h**) NNDiffuse; (**i**) Ehlers.

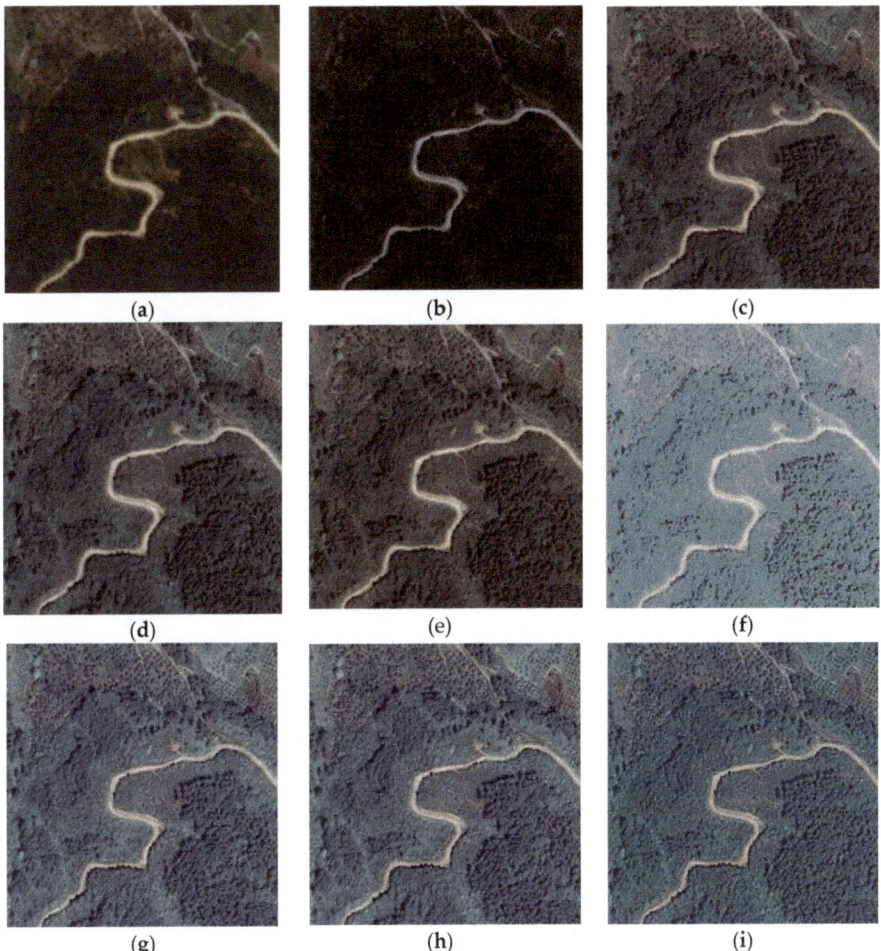

Figure A4. Result and comparison of the proposed Pan sharpening method for the F6 area (zoomed), which is represented in a true color (RGB) combination. (**a**) MS; (**b**) Pan; (**c**) Lab; (**d**) GIHS; (**e**) GS; (**f**) HCS; (**g**) IHS; (**h**) NNDiffuse; (**i**) Ehlers.

Table A1. Numeric results of spectral quality metrics of the Pan-sharpened images produced by selected algorithms for rural test sites (blue: highest accuracy; red: lowest accuracy).

		ERGAS	QAVG	RASE	RMSE	SAM	PSNR	SSIM
F1	Ehlers	8.35973	0.70345	31.03779	0.00169	3.64069	55.45895	0.99423
	GS	3.53280	0.72884	12.85721	0.00070	2.17343	63.81712	0.99854
	GIHS	9.70735	0.68332	54.94083	0.00299	3.71061	50.49886	0.96170
	HCS	3.30104	0.72804	13.12935	0.00071	3.07602	62.93191	0.99913
	IHS	10.74394	0.67747	60.82506	0.00331	3.74898	49.61512	0.95743
	CIELab	2.07704	0.83561	11.24036	0.00061	1.33832	69.28116	1
	NNDiffuse	6.01008	0.68762	29.32491	0.00159	1.68020	55.95203	0.99065
F5	Ehlers	7.62863	0.67932	30.11675	0.00136	2.76553	57.32630	0.99653
	GS	3.43803	0.70832	15.06442	0.00069	1.96874	64.58066	0.99909
	GIHS	4.68240	0.70403	20.21354	0.00091	1.71451	60.78961	0.99738
	HCS	6.04601	0.67023	24.66611	0.00111	1.64450	59.06045	0.98721
	IHS	7.58878	0.66419	32.80574	0.00148	2.31403	56.58346	0.98436
	CIELab	3.1501	0.81033	12.37956	0.00056	1.25643	75.04835	1
	NNDiffuse	6.05444	0.69039	25.02772	0.00117	1.64355	59.53192	0.99658
F6	Ehlers	12.35511	0.68485	44.42476	0.00133	5.60838	57.50393	0.99650
	GS	4.95180	0.73240	18.30183	0.00059	2.46646	66.21170	0.99918
	GIHS	8.96652	0.71253	36.05239	0.00108	3.84187	59.31775	0.99551
	HCS	5.56829	0.71320	22.52386	0.00068	3.70496	63.40357	0.98920
	IHS	12.47236	0.68690	50.19509	0.00151	5.41973	56.44320	0.98278
	CIELab	4.53026	0.83580	16.05962	0.00048	1.86814	66.34172	1
	NNDiffuse	7.74954	0.69166	32.23618	0.00097	2.70472	60.28956	0.99680
F10	Ehlers	9.22107	0.61404	36.48889	0.00316	4.44999	49.99698	0.98567
	GS	4.78197	0.63099	18.07030	0.00157	2.86307	56.10088	0.99517
	GIHS	6.60284	0.62945	32.99550	0.00286	2.41971	50.87109	0.97682
	HCS	9.96965	0.57631	40.17887	0.00348	2.10395	49.16024	0.98781
	IHS	9.49649	0.60973	47.55454	0.00412	3.41879	47.69635	0.96361
	CIELab	4.3611	0.6478	17.14994	0.00149	1.77264	57.55494	1
	NNDiffuse	4.46541	0.63385	17.77395	0.00154	1.50089	56.24451	0.99540

Table A2. Numeric results of spatial quality metrics of the Pan-sharpened images produced by select algorithms for the rural test sites (blue: highest accuracy; red: lowest accuracy).

		CC	Zhou's SP	SRMSE	SP ERGAS
F1	Ehlers	0.876695	0.939608	0.006527	26.540923
	GS	0.970317	0.973490	0.002298	25.222656
	GIHS	0.978149	0.979959	0.005213	25.699874
	HCS	0.939252	0.963691	0.00293	25.531640
	IHS	0.869487	0.929827	0.006592	26.040642
	CIELab	0.982436	0.998617	5.19E-08	17.345011
	NNDiffuse	0.944022	0.967511	0.003237	24.580730
F5	Ehlers	0.926486	0.92948	0.006241	26.658944
	GS	0.989994	0.98932	0.003323	25.503829
	GIHS	0.990875	0.989946	0.004153	25.881689
	HCS	0.869709	0.914225	0.00467	26.457399
	IHS	0.927104	0.989560	0.006261	26.460988
	CIELab	0.996861	0.994414	2.22E-08	4.9495726
	NNDiffuse	0.971652	0.989410	0.004303	25.740781
F6	Ehlers	0.891415	0.929872	0.006123	29.084361
	GS	0.989992	0.989450	0.002473	26.047215
	GIHS	0.989997	0.989974	0.004425	28.173902
	HCS	0.912241	0.972654	0.002903	26.946861
	IHS	0.95928	0.969886	0.006141	29.301514
	CIELab	0.997273	0.996194	3.40E-08	11.968807
	NNDiffuse	0.969999	0.979946	0.003062	27.901263
F10	Ehlers	0.923442	0.919671	0.014214	28.001920
	GS	0.989619	0.989061	0.008828	26.488351
	GIHS	0.971429	0.969959	0.008738	26.263696
	HCS	0.799403	0.694767	0.012855	28.756548
	IHS	0.914264	0.929730	0.014267	27.019798
	CIELab	0.997258	0.996956	2.69E-08	8.0781533
	NNDiffuse	0.929999	0.929405	0.0067663	26.362095

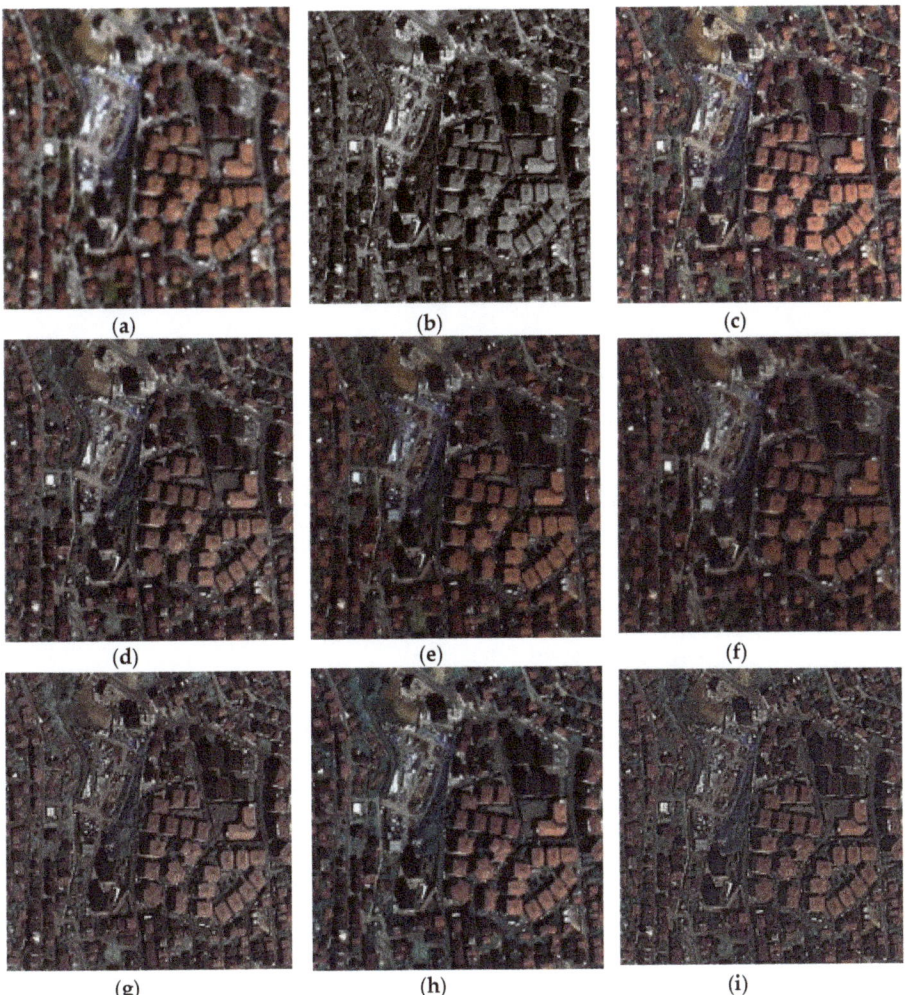

Figure A5. Result and comparison of the proposed Pan sharpening method for the F2 test frame, zoomed areas, which are represented in a true color (RGB) combination. (**a**) MS; (**b**) Pan; (**c**) Lab; (**d**) GIHS; (**e**) GS; (**f**) HCS; (**g**) IHS; (**h**) NNDiffuse; (**i**) Ehlers.

Figure A6. Result and comparison of the proposed Pan sharpening method for the F4 test frame, zoomed areas, which are represented in a true color (RGB) combination. (**a**) MS; (**b**) Pan; (**c**) Lab; (**d**) GIHS; (**e**) GS; (**f**) HCS; (**g**) IHS; (**h**) NNDiffuse; (**i**) Ehlers.

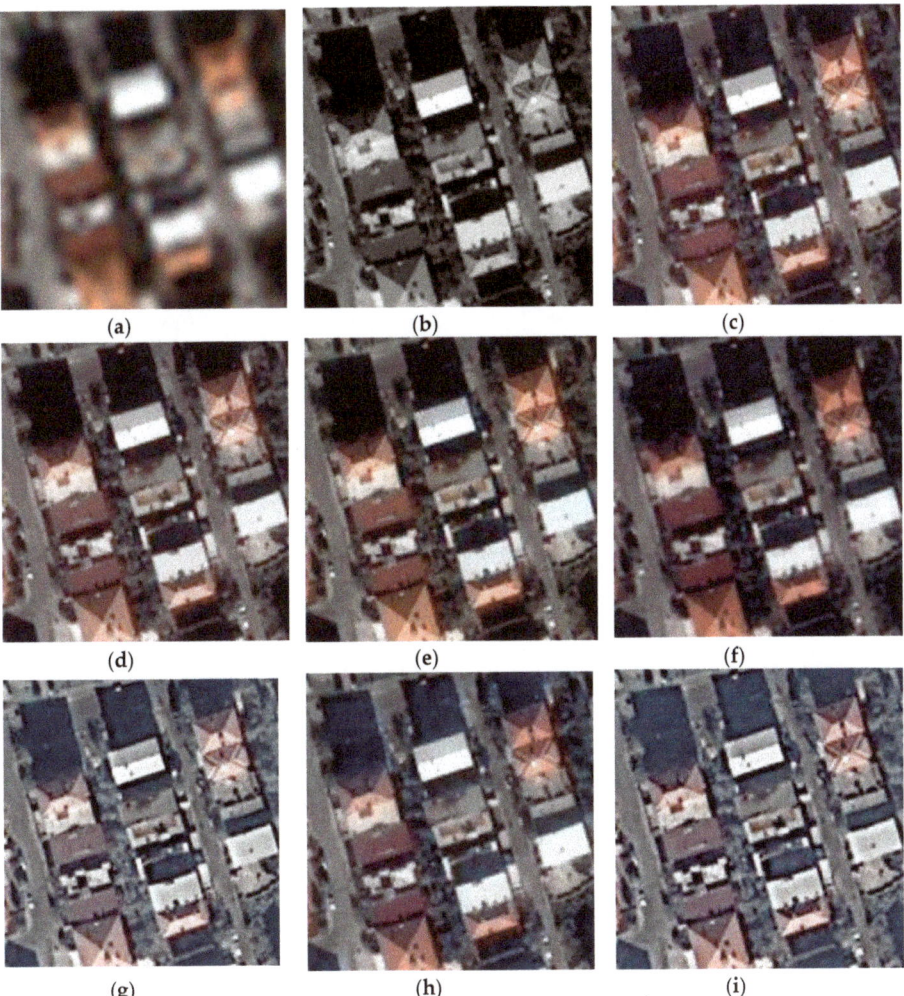

Figure A7. Result and comparison of the proposed Pan sharpening method for the F9 test frame, zoomed areas, which are represented in a true color (RGB) combination. (**a**) MS; (**b**) Pan; (**c**) Lab; (**d**) GIHS; (**e**) GS; (**f**) HCS; (**g**) IHS; (**h**) NNDiffuse; (**i**) Ehlers.

Table A3. Numeric results of spectral quality metrics of the Pan-sharpened images produced by select algorithms for urban test sites (blue: highest accuracy; red: lowest accuracy).

		ERGAS	QAVG	RASE	RMSE	SAM	PSNR	SSIM
F2	Ehlers	11.86921	0.53991	47.33854	0.00401	4.71053	47.94083	0.97725
	GS	5.23770	0.58263	22.61594	0.00195	2.64855	55.16107	0.99458
	GIHS	7.34063	0.57639	33.87054	0.00287	2.46540	50.84869	0.98449
	HCS	15.71881	0.48541	62.43752	0.00529	2.73988	45.53622	0.97461
	IHS	11.04969	0.54971	51.03739	0.00432	3.46087	47.28736	0.95942
	CIELab	4.22351	0.68629	20.75741	0.00176	1.36201	65.10167	1
	NNDiffuse	9.43220	0.56867	49.55085	0.00420	3.40818	47.54411	0.96330
F4	Ehlers	22.84143	0.52356	89.68352	0.00405	7.95294	47.84821	0.95598
	GS	12.57253	0.42386	65.56001	0.00296	6.13381	50.56968	0.96821
	GIHS	15.81385	0.63109	90.10525	0.00407	3.15646	47.80746	0.94837
	HCS	23.98628	0.28239	121.71057	0.00550	8.28181	45.19589	0.93994
	IHS	19.50133	0.38961	111.13086	0.00502	8.99373	45.98577	0.92838
	CIELab	6.86913	0.70144	26.93926	0.00122	1.89738	58.29474	1
	NNDiffuse	19.72400	0.63077	98.22609	0.00441	6.13952	50.53176	0.97519
F9	Ehlers	9.89595	0.51189	39.61836	0.00495	4.27519	46.10242	0.97015
	GS	4.96528	0.55533	18.29249	0.00256	2.20216	51.30320	0.99273
	GIHS	5.40401	0.53562	24.49466	0.00306	1.92496	50.27892	0.98486
	HCS	10.02627	0.47659	39.67119	0.00496	2.02550	46.09085	0.93648
	IHS	9.55051	0.51220	43.30832	0.00541	3.25101	45.32893	0.92951
	CIELab	4.2936	0.6402	17.16686	0.00215	1.12493	54.36654	1
	NNDiffuse	8.25412	0.58294	18.91789	0.01112	1.80691	39.08057	0.94984

Table A4. Numeric results of spatial quality metrics of the Pan-sharpened images produced by select algorithms for urban test sites (blue: highest accuracy; red: lowest accuracy).

		CC	Zhou's SP	SRMSE	SP ERGAS
F2	Ehlers	0.923124	0.939587	0.027718	28.484374
	GS	0.985504	0.968697	0.008643	25.816466
	GIHS	0.986114	0.989954	0.012513	26.611553
	HCS	0.937058	0.949630	0.019802	21.018918
	IHS	0.913914	0.929653	0.027772	27.734556
	CIELab	0.996129	0.995455	7.17E-08	6.2709053
	NNDiffuse	0.960443	0.961942	0.012853	22.490210
F4	Ehlers	0.820014	0.939655	0.017949	31.953533
	GS	0.989999	0.989842	0.009369	26.949381
	GIHS	0.992001	0.989953	0.012168	28.452035
	HCS	0.775576	0.688826	0.018171	33.941348
	IHS	0.919941	0.989666	0.018000	31.259808
	CIELab	0.997280	0.996187	5.44E-08	5.8158174
	NNDiffuse	0.914590	0.888001	0.012253	27.737860
F9	Ehlers	0.924923	0.949622	0.024424	28.179705
	GS	0.989237	0.982593	0.014115	26.132656
	GIHS	0.978923	0.989960	0.015724	26.434713
	HCS	0.860205	0.794738	0.023803	28.880067
	IHS	0.912546	0.969662	0.024479	27.533331
	CIELab	0.99848	0.998002	5.26E-08	4.4340045
	NNDiffuse	0.929067	0.958606	0.021917	25.926934

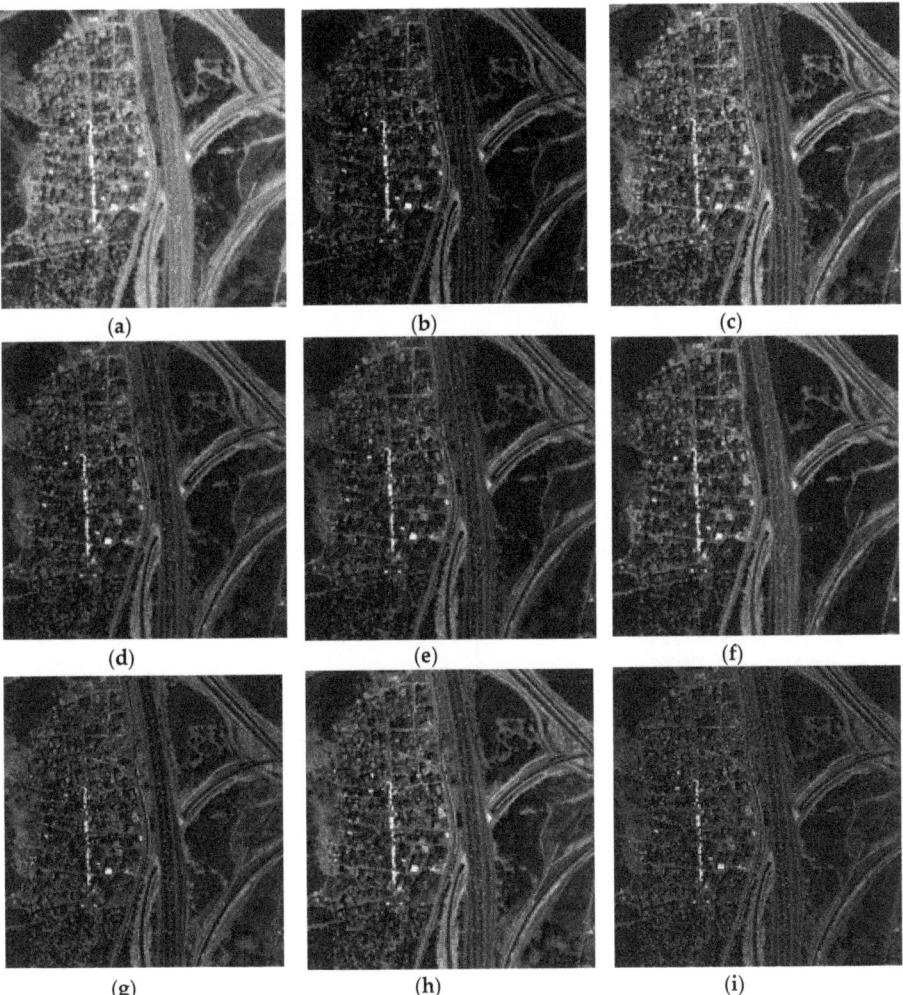

Figure A8. Result and comparison of the proposed Pan sharpening method for the F3 test frame, zoomed areas, which are represented in a true color (RGB) combination. (**a**) MS; (**b**) Pan; (**c**) Lab; (**d**) GIHS; (**e**) GS; (**f**) HCS; (**g**) IHS; (**h**) NNDiffuse; (**i**) Ehlers.

Figure A9. Result and comparison of the proposed Pan sharpening method for the F7 test frame, zoomed areas, which are represented in a true color (RGB) combination. (**a**) MS; (**b**) Pan; (**c**) Lab; (**d**) GIHS; (**e**) GS; (**f**) HCS; (**g**) IHS; (**h**) NNDiffuse; (**i**) Ehlers.

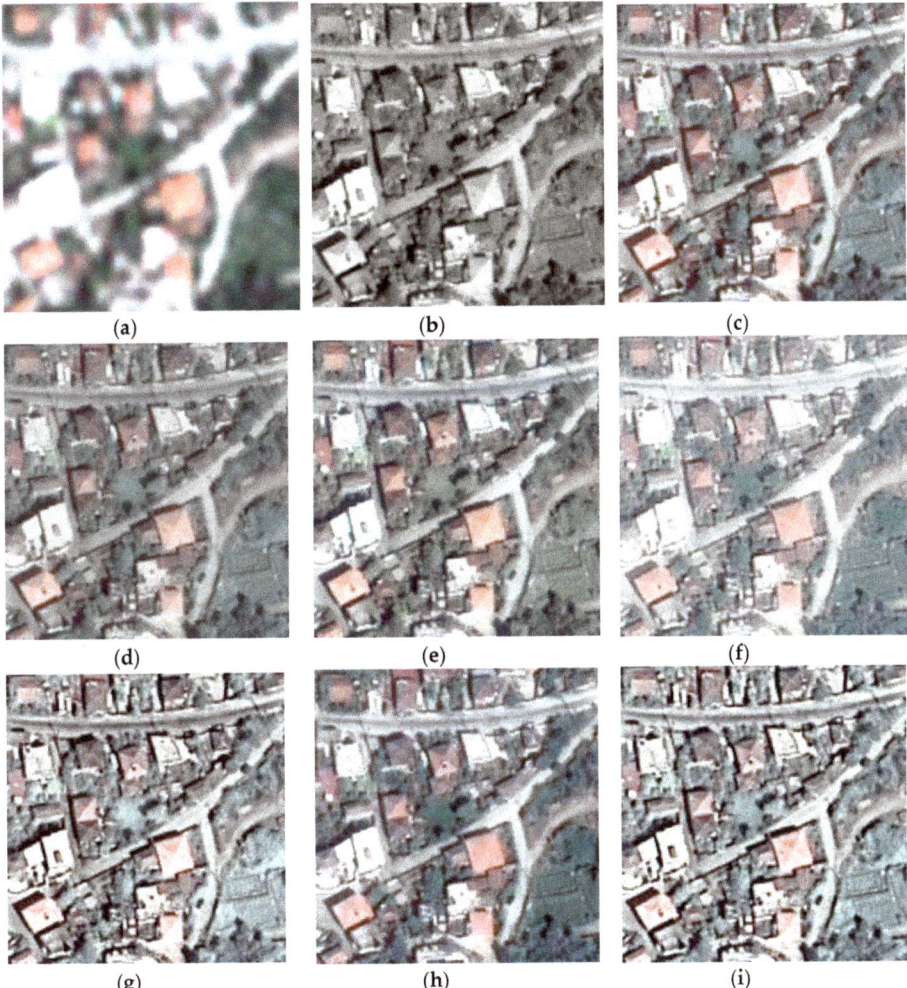

Figure A10. Result and comparison of the proposed Pan sharpening method for the F8 test frame, zoomed areas, which are represented in a true color (RGB) combination. (**a**) MS; (**b**) Pan; (**c**) Lab; (**d**) GIHS; (**e**) GS; (**f**) HCS; (**g**) IHS; (**h**) NNDiffuse; (**i**) Ehlers.

Table A5. Numeric results of spectral quality metrics of the Pan-sharpened images produced by select algorithms for suburban test sites.

		ERGAS	QAVG	RASE	RMSE	SAM	PSNR	SSIM
F3	Ehlers	10.98399	0.63217	43.08140	0.00301	4.48411	50.43809	0.98554
	GS	5.51194	0.66128	23.69334	0.00154	2.84298	56.80727	0.99542
	GIHS	6.97787	0.65746	33.45619	0.00233	2.40080	52.63436	0.98413
	HCS	9.58868	0.62070	38.29194	0.00267	2.67967	51.46174	0.99176
	IHS	10.61170	0.63204	50.97203	0.00356	3.52966	48.97725	0.97134
	CIELab	4.14506	0.77127	20.06662	0.00140	1.84331	67.07440	1
	NNDiffuse	6.93153	0.68589	30.69262	0.00214	2.67079	53.38321	0.99047
F7	Ehlers	9.66602	0.58842	38.60687	0.00252	5.34836	51.98700	0.98848
	GS	4.43979	0.64207	28.36296	0.00183	2.15986	58.92781	0.99695
	GIHS	4.86275	0.61769	19.90348	0.00130	2.39510	57.74171	0.99608
	HCS	6.21293	0.59860	24.68755	0.00161	6.57336	55.87073	0.99479
	IHS	9.99170	0.58440	40.96218	0.00267	5.54742	51.47263	0.98461
	CIELab	3.3780	0.72134	17.43123	0.00114	1.88890	68.89373	1
	NNDiffuse	6.00374	0.60227	28.30174	0.00184	2.87237	54.68403	0.98907
F8	Ehlers	7.61492	0.68151	29.46707	0.00217	3.58878	53.26597	0.99194
	GS	4.02694	0.70121	14.48671	0.00107	2.77359	59.43332	0.99737
	GIHS	5.76109	0.70009	27.24384	0.00201	2.20337	53.94734	0.98655
	HCS	6.82371	0.68186	27.87873	0.00205	1.32168	53.74725	0.99579
	IHS	8.13416	0.68201	38.54293	0.00284	2.97812	50.93381	0.97920
	CIELab	3.5084	0.7133	13.48278	0.00099	1.20401	60.05712	1
	NNDiffuse	5.70992	0.69899	14.95033	0.00110	1.31369	59.15970	0.99740

Table A6. Numeric results of spatial quality metrics of the Pan-sharpened images produced by select algorithms for suburban test sites.

		CC	Zhou's SP	SRMSE	SP ERGAS
F3	Ehlers	0.922299	0.949657	0.012645	28.478359
	GS	0.989999	0.979878	0.007121	26.395064
	GIHS	0.988664	0.989955	0.00808	26.561586
	HCS	0.942661	0.979506	0.01034	26.580025
	IHS	0.920211	0.929723	0.012687	27.542710
	CIELab	0.996151	0.996340	3.22E-08	7.7739934
	NNDiffuse	0.940385	0.972273	0.00683	26.669404
F7	Ehlers	0.940410	0.929782	0.013524	30.304598
	GSc	0.989997	0.989956	0.008056	28.497749
	GIHS	0.973639	0.978996	0.008367	29.121990
	HCS	0.968484	0.962481	0.009486	29.539885
	IHS	0.939801	0.964973	0.013591	30.416119
	CIELab	0.998630	0.996223	1.66E-08	3.1299142
	NNDiffuse	0.996187	0.989929	0.008685	28.273530
F8	Ehlers	0.918887	0.919399	0.009181	26.935703
	GS	0.989998	0.989753	0.005542	25.948199
	GIHS	0.972152	0.989942	0.005759	25.943732
	HCS	0.800374	0.700073	0.006954	27.084421
	IHS	0.921523	0.995543	0.009236	26.447253
	CIELab	0.997412	0.997655	2.26E-08	8.2907935
	NNDiffuse	0.989999	0.969353	0.004198	26.011647

Table A7. Band-by-band calculation results of spectral quality metrics belonging to test site F3.

Method	Band	Ehlers	GC	GIHS	HCS	IHS	CIELab	NNDIF
ERGAS	Band 1	13.23542	6.28494	7.53986	11.51714	14.68644	6.19922	9.43229
	Band 2	10.86379	5.49824	6.73039	10.62880	10.07883	4.07797	7.66444
	Band 3	6.52447	4.08371	4.97720	5.58341	7.75358	2.07075	2.81246
	Average	10.98399	5.51194	6.97787	9.58868	10.6117	4.14506	6.93153
QAVG	Band 1	0.86547	1.02826	0.95928	1.02387	0.87788	1.0607	1.03723
	Band 2	0.57607	0.65720	0.69449	0.52406	0.56826	0.70848	0.60802
	Band 3	0.48901	0.30277	0.36560	0.31617	0.45130	0.54621	0.41064
	Average	0.63217	0.66128	0.65746	0.62070	0.63204	0.77127	0.68589
RASE	Band 1	49.91752	30.04186	39.39898	42.79105	54.69452	25.33830	34.82911
	Band 2	46.79656	22.35778	35.26309	37.59033	52.26805	21.10608	31.65890
	Band 3	34.19874	18.59234	25.44349	36.19742	45.77826	13.75556	25.58183
	Average	43.08140	23.69334	33.45619	38.29194	50.97203	20.06662	30.69262
RMSE	Band 1	0.00833	0.00450	0.00525	0.00625	0.01033	0.00413	0.00525
	Band 2	0.00040	0.00010	0.00186	0.00156	0.00042	0.00008	0.00106
	Band 3	0.00031	0.00002	0.00001	0.00009	0.00001	0.00001	0.00009
	Average	0.00301	0.00154	0.00233	0.00267	0.00356	0.00140	0.00214
SAM	Band 1	4.86237	3.61186	3.40619	3.10669	4.08712	2.22633	3.13166
	Band 2	4.42003	2.42682	2.50814	2.87424	3.16997	1.82082	2.55769
	Band 3	3.95193	2.35714	1.78239	2.20364	3.05983	1.53200	2.21219
	Average	4.48411	2.84298	2.4008	2.67967	3.52966	1.84331	2.67079
PSNR	Band 1	56.42695	60.52591	54.16646	54.15527	51.81649	69.90153	57.27461
	Band 2	48.08904	59.45342	51.82179	51.08538	47.59585	67.71639	57.20947
	Band 3	47.47481	50.38406	50.63450	49.28219	46.97046	65.36066	45.98168
	Average	50.43809	56.80727	52.63436	51.46174	48.97725	67.07440	53.383210
SSIM	Band 1	0.99888	0.99702	0.99417	0.99251	0.98071	1	0.99051
	Band 2	0.98443	0.99539	0.98407	0.99175	0.97231	1	0.99048
	Band 3	0.97331	0.99385	0.97415	0.99108	0.96142	0.9999	0.99042
	Average	0.98554	0.99542	0.98413	0.99176	0.97134	1	0.99047

List A1. Definition of Terms in Table 2

RMSE: MN is the image size, PS(i,j) and MS(i,j) represent pixel digital number (DN) at (i,j)'th position of Pan-sharpened and MS image.

ERGAS: $\frac{dh}{dl}$ represents the ratio between the pixel size of high resolution and low resolution images; e.g., $\frac{1}{4}$ for Pléiades data, and n number of bands. The RMSE represents root mean square error of band i.

SAM: The spectral vector $V = \{V_1, V_2, \ldots, V_n\}$ stands for reference MS image pixels and $\hat{V} = \{\hat{V}_1, \hat{V}_2, \ldots, \hat{V}_n\}$ stands for Pan-sharpened image pixels rep reference and both have L components.

RASE: The μ represnts the mean of bth band; b is the number of bands and RMSE represents root mean square error.

PSNR: The L represents the number of gray levels in the image; MN is the image size, $I_r(i,j)$ is pixel value of reference image and $I_p(i,j)$ is the pixel value of Pan-sharpened image. A higher PSNR value indicates more similarity between the reference MS and Pan-sharpened images.

QAVG: The $\bar{x}$ and $\bar{y}$ are the means of reference and Pan-sharpened images, respectively; σ_{xy} is the covariance and σ_x^2 and σ_y^2 are variances. As QI can only be applied to one band, the average value of three or more bands (QAVG) is used for calculating a global spectral quality index for multi-bands images. QI values range between −1 and 1. A higher value indicates more similarity between reference and Pan-sharpened image.

SSIM: The μ stands for mean, σ stands for standard deviation; I_r and I_p represent reference and Pan-sharpened image respectively. The C1 and C2 are two necessary constants to avoid the index from a division by zero. These constants depend on the dynamic range of the pixel values. A higher value of the measured index shows the better quality of Pan-sharpened algorithm.

CC: $C_{r,f}$ is the cross-correlation between reference and fused images, while C_r and C_f are the correlation coefficients belonging to reference and fused images respectively.

SRMSE: Edge magnitude (M) is calculated via spectral distance of horizontal and vertical (M_x and M_y) edge intensities.

Sp-ERGAS: $\frac{dh}{dl}$ represents the ratio between the pixel size of MS and Pan images, and n is the number of bands. Spatial RMSE is represented as below:

$$\text{Spatial RMSE} = \sqrt{\frac{1}{MN}\sum_{i=1}^{M}\sum_{j=1}^{N}(\text{Pan}(i,j) - \text{PS}(i,j))^2}, \quad (A1)$$

where MN is the image size, $\text{PS}(i,j)$ and $\text{Pan}(i,j)$ represents the pixel digital number (DN) at (i,j) 'th position of Pan-sharpened and Pan image.

References

1. Aplin, P.; Atkinson, P.M.; Curran, P.J. Fine spatial resolution satellite sensors for the next decade. *Int. J. Remote Sens.* **1997**, *18*, 3873–3881. [CrossRef]
2. Pohl, C.; van Genderen, J. *Remote Sensing Image Fusion: A Practical Guide*; CRC Press: Boca Raton, FL, USA, 2016; ISBN 9781498730020.
3. Vivone, G.; Alparone, L.; Chanussot, J.; Mura, M.D.; Garzelli, A.; Member, S.; Licciardi, G.A.; Restaino, R.; Wald, L. A critical comparison among pansharpening algorithms. *IEEE Trans. Geosci. Remote Sens.* **2014**, *53*, 2565–2586. [CrossRef]
4. Thomas, C.; Ranchin, T.; Wald, L.; Chanussot, J. Synthesis of multispectral images to high spatial resolution: A critical review of fusion methods based on remote sensing physics. *IEEE Trans. Geosci. Remote Sens.* **2008**, *46*, 1301–1312. [CrossRef]
5. Aiazzi, B.; Baronti, S.; Selva, M. Improving component substitution pansharpening through multivariate regression of MS+Pan data. *IEEE Trans. Geosci. Remote Sens.* **2007**, *45*, 3230–3239. [CrossRef]
6. Amro, I.; Mateos, J.; Vega, M.; Molina, R.; Katsaggelos, A.K. A survey of classical methods and new trends in pansharpening of multispectral images. *EURASIP J. Adv. Signal Process.* **2011**, *1*, 1–22. [CrossRef]
7. Chien, C.-L.; Tsai, W.-H. Image fusion with no gamut problem by improved nonlinear IHS transforms for remote sensing. *IEEE Trans. Geosci. Remote Sens.* **2014**, *52*, 651–663. [CrossRef]
8. Mohammadzadeh, A.; Tavakoli, A.; Zoej, M.J. V Road extraction based on fuzzy logic and mathematical morphology from pan-sharpened IKONOS images. *Photogramm. Rec.* **2006**, *21*, 44–60. [CrossRef]
9. Souza, C.; Firestone, L.; Silva, L.M.; Roberts, D. Mapping forest degradation in the Eastern Amazon from SPOT 4 through spectral mixture models. *Remote Sens. Environ.* **2003**, *87*, 494–506. [CrossRef]
10. Rahimzadeganasl, A.; Sertel, E. Automatic building detection based on CIE LUV color space using very high resolution pleiades images. In Proceedings of the 25th Signal Processing and Communications Applications Conference (SIU), Antalya, Turkey, 15 May 2017; pp. 6–9.
11. Rahkar Farshi, T.; Demirci, R.; Feizi-Derakhshi, M. Image clustering with optimization algorithms and color space. *Entropy* **2018**, *20*, 296. [CrossRef]
12. Laporterie-Dejean, F.; De Boissezon, H.; Flouzat, G.; Lefevre-Fonollosa, M.J. Thematic and statistical evaluations of five panchromatic/multispectral fusion methods on simulated PLEIADES-HR images. *Inf. Fusion* **2005**, *6*, 193–212. [CrossRef]
13. Pohl, C. Challenges of remote sensing image fusion to optimize earch observation data exploration. *Eur. Sci. J.* **2013**, *4*, 355–365.
14. Zhang, J. Multi-source remote sensing data fusion: Status and trends. *Int. J. Image Data Fusion* **2010**, *1*, 5–24. [CrossRef]
15. Yang, S.; Wang, M.; Jiao, L. Fusion of multispectral and panchromatic images based on support value transform and adaptive principal component analysis. *Inf. Fusion* **2012**, *13*, 177–184. [CrossRef]

16. Chavez, P.S., Jr.; Kwarteng, A.Y. Extracting spectral contrast in Landsat Thematic Mapper image data using selective principal component analysis. *Photogramm. Eng. Remote Sens.* **1989**, *55*, 339–348.
17. Carper, W.J.; Lillesand, T.M.; Kiefer, R.W. The use of intensity-hue-saturation transformations for merging SPOT panchromatic and multispectral image data. *Photogramm. Eng. Remote Sensing* **1990**, *56*, 459–467.
18. Laben, C.; Brower, B. Process for Enhancing the Spatial Resolution of Multispectral Imagery Using Pan-Sharpening. United States Patent US6011875A, 4 January 2000.
19. Aiazzi, B.; Baronti, S.; Selva, M.; Alparone, L. Enhanced gram-schmidt spectral sharpening based on multivariate regression of MS and pan data. In Proceedings of the International Geoscience and Remote Sensing Symposium (IGARSS), Denver, CO, USA, 31 July–4 August 2006; pp. 3806–3809.
20. Choi, J.; Yu, K.; Kim, Y. A new adaptive component-substitution-based satellite image fusion by using partial replacement. *IEEE Trans. Geosci. Remote Sens.* **2011**, *49*, 295–309. [CrossRef]
21. Maurer, T.; Street, N.Y. How to pan-sharpen images using the Gram-Schmidt pan-sharpen method—A recipe. In Proceedings of the ISPRS Hannover Workshop 2013, Hannover, 21–24 May 2013; Volume XL, pp. 21–24.
22. Grochala, A.; Kedzierski, M. A method of panchromatic image modification for satellite imagery data fusion. *Remote Sens.* **2017**, *9*, 639. [CrossRef]
23. Schanda, J. *Colorimetry: Understanding the CIE System*; Wiley-Interscience: Hoboken, NJ, USA, 2007; ISBN 9780470049044.
24. Wirth, M.; Nikitenko, D. The effect of colour space on image sharpening algorithms. In Proceedings of the CRV 2010—7th Canadian Conference on Computer and Robot Vision, Ottawa, ON, Canada, 31 May–2 June 2010; pp. 79–85.
25. Singha, M.; Hemachandran, K. Performance analysis of color spaces in image retrieval. *Assam Univ. J. Sci. Technol.* **2011**, *7*.
26. Ganesan, P.; Rajini, V.; Sathish, B.S.; Shaik, K.B. CIELAB color space based high resolution satellite image segmentation using modified fuzzy c-means clustering. *MAGNT Res. Rep.* **2014**, *2*, 199–210.
27. Bora, D.J.; Gupta, A.K.; Khan, F.A. Comparing the performance of L*A*B* and HSV color spaces with respect to color image segmentation. *Int. J. Emerg. Technol. Adv. Eng.* **2015**, *5*, 192–203.
28. Baisantry, M.; Khare, A. Pan sharpening for hyper spectral imagery using spectral mixing-based color preservation model. *J. Indian Soc. Remote Sens.* **2017**, *45*, 743–748. [CrossRef]
29. Jin, X.; Zhou, D.; Yao, S.; Nie, R.; Yu, C.; Ding, T. Remote sensing image fusion method in CIELab color space using nonsubsampled shearlet transform and pulse coupled neural networks. *J. Appl. Remote Sens.* **2016**, *10*, 025023. [CrossRef]
30. Shettigara, V.K. A generalized component substitution technique for spatial enhancement of multispectral images using a higher resolution data set. *Photogramm. Eng. Remote Sens.* **1992**, *58*, 561–567.
31. Pohl, C.; Van Genderen, J.L. Multisensor image fusion in remote sensing: Concepts, methods and applications. *Int. J. Remote Sens.* **1998**, *19*, 823–854. [CrossRef]
32. Ehlers, M.; Madden, M. FFT-enhanced IHS transform for fusing high-resolution satellite images FFT-enhanced IHS transform method for fusing high-resolution satellite images. *ISPRS J. Photogramm. Remote Sens.* **2007**, *61*, 381–392.
33. Sun, W.; Chen, B.; Messinger, D. Nearest-neighbor diffusion-based pansharpening algorithm for spectral images. *Opt. Eng.* **2014**, *53*, 013107. [CrossRef]
34. Perona, P.; Malik, J. Scale-space and edge detection using anisotropic diffusion. *IEEE Trans. Pattern Anal. Mach. Intell.* **1990**, *12*, 629–639. [CrossRef]
35. Tu, T.; Su, S.; Shyu, H.; Huang, P.S. A new look at IHS-like image fusion methods. *Inf. Fusion* **2001**, *2*, 177–186. [CrossRef]
36. Li, H.; Jing, L.; Tang, Y.; Liu, Q.; Ding, H.; Sun, Z.; Chen, Y. Assessment of pan-sharpening methods applied to WorldView-2 image fusion. *Sensors* **2017**, *17*, 89. [CrossRef]
37. Padwick, C.; Scientist, P.; Deskevich, M.; Pacifici, F.; Smallwood, S. WorldView-2 pan-sharpening. *ASPRS 2010* **2010**, *48*, 26–30.
38. León, K.; Mery, D.; Pedreschi, F.; León, J. Color measurement in L∗A∗B∗ units from RGB digital images. *Food Res. Int.* **2006**, *39*, 1084–1091. [CrossRef]
39. Hammond, D.L. Validation of LAB color mode as a nondestructive method to differentiate black ballpoint pen inks. *J. Forensic Sci.* **2007**, *52*, 967–973. [CrossRef] [PubMed]

40. Hubel, D. David Hubel's Eye, Brain, and Vision. Available online: http://hubel.med.harvard.edu/book/b44.htm (accessed on 25 August 2019).
41. Gilchrist, A.; Nobbs, J. Colorimetry, theory. In *Encyclopedia of Spectroscopy and Spectrometry*, 3rd ed.; Lindon, J.C., Tranter, G.E., Koppenaal, D.W., Eds.; Academic Press: Oxford, UK, 2017; pp. 328–333. ISBN 978-0-12-803224-4.
42. Yuan, D.; Elvidge, C.D. Comparison of relative radiometric normalization techniques. *ISPRS J. Photogramm. Remote Sens.* **1996**, *51*, 117–126. [CrossRef]
43. Dou, W.; Chen, Y. An improved IHS image fusion method. In Proceedings of the The International Archives of the Photogrammetry, Remote Sensing and Spatial Information Sciences, Calgary, AB, Canada, 5–8 August 2008; ISPRS: Hanover, Germany, 2008; Volume XXXVII, pp. 1253–1256.
44. Airbus, Pleiades Products. 2017. Available online: http://www.intelligence-airbusds.com/en/3027-pleiades-50-cmresolution-products (accessed on 5 September 2017).
45. Jagalingam, P.; Vittal, A. A Review of quality metrics for fused image. *Aquat. Procedia* **2015**, *4*, 133–142. [CrossRef]
46. Helmy, A.K.; El-Tawel, G.S. An integrated scheme to improve pan-sharpening visual quality of satellite images. *Egypt. Inform. J.* **2015**, *16*, 121–131. [CrossRef]
47. Naidu, V.P.S. Discrete cosine transform based image fusion techniques. *J. Commun. Navig. Signal Process.* **2012**, *1*, 35–45.
48. Otazu, X.; González-Audícana, M.; Fors, O.; Núñez, J. Introduction of sensor spectral response into image fusion methods. Application to wavelet-based methods. *IEEE Trans. Geosci. Remote Sens.* **2005**, *43*, 2376–2385. [CrossRef]
49. Li, S.; Kwok, J.T.; Wang, Y. Using the discrete wavelet frame transform to merge Landsat TM and SPOT panchromatic images. *Inf. Fusion* **2002**, *3*, 17–23. [CrossRef]
50. Zhou, J.; Civco, D.L.; Silander, J.A. A wavelet transform method to merge Landsat TM and SPOT panchromatic data. *Int. J. Remote Sens.* **1998**, *19*, 743–757. [CrossRef]
51. Ashraf, S.; Brabyn, L.; Hicks, B.J. Image data fusion for the remote sensing of freshwater environments. *Appl. Geogr.* **2012**, *32*, 619–628. [CrossRef]
52. Gonzalo-Martin, C.; Lillo, M. Balancing the spatial and spectral quality of satellite fused images through a search algorithm. *InTechOpen* **2011**. [CrossRef]
53. Wald, L. *Definitions and Architectures: Fusion of Images of Different Spatial Resolutions*; Les Presses de l'Ecole des Mines: Paris, France, 2002.
54. Gitelson, A.A.; Stark, R.; Grits, U.; Rundquist, D.; Kaufman, Y.; Derry, D. Vegetation and soil lines in visible spectral space: A concept and technique for remote estimation of vegetation fraction. *Int. J. Remote Sens.* **2002**, *23*, 2537–2562. [CrossRef]

© 2019 by the authors. Licensee MDPI, Basel, Switzerland. This article is an open access article distributed under the terms and conditions of the Creative Commons Attribution (CC BY) license (http://creativecommons.org/licenses/by/4.0/).

Article

The Classification of Inertinite Macerals in Coal Based on the Multifractal Spectrum Method

Man Liu [1], Peizhen Wang [1,2,*], Simin Chen [1] and Dailin Zhang [3]

1 School of Electrical and Information Engineering, Anhui University of Technology, Ma'anshan 243002, China; lmdyne@163.com (M.L.); csmydd@163.com (S.C.)
2 Key Laboratory of Metallurgical Emission Reduction & Resources Recycling, Ministry of Education, Anhui University of Technology, Ma'anshan 243002, China
3 Anhui Key Laboratory of Clean Conversion and Utilization, Anhui University of Technology, Ma'anshan 243002, China; agdzdl@ahut.edu.cn
* Correspondence: pzhwang@ahut.edu.cn

Received: 12 November 2019; Accepted: 8 December 2019; Published: 14 December 2019

Abstract: Considering the heterogeneous nature and non-stationary property of inertinite components, we propose a texture description method with a set of multifractal descriptors to identify different macerals with few but effective features. This method is based on the multifractal spectrum calculated from the method of multifractal detrended fluctuation analysis (MF-DFA). Additionally, microscopic images of inertinite macerals were analyzed, which were verified to possess the property of multifractal. Simultaneously, we made an attempt to assess the influences of noise and blur on multifractal descriptors; the multifractal analysis was proven to be robust and immune to image quality. Finally, a classification model with a support vector machine (SVM) was built to distinguish different inertinite macerals from microscopic images of coal. The performance evaluation proves that the proposed descriptors based on multifractal spectrum can be successfully applied in the classification of inertinite macerals. The average classification precision can reach 95.33%, higher than that of description method with gray level co-occurrence matrix (GLCM; about 7.99%).

Keywords: coal; inertinite macerals; classification; multifractal analysis; support vector machine

1. Introduction

Macerals of coking coal closely relate to its characteristics, such as coke ability, caking ability, and thermal crushing performance, which directly influence the optical texture component distribution and quality of the coke [1–3]. Automatic classification and identification of different macerals in coal are of great significance for the effective evaluation of coal process properties [4]. Inertinite is one of the main groups in coal, and the classification of its macerals is of theoretical significance and application value for the efficient cleaning utilization of coal.

In view of the computational complexity, and the heavy workload, along with the subjective factors of the conventional manual and semi-manual method for maceral analysis, the methods of image processing and pattern recognition have been employed to analyze the components in coal [5,6]. Besides, based on the advantages of data analysis and processing, the machine learning approach is widely used in various fields [7]. Edward Lester [8] developed an image analysis technique to separate the major maceral groups of liptinite, vitrinite, fusinite, and semi-fusinite from the background resin according to the gray scales of the surface images captured with suitable camera exposure times. Nonetheless, even though the foregoing technique can work in some situations, it has not been implemented for a deep identification of macerals. There exists a fact that the characteristics of shape, color, contour, and texture of the microscopic image are essential for information expression of macerals in coal. Some related references have been published. To name a few, the authors of [9] completed the detection of approximately circular particles in the microscopic image of coal by the contour features, and the authors of [10] proposed a method to extract the outline of the maceral area by using structural elements. The texture features of local binary patterns (LBP) and the gray level co-occurrence matrix (GLCM) were combined to identify three major groups in coal macerals [11]. Grey scale, GLCM, Tamura, contourlet transform, and supervised locality preserving projections methods were employed by the authors in the previous work [12–15] to describe features of macerals. However, because the complex construction of macerals and similar morphological features among some different macerals exist, these techniques may not characterize them perfectly, especially for the features of texture.

In recent years, the fractal theory, first coined in [16], has been rapidly developed as a powerful analytical tool, which can reflect the heterogeneity and irregularities of a physical surface. There are several published techniques for characterizing the surface irregularity of coal with the mono-fractal method [17–21]. Nevertheless, it can not provide a comprehensive and accurate description of the details of image changes at different scales owing to the single scale of fractal dimensions. Coal's surface is known to be non-stationary and heterogeneous as a consequence of the long-term and multi-stage effects of geological processes. Some local trends in texture and dramatic changes in gray value are universal in microscopic images of macerals. Fortunately, a method named multifractal detrended fluctuation analysis (MF-DFA) can quickly eliminate local trends [22], making itself more suitable for describing the texture characteristics of the microscopic images of macerals. Given the superiority in solving non-stationary problems, the MF-DFA method has applications in quite a few fields [23–26]. Nevertheless, it was the first attempt that the approach was applied for the purpose of the classification of macerals in coal.

The major goal of our work was to find an artificial intelligence method to distinguish eight groups of inertinite macerals with few but stable and effective texture features. We analyzed and verified the multifractal properties of inertinite macerals by the method of MF-DFA. Additionally, multifractal descriptors of microscopic images were proposed based on the multifractal spectrum. In order to demonstrate the effectiveness of the multifractal descriptors, a comparison experiment of stability was implemented. Finally, we built an automatic classification model with support vector machine (SVM) to identify the inertinite macerals.

2. Materials

According to International Commission for Coal Petrology (ICCP) standard, coal is classified across three main maceral groups; i.e. vitrinite, liptinite, and inertinite [27]. Macerals of inertinite mainly come from woody fiber of plant or fungus [28]. The plant cellular structure of fusinite is relatively complete, and some of them have clear intercellular space and cellular wall. The cells of the pyrofusinite are crushed and shattered to present the shape of "arc" or "star-like", while the oxyfusinite has an unbroken cellular structure that exhibits a sieve shape. Semifusinite, the transitional maceral between telinite and fusinite, is located in the form of irregular strips. Secretinite is generally a product of silk carbonization reaction of secretions (tannin, resin, etc.), and few of them are derived from gelation of humus coal. Besides, the microscopic images are irregularly elliptical. Funginite is mainly derived from the remains of fungi or the secretions of higher plants, and has a honeycomb-like or reticulated multicellular structure inside. Additionally, the outer shape is flattened circular or ring-shaped due to extrusion. The cellular structure of the macrinite has a high protrusion and is generally an irregular matrix. A fragment of the inertinite group of particles have a particle size of less than 30 μm, angular or irregular in shape, and has no generally cellular structure. Most of the micrinites are distributed in asphaltene or mineral asphaltene with minor particle size and often small, nearly circular particles. Note that for fusinite, the two sub-macerals named pyrofusinite and oxyfusinite will be analyzed together with other six types of macerals in our work, as the texture differences are significant and obvious.

From Figure 1, we can observe that there are some morphological differences among different macerals of inertinite in coal. However, their textures are fairly clear with singularity and conspicuous self-similarity. For such non-stationary structures, MF-DFA analysis can characterize them more effectively and show better processing power. In view of this, this paper performed the method of MF-DFA on each maceral image. For implementation, we used inertinite image data with 60 grayscale microscopic images of 227 × 227 pixels in size per group. The size was chosen to ensure that each image contained only one specific component, which is beneficial for subsequent feature extraction and classification experiments.

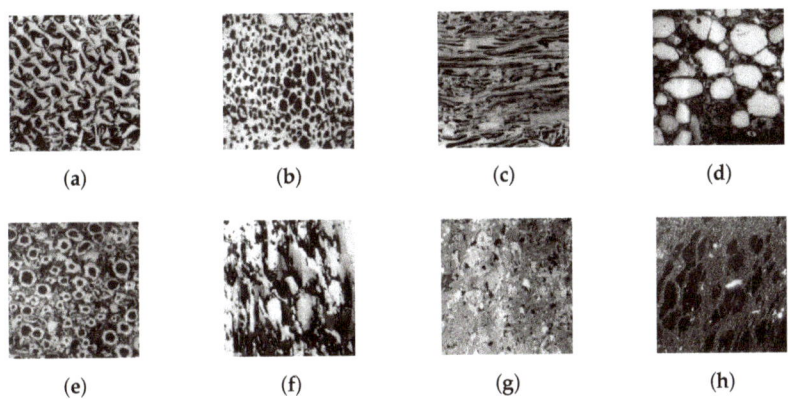

Figure 1. Typical microscopic images of inertinite in coal. (**a**) Pyrofusinite; (**b**) oxyfusinite; (**c**) semifusinit; (**d**) secretinite; (**e**) funginite; (**f**) macrinite; (**g**) inertodetrinite; (**h**) micirinite.

3. Methods

3.1. Multifractal Spectrum Based on MF-DFA

The method of MF-DFA is widely applied in scaling analysis due to its high accuracy and easy implementation. For grayscale images, it is not appropriate to calculate the multifractal spectrum with a gray series by the approach of one-dimensional MF-DFA. Generalizing the one-dimensional method to two-dimensional one can better express the information of the surface with self-similar properties [29]. Specifically, the process of calculating the multifractal spectrum of the grayscale image by using the two-dimensional MF-DFA method is determined as follows.

Step 1. Regard a microscopic image as a self-similar surface with a size of $M \times N$, which is represented by a matrix $X(i,j)$, $i = 1, 2, ..., M$ and $j = 1, 2, ..., N$. Partition the surface into $M_s \times N_s$ ($M_s \equiv [M/s]$, $N_s \equiv [N/s]$) none-overlapping square subdomains of equal length s. Each subdomain is denoted by $X_{m,n} \equiv X_{m,n}(i,j)$ with $X_{m,n}(i,j) = X(r+i, t+j)$ for $1 \leq i, j \leq s$ where $r = (m-1)s$, $t = (n-1)s$.

Step 2. For each subdomain $X_{m,n}$, the cumulative sum is constructed as follows

$$G_{m,n}(i,j) = \sum_{k_1=1}^{i} \sum_{k_2=1}^{j} X_{m,n}(k_1, k_2), \qquad (1)$$

where $1 \leq i, j \leq s$, $m = 1, 2, ..., M_s$, $n = 1, 2, ..., N_s$. Note that $G_{m,n} = G_{m,n}(i,j) (i,j = 1, 2, .., s)$ is a surface.

Step 3. The local trend $\tilde{G}_{m,n}$ for each surface $G_{m,n}$ can be obtained by fitting it with a pre-chosen bivariate polynomial function. In this paper, we adopt the trending function as

$$\tilde{G}_{m,n}(i,j) = ai + bj + c \qquad (2)$$

where a, b, and c are free parameters to be estimated by the least-squares method. We can determine the residual matrix $y_{m,n}(i,j)$ with

$$y_{m,n}(i,j) = G_{m,n}(i,j) - \tilde{G}_{m,n}(i,j). \tag{3}$$

Step 4. The detrended fluctuation $F(m,n,s)$ for each subdomain $X_{m,n}$ can be defined via the variance of $y_{m,n}(i,j)$ as follows

$$F^2(m,n,s) = \frac{1}{s^2} \sum_{i=1}^{s} \sum_{j=1}^{s} y^2_{m,n}(i,j). \tag{4}$$

Step 5. The $q-th$ order fluctuation is obtained by averaging over all the subdomain

$$F_q(s) = \exp\left\{ \frac{1}{M_s N_s} \sum_{m=1}^{M_s} \sum_{n=1}^{N_s} \ln[F(m,n,s)] \right\}, q = 0 \tag{5}$$

$$F_q(s) = [\frac{1}{M_s N_s} \sum_{m=1}^{M_s} \sum_{n=1}^{N_s} [F(m,n,s)]^q]^{1/q}, q \neq 0. \tag{6}$$

Step 6. The scaling relation of the fluctuation can be determined by analyzing the log-log $F_q(s)$ versus the s for different values of s ranging from 6 to $(M,N)/4$, which reads

$$F_q(s) \propto s^{h(q)}. \tag{7}$$

The scaling exponent $h(q)$ can be obtained by the linear regression of $\ln F_q(s)$ to $\ln s$, which is also called the generalized Hurst index. For each q, the corresponding traditional scaling exponent as $\tau(q)$

$$\tau(q) = qh(q) - D_f. \tag{8}$$

Note that, D_f represents the fractal dimension of the geometric support. For the two-dimensional microscopic image of this paper, we take the value of $D_f = 2$.

Step 7. The multifractal surface can be characterized by Hölder exponent $\alpha(q)$ and singularity spectrum $f(\alpha)$, which are given by the Legendre transform [30].

$$\alpha(q) = \tau'(q) = h(q) + qh'(q) \tag{9}$$

$$f(\alpha) = q\alpha(q) - \tau(q) = q[\alpha - h(q)] + 2. \tag{10}$$

Here, the multifractal singularity spectrum $f(\alpha)$ is a continuous exponential spectrum used to characterize multiple fractal sets, which provides a complete statistical description of the internal inconsistencies of fractals.

3.2. Multifractal Analysis and Feature Extraction

We express grayscale images of inertinite macerals as two-dimensional matrices and analyze them in accordance with the multifractal detrended fluctuation analysis introduced previously. It is worth mentioning that in the partitioning process, the upper-right and bottom areas are ignored since the image sizes of M and N are not particular multiples of the small square s. Hence, we can repeat the partitioning process in the other three directions. Taking the typical microscopic images in Figure 1 as examples, we calculate the scaling exponent $h(q)$ with different values of q in the range from -6 to 6; then, the corresponding function $\tau(q)$ can be obtained according to Equation (8). The result $\tau(q)$ is given in Figure 2, and the inset displays the scaling exponent $h(q)$. We can find that the function $\tau(q)$

is nonlinear with respect to q, which indicates that the exponent $\tau(q)$ is dependent on q. Nonlinearity also confirms that the microscopic images of inertinite do possess multifractal nature.

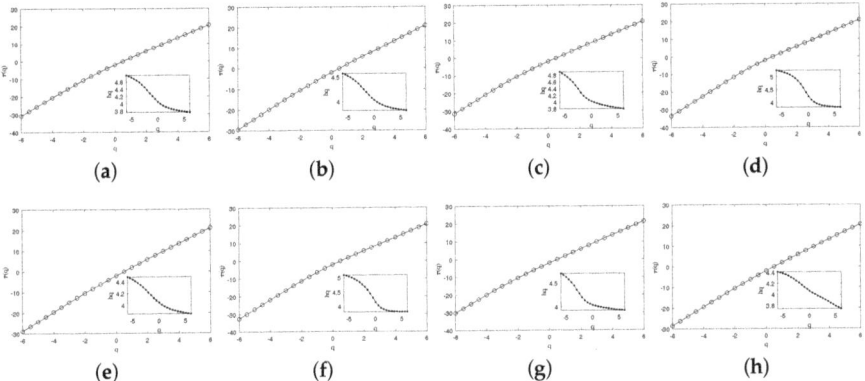

Figure 2. Dependence of $\tau(q)$ and $h(q)$ on q for the typical microscopic images of inertinite macerals. (**a**) Pyrofusinite; (**b**) oxyfusinite; (**c**) semifusinit; (**d**) secretinite; (**e**) funginite; (**f**) macrinite; (**g**) inertodetrinite; (**h**) micirinite.

According to Equations (9) and (10), we calculate the multifractal spectra of the macerals of inertinite, which are displayed in Figure 3. Their graphs are typically barbed, indicating that different parts with different singularities have different fractal dimensions, confirming the multifractal properties of our microscopic images. The multifractal singularity spectrum is a single-peak map normally, and several important multifractal feature parameters can be extracted as the texture descriptors of the corresponding image, such as the minimum value of the local singularity α_{min}, the maximum value of the local singularity α_{max}, and the maximum value of the spectrum f_{max}.

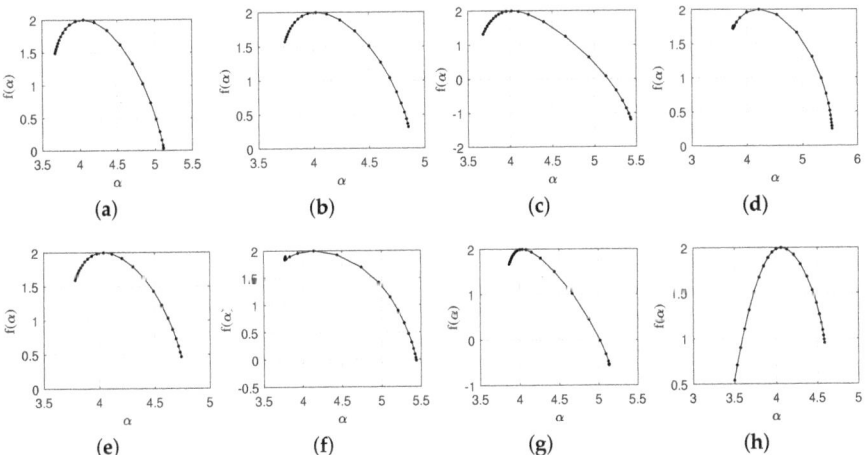

Figure 3. Multifractal spectra of microscopic images of the typical inertinite macerals. (**a**) Pyrofusinite; (**b**) oxyfusinite; (**c**) semifusinite; (**d**) secretinite; (**e**) funginite; (**f**) macrinite; (**g**) inertodetrinite; (**h**) micirinite.

Additionally, the multifractal descriptors of α_{min}, α_{max}, and f_{max} are used to build a three-dimensional space to test the distinguishing ability of each of the two groups. We calculated the multifractal spectra of 480 grayscale images in the inertinite data set, and their corresponding multifractal descriptors are plotted in Figure 4, respectively. We can find that it is not difficult to distinguish different groups due to the fact that the same components are clustered together and different macerals are separated in the space. It is worth mentioning that a small number of combinations of macerals have a certain degree of overlap due to a high similarity between their textures. However, the majority of combinations are separable in our three-dimensional space.

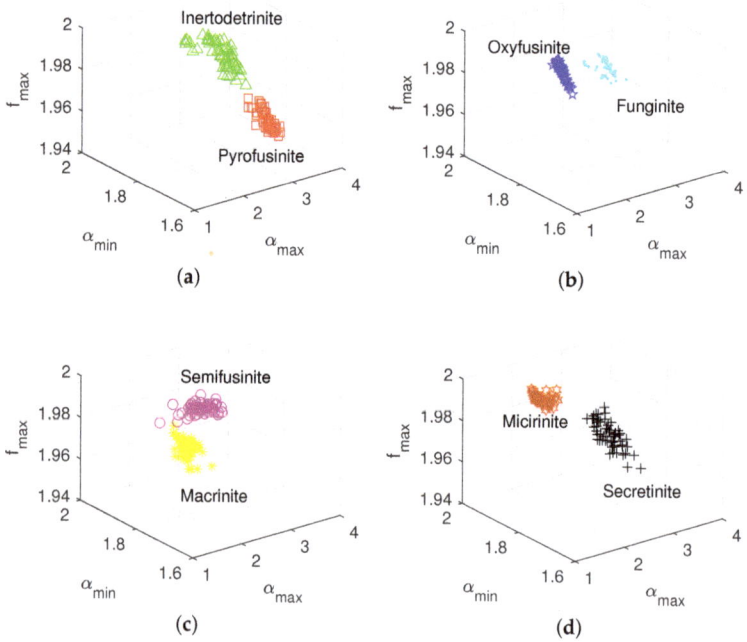

Figure 4. The three-dimensional space with multifractal descriptors for every pair of groups of intertinite macerals. (a) inertodetrinite Vs pyrofusinite; (b) oxyfusinite Vs funginite; (c) semifusinite Vs macrinite; (d) micrinite Vs secretinite.

4. Stability Analysis of Multifractal Feature Descriptors

The feature descriptors (α_{min}, α_{max}, f_{max}) extracted from the multifractal spectrum should be able to characterize the significant textural information of the inertinite macerals. As is well known, effective texture features for image recognition are supposed to be robust and not subject to image quality. In this section, we consider the stability of our multifractal descriptors in terms of noise immunity and anti-blurring ability, and then illustrate the superiority of multifractal descriptors compared to the traditional feature descriptors.

4.1. Stability to Image Noise

Textural features of images can be disturbed by noise to a great extent. In this paper, Gaussian noise, speckle noise, and salt and pepper noise are added to the inertinite microscopic images to investigate the influence of noise on the multifractal spectrum. Figure 5 gives the images of pyrofusinite with the addition of Gaussian noise (0-mean and variance of 0.05), speckle noise (variance of 0.05), and salt and pepper noise (density of 2%), respectively.

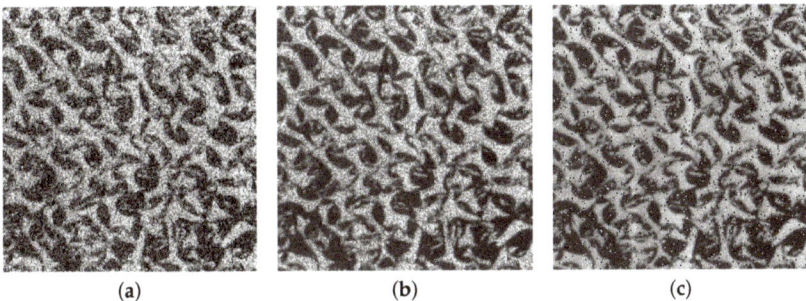

Figure 5. Typical images of pyrofusinite with different noises. (a) Gaussian noise; (b) speckle noise; (c) salt and pepper noise.

The multifractal spectra $f(\alpha)$ of the pyrofusinite images with various noises were calculated and the comparisons with the original image were done. As shown in Figure 6, the spectrum of pyrofusinite image with speckle noise is almost identical to the original one, which illustrates that the speckle noise has a slight influence on pyrofusinite image. In addition, we extract and report the values of multifractal descriptors of eight groups of inertinite macerals with different noises in Table 1. For comparisons, the statistical features, such as angular second moment (ASM), entropy, moment of inertia (IM), and correlation based on GLCM, were calculated and listed in Table 2. From Tables 1 and 2, we can find that the multifractal descriptors are relatively stable, while the GLCM-based texture descriptors are sensitive to noise, and the value of IM fluctuates significantly with different noises.

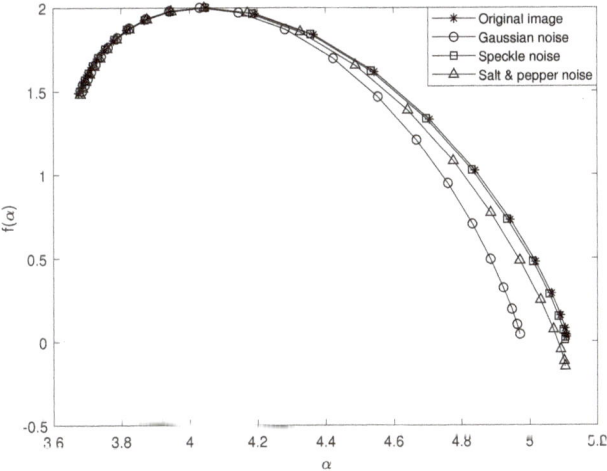

Figure 6. Multifractal spectra of the microscopic images of pyrofusinite with different noises.

Table 1. Multifractal descriptors of typical microscopic images of inertinite with different noises. Sample labels (a)–(h) are consistent with the labels of typical images in Figure 1.

Sample Label	Original Image			Gaussian Noise			Speckle Noise			Salt & Pepper Noise		
	α_{min}	α_{max}	f_{max}	α_{min}	α_{max}	f_{max}	α_{min}	α_{max}	f_{max}	α_{min}	α_{max}	f_{max}
(a)	1.8717	2.4682	1.9974	1.8776	2.3777	1.9978	1.8731	2.4640	1.9975	1.8760	2.4406	1.9976
(b)	1.9019	2.3411	1.9982	1.9066	2.3093	1.9985	1.9101	2.3239	1.9984	1.9060	2.3163	1.9984
(c)	1.8987	2.5650	1.9985	1.8986	2.2927	1.9987	1.8970	2.5879	1.9985	1.9018	2.3932	1.9987
(d)	1.8810	2.7293	1.9946	1.8879	2.4767	1.9959	1.8869	2.7477	1.9948	1.8825	2.5918	1.9953
(e)	1.9213	2.2807	1.9985	1.9221	2.2545	1.9987	1.9211	2.2808	1.9986	1.9240	2.2550	1.9987
(f)	1.8868	2.7113	1.9948	1.8959	2.4883	1.9961	1.8926	2.7285	1.9952	1.8881	2.6409	1.9954
(g)	1.9615	2.4384	1.9992	1.9607	2.2565	1.9993	1.9635	2.4191	1.9992	1.9608	2.3784	1.9993
(h)	1.8924	2.2427	1.9986	1.9075	2.2099	1.9989	1.9003	2.2446	1.9986	1.9023	2.2149	1.9988

To further clarify that our multifractal descriptors of α_{min}, α_{max} and f_{max} possess better anti-noise stability than that of GLCM-based texture parameters, the average relative errors of feature descriptors from typical microscopic images with different noises are calculated and displayed in Figure 7. We can see that three types of noises all have a great influence on GLCM-based texture parameters, especially for the moment of inertia, whose relative error is much higher than 100% for each maceral of inertinite. The parameter of IM of secretinite is highly sensitive to different noise with a relative error close to 400%. Furthermore, the relative errors of the three multifractal texture descriptors are particularly low among the seven parameters, none of which exceeds 15%, and that of f_{max} even closes in on zero. From the results of noise immunity experiment, it is clear that our descriptors of α_{min}, α_{max}, and f_{max} possess great stability to various noises.

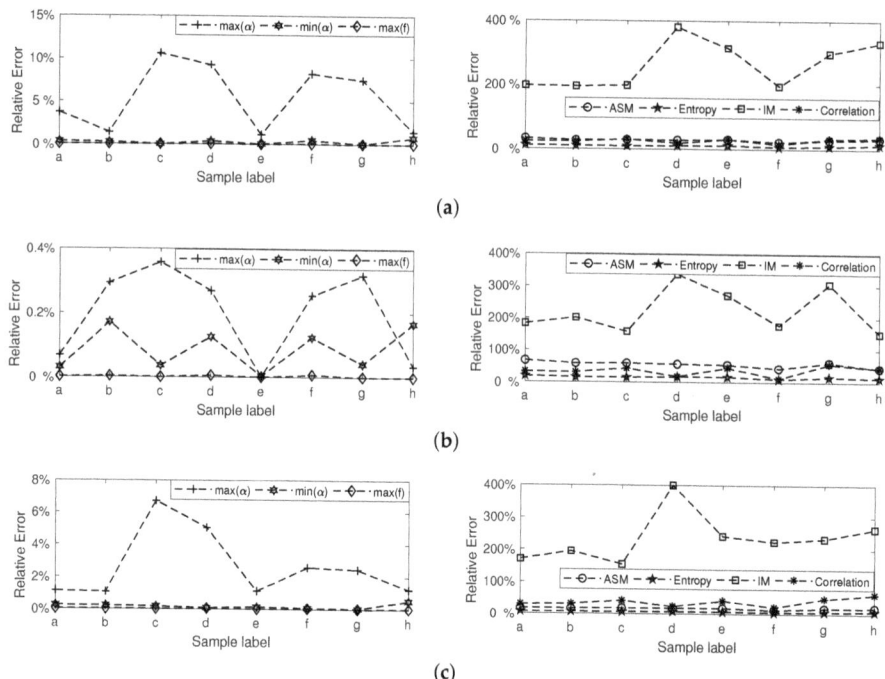

Figure 7. Relative errors of texture descriptors of typical inertinite microscopic images with different noises. (**a**) Gaussian noise; (**b**) speckle noise; (**c**) salt and pepper noise.

Table 2. GLCM-based descriptors of typical microscopic images of inertinite with different noises. Sample labels (a)–(h) are consistent with the labels of typical images in Figure 1.

Sample Label	Original Image				Gaussian Noise				Speckle Noise				Salt & Pepper Noise			
	ASM	Entropy	IM	Correlation	ASM	Entropy	IM	Correlation	ASM	Entropy	IM	Correlation	ASM	Entropy	IM	Correlation
(a)	0.0311	4.1129	3.8208	0.1583	0.0057	5.3468	22.6266	0.0221	0.0103	4.8912	10.8139	0.0393	0.0257	4.4021	10.3217	0.0410
(b)	0.0275	4.1562	3.6523	0.1577	0.0086	5.2229	21.4380	0.0233	0.0115	4.8042	11.0043	0.0399	0.0228	4.4171	10.7620	0.0396
(c)	0.0196	4.3374	4.0526	0.2813	0.0051	5.3947	24.1092	0.0187	0.0160	4.6026	10.3152	0.0474	0.0080	5.0158	10.4514	0.0462
(d)	0.0280	4.0889	1.8521	0.0467	0.0082	5.2103	19.4783	0.0245	0.0121	4.7789	8.0808	0.0382	0.0231	4.3789	9.2544	0.0356
(e)	0.0212	4.1389	2.6026	0.0895	0.0050	5.3962	23.1238	0.0203	0.0097	4.8445	9.6475	0.0490	0.0175	4.4307	8.9111	0.0523
(f)	0.0239	4.3333	3.2983	0.0395	0.0105	5.1325	19.5031	0.0240	0.0135	4.7792	9.1217	0.0348	0.0209	4.5520	10.7023	0.0313
(g)	0.0212	4.2299	2.7384	0.1043	0.0059	5.3177	23.1227	0.0186	0.0082	4.9513	11.1185	0.0449	0.0175	4.4992	9.1495	0.0538
(h)	0.0327	3.8546	2.4882	0.1421	0.0066	5.2311	23.1091	0.0153	0.0181	4.3865	6.2596	0.0786	0.0267	4.1566	9.0840	0.5460

4.2. Stability to Image Blurring

Due to the limitations of objective conditions and the interference from human factors, some inevitable phenomena may occur in the process of microscopic image acquisition, such as motion blur caused by lens jitter and defocusing blur caused by inaccurate focusing, while stable texture parameters should have good immunity to these kinds of fuzzy degradation [31].

Taking the image of pyrofusinite as an example, motion blur and defocusing blur degradation are processed as shown in Figure 8. We plot their multifractal spectra in Figure 9 and compare the spectra with the original one. As can be seen from the multifractal spectra, after image blurring, the value of f_{max} fluctuates slightly between 2 and 2.05, indicating the extracted texture parameter f_{max} is not sensitive to blurring.

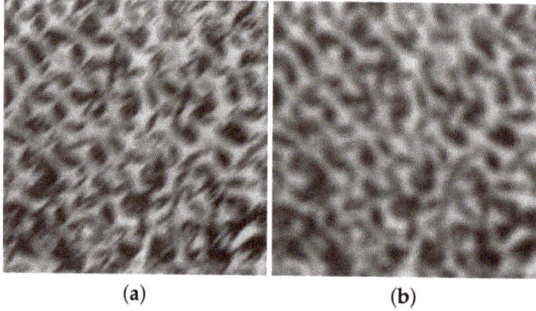

Figure 8. Typical images of pyrofusinite with different blurred processing methods. (**a**) Motion blurred image; (**b**) defocus blurred image.

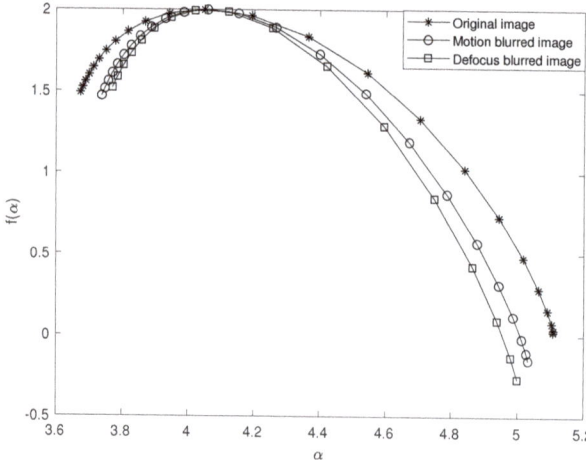

Figure 9. Multifractal spectra of the microscopic images of pyrofusinite with different blurring.

In order to demonstrate the robustness of the multifractal descriptors to image blurring more convincingly, we perform motion blur and defocus blur on all microscopic images labeled (a)–(h) form Figure 1. Then the parameters of α_{min}, α_{max}, and f_{max} are calculated; besides, the GLCM-based texture features are also calculated for comparison. Figure 10 shows the average error of these texture features. For eight types of inertinite macerals, the relative error of f_{max} is close to 0, α_{min} and α_{max} are between 0% and 15%, which indicates that the multifractal features have excellent robustness and are insensitive to blurring. However, GlCM-based features are susceptible to image blurring. For example, the relative error of the second-order moment of the semifusinite with defocus blurring is even higher than 300%; the parameter of energy is relatively stable in the microscopic images of inertinite macerals, all of which are less than 40%. The above analysis depicts that the three multifractal descriptors possess great stability to different kinds of blurring.

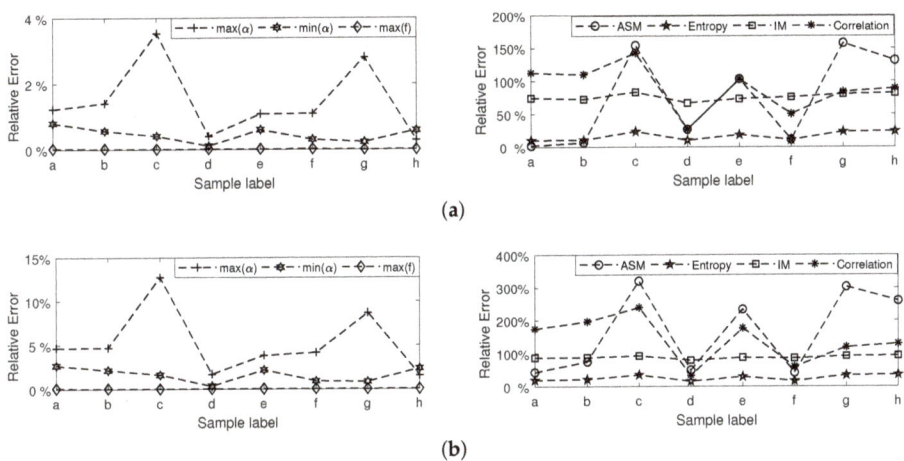

Figure 10. The relative errors of textural descriptors of typical inertinite microscopic images with different blurring types. (**a**) Motion blurred image; (**b**) defocus blurred image.

5. Classification Experiment

5.1. Experiment Design

Considering small samples, SVM is employed to build a classifier for the classification of inertinite macerals [32]. To address the non-linear and the multi-classes problem in this paper, the input data are mapped into high-dimensional space with a non-linear mapping, and the relevant classification function can be expressed as

$$F(x) = \text{sgn}[\sum_{i=1}^{n} a_i y_i K(x_i, x) + b_0], \quad (11)$$

where $a_i, i = 1, ..., n$ are Lagrange multipliers, the class to which a sample is assigned is labeled y_i, and $K(x_i, x)$ represents a kernel function, which is the radial basis function (RBF) kernel function here.

The classification model for inertinite macerals with the SVM-based classifiers is illustrated in Figure 11. To implement the multi-classification, we construct a classifier group with 28 RBF-SVM classifiers to distinguish eight groups of inertinite macerals based on the one-against-one (1A1) technique and optimize the error parameter (usually designated c) and parameter γ in RBF kernel function by a grid search [33,34]. Besides, 40 of the microscopic samples per group are used for training, and the remaining 20 samples for testing and each classifier is used to distinguish two different classes of inertinite macerals. Then, the remaining testing samples per group are input into the trained classifiers. The specific testing process is as follows.

Step 1. Calculate the texture descriptors of α_{min}, α_{max} and f_{max} for each image in the testing set.
Step 2. Input the texture data obtained in the previous step into the classifier group in turn.
Step 3. Count the votes in eight groups; the testing image is classified into the group with the best poll numbers.

Step 4. Repeat the above steps for the remaining images, and finally, get the category for each training images.

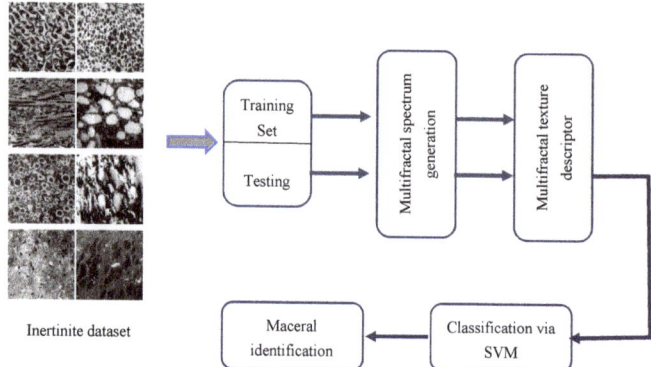

Figure 11. Classification model for inertinite macerals with the SVM-based classifiers.

5.2. Evaluation Measures

The results of the automatic classification method are quantitatively evaluated by ensemble of popular measures. The measures used in our work comprise precision, recall, and F-measure.

The class agreement of the predicted labels with the positive labels given by the classifier is estimated by precision, and the validity of the positive label recognition is measured by recall. The F-measure is defined as a scaled harmonic mean of precision and recall.

$$\text{precision}_i = \frac{tp_i}{tp_i + fp_i} \quad (12)$$

$$\text{recall}_i = \frac{tp_i}{tp_i + fn_i} \quad (13)$$

$$\text{F-measure}_i = \frac{2 * \text{precision}_i * \text{recall}_i}{\text{precision}_i + \text{recall}_i}, \quad (14)$$

where tp_i, fp_i, tn_i, and fn_i denote the values of true positives, false positives, true negatives, and false negatives for class i, respectively. Using the above measurements, the performance of proposed classification model can be conducted for comparison purposes. Additionally, for the purpose of comprehensively evaluating the average performance of eight groups of inertinite macerals, we consider the average values of precision (macro-precision), the average values of recall (macro-recall), and macro-F, which is a scaled harmonic mean of macro-precision and macro-recall.

5.3. Experimental Results

Based on the classification model, each RBF-SVM classifier is trained with the training samples to get specific values of parameters c and γ, as summarized in Table 3. For the testing samples, the previous evaluation performance of classifying inertinite macerals using multifractal descriptors is reported in Table 4. For each maceral, the classification result has achieved satisfactory performance in terms of precision, recall, and F-measure. We notice that the precision performances of oxyfusinite, secretinite, and funginite are slightly lower than those of the best performances of about 0.1304, 0.9520, and 0.1000, which may be due to their fractal similarity corresponding to the distribution of multifractal spectra, as shown in Figure 3. Remarkably, the result for macrinite presents the most appealing performance with three full marks. This may be attributed to the fact that the MF-DFA method can effectively eliminate the local trends of non-stationary images and detect their multifractal features more accurately. These data from the evaluation matrices indicate that our multifractal features are effective in representing texture information of microscopic images of inertinite macerals.

Table 3. Objects and parameters of different classifiers. (**a**) Pyrofusinite; (**b**) oxyfusinite; (**c**) semifusinite; (**d**) secretinite; (**e**) funginite; (**f**) macrinitee; (**g**) inertodetrinite; (**h**) micirinite.

Classifier	Objects	c	γ	Classifier	Objects	c	γ
RBF-SVM1	(a) Vs (b)	0.5000	2.0000	RBF-SVM15	(c) Vs (e)	0.0313	0.0313
RBF-SVM2	(a) Vs (c)	0.0313	0.0313	RBF-SVM16	(c) Vs (f)	0.0313	0.0313
RBF-SVM3	(a) Vs (d)	0.2500	32.0000	RBF-SVM17	(c) Vs (g)	0.0313	0.0313
RBF-SVM4	(a) Vs (e)	4.0000	32.0000	RBF-SVM18	(c) Vs (h)	0.0313	0.0313
RBF-SVM5	(a) Vs (f)	16.0000	32.0000	RBF-SVM19	(d) Vs (e)	2.0000	16.0000
RBF-SVM6	(a) Vs (g)	0.0313	2.0000	RBF-SVM20	(d) Vs (f)	0.0313	0.0313
RBF-SVM7	(a) Vs (h)	1.0000	32.0000	RBF-SVM21	(d) Vs (g)	0.0313	0.5000
RBF-SVM8	(b) Vs (c)	0.0313	0.0313	RBF-SVM22	(d) Vs (h)	0.0313	8.0000
RBF-SVM9	(b) Vs (d)	0.0313	0.0313	RBF-SVM23	(e) Vs (f)	0.0313	32.0000
RBF-SVM10	(b) Vs (e)	0.0625	8.0000	RBF-SVM24	(e) Vs (g)	0.0313	0.0313
RBF-SVM11	(b) Vs (f)	0.0313	0.0313	RBF-SVM25	(e) Vs (h)	16.0000	2.0000
RBF-SVM12	(b) Vs (g)	0.0313	1.0000	RBF-SVM26	(f) Vs (g)	0.0313	0.5000
RBF-SVM13	(b) Vs (h)	0.0313	0.2500	RBF-SVM27	(f) Vs (h)	0.0313	32.0000
RBF-SVM14	(c) Vs (d)	0.0313	0.2500	RBF-SVM28	(g) Vs (h)	0.0313	0.0313

As a comparison, the performance evaluation of the classification of GLCM-based descriptors is reported in Table 5. It is not surprising to find that the GLCM-based descriptors always lead to unsatisfactory performance when compared to multifractal descriptors. This may be explained by the fact that the statistical features based on GLCM are not applicable for describing texture images with complex and heterogeneous naturals. Especially for the maceral of inertodetrinite, the three evaluation values are as low as 0.667, 0.5000, and 0.667, nearly half of the corresponding evaluation values of our method, which are far from satisfying our classification purpose. Overall, we give the average performance evaluation in Figure 12. The macro-precision of the GLCM-based descriptors can be improved by means of the proposed multifractal descriptors up to 7.99%. This holds in both micro-recall and macro-F with improvements of 10.00% and 9.02%, respectively. These data present report the effectiveness and feasibleness of our proposed method.

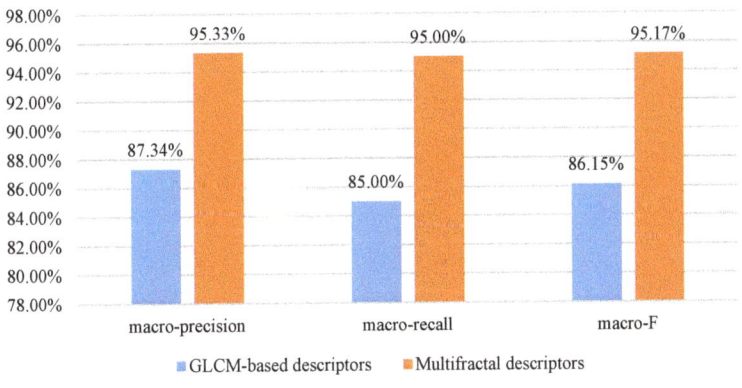

Figure 12. Average performance evaluation of different texture descriptors.

Table 4. Performance of inertinite macerals' classification with multifractal descriptors.

	Pyrofusinite	Oxyfusinite	Semifusinite	Secretinite	Funginite	Macrinite	Inertodetrinite	Micinite
precision	1.0000	0.8696	1.0000	0.9048	0.9000	1.0000	0.9524	1.0000
recall	0.8500	1.0000	0.9500	0.9500	0.9000	1.0000	1.0000	0.9500
F-measure	0.9189	0.9302	0.9744	0.9268	0.9000	1.0000	0.9756	0.9744

Table 5. Performance of inertinite macerals' classification with GLCM-based descriptors.

	Pyrofusinite	Oxyfusinite	Semifusinite	Secretinite	Funginite	Macrinite	Inertodetrinite	Micinite
precision	0.8182	0.9756	0.9231	0.7368	0.7083	0.9756	0.6667	0.9744
recall	0.9000	1.0000	0.9000	0.7000	0.8500	1.0000	0.5000	0.9500
F-measure	0.8182	0.9756	0.9231	0.7368	0.7083	0.9756	0.6667	0.9744

6. Conclusions

Considering the fact that the petrological properties of coal are complex and widely distributed, in this paper, the microscopic images with heterogeneous natural have been analyzed by the MF-DFA method. We verified the multifractal properties of the microscopic image by the function of $\tau(q)$ and $h(q)$. In addition, with the multifractal spectrum, we have proposed three important texture descriptors for characterizing image information, such as α_{min}, α_{max}, and f_{max}. It is well known that the texture descriptor of an image should be robust and immune to image quality; thus, the stability experiments have been implemented and the results have verified the anti-noise ability and anti-blur capability of the multifractal descriptors.

A classification model with RBF-SVM classifier has been built to distinguish the 160 microscopic images of inertinite macerals in coal. Our multifractal descriptors have represented the most appealing results in terms of performance metrics of precision, recall, and F-measure, providing excellent performance compared with GLCM-based texture descriptors. The successful implementation of our proposed method in the identification of inertinite materials can assist petrologists to make correct decisions and reduce the influences of subjective factors in practical scenarios, which is particularly beneficial to geologists with less experience. In view of the fact that there are some similarities of structural complicacy and non-linear multi-classification, we will investigate the classification of other maceral groups with a reference to our proposed method in the future. Simultaneously, in order to be more suitable for industrial applications, we will also develop a cross platform software for maceral image recognition and classification in the future work.

Author Contributions: Conceptualization, P.W. and M.L.; formal analysis, M.L.; investigation, M.L and S.C.; resources, D.Z.; data curation, D.Z.; writing—original draft preparation, M.L.; writing—review and editing, P.W.; supervision, S.C.; project administration, P.W.; funding acquisition, P.W.

Funding: This research was funded by the National Natural Science Foundation of China (number 51574004); Natural Science Foundation of the Higher Education Institutions of Anhui Province, China (number KJ2019A0085); Academic Foundation for Top Talents of the Higher Education Institutions of Anhui Province, China (number 2016041).

Conflicts of Interest: The authors declare no conflict of interest.

References

1. Flores, B.D.; Borrego, A.G.; Diez, M.A.; da Silva, G.L.; Zymla, V.; Vilela, A.C.; Osório, E. How coke optical texture became a relevant tool for understanding coal blending and coke quality. *Fuel Process. Technol.* **2017**, *164*, 13–23. [CrossRef]
2. Piechaczek, M.; Mianowski, A.; Sobolewski, A. Reprint of "The original concept of description of the coke optical texture". *Int. J. Coal Geol.* **2015**, *139*, 184–190. [CrossRef]
3. Chalmers, G.R.; Bustin, R.M. A multidisciplinary approach in determining the maceral (kerogen type) and mineralogical composition of Upper Cretaceous Eagle Ford Formation: Impact on pore development and pore size distribution. *Int. J. Coal Geol.* **2017**, *171*, 93–110. [CrossRef]

4. Yang, J.; Stansberry, P.G.; Zondlo, J.W.; Stiller, A.H. Characteristics and carbonization behaviors of coal extracts. *Fuel Process. Technol.* **2002**, *79*, 207–215. [CrossRef]
5. Wang, H.; Lei, M.; Chen, Y.; Li, M.; Zou, L. Intelligent identification of maceral components of coal based on image segmentation and classification. *Appl. Sci.* **2019**, *9*, 3245. [CrossRef]
6. Mlynarczuk, M.; Skiba, M. The application of artificial intelligence for the identification of the maceral groups and mineral components of coal. *Comput. Geosci.* **2017**, *103*, 133–141. [CrossRef]
7. D'Angelo, G.; Palmieri, F.; Rampone, S. Detecting unfair recommendations in trust-based pervasive environments. *Inf. Sci.* **2019**, *486*, 31–51. [CrossRef]
8. Lester, E.; Watts, D.; Cloke, M. A novel automated image analysis method for maceral analysis. *Fuel* **2002**, *81*, 2209–2217. [CrossRef]
9. Ruan, X.D.; ZHAO, W.F. Recognizing of overlapped coal particles in microscope images. *J. China Coal Soc.* **2005**, *30*, 769–771.
10. Wang, P.Z.; Ding, H.T.; Liu, C.L. Coal microscope image contour extraction algorithm based on structuring elements. *J. China Coal Soc.* **2014**, *39*, 285–288. [CrossRef]
11. Wang, S.; Zhu, X.K.; Lyu, Q. Coal rock macerals recognition based on RILBP-GLCM algorithm. *J. China Coal Soc.* **2017**, *36*, 142–144.
12. Wang, P.Z.; Yin, Z.H.; Wang, G. A classification method of vitrinite for coal macerals based on the PCA and RBF-SVM. *J. China Coal Soc.* **2017**, *42*, 977–984.
13. Wang, P.Z.; Reng, J.; Du, C.L. Classification of macerals in exinite of coal based on Tamura features. *J. Anhui Univ. Technol. (Nat. Sci. Ed.)* **2018**, *35*, 131–136.
14. Wang, P.Z.; Liu, J.M.; Wang, W.Y. Classification of macerals in exinite of coal based on contourlet transform. *J. China Coal Soc.* **2018**, *43*, 641–645.
15. Wang, P.Z.; Wang, H.; Liu, M. A PCA-SLPP dimensionality reduction method based on manifold learning. *J. Anhui Univ. Technol. (Nat. Sci. Ed.)* **2018**, *35*, 352–359.
16. Mandelbrot, B. How long is the coast of Britain? Statistical self-similarity and fractional dimension. *Science* **1967**, *156*, 636–638. [CrossRef] [PubMed]
17. Mahamud, M.; Óscar, L.; Pis, J.J.; Pajares, J.A. Textural characterization of coals using fractal analysis. *Fuel Process. Technol.* **2003**, *86*, 135–149. [CrossRef]
18. Nie, B.; Liu, X.; Yang, L.; Meng, J.; Li, X. Pore structure characterization of different rank coals using gas adsorption and scanning electron microscopy. *Fuel* **2015**, *158*, 908–917. [CrossRef]
19. Liu, X.F.; Nie, B.S. Fractal characteristics of coal samples utilizing image analysis and gas adsorption. *Fuel* **2016**, *182*, 314–322. [CrossRef]
20. Li, Y.Y.; Zhang, S.C.; Xin, Z. Classification and fractal characteristics of coal rock fragments under uniaxial cyclic loading conditions. *Arabian J. Geosci.* **2018**, *11*, 201. [CrossRef]
21. Pandey, R.; Harpalani, S. An imaging and fractal approach towards understanding reservoir scale changes in coal due to bioconversion. *Fuel* **2018**, *230*, 282–297. [CrossRef]
22. Kantelhardt, J.W. Multifractal detrended fluctuation analysis of nonstationary time series. *Phys. A* **2002**, *316*, 87–114. [CrossRef]
23. Zhao, H.; He, S. Analysis of speech signals' characteristics based on MF-DFA with moving overlapping windows. *Phys. A* **2016**, *442*, 343–349. [CrossRef]
24. Rizvi, S.A.R.; Dewandaru, G.; Bacha, O.I.; Masih, M. An analysis of stock market efficiency: Developed vs Islamic stock markets using MF-DFA. *Phys. A* **2014**, *407*, 86–99. [CrossRef]
25. Mensi, W.; Tiwari, A.K.; Yoon, S.M. Global financial crisis and weak-form efficiency of Islamic sectoral stock markets: An MF-DFA analysis. *Phys. A* **2017**, *471*, 135–146. [CrossRef]
26. Mukhopadhyay, S.; Mandal, S.; Das, N.K.; Dey, S.; Mitra, A.; Ghosh, N.; Panigrahi, P.K. Diagnosing heterogeneous dynamics for CT scan images of human brain in wavelet and MFDFA domain. In *Advances in Optical Science and Engineering*; Springer: Berlin, Germany, 2015; pp. 335–340.
27. Sýkorová, I.; Pickel, W.; Christanis, K.; Wolf, M.; Taylor, G.; Flores, D. Classification of huminite—ICCP System 1994. *Int. J. Coal Geol.* **2005**, *62*, 85–106. [CrossRef]
28. Scott, A.C.; Glasspool, I.J. Observations and experiments on the origin and formation of inertinite group macerals. *Int. J. Coal Geol.* **2007**, *70*, 53–66. [CrossRef]
29. Gu, G.F.; Zhou, W.X. Detrended fluctuation analysis for fractals and multifractals in higher dimensions. *Phys. Rev. E Stat. Nonlinear Soft Matter Phys.* **2006**, *74*, 061104. [CrossRef]

30. Meakin, P. *Fractals, Scaling and Growth Far from Equilibrium*; Cambridge University Press: London, UK, 1998; Volume 5.
31. Chen, Y.X.; Wang, J.Z. A region-based fuzzy feature matching approach to content-based image retrieval. *IEEE Trans. Pattern Anal. Mach. Intell.* **2002**, *24*, 1252–1267. [CrossRef]
32. Zhu, X.; Li, N.; Pan, Y. Optimization Performance Comparison of Three Different Group Intelligence Algorithms on a SVM for Hyperspectral Imagery Classification. *Remote Sens.* **2019**, *11*, 734. [CrossRef]
33. Wang, T.Y.; Chiang, H.M. One-against-one fuzzy support vector machine classifier: An approach to text categorization. *Expert Syst. Appl.* **2009**, *36*, 10030–10034. [CrossRef]
34. Kang, S.; Cho, S.; Kang, P. Constructing a multi-class classifier using one-against-one approach with different binary classifiers. *Neurocomputing* **2015**, *149*, 677–682. [CrossRef]

© 2019 by the authors. Licensee MDPI, Basel, Switzerland. This article is an open access article distributed under the terms and conditions of the Creative Commons Attribution (CC BY) license (http://creativecommons.org/licenses/by/4.0/).

Article

Optical Flow-Based Fast Motion Parameters Estimation for Affine Motion Compensation

Antoine Chauvet *, Yoshihiro Sugaya and Tomo Miyazaki and Shinichiro Omachi

Graduate School of Engineering, Tohoku University, Sendai, Miyagi 980-8579, Japan; sugaya@iic.ecei.tohoku.ac.jp (Y.S.); tomo@iic.ecei.tohoku.ac.jp (T.M.); machi@ecei.tohoku.ac.jp (S.O.)
* Correspondence: achauvet@iic.ecei.tohoku.ac.jp

Received: 14 December 2019; Accepted: 18 January 2020; Published: 20 January 2020

Abstract: This study proposes a lightweight solution to estimate affine parameters in affine motion compensation. Most of the current approaches start with an initial approximation based on the standard motion estimation, which only estimates the translation parameters. From there, iterative methods are used to find the best parameters, but they require a significant amount of time. The proposed method aims to speed up the process in two ways, first, skip evaluating affine prediction when it is likely to bring no encoding efficiency benefit, and second, by estimating better initial values for the iteration process. We use the optical flow between the reference picture and the current picture to estimate quickly the best encoding mode and get a better initial estimation. We achieve a reduction in encoding time over the reference of half when compared to the state of the art, with a loss in efficiency below 1%.

Keywords: block-based coding; video coding; H.265/HEVC; affine motion compensation

1. Introduction

High Efficiency Video Coding (HEVC) [1] is a standard of video coding that is used extensively for High Definition content. It has provided very large gains in coding efficiency compared to previous standards like Advanced Video Coding (AVC) [2].

Most of the efficiency in modern video encoding methods comes from exploiting the similarity between the pictures that form the video sequence, also known as frames. Currently, this works by dividing the current picture into blocks of various sizes and giving them a motion vector and one (or two in case of bi-directional prediction) already decoded pictures to use as source data. The error resulting from prediction, also known as residual, has its entropy further reduced using transforms and quantization. Quantization introduces errors, making the step non-reversible, but it allows for a greatly reduced entropy in the result. Various methods are used to code the prediction modes used and the transformed residual coefficients.

This process works very well when the only changes in the picture can be represented by translations. However, for complex movements, it requires approximating a higher order motion with a translation, leading to prediction error. In most cases, the encoder will decide to use smaller prediction blocks to limit the error for each block, as a larger block would have a more inaccurate motion vector. On the other hand, the high order transform can represent accurately the motion even with a large block. So while additional parameters need to be coded, the reduced amount of blocks means that there are less parameters overall that need to be coded, reducing the cost of coding the motion parameters. Furthermore, this prediction can be more accurate than the translation approximation using many small blocks. The potential of higher order motion models for video coding has been known for a long time, and several papers have demonstrated significant gains, such as Reference [3]. Using affine prediction, they showed an improvement of 6.3% coding efficiency on sequences using non-translational motion, further increased to 7.6% when using larger blocks up to 128 × 128. However, when using smaller blocks, such as 16 × 16 like in the previous standard AVC, the gain is reduced to 0.1%. This shows that using large blocks is a critical aspect for higher order motion compensation.

Because affine motion prediction showed very impressive gains on some sequences, it was one of the tools added in the Joint Exploration Model (JEM) [4]. JEM was an experiment to evaluate new proposals for a future encoding standard after HEVC. As affine motion compensation proved it could achieve significant gains, it has been included in the currently being developed future standard Versatile Video Coding (VVC). Several improvements over the original JEM implementation were proposed [5]. While the original implementation supported only a 4-parameter model, it is possible to allow a 6-parameter model as well and let the encoder decide the best model for each block. There are also possible improvements on the entropy coding, based on better motion vector prediction and coding of motion vector differences.

However, this improvement, as most improvements in video encoding, comes with a cost. Most new tools in recent encoding standards work by giving more options to the encoder. For example, allowing larger blocks in HEVC was the source of many improvements in coding efficiency, but this also required much more processing on the encoder side, as to find the best possible block sizes, the encoder needs to try everything. There are 341 possible block partitionings in a given Coding Tree Unit (CTU) [6], and an optimal encoder would need to test all of them to find the most efficient partitioning, which is too demanding for fast encoding, so fast estimation methods are desired. In VVC, the maximum block size is even further increased, increasing even further the amount of possible block partitionings. Higher order motion compensation, like affine motion compensation, is another mode that requires to be evaluated. But the additional encoding time cost is even bigger, as unlike the translation-based motion vectors using two parameters, an affine transform requires six parameters. Classical block-matching approaches do not scale well with more parameters, making them unpractical for this case.

To solve the problem of fast parameter estimation, different methods were designed. In the recent years, the most common implementation for obtaining the parameters is gradient-based. This gradient process is used in many methods, including the affine motion compensation in JEM [7], and methods based on HEVC [8,9]. Typically, the process starts with an initial estimation. The most simple initial estimator is the best translational motion vector, as the motion estimation for translation is performed before the affine motion compensation. If neighbors are available, it is possible to use their affine parameters for the initial estimation. To find a better value, a gradient is computed at the current estimation. The process is repeated either until no improvement is found or a maximum iteration count has been reached. The process is costly as it requires to solve linear equations at each step, but is still much faster than block-matching.

Another method is to reduce the number of parameters of the transform to make the traditional approaches to parameter estimation work in a reasonable time. In Reference [10], the authors have replaced the 4-parameter (also known as zoom&rotation model) transform by two 3-parameter models that can be used depending on the movement. As in most cases, the video is mostly either a rotation or a zoom, it is very common than one of the two parameters is very small or even zero. In those cases, using a model with fewer parameters allows a similar efficiency, and even more in some cases as coding becomes easier. The main drawback is that it requires evaluating the parameters twice. However, this method allows the implementation to use standard block matching techniques that can reuse existing hardware or already implemented methods in software, while solving linear equations in the gradient-based approach requires a completely new implementation. They show a similar time and efficiency compared to Reference [9], but with fewer changes to the existing encoder.

In our proposed method, we decide to use the estimated displacement for each sample in the picture from optical flow to get a faster encoding than the current methods. The displacement can be used to estimate transform parameters for a given affine model. We use this estimation and the variance of the displacements in a given block to decide what transform model is the most appropriate between zooming, rotation and skipping affine mode parameter estimation entirely. This saves encoding time as fewer affine parameter estimations will be performed. In standard encoding, the parameter estimation for the translation is fast, so optical flow would introduce too much overhead, but the complexity of the affine transform makes motion estimation much slower. We believe the overhead is smaller than the time savings it allows.

In the following section, the current state of the art for affine motion compensation and optical flow will be presented. The methods section will present and explain how our proposed method works. In the results section, we will evaluate the accuracy of the heuristics of the proposed method and compare it with the state of the art.

2. Related Works

As mentioned in the introduction, HEVC, by allowing a larger block size compared to AVC, has made affine motion compensation more usable, allowing for very large efficiency gains in sequences that present non-translational motion.

We focus on the implementations on top of HEVC as the proposed implementations in JEM in VVC are not true affine motion compensation, as they compute a standard translational motion vector for 4×4 subblocks.

2.1. Higher Order Motion Prediction Models

In all existing video encoding standards, translation-based prediction is supported. It can be defined mathematically by the following equation:

$$\begin{bmatrix} x' \\ y' \end{bmatrix} = \begin{bmatrix} x \\ y \end{bmatrix} + \begin{bmatrix} v_x \\ v_y \end{bmatrix} \qquad (1)$$

where $\begin{bmatrix} x' & y' \end{bmatrix}^t$ represent the coordinates of the points on the reference picture, $\begin{bmatrix} x & y \end{bmatrix}^t$ the coordinates of the points on the current picture, and $\begin{bmatrix} v_x & v_y \end{bmatrix}^t$ the motion vector.

Higher order motion prediction models are models that use more than two parameters to represent motion. While it is possible to define motion models with an arbitrarily high amount of parameters, in practice two models have been used the most: the affine motion model, that uses six parameters, defined by Equation (2), and the zoom and rotation model, that uses four parameters, defined by Equation (3).

$$\begin{bmatrix} x' \\ y' \end{bmatrix} = \begin{bmatrix} a & b \\ c & d \end{bmatrix} \begin{bmatrix} x \\ y \end{bmatrix} + \begin{bmatrix} v_x \\ v_y \end{bmatrix} \qquad (2)$$

$$\begin{bmatrix} x' \\ y' \end{bmatrix} = \begin{bmatrix} a & b \\ -b & a \end{bmatrix} \begin{bmatrix} x \\ y \end{bmatrix} + \begin{bmatrix} v_x \\ v_y \end{bmatrix} \qquad (3)$$

In these equations, a and b are the affine motion parameters, v_x and v_y are the translational motion parameters. By comparing with Equation (1), we can see that they are very similar, with an additional two or four parameters added.

Tsutake et al. [10] proposed using two 3-parameter models for affine motion compensation to replace the zoom and rotation model, that are defined as follows:

$$\begin{bmatrix} x' \\ y' \end{bmatrix} = \begin{bmatrix} 1+s & 0 \\ 0 & 1+s \end{bmatrix} \begin{bmatrix} x \\ y \end{bmatrix} + \begin{bmatrix} v_x \\ v_y \end{bmatrix} \quad (4)$$

$$\begin{bmatrix} x' \\ y' \end{bmatrix} = \begin{bmatrix} 1 & -r \\ r & 1 \end{bmatrix} \begin{bmatrix} x \\ y \end{bmatrix} + \begin{bmatrix} v_x \\ v_y \end{bmatrix} \quad (5)$$

The two 3-parameter models are simplifications of the 4-parameter zoom and rotation model. The first model, described in Equation (4), sets b to 0 and a to $1+s$, as a value of 0 for s represents a translation. The second model, described in Equation (5), sets b to r and a to 1, so a value of 0 for r represents a translation.

Because it is common that the movement is either zooming or rotation rather than a combination of both, it is common that one of the two affine parameters is much smaller than the other. In this case, reducing the number of parameters will reduce the coding cost of the prediction without losing much accuracy.

Using this dual model option allows for good efficiency, but it requires doing the parameter estimation process twice.

2.2. Transform Computation

As seen in the previous equations that represent higher-order motions, they result in a motion vector that depends on the position within the block. While implementations are very good at computing predictions with a constant motion vector (and especially for integer motion vectors as they are simple copy and paste), they are not designed for a constantly changing motion vector.

In the proposed affine motion compensation in JEM [7], this problem is avoided by using constant motion vectors for blocks of 4 × 4 samples. However, this also means it is not true affine motion compensation.

In Reference [8,9], the authors suggest doing a $1/16^{th}$ sample interpolation using a eight-tap filter. While it is quite slow, as the gradient method converges quickly towards the optimal value, it does not add too much additional burden to the encoder.

In Reference [10], because the method requires to evaluate more transforms, the interpolation is faster, using the quarter sample interpolation from HEVC and using bilinear interpolation between the four surrounding samples. To avoid the need for computing the interpolation many times, the interpolated samples are stored in a buffer for each reference picture.

2.3. Gradient-Based Parameter Estimation

In Reference [5,7–9], a gradient method is used to estimate the affine motion parameters. This method is based on the Newton–Raphson method, which is a method that allows finding the root of a function with an iterative process. The general form is given by the following equation:

$$x_1 = x_0 - \frac{f(x_0)}{f'(x_0)} \quad (6)$$

It is possible to generalize this equation to multi-dimensional problems. With affine motion compensation, we have the following error function:

$$E = \sum_{(x,y)} (org(x,y) - ref(x',y')) \quad (7)$$

where $org(x,y)$ refers to the original value of the sample at coordinates $\begin{bmatrix} x & y \end{bmatrix}^t$ in the current picture, $ref(x,y)$ refers to the sample value at coordinates $\begin{bmatrix} x & y \end{bmatrix}^t$ in the reference picture.

2.4. Block-Matching-Based Estimation

Reference [10] use a different method than the others to find the affine parameters. Because they use less parameters, the complexity increase is lower. However, even with only three parameters, the search around neighbors, if using a standard diamond or square pattern, goes from 8 transform computations to 26, and affine prediction is also more costly to compute.

Their idea is to decouple the search for the parameters. As with other methods, they start with an initial estimation based on the classical translation-based motion estimation. Then, they try values in the entire search range, with a step size of 4Δ, where Δ represents the quantization step for the affine parameter. They use the best value they found during this search for the next iterations. The first iteration checks the neighbors at a distance of 2Δ, then the second with a distance of Δ. This will give the best affine parameter for the given translation parameters. But the best translation parameters might be different in case of affine prediction, so the second step, the parameter refinement, is performed.

The parameter refinement works by alternating translation parameter refinement and affine parameter refinement. In both cases, the encoder will look for the closest neighbors, at a quarter sample distance for the translation and Δ for the affine parameter. The refinement stops when either a maximum number of iterations or no more improvement happens.

2.5. Motion Parameter Prediction and Entropy Coding

To achieve optimal efficiency when using affine motion prediction, it is important to signal the affine motion parameters with as few bits as possible. Every method uses the same coding as HEVC for the translational parameters, making full use of the motion vector prediction coding.

Reference [9] improves the translational motion vector coding by estimating the change in the translation parameter between blocks. Block-to-block translational shift compensation (BBTSC) corrects the translational shift, allowing merge mode to be used much more often as there is no need to signal the motion vector difference. This results in an improvement of 6% in the tested sequences.

Coding the affine motion parameters is difficult, as it is more difficult to predict them from neighboring blocks. The first limitation is not all blocks are going to use affine prediction, so it may be often necessary to code them without a prediction, but even in the case where a neighbor uses affine prediction, it may use a different reference picture, and scaling the motion parameters is challenging, as simply multiplying every value by the distance ratio does not work. Reference [11] tackles this problem by allowing motion scaling to work on affine parameters. They propose decomposing the transform into separate transforms, for example a rotation and a zoom operation, and scale each matrix appropriately, then combine them again to get the new parameters.

For the quantization, the most common, used in References [3,8,9], is a quantization step of $1/512$. Reference [10] evaluates different quantization step sizes, from $1/16$ to $1/512$. They find that using such a fine quantization step gives no coding efficiency benefit, and that $1/256$ is enough to get the best efficiency. As their method is a semi-exhaustive search, reducing the number of possible values is also good for encoding speed. They also choose to limit the maximum quantized parameter to 16, as higher values are too rare and seldom used.

2.6. Optical Flow

Estimating the movement between two pictures has been a subject of research for a long time, as it has numerous applications. For video coding, it is necessary for finding motion vectors, and is often done through computationally expensive methods that check the error for each possible motion vector, with more recent methods improving the search algorithms to keep the encoding time reasonable. In those cases, only the cost for the whole block is considered, so the movement estimation is often not accurate at a more granular level.

However, in many applications, the movement for each pixel is desired. This is typically referred to as optical flow. One of the most famous and popular methods for estimating optical flow is the Lucas-Kanade method [12]. It has been used a lot and gives satisfying results for simple movements. It is quite fast, which is one of the reasons for its popularity. Because it is included in the OpenCV library, it is also very easy to use, while many methods do not release their code, which adds the additional burden of implementation to potential users.

A recent application that also shows potential for video coding is frame interpolation, where by computing the movement for each pixel between the two frames, it is possible to estimate the missing frame with remarkable accuracy, which was demonstrated in EpicFlow [13]. To speed up the process, it is possible to use the motion vectors that are used for encoding the frames as estimators of the motion for a given block, then refine the optical flow to a pixel level, as was proposed in HEVC-Epic [14], which offers a good increase in speed compared to EpicFlow, but is still very slow, taking several seconds for estimating a single frame.

While the computed interpolated frame could be used in encoding with a new kind of prediction, it would make decoding too slow. Decoding needs to be possible on inexpensive hardware to see any large scale adoption.

While the state of the art optical flow methods achieve impressive accuracy, this comes at the cost of increased computation, and depending on the methods the time required varies depending on the picture. When considering hardware implementations and real time constraints, as is the case in encoding, it is important to ensure that the computations will always be bounded as to avoid the need for additional circuitry that will be used only in few cases. In this paper, the optical flow method from Ce Liu [15] was considered because the computation cost varies solely on the size of the input picture and the parameters for the number of iterations.

It also offers very nice properties for hardware implementation, as all the operations are highly parallel in nature, which makes them very easy to implement in hardware. While the software implementation is not parallelized, it would be possible to improve the speed relatively easily.

3. Proposed Method

3.1. Optical Flow Estimation

For each picture using inter-picture prediction, optical flow is computed using the current picture and the first picture in the reference picture list. While computing it for every picture in the reference picture list leads to better approximations, the required time is much higher, and the proposed method aims to provide good encoding efficiency with a faster encoding than similar methods. For the reference picture, the picture before encoding is used. This offers two advantages: first, this allows optical flow to be computed before the picture is encoded, and second, the motion estimation is more accurate and follows the real movement better, especially when the quantization parameter is large and the reconstructed picture is of lower quality.

After obtaining an approximate displacement for each pixel in the current picture, the estimation is performed for each CTU. As in Reference [3], using smaller blocks improves only slightly the encoding efficiency, but it would require a lot more time. The estimation is based on resolving the linear equation for the 4-parameter model transform with two points in the block.

As the translation parameter can be more accurately estimated with the standard motion estimation technique, only the parameters a and b are considered. Using x and y as the distance between the input points and x' and y' as the distance between the output points, we can estimate a and b with the following equation:

$$a = 1 + s = \frac{xx' + yy'}{x^2 + y^2}$$
$$b = -r = \frac{x'y - xy'}{x^2 + y^2}$$

(8)

To get good results, the points should be far enough apart, so points around the edge of the current block are used. If the points are too close together, cancellation is likely to occur, as the subpixel motion estimation through optical flow is imprecise. To remove the risk of bad estimations from outliers, the values of a and b are estimated for multiple couples of points, and the median value is retained. When the block is on the edges of the picture and contains pixels outside the reconstructed picture, we cannot compute optical flow on these samples. This happens when the input size is not a multiple of the largest coding block size. In this case, we use samples that are within the reconstructed picture for the computations.

3.2. Fast Mode Selection

In other methods, affine prediction is evaluated for each block, which takes a significant amount of time. In Reference [10], there are two affine prediction modes, which take even more time. We propose heuristics to avoid computing all possible modes and save on encoding time.

We decide if affine models should be used over translation first by looking at the variance of the optical flow in a given block. The variance is computed as in Equation (13).

$$\bar{x} = \sum_{i=0}^{N}\sum_{j=0}^{N} \frac{flow_x(i,j)}{N^2} \tag{9}$$

$$\sigma_x^2 = \sum_{i=0}^{N}\sum_{j=0}^{N} \frac{(flow_x(i,j) - \bar{x})^2}{N^2} \tag{10}$$

$$\bar{y} = \sum_{i=0}^{N}\sum_{j=0}^{N} \frac{flow_y(i,j)}{N^2} \tag{11}$$

$$\sigma_y^2 = \sum_{i=0}^{N}\sum_{j=0}^{N} \frac{(flow_y(i,j) - \bar{y})^2}{N^2} \tag{12}$$

$$\sigma_{xy} = \sqrt{\sigma_x^2 + \sigma_y^2} \tag{13}$$

In these equations, $flow_x(i,j)$ and $flow_y(i,j)$ represent the optical flow at the position (i,j). When the resulting variance σ_{xy} is very small, translation for the whole block is likely to be very accurate, as every pixel has the same displacement. The opposite case, where the variance is very high, mostly represents large discontinuities in the motion vector we should use to predict the current block. It is very likely that splitting the block into smaller subblocks is preferable.

We decide on two threshold values for these cases, resulting in the following:

1. translation if $\sigma_{xy} < 0.01$
2. affine if $0.01 < \sigma_{xy} < 4$
3. split block if $\sigma_{xy} > 4$

To determine the best threshold values, we ran tests on a few sequences. For the lower bound, 0.01 was determined experimentally to avoid skipping the numerous cases where the best parameter is 1 and the variance would be around 0.05. For the higher bound, we checked the variance of the sequences and values over 1 correlated heavily with object boundaries, but setting the threshold to 1 made the skipping too eager, so we increased it to 4 to allow for some margin of error.

Then, to see which 3-parameter model would fit best, the absolute values of s and r are compared, and the model corresponding with the highest value is selected. In case neither is bigger than a small threshold, set to a tenth of the minimal non-zero value for the affine parameter, affine motion estimation is skipped for the current block. While in most cases the variance heuristics catch those blocks, some outliers can affect the variance greatly.

To predict values for other pictures in the picture reference list, the displacement is scaled proportionally to the temporal distance between the frames. This approximation is typically accurate enough when the movement stays similar. For example, if the first reference picture is at a distance of 1 and the second at a distance of 2, the displacement values are doubled.

3.3. Parameter Refinement

We also propose a very fast refinement algorithm inspired by Tsutake et al. [10]. It is very simplified to reduce the number of iterations. Instead of going over every 4 possible values for the affine parameter, the proposed method encoder only checks the neighbors with a step size of 2Δ, refines to Δ and then refines the quarter pixel translation parameter only once. In case the best value for the affine parameter is zero after the initial neighbor check, the refinement is aborted. In this case, only four affine prediction estimations had to be performed, much fewer than in Tsutake et al. even in the cases of an early abort.

3.4. Parallel Processing

The optical flow method requires no encoding information and can be performed while other frames are being encoded. In a typical situation, while the first frame, which has to be Intra, is being encoded, there is enough time for the optical flow computation for the second frame, so if enough CPU cores are available, it can be computed before the need for it arises. If a single frame delay is acceptable, this method will allow saving a significant amount of time in the main encoding loop, which has to iterate over all blocks in order. Even in the case where this one frame delay would be unacceptable, the optical flow method used can be parallelized very well, and as it performs only basic mathematical operations, can easily run on a GPU or dedicated hardware.

4. Experimental Results

4.1. Testing Conditions

The HEVC reference encoder HM14 [16] is used as the anchor to estimate the Bjøntegaard Delta Bitrate (BD-R) [17] estimated bitrate savings and relative encoding time to compare the various methods.

We used the code from Tsutake et al. [10] to compare our proposed method with the existing state of the art. We also used their implementation of the gradient method from Reference [9] and a 3-parameter variant of the gradient approach that uses the same entropy coding as their method.

We used the same code for the entropy coding and transform calculations. We wrote the parameter estimation of the proposed method to replace theirs. This allows us to compare the parameter estimation process without other variables making the comparison difficult.

We compare our method to Reference [10], their implementation of Reference [9], and the 3-parameter variant of the gradient method.

For the encoding settings, the same settings as Reference [10] are used: The encoding mode is set to Low Delay P, and the quantization parameter (QP) values are 22, 27, 32, 37.

A total of seven sequences that show various motions were encoded with HM14 [16], Tsutake [10], Heithausen [9], the 3-parameter gradient and the proposed method. The sequences used are from two datasets, the ITE/ARIB Hi-Vision Test Sequence 2nd Edition [18] and Derf's collection [19]. Table 1 lists the sequences that were used, with the sequence number for the sequences from Reference [18]. To compute the encoding time, we used the following formula:

$$\Delta T = \frac{T_{target} - T_{HM_{14}}}{T_{HM_{14}}} \tag{14}$$

Table 1. Video Sequences.

Sequence Name	Motion
Twilight Scene (s215)	Zoom
Rotating Disk (s251)	Rotation
Fountain (s265)	Rotation
Station	Zoom
Blue Sky	Rotation
Fungus Zoom	Zoom
Tractor	Rotation + Zoom

In the following tables, the encoding time shown is the average over all QP values.

4.2. Mode Prediction Accuracy Evaluation

To evaluate the accuracy of our mode selection method, we compared the decisions made with Tsutake [10] with the decision made by the proposed method. We computed how often each affine transform model was used and how accurately the proposed method estimated the correct model. We consider the correct model the one that was used in the final coding, so if a given model was found better than the translation of the full block during the motion estimation phase but was inferior to a split block with different translation, skipping affine is classified as correct choice. We also evaluated the accuracy of the early skipping based on the variance that skips evaluating affine prediction entirely. The results are shown in Table 2.

Table 2. Evaluation of mode prediction accuracy of the proposed method compared to Reference [10].

Sequence Name	Sensitivity		Best Block Rate		Correct	Affine Skip	
	Rotation[%]	Zoom[%]	Rotation[%]	Zoom[%]	Model[%]	Bad[%]	Missed[%]
Station	14.6	90.8	0.5	33.4	89.7	3.3	70.2
Fountain	71.2	8.0	2.0	0.4	59.8	35.3	59.8
Fungus Zoom	0.0	99.2	0.3	35.6	98.4	0.0	100.0
Rotating Disk	86.9	30.9	21.6	1.3	83.9	4.5	89.7
Blue Sky	92.8	20.4	10.2	0.7	88.2	4.5	93.6
Tractor	27.4	58.6	0.9	16.7	57.0	29.3	48.6
Twilight Scene	30.8	38.6	0.8	1.2	35.5	34.4	83.3

Sensitivity represents how often the proposed method predicted this model correctly compared to how often this model was the best when evaluating both. It is calculated with the following formula:

$$\text{sensitivity}_{model} = \frac{\text{TP}_{model}}{\text{TP}_{model} + \text{FN}_{model}} \quad (15)$$

where TP_{model} is the true positives for a given model (prediction said to use the model and the model was used), and FN_{model} the false negatives (prediction said to use the other model or to skip while this model was correct).

The best block rate is the percentage of encoded blocks that use that model. The correct model represents how often the proposed method chose the right affine prediction model. It is the weighed average between the sensitivity values for both models, weighed by the prevalence of each model. The skip statistics represent how often the proposed method decided to skip evaluating affine parameters wrongly, and the rate of missed opportunities for skipping affine prediction.

While the accuracy appears to be low for many cases, the accuracy is not weighed with the loss of coding efficiency. While one could measure the efficiency gains estimated for a single block, it is not perfect, as the state of the entropy coder influences the coding of the following blocks. However, according to our results detailed in the following subsection, the blocks that were predicted incorrectly offered little benefit.

On some sequences where a type of motion is very dominant, like Fungus Zoom where zooming is used much more than rotation, the encoder will often predict the most common model even when it is not the best. This leads to a very low sensitivity for this model, but has a limited effect on the encoding efficiency since that model is not used much. This can be seen with the correct model value that is very high in this case. In the opposite case where rotation is dominant, like Blue Sky, the sensitivity for the zoom models is limited, but it also has a limited effect overall because of the rarity of the other mode.

For some sequences, especially Twilight Scene, the accuracy when compared to the alternative trying every possible transform is very low. However, in this case skipping wrongly according to the reference leads to better results that will be explained in the following subsection. To better investigate why the mispredictions were so common for some sequences, we recorded the affine parameters that were used both when our proposed method predicted accurately and when it gave a bad prediction. The results for the Rotating Disk sequence are presented in Figure 1. It appears that while for all cases smaller (in absolute value) parameters are more common, the wrong predictions have an even higher percentage of small values than the accurate prediction. This suggests that in these cases, the transform brings a smaller gain. As differentiating between the different motions for smaller movements is more complex, the limited accuracy for mode prediction can be understood.

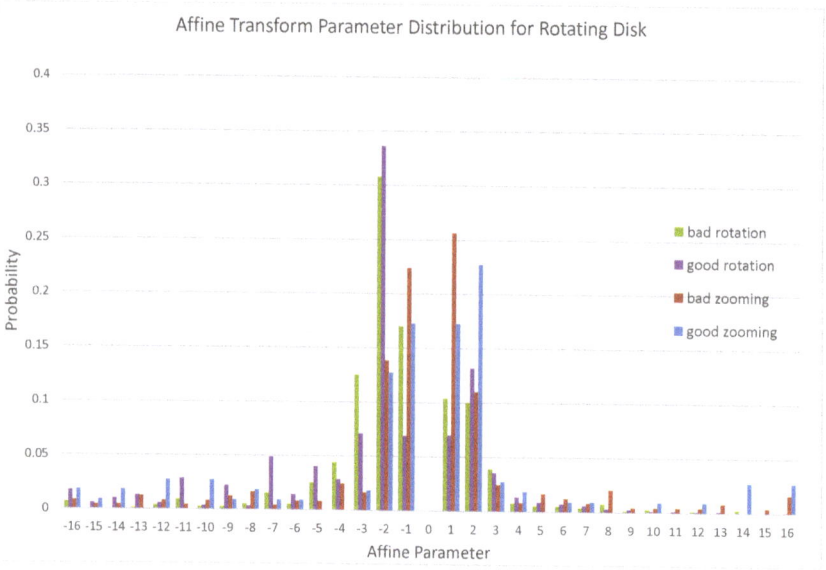

Figure 1. Distribution of the affine parameter (quantization levels) in the Rotating Disk sequence for accurately and incorrectly predicted transform models.

4.3. Comparison of Variants of the Proposed Method

We evaluated the encoding time and coding efficiency effects of our proposed model prediction, affine mode skip and fast parameter estimation. We compare three variants of the proposed method. The differences between the variants are presented in Table 3.

Table 3. Overview of proposed method variants.

Method Name	Affine Model Prediction	Affine Skip	Fast Parameter Refinement
Model prediction	✓	×	×
Model + Skip	✓	✓	×
Fast estimation	✓	✓	✓

Table 4 shows the results of the three variants. While the fast estimation variant is able to achieve the fastest encoding, this comes at the cost of greatly reduced efficiency. If more time is available, on of the other two methods is preferable, as they are able to achieve a better efficiency for a little more time. On some more complex sequences like Tractor, while the encoding speed increases significantly with the fast estimation method, the efficiency is more affected. This sequence is very challenging and the optical flow scaling fails to work on the wheels because of the fast rotation. While optical flow can estimate with some accuracy the motion for the first reference picture, the scaling does not work. As the wheel follows a rotational symmetry, in most cases the correct motion vector does not represent the real movement of the wheel. It will match a similar part of the wheel that has moved less compared to the current picture. Figure 2 illustrates this.

Table 4. Comparison of Coding Efficiency and Encoding Speed of the Proposed Method Variants.

Sequence Name	Model Prediction		Model + Skip		Fast Estimation	
	BD-R[%]	ΔT[%]	BD-R[%]	ΔT[%]	BD-R[%]	ΔT[%]
Station	−23.75	14.54	−23.68	13.25	−18.03	14.32
Fountain	−0.15	7.38	−0.15	5.10	−0.10	5.28
Fungus Zoom	−16.18	19.77	−16.42	19.92	−11.38	16.77
Rotating Disk	−24.07	10.23	−23.74	10.01	−13.22	6.98
Blue Sky	−4.74	8.78	−4.69	8.93	−3.76	5.90
Tractor	−3.71	8.44	−3.38	5.79	−1.66	5.79
Twilight Scene	−0.26	11.05	−0.42	10.65	−0.27	8.01
Average	−10.41	11.46	−10.35	10.52	−6.92	9.01

(a)

(b)

(c)

Figure 2. Three frames extracted from the Tractor sequence: (a) Current picture (POC N), wheel angle 136; (b) reference picture 0 (POC N-1), wheel angle 132; (c) reference picture 1 (POC N-4), wheel angle 118. While the wheel is in a more distant position in (c) than (b), an acceptable prediction can be done with (c) using the wheel rotational symmetry

There are two interesting results for the method using variance to skip affine mode, Twilight Scene and Fungus Zoom, where the efficiency increases with checking the affine mode less often. This happens because the Rate Distortion Optimization (RDO) process is not perfect. While we do not have a certain explanation, we have two hypotheses: First, not using affine coding at a place where it offered a negligible benefit changed the state of the context in the Context Adaptive Binary Arithmetic Coding (CABAC) enough to improve the coding of future blocks. Second, the tradeoff between quality and bitrate using the Lagrange multiplier is fallible, resulting in a better encoding with an apparently wrong decision. In the present case, for Fungus Zoom, skipping affine resulted in a loss of PSNR of 0.0019dB, for an decrease in bitrate of 0.74% for the quality parameter 27. While the mode accuracy seemed low in Table 2, it seems that it was actually able to remove affine prediction use when it was not beneficial. This suggests that the proposed method is accurate at predicting affine prediction when there is a significant benefit.

On average, the speed is improved by about 1% but in some cases, the required time goes up a little. Some might be caused by the processing of the variance, but we believe it is likely some is from measurement error, as variations of a percent are possible when repeating the same experiment and we only encoded the sequences once for each setting.

Because the efficiency on average decreases only slightly but the encoding time improves, we decided to use this method to compare to the state of the art, as the faster estimation variant reduces efficiency too much.

4.4. Comparison with the State of The Art

Table 5 shows how the proposed method compares to Reference [9,10] and the 3-parameter gradient. Table 6 shows the advantages and disadvantages of each method. Each method is able to offer significant improvement for sequences that present affine motion. The current three-parameter model implementations require significant time for encoding, making them difficult to use in practice. Both the proposed and the gradient approach are able to encode sequences with an acceptable overhead. For hardware implementation, gradient methods require many changes, including a more precise sample interpolation scheme, also increasing decoding costs, and a completely different architecture for motion vector parameters estimation. The former is no longer an issue with VVC that made 1/16 sample interpolation the standard for all prediction. However, gradient estimation will still require entirely different circuits. Tsutake [10] is able to provide a solution with minimal hardware changes, but the number of transform evaluations is too important. In our proposed method, there is some additional processing required for the optical flow, but it is possible to implement it at minimal cost, and alternatives for the optical flow method are possible. We believe that overall the total implementation cost is smaller for our proposed method. The last aspect to consider is performance when using content with mostly translation, like the Fountain sequence. In those cases, the proposed method classifies the block as requiring translation, which skips the affine parameter estimation, reducing the encoding speed cost for those sequences where affine prediction offers little encoding efficiency gains. The gradient method performs better than Tsutake here, as it will compute only one transform before giving up, while Tsutake will search many different values first.

On average, the proposed method loses less than 1% in BD-R, but the required encoding time goes down from over 20% in Reference [10] to just over 10%, about half of the time, which is expected from having to evaluate only one of the two affine prediction models, and also skip evaluating both in some cases. In sequences that use mostly translation, like Fountain, skipping many affine prediction blocks reduces the encoding time greatly, from 16.2% overhead to 5.1% with almost no change in efficiency.

However, when comparing with the gradient approach, the encoding time gains are much smaller. Reference [10] shows that their code offers a similar speed to Reference [9], but our experiments show that the gradient approach is much faster. Even the 3-parameter gradient variant that needs to perform the parameter estimation twice is faster than Tsutake. We believe the significant improvement in the speed of the gradient approach comes from the modern compiler used with many optimizations using vector instructions, that were for some reason optimized very well, while the block-matching approach did not get this advantage. However, the block-matching approach still has the advantages described in Reference [10] for hardware implementations as they can reuse more easily existing parts of encoders.

While the optimized version using vector instructions is faster in the software implementation, in hardware it would require a lot more silicon, as there are more operations to perform.

Even with the gradient method being optimized very well for our testing environment, the proposed method is still slightly faster than the 4-parameter gradient method, and significantly faster when compared to the 3-parameter variant. We believe it is possible to use the code of the gradient method to improve our proposed method for both speed and accuracy. On average, the gradient method, even when restricted to fewer parameters, finds slightly better parameters than the block matching approach from Reference [10]. When comparing with the proposed method, the gradient approach offers a better encoding for a limited cost in encoding time but we believe we have a lot of margin left in optimizations.

Table 5. Comparison of Coding Efficiency and Encoding Speed.

Sequence Name	Proposed		Tsutake [10]		Gradient [9]		Gradient 3-Parameter	
	BD-R[%]	ΔT[%]	BD-R[%]	ΔT[%]	BD-R[%]	ΔT[%]	BD-R[%]	ΔT[%]
Station	−23.68	13.25	−24.76	24.60	−25.62	12.81	−24.61	22.22
Fountain	−0.15	5.10	−0.16	16.20	−0.24	10.49	−0.17	10.07
Fungus Zoom	−16.42	19.92	−16.37	26.70	−15.23	17.35	−16.64	23.15
Rotating Disk	−23.74	10.01	−26.77	20.42	−29.28	11.24	−27.28	17.06
Blue Sky	−4.69	8.93	−5.13	19.18	−5.52	9.23	−5.78	15.52
Tractor	−3.38	5.79	−4.59	15.24	−4.82	7.68	−4.09	11.94
Twilight Scene	−0.42	10.65	−0.39	20.48	−0.51	10.15	−0.65	16.43
Average	−10.35	10.52	−11.17	20.40	−11.61	11.28	−11.32	16.62

Table 6. Overview of Advantages and Disadvantages of Each Method. ○ marks when the method is effective, △ when it is acceptable, and × when it is inadequate for this aspect.

	Proposed	Tsutake [10]	Gradient [9]	Gradient 3-Parameter
Encoding Efficiency	○	○	○	○
Encoding Speed (affine motion)	○	×	○	△
Encoding Speed (translation)	○	×	△	△
Hardware implementation	△	○	×	×

On some videos, like Blue Sky and Station the efficiency of the proposed method is very close to the existing state of the art, with a increase in time halved compared to Tsutake et al. If there are time constraints, the proposed method can offer superior encoding to HM and close to state of the art while maintaining the encoding time low.

In two sequences, Fungus Zoom and Twilight scene, the efficiency is higher than Tsutake et al., but fails to attain the efficient from the gradient approach using 3 parameters. However, it beats the gradient approach using 4 parameters in the Fungus Zoom case, as the additional unused parameter (rotation being almost inexistent) incurs a coding cost overhead.

Two sequences are very challenging for our proposed method. Tractor was previously mentioned for the limited accuracy for motion estimation, and when compared to the state of the art the effects of the limited accuracy in model estimation are significant. Figure 2 illustrates only one aspect of the challenges in encoding this sequence. Rotating wheel is difficult because of the black background, that optical flow is unable to track, making areas at the edge of the rotating objects hard to estimate. However, as it is a very artificial sequence that is unlikely to appear in more common sequences, we do not believe optimizing for this specific sequence to be sensible.

We can see that while the proposed method does not achieve an efficiency as high as the existing state of the art, it is able to encode in a much faster time, so if time is limited, it could be preferable to use the proposed method as the best compromise between speed and efficiency.

5. Conclusions

We presented a solution for the slow encoding when using affine motion compensation by changing the motion estimation algorithm. We proposed three improvements: a fast affine transform model estimation, a skip affine prediction and a fast parameter estimation algorithm. The proposed method is able to predict the correct affine model with good accuracy, and also skip evaluating affine prediction in some cases, saving significant encoding time. When compared to the state of the art, the reduction in bitrate according to the BD-R metric is below 1% on average, with a reduction of the encoding overhead in half compared to Reference [10], and slightly faster than the gradient approach from Reference [9] with less complexity when it comes to hardware implementations. In future work, we plan to investigate ways to make the implementation of the transform faster to reduce further the overhead of affine motion compensation. We also plan to use the optical flow information for block splitting decisions and stop the costly evaluation of smaller blocks when they would bring no benefit.

Author Contributions: Methodology, A.C.; Software, A.C.; Validation, Y.S. and T.M.; Writing—Original Draft Preparation, A.C.; Writing—Review & Editing, Y.S. and T.M.; Supervision, S.O.; Project Administration, S.O.; Funding Acquisition, S.O. All authors have read and agreed to the published version of the manuscript.

Funding: This study was partially supported by JSPS KAKENHI Grant Number 18K19772 and Yotta Informatics Project by MEXT, Japan

Acknowledgments: We would like to thank Tsutake and Yoshida for sharing the code of their method [10], and also their implementation of the other methods they used in their paper.

Conflicts of Interest: The authors declare no conflict of interest.

References

1. Sullivan, G.J.; Ohm, J.; Han, W.; Wiegand, T. Overview of the High Efficiency Video Coding (HEVC) Standard. *IEEE Trans. Circuits Syst. Video Technol.* **2012**, *22*, 1649–1668. [CrossRef]
2. Wiegand, T.; Sullivan, G.J.; Bjontegaard, G.; Luthra, A. Overview of the H.264/AVC video coding standard. *IEEE Trans. Circuits Syst. Video Technol.* **2003**, *13*, 560–576. [CrossRef]
3. Narroschke, M.; Swoboda, R. Extending HEVC by an affine motion model. In Proceedings of the 2013 Picture Coding Symposium (PCS), San Jose, CA, USA, 8–11 December 2013; pp. 321–324. PCS.2013.6737748. [CrossRef]
4. Lin, S.; Chen, H.; Zhang, H.; Maxim, S.; Yang, H.; Zhou, J. *Affine Transform Prediction for Next Generation Video Coding*; Technical report; Document ITU-T SG 16; ITU: Geneva, Switzerland, 2015.
5. Zhang, K.; Chen, Y.; Zhang, L.; Chien, W.; Karczewicz, M. An Improved Framework of Affine Motion Compensation in Video Coding. *IEEE Trans. Image Process.* **2019**, *28*, 1456–1469. TIP.2018.2877355. [CrossRef] [PubMed]
6. Sharabayko, M.; Ponomarev, O. Fast rate estimation for RDO mode decision in HEVC. *Entropy* **2014**, *16*, 6667–6685. [CrossRef]
7. Li, L.; Li, H.; Liu, D.; Li, Z.; Yang, H.; Lin, S.; Chen, H.; Wu, F. An Efficient Four-Parameter Affine Motion Model for Video Coding. *IEEE Trans. Circuits Syst. Video Technol.* **2018**, *28*, 1934–1948. TCSVT.2017.2699919. [CrossRef]
8. Heithausen, C.; Vorwerk, J.H. Motion compensation with higher order motion models for HEVC. In Proceedings of the 2015 IEEE International Conference on Acoustics, Speech and Signal Processing (ICASSP), Brisbane, QLD, Australia, 19–24 April 2015; pp. 1438–1442. [CrossRef]
9. Heithausen, C.; Bläser, M.; Wien, M.; Ohm, J. Improved higher order motion compensation in HEVC with block-to-block translational shift compensation. In Proceedings of the 2016 IEEE International Conference on Image Processing (ICIP), Phoenix, AZ, USA, 25–28 September 2016; pp. 2008–2012. [CrossRef]
10. Tsutake, C.; Yoshida, T. Block-Matching-Based Implementation of Affine Motion Estimation for HEVC. *IEICE Trans. Inf. Syst.* **2018**, *E101.D*, 1151–1158. [CrossRef]
11. Heithausen, C.; Bläser, M.; Wien, M. Distance scaling of higher order motion parameters in an extension of HEVC. In Proceedings of the 2016 Picture Coding Symposium (PCS), Nuremberg, Germany, 4–7 December 2016; pp. 1–5. [CrossRef]

12. Lucas, B.D.; Kanade, T. An Iterative Image Registration Technique with an Application to Stereo Vision. In Proceedings of the 7th International Joint Conference on Artificial Intelligence, Vancouver, BC, Canada, 24–28 August 1981; Morgan Kaufmann Publishers Inc.: San Francisco, CA, USA, 1981; Volume 2, pp. 674–679.
13. Revaud, J.; Weinzaepfel, P.; Harchaoui, Z.; Schmid, C. EpicFlow: Edge-Preserving Interpolation of Correspondences for Optical Flow. In Proceedings of the IEEE Conference on Computer Vision & Pattern Recognition (CVPR), Boston, MA, USA, 7–12 June 2015; pp. 1164–1172. [CrossRef]
14. Rüfenacht, D.; Taubman, D. HEVC-EPIC: Fast Optical Flow Estimation From Coded Video via Edge-Preserving Interpolation. *IEEE Trans. Image Process.* **2018**, *27*, 3100–3113. [CrossRef] [PubMed]
15. Liu, C. Beyond Pixels: Exploring New Representations and Applications for Motion Analysis. Ph.D. Thesis, Massachusetts Institute of Technology, Cambridge, MA, USA, 2009.
16. JCT-VC. *High Efficiency Video Coding (HEVC) Test Model 14 (HM 14.0)*; Fraunhofer Heinrich Hertz Institute: Berlin, Germany, 2014.
17. Bjøntegaard, G. Calculation of Average PSNR Differences between RD-curves. In Proceedings of the ITU—Telecommunications Standardization Sector STUDY GROUP 16 Video Coding Experts Group (VCEG), 13th Meeting, Austin, TX, USA, 2–4 April 2001.
18. Institute of Image Information and Television Engineers. *ITE/ARIB Hi-Vision Test Sequence*, 2nd ed.; NHK Engineering Services, Inc.: Tokyo, Japan, 2009.
19. Derf. Xiph.org Video Test Media [Derf's Collection]. 2018. Available online: https://media.xiph.org/video/derf/ (accessed on 10 October 2018).

© 2020 by the authors. Licensee MDPI, Basel, Switzerland. This article is an open access article distributed under the terms and conditions of the Creative Commons Attribution (CC BY) license (http://creativecommons.org/licenses/by/4.0/).

Article

Image Registration Algorithm Based on Convolutional Neural Network and Local Homography Transformation

Yuanwei Wang, Mei Yu, Gangyi Jiang *, Zhiyong Pan and Jiqiang Lin

Faculty of Information Science and Engineering, Ningbo University, Ningbo 315211, China; jgyvciplab@126.com (Y.W.); yumei2@126.com (M.Y.); zhiyong_pan@126.com (Z.P.); jiqiang_lin@126.com (J.L.)
* Correspondence: jianggangyi@nbu.edu.cn; Tel.: +86-574-8760-0017

Received: 18 December 2019; Accepted: 16 January 2020; Published: 21 January 2020

Abstract: In order to overcome the poor robustness of traditional image registration algorithms in illuminating and solving the problem of low accuracy of a learning-based image homography matrix estimation algorithm, an image registration algorithm based on convolutional neural network (CNN) and local homography transformation is proposed. Firstly, to ensure the diversity of samples, a sample and label generation method based on moving direct linear transformation (MDLT) is designed. The generated samples and labels can effectively reflect the local characteristics of images and are suitable for training the CNN model with which multiple pairs of local matching points between two images to be registered can be calculated. Then, the local homography matrices between the two images are estimated by using the MDLT and finally the image registration can be realized. The experimental results show that the proposed image registration algorithm achieves higher accuracy than other commonly used algorithms such as the SIFT, ORB, ECC, and APAP algorithms, as well as another two learning-based algorithms, and it has good robustness for different types of illumination imaging.

Keywords: image registration; homography matrix; local homography transformation; convolutional neural network; moving direct linear transformation

---

1. Introduction

Image registration is a process of image matching and transformation of two or more different images. It is widely used in such fields as panoramic image splicing [1,2], high dynamic range imaging [3], simultaneous localization and mapping (SLAM) [4], and so on.

Traditional image registration algorithms are mainly classified into pixel-based algorithms and feature-based algorithms [5,6]. In pixel-based image registration algorithms, the original pixel values are directly used to estimate the transformation relationship between images [7,8]. Firstly, the homography matrix between a pair of images is initialized. Then, the homography matrix is used to transform the image, and the errors of pixel values of the transformed image are calculated. Finally, the optimization technique is used to minimize the error function to achieve image registration. The pixel-based algorithms usually run slowly and are effective to low-texture scenes, but have poor robustness to scale, rotation and brightness.

In feature-based image registration algorithms [9,10] such as SIFT [11], ORB [12], etc., feature points of images are generally extracted first, and the corresponding relationship between feature points of the two images is established by feature matching, and the optimal homography matrix is estimated by algorithms such as RANSAC [13], etc. Feature-based image registration algorithms are generally better and faster than pixel-based image registration, but feature-based algorithms require that there must be enough matching points between the two images and that the accuracy of matching points is higher and the location distribution of matching points is uniform. Otherwise, the registration accuracy will be greatly reduced. Feature-based image registration algorithms generally have good robustness to scale and rotation and have robustness to brightness to some extent, but are not suitable for low-texture images.

Recently, some deep learning-based image registration algorithms have been proposed. DeTone et al. [14] proposed a homography matrix estimation algorithm with supervised learning. A 128 × 128 image I_A was generated by randomly clipping from an image I, and then random perturbation values were added to the coordinates of the four corners of the image I_A to generate four perturbation points, so that four pairs of matching points were obtained. The homography matrix corresponding to the four pairs of points was calculated by using the coordinates of the four corners of image I_A and their corresponding perturbation points. The homography matrix was used to transform image I_A into image I_B. Then, the images I_A and I_B were converted into grayscale images as samples, and the coordinate differences between the four corner points of I_A and their corresponding perturbation points in I_B were used as labels, with which a 10-layer VGG (Visual Geometry Group) network was trained, and finally a homography matrix estimation model that could be used for image registration was obtained. The algorithm has better robustness to brightness, scale, rotation, and texture. On the basis of DeTone's work, Nguyen et al. [15] proposed a homography matrix estimation algorithm with unsupervised learning to solve the shortcoming of artificially generated labels in supervised learning, but this algorithm had weak robustness to illumination. The samples used in these two algorithms were mainly artificially generated samples. The artificial samples ensured that the accuracy of the samples and labels was high enough, which was a beneficial exploration for deep learning to solve the actual image registration problem. However, the artificial samples adopted by these two works default to no parallax between the images to be registered, so only four pairs of corresponding points are used to represent the registration relationship between the two images. However, in practice, there is parallax between the images to be registered, and the relationship between such kinds of images is often not exact homography transformation.

In image registration, it is necessary to estimate the homography matrix between the target image and the reference image. The homography matrix is used to transform the target image to achieve the alignment of the target image and the reference image in spatial coordinates. The transformation process is called image mapping or image transformation. According to the application scope of the homography matrix, image transformation can be divided into global homography transformation and local homography transformation. Global homography transformation [7,11,12,14,16] uses the same homography matrix to transform the whole image. It requires that the target image and the reference image contain basically the same image information in the overlapping region. It is only suitable for images with small or no parallax. When this condition is not satisfied, the accuracy of image registration will be reduced significantly. Local homography transformation algorithm [17–19] maps different regions of an image using different transformation matrices, which can better overcome the shortcomings of the global homography transformation algorithm. As-Projective-As-Possible (APAP) algorithm [19] is a representative local homography transformation algorithm. It first extracts the feature matching points between the images and then divides the images into a uniform grid. Moving direct linear transform (MDLT) is used to estimate the homography matrix of each grid. Finally, the homography matrix of each grid is used to implement local homography transformation on the image to be registered. For images that do not satisfy the condition of global homography transformation, the image registration accuracy achieved by APAP algorithm is higher than that achieved by the global homography transformation algorithm [20]. APAP algorithm is also a feature-based image registration algorithm in essence. It also has the characteristics of a feature-based image registration algorithm and has higher accuracy than the general feature-based image registration algorithm. The general image registration algorithm based on global homography transformation only uses one homography matrix estimation and one homography transformation, while APAP algorithm needs multiple homography matrix estimations and homography transformations, so the speed of the APAP algorithm is slower than that of the general feature-based image registration algorithm.

The above two deep learning-based image registration algorithms are both for global homography transformation, and the used samples cannot be adopted to estimate the local homography matrix. Therefore, based on the above researches, an image registration algorithm based on deep learning and local homography transformation is proposed in this paper. An image sample and label generation method suitable for local homography transformation is designed so as to train the image registration model with convolutional neural network (CNN) effectively. The resulted image registration model can effectively reduce the error of image registration and overcome the defects of poor robustness of traditional image registration algorithms and low accuracy of existing deep learning-based image registration algorithms.

The main contributions of this paper are as follows: (1) A CNN and local homography transformation-based algorithm are proposed to solve the problem of image registration, which is a useful exploration for deep learning to solve the problem of image registration; (2) an image sample and label generation method suitable for local homography transformation is proposed, and the generated samples have good diversity and can simulate the actual image registration situation.

The rest of this paper is organized as follows. Section 2 mainly introduces the basic theory of the proposed algorithm, focusing on the image sample, label generation, CNN model, and loss function. Section 3 shows the experimental results, which verify the effectiveness of the proposed algorithm. The conclusion is given in Section 4, which summarizes the main work of this paper and analyses the shortcomings of the algorithm and possible improvement aspects.

2. Image Registration Algorithm Based on Deep Learning and Local Homography Transformation

In supervised learning-based image registration, sample labeling is required first. However, the cost of labeling samples manually is too high, and it is usually difficult to ensure the labeling accuracy, as well as to collect enough diverse images for registration. To solve this problem, an image registration algorithm based on deep learning and local homography transformation is proposed in this paper. Firstly, a sample and label generation method for deep learning is designed. In this method, direct linear transformation (DLT) and moving direct linear transformation (MDLT) are used to automatically generate more reasonable and effective samples and labels for deep learning, and then supervised learning is used to train CNN so as to obtain the image registration model, with which the local homography transformation-based image registration can be achieved.

2.1. Direct Linear Transformation (DLT)

If there is no parallax between the reference and target images, the mapping relationship between the two images is simple homographic, which can be described by the homography matrix. Suppose that two points with coordinates $\mathbf{x}' = [x', y']^T$ and $\mathbf{x} = [x, y]^T$ are the corresponding matching points on the reference image I' and the target image I respectively, and the corresponding relationship between these two points can be expressed as

$$\tilde{\mathbf{x}}' = \mathbf{H}\tilde{\mathbf{x}} \qquad (1)$$

where $\tilde{\mathbf{x}}'$ and $\tilde{\mathbf{x}}$ are the homogeneous coordinates of the two points respectively, and $\tilde{\mathbf{x}}' = \begin{pmatrix} x'' \\ y'' \\ z'' \end{pmatrix}$,

$\tilde{\mathbf{x}} = \begin{pmatrix} x \\ y \\ 1 \end{pmatrix}$, $\mathbf{H}$ is the homography matrix between the two images, $\mathbf{H} = \begin{pmatrix} h_{11} & h_{12} & h_{13} \\ h_{21} & h_{22} & h_{23} \\ h_{31} & h_{32} & h_{33} \end{pmatrix}$.

In the non-homogeneous coordinates, the corresponding relationship between matching points $\mathbf{x}$ and $\mathbf{x}'$ can be expressed as

$$x' = \frac{x''}{z''} = \frac{h_{11}x + h_{12}y + h_{13}}{h_{31}x + h_{32}y + h_{33}} \quad y' = \frac{y''}{z''} = \frac{h_{21}x + h_{22}y + h_{23}}{h_{31}x + h_{32}y + h_{33}} \qquad (2)$$

Transform Equation (1) into the form of $0_{3\times 1}=\widetilde{\mathbf{x}}' \times \mathbf{H}\widetilde{\mathbf{x}}$ and obtain

$$\begin{pmatrix} 0 \\ 0 \\ 0 \end{pmatrix} = \begin{pmatrix} 0 & 0 & 0 & -x & -y & -1 & xy' & yy' & y' \\ x & y & 1 & 0 & 0 & 0 & -xx' & -yx' & -x' \\ -xy' & -yy' & -y' & xx' & yx' & x' & 0 & 0 & 0 \end{pmatrix} \mathbf{h} \qquad (3)$$

where $\mathbf{h} = (h_{11}\ h_{12}\ h_{13}\ h_{21}\ h_{22}\ h_{23}\ h_{31}\ h_{32}\ h_{33})^{\mathrm{T}}$.

When estimating $\mathbf{H}$, more matching point information can be used to reduce the estimation error. In Equation (3), only two rows of the 3×9 coefficient matrix on the right side of the equation are independent. By selecting the first two rows to form an independent coefficient matrix $\mathbf{A}_i$, and taking all matching points into account, a $2N \times 9$ coefficient matrix $\mathbf{A}$ can be formed. By using the least square method, the solution of $\mathbf{h}$ can be expressed as

$$\hat{\mathbf{h}} = \underset{\mathbf{h}}{\mathrm{argmin}} \sum_{i=1}^{N} \|\mathbf{A}_i \mathbf{h}\|^2 = \underset{\mathbf{h}}{\mathrm{argmin}} \|\mathbf{A}\mathbf{h}\|^2 \qquad (4)$$

where $\hat{\mathbf{h}}$ is an estimation of $\mathbf{h}$, $\|\mathbf{A}\mathbf{h}\|$ denotes the two norms of vector $\mathbf{A}\mathbf{h}$, $\mathbf{h}$ is the normalized unit vector, N denotes the total number of pairs of matching points, and $\mathbf{A}_i$ denotes the independent coefficient matrix corresponding to the ith pair of matching points. Singular value decomposition (SVD) can be used to calculate $\hat{\mathbf{h}}$. The right singular vector corresponding to the minimum singular value of $\mathbf{A}$ is the result. The estimation of homography matrix $\mathbf{H}$ is obtained by arranging the elements of vector $\hat{\mathbf{h}}$ in a certain order.

Considering that SVD is time-consuming, which will affect the training speed of the neural network, Equation (3) is transformed into the form of non-homogeneous linear least squares. Let $h_{33} = 1$, two independent non-homogeneous linear equations can be obtained as

$$\mathbf{A}'_i \mathbf{h}' = \mathbf{b}'_i \qquad (5)$$

$$\mathbf{A}'_i = \begin{pmatrix} 0 & 0 & 0 & -x & -y & -1 & xy' & yy' \\ x & y & 1 & 0 & 0 & 0 & -xx' & -yx' \end{pmatrix} \qquad (6)$$

$$\mathbf{h}' = (h_{11}\ h_{12}\ h_{13}\ h_{21}\ h_{22}\ h_{23}\ h_{31}\ h_{32})^{\mathrm{T}} \qquad (7)$$

$$\mathbf{b}'_i = \begin{pmatrix} -y' \\ x' \end{pmatrix} \qquad (8)$$

If all N matching points are included, then Equation (4) can be represented as

$$\hat{\mathbf{h}}' = \underset{\mathbf{h}'}{\mathrm{argmin}} \sum_{i=1}^{N} \|\mathbf{A}'_i \mathbf{h}' - \mathbf{b}'_i\|^2 = \underset{\mathbf{h}'}{\mathrm{argmin}} \|\mathbf{A}' \mathbf{h}' - \mathbf{b}'\|^2 \qquad (9)$$

where $\hat{\mathbf{h}}'$ is the estimation of $\mathbf{h}'$, and $\mathbf{A}'$ is the coefficient matrix of $2N \times 8$ obtained by arranging all coefficient matrices $\mathbf{A}'_i$ in the vertical direction. $\mathbf{b}'$ is a constant column matrix of $2N \times 1$ obtained by arranging all the constant column matrices $\mathbf{b}'_i$ in the vertical direction.

Let $E = \|\mathbf{A}'\mathbf{h}' - \mathbf{b}'\|^2$; $\hat{\mathbf{h}}'$ can be calculated through $\frac{dE}{d\mathbf{h}'} = 0$

$$\hat{\mathbf{h}}' = \left(\mathbf{A}'^{\mathrm{T}} \mathbf{A}'\right)^{-1} \mathbf{A}'^{\mathrm{T}} \mathbf{b}' \qquad (10)$$

2.2. Moving Direct Linear Transformation (MDLT)

For an image with a certain parallax, the relationship between the reference and target images is no longer a simple homography transformation. In this case, the global homography transformation cannot ensure the accuracy of image registration, and simple local homography transformation will cause a blocking effect, which destroys the visual quality of the image. It is a good choice to use the MDLT algorithm for local homography transformation. The MDLT algorithm not only has high accuracy of image registration, but also can smooth different image blocks, taking into account the accuracy of image registration and the overall visual quality of the image.

Firstly, the image to be transformed is divided into several image blocks, and then all matching points of the two images are taken into account. For each of the image blocks, according to the central position of the image block, the weights are assigned to all matching points so as to estimate the homography matrix corresponding to this image block. Accordingly, Equation (4) can be rewritten as

$$\hat{h}_j = \underset{h_j}{\operatorname{argmin}} \sum_{i=1}^{N} \|\omega_{ij}(A_i h - b)\|^2 = \underset{h_j}{\operatorname{argmin}} \|W_j(A'h' - b')\|^2 \quad (11)$$

where $\hat{h}_j$ represents an estimation of the homography matrix of the jth image block, ω_{ij} is a weight that changes with the coordinate of the center point of the current image block, and W_j is a diagonal matrix that represents the weights of all matching points, and

$$W_j = \operatorname{diag}\left(\begin{bmatrix} \omega_{1j} & \omega_{1j} & \cdots & \omega_{ij} & \omega_{ij} & \cdots & \omega_{Nj} & \omega_{Nj} \end{bmatrix}\right) \quad (12)$$

The weight ω_{ij} is determined by the distance between the ith matching point and the center point of the jth image block. The smaller the distance, the larger the weight. Zaragoza et al. [19] used Gaussian function to calculate the weight

$$\omega_{ij} = \max\left(\exp\left(-\frac{\|x_i - x_j^*\|^2}{\sigma^2}\right), \gamma\right) \quad (13)$$

where x_j^* represents the coordinate of the center point of the jth image block, x_i represents the coordinate of the ith matching point of the image to be transformed, σ is the scale factor, and γ is the minimum weight value, which prevents the weight of some matching points far from the current image block from being too small.

Lin et al. [21] proposed another method of calculating weights, using Student-t distribution function instead of Gaussian distribution function, which is represented as

$$\omega_{ij} = \left(1 + \frac{\|x_i - x_j^*\|^2}{\nu\sigma^2}\right)^{-\frac{\nu+1}{2}} \quad (14)$$

Because the student t-distribution function is smoother than the Gaussian distribution function, it is not easy for the block effect caused by local homography transformation to appear, so the student-t distribution function is adopted in this paper. By using the same analysis method of the DLT algorithm, the estimation of the local homography matrix is finally calculated as follows:

$$\hat{h}_j = \left(A'^T W_j^2 A'\right)^{-1} A'^T W_j^2 b' \quad (15)$$

2.3. Sample and Label Generation Method Based on Local Homography Transformation

In the homography matrix, the rotational and shear components are often much smaller than the translation components, so it is difficult for a model to converge if the homography matrix is used as a label directly. Therefore, DeTone et al. proposed a method of substituting four pairs of corresponding points for the homography matrix [14]. The algorithm uses global homography transformation and is only suitable for the registration of an image without parallax. However, the actual images usually have parallax.

To overcome the shortcomings of DeTone's method, an improved sample generation method based on local homography transformation is proposed to generate sample images with parallax, as illustrated in Figure 1. The sample and label generation process is described in detail as follows:

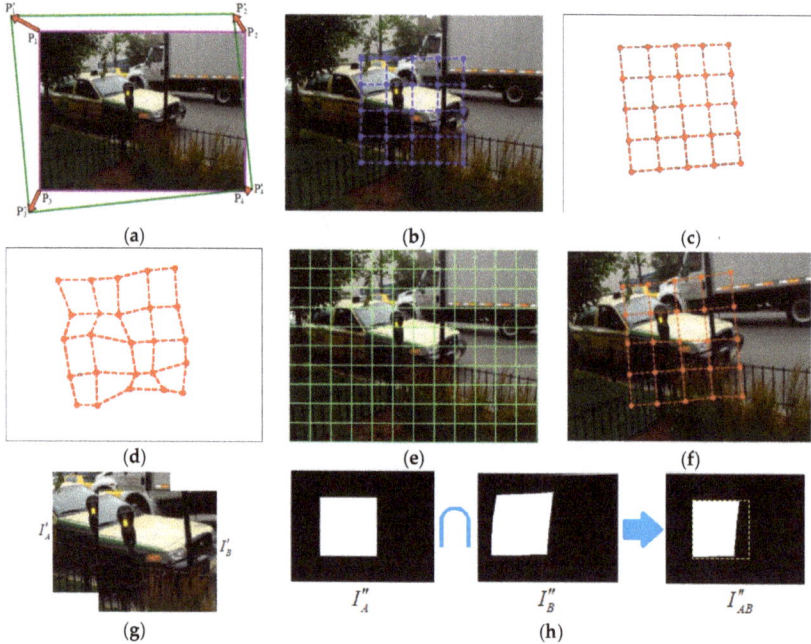

Figure 1. The process of the proposed sample and label generation method: (**a**) Generate four pairs of points and obtain the corresponding homography matrix $\mathbf{H}_{4pt'}^{AB}$ (**b**) randomly cut out the original image to generate an $M \times N$ uniform grid G_A; (**c**) $M \times N$ points G'_A transformed from G_A by using $\mathbf{H}_{4pt'}^{AB}$ (**d**) $M \times N$ perturbation points $\widetilde{G}'_A$ generated from G'_A; (**e**) adaptively generate $m \times n$ uniform grid; (**f**) image I_B transformed from I_A using local homography matrices $\mathbf{H}_L^{AB}$; (**g**) generated alternative samples; (**h**) calculation of overlap degree of two sample images.

Step 1: Firstly, add random perturbation values to the coordinates of the four corners {P_1, P_2, P_3, P_4} of the original image I_A to obtain four new points {P'_1, P'_2, P'_3, P'_4}, where the ranges of the random perturbation values in horizontal and vertical directions are $[-\rho_x, \rho_x]$ and $[-\rho_y, \rho_y]$, respectively. The two points before and after the perturbation form a pair of corresponding points, therefore, a total of four pairs of corresponding points are obtained, as shown in Figure 1a. Then, calculate the homography matrix $\mathbf{H}_{4pt}^{AB}$ corresponding to the four pairs of corresponding points.

Step 2: Randomly select a point p in the original image I_A, cut out a block I'_A with fixed size using p as the upper left corner of the block, and divide the block into a uniform grid to get $M \times N$ grid points G_A, as illustrated in Figure 1b.

Step 3: According to Equations (1) and (2), transform the $M \times N$ grid points G_A into new corresponding $M \times N$ points G'_A by using the homography matrix $\mathbf{H}_{4pt'}^{AB}$ as illustrated in Figure 1c.

Step 4: Add random perturbation values to each of the new corresponding $M \times N$ points G'_A to get $M \times N$ perturbation points $\widetilde{G}'_A$, as illustrated in Figure 1d. The ranges of random perturbation values in horizontal and vertical directions are $\left[-\rho'_x, \rho'_x\right]$ and $\left[-\rho'_y, \rho'_y\right]$, respectively, and $\rho'_x < \rho_x/2$, $\rho'_y < \rho_y/2$, so as to ensure the global consistency of these random perturbation points.

Step 5: Through the $M \times N$ uniform grid points, G_A generated in Step 2 and $M \times N$ corresponding perturbation points $\widetilde{G'}_A$ generated in Step 4, the corresponding global homography matrix $\mathbf{H}_g^{AB}$ is calculated by the DLT algorithm. Then transform the $M \times N$ uniform grid points G_A into new points G''_A by using $\mathbf{H}_g^{AB}$ and calculate the root mean square error (RMSE) between $\widetilde{G'}_A$ and G''_A. After that, divide the original image I_A into an $m \times n$ uniform grid according to the RMSE, as shown in Figure 1e. If the RMSE is large, which means that there is a strong locality between G_A and $\widetilde{G'}_A$, the grid of the original image should be partitioned smaller to improve the local accuracy; conversely, if the RMSE is small, it means that the local homography matrixes have strong global character, therefore, the grid of the original image can be partitioned larger so as to speed up sample generation. The number of rows and columns of the uniform grid can be determined by

$$m = \text{int}\left(\min\left(1 + \frac{H \cdot y_{rmse}}{\rho'_y h_{min}}, \frac{H}{h_{min}}\right)\right), \quad n = \text{int}\left(\min\left(1 + \frac{W \cdot x_{rmse}}{\rho'_x w_{min}}, \frac{W}{w_{min}}\right)\right) \quad (16)$$

where m and n are the number of rows and columns of the uniform grid, W and H are the width and height of the image I_A, x_{rmse} and y_{rmse} represent the RMSE between $\widetilde{G'}_A$ and G''_A in horizontal and vertical directions, and w_{min} and h_{min} represent the minimum width and minimum height of each image block, respectively. w_{min} and h_{min} should not be too small, otherwise, it will cause too many blocks of some samples, which will affect the speed of sample generation; however, it also should not be too large, so as to avoid too few blocks of samples, which will result in an unnatural block effect in the transformed image.

Step 6: Calculate the local homography matrix $\mathbf{H}_j^{AB}$ ($j = 1, 2, \cdots, m \times n$) corresponding to each block of the $m \times n$ uniform grid with the MDLT algorithm, in which the $M \times N$ pairs of corresponding points between G_A and $\widetilde{G'}_A$ are used as the pairs of matching points, so that the $m \times n$ local homography matrixes $\mathbf{H}_L^{AB} = \left\{ \mathbf{H}_j^{AB} \middle| j = 1, 2, \cdots, m \times n \right\}$ are obtained. Then transform the original image I_A into a new image I_B with $\mathbf{H}_L^{AB}$ and calculate the coordinate of the points G_B in image I_B corresponding to G_A in I_A with $\mathbf{H}_L^{AB}$.

Figure 1f shows the image I_B generated from the original image I_A shown in Figure 1a after local homography transformation, and the grid points in Figure 1f represent the new grid points generated by local homography transformation corresponding to the $M \times N$ uniform grid points G_A in Figure 1b.

Step 7: For image I_B, an image block with the same size and coordinates as that of I'_A in image I_A is cropped as I'_B. Image I'_A and image I'_B constitute the alternative sample of the neural network. The coordinate difference G_{AB} between the points G_B in image I_B and its corresponding points G_A in image I_A forms the alternative label of the neural network.

Figure 1g gives a pair of alternative samples cropped from the images in Figure 1b,f.

Step 8: In the process of generation of image I_B, if the overlap degree of two sample images is too low because of the extreme distribution of perturbation point $\widetilde{G'}_A$, the samples are regarded to be invalid and will be discarded.

The calculation of the overlap degree of two sample images is illustrated in Figure 1h. Let I''_A be the corresponding binary mask of sample image I'_A in the original image I_A. Transform the mask image I''_A through the local homography matrix $\mathbf{H}_L^{AB}$ so as to obtain the corresponding binary mask I''_B in the image I_B. Then the binary mask images I''_A and I''_B are intersected to get the binary mask image I''_{AB}, in which the non-zero-pixel region indicates the overlap region of the two sample images, as shown in Figure 1h. Thus, the overlap degree of two sample images is calculated as

$$\partial = \frac{S_{AB}}{S_A} \quad (17)$$

where ∂ denotes the overlap degree, S_A denotes the number of non-zero pixels in I''_A, and S_{AB} denotes the number of non-zero pixels in I''_{AB}. If ∂ of two sample images is lower than a threshold, the two sample images will be discarded.

2.4. Loss Function and Convolutional Neural Network

RMSE can be used as a loss function of CNN, which is defined by

$$L_s = \sqrt{\frac{1}{k}\sum_{i=1}^{k} \|x_i - \hat{x}_i\|^2} \qquad (18)$$

where x_i is the label value of the ith pair of matching points, $\hat{x}_i$ is the corresponding output value of the CNN, and k is the total number of pairs of matching points.

General CNN can be used to obtain the image registration model. In this paper, three network architectures including VGG [22], Googlenet [23] and Xception [24] are compared. The structure of the VGG network is simple and the depth of the network is easily expanded, but its training speed is slow and it requires a lot of hardware resources. For simplicity, we adopted a 10-layer VGG network [14] in the experiments. Googlenet can deepen the depth and width of the neural network, speed up the training speed, and reduce the hardware resources needed by the network. The convergence speed of the Xception network is fast, and the hardware resources required are also less. Additionally, the convergence performance of the Xception network is generally better than that of VGG and Googlenet networks.

3. Experimental Results and Analysis

To test the performance of the proposed algorithm, it is compared with Scale-Invariant Feature Transform (SIFT) algorithm [11], Oriented FAST and Rotated BRIEF(ORB) algorithm [12], Error Checking and Correction (ECC) algorithm [7], APAP [19], the DeTone's algorithm [14], and the Nguyen's algorithm [15]. The experiments are implemented on a computer with Intel i7-6700 CPU, 32 GB memory, one NVIDIA GTX 1080 Ti GPU, and the operating system used is Ubuntu 16.04 LTS.

The performances of different image registration algorithms are compared in terms of accuracy, running time and robustness. The three algorithms of SIFT, ORB and ECC are implemented by using Python OpenCV. The RANdom SAmple Consensus (RANSAC) threshold of SIFT and ORB algorithms is 5. The maximum number of iterations of the ECC algorithm is 1000. The adopted framework of deep learning is TensorFlow [25]. The APAP, DeTone's algorithm and Nguyen's algorithm are implemented with Python programming language on the same platform.

To facilitate comparison with the DeTone's and Nguyen's algorithms, the size of sample images used in this paper is the same as that of DeTone's and Nguyen's algorithms. The used perturbation values consist of components in horizontal and vertical directions, the range of which should not be too small or too large. If the perturbation range is too small, the generated perturbation value will be small, which will reduce the diversity of the samples and weaken the generalization ability of the model. However, if the perturbation range is too large, it may easily generate some samples with extreme deformation, which will make the training of the model more difficult and lead to the reduction of prediction accuracy of the model. The maximum perturbation values ρ_x or ρ_y of corner points in Step 1 of the proposed image sample and label generation method should not exceed half of the width or height of the original image respectively. Generally, taking 1/3~1/10 of the image width or height can ensure that the generated samples have better diversity and visual quality. Similarly, in Step 4, taking 1/3~1/10 of ρ_x for ρ'_x, 1/3~1/10 of ρ_y for ρ'_y can achieve better results.

The original data sets used in the experiments are MS-COCOCO2014 and MS-COCOCO2017 data sets [26]. Firstly, all images in these two data sets are scaled to 320 × 240, on which the proposed sample and label generation method is performed to obtain the gray-scale sample images with the size of 128 × 128. The maximum perturbation values ρ_x and ρ_y in horizontal and vertical directions of the corner points in Step 1 are set to 45, and the number of matching points for each pair of images in Step 2 is set to 5 × 5. The maximum perturbation values ρ'_x and ρ'_y in Step 4 are set to 11. In Step 5, the values of w_{min} and h_{min} are both 5. In Step 8, the threshold of overlap degree is 0.3, that is, when the overlap degree is lower than 0.3, the sample will be discarded. To increase the robustness of the model and reduce the possibility of over-fitting, image augmentation technology [27] is also used in the generation of training samples. The color and brightness of some of the sample images are randomly changed, and some of the sample images are processed with Gamma transformation. Finally, a total of 500,000 pairs of images are generated as a training set, 10,000 pairs of images as a validation set, and 5000 pairs of images as a test set.

In order to prove the generality of the proposed algorithm, three CNNs, including VGG, Googlenet and Xception, are used to train and test each of the learning-based image registration algorithms. The used optimization algorithm is Adam [28], where $\beta_1 = 0.9$, $\beta_2 = 0.999$, $\varepsilon = 10^{-8}$. The batch size is 128. The initial learning rate of the proposed algorithm and supervised learning of DeTone's algorithm is 0.0005, and that of unsupervised learning of Nguyen's algorithm is 0.0001. To prevent over-fitting, dropout [29] is used before the output layer of all neural networks. In the process of training, the test error of the validation set can be observed. When the test error of the validation set is no longer reduced, the training is stopped to prevent under-fitting or over-fitting.

When training the network models of the DeTone's algorithm and Nguyen's algorithm, the perturbation values of their samples are also set to 45, the same optimization techniques and image augmentation techniques as well as the same CNN are adopted. The number of training samples generated is the same as that of the proposed algorithm, and the training methods and observation methods are also the same. All algorithms are tested on the test set generated by the proposed method to ensure the objectivity of the comparison.

3.1. Accuracy of Image Registration

The accuracy of image registration can be measured by RMSE of registration points, which is defined by

$$RMSE(f) = \sqrt{\frac{1}{k}\sum_{i=1}^{k} \|f(x_i) - x'_i\|^2} \tag{19}$$

where x_i denotes the coordinates of grid points G_A in image I_A, and x'_i denotes the coordinates corresponding to x_i in image I_B; f represents different image registration models, and the proposed algorithm and APAP algorithm use the local homography matrix, while the other algorithms use the global homography matrix as their image registration model; $f(x_i)$ denotes the coordinates transformed from x_i by using the image registration model f, which is the estimation of x'_i; k is the total number of matching points in the pair of images, and it is set to 25 in the experiments.

Table 1 shows the average RMSE of registration points achieved by several different image registration algorithms when implemented on the test set generated by the proposed method. To better present the performance of learning-based image registration algorithms, Table 1 gives in detail the registration accuracy of several deep learning-based image registration algorithms using VGG, Googlenet and Xception neural networks, respectively.

Table 1. RMSE comparison of different image registration algorithms.

Algorithmic Type	Algorithm	RMSE
Pixel based	ECC	18.13
Feature based	SIFT	5.077
	ORB	17.751
	APAP	4.458
Learning based	DeTone + VGG	11.844
	DeTone + Googlenet	10.512
	DeTone + Xception	10.011
	Nguyen + VGG	10.455
	Nguyen + Googlenet	9.936
	Nguyen + Xception	9.861
	Proposed + VGG	6.113
	Proposed + Googlenet	4.344
	Proposed + Xception	2.339

From Table 1, it can be seen that the accuracy of the pixel-based ECC image registration algorithm is the lowest, and that of the feature-based SIFT image registration algorithm is higher. The APAP algorithm takes into account the locality of image registration, so it achieves the best result among the pixel-based and feature-based algorithms. The performance of the learning-based image registration algorithms is related to the used CNN models, and more advanced CNN models have higher image registration accuracy. The samples used by the DeTone's algorithm and Nguyen's algorithm are relatively simple, so there is little difference in the accuracy of image registration under different neural networks. These two algorithms do not fully consider the locality of image registration, resulting in low accuracy of image registration. Compared with other algorithms, the proposed algorithm achieves the highest image registration accuracy by using the Xception network model. In addition, from Table 1, it is seen that the effect of the proposed algorithm under Xception network is better than that under Googlenet and VGG networks. This is because the samples and labels used in the proposed algorithm are more complex, and there are obvious differences under different neural networks. When combined with more advanced CNN models, the proposed algorithm can achieve higher accuracy of image registration.

3.2. Running Time

To compare the calculation complexity of different image registration algorithms, Table 2 shows the average running time of each algorithm running for 10 times, where all algorithms are implemented under a computer with Intel i7-6700 CPU, 32 GB memory and one NVIDIA GTX 1080 Ti GPU. It is seen that APAP algorithm runs slowest due to the use of the local homography matrix and ORB algorithm runs fastest among the traditional image registration algorithms. For learning-based image registration algorithms, Table 2 gives the running time when the algorithms are accelerated with one GPU, as well as the running time achieved without the GPU. It is seen that GPU can significantly speed up the learning-based algorithms. The running speed of GPU is much faster than that of CPU, and different neural network models achieve different running speeds, among which Xception runs the slowest and Googlenet runs the fastest. Because the DeTone's and Nguyen's algorithms are only different in loss function and the neural network model is basically the same, the running time of the two algorithms are the same under the same conditions. The proposed algorithm involves the estimation of local homography matrices, so it runs slower than DeTone's and Nguyen's algorithms under the same neural network.

Table 2. Running time comparison of different image registration algorithms.

Algorithmic Type	Algorithm	Running Time of GPU (s)	Running Time of CPU (s)
Pixel based	ECC	-	226
Feature based	SIFT	-	99
	ORB	-	65
	APAP	-	456
Learning based	DeTone + VGG	36.2	123
	DeTone + Googlenet	26.9	57.3
	DeTone + Xception	46.2	208
	Nguyen + VGG	36.2	123
	Nguyen + Googlenet	26.9	57.3
	Nguyen + Xception	46.2	208
	Proposed + VGG	47.2	138
	Proposed + Googlenet	39.7	61
	Proposed + Xception	59.6	213

3.3. Robustness to Illumination, Color and Brightness

In order to compare the robustness of different image registration algorithms to illumination, color, and brightness, the test set in the experiments is augmented, and the used image augmentation method is the same as that of the training set. After image augmentation, the registration accuracy and failure rate of each algorithm are compared. We only randomly augmented some of the images in the test set, but not all of them. The higher the number of augmented images is, the higher the image augmentation degree of the test set is, and the test set has more diversity in illumination, color and brightness. The image augmentation degree can be represented by the probability of an image being augmented in the test set. The test set used in this experiment contains 5000 pairs of test images. Each algorithm runs 10 times repeatedly, during which the image augmentation is randomly implemented at a pre-specified image augmentation degree, and the average result of the 10 runs is taken as the final result of this algorithm with respect to the pre-specified image augmentation degree. Therefore, the image augmentation degree also represents the degree that the test set is affected by image augmentation.

The accuracy and failure rate of image registration can be used to measure the robustness of different image registration algorithms. Since the maximum perturbation values of each grid point in the sample image in the horizontal and vertical directions are ρ_x and ρ_y respectively, when the accuracy of image registration of a pair of images is greater than $\sqrt{\rho^2_x + \rho^2_y}$, the pair can be considered as a registration failure, and the failure rate of image registration on the test set can further be calculated. Considering that the RMSE values of test samples failed to be registered may be too large, and these extreme data may affect the RMSE values of the whole test set greatly, therefore, the RMSE of the whole test set is defined as

$$RMSE'_i = \min(RMSE_i, \sqrt{\rho^2_x + \rho^2_y})$$
$$RMSE = \frac{1}{K}\sum_{i=1}^{K} RMSE'_i \quad (20)$$

where $RMSE_i$ represents the RMSE value of the ith pair of images, and K denotes the total number of image pairs in the test set.

Figures 2–5 show the failure rate and RMSE achieved by different algorithms under different image augmentation degrees. The abscissa is the image augmentation degree of the test set, which changes from 0.0 to 1.0 with a step size of 0.1; the ordinate represents the registration failure rate or RMSE. Figure 2 shows the robustness comparison of seven image registration algorithms, in which the CNN model used by DeTone's and Nguyen's algorithms is VGG, while the model used by the proposed algorithm is Xception. As can be seen from Figure 2, the robustness of the traditional image registration algorithms to illumination, color, and brightness is very poor, and the robustness of the learning-based algorithms, especially the supervised learning-based algorithm, is better than that of the traditional ones. Figures 3–5 further give robustness analysis of the three learning-based image registration algorithms under three different CNN models. The used three CNN models are VGG, Googlenet and Xception, respectively. It can be seen that under the same neural network model, the robustness of Nguyen's algorithm is inferior to the other two algorithms. Nguyen's algorithm uses L1 norm as a loss function in the unsupervised learning algorithm, requiring the same image augmentation parameters for I'_A and I'_B in each pair of samples during the training, otherwise, the model will not converge normally, which results in the poor robustness of the unsupervised learning image registration algorithm. In contrast, DeTone's algorithm and the proposed algorithm do not have this problem, because both of them adopt supervised learning; the label value can supervise the training of the neural network very well, so the model has better robustness.

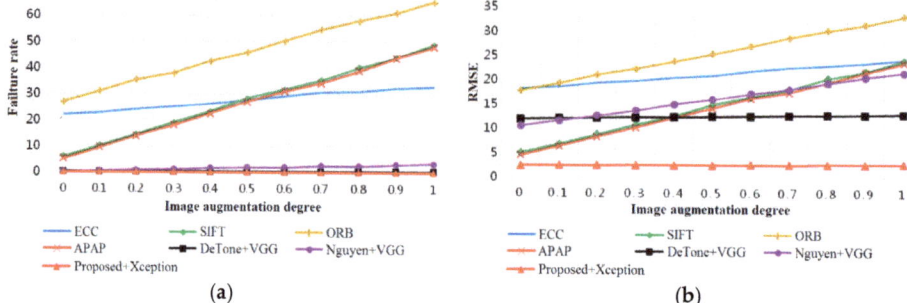

Figure 2. Robustness of seven image registration algorithms under different image augmentation degrees: (**a**) Failure rate; (**b**) RMSE.

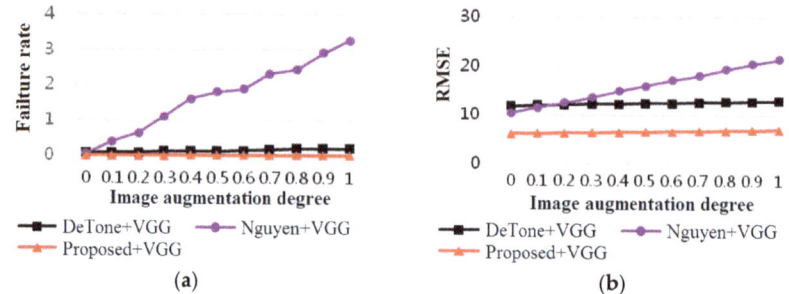

Figure 3. Robustness of DeTone's algorithm, Nguyen's algorithm and the proposed algorithm using VGG: (**a**) Failure rate; (**b**) RMSE.

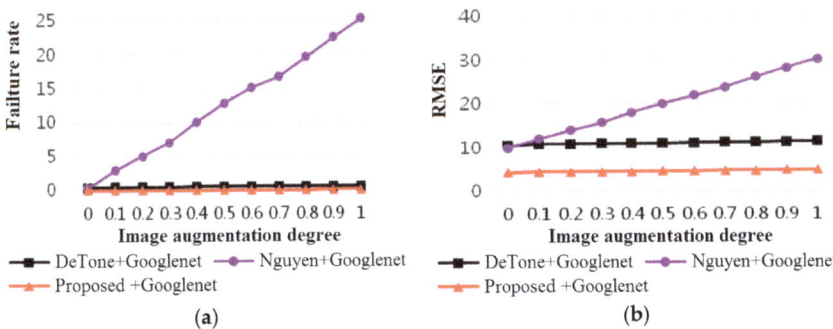

Figure 4. Robustness of DeTone's algorithm, Nguyen's algorithm and the proposed algorithm using Googlenet: (**a**) Failure rate; (**b**) RMSE.

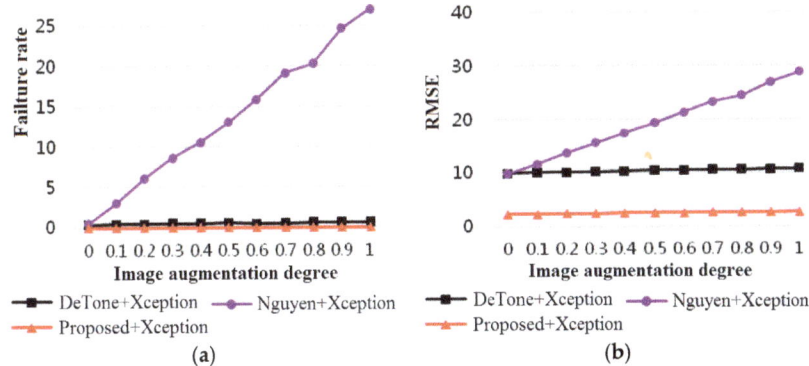

Figure 5. Robustness of DeTone's algorithm, Nguyen's algorithm and the proposed algorithm using Xception: (**a**) Failure rate; (**b**) RMSE.

In order to further analyze the influence of different perturbation values on the accuracy of the proposed algorithm, four maximum perturbation values in Step 1 including 24, 28, 32, and 36 are tested on test sets with different image augmentation degrees, respectively. The experimental results are shown in Figure 6, in which the abscissa and ordinate are the image augmentation degree of the test set and RMSE achieved by different image registration algorithms, respectively. It can be seen that as the maximum perturbation value ρ decreases, the RMSE of image registration also decreases, that is, the higher the accuracy of image registration.

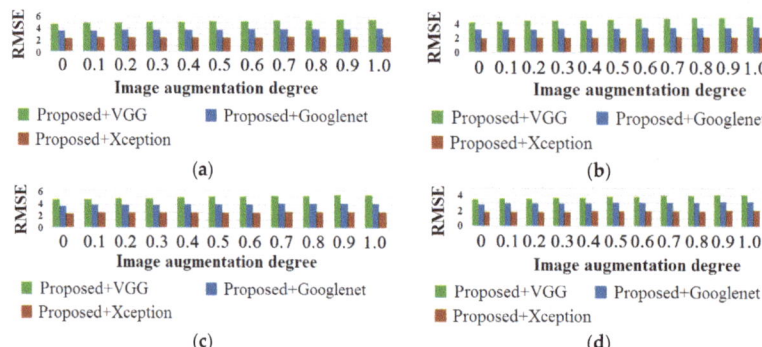

Figure 6. Robustness of the proposed algorithm under different perturbation values and CNNs: (**a**) $\rho = 36$; (**b**) $\rho = 32$; (**c**) $\rho = 28$; (**d**) $\rho = 24$.

Figure 7 gives the visualized homography estimation results. The red boxes in the left images are mapped to the red boxes in the right images. These red boxes are labels, which are generated by the proposed method described in Section 2.3. The yellow boxes in the right images indicate the results of homography estimation. The more the red and yellow boxes in the right images coincide, the higher the accuracy of feature point matching is. From Figure 7, it is also noticed that the proposed algorithm with Xception model is superior to the proposed algorithms with Googlenet and VGG neural network models.

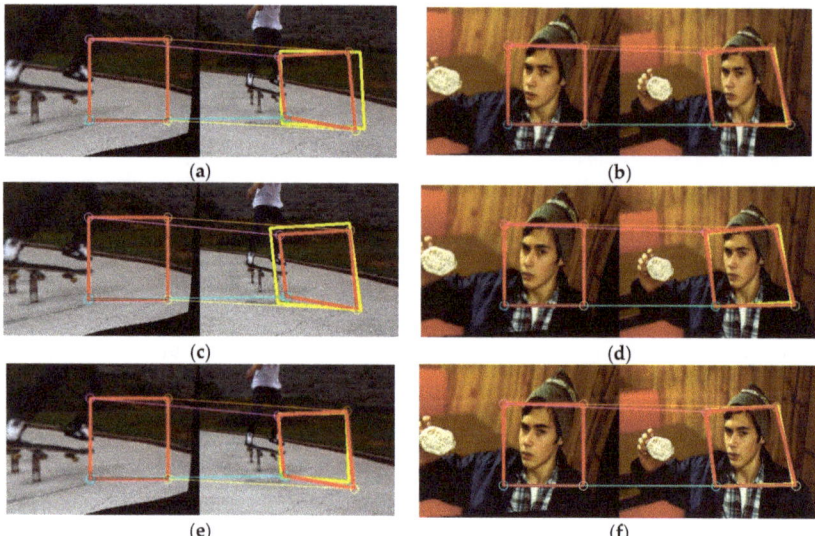

Figure 7. Visualization analysis of the proposed algorithm under different CNNs (The red boxes indicate the ground truth, and the yellow boxes are the estimation results): (**a**) accuracy of image registration under VGG (RMSE = 10.154711); (**b**) accuracy of image registration under VGG (RMSE = 2.240815); (**c**) accuracy of image registration under Googlenet (RMSE = 7.2284245); (**d**) accuracy of image registration under Googlenet (RMSE = 1.9681364); (**e**) accuracy of image registration under Xception (RMSE = 3.1798978); (**f**) accuracy of image registration under Xception (RMSE = 1.4085304).

4. Conclusions

Aiming at the problem of image registration with parallax, an image registration algorithm based on deep learning and local homography transformation is proposed. A sample and label generation method suitable for local homography matrix estimation is designed by using DLT and MDLT, so as to obtain an effective image registration model through supervised learning. The proposed algorithm overcomes the defect that the existing learning-based image registration algorithm cannot be used for local homography matrix estimation and improves the weak robustness of traditional image registration algorithms. Experimental results show that the proposed algorithm achieves high image registration accuracy; low time complexity; and good robustness to illumination, color, and brightness. In particular, the combination of the proposed algorithm and a better CNN architecture can significantly improve the accuracy of image registration.

In this paper, the MDLT algorithm is adopted to generate samples with local matching points. The perturbation value cannot be set very large, otherwise it will cause unnatural deformation and dislocation of the image. Therefore, the proposed algorithm is more suitable for the sample with weak locality. In addition, compared with the traditional algorithms, the proposed algorithm has higher requirements on hardware and takes a longer time to generate samples and train neural networks; this will be improved in further work.

Author Contributions: Conceptualization, Y.W., M.Y. and G.J.; methodology, Y.W., M.Y. and G.J.; software, Y.W.; investigation, Z.P. and J.L.; Writing—Original draft preparation, Y.W., M.Y. and G.J.; Writing—Review and editing, M.Y. and G.J. All authors have read and agreed to the published version of the manuscript.

Funding: This research was funded by the National Natural Science Foundation of China under Grant No. 61671258, 61871247, 61931022. It was also sponsored by the K. C. Wong Magna Fund of Ningbo University.

Conflicts of Interest: The authors declare no conflict of interest.

References

1. Du, C.Y.; Yuan, J.L.; Dong, J.S.; Li, L.; Chen, M.C.; Li, T. GPU based Parallel Optimization for Real Time Panoramic Video Stitching. *Pattern Recognit. Lett.* **2019**. [CrossRef]
2. Zheng, J.; Zhang, Z.; Tao, Q.H.; Shen, K.; Wang, Y. An Accurate Multi-Row Panorama Generation Using Multi-Point Joint Stitching. *IEEE Access* **2018**, *6*, 27827–27839. [CrossRef]
3. Aguerrebere, C.; Delbracio, M.; Bartesaghi, A.; Sapiro, G. A Practical Guide to Multi-Image Alignment. In Proceedings of the 2018 IEEE International Conference on Acoustics, Speech and Signal Processing (ICASSP), Calgary, AB, Canada, 15–20 April 2018.
4. Gomez-Ojeda, R.; Moreno, F.A.; Zuniga-Noel, D.; Scaramuzza, D.; Gonzalez-Jimenez, J. PL-SLAM: A Stereo SLAM System Through the Combination of Points and Line Segments. *IEEE Trans. Robot.* **2019**, *35*, 734–746. [CrossRef]
5. Leng, C.C.; Zhang, H.; Li, B.; Cai, G.R.; Pei, Z.; He, L. Local feature descriptor for image matching: A survey. *IEEE Access* **2019**, *7*, 6424–6434. [CrossRef]
6. Chang, C.H.; Chou, C.N.; Chang, E.Y. CLKN: Cascaded Lucas-Kanade Networks for Image Alignment. In Proceedings of the 2017 IEEE Conference on Computer Vision and Pattern Recognition (CVPR), Honolulu, HI, USA, 21–26 July 2017.
7. Evangelidis, G.; Psarakis, E. Parametric Image Alignment Using Enhanced Correlation Coefficient Maximization. *IEEE Trans. Pattern Anal. Mach. Intell.* **2008**, *30*, 1858–1865. [CrossRef] [PubMed]
8. Baker, S.; Matthews, I. Lucas-Kanade 20 Years On: A Unifying Framework. *Int. J. Comput. Vis.* **2004**, *56*, 221–255. [CrossRef]
9. Li, Y.L.; Wang, S.J.; Tian, Q.; Ding, X.Q. A survey of recent advances in visual feature detection. *Neurocomputing* **2015**, *149*, 736–751. [CrossRef]
10. Salahat, E.; Qasaimeh, M. Recent advances in features extraction and description algorithms: A comprehensive survey. In Proceedings of the 2017 IEEE International Conference on Industrial Technology (ICIT), Toronto, ON, Canada, 23–25 March 2017.

11. Lowe, D.G. Distinctive Image Features from Scale-Invariant Keypoints. *Int. J. Comput. Vis.* **2004**, *60*, 91–110. [CrossRef]
12. Rublee, E.; Rabaud, V.; Konolige, K.; Bradski, G.R. ORB: An efficient alternative to SIFT or SURF. In Proceedings of the 2011 International Conference on Computer Vision, Barcelona, Spain, 6–13 November 2011.
13. Fischler, M.A.; Bolles, R.C. Random sample consensus: A paradigm for model fitting with applications to image analysis and automated cartography. *Commun. ACM* **1981**, *24*, 381–395. [CrossRef]
14. DeTone, D.; Malisiewicz, T.; Rabinovich, A. Deep Image Homography Estimation. Available online: https://arxiv.org/abs/1606.03798 (accessed on 13 June 2016).
15. Nguyen, T.; Chen, S.W.; Shivakumar, S.S.; Taylor, C.J.; Kumar, V.; Skandan, S. Unsupervised Deep Homography: A Fast and Robust Homography Estimation Model. *IEEE Robot. Autom. Lett.* **2018**, *3*, 2346–2353. [CrossRef]
16. Li, N.; Xu, Y.F.; Wang, C. Quasi-Homography Warps in Image Stitching. *IEEE Trans. Multimed.* **2018**, *20*, 1365–1375. [CrossRef]
17. Zhou, E.; Cao, Z.; Sun, J. GridFace: Face rectification via learning local homography transformations. In Proceedings of the 15th European Conference on Computer Vision, Munich, Germany, 8–14 September 2018.
18. Jia, Q.; Fan, X.; Gao, X.K.; Yu, M.Y.; Li, H.J.; Luo, Z.X. Line matching based on line-points invariant and local homography. *Pattern Recognit.* **2018**, *81*, 471–483. [CrossRef]
19. Zaragoza, J.; Chin, T.J.; Tran, Q.H.; Brown, M.S.; Suter, D. As-projective-as-possible image stitching with moving DLT. *IEEE Trans. Pattern Anal. Mach. Intell.* **2014**, *36*, 1285–1298. [PubMed]
20. Chang, C.H.; Sato, Y.; Chuang, Y.Y.; Sato, Y. Shape-Preserving Half-Projective Warps for Image Stitching. In Proceedings of the 2014 IEEE Conference on Computer Vision and Pattern Recognition, Columbus, OH, USA, 23–28 June 2014.
21. Lin, C.C.; Pankanti, S.U.; Ramamurthy, K.N.; Aravkin, A.Y. Adaptive as-natural-as-possible image stitching. In Proceedings of the 2015 IEEE Conference on Computer Vision and Pattern Recognition (CVPR), Boston, MA, USA, 7–12 June 2015.
22. Simonyan, K.; Zisserman, A. Very deep convolutional networks for large-scale image recognition. In Proceedings of the 3rd International Conference on Learning Representations, San Diego, CA, USA, 7–9 May 2015.
23. Szegedy, C.; Liu, W.; Jia, Y.; Sermanet, P.; Reed, S.; Anguelov, D.; Erhan, D.; Vanhoucke, V.; Rabinovich, A. Going deeper with convolutions. In Proceedings of the 2015 IEEE Conference on Computer Vision and Pattern Recognition (CVPR), Boston, MA, USA, 7–12 June 2015.
24. Chollet, F. Xception: Deep Learning with Depthwise Separable Convolutions. In Proceedings of the 2017 IEEE Conference on Computer Vision and Pattern Recognition (CVPR), Honolulu, HI, USA, 21–26 July 2017.
25. Abadi, M.; Barham, P.; Chen, J.; Chen, Z.F.; Davis, A.; Dean, J.; Devin, M.; Ghemawat, S.; Irving, G.; Isard, M.; et al. TensorFlow: A system for large-scale machine learning. In Proceedings of the 12th USENIX Conference on Operating Systems Design and Implementation, Savannah, GA, USA, 2–4 November 2016.
26. Lin, T.Y.; Maire, M.; Belongie, S.; Hays, J.; Perona, P.; Ramanan, D.; Dollár, P.; Zitnick, C.L. Microsoft coco: Common objects in context. In Proceedings of the European Conference on Computer Vision, Zurich, Switzerland, 6–12 September 2014.
27. Howard, A.G. Some improvements on deep convolutional neural network based image classification. In Proceedings of the 2nd International Conference on Learning Representations, Banff, AB, Canada, 14–16 April 2014.
28. Kingma, D.P.; Ba, J.L. Adam: A method for stochastic optimization. In Proceedings of the 3rd International Conference on Learning Representations, San Diego, CA, USA, 7–9 May 2015.
29. Srivastava, N.; Hinton, G.; Krizhevsky, A.; Sutskever, I.; Salakhutdinov, R. Dropout: A simple way to prevent neural networks from overfitting. *J. Mach. Learn. Res.* **2014**, *15*, 1929–1958.

© 2020 by the authors. Licensee MDPI, Basel, Switzerland. This article is an open access article distributed under the terms and conditions of the Creative Commons Attribution (CC BY) license (http://creativecommons.org/licenses/by/4.0/).

Article

Image Super-Resolution Based on CNN Using Multilabel Gene Expression Programming

Jiali Tang [1], Chenrong Huang [2,*], Jian Liu [1] and Hongjin Zhu [1]

[1] College of Computer Engineering, Jiangsu University of Technology, Changzhou 213001, Jiangsu, China; tangjl@jsut.edu.cn (J.T.); lj18816276124@hotmail.com (J.L.); zhuhongjin@jsut.edu.cn (H.Z.)
[2] School of Computer Engineering, Nanjing Institute of Technology, Nanjing 211167, Jiangsu, China
* Correspondence: huangcr@njit.edu.cn

Received: 25 December 2019; Accepted: 23 January 2020; Published: 25 January 2020

Abstract: Current mainstream super-resolution algorithms based on deep learning use a deep convolution neural network (CNN) framework to realize end-to-end learning from low-resolution (LR) image to high-resolution (HR) images, and have achieved good image restoration effects. However, as the number of layers in the network is increased, better results are not necessarily obtained, and there will be problems such as slow training convergence, mismatched sample blocks, and unstable image restoration results. We propose a preclassified deep-learning algorithm (MGEP-SRCNN) using Multilabel Gene Expression Programming (MGEP), which screens out a sample sub-bank with high relevance to the target image before image block extraction, preclassifies samples in a multilabel framework, and then performs nonlinear mapping and image reconstruction. The algorithm is verified through standard images, and better objective image quality is obtained. The restoration effect under different magnification conditions is also better.

Keywords: super-resolution (SR); convolution neural network (CNN); Gene Expression Programming (GEP); deep learning; image preclassification

1. Introduction

Aiming at addressing image degradation during digital image acquisition and processing, Single-Image Super-Resolution (SISR) technology [1,2] enables high-resolution (HR) images to be recovered from low-resolution (LR) ones with high-frequency texture details and edge structure information observations of images to meet people's image quality needs.

Early reconstruction-based SR methods mainly modeled the acquisition process of low-resolution observation images, used the regularization method to construct the prior constraints of high-resolution images, estimated the HR images from the LR observation images, and finally restored the super resolution image. The problem turns into an optimization problem of a cost function under a constraint [3]. Learning-based super-resolution restoration technology was first proposed by Freeman [4]. This type of algorithm uses the similarity of different images in high-frequency details to obtain the relationship between the HR and LR images through the algorithm to guide the reconstruction of the output image. Prior knowledge can be obtained through learning, instead of defining the prior knowledge in the model-based reconstruction method.

In recent years, deep learning has been a hot topic in the field of machine learning, and its related theories have attracted widespread attention from researchers. It has been gradually used in the field of image super-resolution reconstruction and has better effects than shallow learning [5–13]. The most classic of them is an end-to-end deep learning model, the super-resolution convolution neural network (SRCNN), constructed by a three-layer convolutional neural network proposed by Dong et al. [5]. The image is input after Bicubic preprocessing, and it is trained on LR and HR images in pairs. The gradient descent method continuously adjusts the weights to obtain a mapping from LR to HR.

Its simple network structure design and excellent image restoration results created a precedent for deep learning in super-resolution image reconstruction. However, the SRCNN method does not obtain better results when the number of layers in the network is increased. The training convergence rate is slow and it is not suitable for multiscale amplification.

Based on the above problems, we propose an improved deep learning algorithm for Gene Expression Programming (GEP) preclassification. This method uses the GEP multilabeling algorithm to classify the trained image set and select a subset of samples that are related in color and texture feature categories, thereby reducing the complexity of the convolutional neural network parameters. We compare the performance of our approach to that of other state-of-the-art methods and obtain improved objective image quality.

2. Related Work

In recent years, deep learning and artificial intelligence have been widely used in various industries, especially in the field of computer vision, and have achieved better results than traditional methods [14,15]. Using the feed-forward depth network methods of CNN is the mainstream of the current super-resolution reconstruction field after sparse representation. Such methods focus less on the reconstruction speed and more on whether the high-resolution map can be better restored at a large magnification. They have better generalization ability and ability to characterize the high-level characteristics, compared with traditional shallow learning algorithms.

2.1. SRCNN/Fast SRCNN (FSRCNN)

Dong et al. [5] first proposed the use of a convolutional neural network for image super-resolution reconstruction. An LR image was first enlarged to the target size using Bicubic interpolation, and then a nonlinear mapping was performed through a three-layer convolutional network. The obtained results were output as high-resolution images, and good results were obtained. As shown in Figure 1, the network structure design of this method is simple. Compared with previous learning algorithms, it saves a lot of artificial feature extraction steps and post-integration, thus opening up the era of deep CNN super-resolution image processing problems.

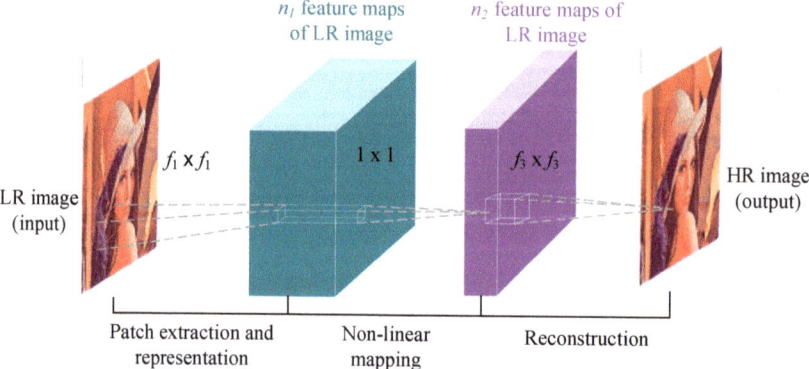

Figure 1. Network architecture of the super-resolution convolution neural network (SRCNN).

After that, Dong et al. [6] improved upon the SRCNN, and the fast SRCNN (FSRCNN) was proposed, which increases the depth of the network and introduces a deconvolution layer to restore features. The deconvolution layer can realize the conversion from low-resolution space to high-resolution space. This feature allows the FSRCNN to directly use the low-resolution image instead of the interpolation result as the network input. Directly using LR images as input can not only reduce the calculation amount of the model, but also avoid the obvious artificial traces introduced by interpolation. FSRCNN offers a great improvement in speed, without any preprocessing, to achieve end-to-end input and output of the network, but the restoration accuracy is somewhat insufficient.

2.2. Sparse-Coding-Based Network (SCN)

The SCN method [9] firstly obtains the sparse prior information of the image through the feature extraction layer, then establishes a feed-forward neural network which can implement sparse encoding and decoding of the image, and finally uses a cascade network to complete the image enlargement. This method can improve the Peak Signal-to-Noise Ratio (PSNR) at a higher magnification, and the algorithm running speed is further improved. Moreover, with the correct understanding of each layer's physical meaning, the SCN method offers a more principled way to initialize the parameters, which helps to improve optimization speed and quality.

2.3. Very Deep Convolutional Networks for Image Super-Resolution (VDSR)

The ultra-deep super-resolution network proposed by Kim et al. [8] extended the SRCNN from a 3-layer shallow network structure to a 20-layer ultra-deep network, and they concluded that the reconstruction effect will be improved as the number of layers increases. Compared to SRCNN, which only depends on the image context in a small area, VDSR, by exploring more contextual information through a larger receptive field, helps to better restore the detailed structure, especially in super-resolution applications with large magnification factors. In addition, in order to solve the problem of slow convergence in SRCNN, VDSR residual learning was introduced, which greatly increased the learning rate.

VDSR accepts image features of different scales by adjusting the size of the filter to produce a fixed feature output. Although VDSR can achieve specific-scale magnification, it cannot achieve free-scale, multiscale magnification, and its parameter storage and retrieval also have obvious shortcomings.

3. The Proposed Method

3.1. Multifeature Representation of Images

Image features include color, texture, shape, and spatial relationships. Features can be extracted from the image after being detected by the computer. The result is called a feature description or feature vector. In this paper, the Multilabel Gene Expression Programming (MGEP) algorithm mainly uses image color and texture features for multilabel recognition.

3.1.1. Color Feature

The color feature is a global feature that describes the surface properties of the scene corresponding to the image or image area, and is also the most direct visual feature in the physical characteristics of the image. Compared with various other image features, the color feature has two obvious advantages: one is stability, low sensitivity to various changes in the image such as translation, scaling, rotation, etc., and strong robustness, the second is that its complicated calculation degree is low. The pixel values in the image are converted, and the corresponding numerical expression is used to obtain the image characteristics [16]. Because of the stability and simple calculation, the color feature has become a widely used image feature.

Shown in Figure 2, the color histogram is widely used in many image retrieval systems. It describes the proportion of different colors in the entire image, and does not pay attention to the spatial location of each color; that is, it cannot describe the objects or objects in the image.

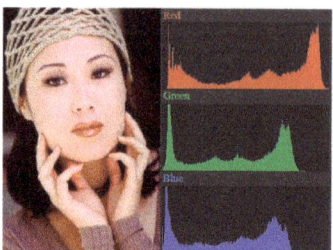

Figure 2. Color histogram of an image (RGB channel).

The color histogram can be defined as the joint probability density function of the three color channels (RGB) in the image:

$$h_{R,G,B}(a,b,c) = N \bullet P(R = a, G = b, B = c) \tag{1}$$

where R, G, and B represent the RGB color channels of the image, N indicates the number of image pixels, P represents the probability density function, and h represents a histogram function, defined as a four-dimensional eigenvector $H(H_R, H_G, H_B, \mu)$. The first three dimensions H_R, H_G, and H_B correspond to the three color channels, and the last dimension μ indicates the proportion of the color in the entire image.

3.1.2. Texture Feature

Texture is a visual feature that reflects homogeneous phenomena in an image, and it reflects the surface structure organization and arrangement properties of an object surface with slow or periodic changes. Texture is a pattern produced by the gray or color of the target image in space in a certain form [17]. From the perspective of texture, the image can be roughly divided into three cases: first, the gray distribution has a certain periodicity (even if the gray change is random, it also has certain statistical characteristics, and may be in a larger area repeatedly); second, the basic components that make up the sequence are regular rather than random; third, the texture of each part in the texture area shows roughly the same size, structure, and image, and is uniformly distributed as a whole.

The Fourier power spectrum method is used to measure the texture characteristics of the image. Let the texture image be $f(x, y)$; its Fourier transform can be expressed by Equation (2).

$$F(u,v) = \int \int_{-\infty}^{\infty} f(x,y) \exp\{-j2\pi(ux + vy)\} dx dy \tag{2}$$

The definition of the power spectrum of the two-dimensional Fourier transform is shown in Equation (3):

$$|F|^2 = FF^* \tag{3}$$

where F^* stands for the conjugate of F. The power spectrum $|F|^2$ reflects the nature of the entire image. If the Fourier transform is expressed in polar form, i.e., $F(r, \theta)$ form, then the energy on the circle r from the origin is

$$\Phi_r = \int_0^{2\pi} [F(r,\theta)]^2 d\theta. \tag{4}$$

From research on the energy in the small fan-shaped region in the angle θ direction, the law of this energy changing with the angle can be obtained by Equation (5):

$$\Phi_\theta = \int_0^\infty |F(r,\theta)|^2 dr. \tag{5}$$

When a texture image runs along θ and there are many lines, edges, etc., in the direction $\theta + \frac{\pi}{2}$, i.e., in a right-angle direction to θ, the energy is concentrated. If the texture does not show directionality, there is no directionality in the power spectrum. Therefore, the $|F|^2$ value reflects the directionality of the texture.

3.2. GEP Network

Gene Expression Programming (GEP) was proposed by Ferreira in 2001. It is a new evolutionary model and belongs to the family of genetic algorithms [18,19]. The GEP algorithm, like the Genetic Algorithm (GA) and Genetic Programming (GP), is a computational model that simulates the evolutionary process of living things. Because GEP chromosomes are simple, linear, and compact; make it easy to carry out genetic operations, etc.; and have stronger problem-solving capabilities, they are 2 to 4 orders of magnitude faster than GA and GP [19]. Because of these advantages, GEP technology has attracted the attention of many researchers and has been used in machine learning fields such as function discovery, symbol regression, classification, clustering, and association rule analysis.

(S, F, T) represents a GEP gene as a 3-tuple, of which S is a fixed-length string, F is the set of calculation functions, and T is the basic terminal set. Sometimes, for convenience, the fixed-length string S is called a gene. The gene is divided into two parts, the head and the tail. The former symbol can be taken from F and T, and the latter must be taken from T. GEP gene coding rules ensure that it can be decoded into an expression tree corresponding to a legal mathematical expression. Suppose its head length is h, tail length is t, and $n_{\max}$ is the maximum number of parameters of a function in the function set; then the relationship between h and t can be expressed by Equation (6).

$$t = h(n_{\max} - 1) + 1 \tag{6}$$

GEP's neural network selective integration process is divided into two stages.

Stage 1: Network group generation.

We use existing methods such as Boosting and Bagging to generate network groups. Assume the output vector of the network population is $Y = (y_1, y_2, \ldots, y_n)$, $y_i \in \{0, 1\}$.

Stage 2: Individual network selection and conclusion generation based on GEP.

For input x, there are the following integrated classification results:

$$y(x) = \text{sign}(f(Y')). \tag{7}$$

Among them, $Y' \subseteq Y$, $Y' = (y_{i_1}, y_{i_2}, \ldots, y_{i_m})$. That is, the final classification result is synthesized from some network outputs in the network group in some way. Because GEP has powerful function discovery and parameter selection functions, it can be discovered using the GEP method $f(Y')$.

Taking the threshold $lamda = 0.5$, the integrated classification result $y(x)$ is calculated as follows:

$$y(x) = \begin{cases} 1 & f(Y') \geq 0.5 \\ 0 & f(Y') < 0.5 \end{cases} \tag{8}$$

3.3. Fitness Function Design

The fitness function is the guideline for the evolution of the GEP algorithm. For feed-forward neural networks, the topology selection and training of weights can be regarded as an optimization process. The purpose of optimization is to design the network so that the fitness function value reaches the maximum value. The performance of the current network for a given training data set is described by a least squares error function.

We use category-based multilabel evaluation indicators. We first measure the classifier's corresponding two-class classification performance on a single class, and then calculate the average performance of the classifier on all classes as the evaluation index value of the classifier. Suppose we have a multilabeled test set with p-many sample data $S = \{(x_i, Y_i) | 1 \le i \le p\}$ for the jth category y_j ($1 \le j \le q$). In terms of the multilabel classifier, the two-class classification performance of $h(\cdot)$ in this category can be described by the four statistics given by Equations (9)–(12).

1. TP_j (#true positive instances)

$$TP_j = |\{x_i \mid y_j \in Y_i \wedge y_j \in h(x_i), (x_i, Y_i) \in S\}| \tag{9}$$

2. FP_j (#false positive instances)

$$FP_j = |\{x_i \mid y_j \notin Y_i \wedge y_j \in h(x_i), (x_i, Y_i) \in S\}| \tag{10}$$

3. TP_j (#true negative instances)

$$TP_j = |\{x_i \mid y_j \notin Y_i \wedge y_j \notin h(x_i), (x_i, Y_i) \in S\}| \tag{11}$$

4. FP_j (#false negative instances)

$$FP_j = |\{x_i \mid y_j \in Y_i \wedge y_j \notin h(x_i), (x_i, Y_i) \in S\}| \tag{12}$$

From Equations (9)–(12), $TP_j + FP_j + TN_j + FN_j = p$ is established. Most classification performance indicators, such as accuracy, precision, and recall, can be derived from the above four statistics—see Equations (13)–(15).

$$\text{Accuracy} = B(TP_j, FP_j, TN_j, FN_j) = \frac{TP_j + TN_j}{TP_j + FP_j + TN_j + FN_j} \tag{13}$$

$$\text{Precision} = B(TP_j, FP_j, TN_j, FN_j) = \frac{TP_j}{TP_j + FP_j} \tag{14}$$

$$\text{Recall} = B(TP_j, FP_j, TN_j, FN_j) = \frac{TP_j}{TP_j + FN_j} \tag{15}$$

Therefore, combined with category-based multilabel classification evaluation index, we design a fitness function for the MGEP classification algorithm.

1. Design of fitness function based on macro-averaging:

$$Fit_i = \left| R - 100 \times \frac{1}{q} \sum_{j=1}^{q} B(TP_j, FP_j, TN_j, FN_j) \right| \tag{16}$$

2. Design of fitness function based on micro-averaging:

$$Fit_i = \left| R - B\left(\sum_{j=1}^{q} TP_j, \sum_{j=1}^{q} FP_j, \sum_{j=1}^{q} TN_j, \sum_{j=1}^{q} FN_j \right) \right| \tag{17}$$

In Equations (16) and (17), Fit_i is the fitness value of the ith individual to the environment, and R is the selected bandwidth.

3.4. MGEP Classification before CNN Image Super-Resolution

In the process of image super-resolution reconstruction, the traditional K-means clustering algorithm [20] is used to classify the trained image set to improve the training effect and reduce the training time. In the K-means clustering algorithm, the value of K needs to be determined in advance, and it cannot be changed during the entire course of the algorithm, which makes it difficult to accurately estimate the value of K when training high-dimensional data sets.

We used the MGEP classification algorithm instead of the K-means clustering algorithm, and its preclassification model is shown in Figure 3.

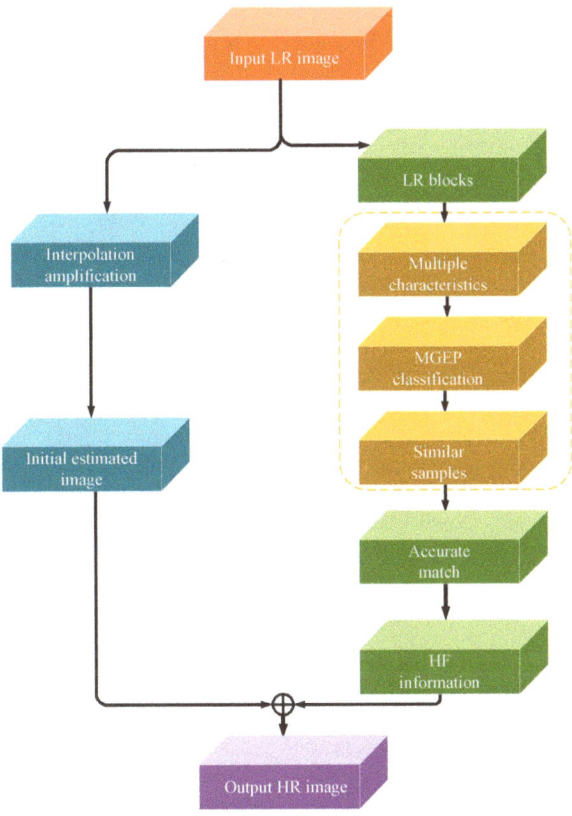

Figure 3. The Multilabel Gene Expression Programming (MGEP) preclassification model.

Let p-many sample pattern pairs (x_k, y_k) constitute the training set, $k = 1, 2, \ldots, p$. According to the definition of the GEP classifier, for sample k, there are $x_k = (x_{k1}, x_{k2}, \ldots, x_{km})$ and $y_k = (y_{k1}, y_{k2}, \ldots, y_{kn})$, where x_{kj} is the sample in the attribute A_j ($j = 1, 2, \ldots, m$) and y_{ki} is the degree of membership of the sample to the category C_i ($i = 1, 2, \ldots, n$). The training set constitutes the set of adaptive instances, and the set of adapted instances of a particular problem forms the adaptive environment of the MGEP algorithm. Under a certain adaptive environment, starting from the initial population, selection, replication, and various genetic operations are performed according to individual fitness to form a new population. This process is repeated until the optimal individual is evolved and decoded to obtain a GEP multilabel classifier. In the MGEP preclassification learning, we find similar samples for LR image blocks in terms of color and texture features, thereby shortening the time of the next precise matching and improving the efficiency and effect of SR image restoration.

In the training of the CNN, the MGEP algorithm is used to classify the trained image set, classify the approximate images into one category, and reduce the parameter scale of the convolutional neural network model, which can reduce the training time of the network to a certain extent and improve the training efficiency of the CNN. The improved algorithm flow based on SRCNN is shown in Figure 4.

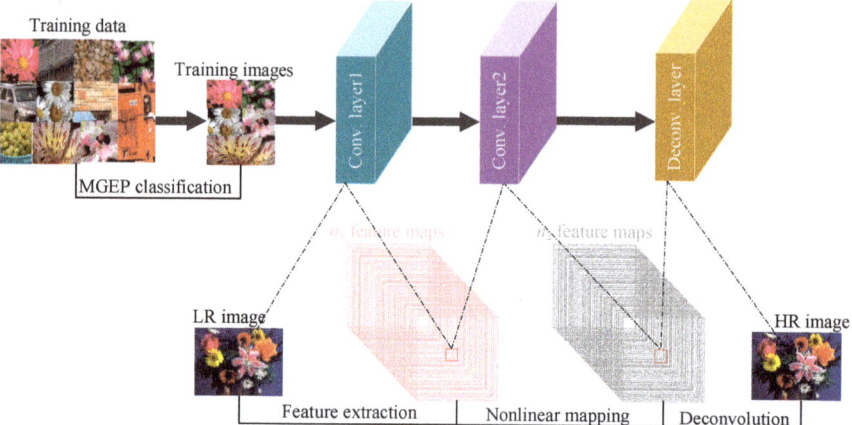

Figure 4. MGEP-SRCNN algorithm flow chart.

The algorithm uses Wiener filtering to construct a deconvolution layer, which is used to implement multiscale image reconstruction. The deconvolution network part adopts the mirror structure of the convolution network. The purpose is to reconstruct the shape of the input target, so the multilevel deconvolution structure can also capture the shape details of different levels like the convolution network. In the model of the convolutional network, low-level features can describe the rough information of the entire target, such as target position and approximate shape, while more complex high-level features have classification characteristics and also contain more detailed target information.

4. Experiments

4.1. Experimental Environment and Parameter Settings

The experimental software environment used was Ubuntu 14.04, Python 2.7, TensorFlow 1.4; the hardware environment was an Intel Core i7-6700K, RAM 16GB, and the GPU was an NVIDIA GTX1080.

As the training set, we used ImageNet-91 [5], and as the test set, we used Set5 [21], Set14 [22], BSD100 [23], and Urban100 [24]. We tested on three commonly used scale factors, 2, 3, and 4, and compared the results with those of the Bicubic, SCN [9], SRCNN [5], VDSR [8], and DRCN [10] algorithms. Two evaluation indexes, PSNR and Structural Similarity (SSIM), were selected as an objective reference basis for the superiority of algorithm reconstruction to measure the effect of image restoration.

4.2. MGEP Preclassification Settings

We used the MGEP algorithm to preclassify the trained image set before deep learning. We selected a subset of samples that were related in color and texture feature categories. Equation (16) was used as the fitness function to implement the MGEP classification algorithm, which was then applied to sample preclassification in the SR image restoration process.

The function set was set to {+, −, ×, /}, the evolution algebra *gen* was set to 1000, and the population size N was set to 100. The total number of genes was set to 10, of which there were 7 common genes and 3 homologous genes. The three homologous genes respectively output the color category calculated according to Equation (1), the texture category calculated according to Equation (18), and the texture category calculated according to Equation (19) of the input LR image block.

$$T(j,k) = \sum_{\varepsilon=-T}^{j} \sum_{n=-T}^{k} \varepsilon^2 \eta^2 C(\varepsilon, \eta, j, k) \tag{18}$$

$$\text{MEAN} = \frac{1}{m}\sum_i ip_\Delta(i) \tag{19}$$

Each gene had a head length of 5 and a chromosome length of 110. The genetic manipulation probability was set to 0.1.

The MGEP preclassification effect is shown in Figure 4. The training samples "Car", "Building", and "Cobblestone" in ImageNet-91 that have little correlation with the color texture features of the input image "Flowers" were excluded, thereby improving the training effect and matching accuracy.

4.3. Image Restoration Results

CNN deep learning was performed after MGEP preclassification. All convolutional layer filters were 3 × 3 in size and the number of filters was 64. We used the method of He et al. [25] to initialize the convolutional layer. The convolution kernel moved in steps of 1. In order to keep the size of all feature maps the same as the input of each layer, 0 was filled around the boundary before applying the convolution. The learning rate of all layers was initialized to 5×10^{-4}, and the learning rate dropped by 2 times every 15 epochs until the learning rate was less than 5×10^{-9}.

Tables 1–4 show the PSNR/SSIM values and running times of the six algorithms on the Set5, Set14, BSD100, and Urban100 test sets when the upscale factors were 2, 3, and 4, respectively.

Table 1. Average Peak Signal-to-Noise Ratio (PSNR)/Structural Similarity (SSIM) values for 2× scale. Red color indicates the best and the blue color indicates the second-best performance.

Dataset	Bicubic	SRCNN [5]	SCN [9]	VDSR [8]	DRCN [10]	MGEP-SRCNN
Set5	33.66/0.9299	36.66/0.9542	36.93/0.9552	37.53/0.9587	37.63/0.9588	37.78/0.9594
Set14	30.24/0.8688	32.42/0.9063	32.56/0.9074	33.03/0.9124	33.04/0.9118	33.29/0.9135
BSD100	29.56/0.8431	31.36/0.8879	31.40/0.8884	31.90/0.8960	31.85/0.8942	32.01/0.8979
Urban100	26.88/0.8403	29.50/0.8946	29.50/0.8960	30.76/0.9140	30.75/0.9133	31.19/0.9181

Table 2. Average PSNR/SSIM values for 3× scale. Red color indicates the best and the blue color indicates the second-best performance.

Dataset	Bicubic	SRCNN [5]	SCN [9]	VDSR [8]	DRCN [10]	MGEP-SRCNN
Set5	30.39/0.8682	32.75/0.9090	33.10/0.9144	33.66/0.9213	33.82/0.9226	34.04/0.9250
Set14	27.55/0.7742	29.28/0.8209	29.41/0.8238	29.77/0.8314	29.76/0.8311	29.97/0.8333
BSD100	27.21/0.7385	28.41/0.7863	28.50/0.7885	28.82/0.7976	28.80/0.7963	28.92/0.7972
Urban100	24.46/0.7349	26.24/0.7989	26.21/0.8010	27.14/0.8279	27.15/0.8276	27.24/0.8330

Table 3. Average PSNR/SSIM values for 4× scale. Red color indicates the best and the blue color indicates the second-best performance.

Dataset	Bicubic	SRCNN [5]	SCN [9]	VDSR [8]	DRCN [10]	MGEP-SRCNN
Set5	28.42/0.8104	30.48/0.8628	30.06/0.8732	31.35/0.8838	31.53/0.8851	31.66/0.8899
Set14	26.00/0.7027	27.49/0.7503	27.64/0.7578	28.01/0.7674	28.02/0.7670	28.19/0.8359
BSD100	25.96/0.6675	26.90/0.7101	27.03/0.7161	27.29/0.7251	27.23/0.7233	27.34/0.7238
Urban100	23.14/0.6577	24.52/0.7221	24.52/0.7250	25.18/0.7524	25.14/0.7510	25.21/0.7837

Table 4. Comparison of the running times (sec) for scales 2×, 3×, and 4×. Red color indicates the best performance.

Dataset	Scale	Bicubic	SRCNN [5]	SCN [9]	VDSR [8]	DRCN [10]	MGEP-SRCNN
Set5	×2	-	2.191	0.941	0.054	0.735	0.039
	×3	-	2.235	1.829	0.062	0.748	0.052
	×4	-	2.193	1.245	0.054	0.735	0.044
Set14	×2	-	4.324	1.709	0.113	1.579	0.097
	×3	-	4.402	3.611	0.122	1.569	0.113
	×4	-	4.397	2.377	0.112	1.526	0.101
BSD100	×2	-	2.517	1.015	0.071	0.983	0.069
	×3	-	2.583	2.138	0.071	0.996	0.067
	×4	-	2.516	1.290	0.071	0.984	0.061
Urban100	×2	-	22.123	4.779	0.451	5.010	0.401
	×3	-	19.358	4.012	0.514	5.054	0.484
	×4	-	18.462	3.199	0.448	5.048	0.407

As can be seen from Tables 1–3, the MGEP-SRCNN algorithm achieved the best PSNR effect at different magnifications on the four test sets. Compared with SRCNN, the PSNR evaluation index increased by 0.44–1.69 dB, and the improvement effect obtained in the Set5 dataset was the best. In terms of SSIM indicators, except for the suboptimal data obtained under the 2× and 3× conditions on the BSD100 dataset, other SSIM indicators were all optimal. Compared with SRCNN, the SSIM evaluation index improved by about 0.005–0.062, where 4× showed the best improvement. In addition, from Table 4 we can see that the MGEP-SRCNN algorithm achieved the best performance of running time on the precondition of accuracy.

Then, we subjectively determined the quality of the output image and compared the performance of the six SR algorithms by observing the visual effects of the restored image. For comparison, given a 3× upscale factor, the restoration effects of the different SR algorithms used on the Set5, Set14, BSD100, and Urban100 test sets are shown in Figures 5–8.

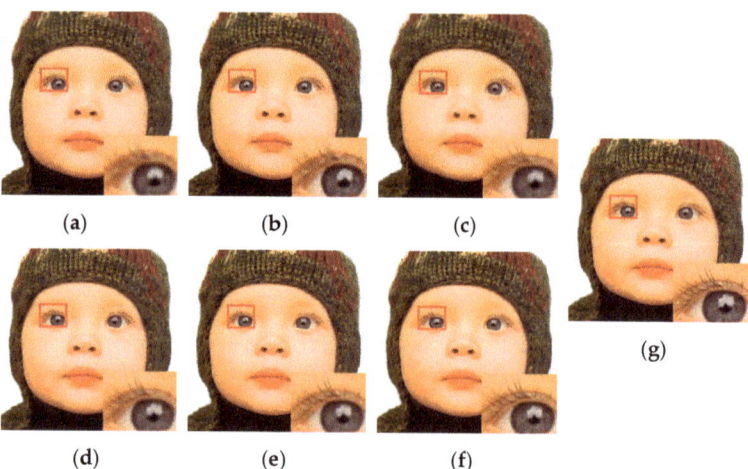

Figure 5. Super-resolution restoration results of the image "Baby" in Set5 [21]. (**a**) Bicubic; (**b**) SRCNN [5]; (**c**) SCN [9]; (**d**) VDSR [8]; (**e**) DRCN [10]; (**f**) MGEP-SRCNN; (**g**) Ground truth.

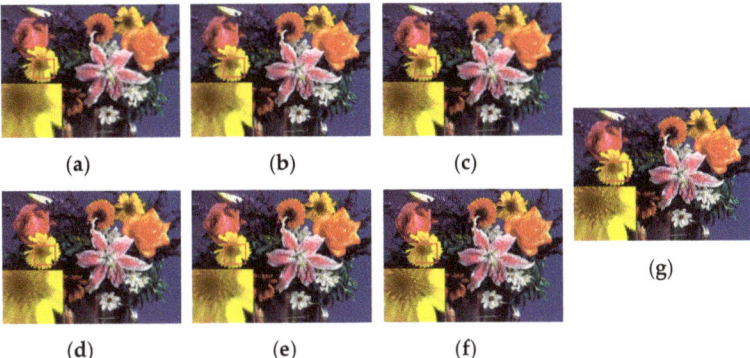

Figure 6. Super-resolution restoration results of the image "Flowers" in Set14 [22]. (**a**) Bicubic; (**b**) SRCNN [5]; (**c**) SCN [9]; (**d**) VDSR [8]; (**e**) DRCN [10]; (**f**) MGEP-SRCNN; (**g**) Ground truth.

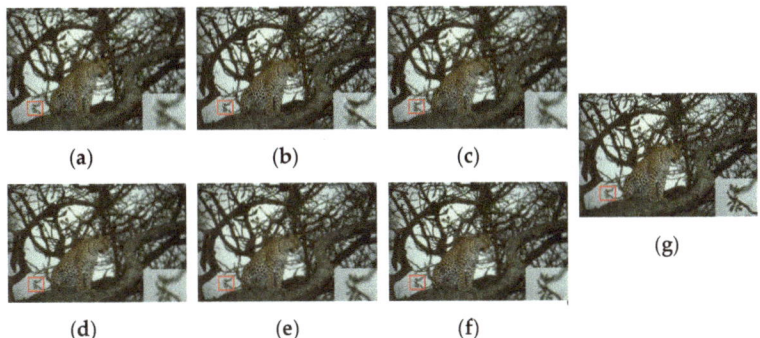

Figure 7. Super-resolution restoration results of the image "016" in BSD100 [23]. (**a**) Bicubic; (**b**) SRCNN [5]; (**c**) SCN [9]; (**d**) VDSR [8]; (**e**) DRCN [10]; (**f**) MGEP-SRCNN; (**g**) Ground truth.

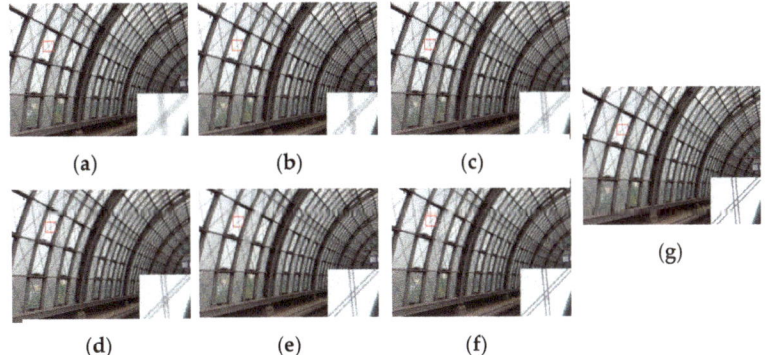

Figure 8. Super-resolution restoration results of the image "002" in Urban100 [24]. (**a**) Bicubic; (**b**) SRCNN [5]; (**c**) SCN [9]; (**d**) VDSR [8]; (**e**) DRCN [10]; (**f**) MGEP-SRCNN; (**g**) Ground truth.

It can be intuitively seen from the figure that the reconstructed images of both traditional Bicubic and SRCNN have aliasing, while the restored image provided by our algorithm is clearer and sharper, and the reconstruction quality is better. In the details, as seen in the baby eye in Figure 5, petal color in Figure 6, branch texture in Figure 7, and building glass in Figure 8, MGEP-SRCNN reconstructed images have clearer features, have no sawtooth texture, and are more in line with the visual needs of the human eye.

Figure 9 shows the PSNR/SSIM values of the six algorithms on the Set5, Set14, BSD100, and Urban100 test sets when the upscale factor was 3. The MGEP-SRCNN algorithm achieved the best PSNR effects in all four datasets. Except for the suboptimal data obtained in BSD100, the SSIM indicators were all optimal.

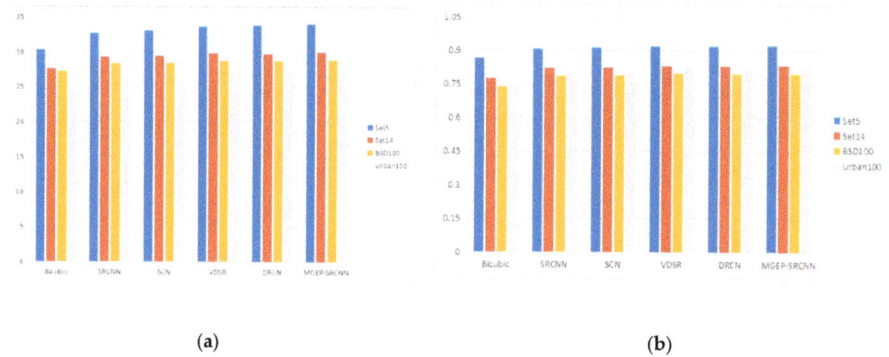

Figure 9. Image restoration results of the six SR algorithms. (**a**) PSNR; (**b**) SSIM.

5. Conclusions

In this work, we presented a super-resolution method using Multilabel Gene Expression Programming. This method uses MGEP to extract a subset of image samples related to color and texture features in advance, and then performs nonlinear mapping and image reconstruction, thereby reducing the complexity of the convolutional neural network parameters so as to avoid the SR problems of slow training convergence and unstable recovery results. It was experimentally verified that the image restoration effect of this method under different magnifications and on training sets is better than that of the commonly used deep learning algorithms, and it also performs well in terms of subjective visual effects.

Author Contributions: Conceptualization, J.T.; methodology, C.H.; software, J.L.; validation, H.Z.; formal analysis, J.T.; investigation, C.H.; resources, J.L.; data curation, J.L.; writing—original draft preparation, J.T.; writing—review and editing, H.Z.; supervision, C.H.; funding acquisition, J.T. and H.Z. All authors have read and agreed to the published version of the manuscript.

Funding: This work was supported by the National Natural Science Foundation of China (61806088), by the Opening Project of Jiangsu Key Laboratory of Advanced Numerical Control Technology (SYKJ201804), by the Project funded by Jiangsu Province Postdoctoral Science Foundation (2019K041), and by Changzhou Sci&Tech Program (CE20195030).

Acknowledgments: We are grateful to our anonymous referees for their useful comments and suggestions. The authors also thank Honghui Fan, Yijun Liu, Yan Wang, Wei Gao and Jie Zhang for their useful advice during this work.

Conflicts of Interest: The authors declare no conflict of interest.

References

1. Freeman, W.T.; Pasztor, E.C.; Carmichael, O.T. Learning Low-Level Vision. *Int. J. Comput. Vision* **2000**, *40*, 25–47. [CrossRef]
2. Glasner, D.; Bagon, S.; Irani, M. Super-resolution from a single image. In Proceedings of the 2009 IEEE 12th International Conference on Computer Vision, Kyoto, Japan, 29 September–2 October 2009; pp. 349–356.

3. Zhang, X.L.; Lam, K.M.; Shen, L.S. Image magnification based on a blockwise adaptive Markov random field model. *Image Vis. Comput.* **2008**, *26*, 1277–1284. [CrossRef]
4. Freeman, W.T.; Jones, T.R.; Pasztor, E.C. Example-based super-resolution. *IEEE Comput. Graph. Appl.* **2002**, *22*, 56–65. [CrossRef]
5. Dong, C.; Loy, C.C.; He, K.M.; Tang, X.O. Image Super-Resolution Using Deep Convolutional Networks. *IEEE Trans. Pattern Anal. Mach. Intell.* **2016**, *38*, 295–307. [CrossRef] [PubMed]
6. Dong, C.; Loy, C.C.; Tang, X. Accelerating the Super-Resolution Convolutional Neural Network. In Proceedings of the Computer Vision—ECCV 2016; Springer: Cham, Switzerland, 2016; pp. 391–407.
7. Hong, P.; Zhang, G. A Review of Super-Resolution Imaging through Optical High-Order Interference. *Appl. Sci.* **2019**, *9*, 1166. [CrossRef]
8. Kim, J.; Lee, J.K.; Lee, K.M. Accurate image super-resolution using very deep convolutional networks. In Proceedings of the 2016 IEEE Conference on Computer Vision and Pattern Recognition, Las Vegas, NV, USA, 27–30 June 2016; pp. 1646–1654.
9. Wang, Z.; Liu, D.; Yang, J.; Han, W.; Huang, T. Deep Networks for Image Super-Resolution with Sparse Prior. In Proceedings of the IEEE International Conference on Computer Vision, Santiago, Chile, 7–13 December 2015; pp. 370–378.
10. Kim, J.; Lee, J.K.; Lee, K.M. Deeply-recursive convolutional network for image super-resolution. In Proceedings of the 2016 IEEE Conference on Computer Vision and Pattern Recognition, Las Vegas, NV, USA, 27–30 June 2016; pp. 1637–1645.
11. Zhang, K.; Zuo, W.; Chen, Y.; Meng, D.; Zhang, L. Beyond a Gaussian Denoiser: Residual Learning of Deep CNN for Image Denoising. *IEEE Trans. Image Process.* **2017**, *26*, 3142–3155. [CrossRef] [PubMed]
12. Zhang, K.; Zuo, W.; Gu, S.; Zhang, L. Learning deep CNN denoiser prior for image restoration. In Proceedings of the IEEE Conference on Computer Vision and Pattern Recognition, Honolulu, HI, USA, 21–26 July 2017; pp. 3929–3938.
13. Lim, B.; Son, S.; Kim, H.; Nah, S.; Lee, K.M. Enhanced deep residual networks for single image super-resolution. In Proceedings of the IEEE Conference on Computer Vision and Pattern Recognition Workshops, Honolulu, HI, USA, 21–26 July 2017; pp. 136–144.
14. Hayat, K. Multimedia super-resolution via deep learning: A survey. *Digit. Signal Process.* **2018**, *81*, 198–217. [CrossRef]
15. Yang, W.; Zhang, X.; Tian, Y.; Wang, W.; Xue, J.; Liao, Q. Deep Learning for Single Image Super-Resolution: A Brief Review. *IEEE Trans. Multimedia* **2019**, *21*, 3106–3121. [CrossRef]
16. Zhang, H.J.; Gong, Y.H.; Low, C.Y.; Smoliar, S.W. Image retrieval based on color features: An evaluation study. In Proceedings of the SPIE, Digital Image Storage and Archiving Systems, Philadelphia, PA, USA, 21 November 1995; pp. 212–220.
17. Haralick, R.M.; Shanmugam, K.; Dinstein, I. Textural Features for Image Classification. *IEEE Trans. Syst. Man. Cybern.* **1973**, *SMC-3*, 610–621. [CrossRef]
18. Ferreira, C. Gene Expression Programming: A New Adaptive Algorithm for Solving Problems. *Complex Syst.* **2001**, *13*, 87–129.
19. Zhou, C.; Xiao, W.M.; Tirpak, T.M.; Nelson, P.C. Evolving accurate and compact classification rules with gene expression programming. *IEEE Trans. Evol. Comput.* **2003**, *7*, 519–531. [CrossRef]
20. Choi, J.; Kim, M. Single Image Super-Resolution Using Global Regression Based on Multiple Local Linear Mappings. *IEEE Trans. Image Process.* **2017**, *26*, 1300–1314. [CrossRef] [PubMed]
21. Bevilacqua, M.; Roumy, A.; Guillemot, C.; Morel, M.L.A. Low-Complexity Single-Image Super-Resolution based on Nonnegative Neighbor Embedding. In Proceedings of the British Machine Vision Conference (BMVC), Guildford, Surrey, UK, 3–7 September 2012; pp. 1–10.
22. Zeyde, R.; Elad, M.; Protter, M. On Single Image Scale-Up Using Sparse-Representations. In *Proceedings of the International Conference on Curves and Surfaces*; Springer: Berlin/Heidelberg, Germany, 2012; pp. 711–730.
23. Martin, D.; Fowlkes, C.; Tal, D.; Malik, J. A database of human segmented natural images and its application to evaluating segmentation algorithms and measuring ecological statistics. In Proceedings of the Eighth IEEE International Conference on Computer Vision (ICCV), Vancouver, BC, Canada, 7–14 July 2001; pp. 416–423.

24. Huang, J.B.; Singh, A.; Ahuja, N. Single image super-resolution from transformed self-exemplars. In Proceedings of the IEEE Conference on Computer Vision and Pattern Recognition (CVPR), Boston, MA, USA, 7–12 June 2015; pp. 5197–5206.
25. He, K.; Zhang, X.; Ren, S.; Sun, J. Delving Deep into Rectifiers: Surpassing Human-Level Performance on ImageNet Classification. In Proceedings of the 2015 IEEE International Conference on Computer Vision (ICCV), Santiago, Chile, 7–13 December 2015; pp. 1026–1034.

© 2020 by the authors. Licensee MDPI, Basel, Switzerland. This article is an open access article distributed under the terms and conditions of the Creative Commons Attribution (CC BY) license (http://creativecommons.org/licenses/by/4.0/).

Article
Temporal Saliency-Based Suspicious Behavior Pattern Detection

Kyung Joo Cheoi

Department of Computer Science, Chungbuk National University, Chungdae-ro 1, Seowon-gu, Cheongju-si, Chungbuk 28644, Korea; kjcheoi@chungbuk.ac.kr

Received: 5 December 2019; Accepted: 29 January 2020; Published: 4 February 2020

Abstract: The topic of suspicious behavior detection has been one of the most emergent research themes in computer vision, video analysis, and monitoring. Due to the huge number of CCTV (closed-circuit television) systems, it is not easy for people to manually identify CCTV for suspicious motion monitoring. This paper is concerned with an automatic suspicious behavior detection method using a CCTV video stream. Observers generally focus their attention on behaviors that vary in terms of magnitude or gradient of motion and behave differently in rules of motion with other objects. Based on these facts, the proposed method detected suspicious behavior with a temporal saliency map by combining the moving reactivity features of motion magnitude and gradient extracted by optical flow. It has been tested on various video clips that contain suspicious behavior. The experimental results show that the performance of the proposed method is good at detecting the six designated types of suspicious behavior examined: sudden running, colliding, falling, jumping, fighting, and slipping. The proposed method achieved an average accuracy of 93.89%, a precision of 96.21% and a recall of 94.90%.

Keywords: suspicious behavior detection; motion; magnitude; gradient; reactivity; saliency

1. Introduction

The vast majority of animals, including humans, get the most information from vision among various sensory organs and with this vision, they recognize and judge the situation [1]. As such, visual information is important to judge not only general circumstances but also special situations [2,3]. Although the technology of image processing and the performance of the computer have dramatically improved, analyzing and judging the situation comprehensively as a human does is still difficult [3]. Today, as various technologies using image processing continue being developed, the scope of intelligent image security technology in the video security market is rapidly expanding; the market share is rapidly expanding from hardware to software, such as intelligent image analysis [4]. The technology used for image security requires suspicious behavior detection technology to prevent public security issues, incidents, and accidents. Attempting to enter a personal property, entering a subway station without paying a ticket, kidnapping a child, beating a person, or an act of sudden collapse of a person who is walking along the road may be examples.

This kind of image analysis technology can cope with security threats to individuals and society at large from terrorism, crime, and disasters. In the wake of recent terrorist accidents in many countries, each country has been actively investing in expanding the video security market and securing security systems for the safety of people all over the world [5,6]. In recent years, the number of CCTV installations in the public sector, such as transportation and crime prevention CCTV, has increased to cope with various accidents, such as safety accidents and violent accidents [7]. While the number of areas being surveilled has increased due to the spread of CCTV, the extent of smart technology application remains insufficient. CCTV is already installed in many areas and records automatically, but the reading and checking of the video still must be done manually by a person. Human evaluation of CCTV is not ideal, because it is a task that requires high levels of concentration over long periods. Therefore, an automated monitoring system should be implemented that can automatically recognize crime such as robbery and violence, as well as other situations that require urgent responses, and then notify the proper parties. To date, in the field of intelligent CCTV research [4–7], relatively few studies on behavior recognition or suspicious behavior detection have been carried out in comparison to the number of studies on the active classification and segmentation of objects. In most cases, CCTV is used for security reasons. In particular, when constructing a public place such as an airport, a train station, or a park, ensuring the safety and security of the people using that place is mandatory. If CCTV can automatically detect people who are acting abnormally rather than simply recording them, it will greatly aid accident prevention and response.

There are various patterns of suspicious behavior that we want to detect through CCTV, but the common factor is that the size of the movement is large and the direction is irregular [8–10]. For example, while violence is being committed, the speed of movement generally increases sharply, and the direction of movement becomes very irregular. When a person bumps something or falls on something, the movement at this moment has a different direction of movement than that of a normal moving person, and the magnitude of motion at that moment becomes irregularly large. Beyond these cases, running or jumping behaviors that occur indoors, such as in a classroom, can be considered to be suspicious behaviors, and they have characteristics similar to those described above.

Suspicious behavior detection is one of the most actively studied areas of computer vision, such as video analysis and surveillance [8–27]. Ordinary behavior refers to actions that do not attract people's attention when people perceive some sort of movement [8]. Therefore, surveillance systems detect suspicious behavior using characteristic patterns for various behaviors, which are generally opposed to ordinary behaviors. There have been many studies on abnormal behavior detection using different approaches such as spatio–temporal features [8–16] and machine learning techniques [17–25].

As a high-dimensional feature is essential to better represent the suspicious behavior pattern, many methods based on spatio–temporal information such as optical flow [8], spatio–temporal gradient [9], the social force model [10], chaotic invariant [11], and sparse representation [12] have been studied. It does not require any training learning process, so it has less computation, which can be used in real-time detection [8]. The method described in [9] extracts moving objects from video sequence first and then tracks moving objects to detect their overlapping. Once an overlapping area is detected, the clutter model is built up based on the changes of spatio–temporal features to detect abnormal behavior. An abnormal pattern detecting method based on spatiotemporal volume has been presented in [13]. It calculated the likelihood by analyzing the area occupying a relatively large part of the periphery and transformed it into the form of a codebook, thereby reducing the time required for the calculation. This method is competitive with other methods because it does not require background/foreground segmentation and tracking calculations. However, it is difficult to use this method in an image in which various kinds of abnormal conditions may exist, because the threshold value necessary for detecting abnormal patterns has to be individually calculated and applied experimentally for each image. The method described in [14] detects abnormal crowd behavior based on a combined approach of energy model and threshold. It used the optical flow method to estimate displacement vectors of moving crowd and the computation of crowd motion energy. The crowd motion energy was further modified by crowd motion intensity. The method described in [15] also extracts the motion vector using the optical flow from the segmented image with foreground and background; then, the motion vector with a large change was detected and learned by principal component analysis (PCA). However, data loss can occur due to noise in the process of separating the foreground and background from actual images. Abnormal behavior detection using an interest point by simply monitoring the change of topological structure has been presented in [16]. Two new methods for the analysis of boundary point structure and the extraction of a critical point from the partial motion fields were introduced and both methods were used to build the global topological structure of the crowd motion.

Machine learning techniques for detecting unusual events have been presented in [17–26]. These methods also employ the feature extraction process but use trained data that came out of the learning process. The method described in [17] detects multiple anomalous activities with key features such as speed, direction, centroid, and dimensions, and these help to track an object in video frames. It also employed problem domain knowledge rules in order to distinguish activities and the dominant behavior of activities. In [18], a video frame is divided into several segments of equal size, and the features that were extracted from each segment were clustered using unsupervised learning. Then, the clusters smaller than this were classified as abnormal behavior. In this method, unusual phenomena that do not follow the general statistics are judged as abnormal behavior. However, when there is only abnormal behavior, not ordinary behavior, it is highly unlikely that abnormal behavior can be detected. In order to solve the above-mentioned problems appearing in the method presented in [18,19], Hamid et al. analyzed the whole structure information using statistical information of behavior class and then defined and detected abnormal behavior based on the subclass. However, there was a scalability problem in applying it to various images because of the discontinuous sequence and the fact that the spatiotemporal patch must be stored in the same form every moment. In addition, since data is processed in a batch process, it cannot cope with real-time environmental change. A method that uses violent flows (ViF) feature points for real-time processing has been presented in [20]. After extracting motion vector, motion vectors whose magnitude value exceeds the threshold value are studied and learned by support vector machine (SVM) [8]. However, this method is not applicable to surveillance cameras used in real life because it deals only with images taken from a distance. Convolutional neural network (CNN)-based algorithms have been presented in [21]. Using fully convolutional neural networks (FCNs) and temporal data, a pre-trained supervised FCN is transferred into an unsupervised FCN ensuring the detection of anomalies in scenes. The method described in [22] considered successive chunks that could be observed in segments made from a database that contained no suspicious behavior to be ordinary behavior. Then, by using these successive chunks for learning, the parts for which the magnitude of the feature is small or those who are not included in the learning are detected as suspicious behavior. However, these methods that use the learning process show weakness in versatility because they cannot detect behaviors that are not used in learning. In [23], a unified framework for anomaly detection in video based on the restricted Boltzmann machine (RBM), a recent powerful method for unsupervised learning and representation learning, has been introduced. Unsupervised learning techniques also employed in the method described in [24], and the Bayesian model is employed in the method described in [25]. More significant related work to abnormal behavior detection is described in the review paper [27].

Such methods of manually applying a threshold value or using a background removal with or without data loss are not versatile. In addition, methods using the learning process are dependent on the training data and also require lots of computation, so it is hard to be used as a real-time surveillance system. In this paper, a new suspicious behavior detection method that can be used in real life by supplementing these matters is presented. The proposed method can infer suspicious behavior patterns by solely using simple motion features for real-time anomaly detection. Generally, as humans, we focus our attention on behaviors that vary in the magnitude or direction of motion and behave differently in terms of the rules of motion compared to other objects. In this paper, this information was used in the proposed method. The developed system with the proposed method attempts to detect significantly different behaviors among other behaviors in order to search for suspicious behaviors. To this end, motion features are extracted using optical flow, and these features are then integrated to create temporal saliency. Finally, abnormal behavior can be detected based on temporal saliency.

This paper is organized as follows. In Section 2, the proposed method is presented. A temporal saliency is made by extracting and combining motion features using optical flow and detects suspicious behavior based on this. Test datasets used in the proposed method are also described here. In Section 3, experimental results and discussions were described so as to evaluate the performance of the method.

Finally, in Section 4, conclusions were drawn with some general observations and recommendations for ongoing work.

2. Materials and Methods

2.1. Data Aquisition

Various kinds of suspicious behavior video sequences are used as a dataset in the proposed method. The UMN (University of Minnesota) crowd dataset and Avenue dataset, which are used in various behavior recognition and detection papers [8,10–12,25,28,29] were collected. The video sequences in the UMN dataset were each filmed from three different backgrounds—lawn, indoor, and plaza—featuring scenes where multiple people ran away simultaneously when they heard explosions. The video sequences in the Avenue dataset were filmed from in front of a building, and in that video, a few people are running or jumping, while most people are walking. The Walk dataset, which does not include any suspicious behavior, was also used. The Walk dataset does not contain any suspicious behaviors and features videos that were just filmed of people walking along the street without any special features. This video sequence was selected to check for false detection of the proposed method. As shown in No. 6 to No. 10 in Table 1, various types of YouTube video sequences on the Internet that contain various kinds of suspicious behaviors that could lead to a real accident were also collected.

Table 1. Dataset and types of suspicious behaviors used in the proposed method.

No	Dataset	Suspicious Behaviors Description
1	UMN dataset: Lawn	Multiple people are running away in multiple directions simultaneously with an explosion sound.
2	UMN dataset: Indoor	
3	UMN dataset: Plaza	
4	Avenue dataset	A few people are jumping and running in front of the building while others are walking.
5	Walk dataset	People are walking normally. There are not any abnormal behaviors.
6	Bump data	A man is smashed against an obstacle.
7	Fall down data	A man is falling over an obstacle.
8	Water data	A man is walking on the road falls into the water.
9	Stairs fall down data	The man who came down the stairs is falling down.
10	CCTV violent robbery data in South Kensington	Two men are assaulting one man.

Table 1 describes what kind of suspicious behavior has been collected as datasets. Actual suspicious behaviors such as violence, tumbling, falling, jumping, and suddenly running behaviors that can be detected in CCTVs installed on the street have been designated as ground truth. All of these behaviors are characterized by large changes in motion or irregular directions of motion.

2.2. Description of Proposed Method

The proposed method has been developed to detect suspicious behavior in real-time using CCTV. This system is designed to detect instantaneous big changes in the size and direction of motion, such as collisions, sudden running, falling, and assault, which can all occur frequently in real life.

Figure 1 shows the overall process of the proposed method. After performing preprocessing such as grayscale image transformation and median filtering, the two kinds of motion vectors, magnitude (size of motion) and gradient (direction of motion), are extracted by optical flow calculation. Then, the two kinds of extracted motion vectors are converted into the polar coordinate system, and the magnitude feature map for the magnitude of the motion vector (F_{mag}) and the gradient feature map for the gradient of the motion vector (F_{grad}) are generated. Then, two reactivity maps (R_{mag}, R_{grad}) are generated using the mean and variance of each feature map and combined into one temporal saliency map (TS). The temporal saliency map shows the area finally detected as suspicious behavior. This described in detail below.

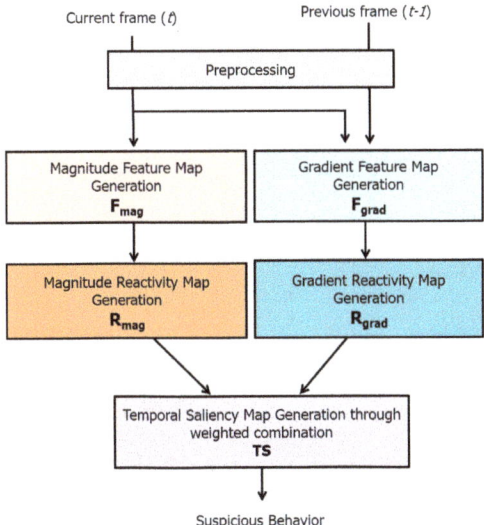

Figure 1. The overall process of the proposed method.

2.2.1. Preprocessing for Denoising

Various preprocessing methods have been used to enhance the performance or efficiency of the experiment in most technical research and process fields as well as image processing fields. In our system, the input image data is converted into a grayscale image, and a median filter is applied to remove noise.

Since only motion information is needed from the input image, color information is not required. Therefore, the input color image is converted into a grayscale image to reduce the dimension of the data. Then, the transformed grayscale image is filtered by a median filter to remove noise. Median filters are often used to remove signal noise. Unlike other smoothing filters, it also preserves the boundary values well in the noise removal process. In the case of the CCTV image, there is much noise due to sunlight or other illumination. Besides, there are many cases where the image quality is low, so it is necessary to enhance the edge. Using the median filter, we can remove noise and enhance the edge.

2.2.2. Feature Map Generation

(1) Motion Vector Extraction with Optical Flow

Optical flow is used to extract the motion of a moving object. Optical flow is an object movement pattern between two consecutive frames caused by the movement of an object or a camera [30]. So, with optical flow, we can obtain important information about how objects are viewed locally and how they move. In other words, optical flow can be said to be a distribution indicating how the brightness pattern has moved. Therefore, optical flow is a good method for detecting the motion of objects moving locally in the continuous frame image [31–33].

Farnebäck [34] proposed a dense optical flow. Unlike sparse optical flow [27], dense optical flow can get a more accurate motion vector because it calculates from all pixels of the image. Since sparse optical flow only calculates some pixels of the image locally, only the partial motion feature of the object is extracted. Therefore, it is less accurate than dense optical flow. For example, suppose that two people are walking. In general, when people walk, they move their arms, legs, head, etc. If their motion information is only calculated from some pixels, it can be misunderstood that one person is moving but the other is moving. In other words, the motion information is not continuous because they are extracted from some pixels, and can be misunderstood as movements from different objects. To get more accurate behavior pattern information, dense optical flow is used in the proposed method.

Figure 2 shows a visualization of the optical flow calculation results. Figure 2 is a scene in which people are walking in different directions. The magnitude and the gradient of the object's motion can be acquired through the optical flow calculation results [30]. Points on the image represent feature points, and lines represent motion vectors. The magnitude of the motion vector is the length of the line, and the gradient of the vector in the direction of the line. In this way, the size and direction of the vector of the object moving through the optical flow can be calculated.

Figure 2. Motion detection through optical flow.

(2) Feature Map Generation: F_{mag}, F_{grad}

Since the information extracted by the optical flow in the preprocessed image is expressed by the magnitude of the movement in the x and y-axes, the extracted information is converted into two feature maps: magnitude and gradient feature maps. The magnitude and the gradient of the motion vector can be calculated through the motion vector obtained using the actual optical flow. The motion vector calculated by the optical flow must be converted into a polar coordinate system to form two feature maps. The polar coordinate system is a coordinate system in which the position of a point is defined as a distance (r) and a direction (θ) from a vertex. In the Cartesian coordinate system, the relationship of the vertices, which are represented in a complicated manner by trigonometric functions, can be easily expressed in the polar coordinate system.

The two-dimensional vector (x, y) calculated as an optical flow is transformed into a value in the polar coordinate system as follows.

$$F_{mag} = \sqrt{x(t)^2 + y(t)^2}, \; F_{grad} = \arctan\left(y(t), x(t)\right)\left[\frac{180}{\pi}\right] \tag{1}$$

where F_{mag} is a feature map of the magnitude of the motion vector converted to the polar coordinate system, and F_{grad} is a feature map of the direction of the motion vector.

Figure 3 shows the visualization image of F_{mag} (Figure 3b) and F_{grad} (Figure 3c) for the input video (Figure 2). Figure 3b is a visualization image of the magnitude feature of the motion of moving people, and Figure 3c is a visualization image of the numerical value of the directional feature using the HSV (Hue-Saturation-Value) color model. Since the direction ranges from 0° to 360°, the size of the H channel of the HSV color model was used to express the angle in the form of a color. In Figure 3c, people walking from the front of the building to the right were represented in red, while people moving to the left were represented in blue.

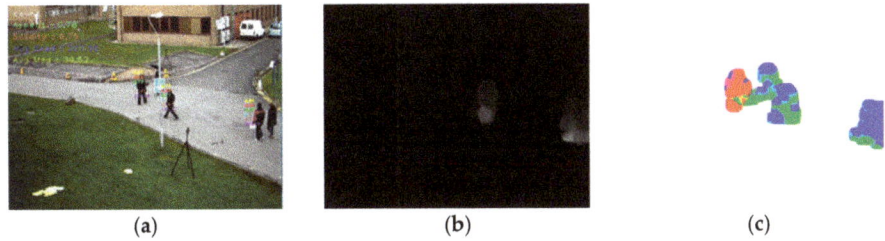

Figure 3. Magnitude and gradient feature map. (a) original frame; (b) F_{mag}; (c) F_{grad}.

2.2.3. Reactivity Map Generation

(1) The distinction between ordinary and suspicious behavior

The statistical value of the magnitude of the motion vector is used to distinguish ordinary motion from suspicious motion in the feature map represented by the polar coordinate system. The statistical value in the region where suspicious behavior occurs is different from the statistical value in the region where ordinary behavior occurs. To determine the statistical value, experiments were performed. Four video sequences were selected among No. 4, No. 5, No. 7, and No. 9 data, which were mentioned in Section 2.1 and were edited to include actual suspicious behaviors such as falling, jumping, violence, and suddenly running behaviors in the 40th frame of each video. Selected video sequences all contain suspicious behaviors. However, for testing purposes, these suspicious behaviors have been edited to appear in the 40th frame. Edited videos are 15 s long, and there are about 15 people in the first video, eight people in the second video, three people in the third video, and about 13 people in the fourth video. After that, motion vectors were calculated, and the results were analyzed.

Figure 4 shows the graphs that show the statistical values of motion vectors of the four kinds of videos after editing the image frame to contain suspicious behavior in the 40th frame. A legend 'value' shown in Figure 4a means the minimum, maximum, and average value of the motion vector, and Figure 4b means the standard deviation value of the motion vector. After the motion vector was extracted from these edited videos, the statistical information of the motion vector was analyzed. As we can see in Figure 4a, the motion vector value was maximized near 40 frames of each video. This was because each video contained suspicious behavior (crashes, drowsiness, falls, etc.) near the 40th frame. Since the sizes of objects showing suspicious behavior are slightly different for each dataset image, there could be a slight difference in the average value. Figure 4b also shows that there is a large increase in the standard deviation near 40 frames. As a result of extracting and experimenting motion vectors for several videos, the average value is different according to the size of the moving region included in the video, while the value of the standard deviation changes a lot when suspicious behavior appears. Through these experiments, the standard deviation is selected as the criterion value for judging the abnormal behavior, and value 1.2 was selected.

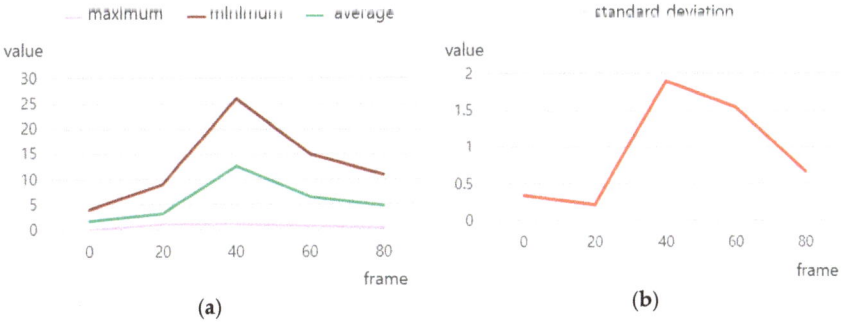

Figure 4. Statistical value of the motion vector. (a) Maximum, minimum, average; (b) standard deviation.

(2) Magnitude Reactivity Map Generation: R_{mag}

The frame was considered that it contains suspicious behavior when a frame with a standard deviation of the motion vector at the time (t) is greater than 1.2, which was calculated experimentally. The region where the magnitude of the vector is calculated by optical flow at the point (x, y) is larger than the summation of the average, and the variance of the whole image was considered to be the suspicious behavior region. Since the movement is slightly different for each person even when performing the same ordinary behavior, the region was detected based on the summation of the average and the variation. Based on these facts, the magnitude reactivity map (R_{mag}) is calculated as follows.

$$R_{mag} = F_{mag}(x,y,t) \times \sigma(F_{mag}(x,y,t))$$
$$\text{where, } \sigma(F_{mag}(x,y,t)) > 1.2 \text{ and } F_{mag}(x,y,t) > \mu(F_{mag}(x,y,t)) + \sigma(F_{mag}(x,y,t)) \quad (2)$$

Figure 5 shows the magnitude reactivity map generated by the proposed method. Figure 5a shows the video of people gathered at the center of the park moving in various directions simultaneously with any signal. In this video, the suspicious behavior is the sudden movement of people. Figure 5b shows the magnitude feature map in polar coordinates, and with this feature map, we can see the moving area of people. Figure 5c shows the generated final magnitude reactivity map. We can see that the area in which people are running away has been properly detected. Figure 5d shows the detection of anomalous regions based on the magnitude reactivity map. In the scene where several people are running away, we can see that the motion vector is greatly increased, and all of the suspicious behavior is detected.

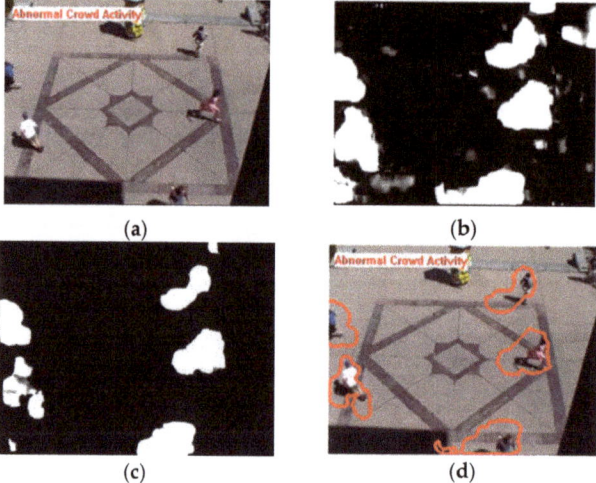

Figure 5. Example result of calculating R_{mag}. (**a**) original frame; (**b**) F_{mag}; (**c**) R_{mag}; (**d**) result of the system.

(3) Gradient Reactivity Map Generation: R_{grad}

Unlike a group of people who are regularly moving in the same direction, if there is an object moving in the opposite direction, this can be considered suspicious behavior. To detect this behavior, a reactivity map for the gradient feature of the motion vector was generated. First, the motion vector calculated for each pixel is divided into object units to prevent the movement direction of the object and the part included in the object from being different directions. For example, when a man moves to the left with his arms and legs shaking up and down, the main movement direction may be misjudged because of the movement direction of the arms and legs, although the main direction of the man's movement is left direction. Based on these, the gradient reactivity map (R_{grad}) is calculated as follows.

$$R_{grad} = grad(x,y,t) + \frac{grad(x,y,t)}{180}$$
$$\text{where, if } \left|\mu(F_{grad}(x,y,t)) - F_{grad}(x,y,t)\right| \leq 180$$
$$grad(x,y,t) = \left|\mu(F_{grad}(x,y,t)) - F_{grad}(x,y,t)\right| \tag{3}$$
$$\text{else}$$
$$grad(x,y,t) = \left|\mu(F_{grad}(x,y,t)) - F_{grad}(x,y,t)\right| - 180$$

The region of the object that moves differently from the average direction of movement becomes a component of the gradient reactivity map.

Figure 6 shows the gradient reactivity map generated by the proposed method. Figure 6a shows the original video of the people walking around the park, and Figure 6b shows the gradient feature map of the motion vector. The circle in the middle represents the average of the angles in the entire image and is displayed on the screen to show the angle of 181°. The rectangle drawn on the right is the area detected by applying Equation (3). Figure 6c is the final generated gradient reactivity map. In the reactivity map, we can see that when the average direction of the people is to the left, weights are added to the object moving in the opposite direction, and the system has responded to it very strongly.

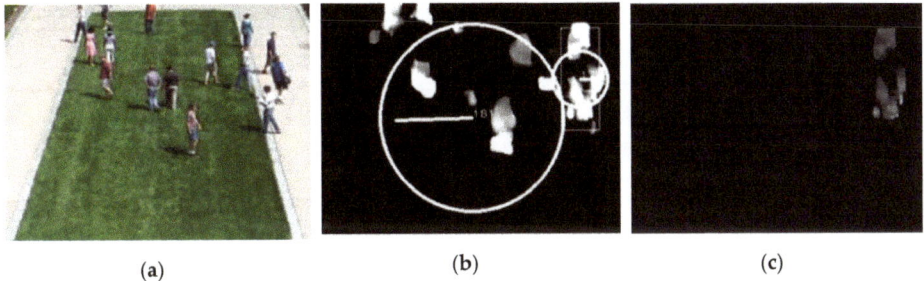

Figure 6. Example result of calculating R_{grad}. (**a**) original frame; (**b**) F_{grad}; (**c**) R_{grad}.

The two reactivity maps described above are incorporated into the temporal saliency map through weighted combinations. Among the feature values constituting the temporal saliency map, a region having a high value is a region that includes noticeable suspicious behavior. Therefore, the presence or absence of suspicious behavior can be determined through the temporal saliency map. The two reactivity maps are combined as follows.

$$S(t) = \alpha \times R_{mag} + (1 - \alpha) \times R_{grad} \tag{4}$$

The weight value α is applied proportionally to the maximum value of the magnitude. In general, the anomalous behaviors to detect are always increased in the magnitude of the motion, but the moving direction is partially applied, so the weight value is calculated proportionally to the magnitude value. In the final generated temporal saliency map, neighboring pixels are clustered, and the area of 30 pixels or more is displayed as the final detection area.

Figure 7 shows the final detected suspicious behavior region using the temporal saliency map. Figure 7a shows the experimental result on a video in which a man is walking to the right and a child is jumping to the left. Figure 7c,d show the reactivity map for the magnitude and gradient of the motion vector, respectively, and Figure 7e shows the temporal saliency map finally generated through weighted combination. At the moment the child jumps, the motion increases greatly, and the reactivity to the magnitude of the motion increases significantly. Additionally, the reactivity to the direction also increased because everyone else moves to the right while the child jumps to the left. Figure 7b shows the final result of the proposed method. Two reactivity maps were combined and finally, a temporal saliency map was generated to detect the suspicious behavior regions.

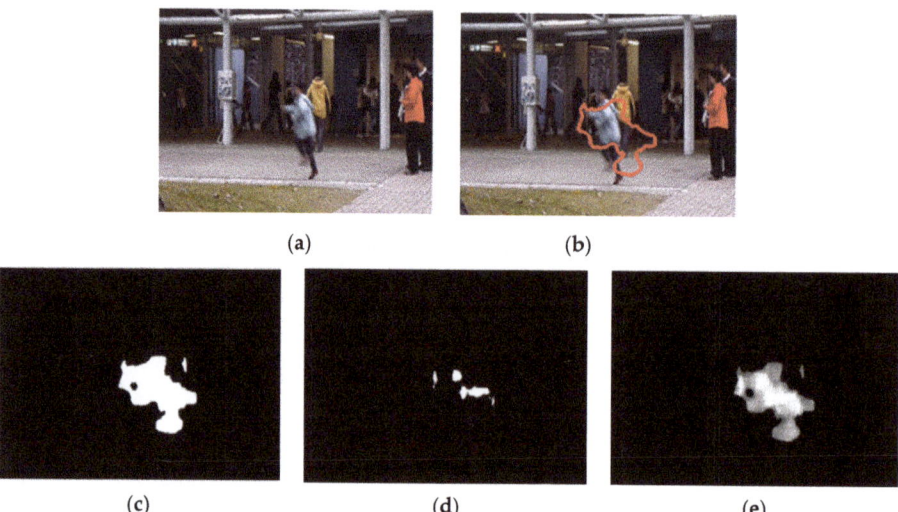

Figure 7. Example result of calculating temporal saliency map. (**a**) original frame; (**b**) result of the system; (**c**) R_{mag}; (**d**) R_{grad}; (**e**) temporal saliency map (*TS*).

3. Results and Discussion

In order to verify that the proposed method detects suspicious behavior region correctly, the experiments were conducted on 10 different types of video sequences mentioned in Section 2.1. In addition, to carry out a quantitative evaluation, the proposed method was compared with the state-of-art methods with the experiments, which were conducted on two different publicly available datasets, namely UMN and Avenue. Although some of the compared methods perform evaluations on videos that are gathered from the Internet, these videos are not available online for comparison. Therefore, comparison evaluations were conducted on the UMN and Avenue datasets, which are publicly available.

3.1. Comparison Results from Experiments with UMN Dataset and Avenue Dataset

For the UMN dataset, the method based on optical flow-based features [8], Bayesian model [25], chaotic invariants [11], the social force model [10], and sparse reconstruction cost [12] were compared with the proposed method. The UMN dataset contains three crowd escaping scenes in both indoor and outdoor environments. The normal events depict people wandering in groups, while abnormal events depict a crowd escaping quickly. The dataset contains 11 video sequences that are captured in three different backgrounds. Scene 1 and Scene 3 are outdoor scenes (lawn, plaza) and Scene 2 is an indoor scene. The accuracy was defined to be the percentage of correctly identified frames that are calculated by comparing with ground truth.

Table 2 demonstrates the accuracy comparison of six methods for three different scenes of the UMN dataset in identifying escape events.

Table 2. Accuracy comparison with state-of-the art methods on the UMN dataset.

UMN Dataset	Proposed Method	[8]	[25]	[11]	[10]	[12]
Scene 1: Lawn	99.20%	99.10%	99.03%	90.62%	84.41%	90.52%
Scene 2: Indoor	97.10%	94.85%	95.36%	85.06%	82.35%	78.48%
Scene 3: Plaza	93.20%	97.76%	96.63%	91.58%	90.83%	92.70%
average	96.50%	96.46%	96.40%	87.91%	85.09%	84.70%

The methods in [8,25] were previously tested on the whole UMN dataset, and the provided results were used to compute the corresponding accuracy. As an evaluation setting, the same evaluation settings as described in [25] were used. Overall, the proposed method achieves the best accuracy with an average of 96.50%, which is higher than that of the other methods. Even though the proposed method did not employ any learning process, the proposed method outperforms the comparison methods. Such methods using the learning process are dependent on the training dataset and also require lots of computation, so it is hard to be used as a real-time surveillance system. The proposed method can be used in real life by supplementing these matters.

Figures 8–10 demonstrate the examples of detection results for abnormality from the UMN dataset (No. 1 to No. 3) in the proposed method. In these videos, the suspicious behavior is the sudden movement of people. When people run away in multiple directions at the same time, the direction of movement appears very irregular and the size of the movement is also dramatically increased. The proposed method responded appropriately to this kind of motion. The area in which people are running away has been properly detected. In the scene where several people are running away, we can see that the motion vector is greatly increased, and all of the suspicious behavior is detected. The proposed method generated reactivity images using feature information extracted from optical flow in the video and detected anomalous regions based on temporal saliency obtained through a weighted combination of them. Feature information using the magnitude and gradient of movement, which is the most important factor that constitutes a behavior, is extracted, and a strongly reactive region is detected through a weighting condition formula. The result demonstrates that the suspicious behavior was reasonably detected.

For the Avenue dataset, the methods described in [21,26,29] were compared with the proposed method. The Avenue dataset contatins 16 training videos and 21 testing videos. The only normal behavior in the dataset is people walking in front of the camera, and the abnormal behaviors are unusual actions such as running and jumping, and walking in the wrong direction. Table 3 demonstrates the AUC (area under the curve) values of both the proposed method and the state-of-the-art comparison methods [21,26,29] for the Avenue dataset. The method in [26] was previously tested on the whole Avenue dataset, and the provided results were used in the comparison. The comparison results of Table 4 shows that the performance of the proposed method outperforms the comparison methods.

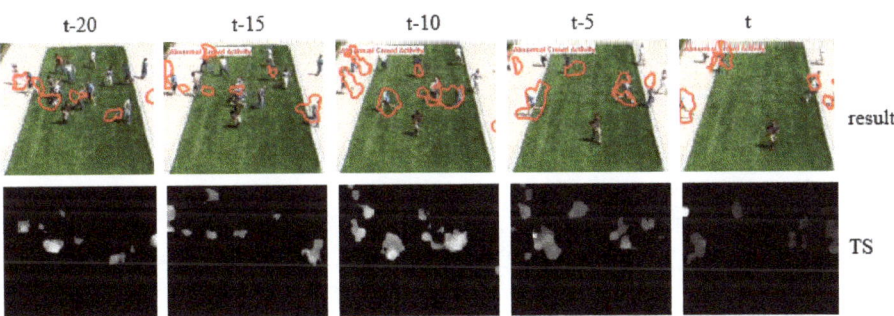

Figure 8. Examples of detection results for abnormality from No. 1 data (UMN Scene 1: Lawn).

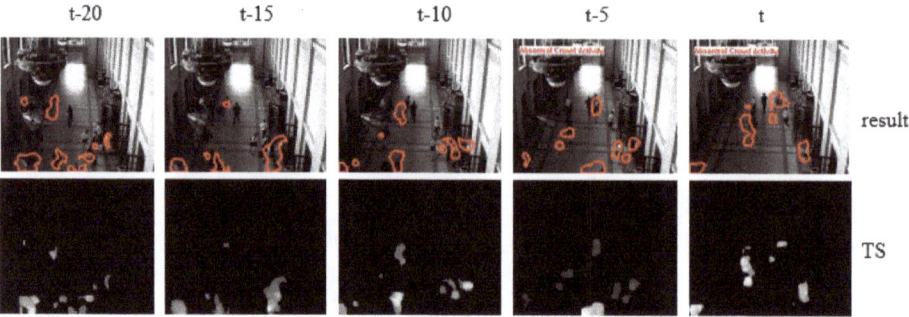

Figure 9. Examples of detection results for abnormality from No. 2 data (UMN Scene 2: Indoor).

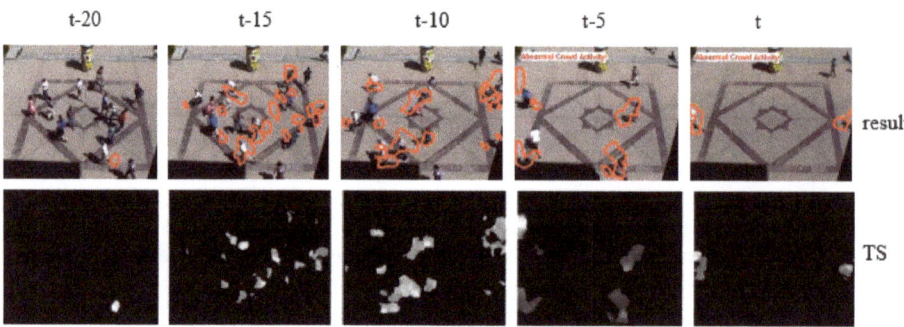

Figure 10. Examples of detection results for abnormality from No. 3 data (UMN Scene 3: Plaza).

Table 3. AUC (area under the curve) comparison with state-of-the art methods on the Avenue dataset.

	Proposed Method	[26]	[29]	[21]
Avenue dataset	90.18%	87.70%	87.19%	80.30%

Table 4. The overall performance evaluation result of the proposed method.

No.	Dataset	Accuracy	Precision	Recall
1	UMN dataset: Lawn	99.2%	99.8%	91.1%
2	UMN dataset: Lobby	97.1%	99.5%	93.7%
3	UMN dataset: Park	93.2%	98.9%	92.5%
4	Avenue dataset	90.1%	93.2%	94.5%
5	Walk dataset	100%	100%	100%
6	Bump data	95.8%	100%	94.4%
7	Fall down data	95%	91.6%	100%
8	Water data	82.7%	79.1%	100%
9	Stairs fall down data	94.4%	100%	84.6%
10	CCTV violent robbery data in South Kensington	91.4%	100%	90.6%
	average	93.89%	96.21%	94.9%

Due to the unpredictability of abnormal events, most previous approaches employ a learning process, and most of them only learn normal event models in an unsupervised or semi-supervised manner, and abnormal events are considered to be patterns that significantly deviate from the created normal event models [29]. The method used in [21] uses spatio–temporal convolutional neural networks to extract and learn various features, and the method in [29] employs the online dictionary learning and sparse reconstruction framework. The method in [26] used both training data and testing data to make a global grid motion template (GGMT). As mentioned before, even though the proposed method did not employ any learning process and uses simple motion features, the proposed method outperforms the comparison methods.

Figure 11 demonstrates the examples of detection results for abnormality from No. 4, which were chosen from the Avenue dataset in the proposed method. In this video sequence, most people in front of the building are walking to the right, while a child jumps to the left. The proposed method properly detected the area where the child jumps. We can see that the percentage of the child occupying the image has increased, because the distance between the child and the camera is much closer than that of the other people. Due to this, the average direction was calculated as the left direction, from the moment the child jumps. Since the child is moving to the left during the jump, the whole direction was calculated correctly. It is seen that different types of abnormality such as running and jumping can be accurately detected and localized.

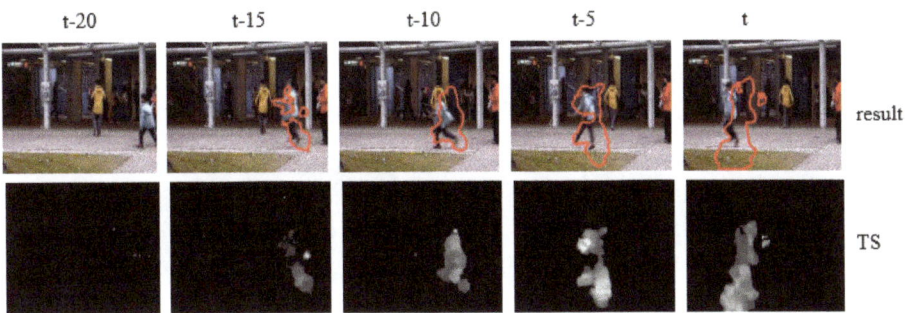

Figure 11. Examples of detection results for abnormality from the No. 4 data (Avenue).

3.2. Analysis of Examples of Detection Results for Abnormalities with 10 Different Types of Video Sequences

Figures 8–17 shows the examples of detection results for abnormalities from 10 different types of video sequences. The results for the No. 1 to No. 4 data are shown in Figures 8–11 and are explained in detail in Section 3.1.

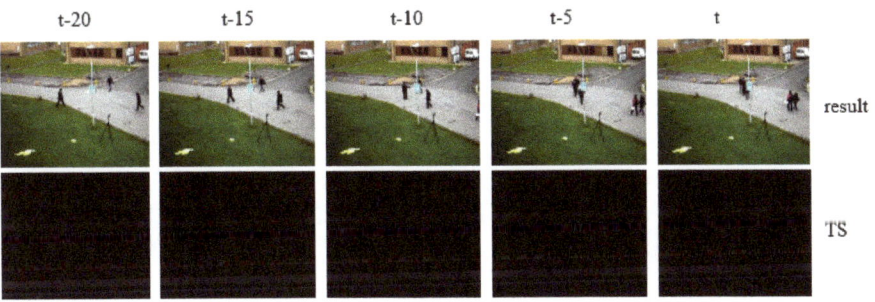

Figure 12. Examples of detection results for abnormality from the No. 5 data.

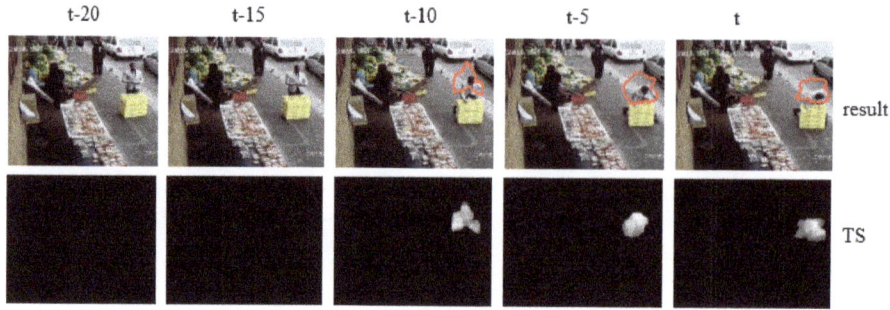

Figure 13. Examples of detection results for abnormality from the No. 6 data.

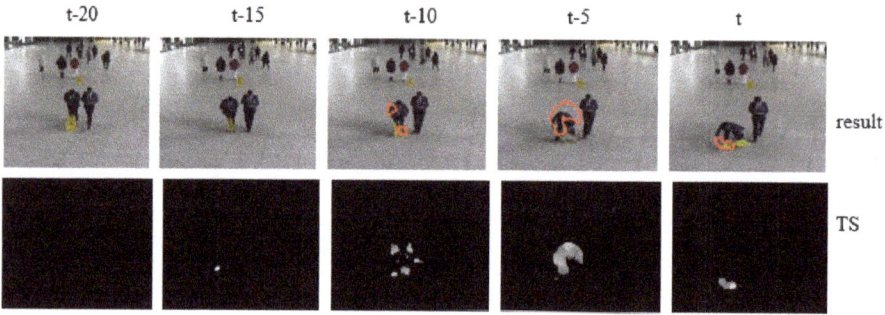

Figure 14. Examples of detection results for abnormality from the No. 7 data.

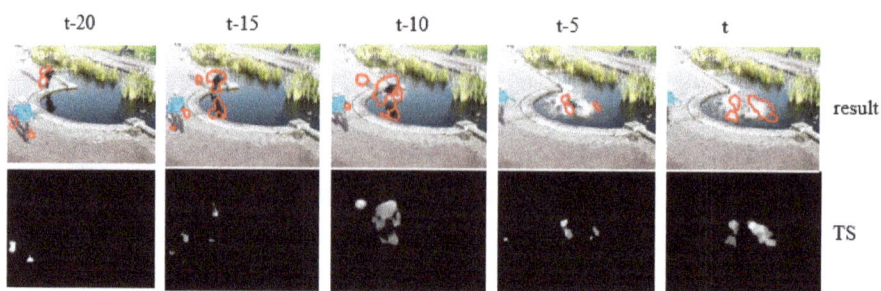

Figure 15. Examples of detection results for abnormality from the No. 8 data.

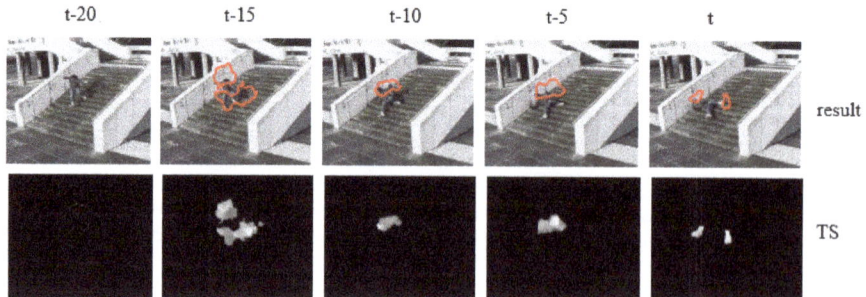

Figure 16. Examples of detection results for abnormality from the No. 9 data.

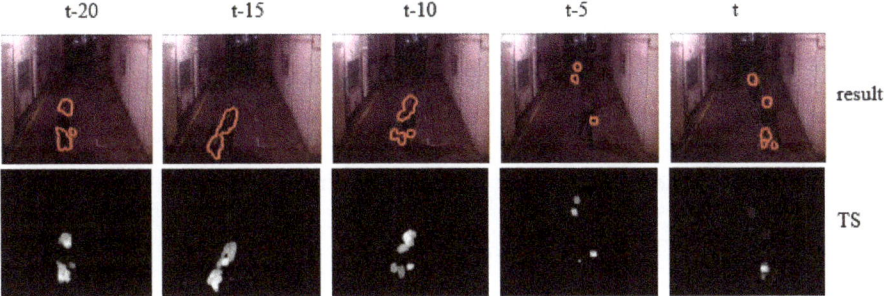

Figure 17. Examples of detection results for abnormality from the No. 10 data.

Figure 12 shows the examples of detection results for abnormality from the No. 5 data. As mentioned before, this video sequence is a video recording of people in which there are no anomalous behaviors and all people are moving normally. This experiment is performed to see if the proposed method responds to ordinary behavior. As a result, it was found it did not react at all to the usual walking behavior (reaction rate 0%).

Figure 13 shows the examples of detection results for abnormality from No. 6 data in which a man is walking while looking at his cell phone and after a while, he falls over an obstacle. This video includes every scene from his usual walking to the falling down. Through the result, we can see that the system does not react at all to the ordinary walking, but it reacts strongly from the moment when the man falls over the obstacle.

The video shown in Figure 14 is similar to the video shown in Figure 13. As two men walk together, the man on the left falls on an obstacle. As a result of the experiment, we can see that the area of the man on the left is correctly detected from the moment he falls. The man on the right was similar in size to the fallen man but was not detected.

Figure 15 shows the examples of detection results for abnormality from the No. 8 data, in which a man is falling into the water. The man falling into the water was correctly detected, but another man's foot moving on the left side was erroneously detected. This is because as the distance from the camera is close to the scene, the magnitude of the motion vector is greatly affected.

Figure 16 shows the examples of detection results for abnormality from the No. 9 data, in which a man is falling down a stairway. Similarly, as the response to the magnitude and direction of the action grows, the behavior that a man is falling is detected.

Figure 17 shows the examples of detection results from the No. 10 data. This is a violent robbery video that happened in South Kensington, which was reported in US news. This video sequence contains a scene in which two men assault one man. Even though the fact that the video is very low in intensity and contains lots of noise due to illumination, the proposed system both detects the scene where one man is running as well as the scene where two men joined together and committed violence on another man.

3.3. Overall Performance Evaluation Results of 10 Different Types of Video Sequences

The actual results of the proposed method are compared with those of the actual suspicious behavior region, which is regarded as a ground truth. Frames that successfully detected a region containing suspicious behaviors are used as a component of a true positive (*tp*), and frames that detected a suspicious behavior region even if there were not any suspicious behaviors in the frame were used as a component of a false positive (*fp*). Frames that did not detect any regions, even if there were suspicious behavior in the frame, were used as a component of false negative (*fn*). The proposed method achieved a 100% true negative (*tn*) rate, because nothing was detected as a suspicious behavior region in experiments with No. 5 data where no suspicious behavior is included. The accuracy, precision, recall, and FNR (False Negative Rate) is calculated as follows.

$$accuracy = \frac{tp+tn}{tp+fp+fn+tn}, precision = \frac{tp}{tp+fp}$$
$$recall(True\ Positive\ Rate) = \frac{tp}{tp+fn}, FNR(False\ Negative\ Rate) = \frac{fp}{fp+tn} \quad (5)$$

Table 4 summarizes the overall performance evaluation result of the proposed method.

The reason for the low performance of the No. 9 data was analyzed as follows. In the No. 9 data, all the motion vectors were not detected and only a part of them was detected because the position of the walking man is too close to the photographing camera. It was a difficult environment to measure the motion vector properly. For this reason, false positives have been increased, resulting in lower performance compared with that of the other data.

As a summary, the proposed system detects various suspicious behaviors captured in various environments with high performance, and it is also robust to differences in brightness depending on the weather and time. However, given the results of the No. 9 data, it is necessary to secure a suitable shooting distance to accurately run the proposed method.

4. Conclusions

In this paper, a new surveillance system for detecting suspicious behavior regions that can be used in real-time was proposed. The proposed method generated reactivity images using feature information extracted from optical flow in CCTV video and detected anomalous regions based on temporal saliency obtained through a weighted combination of them. Feature information using the magnitude and gradient of movement, which is the most important factor that constitutes a behavior, is extracted, and a strongly reactive region is detected through a weighting condition formula.

Extensive experiments on different challenging public datasets as well as on eight various types of video sequences collected online were conducted to demonstrate the effectiveness of the proposed method. Quantitative and qualitative analyses of the experimental results showed that the proposed method outperformed the traditional method in suspicious behavior detection and was comparable to the state-of-the-art methods without using complicated training approaches. In addition, experimental results showed that the proposed system is suitable for detecting suspicious behaviors such as violent actions, fallings, jumping, sudden running, and bumps. The proposed method can detect instantaneous events and accidents.

In the proposed method, two reactivity maps of motion magnitude and motion gradient were generated, and these two maps were weighted and combined to make a temporal saliency map. However, to detect more complex behaviors, it is not enough to combine just the two features used in the proposed method. It is necessary to grasp the relation of existing objects in the video and to grasp the situation before and after based on the time when the event occurred. However, an essential motion pattern is indispensable for detecting such a complicated behavioral relationship. The proposed method is structurally easy to combine with other features. Just adding a new algorithm that extracts other features to the proposed method is not difficult, and with this extension, it can be used not only in the field of detecting more various abnormal behavior but also in various other fields.

Funding: This research received no external funding.

Conflicts of Interest: The author declares no conflict of interest.

References

1. Why Vision Is the Most Important Sense Organ. Available online: https://medium.com/@SmartVisionLabs/why-vision-is-the-most-important-sense-organ-60a2cec1c164 (accessed on 30 October 2019).
2. Beckermann, A. Visual Information Processing and Phenomenal Consciousness. In *Conscious Experience*; Schöningh: Paderborn, Germany, 1995; pp. 409–424.

3. Szeliski, R. *Computer Vision: Algorithms and Applications*; Springer-Verlag: London, UK, 2011.
4. Sage, K.; Young, S. Computer vision for security applications. In Proceedings of the IEEE 32nd Annual 1998 International Carnahan Conference on Security Technology, Alexandria, VA, USA, 12–14 October 1998; pp. 210–215.
5. Stubbington, B.; Keenan, P. Intelligent scene monitoring; technical aspects and practical experience. In Proceedings of the 29th Annual 1995 International Carnahan Conference on Security Technology, Sanderstead, Surrey, UK, 18–20 October 1995; pp. 364–375.
6. Davies, A.; Velastin, S. A Progress Review of Intelligent CCTV Surveillance Systems. In Proceedings of the IDAACS'05 Workshop, Sofia, Bulgaria, 5–7 September 2005; pp. 417–423.
7. Sanderson, C.; Bigdeli, A.; Shan, T.; Chen, S.; Berglund, E.; Lovel, B.C. Intelligent CCTV for Mass Transport Security: Challenges and Opportunities for Video and Face Processing. In *Progress in Computer Vision and Image Analysis*; Bunke, H., Villanueva, J.J., Sanchez, G., Eds.; World Scientific: Singapore, 2010; Volume 73, pp. 557–573.
8. Direkoglu, C.; Sah, M.; O'Connor, N.E. Abnormal crowd behavior detection using novel optical flow-based features. In Proceedings of the 2017 14th IEEE International Conference on Advanced Video and Signal Based Surveillance, Lecce, Italy, 29 August–1 September 2017; pp. 1–6.
9. Xiang, J.; Fan, H.; Xu, J. Abnormal behavior detection based on spatial-temporal features. In Proceedings of the International Conference on Machine Learning and Cybernetics, Tianjin, China, 14–17 July 2013; pp. 871–876.
10. Mehran, R.; Oyama, A.; Shah, M. Abnormal crowd behavior detection using social force model. In Proceedings of the 2009 IEEE Conference on Computer Vision and Pattern Recognition, Miami, FL, USA, 20–25 June 2009; pp. 935–942.
11. Wu, S.; Moore, B.E.; Shah, M. Chaotic invariants of Lagrangian particle trajectories for anomaly detection in crowded scenes. In Proceedings of the 2010 IEEE Computer Society Conference on Computer Vision and Pattern Recognition, San Francisco, CA, USA, 13–18 June 2010; pp. 2054–2060.
12. Cong, Y.; Yuan, J.; Liu, J. Abnormal event detection in crowded scenes using sparse representation. *Pattern Recognit.* **2013**, *46*, 1851–1864. [CrossRef]
13. Roshtkhari, M.J.; Levine, M.D. Online Dominant and Anomalous Behavior Detection in Videos. In Proceedings of the 2013 International Conference on Computer Vision and Pattern Recognition, Portland, OR, USA, 23–28 June 2013; pp. 2611–2618.
14. Halbe, M.; Vyas, V.; Vaidya, Y. Abnormal Crowd Behavior Detection Based on Combined Approach of Energy Model and Threshold. In Proceedings of the 7th International Conference on Pattern Recognition and Machine Intelligence, Kolkata, India, 5–8 December 2017; pp. 187–195.
15. Yu, T.H.; Moon, Y. Unsupervised Abnormal Behavior Detection for Real-time Surveillance Using Observed History. In Proceedings of the 2009 IAPR Conference on Machine Vision Applications, Yokohama, Japan, 20–22 May 2009; pp. 166–169.
16. Li, N.; Zhang, Z. Abnormal Crowd Behavior Detection using Topological Method. In Proceedings of the 12th ACIS International Conference on Software Engineering, Networking and Parallel/Distributed Computing, Sydney, NSW, Australia, 6–8 July 2011; pp. 13–18.
17. Chaudharya, S.; Khana, M.A.; Bhatnagara, C. Multiple Anomalous Activity Detection in Videos. In Proceedings of the 6th International Conference on Smart Computing and Communications, Kurukshetra, India, 7–8 December 2017; pp. 336–345.
18. Zhong, H.; Shi, J.; Visontai, M. Detecting unusual activity in video. In Proceedings of the 2004 IEEE Computer Society Conference on Computer Vision and Pattern Recognition, Washington, DC, USA, 27 June–2 July 2004; pp. 819–826.
19. Hamid, R.; Johnson, A.; Batta, S.; Bobick, A.; Isbell, C.; Coleman, G. Detection and explanation of anomalous activities: Representing activities as bags of event n-grams. In Proceedings of the 2005 IEEE Computer Society Conference on Computer Vision and Pattern Recognition, San Diego, CA, USA, 20–25 June 2005; pp. 1031–1038.
20. Hassner, T.; Itcher, Y.; Kliper-Gross, O. Violent flows: Real-time detection of violent crowd behavior. In Proceedings of the 2012 IEEE Computer Society Conference on Computer Vision and Pattern Recognition Workshops, Providence, RI, USA, 16–21 June 2012; pp. 1–6.

21. Zhou, S.; Shen, W.; Zeng, D.; Fang, M.; Wei, Y.; Zhang, Z. Spatial-temporal convolutional neural networks for anomaly detection and localization in crowded scenes. *Signal Process. Image Commun.* **2016**, *47*, 358–368. [CrossRef]
22. Boiman, O.; Irani, M. Detecting Irregularities in Images and in Video. *Int. J. Comput. Vis.* **2007**, *74*, 11–31. [CrossRef]
23. Vu, H.; Nguyen, T.D.; Travers, A.; Venkatesh, S.; Phung, D. Energy-Based Localized Anomaly Detection in Video Surveillance. In Proceedings of the 21st Pacific-Asia Conference on Knowledge Discovery and Data Mining, Jeju, South Korea, 23–26 May 2017; pp. 641–653.
24. Giorno, D.A.; Bagnell, J.; Hebert, M. A Discriminative Framework for Anomaly Detection in Large Videos. In Proceedings of the 2016 European Conference on Computer Vision, Amsterdam, The Netherlands, 11–14 October 2016; pp. 334–349.
25. Wu, S.; Wong, H.; Yu, Z. A Bayesian Model for Crowd Escape Behavior Detection. *IEEE Trans. Circuits Syst. Video Technol.* **2014**, *24*, 85–98. [CrossRef]
26. Li, S.; Yang, Y.; Liu, C. Anomaly detection based on two global grid motion templates. *Signal Process. Image Commun.* **2018**, *60*, 6–12. [CrossRef]
27. Al-Dhamari, A.; Sudirman, R.; Mahmood, N.H. Abnormal behavior detection in automated surveillance videos: A review. *J. Theor. Appl. Inf. Technol.* **2017**, *95*, 5245–5263.
28. Cong, Y.; Yuan, J.; Liu, J. Sparse reconstruction cost for abnormal event detection. In Proceedings of the 2011 IEEE Conference on Computer Vision and Pattern Recognition, Providence, RI, USA, 20–25 June 2011; pp. 3449–3456.
29. Hu, X.; Huang, Y.; Duan, Q.; Ci, W.; Dai, J.; Yang, H. Abnormal event detection in crowded scenes using histogram of oriented contextual gradient descriptor. *EURASIP J. Adv. Signal Process.* **2018**, *54*. [CrossRef]
30. Using Optical Flow to Find Direction of Motion. Available online: http://www.cs.utah.edu/~{}ssingla/CV/Project/OpticalFlow.html (accessed on 12 November 2019).
31. Lucas, B.D.; Kanade, T. An Iterative Image Registration Technique with an Application to Stereo Vision. In Proceedings of the 1981 DARPA Image Understanding Workshop, 23 April 1981; pp. 121–130.
32. Adelson, E.H.; Anderson, C.H.; Bergen, J.R.; Burt, P.J.; Ogden, J.M. Pyramid methods in image processing. *RCA Eng.* **1984**, *29*, 33–41.
33. Adelson, E.H.; Bergen, J.R. Spatiotemporal energy models for the perception of motion. *J. Opt. Soc. Am. A* **1985**, *2*, 284–299. [CrossRef] [PubMed]
34. Farnebäck, G. Two-Frame Motion Estimation Based on Polynomial Expansion. In Proceedings of the 2003 Scandinavian Conference on Image Analysis, Halmstad, Sweden, 29 June–2 July 2003; pp. 363–370.

© 2020 by the author. Licensee MDPI, Basel, Switzerland. This article is an open access article distributed under the terms and conditions of the Creative Commons Attribution (CC BY) license (http://creativecommons.org/licenses/by/4.0/).

Article

Real-Time Haze Removal Using Normalised Pixel-Wise Dark-Channel Prior and Robust Atmospheric-Light Estimation

Yutaro Iwamoto, Naoaki Hashimoto and Yen-Wei Chen *

College of Information Science and Engineering, Ritsumeikan University, Shiga 525-8577, Japan; yiwamoto@fc.ritsumei.ac.jp (Y.I.); naoaki111.de@gmail.com (N.H.)
* Correspondence: chen@is.ritsumei.ac.jp

Received: 16 December 2019; Accepted: 4 February 2020; Published: 9 February 2020

Abstract: This study proposes real-time haze removal from a single image using normalised pixel-wise dark-channel prior (DCP). DCP assumes that at least one RGB colour channel within most local patches in a haze-free image has a low-intensity value. Since the spatial resolution of the transmission map depends on the patch size and it loses the detailed structure with large patch sizes, original work refines the transmission map using an image-matting technique. However, it requires high computational cost and is not adequate for real-time application. To solve these problems, we use normalised pixel-wise haze estimation without losing the detailed structure of the transmission map. This study also proposes robust atmospheric-light estimation using a coarse-to-fine search strategy and down-sampled haze estimation for acceleration. Experiments with actual and simulated haze images showed that the proposed method achieves real-time results of visually and quantitatively acceptable quality compared with other conventional methods of haze removal.

Keywords: haze removal; dark channel; atmospheric-light estimation; coarse-to-fine search strategy

1. Introduction

In recent years, self-driving vehicles, underwater robots, and remote sensing have attracted attention; such applications employ fast and robust image-recognition techniques. However, images of outdoor or underwater scenes have poor image quality because of haze (Figure 1a), thus affecting image recognition. To solve this problem, many haze removal techniques were proposed, and these techniques can be classified into non-learning-based and learning-based approaches.

Non-learning-based approaches use multiple haze images [1], depth information [2] and prior knowledge from a single haze image [3–5]. Methods employing prior knowledge maximise contrast within the local patch [3], assuming that surface shading and transmission are locally uncorrelated [4], and statistically observe that at least one RGB colour channel within most local patches in a haze-free image has a low-intensity value [5]. Median and guided-image filters [6,7] are used for accelerating haze removal; however, these methods could not achieve real-time processing (defined as 20 fps for our calculations herein). Learning-based approaches employ random forest [8], colour-attenuation and prior-based brightness-saturation relation [9] and deep learning [10,11]. These methods can achieve accurate and fast haze removal compared with conventional non-learning-based approaches. In deep-learning-based methods, large-scale pairs of haze images and corresponding haze-free images must be prepared and their relation must be trained. Image pairs of haze and haze-free images cannot be existed simultaneously in actual situation; therefore, haze images are generated from haze-free images by employing haze-observation model [10] and depth information from the corresponding haze-free images [11]. The haze-removal accuracy of deep-learning-based methods depends on the dataset and preparing large datasets is cumbersome. Deep-learning-based methods [10,11] are faster than conventional methods [5,6]; however, computational times of 1.5 s [10] and 0.61 s [11] are required for haze removal of a 640 × 480 image using 3.4 GHz CPU without GPU acceleration; these methods also could not achieve real-time processing.

This study proposes a real-time haze-removal method using a normalised pixel-wise dark-channel prior (DCP) to enable real-time application (Figure 1b,c). This paper is an extended version of [12]. Contributions of the proposed method are as follows:

(a) Normalised pixel-wise DCP

Original patch-wise DCP method requires high computational cost to refine the transmission map using an image-matting technique. In this paper, we propose a normalised pixel-wise DCP method with no need for refinement of transmission map compared with the patch-wise method.

(b) Accelerating haze removal via down-sampling

We estimate the transmission map and atmospheric light using down-sampled haze image for acceleration. This idea is inspired by [13].

(c) Robust atmospheric-light estimation

To reduce the computational time and improve robustness, we propose a coarse-to-fine search strategy for atmospheric-light estimation.

The remainder of this paper is organized as follows. In Section 2, we introduces He et al.'s method [5] in detail because it forms the basis of the proposed method. Section 3 provides the description of proposed method. The experimental results and discussion are reported in Section 4, and conclusion is drawn in Section 5.

(a) Haze image   (b) Proposed haze removal method   (c) Proposed transmission map

Figure 1. Examples of original haze image and proposed haze-removal image and transmission map ($\gamma = 0.5$).

2. Traditional Dark Channel Prior

This section describes DCP [5], which is the basis of the proposed method. The haze-observation model [1,5] is represented by

$$\mathbf{I}(\mathbf{x}) = t(\mathbf{x})\mathbf{J}(\mathbf{x}) + (1 - t(\mathbf{x}))\mathbf{A}, \tag{1}$$

where $\mathbf{I}(\mathbf{x})$ is the observed RGB colour vector of haze image at coordinate $\mathbf{x}$, $\mathbf{J}(\mathbf{x})$ is the ideal haze-free image at coordinate $\mathbf{x}$, $\mathbf{A}$ is the atmospheric light, $t(\mathbf{x})$ is the value of transmission map at coordinate $\mathbf{x}$. To solve the haze-removal problem, some prior knowledge such as DCP must be applied. The transmission map derivation (Section 2.1), atmospheric-light estimation (Section 2.2) and haze-removal image creation (Section 2.3) are explained as follows.

2.1. Estimation of Transmission Map

Medium transmission $t(\mathbf{x})$ [1,5] is expressed by

$$t(\mathbf{x}) = e^{-\beta d(\mathbf{x})}, \tag{2}$$

where β is the scattering coefficient of the atmosphere and $d(\mathbf{x})$ is the depth at coordinate $\mathbf{x}$. He et al. [5] used DCP, indicating that at least one RGB colour channel within most local patch has a low-intensity value

$$DC\left(\mathbf{J}(\mathbf{x})\right) = \min_{\mathbf{y} \in \Omega(\mathbf{x})} \left(\min_{c \in \{r,g,b\}} \left(J^c(\mathbf{y})\right) \right), \tag{3}$$

where $J^c(\mathbf{y})$ is a colour channel of haze-free image $\mathbf{J}(\mathbf{y})$ at coordinate $\mathbf{y}$ and DC is the dark-channel operator which extracts a mimimum RGB colour channel in a local patch $\Omega(\mathbf{x})$ centered at coordinate $\mathbf{x}$. From Equations (1) and (3) can be rewritten as

$$DC\left(\frac{\mathbf{I}(\mathbf{x})}{\mathbf{A}}\right) = \tilde{t}(\mathbf{x})DC\left(\frac{\mathbf{J}(\mathbf{x})}{\mathbf{A}}\right) + (1 - \tilde{t}(\mathbf{x})), \qquad (4)$$

where $\tilde{t}(\mathbf{x})$ is the coarse transmission map based on patch and the argument $\mathbf{I}(\mathbf{x})/\mathbf{A}$ and $\mathbf{J}(\mathbf{x})/\mathbf{A}$ are to be element-wise division. If $\Omega(\mathbf{x})$ is set to large patch size (e.g., 15 × 15), $DC(\mathbf{J}(\mathbf{x})/\mathbf{A})$ should tend to be zero. Finally, the transmission $\tilde{t}(\mathbf{x})$ can be estimated by Equation (5).

$$\tilde{t}(\mathbf{x}) = 1 - \omega DC\left(\frac{\mathbf{I}(\mathbf{x})}{\mathbf{A}}\right). \qquad (5)$$

where ω is the haze removal rate which is considered to the human perception for depth scene (0.95 in the He et al. [5]). Since $\tilde{t}(\mathbf{x})$ is calculated by each large patch to satisfy the DCP, $\tilde{t}(\mathbf{x})$ is not smooth in edge region and the spatial resolution is lost. To solve the problem, He et al. [5] refined the transmission map $\tilde{t}(\mathbf{x})$ using image-matting processing [14] as post-processing. However, such processing requires high computational cost and several tens of seconds to execute the haze-removal method.

2.2. Estimation of Atmospheric Light

Atmospheric light $\mathbf{A}$ comprises pixels of the observed image for which $t(\mathbf{x}) = 0$ in Equation (1); there is no direct light and the distance is infinity in Equation (2). In the outdoor image, this generally represents the intensity of the sky region. To estimate atmospheric light $\mathbf{A}$, the highest luminance value is considered in the haze image $\mathbf{I}$ [3]. If an image contains a white object, the atmospheric light $\mathbf{A}$ is misestimated, and optimum atmospheric light $\mathbf{A}$ is estimated using dark-channel value [5]. Initially He et al. [5] determined the top 0.1% brightest pixels in the dark-channel image, and chose the highest intensity pixels from those same pixels in haze image $\mathbf{I}$. Although this approach is useful because it can estimate atmospheric light $\mathbf{A}$ by ignoring small white object, the size is limited below the patch size.

2.3. Estimation of Haze-Removal Image

Haze removal can be calculated by modifying Equation (1) as follows:

$$\mathbf{J}(\mathbf{x}) = \frac{\mathbf{I}(\mathbf{x}) - \mathbf{A}}{\max(t(\mathbf{x}), t_0)} + \mathbf{A}, \qquad (6)$$

where $t(\mathbf{x})$ is the refined transmission map from patch-based transmission map $\tilde{t}(\mathbf{x})$, $\mathbf{A}$ is atmospheric light and t_0 is a parameter that is set to 0.1 to avoid division by a small value.

3. Proposed Method

Computer vision tasks, such as self-driving vehicles, under-water robots and remote sensing, employ real-time haze removal to realise fast and robust image recognition. In this section, a real-time and highly accurate haze-removal algorithm is proposed.

3.1. Normalized Pixel-Wise Dark Channel Prior

In the DCP, the spatial resolution of the transmission map $t(\mathbf{x})$ worsens along object edges because of calculating spatial minimisation in a dark-channel image. Therefore, He et al. [5] refined the transmission map via image-matting processing [14]. However, image-matting processing requires a high computational cost and is not acceptable for real-time application. Therefore, they proposed a guided-image filter [7] as a fast image-matting technique. Other researchers also proposed a pixel-wise DCP [15–17] and a method combining original patch-wise DCP in a flat region and pixel-wise DCP around the edge region [18]. Although pixel-wise DCP can estimate the transmission map $t(\mathbf{x})$ without selecting a minimum value spatially, the result tends to be darker than the haze image (Figure 2b). The histogram of medium transmission $t(\mathbf{x})$ in Figure 3 shows that the pixel-wise DCP without normalisation shifts to the left side compared with the histogram of the original patch-wise DCP (He et al. [5]). This is why the $DC(\mathbf{J}(\mathbf{x})/\mathbf{A})$ of Equation (4) cannot be zero by setting the patch size to 1×1 instead of 15×15. Therefore, in the proposed method, the $DC(\mathbf{J}(\mathbf{x})/\mathbf{A})$ of Equation (4) has a small value; the value of $(DC_J(\mathbf{x}))$ is defined by multiplying normalised dark channel of haze image $\mathbf{I}$, which ranges from 0 to 1 and the ratio γ in Equation (8).

$$DC_p\left(\frac{\mathbf{I}(\mathbf{x})}{\mathbf{A}}\right) = \min_{c \in \{r,g,b\}}\left(\frac{I^c(\mathbf{x})}{A^c}\right), \qquad (7)$$

$$DC_J(\mathbf{x}) = \gamma \frac{\min_{c \in \{r,g,b\}}\left(\frac{I^c(\mathbf{x})}{A^c}\right) - \min_{y \in \Omega}\left(\min_{c \in \{r,g,b\}}\left(\frac{I^c(\mathbf{y})}{A^c}\right)\right)}{\max_{y \in \Omega}\left(\min_{c \in \{r,g,b\}}\left(\frac{I^c(\mathbf{y})}{A^c}\right)\right) - \min_{y \in \Omega}\left(\min_{c \in \{r,g,b\}}\left(\frac{I^c(\mathbf{y})}{A^c}\right)\right)}, \qquad (8)$$

where DC_p is a pixel-wise dark channel operator, Ω is the entire image. The transmission map $t(\mathbf{x})$ of normalized pixel-wise DCP can be calculated by

$$t(\mathbf{x}) = \frac{1 - \omega DC_p\left(\frac{\mathbf{I}(\mathbf{x})}{\mathbf{A}}\right)}{1 - DC_J(\mathbf{x})}, \qquad (9)$$

The histogram (Figure 3) of the transmission map $t(\mathbf{x})$ derived by the proposed method shifts towards the right side compared with the histogram of transmission map without normalisation. As a result, the histogram of the proposed method gets close to the original patch-wise DCP. Here, if γ is set to be 0, Equation (9) corresponds to the pixel-wise DCP without normalisation (Figure 2b). Furthermore, setting γ to be a small value (e.g., 0.25) results in a dark image within the yellow dotted rectangle (Figure 2c), but if γ is set to be a large value (e.g., 0.75), the haze-removal effect diminishes within the dashed red rectangle (Figure 2e).

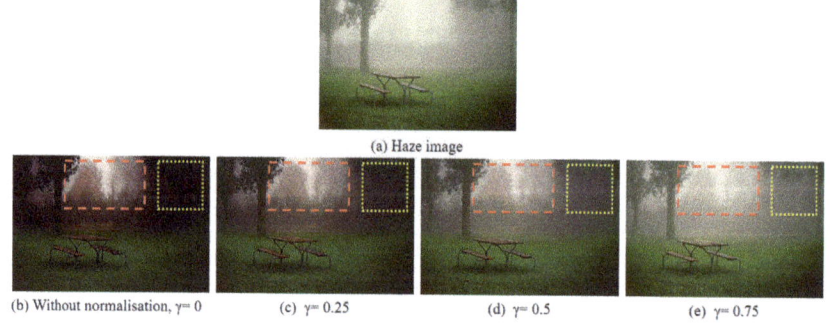

Figure 2. Differences among haze-removal images with each normalisation parameter γ.

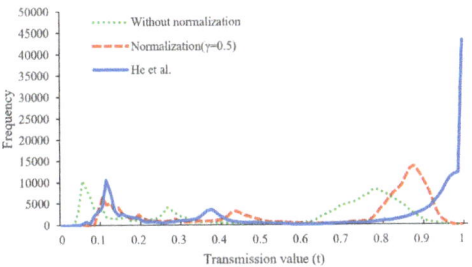

Figure 3. Histogram of medium transmission with each method.

3.2. Acceleration by Down-Sampling

In the haze-removal method, it is necessary to calculate the transmission map $t(\mathbf{x})$ for each pixel. Therefore, the calculation time of haze removal depends on the image size, and thus larger image sizes have higher associated calculation costs. Fortunately, observation of the transmission map $t(\mathbf{x})$ indicates that it is characterised by a relatively low frequency except edges between objects, particularly at different depths. Therefore, we reduced the computation time greatly by down-sampling the input image. It estimated the transmission map $t(\mathbf{x})$ and atmospheric light $\mathbf{A}$ using down-sampled image, and then the haze-removal image $\mathbf{J}$ was estimated by the up-sampled transmission map $t(\mathbf{x})$ using Equation (6). Figure 4 shows the haze-removal results with different down-sampling ratios. The down-sampling ratio set to 1/4 achieved visually acceptable results, but when it was set to 1/8 or 1/16, halo effects were generated along edges such as along the sides of trees and leaves within the dashed red rectangles (second row of Figure 4e,f). Also, significant aliasing occurred along edges of the bench within the yellow dotted rectangle (third row of Figure 4e,f), and uneven colour occurred in the enhancement results in second row of Figure 4e,f. We therefore set the down-sampling ratio to 1/4 in all further experiments. Also, we used box filtering in down-sampling and bicubic interpolation in up-sampling. Too, acceleration by the down-sampling approach helps with noise suppression by spatial smoothing.

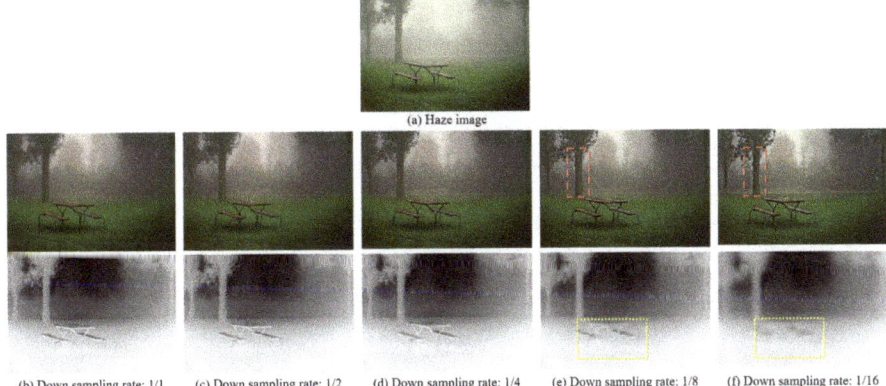

Figure 4. Haze image (first row), different haze-removal images (second row), transmission maps (third row) and corresponding down-sampling ratios.

3.3. Robust Atmospheric Light Estimation

He et al. [5] estimated atmospheric light $\mathbf{A}$ using the original patch-wise DCP, which is a robust method because it ignores small white objects by using a large patch size (e.g., 15×15). In addition, Liu et al.'s method [19] segments the sky region and uses the average value of that region as atmospheric light **A**. In our proposed method, because the dark-channel image is calculated for each pixel, white regions (represented by the blue '+' mark in Figure 5) are misinterpreted as atmospheric light **A**. On the basis of Figure 5, we found that our proposed method cannot use the He et al. [5] approach directly. In addition, their method requires extra computation time for sorting the top 0.1% brightest pixels in the dark channel of haze image **I**. To solve this problem, we propose a method that robustly estimates atmospheric light **A** by using a coarse-to-fine search strategy. Figure 6 shows the flow of the coarse-to-fine search strategy. In this strategy, initially the resolution of the dark-channel image is reduced step by step and the position of the largest dark-channel value is obtained at the lowest resolution; next it recalculates the position of the largest dark-channel value in the second-lowest resolution and continues to recalculate the position of the largest dark-channel value until the original image size is attained. In Figure 5, the red '×' mark (coarse-to-fine search strategy) is the correctly estimated atmospheric light **A**.

Figure 5. Effectiveness of coarse-to-fine search strategy. Blue '+' mark is result of atmospheric-light estimation by pixel-wise dark-channel image without using coarse-to-fine strategy. Red '×' is result of pixel-wise dark-channel image using coarse-to-fine strategy.

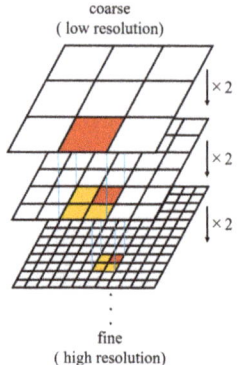

Figure 6. Flow of coarse-to-fine search strategy for estimting atmospheric light **A**.

4. Results and Discussion

In this section, we compare our method with Tarel et al.'s method [6], He et al.'s method [5] and Cai et al.'s method [10] for qualitative visual evaluation and quantitative evaluation. Ref. [10] is used trained network provided by [20]. We used haze and haze-free images downloaded from the Flickr website [21] (all collected images are public domain or creative commons zero license) and MATLAB source codes [20,22,23].

Initially, we generated five uniform and nonuniform haze images (Figures 7b and 8c) from the haze-free image (Figure 7a) by applying Equation (1). In order to do these simulations, we had to set the transmission map, for which we experimented with setting to uniform and nonuniform medium transmissions. In the uniform medium transmission t, it is set to 0.5 directly. On the other hand, in the nonuniform medium transmission $t(\mathbf{x})$, we set depth by manually segmenting four to five classes for the each image (Figure 8b) and then fixing the depth for each class; we determined the medium transmission $t(\mathbf{x})$ by applying Equation (2).

Figure 7. Comparison of proposed method with conventional method using simulated haze images generated with uniform transmission map ($t = 0.5$). (**a**) Original haze-free image, (**b**) Simulated haze image, (**c**) Tarel et al. [6], (**d**) He et al. [5], (**e**) Cai et al. [10], (**f**) Pixel-wise DCP without normalisation, (**g**) Proposed method ($\gamma = 0.9$).

In the quantitative evaluation, peak-signal-to-noise-ratio (PSNR) and structural similarity (SSIM) [24] are calculated

$$MSE = \frac{1}{HWK} \sum_{i=0}^{H-1} \sum_{j=0}^{W-1} \sum_{k=0}^{K-1} (G(i,j,k) - J(i,j,k))^2,$$

$$PSNR = 20 \log_{10} \left(\frac{MAX}{\sqrt{MSE}} \right), \qquad (10)$$

$$SSIM = \frac{1}{HWK} \sum_{i=0}^{H-1} \sum_{j=0}^{W-1} \sum_{k=0}^{K-1} \frac{(2\mu_G(i,j,k)\mu_J(i,j,k) + C_1)}{(\mu_G(i,j,k)^2 + \mu_J(i,j,k)^2 + C_1)} \frac{(2\sigma_{GJ}(i,j,k) + C_2)}{(\sigma_G(i,j,k)^2 + \sigma_J(i,j,k)^2 + C_2)}, \quad (11)$$

where H, W and K are image size as height and width and number of colour channel respectively; G and J are the ground-truth image and haze-removal result, respectively; MAX is maximum possible value of ground-truth image; μ_G and μ_J are gaussian weighted averages of G and J, respectively, within local patch; within local patch, σ_G and σ_J are standard deviations of G and J, respectively, within local patch; σ_{GJ} is a covariance of G and J within local patch; C_1 (set to 0.01^2) and C_2 (set to 0.03^2) are small constants. Secondly, we compared with proposed method and conventional method to actual haze image as qualitative visual evaluation. Finally, we show the comparison of computation time by each method and image size.

In common of qualitative evaluation in results with setting the uniform or the nonuniform medium transmission, the results of Figures 7 and 8 show that both our proposed method (Figures 7g and 8h) and He et al.'s method [5] (Figures 7d and 8e) can obtain highly accurate haze-removal images that are indistinguishable from the original haze-free image. Cai et al.'s method [10] can also obtain highly accurate haze-removal images in outdoor scene such as cityscape and landscape images (Figures 7e and 8f). However, Cai et al.'s method [10] cannot remove the haze in underwater scene. The reason is that underwater images are not included in the training data. The results of pixel-wise DCP without normalisation (Figures 7f and 8g) are darker than their original haze-free images (Figure 7a).

In the quantitative evaluation with uniform setting in Table 1, it is apparent that our proposed method can obtain the highest PSNR and SSIM values compared with conventional methods if the appropriate value for γ is selected. Here, in the case of uniform medium transmission t, $\min_{y \in \Omega}(\min_{c \in \{r,g,b\}}(I^c(y)/A^c))$ is close to $1-t$ because $\min_{y \in \Omega}(\min_{c \in \{r,g,b\}}(J^c(y)/A^c))$ is close to 0, and $\max_{y \in \Omega}(\min_{c \in \{r,g,b\}}(I^c(y)/A^c))$ is close to 1 because $\max_{y \in \Omega}(\min_{c \in \{r,g,b\}}(J^c(y)/A^c))$ is close to 1 in Equation (8). As the result, the appropriate value of γ is close to 1 when the ω equals to 1. From Table 1, the proposed method can obtain the best results when γ is set to a large value. On the other hand, in the quantitative evaluation with nonuniform setting shown in Table 2, some results from He et al.'s method [5] achieved better performance than the proposed method. The main reason is that it is not easy to estimate an appropriate γ in the case of nonuniform medium transmission $t(x)$ because it depends on the haze scene. How to automatically determine an appropriate value from the distribution of haze in the scene is our future work.

Table 1. Quantitative evaluation with PSNR and SSIM [24] for simulated haze images generated using uniform transmission map ($t = 0.5$). First row is PSNR value, and second row is SSIM value in each cell.

	Tarel et al. [6]	He et al. [5]	Cai et al. [10]	Proposed Method (γ)									
				0	0.1	0.2	0.3	0.4	0.5	0.6	0.7	0.8	0.9	1.0
cityscape	13.60	20.58	24.86	11.31	12.25	13.31	14.52	15.94	17.64	19.76	22.57	26.75	**34.77**	32.62
	0.842	0.918	0.966	0.623	0.685	0.743	0.796	0.844	0.887	0.925	0.956	0.981	0.996	**0.997**
crab	10.77	27.22	12.19	15.86	16.86	17.99	19.29	20.80	22.59	24.75	27.32	29.85	**30.40**	25.78
	0.651	0.971	0.705	0.853	0.881	0.905	0.926	0.944	0.958	0.968	0.976	0.979	**0.979**	0.969
coral reef	10.69	22.45	17.89	16.43	17.31	18.28	19.37	20.60	22.01	23.65	25.56	27.68	**29.56**	27.56
	0.661	0.944	0.825	0.817	0.851	0.881	0.907	0.929	0.946	0.960	0.970	0.976	**0.979**	0.977
landscape1	11.41	26.76	23.54	14.99	16.03	17.21	18.57	20.18	22.13	24.52	27.45	**30.27**	30.15	25.06
	0.613	0.947	0.895	0.802	0.833	0.860	0.883	0.904	0.922	0.937	0.950	0.959	**0.962**	0.946
landscape2	12.08	23.73	20.24	14.43	15.40	16.50	17.78	19.30	21.14	23.47	26.59	31.06	**35.53**	27.88
	0.718	0.933	0.884	0.805	0.840	0.870	0.897	0.921	0.941	0.959	0.973	0.982	**0.986**	0.978

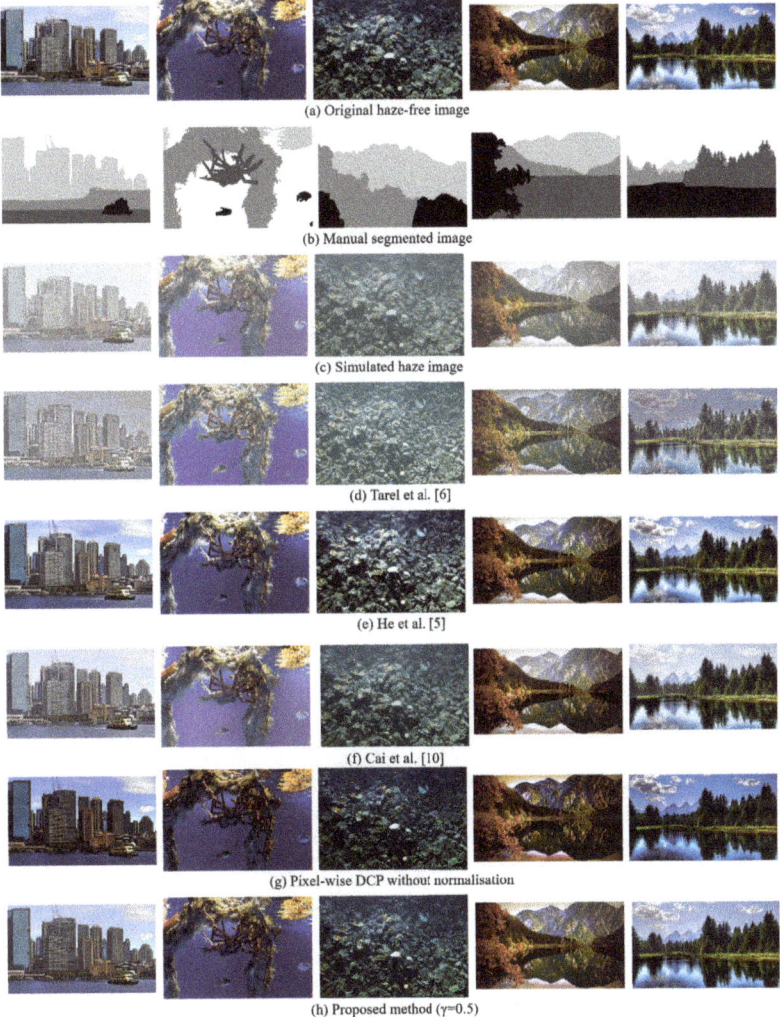

Figure 8. Comparison of proposed method with conventional method using simulated haze image generated with nonuniform transmission map. (**a**) Original haze-free image, (**b**) Manual segmented image, (**c**) Simulated haze image, (**d**) Tarel et al. [6], (**e**) He et al. [5], (**f**) Cai et al. [10], (**g**) Pixel-wise DCP without normalisation, (**h**)Proposed method ($\gamma = 0.5$).

We used the paired t-test to verify whether any performance differences between the proposed method and state-of-the-art methods are statistically significant. The test results are summarized in Table 3. The statistically significant methods ($p < 0.05$) are indicated by "Yes" and others are indicated by "No". As shown in Table 3, the proposed method outperformed Tarel et al.'s method [6] and pixel-wise DCP ($\gamma = 0$) method in both uniform and nonuniform medium transmission cases. On the other hand, the proposed method outperformed He et al.'s method [5] and Cai et al.'s method [10] only in the uniform setting and there are no significant difference in the nonuniform setting.

Table 2. Quantitative evaluation with PSNR and SSIM [24] for simulated haze images generated using nonuniform transmission map. First row is PSNR value, and second row is SSIM value in each cell.

	Tarel et al. [6]	He et al. [5]	Cai et al. [10]	Proposed Method (γ)										
				0	0.1	0.2	0.3	0.4	0.5	0.6	0.7	0.8	0.9	1.0
cityscape	13.58	22.74	19.88	12.89	14.35	16.08	18.12	20.46	22.66	**23.26**	21.60	19.20	16.98	15.06
	0.774	0.941	0.904	0.723	0.799	0.859	0.903	0.934	0.953	**0.958**	0.948	0.920	0.868	0.789
crab	12.10	**27.19**	12.99	15.29	16.28	17.37	18.59	19.95	21.43	22.97	24.32	25.01	24.64	22.64
	0.702	**0.970**	0.743	0.834	0.863	0.889	0.909	0.926	0.938	0.946	0.951	0.951	0.947	0.933
coral reef	11.74	19.78	18.07	16.25	17.22	18.26	19.38	20.53	21.65	22.58	**23.11**	23.04	22.38	20.83
	0.691	0.925	0.837	0.807	0.846	0.877	0.901	0.918	0.929	0.935	**0.937**	0.934	0.927	0.914
landscape1	14.02	**26.47**	25.35	15.29	16.63	18.15	19.88	21.74	23.38	24.01	23.14	21.41	19.53	17.60
	0.667	0.936	**0.937**	0.81	0.852	0.882	0.902	0.916	0.923	0.925	0.919	0.904	0.874	0.824
landscape2	14.63	**23.60**	18.02	15.97	17.23	18.57	19.88	20.90	21.25	20.74	19.61	18.23	16.84	15.54
	0.742	**0.920**	0.848	0.813	0.857	0.885	0.902	0.912	0.914	0.908	0.893	0.865	0.822	0.761

Table 3. Paired *t*-test results between proposed method and conventional methods. The statistically significant methods ($p < 0.05$) are indicated by "Yes" and others are indicated by "No".

			Tarel et al. [6]	He et al. [5]	Cai et al. [10]	pixel-wise DCP w/o normalisation($\gamma = 0$)
uniform	Proposed method($\gamma = 0.9$)	PSNR	Yes	Yes	Yes	Yes
		SSIM	Yes	Yes	Yes	Yes
non-uniform	Proposed method($\gamma = 0.5$)	PSNR	Yes	No	No	Yes
		SSIM	Yes	No	No	Yes

Figure 9 shows that our haze-removal method produced good results for processing actual haze images. Closer qualitative evaluation confirms that the images processed by our proposed method (Figure 9f) are visually similar to those obtained by He et al.'s method [5] (Figure 9c). We can see that the results of pixel-wise DCP without normalisation (Figure 9e) are also unnaturally darker than those obtained by He et al.'s method [5] (Figure 9c) and our proposed method (Figure 9f). Furthermore, although Tarel et al.'s method [6] obtained clearer haze-removal results in the pumpkin, bridge and townscape images compared with our proposed method results, our evaluation confirmed that the colours of the park, bridge and townscape images changed from those of the original haze images. We also noted the occurrence of halo effects in the train image. In addition, Tarel et al.'s method cannot work well in the underwater image. Cai et al.'s method [10] (Figure 9d) can remove haze more naturally than other methods. In particular, it can remove haze uniformly in the sky region and the colour is more natural. On the other hand, it cannot work well in the underwater image.

Figure 10 shows computation time for each image size for each method, assuming a i7-5557U (3.1 GHz, 2 cores, 4 threads) without GPU acceleration and main memory size is 16 GB. All methods are implemented in MATLAB. Using conventional methods, it takes several tens of seconds, and they cannot achieve real-time calculation. However, our proposed method can achieve real-time calculation until image size exceeds 1024 × 680 pixels.

Figure 9. Comparison of haze-removal results by our proposed method with conventional methods applied to actual haze images. (**a**) Haze image, (**b**) Tarel et al. [6], (**c**) He et al. [5], (**d**) Cai et al. [10], (**e**) Pixel-wise DCP without normalisation, (**f**) Proposed method ($\gamma = 0.5$).

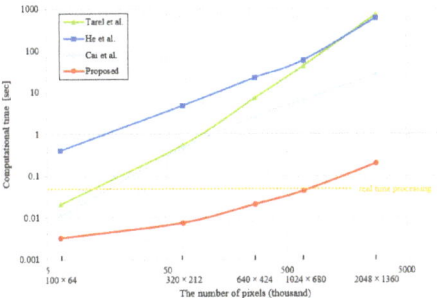

Figure 10. Comparison of computation time for each image size and each method.

5. Conclusions

In this paper, we propose a haze-removal method using a normalised pixel-wise DCP method. We also propose a fast transmission map estimation by down-sampling and robust atmospheric-light estimation using a coarse-to-fine search strategy. Experimental results show that the proposed method can achieve haze removal with acceptable accuracy and greater efficiency than can conventional methods. The advantage of the proposed method is its fast computation with acceptable visual quality compared with state-of-the-art-methods. On the other hand, its disadvantage is that the user must set an appropriate γ manually for each different haze scene. How to systematically determine the appropriate γ value from the distribution of haze in the scene is our future work. In addition, we are going to apply the method to real applications, such as automatic-driving, underwater-robot and remotely sensed imaging [25].

Author Contributions: Conceptualization, methodology, software and analysis, Y.I.; investigation and software, N.H.; Conceptualization and validation, Y.-W.C. All authors have read and agree to the published version of the manuscript.

Funding: This research received no external funding

Acknowledgments: The authors would like to thank Enago (www.enago.jp) for the English language review.

Conflicts of Interest: The authors declare no conflict of interest.

References

1. Narasimhan, S.G.; Nayar, S.K. Chromatic framework for vision in bad weather. In Proceedings of the IEEE Conference on Computer Vision and Pattern Recognition (CVPR), Hilton Head, SC, USA, 13–15 June 2000; Volume 1, pp. 598–605.
2. Kopf, J.; Neubert, B.; Chen, B.; Cohen, M.; Cohen-Or, D.; Deussen, O.; Uyttendaele, M.; Lischinski, D. Deep photo: model-based photograph enhancement and viewing. *ACM Trans. Graph. (TOG)* **2008**, *27*, 116 . [CrossRef]
3. Tan, R.T. Visibility in Bad Weather from a Single Image. In Proceedings of the IEEE Conference on Computer Vision and Pattern Recognition (CVPR), Anchorage, Alaska, 23–28 June 2008; pp. 1–8.
4. Fatal, R. Single Image Dehazing. *ACM Trans. Graph. (TOG)* **2008**, *27*. [CrossRef]
5. He, K.; Sun, J.; Tang, X. Single image haze removal using dark channel prior. *IEEE Trans. Pattern Anal. Mach. Intell.* **2011**, *33*, 2341–2353. [PubMed]
6. Tarel, J.P.; Hautière, N. Fast visibility restoration from a single color or gray level image. In Proceedings of the IEEE 12th International Conference on Computer Vision (ICCV), Kyoto, Japan, 27 September–4 October 2009; pp. 2201–2208.
7. He, K.; Sun, J.; Tang, X. Guided image filtering. *IEEE Trans. Pattern Anal. Mach. Intell.* **2013**, *35*, 1397–1409. [CrossRef] [PubMed]
8. Tang, K.; Yang, J.; Wang, J. Investigating Haze-relevant Features in A Learning Framework for Image Dehazing. In Proceedings of the IEEE Conference on Computer Vision and Pattern Recognition (CVPR), Columbus, OH, USA, 23–28 June 2014; pp. 2995–3000.
9. Zhu, Q.; Mai, J.; Shao, L. A Fast Single Image Haze Removal Algorithm Using Color Attenuation Prior. *IEEE Trans. Image Process.* **2015**, *24*. [CrossRef]
10. Cai, B.; Xu, X.; Jia, K.; Qing, C.; Tao, D.. DehazeNet: An End-to-End System for Single Image Haze Removal. *IEEE Trans. Image Process.* **2016**, *25*, 5187–5198. [CrossRef] [PubMed]
11. Ren, W.; Liu, S.; Zhang, H.; Pan, J.; Cao, X.; Yang, M.H. Single Image Dehazing via Multi-scale Convolutional Neural Networks. In Proceedings of the European Conference on Computer Vision (ECCV), Amsterdam, The Netherlands, 11–14 October 2016; pp. 154–169.
12. Iwamoto, Y.; Hashimoto, N.; Chen, Y.W. Fast Dark Channel Prior Based Haze Removal from a Single Image. In Proceedings of the 14th International Conference on Natural Computation, Fuzzy Systems and Knowledge Discovery (ICNC-FSKD2018), Huangshan, China, 28–30 July 2018.
13. He, K.; Sun, J. Fast Guided Filter. *arXiv* **2015**, arXiv:1505.00996.
14. Levin, A.; Lischinski, D.; Weiss, Y. A closed-form solution to natural image matting. *IEEE Trans. Pattern Anal. Mach. Intell.* **2008**, *30*, 228–242. [CrossRef] [PubMed]
15. Long, J.; Shi, Z.; Tang, W. Fast Haze Removal for a Single Remote Sensing Image Using Dark Channel Prior. In Proceedings of the IEEE 2012 International Conference on Computer Vision in Remote Sensing (CVRS), Xiamen, China, 16–18 December 2012; pp. 132–135.
16. Hsieh, C.H.; Weng, Z.M.; Lin, Y.S. Single image haze removal with pixel-based transmission map estimation. In *WSEAS Recent Advances in Information Science*; World Scientific: Singerpore, 2016; pp. 121–126.
17. Kotera, H. A color correction for degraded scenes by air pollution. *J. Color Sci. Assoc. Jpn.* **2016**, *40*, 49–59.
18. Han, T.; Wan, Y. A fast dark channel prior-based depth map approximation method for dehazing single images. In Proceedings of the IEEE Third International Conference on Information Science and Technology (ICIST), Yangzhou, Jiangsu, China, 23–25 March 2013; pp. 1355–1359.
19. Liu, W.; Chen, X.; Chu, X.; Wu, Y.; Lv, J. Haze removal for a single inland waterway image using sky segmentation and dark channel prior. *IET Image Process.* **2016**, *10*, 996–1006. [CrossRef]

20. The Matlab Source Code of Cai's Method. Available online: https://github.com/caibolun/DehazeNet (accessed on 9 January 2020).
21. Flickr Webpage. Available online: https://www.flickr.com/ (accessed on 25 May 2018).
22. The Matlab Source Code of Tarel's Method. Available online: http://perso.lcpc.fr/tarel.jean-philippe/publis/iccv09.html (accessed on 25 May 2018).
23. The Matlab Source Code of He's Method. Available online: https://github.com/sjtrny/Dark-Channel-Haze-Removal (accessed on 25 May 2018).
24. Wang, Z.; Bovik, A.C.; Sheikh, H.R.; Simoncelli, E.P. Image quality assessment: from error visibility to stuctural similarity. *IEEE Trans. Image Process.* **2004**, *13*, 600–612. [CrossRef] [PubMed]
25. Ahmad, M.; Khan, A.M.; Mazzara, M.; Distefano, S. Multi-layer Extreme Learning Machine-based Autoencoder for Hyperspectral Image Classification, In Proceedings of the the 14th International Conference on Computer Vision Theory and Applications (VISAPP' 19), Valletta, Malta, 27–29 February 2019; pp. 25–27.

© 2020 by the authors. Licensee MDPI, Basel, Switzerland. This article is an open access article distributed under the terms and conditions of the Creative Commons Attribution (CC BY) license (http://creativecommons.org/licenses/by/4.0/).

Article

Stable Sparse Model with Non-Tight Frame

Min Zhang [1], Yunhui Shi [1,*], Na Qi [1] and Baocai Yin [1,2]

1. Beijing Key Laboratory of Multimedia and Intelligent Software Technology, Faculty of Information Technology, Beijing University of Technology, Beijing 100124, China; lengyuewuyan@yeah.net (M.Z.); qina@bjut.edu.cn (N.Q.); ybc@bjut.edu.cn (B.Y.)
2. Computer Science and Technology, Dalian University of Technology, Dalian 116023, China
* Correspondence: syhzm@bjut.edu.cn

Received: 17 January 2020; Accepted: 25 February 2020; Published: 4 March 2020

Abstract: Overcomplete representation is attracting interest in image restoration due to its potential to generate sparse representations of signals. However, the problem of seeking sparse representation must be unstable in the presence of noise. Restricted Isometry Property (RIP), playing a crucial role in providing stable sparse representation, has been ignored in the existing sparse models as it is hard to integrate into the conventional sparse models as a regularizer. In this paper, we propose a stable sparse model with non-tight frame (SSM-NTF) via applying the corresponding frame condition to approximate RIP. Our SSM-NTF model takes into account the advantage of the traditional sparse model, and meanwhile contains RIP and closed-form expression of sparse coefficients which ensure stable recovery. Moreover, benefitting from the pair-wise of the non-tight frame (the original frame and its dual frame), our SSM-NTF model combines a synthesis sparse system and an analysis sparse system. By enforcing the frame bounds and applying a second-order truncated series to approximate the inverse frame operator, we formulate a dictionary pair (frame pair) learning model along with a two-phase iterative algorithm. Extensive experimental results on image restoration tasks such as denoising, super resolution and inpainting show that our proposed SSM-NTF achieves superior recovery performance in terms of both subjective and objective quality.

Keywords: sparse dictionary; stable recovery; frame; RIP

1. Introduction

Sparse representation of signals in dictionary domains has been widely studied and has provided promising performance in numerous signal processing tasks such as image denoising [1–5], super resolution [6–8], inpainting [9,10] and compression [11,12]. It is well known that images are represented by a linear combination of certain atoms of a dictionary. Overcomplete sparse representation is the overcomplete system with a sparse constraint. Common overcomplete systems differ from the traditional bases, such as DCT, DFT and Wavelet, because they offer a wider range of generating elements; potentially, this wider range allows more flexibility and effectiveness in signal sparse representation. However, it is a severely under-constrained illposed problem to find the underlying overcomplete representation due to the redundancy of the systems. When the underlying representation is sparse and the overcomplete systems have stable properties, the ill-posedness will disappear [13]. Sparse models are generally classified into two categories: Synthesis sparse models and analysis sparse model [14]. The commonly referred to sparse models are synthesis sparse models. The analysis ones characterize the signal by multiplying it with an analysis overcomplete dictionary, leading to a sparse outcome. A variety of effective sparse models have been investigated and established such as the classical synthesis sparse model [9,15], the classical analysis sparse model [14], the nonlocal sparse model [16,17] and the 2D sparse model [18]. Unfortunately, these models ignore the stability recovery property which claims that once a sufficient sparse solution is found, all alternative solutions necessarily reside very close to it [9]. Recently, the stable recovery of sparse representation has drawn attention in signal processing theory. Generally speaking, stable recovery can be guaranteed by two properties: Sufficient sparsity and a favorable structure of the dictionary [19]. Donoho defines the concept of mutual incoherence of the dictionary and applies it to prove some possibility of stable recovery [19]. The authors of [20] proposea sparsity-based orthogonal dictionary learning method to minimize the mutual incoherence. The authors of [21] propose an incoherent dictionary learning scheme by integrating a low rank gram matrix of the dictionary into the dictionary learning model.

A more powerful stable recovery guarantee developed by Candes and Tao, termed Restricted Isometry Property (RIP), makes consequent analysis easy [22]. A matrix Φ is said to satisfy the RIP of order k if there exists a constant $\delta_k \in (0, 1)$ such that

$$(1 - \delta_k)\|\mathbf{y}\|_2^2 \leq \|\Phi\mathbf{y}\|_2^2 \leq (1 + \delta_k)\|\mathbf{y}\|_2^2 \tag{1}$$

holds for all k-sparse vectors $\mathbf{y}$. δ_k is defined as the smallest constant which satisfies the above inequalities and is called the restricted isometry constant of Φ.

Most RIP research substantially investigates applying RIP as a stability analysis instrument [17,23,24] or finding optimal RIP constant [25,26] which are all theoretical analyses rather than practical applications. According to the research of [21], the intrinsic property of a dictionary has a direct influence on its performance. All familiar algorithms are staggeringly unstable with a coherent or degenerate dictionary [19]. Recognizing the gap between theoretical analyses and practical applications of RIP, this paper aims to build a stable sparse model satisfying the RIP.

Recently, the frame as a stable overcomplete system has drawn some attention in signal processing as the given signal can be represented by its canonical expansion in a manner similar to conventional bases under the frame. Some data-driven approaches are proposed in [1,27–30]. The authors of [27,29,30] utilize redundant tight frame in compressed sensing and [28] applies tight frame to few-view image reconstruction. Study [1] presents a data-driven method that the dictionary atoms associated with the tight frame are generated by filters. These approaches achieve much better image processing performance than previous methods, and meanwhile the tight frame condition which requires the frame almost-orthogonality will limit the flexibility in sparse representation. Study [31] derives stable recovery result for l_1-analysis minimization in redundant, possibly non-tight frames. Inspired by this result and the relationship between RIP and frame, we aim to establish a stable sparse model with RIP based on non-tight frame.

We call a sequence $\{\boldsymbol{\phi}_i\}_{i=1}^{M} \in \mathbf{H}$ a frame if and only if there exist two positive numbers A and B such that

$$A\|\mathbf{x}\|_2^2 \leq \sum_{i=1}^{M} |<\mathbf{x}, \boldsymbol{\phi}_i>|^2 \leq B\|\mathbf{x}\|_2^2 \quad \forall \mathbf{x} \in \mathbf{H}^N \tag{2}$$

Here, A and B are called the bounds of the frame. We find that every submatrix Φ_k satisfied RIP is a non-tight frame with $(1 - \delta_k)$ and $(1 + \delta_k)$ as its frame bounds with a given k. Obviously, there is an essential connection between the non-tight frame and the RIP.

In this paper we focus on a stable sparse model and more specifically on the development of an algorithm that would learn a pair of non-tight frame based dictionaries from a set of signal examples. We propose a stable sparse model via applying the non-tight frame condition to approximate the RIP. This model shares the favorite overcomplete structures with the common sparse models, and meanwhile it contains RIP and closed-form sparse coefficient expression which ensure stable recovery. Recognizing that the optimal framebounds are essentially the maximum and minimum singular values of the frame, RIP is actually enforced on the dictionary pair (the frame and its dual frame) by constraining the singular values of them. We also formulate a dictionary pair learning model via applying the second-order truncated Taylor series to approximate the inverse frame operator. Then we present an efficient algorithm to learn the dictionary pair via a two-phase iterative approach. To summarize, this paper makes the following contributions:

1. We propose a stable sparse model along with a dictionary pair learning model. Non-tight frame condition is utilized to develop a relaxation of RIP to guarantee stable recovery of sparse representation. Moreover, the sparse coefficients are also modeled, which leads to a more stable recovery especially for seriously noisy image.
2. It is nearly impossible to solve the dictionary pair learning model in a straightforward way since the inverse frame operator is involved. We provide an effective way to modify the model via applying a second-order truncated Taylor series to approximate the inverse frame operator, and provide an efficient algorithm for the modified one.
3. We present the stability analysis of the proposed model and demonstrate it on natural and synthetic image denoising, super resolution and image inpainting. The denoising results show that the proposed approach outperforms synthesis models such as the KSVD and the data-driven tight frame based methods for natural image case in terms of average PSNR. Moreover, it also gains comparable performance to the Analysis KSVD for a piecewise-constant (PWC) image in terms of average PSNR. The meaningful structures in the trained dictionary pairs for natural images and a PWC image are observed. The super resolution results show that the SSM-NTF produces better performance than the Bicubic interpolation method and the method in [32]. The inpainting results show that our model is able to eliminate text of fonts completely.

This paper is organized as follows: Section 2 reviews the related work on frame, synthesis sparse model and analysis sparse model. Section 3 presents our stable sparse model with non-tight frame SSM-NTF along with a dictionary pair learning model. Section 4 proposes the corresponding dictionary pair learning algorithm. Section 5 proposes the image restoration method of our proposed SSM-NTF model. In Section 6 we analyze the computational complexity of our proposed algorithm. In Section 7, we demonstrate the the effectiveness of our SSM-NTF model by analyzing the convergence of the corresponding algorithm, denoising natural and piecewise constant images, super resolution and image inpainting. Finally, Section 8 concludes this paper.

2. Related Work

In this section, we briefly review the related work on frame, synthesis sparse model and analysis sparse model.

Frame: A frame Φ is called a tight frame if the frame bounds are equal in the Equation (2) [32]. There are two associated operators can be defined between the Hilbert space $\mathbf{H}^N$ and Square Integrable Space $l_2^M(\cdot)$ once a frame is defined. One is the analysis operator $\mathbf{T}$ defined by

$$(\mathbf{T}\mathbf{x})_i = <\mathbf{x}, \boldsymbol{\phi}_i>, \quad \forall \mathbf{x} \in \mathbf{H}^N \tag{3}$$

and the other is its adjoint operator $\mathbf{T}^*$ which is called the synthesis operator

$$\mathbf{T}^*\mathbf{c} = \sum_{i=1}^{M} \mathbf{c}\boldsymbol{\phi}_i \quad \forall \mathbf{c} = (\mathbf{c}_i)_{i \in J} \in l_2^M(\mathbf{T}) \tag{4}$$

then, the frame operator can be defined as the following canonical expansion

$$\mathbf{F}\mathbf{x} = \mathbf{T}^*\mathbf{T}\mathbf{x} = \sum_{i=1}^{M} <\mathbf{x}, \boldsymbol{\phi}_i> \boldsymbol{\phi}_i \tag{5}$$

In Euclidean space, a given frame Φ can be represent in manner of matrix with its columns of it as the frame elements. Then one of its adjoint operator can be represented as $\boldsymbol{\psi}_i = \mathbf{F}^{-1}\boldsymbol{\phi}_i$ [32]. Let $\mathbf{x} \in \mathbb{R}^N$ be an arbitrary vector, a reconstruction function can be expressed as the following form

$$\mathbf{x} = \sum_{i=1}^{M} <\mathbf{x}, \boldsymbol{\psi}_i> \boldsymbol{\phi}_i \tag{6}$$

Synthesis sparse model: The conventional synthesis sparse model represents a vector **x** by the linear combination of a few atoms from a large dictionary **Φ**, denoted as $\mathbf{x} = \mathbf{\Phi y}, \|\mathbf{y}\|_0 \leq L$, where L is the sparsity of **y**. The computational techniques for approximating sparse coefficient **y** under a given dictionary **Φ** and **x** includes greedy pursuit (e.g., OMP [9]) and convex relaxation optimization, such as Lasso [33] and FISTA [8]. In order to improve the performance of sparse representation, some modified models such as the nonlocal sparse model [16], the frame based sparse model [21], and the MD sparse model [18] are also investigated.

Analysis sparse model: The analysis sparse model is defined as: $\mathbf{y} = \mathbf{\Omega x}, \|\mathbf{y}\|_0 = p - l$ where $\mathbf{\Omega} \in \mathcal{R}^{p \times d}$ is a linear operator (also called as a dictionary), and l denotes the co-sparsity of the signal **x**. The analysis representative vector **y** is sparse with l zeros. The zeros in **y** denote the low-dimensional subspace to which the signal **x** belongs. The analysis sparse coding [14] and dictionary learning [34] approach are also been proposed.

However, all these models ignore the stability recovery property which provides stable reconstruction of the signals in presence of noise.

Dictionary learning methods: The dictionaries include analytical dictionaries, such as DCT, DWT, curvelets and contourlets and learned dictionaries. Some dictionary learning method are proposed, such as the classical KSVD [9] algorithm, the efficient sparse coding which convert the original dictionary learning problem to two least squares problem by applying the Lagrange dual [3], the non-local sparse model [16] which learns a set of PCA sub-dictionaries by cluster the samples into K clusters using image nonlocal self-similarity prior and its improved version which using the l_q-norm to instead the l_2-norm in order to handle different image contents. With the realization of stability, some mutual-coherence based methods are proposed. In [20] a sparsity-based orthogonal dictionary learning method is proposed to minimize the mutual-coherence of the dictionary. The authors of [21] propose an in coherent dictionary learning scheme by integrating a low rank gram matrix of the dictionary into the dictionary learning model. However, these methods only concern the capability of the dictionary without modeling the sparse coefficients which still has some probability of instability.

3. The Proposed SSM-NTF

In this section, we present the stable sparse model with non-tight frame, (Section 3.1), the stability analysis of the proposed model, (Section 3.2) and the dictionary pair (the frame pair) learning model, (Section 3.3).

3.1. Stable Sparse Model with Non-Tight Frame

In this section, we derive our stable sparse model with non-tight frame where the non-tight frame condition serves as an approximation to the RIP.

According to [35], a k-th RIP constant can be express as

$$\delta_k(\mathbf{\Phi}) = \frac{\Gamma_k(\mathbf{\Phi}) - 1}{\Gamma_k(\mathbf{\Phi}) + 1} \quad (7)$$

where

$$\Gamma_k(\mathbf{\Phi}) = \frac{\theta_{max}^k}{\theta_{min}^k} \quad (8)$$

$$\theta_{max}^k = \max_{\|\mathbf{y}\|_0 = k} \frac{\|\mathbf{\Phi y}\|_2^2}{\|\mathbf{y}\|_2^2}, \theta_{min}^k = \min_{\|\mathbf{y}\|_0 = k} \frac{\|\mathbf{\Phi y}\|_2^2}{\|\mathbf{y}\|_2^2} \quad (9)$$

The Equation (7) provides a new perspective in integrating the RIP to sparse model via applying θ_{max}^k and θ_{min}^k instead of the RIP constant $\delta_k(\mathbf{\Phi})$. The difficulty in building a stable sparse model decreases. However, the sparsity k varies with the noise level, and also, in a feasible numerical calculation method, it is impossible to sweep through all the samples satisfying $\|\mathbf{x}\|_0 = k$ to pursue an unknown dictionary **Φ**.

Let $\mathbf{x}$ be a signal vector, the frame reconstruction function can be formulated as $\mathbf{x} = \mathbf{\Phi}\mathbf{\Psi}^T\mathbf{x}$ where $\mathbf{\Psi}$ is a dual frame of $\mathbf{\Phi}$. Adding a reasonable sparsity prior to the signal $\mathbf{x}$ over $\mathbf{\Psi}$ domain, we can derive

$$\frac{\|\mathbf{\Phi}(\mathbf{\Psi}^T\mathbf{x})\|_2^2}{\|\mathbf{\Psi}^T\mathbf{x}\|_2^2} = \frac{\|\mathbf{x}\|_2^2}{\|\mathbf{\Psi}^T\mathbf{x}\|_2^2} = \frac{1}{\frac{\|\mathbf{\Psi}^T\mathbf{x}\|_2^2}{\|\mathbf{x}\|_2^2}} \tag{10}$$

Denoting the optimal frame bounds of $\mathbf{\Phi}$ as A and B, the frame condition of $\mathbf{\Psi}$ can be formulated as $\frac{1}{B} \leq \frac{\|\mathbf{\Psi}^T\mathbf{x}\|_2^2}{\|\mathbf{x}\|_2^2} \leq \frac{1}{A}$. Then a pair of bounds for Equation (10) can be obtained as $A \leq \frac{\|\mathbf{\Phi}(\mathbf{\Psi}^T\mathbf{x})\|_2^2}{\|\mathbf{\Psi}^T\mathbf{x}\|_2^2} \leq B$. A formula similar to Equation (9) is derived as $B = \max_{\mathbf{x}\in\mathcal{J}} \frac{\|\mathbf{\Phi}(\mathbf{\Psi}^T\mathbf{x})\|_2^2}{\|\mathbf{\Psi}^T\mathbf{x}\|_2^2}$, $A = \min_{\mathbf{x}\in\mathcal{J}} \frac{\|\mathbf{\Phi}(\mathbf{\Psi}^T\mathbf{x})\|_2^2}{\|\mathbf{\Psi}^T\mathbf{x}\|_2^2}$ where $\mathcal{J}$ is the data set. Imitating Equation (7), we can obtain a RIP-like constant expression

$$\hat{\delta}(\mathbf{\Phi}) = \frac{\hat{\Gamma}(\mathbf{\Phi}) - 1}{\hat{\Gamma}(\mathbf{\Phi}) + 1} \tag{11}$$

where $\hat{\Gamma}(\mathbf{\Phi}) = \frac{B}{A}$. Obviously, $\hat{\delta}(\mathbf{\Phi})$ can be regarded as an approximation of the RIP constant which benefits the computation due to the ignorance on sparsity degree. In a word, the RIP constraint can be satisfied by constraining the frame bounds. Thus, a stable overcomplete system with a sparsity prior can be established.

Now we discuss the characteristic of the frame bounds A and B. The Frame Condition (2) has a more compact form $\sqrt{A} \leq \eta_{\mathbf{\Phi}} \leq \sqrt{B}$ where $\eta_{\mathbf{\Phi}}$ denotes any singular value of $\mathbf{\Phi}$. More specifically, $\sqrt{A} = \eta_{min}$, $\sqrt{B} = \eta_{max}$ where η_{max} and η_{min} denote the maximum and minimum singular values of $\mathbf{\Phi}$, respectively. Then, we can obtain $\eta_{max} \geq \theta_{max}^k$, $\eta_{min} \leq \theta_{min}^k$. It is easy to know that $\hat{\delta}(\mathbf{\Phi}) \geq \delta_k(\mathbf{\Phi})$. Obviously, $\hat{\delta}(\mathbf{\Phi})$ is a reasonable relaxation of $\delta_k(\mathbf{\Phi})$ as $\hat{\delta}(\mathbf{\Phi})$ is slightly exceed $\delta_k(\mathbf{\Phi})$ but resides very close to it as long as the data is not seriously degraded. Therefore, the RIP constraint can be enforced on the frames by limiting the maximum and minimum singular values.

In this paper, we integrate non-frame to traditional sparse model to establish a stable sparse model with RIP. Let $\mathbf{x}$ be a signal vector. Under the assumption of the sparsity prior of $\mathbf{\Psi}^T\mathbf{x}$, we apply a soft thresholding operator $\mathcal{S}_\lambda(\cdot)$ (which shall be defined in the next subsection) on it such that

$$\mathbf{x} = \mathbf{\Phi}\mathcal{S}_\lambda(\mathbf{\Psi}^T\mathbf{x}) \tag{12}$$

where λ is a vector with elements λ_i corresponding to ψ_i, $i = 1, 2, \ldots, M$. Therefore, we propose the stable sparse model with non-tight frame (SSM-NTF) as follows

$$\mathbf{y} = \mathcal{S}_\lambda(\mathbf{\Psi}^T\mathbf{x}), \quad \mathbf{x} = \mathbf{\Phi}\mathbf{y}, \tag{13}$$
$$\text{s.t. } \|\mathbf{y}\|_0 \leq s.$$

Here, the correlation between the frame $\mathbf{\Phi}$ and its dual frame $\mathbf{\Psi}$ is formulated as $\mathbf{\Psi} = \mathbf{F}^{-1}\mathbf{\Phi}$. The frame operator $\mathbf{F}$ is formulated as $\mathbf{\Phi}\mathbf{\Phi}^T$ which is indeed a gram matrix of $\mathbf{\Phi}$. The singular values of $\mathbf{\Phi}$ are constrained by $\sqrt{A} \leq \eta_{\mathbf{\Phi}} \leq \sqrt{B}$ to satisfy the RIP. Actually, by constraining the singular values of $\mathbf{\Phi}$, the elements of the gram matrix are also bounded which meets the theory of mutual coherence.

In order to be consistent with the traditional sparse models, we refer to the frame $\mathbf{\Phi}$ and its dual frame $\mathbf{\Psi}$ as dictionary and its dual dictionary.

3.2. The Stability Analysis of the Proposed Model

In sparse representation problem, a given noiseless signal $\mathbf{x}$, can be formulated formulated as

$$(P_0): \min_{\mathbf{x}} \|\mathbf{y}\|_0 \quad s.t. \ \mathbf{x} = \mathbf{\Phi}\mathbf{y} \tag{14}$$

where $\mathbf{\Phi}$ is the sparse representation dictionary and $\mathbf{y}$ is the sparse coefficients. While $\mathbf{x} = \mathbf{\Phi y}$ is an underdetermined linear system, the problem (P_0) has the unique solution $\mathbf{y}_0$ as soon as it satisfies the uniqueness property which is formulated as

$$\|\hat{\mathbf{y}}\|_0 < \frac{1}{2}(1 + 1/\mu) \tag{15}$$

where μ is the mutual-coherence of $\mathbf{\Phi}$ [9]. However, the signals are usually acquired with noise, then the problem (P_0) should be relaxed to the problem (P_ϵ) which is expressed as

$$(P_\epsilon): \quad \min_{\mathbf{x}} \|\mathbf{y}\|_0 \quad s.t. \quad \|\mathbf{x} - \mathbf{\Phi y}\|_F^2 \le \epsilon \tag{16}$$

where ϵ is an error-tolerant which exists due to the noise. The problem (P_ϵ) will no longer maintain the uniqueness of solution as $\mathbf{x} = \mathbf{\Phi y} + \epsilon$ is an inequality system. Thus, the notion of Uniqueness Property (15) is replaced by the notion of stability which claims that all the alternative solutions reside very close to the ideal solution. Under the stable guarantee, we can yet ensure that the recovery results of our methods produce meaningful solutions. Assume that $\mathbf{y}_0$ is the ideal solution to the problem (P_ϵ) and $\hat{\mathbf{y}}$ is the candidate one, the traditional sparse model has a stability claim of the form [9]

$$\|\hat{\mathbf{y}} - \mathbf{y}_0\|_2^2 \le \frac{4\epsilon^2}{1 - (2s_0 - 1)\mu}, \tag{17}$$

where μ is the mutual coherence which is formulated as $\mu = \max_{i \ne j} | < \boldsymbol{\phi}_i, \boldsymbol{\phi}_j > |, i, j = 1, 2, \cdots, M$. Apparently, the error bound of Equation (17) can only be determined with given sparsity s_0 and the mutual coherence μ. However, the mutual coherence of an unknown dictionary is very difficult to calculate which lead to a result that we can not ensure the stability in the dictionary learning case. In contrast, we derive a similar stability claim of our proposed SSM-NTF model.

Defining $\mathbf{d} = \hat{\mathbf{y}} - \mathbf{y}_0$ with $\mathbf{y}_0$ as the ideal solution to the model, we have that $\|\mathbf{\Phi}\hat{\mathbf{y}} - \mathbf{\Phi y}_0\|_2 = \|\mathbf{\Phi d}\|_2 \le 2\epsilon$. From the previous subsection, we have know that the frame $\mathbf{\Phi}$ satisfies the RIP with the corresponding parameter $\hat{\delta}(\mathbf{\Phi})$. Thus, using this property and exploiting the lower-bound part in Equation (1), we get

$$(1 - \hat{\delta}(\mathbf{\Phi}))\|\mathbf{d}\|_2^2 \le \|\mathbf{\Phi d}\|_2^2 \le 4\epsilon^2 \tag{18}$$

where $\hat{\delta}(\mathbf{\Phi}) = \frac{\hat{\Gamma}(\mathbf{\Phi}) - 1}{\hat{\Gamma}(\mathbf{\Phi}) + 1} = \frac{\frac{B}{A} - 1}{\frac{B}{A} + 1}$. Thus, we get a stability claim of the form

$$\|\mathbf{d}\|_2^2 = \|\hat{\mathbf{y}} - \mathbf{y}_0\|_2^2 \le \frac{4\epsilon^2}{1 - \frac{\frac{B}{A} - 1}{\frac{B}{A} + 1}} \tag{19}$$

Obviously, the error bound of the SSM-NTF is determined by $\frac{B}{A}$, the ratio of the upper bound to the lower bound of the frame, rather than the specific values of A and B. Thus, for the convenience of numerical experiments, we usually set A to a fixed value. A main advantage of standard orthogonal transformations is that they maintain the energy of the signals in the transform domain as its frame bounds A and B are equal to 1. However, the standard orthogonal basis is non-redundant that limits its performance in sparse representation. In order to make a trade off between the represent accuracy and the degree of redundant, we usually set the lower frame bound A to a value a little smaller than 1 but not over-small as A is the minimum singular value of $\mathbf{\Phi}$ which determines the condition number of $\mathbf{\Phi}$. Thus, once the tolerance error is given, the value of B can be easily calculated. Further, a pair of dictionaries conform to the given error can be obtained using the proposed SSM-NTF model. On the other hand, if the value of B is given by experience, the error bound of our model can be measured.

3.3. Learning Model of Dictionary Pair

Assuming $\mathbf{X} \in \mathbb{R}^{N \times L}$ is the training data with signal vectors $\mathbf{x}_i \in \mathbb{R}^N, i = 1, 2, \ldots, L$, as its columns. The dictionary pair learning model can be written as

$$\min_{\mathbf{\Phi},\mathbf{\Psi},\lambda,\mathbf{Y}} \|\mathbf{X} - \mathbf{\Phi}\mathbf{Y}\|_F^2 + \gamma_1 \|\mathbf{Y} - \mathcal{S}_\lambda(\mathbf{\Psi}^T\mathbf{X})\|_F^2 + \gamma_2 \|\mathbf{Y}\|_0 + \gamma_3 \|\mathbf{\Psi} - \mathbf{F}^{-1}\mathbf{\Phi}\|_F^2 \quad (20)$$

$$\text{s.t. } \sqrt{A} \leq \eta_\mathbf{\Phi} \leq \sqrt{B}$$

However, the Problem (20) is difficult to solve. First, the inverse of the frame operator $\mathbf{F}$ has no closed-form explicit expression. Secondly, the thresholding operator is a highly nonlinear operator which makes the optimization with respect to λ hard to optimize.

Apparently, the Problem (20) is difficult to solve as the existence of the inverse of $\mathbf{F}$. Fortunately, the matrix $\mathbf{F}^{-1}$ can be expressed as a convergent series [36] which is formulated as

$$\mathbf{F}^{-1} = \frac{2}{A+B} \sum_{k=0}^{\infty} (\mathbf{I} - \frac{2\mathbf{F}}{A+B})^k \quad (21)$$

Here, we truncated the series at $k = 1$ to make a tradeoff between computational complexity and approximation accuracy. It is formulated as

$$\mathbf{F}^{-1} \approx \frac{2}{A+B} + \frac{2}{A+B}(\mathbf{I} - \frac{2\mathbf{F}}{A+B}) = \frac{2}{A+B}(2\mathbf{I} - \frac{2\mathbf{F}}{A+B}) \quad (22)$$

In this way, once the frame bounds are given, the inverse of $\mathbf{F}$ can be calculated easily. Then the optimization problem for training RIP-dictionary pair is formulated as

$$\min_{\mathbf{\Phi},\mathbf{\Psi},\lambda,\mathbf{Y}} \|\mathbf{X} - \mathbf{\Phi}\mathbf{Y}\|_F^2 + \gamma_1 \|\mathbf{Y} - \mathcal{S}_\lambda(\mathbf{\Psi}^T\mathbf{X})\|_F^2 + \gamma_2 \|\mathbf{Y}\|_0 + \gamma_3 \|\mathbf{\Psi} - \frac{2}{A+B}(2\mathbf{I} - \frac{2\mathbf{F}}{A+B})\mathbf{\Phi}\|_F^2 \quad (23)$$

$$\text{s.t. } \sqrt{A} \leq \sigma_\mathbf{\Phi} \leq \sqrt{B}$$

where $\mathcal{S}_\lambda(\cdot)$ is the elementwise thresholding operator. There are two basic thresholding methods: The hard thresholding method whose thresholding operator defines as $\mathcal{S}_\lambda(\cdot) \rightarrow max(|\cdot| - \lambda, 0)$ and the soft thresholding whose operator is defined as $\mathcal{S}_\lambda(\cdot) \rightarrow sgn(\cdot)max(|\cdot| - \lambda, 0)$. Both of the two operator are are non-convex and highly discontinuous which lead to big challenges to solve Problem (23). The mean reason is the fact that the update of the thresholding values λ causing non-smooth changes to the cost function. To solve this difficulty, we design an alternative direction method via global search and least square that will be introduce in Section 4.1.

4. Dictionary Pair Learning Algorithm

In this subsection, we propose the two-phase iterative algorithm for dictionary pair learning by dividing Problem (23) into two subproblems: The sparse coding phase which updates the sparse coefficients $\mathbf{Y}$ and thresholding values λ, and the dictionary pair update phase which computes $\mathbf{\Phi}$ and $\mathbf{\Psi}$.

4.1. Sparse coding phase

In this subsection, we discuss how to calculate the sparse coefficients $\mathbf{Y}$ and the threshold values λ with given $\mathbf{\Phi}$ and $\mathbf{\Psi}$ under our SSM-NTF model.

Given a pair of dictionaries $\mathbf{\Phi}$ and $\mathbf{\Psi}$, calculating $\mathbf{Y}$ and λ from $\mathbf{X}$ is formulated as:

$$\{\hat{\mathbf{Y}}, \hat{\lambda}\} = \min_{\mathbf{Y},\lambda} \|\mathbf{X} - \mathbf{\Phi}\mathbf{Y}\|_F^2 + \gamma_1 \|\mathbf{Y} - \mathcal{S}_\lambda(\mathbf{\Psi}^T\mathbf{X})\|_F^2 + \gamma_2 \|\mathbf{Y}\|_0 \quad (24)$$

We pursue the two variables alternatively. Firstly, with fixed λ, we obtain the sparse coefficients $\mathbf{Y}$ by solving Problem (24) through OMP [9] as it can be easily convert to the classical synthesis sparse expression $\min \|\mathbf{Z} - \mathbf{D}\mathbf{Y}\|_F^2$, s.t. $\|\mathbf{Y}\|_0$ where $\mathbf{Z} = [\mathbf{X} \sqrt{\gamma_1}\mathcal{S}_\lambda(\mathbf{\Psi}^T\mathbf{X})]$ and $\mathbf{D} = [\mathbf{\Phi} \sqrt{\gamma_1}\mathbf{I}]$.

Secondly, the pursue of λ is equivalent to solving the following problem

$$\hat{\lambda} = \arg\min_\lambda \|\mathbf{Y} - \mathcal{S}_\lambda(\mathbf{\Psi}^T\mathbf{X})\|_F^2 \tag{25}$$

which can be decomposed into M individual optimization problems

$$\hat{\lambda}_i = \arg\min_{\lambda_i} \|\bar{\mathbf{y}}_i - \mathcal{S}_{\lambda_i}(\boldsymbol{\psi}_i^T\mathbf{X})\|_2^2, i = 1, \ldots, M. \tag{26}$$

where $\boldsymbol{\psi}_i$ is the column of $\mathbf{\Psi}$. From the definition of soft thresholding operator, we can know that the function of Problem (26) is discrete. By denoting the data indices set that remains intact after the thresholding as $\mathcal{J}_i$, we split the data $\mathbf{X}$ into two parts: $\mathbf{X}^{\mathcal{J}_i}$ and $\mathbf{X}^{\hat{\mathcal{J}}_i}$ such that

$$\mathcal{S}_{\lambda_i}(\boldsymbol{\psi}_i^T\mathbf{X}^{\mathcal{J}_i}) = \boldsymbol{\psi}_i^T\mathbf{X}^{\mathcal{J}_i} - sgn(\boldsymbol{\psi}_i^T\mathbf{X}^{\mathcal{J}_i})\lambda_i \tag{27}$$

$$\mathcal{S}_{\lambda_i}(\boldsymbol{\psi}_i^T\mathbf{X}^{\hat{\mathcal{J}}_i}) = 0. \tag{28}$$

where $\hat{\mathcal{J}}_i$ is a supplementary to the intact indices $\mathcal{J}_i$ which turn the all elements to zero. It is clear to know that the variables $\mathcal{J}_i$ and $\hat{\mathcal{J}}_i$ are both functions of λ_i without explicit expressions which leads to a large challenge in optimization.

In order to solve Problem (26), an intermediate variable μ_i is necessarily to introduced to separate the whole problem into two parts: The update of the indices $\mathcal{J}_i$ and $\hat{\mathcal{J}}_i$ (determined by μ_i) and the update of the explicit thresholding value λ_i. Then Problem (26) can be transformed to another optimization problem:

$$\{\hat{\lambda}_i, \hat{\mu}_i\} = \arg\min_{\lambda_i} \|\bar{\mathbf{y}}_i^{\hat{\mathcal{J}}_i}\|_2^2 + \|\bar{\mathbf{y}}^{\mathcal{J}_i} - [\boldsymbol{\psi}_i^T\mathbf{X}^{\mathcal{J}_i} - sgn(\boldsymbol{\psi}_i^T\mathbf{X}^{\mathcal{J}_i})\lambda_i]\|_2^2 + \tau/2\|\lambda_i - \mu_i\|_2^2 \tag{29}$$

where $\mathcal{J}_i$ and $\hat{\mathcal{J}}_i$ are two functions of the intermediate variable μ_i.

At the k-th step, to obtain μ_i, we solve Problem (29) with λ_i fixed and denote the functions as $f(\mu_i) + g(\mu_i) + l(\mu_i)$ where $f(\mu_i) = \|\bar{\mathbf{y}}_i^{\hat{\mathcal{J}}_i}\|_2^2$, $g(\mu_i) = \|\bar{\mathbf{y}}^{\mathcal{J}_i} - [\boldsymbol{\psi}_i^T\mathbf{X}^{\mathcal{J}_i} - sgn(\boldsymbol{\psi}_i^T\mathbf{X}^{\mathcal{J}_i})\lambda_i]\|_2^2$, $l(\mu_i) = \tau/2\|\lambda_i - \mu_i\|_2^2$. Optimizing this expression is obviously non-trivial as the target function is non-convex and highly discontinuous. Actually, with λ_i fixed, the minimization of $f(\mu_i) + g(\mu_i)$ can be globally solved due to its discrete finite nature. In another word, if a series of candidate terms of μ_i are given, the global search is guaranteed to succeed.

Once a λ_i is given, the $f(\mu_i) + g(\mu_i)$ will be a piecewise constant function. It means that the function values remain unchanged within a series of intervals which are determined by $|\boldsymbol{\psi}_i^T\mathbf{x}_i|, i = i_1, i_2, \ldots, i_l$. Therefore, $|\boldsymbol{\psi}_i^T\mathbf{x}_i|, i = 1, 2, \ldots, L$ can be taken as a portion of candidate terms of μ_i. For the function $l(\mu_i)$, it is clear that it minimizes at $\mu_i = \lambda_i$ and monotonically increases with the increasing distance between $l(\mu_i)$ and the given $l(\lambda_i)$. So, to minimize $l(\mu_i)$, we only need to choose the closest point in the feasible region.

Without loss of generality, we assume that all the $|\boldsymbol{\psi}_i^T\mathbf{x}_i|, i = 1, 2, \ldots, L$ are ascending ordered and the corresponding signals are in the same order. We compute all the possible values of $f(\mu_i) + g(\mu_i)$ by

$$f(\boldsymbol{\psi}_i^T\mathbf{X}_{j+1}) = f(\boldsymbol{\psi}_i^T\mathbf{X}_j) + y_{i(j+1)}^2$$

$$g(\boldsymbol{\psi}_i^T\mathbf{X}_{j+1}) = \|\bar{\mathbf{y}}_i - \boldsymbol{\psi}_i^T\mathbf{X} + sgn(\boldsymbol{\psi}_i^T\mathbf{X})\lambda_i\|_2^2 - \beta_{k+1} \tag{30}$$

where $\beta_{k+1} = \beta_k + [y_{i(k+1)} - \boldsymbol{\psi}_i^T \mathbf{x}_{k+1} + sgn(\boldsymbol{\psi}_i^T \mathbf{x}_{k+1})\lambda_i]^2$, $\beta_1 = [y_{i1} - \boldsymbol{\psi}_i^T \mathbf{x}_1 + sgn(\boldsymbol{\psi}_i^T \mathbf{x}_1)\lambda_i]^2$. Sort $|\boldsymbol{\psi}_i^T \mathbf{x}_i|, i = 1, 2, \ldots, L$ in descending order of $f(\mu_i) + g(\mu_i)$, and every two adjacent values form an interval on which the function value remains unchanged. In another word, the objective function $f(\mu_i) + g(\mu_i) + l(\mu_i)$ is minimized at the point closest to λ_i in the interval. Thus, compute all the minimizer values on every interval and the minimum must be the optimal result.

With μ_i fixed, we solve the following problem in order to pursue λ_i:

$$\{\hat{\lambda}_i\} = \arg\min_{\lambda_i} \|\bar{\mathbf{y}}^{\mathcal{J}_i} - [\boldsymbol{\psi}_i^T \mathbf{X}^{\mathcal{J}_i} - sgn(\boldsymbol{\psi}_i^T \mathbf{X}^{\mathcal{J}_i})\lambda_i]\|_2^2 + \tau/2\|\lambda_i - \mu_i\|_2^2 \tag{31}$$

This is a standard continuous convex function that can be easily sovled by least square.

We summarize our sparse coding method in Algorithm 1.

Algorithm 1 Sparse coding algorithm

Input and Initialization:

  Training data $\mathbf{X} \in \mathcal{R}^{N \times L}$, iteration number r, initial value $\lambda_i = 0$.

Output:

  Sparse coefficients $\mathbf{y}$, and thresholding values λ_i

1: Compute the sparse coefficients $\mathbf{y}$ via Problem (24) according to the OMP algorithm.
2: Sort the columns of $\mathbf{X}$ and $\mathbf{y}$ in increasing order of $|\boldsymbol{\psi}_i^T \mathbf{X}|$.
3: **For** p=1:r

  For j=1:L

  Compute all the possible values for $f(\mu_i) + g(\mu_i)$ by

$$f(\boldsymbol{\psi}_i^T \mathbf{X}_{j+1}) = f(\boldsymbol{\psi}_i^T \mathbf{X}_j) + y_{i(j+1)}^2$$
$$g(\boldsymbol{\psi}_i^T \mathbf{X}_{j+1}) = \|\bar{\mathbf{y}}_i - \boldsymbol{\psi}_i^T \mathbf{X} + sgn(\boldsymbol{\psi}_i^T \mathbf{X})\lambda_i\|_2^2 - \beta_{k+1}$$

  where $\beta_{k+1} = \beta_k + [y_{i(k+1)} - \boldsymbol{\psi}_i^T \mathbf{x}_{k+1} + sgn(\boldsymbol{\psi}_i^T \mathbf{x}_{k+1})\lambda_i]^2$, $\beta_1 = [y_{i1} - \boldsymbol{\psi}_i^T \mathbf{x}_1 + sgn(\boldsymbol{\psi}_i^T \mathbf{x}_1)\lambda_i]^2$.

  Denote them as a vector v.

  End for

4: Sort the elements of $|\boldsymbol{\psi}_i^T \mathbf{X}|$ in descending order of v. Denote the intervals bounded as $\xi_q, q = 1, 2, L-1$.
5: compute every $v_q + l(\hat{\mu}_i)$ where $\hat{\mu}_i$ is the point closest to λ_i in ξ_{j-1}.
6: $\hat{\mu}_i = \arg\min_{\mu_i} v_q + l(\mu_i)$.
7: Compute λ_i via Problem (31).

  End for

4.2. Dictionary Pair Update Phase

To obtain $\boldsymbol{\Psi}$, we solve the following problem with all other variables fixed:

$$\hat{\boldsymbol{\Psi}} = \arg\min_{\boldsymbol{\Psi}} \|\mathbf{Y} - \mathcal{S}_\lambda(\boldsymbol{\Psi}^T \mathbf{X})\|_F^2 + \frac{\gamma_3}{\gamma_1}\|\boldsymbol{\Psi} - \mathbf{F}^{-1}\boldsymbol{\Phi}\|_F^2 \tag{32}$$

Such problem is a highly nonlinear optimization due to the definition of $\mathcal{S}_\lambda$. Here we solve $\boldsymbol{\Psi}$ columnwisely by updating each column of $\boldsymbol{\Psi}$.

For each $\boldsymbol{\psi}_i$, we solve the following subproblem:

$$\hat{\boldsymbol{\psi}}_i = \arg\min_{\boldsymbol{\psi}_i} \|\bar{\mathbf{y}}_i - \mathcal{S}_{\lambda_i}(\boldsymbol{\psi}_i^T \mathbf{X})\|_2^2 + \frac{\gamma_3}{\gamma_1}\|\boldsymbol{\psi}_i - \mathbf{F}^{-1}\boldsymbol{\phi}_i\|_2^2 \tag{33}$$

We denote $\mathcal{J}_i$ and $\hat{\mathcal{J}}_i$ as the indices set as before. Set the elements of $\overline{\mathbf{y}}_i$ corresponding to the indices $\hat{\mathcal{J}}_i$ to be zeros and denote the new vector as $\overline{\mathbf{z}}_i$. This operation leads to a consequence that $\boldsymbol{\psi}_i^T \mathbf{X}^{\hat{\mathcal{J}}_i} \approx 0$. Then we solve the following quadratic optimization problem that is easy to solve with least squares.

$$\hat{\boldsymbol{\psi}}_i = \arg\min_{\boldsymbol{\psi}_i} \|\overline{\mathbf{z}}_i - \boldsymbol{\psi}_i^T \mathbf{X}\|_2^2 + \frac{\gamma_3}{\gamma_1}\|\boldsymbol{\psi}_i - \mathbf{F}^{-1}\boldsymbol{\phi}_i\|_2^2 \tag{34}$$

The optimization problem to pursue $\boldsymbol{\Phi}$ is formulated as

$$\hat{\boldsymbol{\Phi}} = \arg\min_{\boldsymbol{\Phi}} \|\mathbf{X} - \boldsymbol{\Phi}\mathbf{Y}\|_F^2 + \gamma_3 \|\boldsymbol{\Psi} - \mathbf{F}^{-1}\boldsymbol{\Phi}\|_F^2 \tag{35}$$

$$\text{s.t. } \sqrt{A} \leq \delta_{\boldsymbol{\Phi}} \leq \sqrt{B} \tag{36}$$

where the frame operator $\mathbf{F}$ is given by $\boldsymbol{\Phi}\boldsymbol{\Phi}^T$ and $\mathbf{F}^{-1}$ is defined as Equation (22). The target function then becomes

$$\|\mathbf{X} - \boldsymbol{\Phi}\mathbf{Y}\|_F^2 + \eta_3 \|\boldsymbol{\Psi} - \frac{2}{A+B}(2\mathbf{I} - \frac{2\boldsymbol{\Phi}\boldsymbol{\Phi}^T}{A+B})\boldsymbol{\Phi}\|_F^2 \tag{37}$$

which is denoted by $h(\boldsymbol{\Phi})$. We apply the gradient descent method to unconstraint version of Problem (35) and then project the solution to the feasible space. The gradient is given by a very complicated form as follows

$$\nabla h(\boldsymbol{\Phi}) = (\mathbf{X} - \boldsymbol{\Phi}\mathbf{Y})\mathbf{Y}^T - \gamma_3 \{\frac{4}{\alpha}h(\boldsymbol{\Phi}) + \frac{4}{\alpha^2}[\boldsymbol{\Phi}\boldsymbol{\Phi}^T h(\boldsymbol{\Phi}) + \boldsymbol{\Phi}h(\boldsymbol{\Phi})^T \boldsymbol{\Phi} + h(\boldsymbol{\Phi})\boldsymbol{\Phi}\boldsymbol{\Phi}^T]\}. \tag{38}$$

In order to reduce the complexity, the gradient can also be computed with the fixed $\mathbf{F}$ calculated in the previous step of the ADM. Then at the k-th iteration, the gradient can be written as

$$\nabla h(\boldsymbol{\Phi}^k) = (\mathbf{X} - \boldsymbol{\Phi}^{k-1}\mathbf{Y})\mathbf{Y}^T - \gamma_3 \mathbf{F}^{(-1)^T}(\boldsymbol{\Psi}^k - \mathbf{F}^T \boldsymbol{\Phi}^{k-1}) \tag{39}$$

where $\mathbf{F} = \boldsymbol{\Phi}^{k-1}\boldsymbol{\Phi}^{(k-1)^T}$. The descent step length can be obtained by optimizing the problem $\min_{\theta} h(\boldsymbol{\Phi} + \theta \nabla h(\boldsymbol{\Phi}))$ with fixed $\mathbf{F}$, which is given by

$$\hat{\theta} = \frac{<\mathbf{a}, \mathbf{b}> + \gamma_3 <\mathbf{c}, \mathbf{d}>}{\|\mathbf{a}\|_F^2 + \gamma_3\|\mathbf{c}\|_F^2} \tag{40}$$

where $\mathbf{a} = \nabla h(\boldsymbol{\Phi})\mathbf{Y}, \mathbf{b} = \mathbf{X} - \boldsymbol{\Phi}\mathbf{Y}, \mathbf{c} = \mathbf{F}^{-1}\nabla h(\boldsymbol{\Phi}), \mathbf{d} = \boldsymbol{\Psi} - \mathbf{F}^{-1}\boldsymbol{\Phi}$. For the frame condition $\sqrt{A} \leq \delta_{\boldsymbol{\Phi}} \leq \sqrt{B}$, we apply a SVD decomposition $\boldsymbol{\Phi} = \mathbf{U}\boldsymbol{\Sigma}\mathbf{V}^T$ and map the singular values to the interval $[\sqrt{A}, \sqrt{B}]$ linearly. We denote the mapped singular matrix as $\hat{\boldsymbol{\Sigma}}$ and reconstruct $\boldsymbol{\Phi}$ by $\boldsymbol{\Phi} = \mathbf{U}\hat{\boldsymbol{\Sigma}}\mathbf{V}^T$.

We summarize our algorithm in Algorithm 2.

Algorithm 2 Dictionary pair learning algorithm

Input and Initialization:

Training data **X**, frame bound A,B, iteration *num*, gradient descent iterations *r*.

Build frame $\boldsymbol{\Phi} \in \mathbb{R}^{N \times M}$ and $\boldsymbol{\Psi} \in \mathbb{R}^{N \times M}$, either by using random entries, or using M randomly chosen data.

Output:

Frame $\boldsymbol{\Phi}, \boldsymbol{\Psi}$, Sparse coefficients **Y**, and thresholding values λ

For l=1:*num*

Sparse Coding Step:

1: Compute the sparse coefficients **Y** and the thresholding values λ via Algorithm 1.

Frame Update Step:

2: Update $\boldsymbol{\Psi}$ in column-wise. Compute $\mathbf{W} = \mathcal{S}(\boldsymbol{\Psi}^T \mathbf{X})$.

For $i = 1 : M$

Denote $\hat{\mathcal{J}}_i$ as the indices of zeros in the *i*-th column of W. Set $\boldsymbol{\psi}_i^T \mathbf{X}^{\hat{\mathcal{J}}_i} = 0$. Compute $\boldsymbol{\psi}_i$ via Equation (34).

End For

3: Update $\boldsymbol{\Phi}$ via Gradient Descent and singular value map.

For k=1:*r*

Calculate Gradient via Equation (39) and calculate the descent step via Equation (40).

End for

4: Apply SVD decomposition $\boldsymbol{\Phi} = \mathbf{U}\boldsymbol{\Sigma}\mathbf{V}^T$, map $\boldsymbol{\Sigma}$ to obtain $\hat{\boldsymbol{\Sigma}}$ and reconstruct $\boldsymbol{\Phi} = \mathbf{U}\hat{\boldsymbol{\Sigma}}\mathbf{V}^T$.

End for
---

5. Restoration

The image restoration aims to reconstruct a high-quality image $\mathcal{I}$ from its degraded (e.g., noisy, blurred and/or downsampled) version $\mathcal{L}$, denoted by $\mathcal{L} = SH\mathcal{I} + \mathbf{n}$, where H represents a blurring filter, S the downsampling operator, and **n** is a noisy signal. For the signal satisfies the SSM-NTF, the restoration model based on SSM-NTF is formulated as

$$\{\hat{\mathcal{I}}, \hat{\mathbf{Y}}, \hat{\lambda}\} = \min_{\mathcal{I}, \{\mathbf{y}_i\}_{i=1}^N, \lambda} \|\mathcal{L} - SH\mathcal{I}\|_F^2 + \gamma \sum_i \|\mathbf{R}_i \mathcal{I} - \boldsymbol{\Phi}\mathbf{y}_i\|_F^2 + \gamma_1 \sum_i \|\mathbf{y}_i - \mathcal{S}_\lambda(\boldsymbol{\Psi}^T \mathbf{R}_i \mathcal{I})\|_F^2 + \gamma_2 \sum_i \|\mathbf{y}_i\|_0 \quad (41)$$

where $\mathbf{R}_i$ is an operator that extracts the *i*-th patch of the image $\mathcal{I}$ and $\mathbf{y}_i$ is the *i*-th column of **Y**. λ denotes a vector $[\lambda_1, \lambda_2, \cdots, \lambda_M]$ with λ_j operating on the *j*-th element of $\boldsymbol{\Psi}^T \mathbf{R}_i \mathcal{I}$. On the right side of Equation (41), the first term is the global force that demands the proximity between the degraded image $\mathcal{L}$, and its high-quality version $\mathcal{I}$. The rest terms are the local constraints to make sure every patch at location *i* satisfies the SSM-NTF.

To solve Problem (41), we apply Algorithm 1 to obtain the sparse coefficients **Y** and the threshold values λ. We mainly state the iterative method to obtain $\mathcal{I}$. Assume the sign of $\boldsymbol{\Psi}^T \mathbf{R}_i \mathcal{I}^k$ will not change much between two steps, we set it in the *k*-th step by $\mathbf{c}^k = sign(\boldsymbol{\Psi}^T \mathbf{R}_i \mathcal{I}^{k-1})$, where *sign* is the sign function. Denote $\mathbf{d}^k = \boldsymbol{\Psi}^T \mathbf{R}_i \mathcal{I}^{k-1}$. We set $\mathbf{O}^k$ as an index set that satisfies $|d_l| \leq \lambda_l, l \in \mathbf{O}^k$. Set $\mathbf{u}^k \in \mathcal{R}^M$ as a vector with elements $\mathbf{u}_l = \begin{cases} \lambda_l & l \in \mathbf{O}^k, \\ 0 & otherwise. \end{cases}$ Then the non-convex and non-smooth threshold can be removed with the substitution that $\mathbf{y}_i - \mathcal{S}_\lambda(\mathbf{\Psi}^T \mathbf{R}_i \mathcal{I}^k) \approx \mathbf{y}_i + \mathbf{c}^k \odot \mathbf{u} - \mathbf{\Psi}^T \mathbf{R}_i \mathcal{I}^k$ Thus, in the k-th step, the problem needs to be solved is expressed as

$$\{\hat{\mathcal{I}}^k\} = \min_{\mathcal{I}^{k-1}} \|\mathcal{L} - SH\mathcal{I}^{k-1}\|_F^2 + \gamma \sum_i \|\mathbf{R}_i \mathcal{I}^{k-1} - \mathbf{\Phi} \mathbf{y}_i\|_F^2 + \gamma_1 \sum_i \|\mathbf{y}_i + \mathbf{c}^k \odot \mathbf{u}^k - \mathbf{\Psi}^T \mathbf{R}_i \mathcal{I}^{k-1}\|_F^2 \quad (42)$$

where $\odot$ is point multiplication. This convex problem can be easily solved by gradient descent algorithm.

We summarized the restoration algorithm in Algorithm 3.

Algorithm 3 Restoration algorithm

Input

Training dictionaries $\mathbf{\Phi}$, $\mathbf{\Psi}$, iteration number r, a degraded image $\mathcal{L}$, set $\mathcal{I}_0 = \mathcal{L}$.

Output:

The high quality image $\hat{\mathcal{I}}$

1: Compute $\mathbf{Y}$ and λ via the method in Algorithm 1.

   For k=1:r

2: compute $\mathbf{d}^k = \mathbf{\Psi}^T \mathbf{R}_i \mathcal{I}^{k-1}$. Set $\mathbf{c}^k = sign(\mathbf{d}^k)$. set $\mathbf{O}^k$ as an index set that satisfies $|\mathbf{d}_l^k| \leq \lambda_l, l \in \mathbf{O}^k$.

   Set $\mathbf{u}_l^k = \begin{cases} \lambda_l & l \in \mathbf{O}^k, \\ 0 & otherwise. \end{cases}$

3: Solving the Problem (42) via gradient descent algorithm.

   End for

---

6. Complexity Analysis

In this section, we discuss the computational complexity of our sparse coding and dictionary pair learning algorithms with regard to those of conventional sparse model counterparts.

We first analyze complexities of the main components of the sparse coding (SC) and dictionary updating (DU) algorithms. In terms of SC, given a set of training samples, $\mathbf{X} \in \mathcal{R}^{N \times L}$, the complexity of BtOMP of calculating $\hat{\mathbf{Y}} = \min_{\mathbf{Y}} \|\mathbf{X} - \mathbf{\Phi} \mathbf{Y}\|_F^2 + \gamma_1 \|\mathbf{Y} - \mathcal{S}_\lambda(\mathbf{\Psi}^T \mathbf{X})\|_F^2 + \gamma_2 \|\mathbf{Y}\|_0$ is $O(K^2 ML)$ where K is the target sparsity and the complexity of threshold of calculating $\hat{\lambda} = \min_\lambda \|\mathbf{Y} - \mathcal{S}_\lambda(\mathbf{\Psi}^T \mathbf{X})\|_F^2$ is $O(NML)$, which cost most of time in SC step at each iteration. The sparse coefficients $\mathbf{Y} \in N \times L$ and the the threshold values λ are computed with fixed dictionaries $\mathbf{\Phi} \in \mathcal{R}^{N \times M}$ and $\mathbf{\Psi} \in \mathcal{R}^{N \times M}$. Correspondingly, the traditional sparse coefficients $\mathbf{B} \in N \times L$ is sparse approximated by dictionary $\mathbf{D} \in \mathcal{R}^{N \times M}$ and the computational complexity is $O(K^2 ML)$.

In terms of DU, with the given training samples $\mathbf{X} \in \mathcal{R}^{N \times L}$, we learn a pair of dictionary $\mathbf{\Phi} \in \mathcal{R}^{N \times M}$ and $\mathbf{\Psi} \in \mathcal{R}^{N \times M}$. We update $\mathbf{\Psi}$ via Problem (34) with a computational complexity of $O(N^2 L)$. In order to update $\mathbf{\Phi}$. we need to calculate the gradient via Equation (39) with a computational complexity of $O(NML)$ and the step size via Equation (40) with a computational complexity of $O(rNML)$ where r is the iteration number of the gradient descent. For the traditional dictionary learning, the corresponding training set is $\mathbf{X} \in \mathcal{R}^{N \times L}$ and the dictionary $\mathbf{D} \in \mathcal{R}^{N \times M}$ is updated by SVD decomposition of rank-1 with a computational complexity of $O(KML)$.

7. Experimental Results

We demonstrate the effectiveness of our SSM-NTF model by first discussing the convergence of our dictionary pair learning algorithm and then evaluating the performance on natural and piecewise constant image denoising, super resolution and image inpainting.

7.1. Convergence Analysis

The convergence of the presented dictionary pair learning algorithm is evaluated in Figure 1. Here, we train a pair of dictionaries Φ and Ψ of size 100×200 from 65,000 patches, which are of size 10×10 randomly sampled from six natural images. We apply the frame reconstruction function $\Phi \mathcal{S}_\lambda(\Psi^T x)$ to reconstruct the patches. The convergence of the presented dictionary pair learning algorithm is evaluated in Figure 1. The dictionary pair is illustrated in Figure 2. They exhibit that our dictionary pair learning method is able to capture the feature of the image along with the convergence property.

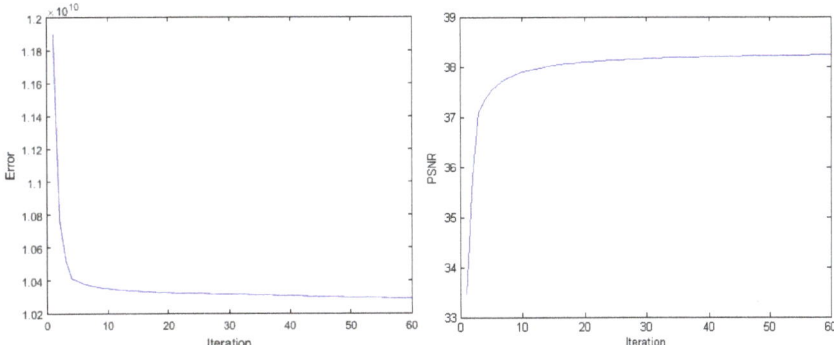

Figure 1. Convergence analysis. The X-labels are the iteration number. The Y-labels are the is the objective function of System (20) (left) and the restoration result (measured by 'PSNR') (right). It is shown that our dictionary pair learning algorithm is a convergence one.

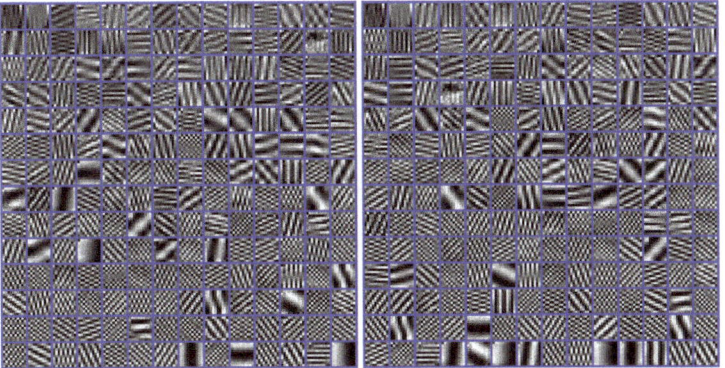

Figure 2. The exemplified dictionary pair (Φ, Ψ) in our stable sparse model with non-tight frame (SSM-NTF) model training by natural images.

7.2. Image Denoising

In this subsection, we evaluate the performance of our proposed SSM-NTF model on image denoising. Benefitting from the concept of non-tight frame, the proposed SSM-NTF model contains a pair of dictionaries: The frame and its dual frame. As a result, our proposed SSM-NTF model contains an analysis system and a synthesis system. The analysis-like system is denoted as

$$\mathbf{y} = \mathcal{S}_\lambda(\Psi^T \mathbf{x}), \quad \|\mathbf{y}\| \leq s \tag{43}$$

which analyzes the signals in $\boldsymbol{\Psi}$ domain. The synthesis system is denoted as

$$\mathbf{x} = \boldsymbol{\Phi}\mathbf{y}, \quad \|\mathbf{y}\| \leq s \tag{44}$$

which reconstructs the analyzed signals. The two systems share the same sparse coefficients $\mathbf{Y}$.

Therefore, we compare our proposed SSM-NTF with synthesis and analysis models, respectively. It is well known that the synthesis sparse model has advantage in dealing with the natural image while the analysis sparse model is mostly used to address the piecewise constant image. Therefore, we respectively, perform the denoising experiments on natural images and piecewise images comparing with the most related approaches.

7.2.1. Natural Image Denoising

We now turn to present experimental results on six classical natural images named 'Barbara', 'Boat', 'Couple', 'Hill', 'Lena' and 'Man' which are shown in [1], to evaluate the performance of the training algorithm. The denoising problem which has been widely studied in sparse representation is used as the target application. We add Gaussian white noise to these images at different noise levels $\sigma = 20, 30, 40, 50, 60, 70, 80, 90, 100$. Then we use the learned dictionary pair to denoise the natural images, with overlap of 1 pixel between adjacent patches of size 10×10. The patch denoising stage is followed by weighted averaging the overlapping patch recoveries to obtain the final clean image. The parameters in our scheme are $\gamma_1 = 1.1$ and $\gamma_3 = 1.2(L/M)^2$ where L and M are the sample and dictionary size, respectively. We have stated in Section 3.2 that we usually set A to a positive number around but smaller than 1. In fact, we set A from 0.6 to 1 by a step of 0.03 to test the denoising performance to determine the specific value of it. Then, with fixed A, we set B from 1 to 4 with a step length of 0.3 to run experiments on every noise level to determine the values of B. The values of frame bounds A and B are shown in Table 1. For example, when the noise level $\sigma = 40$, A and B are set to be 0.8 and 1.8, respectively.

Table 1. The values of A and B.

σ	20	30	40	50	60	70	80	90	100
A	0.8	0.8	0.8	0.8	0.8	0.8	0.8	0.8	0.8
B	1.8	1.8	1.8	2.4	3.0	3.3	3.3	3.6	3.6

Table 2 shows the comparison results in terms of PSNR. There are three related image denoising methods involved, including the classical dictionary learning algorithm KSVD [9], the data-driven tight frame based denoising method [1] and the incoherent dictionary learning based method [21]. The patch size of KSVD [9] and the method in [21] are 8×8 with stripe 1 and the dictionaries are of size 64×256 at their optimal state according to the previous work. We point out that [1] works on filters of size 16×16 instead of image patches and initialized by 64 3-level Harr wavelet filters in size 16×16. All the three compared methods can achieve their best performance with 50 iterations.

Table 2 shows that the incoherent dictionary learning method [21] outperforms the KSVD [9] in average as the mutual incoherent of dictionary can provide stable recovery. That [1] outperforms [21] implies that the tight frame is a more stable system. Then our stable sparse model based method outperforms [1] in average suggests that applying non-tight frame to approximate RIP can provide even better and more stable reconstruction results. Figure 3 shows two exemplified visual results on images 'Man' and 'Couple' at noise levels $\sigma = 50$ and $\sigma = 40$, respectively. The proposed method shows much clearer and better visual results than the other competing methods.

Figure 3. Visual comparison of reconstruction results by different methods on 'Man' ($\sigma = 50$) and 'Couple' ($\sigma = 40$). From left to right: original image, noise image, KSVD [9], method of [1], method of [21] and our proposed method.

Table 2. PSNR (dB) for nature image denoising results.

σ	Image	Barbara	Boat	Couple	Hill	Lena	Man	Average
20	KSVD [9]	31.01	30.50	30.15	30.27	32.51	30.26	30.78
	[21]	31.03	30.45	30.16	30.30	32.52	30.30	30.79
	[1]	**31.07**	30.35	30.20	30.31	32.56	30.07	30.76
	SSM-NTF	31.06	**30.56**	**30.32**	**30.42**	**32.60**	**30.33**	**30.88**
30	KSVD [9]	28.75	28.60	28.07	28.51	30.59	28.43	28.83
	[21]	28.78	28.63	28.06	28.53	30.60	28.47	28.85
	[1]	**29.07**	28.48	28.22	28.64	30.60	28.26	28.88
	SSM-NTF	29.03	**28.71**	**28.32**	**28.74**	**30.82**	**28.59**	**29.04**
40	KSVD [9]	27.03	27.23	26.54	27.23	29.13	27.17	27.39
	[21]	27.05	27.18	26.59	27.21	29.10	27.12	27.38
	[1]	**27.58**	27.20	26.87	27.49	29.25	26.99	27.56
	SSM-NTF	27.52	**27.49**	**27.07**	**27.65**	**29.43**	**27.41**	**27.76**
50	KSVD [9]	25.71	26.05	25.42	26.29	27.92	26.18	26.26
	[21]	25.77	26.08	25.40	26.31	27.87	26.23	26.28
	[1]	**26.45**	26.15	25.84	26.63	28.15	26.09	26.55
	SSM-NTF	26.40	**26.41**	**26.04**	**26.88**	**28.49**	**26.49**	**26.79**
60	KSVD [9]	24.45	25.18	24.57	25.69	27.01	25.40	25.38
	[21]	24.45	25.20	24.50	25.65	27.03	25.42	25.38
	[1]	**25.64**	25.33	25.04	25.91	27.22	25.38	25.75
	SSM-NTF	25.52	**25.55**	**25.22**	**26.11**	**27.41**	**25.74**	**25.93**
70	KSVD [9]	23.40	24.46	23.90	25.10	26.18	24.77	24.63
	[21]	23.46	24.46	23.93	25.15	26.19	24.79	24.66
	[1]	**24.88**	24.67	24.36	25.30	26.44	24.78	25.07
	SSM-NTF	24.74	**25.05**	**24.60**	**25.50**	**26.61**	**25.06**	**25.26**

Table 2. Cont.

	KSVD [9]	22.80	23.85	23.44	24.69	25.34	24.19	24.05
80	[21]	22.87	23.93	23.47	24.76	25.40	24.27	24.09
	[1]	**24.18**	24.09	23.79	24.77	25.74	24.25	24.47
	SSM-NTF	24.11	**24.42**	**24.02**	**24.91**	**26.02**	**24.58**	**24.68**
	KSVD [9]	22.31	23.34	22.98	24.31	24.96	23.78	23.61
90	[21]	22.31	23.38	23.01	24.36	24.97	23.84	23.64
	[1]	**23.50**	23.56	23.27	24.30	25.14	23.79	23.93
	SSM-NTF	23.41	**23.84**	**23.47**	**24.58**	**25.43**	**24.13**	**24.14**
	KSVD [9]	21.88	22.92	22.64	23.96	24.44	23.39	23.21
100	[21]	21.89	22.95	22.67	23.99	24.47	23.43	23.23
	[1]	**23.01**	23.11	22.83	23.86	24.59	23.38	23.46
	SSM-NTF	22.90	**23.46**	**23.05**	**24.16**	**24.90**	**23.68**	**23.69**

7.2.2. Piecewise Constant Image Denoising

In this subsection, we demonstrate the analytical property of our SSM-NTF model using a synthetic image. The denoising problem which has been widely studied in sparse representation is used as the target application. We start with a piecewise constant of size 256×256 contaminated by Gaussian white noise with noise level $\sigma = 5$ and extract all possible 5×5 image pathes. For the denoising we apply the dictionary pair learning algorithm with the parameters $\gamma_1 = 1.5, \gamma_3 = 1.2\, L/M, A = 0.8$ and $B = 1.8$ in parallel with patch denosing with the synthesis KSVD [9] and the analysis KSVD [14]. We apply 100 iterations of the our dictionary learning method on this training set, and learning dictionary pair of size 25×50. The experimental set of the synthesis KSVD [9] and the analysis KSVD [14] are at their optimal state according to the previous work.

The learned dictionary pair Φ which exhibits much like the synthesis dictionary and Ψ which exhibits a high resemblance to the analysis dictionary are illustrated in Figure 4. The resulting PSNRs of the denoised images are 45.32 dB for Analysis KSVD, 43.60 dB for Synthesis KSVD, and 45.17 dB for our proposed algorithm. The figure shows that our dictionary pair learning method is able to capture the features of the piecewise constant image. Figure 5 shows the absolute difference images for each of the three methods. Note that these images are displayed in the dynamic range $[0, 20]$ to make the differences more pronounced. Our proposed approach leads to a much better denoising result than the synthesis KSVD and is comparable with the analysis KSVD.

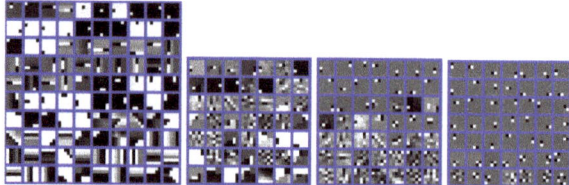

Figure 4. The exemplified dictionaries training by the piecewise constant. From left to right: Synthesis KSVD (25×100), our proposed dictionary pair (25×50) and analysis KSVD (25×50).

Figure 5. Visual quality comparison of denoising results for piecewise constant image. Images of the absolute errors are displayed in the dynamic range [0,20] (from left to right): Original image, noise image, analysis KSVD [14], synthesis KSVD [9], our proposed method.

7.3. Super Resolution

We evaluate our SSM-NTF in comparison with two examplar-based scheme [37] for image Super Resolution (SR) Problem (41) with a bicubic filter. Figure 6 shows the 15 test natural images [18] with both rich texture and structure. All the schemes are applied to the illumination channel, where the scale factor is 3, we always use 3×3 low-resolution patches with overlap of 1 pixel between adjacent patches, corresponding to 9×9 patches with overlap of 3 pixels for the high-resolution patches. In these experiments, we have used the following parameters: $A = 0.8, B = 1.8, \gamma_1 = 1.1$ and $\gamma_3 = 1.2\, L/M$ where L and M are the sample and dictionary size, respectively. In our scheme, dictionary learning is performed between HR and middle-level (MR) images which are the first-, and second-order derivatives of the upsampled version of one LR image by a factor of 2. The four 1D filters used to extract the derivatives are:

$$\begin{aligned}\mathbf{f}_1 &= [-1,0,1], & \mathbf{f}_2 &= \mathbf{f}_1^T \\ \mathbf{f}_3 &= [1,0,-2,0,1], & \mathbf{f}_4 &= \mathbf{f}_3^T\end{aligned} \qquad (45)$$

We train two pairs of HR/LR dictionaries $\{\mathbf{\Phi}_h, \mathbf{\Psi}_h\}$ and $\{\mathbf{\Phi}_l, \mathbf{\Psi}_l\}$ from 100,000 HR/LR patch pairs $[\mathbf{X}_h, \mathbf{X}_l]$ randomly sampled from the collected natural images which are also used in [37] where $\mathbf{X}_h$ is sampled from the HR images and $\mathbf{X}_l$ is sampled from the four feature images. The feature images are obtained by applying the four filters to the upsampled LR image. Given $\mathbf{\Phi}$ and $\mathbf{\Psi}$ and the four MR feature images, the sparse coefficients $\mathbf{Y}$ and threshold value λ can be calculated by Algorithm 1. With the theory in [37], the HR image can be recovered via Algorithm 3. In the experiment, our HR dictionary pair are of size 81×450 and MR ones are of size 144×450. The dictionary size of [37] is 81×1024 (HR) and 144×1024 (MR) at its best performance as stated in the paper. Thus, the dictionary size of [37] is larger than the sum of our dictionaries. Table 3 shows the objective evaluation results of our proposed SSM-NTF compared with bicubic interpolation and [37]. On average, our SSM-NTF presents best in PSNR. Figure 7 presents the corresponding visual comparison of the illumination SR results of Image 12. We can observe that the result of bicubic interpolation is too smooth and the result of [37] suffers from obvious ringing artifact and noises. The HR reconstruction of our SSM-NTF method provides more clear details.

Figure 6. Test images for image super-resolution performance evaluation [18].

Figure 7. Visual quality comparison of SR results for Image 12 corresponding to Table 3. From left to right: Original image, result of bicubic interpolation ($PSNR = 30.28$), [32] ($PSNR = 30.62$) and our SSM-NTF method ($PSNR = 30.99$), respectively.

Table 3. PSNR (dB) for 3× SR reconstructions results.

Image	1	2	3	4	5	6	7	8
Bicubic [37]	32.69	26.32	26.04	28.39	28.70	25.81	37.21	24.40
SC [37]	32.89	26.53	26.16	28.51	29.09	26.25	37.59	24.61
SSM − NTF	**33.10**	**26.75**	**26.41**	**28.82**	**29.31**	**26.40**	37.49	**24.77**
Image	9	10	11	12	13	14	15	Average
Bicubic [37]	31.40	28.72	33.24	30.28	26.49	28.11	31.90	29.31
SC [37]	31.73	**29.35**	33.50	30.62	26.75	28.74	32.13	29.63
SSM − NTF	**31.90**	**29.49**	**33.66**	**30.99**	**26.95**	**29.02**	**32.19**	**29.82**

7.4. Image Inpainting

To illustrate the potential applicability of our proposed SSM-NTF model on image inpainting, we apply it to the applications of text removal. In these experiments, we have used the following parameters: $A = 0.8$, $B = 1.8$, $\gamma_1 = 1.1$ and $\gamma_3 = 1.2\, L/M$ where L and M are the sample and dictionary size, respectively. We operate on the image 'Adar','Lena', 'Couple', 'Hill' with super-imposed text of various fonts.

In this experiment, we applied our SSM-NTF model to image inpainting in a way similar to the non-blind KSVD inpainting algorithm [9], which requires the knowledge of which pixels are corrupted and required inpainting. Actually, only the non-corrupted pixels are used to training the dictionary pair and inpainting the images. We operate our method on pathes of size 10×10 that extract from the images with overlap of 1 pixel between adjacent. The trained dictionary pair are of size 100×200. The KSVD algorithm in this experiment is dealing with patches of size 8×8 that extract from the images with overlap of 1 pixel between adjacent. The dictionary size is 64×256 at its best performance according to [9]. The patch inpainting stage is followed solving Problem (41). Table 4 shows the objective evaluation results of our proposed SSM-NTF compared with DCT and KSVD [9]. The visual comparisons are shown in Figures 8 and 9. We find that the proposed SSM-NTF method is able to eliminate text of fonts completely while the KSVD is dull. Our SSM-NTF method achieves better performance in terms of both subjective and objective quality.

Figure 8. Visual quality comparison of text image inpainting results. From left to right: Original image, text image, result of DCT ($PSNR = 27.11$), KSVD ($PSNR = 28.01$) and our SSM-NTF method ($PSNR = 28.95$), respectively.

Figure 9. Visual quality comparison of scratch image inpainting results. From left to right: Original image, scratch image, result of DCT ($PSNR = 30.81$), KSVD ($PSNR = 31.69$), and our SSM-NTF method ($PSNR = 32.02$), respectively.

Table 4. PSNR (dB) for image inpainting results.

Image	Adar	Lena	Hill	Couple	Average
DCT [9]	27.11	31.30	28.53	29.21	29.04
$KSVD$ [9]	28.01	31.69	28.90	29.50	29.53
$SSM - NTF$	**28.95**	**32.02**	**29.31**	**29.87**	**30.04**

8. Conclusions

In this paper, we propose a stable sparse model with non-tight frame (SSM-NTF) and further formulate a dictionary pair learning model to stably recover the signals. We theoretically analyze the rationality of the approximation for RIP with the non-tight frame condition. The proposed SSM-NTF has RIP and the closed-form expression of the sparse coefficients that ensure the stable recovery especially for seriously noise images. The proposed SSM-NTF contains both a synthesis sparse and an analysis system which share the common sparse coefficients without taking into account the thresholding. We also propose an efficient dictionary pair learning algorithm via developing an explicit analytical expression of the inherent relation between the dictionary pair. The proposed algorithm is capable of approximating structures of signals via a pair of adaptive dictionaries. The effectiveness of our proposed SSM-NTF and its corresponding algorithms are demonstrated in image denoising, image super-resolution and image inpainting. The results of numerical experiments show that the proposed SSM-NTF achieves superior to the compared methods in objective and subjective quality on most of the cases.

On the other hand, our proposed SSM-NTF is actually a 1D sparse model. The 1D sparse model suffers from high memory as well as high computational costs especially when handling high dimensional data. MD frame can be expressed as the kronecker product of a series of 1D frames. Benefitting from this good characteristic, in future work, we will extend our stable sparse model to propose an MD stable sparse model. Moreover, the proposed SSM-NTF is not effective enough to remove other kinds of noise (e.g., salt and pepper noise) as the loss function of SSM-NTF is gaussian. We would like to improve the performance of our model by changing the loss function.

Author Contributions: M.Z. derived the theory, analyzed the data, performed the performance and wrote the original draft; Y.S. and N.Q. researched the relevant theory, participated in discussions of the work and revised the manuscript; B.Y. supervised the project. All authors have read and agreed to the published version of the manuscript.

Funding: This work was supported by NSFC (No.61672066,61976011, U1811463, U19B2039, 61906008, 61906009), Beijing municipal science and technology commission (No.Z171100004417023) and the Scientific Research Common Program of Beijing Municipal Commission of Education (KM202010005018).

Acknowledgments: This work was supported by Beijing Advanced Innovation Center for Future Internet Technology, Beijing Key Laboratory of Multimedia and Intelligent Software Technology. We deeply appreciate the organizations mentioned above.

Conflicts of Interest: The authors declare no conflict of interest.

References

1. Cai, J.F.; Ji, H.; Shen, Z.; Ye, G.B. Data-driven tight frame construction and image denoising. *Appl. Comput. Harmon. Anal.* **2014**, *37*, 89–105. [CrossRef]
2. Xie, J.; Feris, R.S.; Yu, S.S.; Sun, M.T. Joint super resolution and denoising from a single depth image. *IEEE Trans. Multimed.* **2015**, *17*, 1525–1537, . [CrossRef]
3. Rubinstein, R.; Zibulevsky, M.; Elad, M. *Efficient Implementation of the KSVD Algorithm and the Batch-OMP Method*; Tech. Rep.; Department of Computer Science, Technion: Haifa, Israel, 2008.
4. Fadili, M.J.; Starck, J.-L.; Murtagh, F. Inpainting and zooming using sparse representations. *Comput. J.* **2009**, *52*, 64–79.
5. Liu, Y.; Zhai, G.; Gu, K.; Liu, X.; Zhao, D.; Gao, G. Reduced-reference image quality assessment in free-energy principle and sparse representation. *IEEE Trans. Multimed.* **2018**, *20*, 379–391. [CrossRef]
6. Zhao, J.; Hu, H.; Cao, F. Image super-resolution via adaptive sparse representation. *Knowl. Based Syst.* **2017**, *124*, 23–33. [CrossRef]
7. Zhu, Z.; Guo, F.; Yu, H.; Chen, C. Fast single image super-resolution via self-example learning and sparse representation. *IEEE Trans. Multimed.* **2014**, *16*, 2178–2190. [CrossRef]
8. Beck, A.; Teboulle, M. A fast iterative shrinkage thresholding algorithm for linear inverse problems. *SIAM J. Imag. Sci.* **2009**, *2*, 183–202. [CrossRef]
9. Elad, M. Sparse and Redundant Representations. In *From Theory to Applications in Signal and Image Processing*; Springer: Berlin, Germany, 2010.
10. Zhang, L.; Bioucas-Dias, J.M. Fast hyperspectral image denoising and inpainting based on low-rank and sparse representations. *IEEE J. Sel. Top. Appl. Earth Obs. Remote. Sens.* **2018**, *11*, 730–742. [CrossRef]
11. Kalluri, M.; Jiang, M.; Ling, N.; Zheng, J.; Zhang, P. Adaptive RD optimal sparse coding with quantization for image compression. *IEEE Trans. Multimed.* **2019**, *21*, 39–50. [CrossRef]
12. Liu, Y.; Dimitris A. Pados, Compressed-sensed-domain l_1-pca video surveillance. *IEEE Trans. Multimed.* **2016**, *18*, 351–363. [CrossRef]
13. Babaie-Zadeh, M.; Jutten, C. Corrections to on the stable recovery of the sparsest overcomplete representations in presence of noise [oct 10 5396–5400]. *IEEE Trans. Signal Process.* **2011**, *59*, 1913. [CrossRef]
14. Rubinstein, R.; Peleg, T.; Elad, M. Analysis KSVD: A dictionary-learning algorithm for the analysis sparse model. *IEEE Trans. Signal Process.* **2012**, *61*, 661–677. [CrossRef]
15. Elad, M.; Aharon, M. Image denoising via sparse and redundant representations over learned dictionaries. *IEEE Trans. Image Process* **2006**, *15*, 3736–3745. [CrossRef] [PubMed]
16. Dong, W.; Zhang, L.; Shi, G.; Li, X. Nonlocally centralized sparse representation for image restoration. *IEEE Trans. Image Process.* **2013**, *22*, 1620–1630, . [CrossRef] [PubMed]
17. Song, X.; Peng, X.; Xu, J.; Shi, G.; Wu, F. Distributed compressive sensing for cloud-based wireless image Transmission. *IEEE Trans. Multimed.* **2017**, *19*, 1351–1364. [CrossRef]
18. Qi, N.; Shi, Y.; Sun, X.; Yin, B. Tensr: Multi-dimensional tensor sparse representation. In Proceedings of the IEEE Conference on Computer Vision and Pattern Recognition, CVPR 2016, Las Vegas, NV, USA, 27–30 June 2016; pp. 5916–5925.
19. Donoho, D.L.; Elad, M.; Vladimir, N. Temlyakov, Stable recovery of sparse overcomplete representations in the presence of noise. *IEEE Trans. Inf. Theory* **2006**, *52*, 6–18. [CrossRef]

20. Bao, C.; Cai, J.-F.; Ji, H. Fast sparsity-based orthogonal dictionary learning for image restoration. In Proceedings of the IEEE International Conference on Computer Vision, ICCV 2013, Sydney, Australia, 1–8 December 2013; pp. 3384–3391.
21. Wang, J.; Cai, J.-F.; Shi, Y.; Yin, B. Incoherent dictionary learning for sparse representation based image denoising. In Proceedings of the IEEE International Conference on Image Processing, ICIP 2014, Paris, France, 27–30 October 2014; pp. 4582–4586.
22. Candès, E.J.; Tao, T. Decoding by linear programming. *IEEE Trans. Inf. Theory* **2005**, *51*, 4203–4215. [CrossRef]
23. Wang, J.; Li, G.; Rencker, L.; Wang, W.; Gu, Y. An rip-based performance guarantee of covariance-assisted matching pursuit. *IEEE Signal Process. Lett.* **2018**, *25*, 828–832. [CrossRef]
24. Akbari, A.; Trocan, M.; Granado, B. Sparse recovery-based error concealment. *IEEE Trans. Multimed.* **2017**, *19*, 1339–1350. [CrossRef]
25. Zhang, R.; Li, S. A proof of conjecture on restricted isometry property constants δ_t (0<t<4/3). *IEEE Trans. Inf. Theory* **2018**, *64*, 1699–1705.
26. Lin, J.; Li, S.; Shen, Y. New bounds for restricted isometry constants with coherent tight frames. *IEEE Trans. Signal Process.* **2013**, *61*, 611–621. [CrossRef]
27. Cao, C.; Gao, X. Compressed sensing image restoration based on data-driven multi-scale tight frame. *J. Comput. Appl. Math.* **2017**, *309*, 622–629. [CrossRef]
28. Li, J.; Zhang, W.; Zhang, H.; Li, L.; Yan, B. Data driven tight frames regularization for few-view image reconstruction. In Proceedings of the 13th International Conference on Natural Computation, Fuzzy Systems and Knowledge Discovery, ICNC-FSKD 2017, Guilin, China, 29–31 July 2017; pp. 815–820.
29. Liu, Y.; Zhan, Z.; Cai, J.-F.; Guo, D.; Chen, Z.; Qu, X. Projected iterative softthresholding algorithm for tight frames in compressed sensing magnetic resonance imaging. *IEEE Trans. Med. Imaging* **2016**, *35*, 2130–2140. [CrossRef]
30. Bai, H.; Li, S.; He, X. Sensing matrix optimization based on equiangular tight frames with consideration of sparse representation error. *IEEE Trans. Multimed.* **2016**, *18*, 2040–2053. [CrossRef]
31. Haltmeier, M. Stable signal reconstruction via l_1-minimization in redundant, non-tight frames. *IEEE Trans. Signal Process.* **2013**, *61*, 420–426. [CrossRef]
32. Li, D.F.; Sun, W.C. Expansion of frames to tight frames. *Acta Mathematica Sinica Eng. Ser.* **2009**, *25*, 287–292. [CrossRef]
33. Tibshirani, R. Regression Shrinkage and Selection Via the Lasso. *J. R. Statist. Soc. Ser. B* **1996**, *58*, 267–288. [CrossRef]
34. Nam, S.; Davies, M.E.; Elad, M.; Gribonval, R. The cosparse analysis model and algorithms. *Appl. Comput. Harmon. Anal.* **2013**, *34*, 205–229. [CrossRef]
35. Zhang, Y. Theory of compressive sensing via l_1-minimization: A non-rip analysis and extensions. *J. Opt. Res. Soc. China* **2013**, *1*, 79–105. [CrossRef]
36. Christensen, O. Finite dimensional approximation of the inverse frame operator and applications to wavelet frames and Gabor frames. *J. Fourier Anal. Appl.* **2000**, *1*, 79–90. [CrossRef]
37. Yang, J.; Member, J.W.; Huang, T.S.; Ma, Y. Image Super-Resolution Via Sparse Representation. *IEEE Trans. Image Process.* **2010**, *19*, 2861–2873. [CrossRef]

© 2020 by the authors. Licensee MDPI, Basel, Switzerland. This article is an open access article distributed under the terms and conditions of the Creative Commons Attribution (CC BY) license (http://creativecommons.org/licenses/by/4.0/).

Article

A Stronger Aadaptive Local Dimming Method with Details Preservation

Tao Zhang, Wenli Du, Hao Wang *, Qin Zeng and Long Fan

School of Electrical and Information Engineering, Tianjin University, Tianjin 300072, China; zhangtao@tju.edu.cn (T.Z.); duwenli0210@tju.edu.cn (W.D.); zengqin@tju.edu.cn (Q.Z.); fl0228@tju.edu.cn (L.F.)
* Correspondence: wanghao47@tju.edu.cn

Received: 9 February 2020; Accepted: 2 March 2020; Published: 6 March 2020

Abstract: Local dimming technology focuses on improving the contrast ratio of the displayed images for a great visual perception. It consists of backlight extraction and pixel compensation. Considering a single existing backlight extraction algorithm can hardly adapt to images with diverse characteristics and rich details, we propose a stronger adaptive local dimming method with details preservation in this paper. This method, combining the advantages of some existing methods and introducing the combination of the subjective evaluation and the objective evaluation, obtains a stronger adaptation compared with others. Besides, to offset the luminance reduction caused in the backlight extraction process, we improve the bi-histogram equalization algorithm and propose a new pixel compensation method. To preserve image details, the Retinex theory is adopted to separate details. Experimental results demonstrate the effect of the proposed method on contrast ratio improvement and details preservation.

Keywords: local dimming; retinex theory; bi-histogram equalization; contrast ratio; details preservation

1. Introduction

High Dynamic Range (HDR) display is developed for HDR images and videos that convey vastly more color shades and nuances than previous standards. However, these devices are expensive for their complex technology, which limits their promotion. Liquid Crystal Display (LCD) is still the current technology for most devices such as computers and TVs.

LCD consists of a Liquid Crystal (LC) panel and a backlight panel with arrayed Back-Light Units (BLUs). The LC panel is light-modulated instead of self-luminous directly. Hence, an image is displayed by it with the backlight produced by BLUs. In early LCD technology, BLUs are always-on with the maximum luminance level, leading to high power consumption and low contrast ratio. In addition, the image quality is deteriorated due to the light leakage problem [1] in the dark state. Local dimming technology is developed to alleviate these weaknesses. As shown in Figure 1, the technology consists of the backlight extraction and the pixel compensation, which are, respectively, used in obtaining the luminance level for each BLU in backlight panel and the compensated image for the LC panel. In the process of backlight extraction, the luminance of each BLU is controlled dynamically according to the corresponding image content. The power consumption is reduced while the contrast ratio is improved effectively. Backlight smoothing is used to simulate the process of light diffusion, which is a solution to alleviate block artifacts [2,3]. Pixel compensation offsets the luminance reduction caused by the backlight dimming in the backlight extraction process.

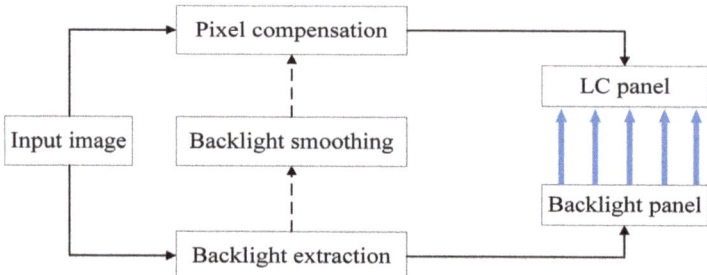

Figure 1. The flowchart of local dimming technique. The dotted line means optional.

The resolution of the displayed image in LC panel is larger than that of the backlight array in backlight panel. The diagram of backlight extraction is shown in Figure 2; the luminance of a BLU is determined by the corresponding block of the input image.

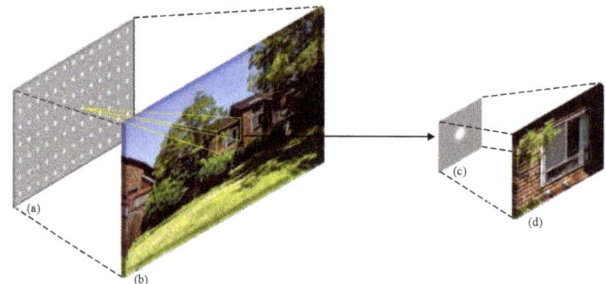

Figure 2. The diagram of backlight extraction: (**a**) backlight panel; (**b**) Liquid Crystal (LC) panel; (**c**) a Back-Light Unit (BLU); and (**d**) the corresponding image block of (**c**).

Many approaches for backlight extraction have been proposed. They determine the luminance level for BLUs from different characteristics of the image. The early method in [4] explores the maximum and the average luminance of the corresponding image block to determine the luminance level of each BLU. The following methods [5–16] extract luminance for BLUs from many other perspectives, such as image histogram, image details, and image quality. However, each method can hardly handle images with diverse and complicated contents. It makes sense to broaden the adaptive scope for a single backlight extraction method. To this end, we propose a method to extract backlight that adapts to images with diverse contents by combining the advantages of some existing methods [4,6–8,10–12], to which previous approaches have paid rare attention. Besides, we introduce subjective evaluation for a better visual perception. Specifically, our method takes three steps to obtain backlight luminance. First, a target backlight is selected from base backlights generated by existing methods. Second, we design a group of constraint conditions and adjust the target backlight under them to obtain several alternative backlights. Finally, the optimal backlight is determined by both the objective evaluation and the display quality of subjective evaluation.

Luminance overcompensation in pixel compensation process will cause image distortion, decreasing its contrast ratio and visual perception. Hence, we take both the backlight information and the luminance information of original image into account to address the overcompensation. Besides, we propose an Improved Bi-Histogram Equalization (IBHE) to further enhance the image. Specifically, Bi-Histogram Equalization (BHE) [17] applies a histogram equalization on two sub-images segmented from one image, obtaining a tradeoff between brightness enhancement and details preservation. Kim, Y.T. [17] adopted the mean luminance of the image as the breakpoint to make segmentation. However, the method lacks effectiveness in details preservation as it simply adopts the image mean luminance as the breakpoint for segmentation. To this end, we improve the method from the view of taking more image details in breakpoint selection. We make the IBHE a part of pixel compensation.

Combing the proposed backlight extraction with pixel compensation methods, a stronger adaptive local dimming method with details preservation is proposed. Our contributions can be summarized as:

- A backlight extraction method is proposed to acquire a stronger adaption in processing images with diverse contents by combining advantages of several existing methods.
- An IBHE method with Retinex theory is proposed to enhance image quality by preserving abundant details.
- A pixel compensation method is proposed to alleviate overcompensation by leveraging information of both the extracted backlight and the original image based on IBHE.

Experimental results demonstrate the effect of the proposed approach in improving contrast ratio, preserving image details, and enhancing image quality in the real display.

The rest of the paper is structured as follows. Section 2 details the related work of local dimming. Section 3 documents the specific process of the proposed method elaborately. Section 4 describes the experiments and results, and analysis of the results is made in this section. Finally, we conclude the paper in Section 5.

2. Related Work

In this section, existing local dimming approaches are described in detail. For clarity, we organize this section into backlight extraction and pixel compensation, as they are the two parts of local dimming.

2.1. Backlight Extraction

As an early and fundamental approach, the max method [4] employs the maximum luminance of an image block to determine the luminance level of the corresponding BLU. It also explores replacing the maximum luminance with the average luminance. However, the former is sensitive to noise and suffers from light leakage [1] problem. The latter reduces image luminance and suffers from losing details in bright areas. To achieve a trade-off between the above two methods, the methods proposed in [1,5,6] consider both the maximum luminance and the average luminance to improve display quality. In [1], a decision rule is proposed to determine optimal backlight by comparing the light leakage and the clipping of image blocks. This method is effective for images with bright objects in a dark area. In [5,6], the difference between the maximum and the average luminance value of a block is used to adjust backlight based on the average value. In [7], the global information of the image is used to extract backlight. It proposes a threshold method using a Cumulative Distribution Function (CDF) to ensure the distortion of the compensated image within a certain range. Besides, the methods proposed in [8,9] are effective to reduce power consumption. Based on Otsu [18], Zhang, T.; Wang, Y.F. [10] introduced a local dimming algorithm to separate foreground and background pixels for backlight extraction. In [11], the Peak Signal to Noise Ratio (PSNR) = 30 is considered as the lowest standard to guarantee the image quality. In [12], a Gaussian distribution model is proposed to reduce power consumption and improve image quality. In Swarm Intelligence (SI), the authors of [13,14] transformed the local backlight dimming to an optimization problem to preserve the image quality with low power consumption. A guided firework algorithm proposed in [14] achieves higher performance than the one in [13]. Although there are other local dimming algorithms [15,16], most of them favor only specific characteristic of an image. Therefore, we propose a backlight extraction method to adapt to images with diverse characteristics, acquiring preferable display quality.

2.2. Pixel Compensation

A backlight extraction method is commonly followed with a corresponding pixel compensation method to offset the luminance reduction. In this section, we document the representative method [5] and the closest related method [10] to ours for readability. In [5], the compensated luminance is obtained using the nonlinear relationship between the maximum backlight and the extracted backlight.

However, image distortion caused by overcompensation in this method decreases the image quality. In [10], the logarithm function is used to compensate for luminance based on the input image and the smoothed backlight image. It is effective to prevent overcompensation but less effective for bright images.

Our pixel compensation method aims to alleviate the overcompensation problem by adjusting the luminance of the pixel in the input image according to the backlight value. Besides, by the proposed IBHE, this method is effective for improving the quality of display images.

3. Method

In this section, we document our local dimming method elaborately. We first introduce the holistic structure of the method. Then, the proposed backlight extraction method and the compensation method are described, respectively.

The diagram of the proposed method is shown in Figure 3. The whole architecture consists of two modules: an Adjustable Backlight Extraction (ABE) module and a pixel compensation module. Furthermore, the ABE module consists of base backlights extraction and optimal backlight selection.

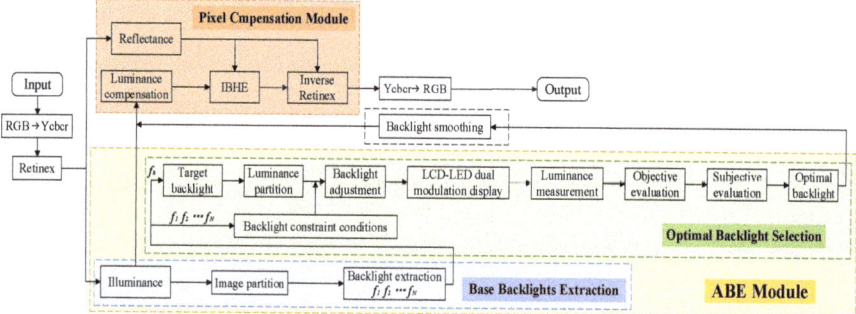

Figure 3. The diagram of the proposed method. It is better to look at it in color: orange block, adjustable backlight extraction module; white block, backlight smoothing module; and pink block, pixel compensation module.

To avoid color distortion, most of the existing local dimming algorithms are performed on the luminance rather than the chroma component. Following this, we separate the luminance information by converting the color space from RGB into $YCbCr$ [19] before all of the succeeding operations. The conversion formula is

$$\begin{cases} [Y \quad Cb \quad Cr]^T = \mathbf{M_{sRGB}} \times [R \quad G \quad B]^T + [16 \quad 128 \quad 128]^T \\ \mathbf{M_{sRGB}} = \begin{bmatrix} 0.257 & 0.564 & 0.098 \\ -0.148 & -0.291 & 0.439 \\ 0.439 & -0.368 & -0.071 \end{bmatrix} \end{cases} \quad (1)$$

According to the Retinex theory [20], which is widely used in image processing [21], an image is composed of reflectance and illuminance. The former presents the detail information and the latter determines the dynamic range. This is represented as:

$$\mathbf{S}(x,y) = \mathbf{R_c}(x,y) \times \mathbf{I}(x,y) \quad (2)$$

where (x, y) is the coordinate of the pixel in the image, $\mathbf{S}$ is the image perceived by human eyes, $\mathbf{R_c}$ is the reflectance, and $\mathbf{I}$ is the illuminance. In our method, $\mathbf{Y}$ component in $YCbCr$ color space is considered as $\mathbf{S}$. $\mathbf{I}$ is obtained by:

$$\mathbf{I}(x, y) = \mathbf{F}(x, y) \otimes \mathbf{Y}(x, y) \tag{3}$$

where $\mathbf{F}$ is the Weighted Least Squares (WLS) filter [22], which is known as an edge-preserving filter; $\otimes$ is the convolution operation; and $\mathbf{Y}$ is the $\mathbf{Y}$ component in $YCbCr$ color space.

Image edge is the most concentrated part of image information such as the change of gray level and the mutation of texture structure, which contains rich details. Therefore, the edge information must be decomposed and kept to improve image quality in image processing. An alternative filter is bilateral filtering, which has been used in many previous works as a base-detail decomposition technique. However, WLS filter is chosen in this paper because of its better performance, especially for increased blur level compared with bilateral filtering. WLS filter is well suited for progressive coarsening of images and for multi-scale detail extraction. For an input image g, an image u is expected to be as close to g as possible and be smoother except for some places where the gradient of the edge of g changes greatly. Formally, the solution to minimize the objective function in Equation (4) is the result of filtering u.

$$\sum_p \left((u_p - g_p)^2 + \lambda \left(a_{x,p(g)} \left(\frac{\partial u}{\partial x}\right)^2 + a_{y,p(g)} \left(\frac{\partial u}{\partial y}\right)^2 \right) \right) \tag{4}$$

where the subscript p represents the coordinate of the pixel. The first term $(u_p - g_p)^2$ is used to measure the similarity between g and u. The second term is a regular term, and λ is a weight coefficient of the regular term. The larger λ is, the smoother the image will be. The image g is smoothed by minimizing the partial derivative of u, and the weights of smoothing terms are $a_{x,p(g)}$ and $a_{y,p(g)}$, respectively. The definitions of $a_{x,p(g)}$ and $a_{y,p(g)}$ are shown in Equation (5).

$$\begin{cases} a_{x,p(g)} = \left(\left|\frac{\partial l}{\partial x}(p)\right|^\alpha + \epsilon \right)^{-1} \\ a_{y,p(g)} = \left(\left|\frac{\partial l}{\partial y}(p)\right|^\alpha + \epsilon \right)^{-1} \end{cases} \tag{5}$$

where l is the logarithmic transformation of g, the exponential parameter α is used to determine the gradient sensitivity, and ϵ is the offset for avoiding invalid division when $\frac{\partial l}{\partial x}(p)$ or $\frac{\partial l}{\partial y}(p)$ is zero. From the above equations, $a_{x,p(g)}$ and $a_{y,p(g)}$ decrease when the gradient of l increases, by which the edge information is kept and unnecessary details is smoothed.

Backlight extraction and pixel compensation are processed on the illuminance $\mathbf{I}$. Then, the logarithm of $\mathbf{R_c}$ is defined in Equation (6).

$$\mathbf{r}(x, y) = \log(\mathbf{R_c}(x, y)) = \log(\mathbf{Y}(x, y)) - \log(\mathbf{I}(x, y)) \tag{6}$$

where $\mathbf{r}$ is the logarithmic result of $\mathbf{R_c}$, and it is used in IBHE in Section 3.2.

3.1. Adjustable Backlight Extraction Module

To respect the image content and avoid drawbacks of a single algorithm, we propose a three-step backlight extraction method to determine an optimal backlight, making displayed images perceived vividly. We document the first step in Section 3.1.1 and the second and the third steps in Section 3.1.2.

3.1.1. Base Backlights Extraction

The first step is to extract base backlights. As mentioned above, each single existing backlight extraction method is not enough to adapt to images with diverse characteristics and contents. However, their respective strengths are complementary and compatible. Each of them can be a base backlight from which we absorb advantages. Assuming that N is the number of base backlights, the base backlights extraction in Figure 3 is defined as follows.

$$\mathbf{BL}^t = f^t(I) \qquad t = 1, 2, \cdots, N \tag{7}$$

where f^t is the t_{th} base backlight algorithm and $\mathbf{BL}^t$ is the t_{th} base backlight.

3.1.2. Optimal Backlight Selection

Optimal backlight constraint conditions are constructed by all of the base backlights extracted above. One of the base backlights is selected as the target backlight for its ability in reducing power consumption and improving the contrast ratio.

The second step of our method is to adjust the selected target backlight. Specifically, we adjust it based on the segmentation method in [23] and the obtained constraint conditions.

Based on our self-developed LCD-LED dual modulation display [10], the optimal backlight is selected from adjusted backlights by objective evaluation as well as subjective evaluation in the third step.

- Backlight constraint conditions

We change specific values of the target backlight to obtain several adjusted backlights as alternations of the optimal backlight. The change needs to be within the effective range of backlight to prevent the deterioration of image quality. For an image block, we go through all base backlights for its corresponding maximum and minimum values. The maximum and minimum matrices are denoted as $\mathbf{P}_{max}$ and $\mathbf{P}_{min}$. This process is defined as:

$$\begin{cases} \mathbf{P}_{max} = max\left(\mathbf{BL}^t(m,n)\right) \\ \mathbf{P}_{min} = min\left(\mathbf{BL}^t(m,n)\right) \end{cases} \tag{8}$$

where (m, n) is the coordinate of each backlight value in the backlight image.

Considering that limited backlight extraction algorithms are used to construct backlight constraint conditions, $\mathbf{P}_{max}$ is increased by 10% with an upper boundary 255 and $\mathbf{P}_{min}$ is decreased by 10% with a lower boundary 0. The adjusted $\mathbf{P}_{max}$ and $\mathbf{P}_{min}$ are represented as $\mathbf{PA}_{max}$ and $\mathbf{PA}_{min}$, and they form the constraint conditions for obtaining the optimal backlight.

- Backlight adjustment and optimal backlight selection

Just Noticeable Difference (JND) [24] reflects the sensitivity of human vision. As shown in Figure 4, under different background luminance, JND is different.

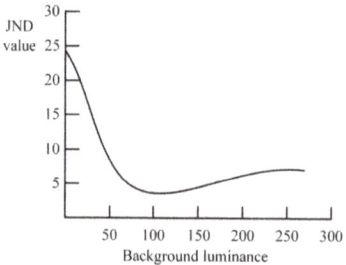

Figure 4. JND curve.

In image quality evaluation, if the luminance of details is too close to the neighboring pixels, that is, the difference is less than JND, then the details of this image are not well-displayed. In real display, the background luminance may be changed due to light diffusion between different backlights, leading to the change of JND. Therefore, the image quality in real display may be degraded. To this end, we adjust the target backlight to change the background luminance and select the backlight that presents the details effectively based on display quality as the optimal backlight.

Assume that target backlight is the k_{th} base backlight denoted as $\mathbf{BL_0}$.

$$\mathbf{BL_0} = f^k(I) \quad k \in \{1, 2, \cdots, N\} \quad (9)$$

where f^k is the k_{th} base backlight extraction method. Improving the dynamic range is important in local dimming. Hence, for $\mathbf{BL_0}$, we strengthen the luminance in bright area and weaken it in dark area to improve its dynamic range. Specifically, the bright and the dark area are selected by mean and variance of the backlight image. The process is expressed as Equations (10) and (11).

$$\begin{cases} M = \left(\sum_{m=1}^{W} \sum_{n=1}^{H} \mathbf{BL_0}(m,n) \right) \div (W \times H) \\ V = \left(\sum_{m=1}^{W} \sum_{n=1}^{H} (\mathbf{BL_0}(m,n) - M)^2 \right) \div (W \times H) \end{cases} \quad (10)$$

$$\begin{cases} P_1 = M - V \\ P_2 = M + V \end{cases} \quad (11)$$

where W, H, M, and V are the width, height, mean, and variance of $\mathbf{BL_0}$, respectively. P_1 and P_2 are the breakpoints to partition areas of different luminance. The pixel with luminance less than P_1 is considered as dark area and the pixel with luminance larger than P_2 is considered as bright area,

Since the backlight value ranges in 0–255, we use the exponent of 2 as the adjustment step to adjust the target backlight $\mathbf{BL_0}$. The process is expressed as Equation (12).

$$\begin{cases} \mathbf{BL}_i(m,n) = \begin{cases} \mathbf{BL_0}(m,n) - 2^i & \mathbf{BL_0}(m,n) < P_1 \\ \mathbf{BL_0}(m,n) + 2^i & \mathbf{BL_0}(m,n) > P_2 \end{cases} \\ \mathbf{BL}_i(m,n) = \begin{cases} \min(\mathbf{PA_{max}}(m,n), \mathbf{BL}_i(m,n)) & \mathbf{BL}_i(m,n) > \mathbf{PA_{max}}(m,n) \\ \max(\mathbf{PA_{min}}(m,n), \mathbf{BL}_i(m,n)) & \mathbf{BL}_i(m,n) < \mathbf{PA_{min}}(m,n) \end{cases} \end{cases} \quad (12)$$

where $i = 1, 2, \cdots, 8$, $\mathbf{BL}_i$ means the i_{th} adjusted backlight based on $\mathbf{BL_0}$. $\mathbf{PA_{max}}$ and $\mathbf{PA_{min}}$ are used to prevent the adjusted backlight from making poor display quality.

Contrast Ratio (CR) and Dynamic Range (DR) are two objective indicators of display quality. Both reflect the change of brightness ranging from dark to bright, and the higher are CR and DR, the wider is the brightness range. To select the optimal backlight, the display luminance is first measured under all adjusted backlights. Then, CR and DR of each measured luminance are calculated. The adjusted backlights with the top three performances based on the results of CR and DR are selected. Finally, the optimal backlight is selected from the three adjusted backlights by display quality subjectively. The process is shown in Figure 5.

The subjective evaluation is set as follows. The three selected adjusted backlights are demonstrated on the display prototype. Observers are asked to vote for the optimal backlight based on visual perception over details, contrast, and brightness. The backlight with the largest number of votes is determined to be the optimal backlight. Given that subjective feeling is susceptible to factors such as gender, age, occupation, and surroundings, the selection was done by 16 observers who are non-experts in image and video processing field. Their ages range from 22 to 30, with eight males and eight females. All of them have normal visual ability, that is, none of them have eye problems such as color blindness, color weakness, shortsighted, etc.

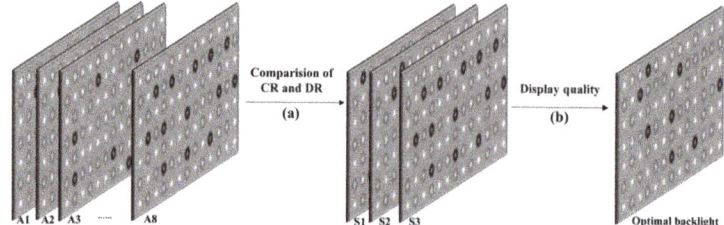

Figure 5. Process of selecting the optimal backlight: (**a**) objective evaluation using Contrast Ratio (CR) and Dynamic Range (DR); and (**b**) subjective evaluation via voting based on display quality. A_i (i = 1, 2 ··· 8) means adjusted backlight; S_j (j = 1, 2, 3) means backlights with top three objective indicators.

3.2. Pixel Compensation Module

In this work, we compensate luminance according to the optimal backlight described as **BL$_{op}$** and the luminance of the input image. Before the compensation, we use Improved Blur Mask Approach (IBMA) [10] to smooth optimal backlight to removes the block artifacts. Specifically, Zhang, T.; Wang, Y.F. [10] divided the points of **BL$_{op}$** into three categories. The first category includes the corner points, the second category includes the peripheral points except for the cornet points, and the third category includes the internal points of **BL$_{op}$**. Different Low Pass Filter (LPF) templates are used to smooth points of **BL$_{op}$** in different categories. IBMA uses the smoothing process to simulate the light diffusion, and **BL$_{op}$** is resized after each smoothing operation. By several smoothing operations, the smoothed backlight has the same size as the input image. The process is expressed in Equation (13).

$$\mathbf{BL_{sm}} = IBMA\left(\mathbf{BL_{op}}\right) \tag{13}$$

where **BL$_{sm}$** represents the backlight after IBMA and **BL$_{op}$** is the optimal backlight. The comparison results of using or not using IBMA are shown in Figure 6.

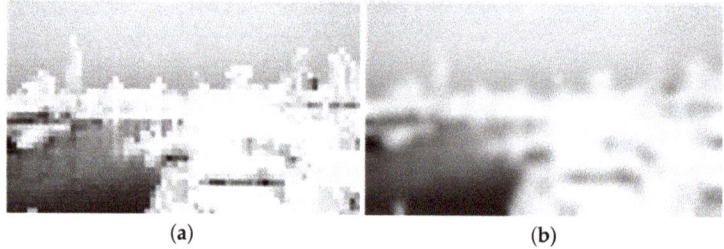

Figure 6. (**a**) Backlight without Improved Blur Mask Approach; and (**b**) backlight with Improved Blur Mask Approach.

Compared with Figure 6a, artifacts are removed obviously in Figure 6b by applying IBMA.

We use a compensation coefficient k to control the compensation degree, which is determined by the smoothed backlight and the luminance of the input image. The process is formulated as Equations (14) and (15).

$$\mathbf{k}\left(x,y\right) = \left(\mathbf{BL_{sm}}\left(x,y\right) \div \mathbf{I}\left(x,y\right)\right)^{\gamma} \tag{14}$$

$$\mathbf{I_p}\left(x,y\right) = \mathbf{k}\left(x,y\right) \times \mathbf{I}\left(x,y\right) + \left(1 - \mathbf{k}\left(x,y\right)\right) \times \mathbf{BL_{sm}}\left(x,y\right) \tag{15}$$

where $\gamma = 0.125$ is selected from multiple experimental results to prevent overcompensation problem and enhance the overall luminance of the image effectively. **I$_p$** is the compensated luminance.

Next, IBHE is used to further enhance the compensated luminance. In BHE, an image is decomposed into two sub-images based on its mean, and then the sub-images are equalized independently to improve CR while maintaining the luminance of the image. Different from this, we rely on the Otsu method and the histogram of **r** in Equation (6) to obtain two sub-images. Algorithm 1 is devised to acquire the breakpoint for the image segmentation.

Algorithm 1 Proposed algorithm for breakpoint acquisition.

Input: r, I_P;
Output: the breakpoint T;
1: $[z_1, z_2]$ = size (r);
2: $num = 0$;
3: $I_m = I_P$;
4: **for** $i = 1$ to z_1 **do**
5:     **for** $j = 1$ to z_2 **do**
6:         **if** $r(i,j) == 0$ **then**
7:             $num+ = 1$;
8:         **else**
9:             $I_m(i,j) = 0$;
10:        **end if**
11:     **end for**
12: **end for**
13: $T1 = (sum(sum(I_m))) \div num$;
14: $T2 = Otsu((I_m))$;   the breakpoint obtained by Otsu method
15: $T = floor((T1 + T2) \div 2)$;   the average value of T_1 and T_2
16: **return** T;

By the breakpoint T, the CDF curves of the two sub-images are obtained to perform BHE [17]. The process is expressed as Equation (16).

$$\mathbf{I_{out}}(k) = \begin{cases} (T - I_{pmin}) \times CDF_1(k) + I_{pmin} & 0 < k < T \\ (I_{pmax} - T) \times CDF_2(k) + T & T + 1 < k < 255 \end{cases} \quad (16)$$

where I_{pmin} and I_{pmax} are the minimum and the maximum of compensated luminance $\mathbf{I_p}$, respectively. CDF_1 and CDF_2 are respective CDF curves of the two sub-images.

Finally, $\mathbf{I_{out}}$ and **r** in Equation (6) are combined to reconstruct final luminance image by Equation (17), and color transformation from $YCbCr$ to RGB [25] is employed to generate the final image.

$$\mathbf{Y_{out}}(x,y) = \mathbf{I_{out}}(x,y) \times e^{\mathbf{r}(x,y)} \quad (17)$$

4. Experiment

In this section, we describe the settings and the results of our experiments. In backlight extraction, the base backlight extraction methods in our experiment consisted of the max method [4], the average method [4], LUT method [6], CDF method [7], IMF method [8], the method based on Otsu [10], PSNR method [11], and Gaussian method [12]. The method based on Otsu in [10] was considered as the target algorithm, extracted by which the backlight is taken as the target backlight. The sizes of the input image and the backlight are 1920 × 1080 and 66 × 36, respectively.

4.1. Hardware

A self-designed LED-LCD prototype display [10] was adopted to verify display quality with the optimal backlight and compensated image that is the output in Figure 3. The display principle of the prototype is shown in Figure 7a. The measure environment in our experiment was a dark room to prevent interference from light. The luminance meter used in our experiment is CX-2B color brightness meter, for which the luminance ranges in 0.001–200 kcd/m².

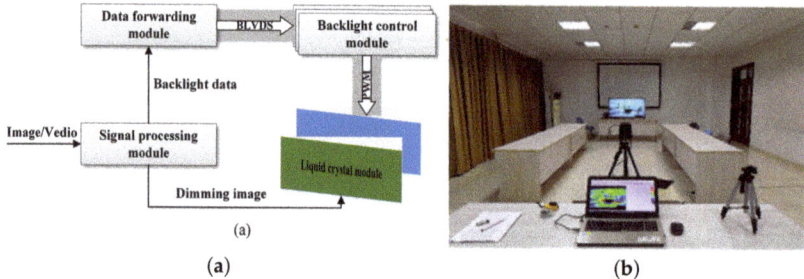

Figure 7. Hardware support: (**a**) display principle of LED-LCD prototype; and (**b**) measurement environment (the lights were off when we measured the luminance).

4.2. Experiment of Improved Bi-Histogram Equalization

To illustrate the effectiveness of the proposed IBHE method in segmenting image, the breakpoint by Kim, Y.T. [17] was used to make comparison. The results are shown in Figure 8.

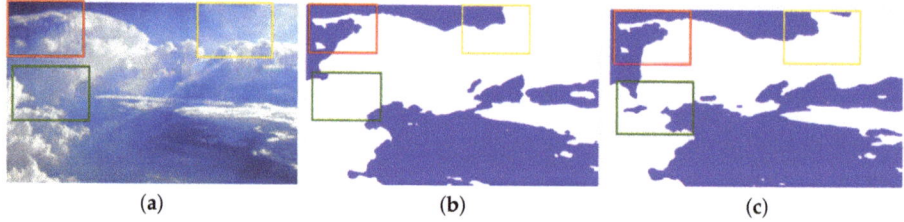

Figure 8. Segmentation results with different breakpoints: (**a**) test image; (**b**) breakpoint by the method in [17]; and (**c**) breakpoint by the proposed Improved Bi-Histogram Equalization (IBHE).

As shown in the red square of Figure 8b,c, the segmentation effect is basically the same, while, in the yellow as well as green squares, the segmentation is more accurate by the proposed IBHE method than by the method in [17] according to the test image.

4.3. Experiment of Adjustable Backlight Extraction

4.3.1. Subjective Experiment

The comparison of image display quality under the target backlight and the optimal backlight is shown in Figure 9.

The images were taken by an optical recorder. Obviously, the image recorders can hardly reproduce the visual perception of eyes. However, we can still distinguish that the visual perception of the optimal backlight is more vivid than that of the target backlight. For clarity, the detail with obvious difference is marked. In the above two images in Figure 9, we observe that the dark areas are enhanced under optimal backlight to improve CR of the displayed image. In the other two images, the marked areas illustrate a higher color saturation to improve display quality under optimal backlight. These demonstrate that the proposed backlight extraction method has stronger adaption in an image with different brightness and rich details in the real display.

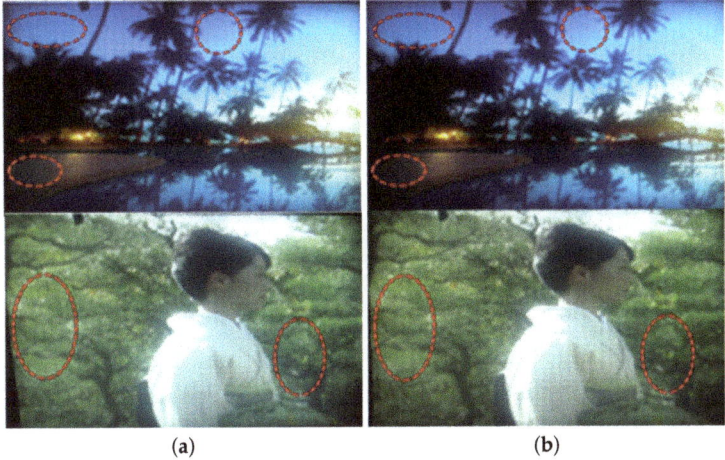

Figure 9. Display effects with target backlight and optimal backlight: (**a**) target backlight; and (**b**) optimal backlight.

4.3.2. Objective Experiment

Tong, H. [26] defined a group of conditions to separate low/high luminance and low/high CR images with CDF curve. We selected one image from each category to evaluate the proposed method according to the conditions. The images chosen for the experiment and their corresponding CDF curves are illustrated in Figure 10.

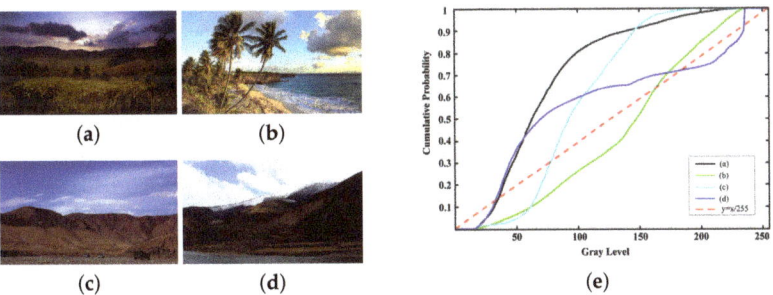

Figure 10. Images used for objective experiment and corresponding Cumulative Distribution Function (CDF) curves: (**a**) low luminance image; (**b**) high luminance image; (**c**) low contrast ratio image; (**d**) high contrast ratio image; and (**e**) CDF curves of the images.

Assuming that h denotes the histogram of the measured luminance using luminance meter, $h(x)$ denotes the number of pixels whose luminance is x. Inspired by the method of calculating CR in [10], we calculated the average values of luminance that are greater than P_{90} and lower than P_{10}, respectively, to calculate CR to reduce the influence of the measurement error. P_{10} and P_{90} are the luminance of which the cumulative numbers account for 10% and 90% of the total pixels, respectively. M_{max} and M_{min} are the maximum and minimum of the measured luminance. CR and DR are calculated as follows.

$$\begin{cases} Avg_{10} = \sum_{x<P_{10}} (h(x) \times x) \div \sum_{x<P_{10}} h(x) \\ Avg_{90} = \sum_{x>P_{90}} (h(x) \times x) \div \sum_{x>P_{90}} h(x) \\ CR = Avg_{90} \div Avg_{10} \\ DR = M_{max} \div M_{min} \end{cases} \qquad (18)$$

The objective evaluations are shown in Table 1. We can observe that all CR values of optimal backlights are better than that of the target backlights. DR values in Images (b) and (d) under optimal backlights are slightly lower than those under target backlights. The reason lies in that the luminance of the bright area is almost 255, which cannot be increased. In contrast, the luminance of the dark area is still decreased, resulting in a reduction in overall luminance. For most cases, the comparisons confirm the effectiveness of the proposed method.

Table 1. Objective evaluation comparisons of CR and DR. **BL$_0$**, the target backlight; **BL$_i$**, the optimal backlight; (a)–(d), images in Figure 10. The better performance is marked in bold.

Image	Backlight	CR	DR
(a)	BL$_0$	11,209.24	1,630,700
	BL$_3$	**11,284.18**	**1,631,900**
(b)	BL$_0$	8.97	**2,059,400**
	BL$_4$	**9.14**	1,974,200
(c)	BL$_0$	3228.41	1,056,333
	BL$_4$	**3272.41**	**1,156,091**
(d)	BL$_0$	1913.71	**1,659,500**
	BL$_3$	**5464.29**	1,656,385

4.4. Experiment of Simulated Images

4.4.1. Subjective Experiment

The simulated comparisons of the proposed local dimming method with LUT method, CDF method, and the method based on Otsu [10] are shown in Figure 11.

For Figure 11a, the dark areas in red rectangles of CDF and LUT algorithms are brighter, leading to a lower CR than the other two methods. In contrast, the method in [10] missed details caused by reducing luminance. The proposed method is a balance between improving CR and preserving details.

For Figure 11b, the clouds in the red circles of CDF and LUT methods are brighter than Figure 10b, which should be darker. For the clouds in the red rectangle by the method in [10], the image distortion is caused by overcompensation. For the image by the proposed method, the image contents in both the red circle and the red rectangle are well-compensated to improve CR and preserve details.

For Figure 11c, CDF and LUT methods simply improve the overall image luminance but without improvement of CR and image quality. The method in [10] improved the luminance of bright areas and decreased that of dark areas, which shows a preferable image. The image of the proposed method shows a higher CR with a higher saturation. However, the mountain part is slightly unsatisfactory compared with the image obtained by the method in [10]. This may be because the low luminance is mapped to smaller by histogram equalization.

Figure 11. Simulation results. From left to right: Images (**a–d**).

For Figure 11d, the images of CDF and LUT methods are bright to show rich details. In contrast, the image obtained by the method in [10] is distorted. Note that the red rectangle, seen as a high spatial-frequency part, retains more details by the proposed method compared with the image obtained by the method in [10].

4.4.2. Objective Experiment

In our experiments, in addition to for CR [10], Peak Signal-to-Noise Ratio (PSNR) [27], Structural Similarity Index (SSIM) [14], and Color Difference (CD) [28] were further applied to evaluate the simulated image comprehensively.

CR, used to evaluate the dynamic range of luminance, is an important metrics in image processing. Generally, an image with a high CR presents vivid and rich colors. Note that the CR used to evaluate the simulated images is calculated differently compared with the CR in Section 4.3.2. To distinguish them, the CR calculated by the simulated image is defined as CR_{SI} and obtained by Equation (19).

$$CR_{SI} = P_{90}/P_{10} \tag{19}$$

where P_{10} and P_{90} are the luminance of which the cumulative numbers account for 10% and 90% of the total number of pixels in simulated image, respectively.

PSNR was employed to evaluate the distortion between signal and noise. A higher PSNR indicates a lower distortion. The definition of PSNR is described in Equation (20).

$$\begin{cases} PSNR\left(C_{1}, C_{2}\right) = 10 \times \log \left(\dfrac{255^{2}}{MSE\left(C_{1}, C_{2}\right)}\right) \\ MSE\left(C_{1}, C_{2}\right) = \dfrac{1}{w \times h} \sum_{i=1}^{w} \sum_{j=1}^{h} \left(C_{1}\left(i, j\right) - C_{2}\left(i, j\right)\right)^{2} \end{cases} \tag{20}$$

where C_1 and C_2 are the original image and the simulated image, respectively, while w and h mean the width and the height of the simulated image.

SSIM is widely used in realizing structural similarity theory. SSIM ranges from 0 to 1 and a better image quality leads to a higher SSIM. The definition of SSIM is described in Equation (21)

$$SSIM\left(C_{1}, C_{2}\right) = \dfrac{\left(2\mu_{C_{1}}\mu_{C_{2}} + \epsilon_{1}\right)\left(2\sigma_{C_{1}C_{2}} + \epsilon_{2}\right)}{\left(\mu_{C_{1}}^{2} + \mu_{C_{2}}^{2} + \epsilon_{1}\right)\left(\sigma_{C_{1}}^{2} + \sigma_{C_{2}}^{2} + \epsilon_{2}\right)} \tag{21}$$

where μ_{C_1} and μ_{C_2} are the mean values of C_1 and C_2 respectively; σ_{C_1} and σ_{C_2} are the variance of C_1 and C_2, respectively; $\sigma_{C_1 C_2}$ is the covariance of C_1 and C_2; and ϵ_1 and ϵ_2 are two constants to avoid invalid division.

Besides, from the perspective of color information, we adopted CD to evaluate the color distortion by applying weighted Euclidean distance in RGB color space. The process to obtain the CD is expressed in Equation (22).

$$\begin{cases} \Delta C = \sqrt{\left(2 + \dfrac{\bar{r}}{256}\right) \times \Delta R^2 + 4 \times \Delta G^2 + \left(2 + \dfrac{255 - \bar{r}}{256}\right) \times \Delta B^2} \\ CD = \dfrac{\Delta C}{w \times h} \end{cases} \quad (22)$$

where $\bar{r} = (C_{1,R} + C_{2,R})/2$, $\Delta R = C_{1,R} - C_{2,R}$, $\Delta G = C_{1,G} - C_{2,G}$, and $\Delta B = C_{1,B} - C_{2,B}$; $C_{1,R}$, $C_{1,G}$, and $C_{1,B}$ represent the normalized components of original image, respectively; and $C_{2,R}$, $C_{2,G}$, and $C_{2,B}$ represent the normalized components of simulated image; respectively. The comparisons of the above four metrics are shown in Table 2.

Table 2. Comparisons of algorithmic processing. The best performance is marked in bold.

Image	Evaluation Metrics	CDF Method	LUT Method	[10]	the Proposed Method
(a)	CR_{SI}	4.88	4.93	7.00	**7.50**
	PSNR	18.40	19.43	24.78	**33.19**
	SSIM	0.87	0.89	0.94	**0.97**
	CD	0.32	0.28	0.15	**0.06**
(b)	CR_{SI}	4.32	4.28	7.68	**8.42**
	PSNR	24.10	25.49	24.24	**27.00**
	SSIM	0.98	**0.99**	0.97	0.98
	CD	0.13	**0.12**	0.16	**0.12**
(c)	CR_{SI}	5.88	5.76	6.08	**7.71**
	PSNR	20.32	21.49	23.44	**24.39**
	SSIM	0.91	0.92	**0.93**	0.90
	CD	0.26	0.23	**0.19**	**0.19**
(d)	CR_{SI}	5.69	6.00	6.50	**8.00**
	PSNR	19.81	20.49	**25.85**	24.80
	SSIM	0.83	0.84	0.90	**0.93**
	CD	0.23	0.21	**0.13**	0.14

In Table 2, CR_{SI} obtained by the proposed method is higher than that of the three other top algorithms by 7.0%, 10.0%, 26.8%, and 23.1%, respectively. PSNR is improved by 33.9%, 11.4%, 4.1%, and −4.1%, respectively. PSNR of high contrast ratio image by the proposed method follows the highest one by the method in [10] closely. For SSIM, the performance of the proposed method is slightly inferior for low contrast ratio image. However, it is still competitive to other algorithms, especially for low luminance image. For CD, images processed by the proposed method reduce the distortion of chroma information effectively, especially for the low luminance image and the high contrast ratio image. In other words, the objective evaluation values are consistent with the subjective quality of the simulated images.

5. Conclusions

In this paper, a stronger adaptive local dimming method with details preservation is proposed to alleviate the disadvantage of a single algorithm. A three-step backlight extraction method is applied to determine the optimal backlight to improve display quality. In the pixel compensation, we compensate the luminance of the input image according to the smoothed backlight information. In addition, IBHE is proposed to enhance the luminance of an image and realize details preservation. Both the objective and subjective evaluation results demonstrate the effectiveness of the proposed local dimming method in keeping chroma information, and improving CR as well as PSNR, SSIM.

Author Contributions: Conceptualization, T.Z., W.D., and H.W.; methodology, T.Z., W.D., and H.W.; software, W.D.; validation, W.D., Q.Z., and L.F.; formal analysis, W.D.; investigation, H.W., W.D., Q.Z., and L.F.; resources, T.Z.; data curation, H.W.; writing—original draft preparation, T.Z. and W.D.; writing—review and editing, H.W., Q.Z., and L.F.; visualization, W.D.; supervision, T.Z.; project administration, T.Z.; and funding acquisition, T.Z. All authors have read and agreed to the published version of the manuscript.

Funding: This work was supported by the Research on HDR Backlight Liquid Crystal Processing Technology Based on Depth Neural Network under Contract HO2018085418.

Conflicts of Interest: The authors declare no conflict of interest.

References

1. Kim, S.E.; An, J.Y.; Hong, J.J. How to reduce light leakage and clipping in local-dimming liquid-crystal displays. *J. Soc. Inf. Disp.* **2009**, *17*, 1051–1057. [CrossRef]
2. Chen, H.; Ha, T.H.; Sung, J.H. Evaluation of LCD local dimming backlight system. *J. Soc. Inf. Disp.* **2012**, *18*, 57–65. [CrossRef]
3. Nam, H.; Song, E.; Kim, S.K. Weighted roll-off scheme to remove block artifacts for low power local dimming liquid crystal displays. *Opt. Laser Technol.* **2014**, *58*, 8–15. [CrossRef]
4. Funamoto, T.; Kobayashi, T.; Murao, T. High-picture-quality technique for LCD televisions: LCD-AI. In Proceedings of the International Display Workshops, Kobe, Japan, 29 December 2000; pp. 1157–1158.
5. Zhang, X.B.; Wang, R.; Dong, D. Dynamic Backlight Adaptation Based on the Details of Image for Liquid Crystal Displays. *J. Disp. Technol.* **2012**, *8*, 108–111. [CrossRef]
6. Cho, H.; Kwon, O.K. A backlight dimming algorithm for low power and high image quality LCD applications. *IEEE Trans. Consum. Electron.* **2009**, *55*, 839–844. [CrossRef]
7. Liu, Y.Z.; Zheng, X.R.; Chen, J.B. Dynamic Backlight Signal Extraction Algorithm Based on Threshold of Image CDF for LCD-TV and its Hardware Implementation. *Chin. J. Liq. Cryst. Disp.* **2010**, *25*, 449–453.
8. Lin, F.C.; Liao, C.Y.; Liao, L.Y. Inverse of Mapping Function (IMF) Method for Image Quality Enhancement of High Dynamic Range LCD TVs. *SID Symp. Dig. Tech. Pap.* **2007**, *38*, 1343–1346. [CrossRef]
9. Nadernejad, E.; Burini, N.; Korhonen, J. Adaptive local backlight dimming algorithm based on local histogram and image characteristics. In Proceedings of the IS&T/SPIE Electronic Imaging, Burlingame, CA, USA, 3–7 February 2013.
10. Zhang, T.; Wang, Y.F. High-Performance Local Dimming Algorithm Based on Image Characteristic and Logarithmic Function. *J. Soc. Inf. Disp.* **2019**, *27*, 85–100. [CrossRef]
11. Zhang, X.B.; Liu, X.; Liu, B. A Control Algorithm of LCD Dynamic Backlight Based on PSNR. *Appl. Mech. Mater.* **2012**, *241–244*, 3014–3019. [CrossRef]
12. Chen, S.L.; Tsai, H.J. A Novel Adaptive Local Dimming Backlight Control Chip Design Based on Gaussian Distribution for Liquid Crystal Displays. *J. Disp. Technol.* **2016**, *99*, 1494–1505. [CrossRef]
13. Zhang, T.; Zhao, X.; Pan, X.H. Optimal Local Dimming Based on an Improved Shuffled Frog Leaping Algorithm. *IEEE Access* **2018**, *6*, 40472–40484. [CrossRef]
14. Zhang, T.; Zhao, X. Using the Guided Fireworks Algorithm for Local Backlight Dimming. *Appl. Sci.* **2019**, *9*, 129. [CrossRef]
15. Yeo, D.M.; Kwon, Y.H.; Kang, E.J. Smart Algorithms for Local Dimming LED Backlight. *SID Symp. Dig. Tech. Pap.* **2008**, *39*, 1343–1346. [CrossRef]
16. Wang, X.; Su, H.S.; Li, C.L. HDR image display algorithm based on LCD-LED dual modulation HDR display. *Chin. J. Liq. Cryst. Disp.* **2019**, *34*, 18–27.
17. Kim, Y.T. Contrast enhancement using brightness preserving bi-histogram equalization. *IEEE Trans. Consum. Electron.* **1997**, *43*, 1–8.
18. Otsu, N. A Threshold Selection Method from Gray-Level Histograms. *IEEE Trans. Syst. Man Cybern.* **2007**, *9*, 62–66. [CrossRef]
19. Genesis Microchip. *gm6010/gm6015 Programming Guide*; Genesis Microchip Company: Anaheim, CA, USA, 2002; pp. 85–90.
20. LAND, E.H. Lightness and retinex theory. *J. Opt. Soc. Am.* **1971**, *61*, 2032–2040. [CrossRef]

21. Tang, L.; Chen, S.; Liu, W. Improved Retinex Image Enhancement Algorithm. *Procedia Environ. Sci.* **2011**, *11*, 208–212. [CrossRef]
22. Farbman, Z.; Fattal, R.; Lischinski, D. Edge-preserving decompositions for multi-scale tone and detail manipulation. *ACM Trans. Graph.* **2008**, *27*, 1–10. [CrossRef]
23. Lu, X.M.; Zhu, X.Y.; Li, Z.W. A Brightness-scaling and Detail-preserving Tone Mapping Method for High Dynamic Range Images. *Acta Autom. Sin.* **2015**, *41*, 1080–1092.
24. Li, J.X. Research on Image Enhancement Based on JND Curve Property. Master's Thesis, Lanzhou Jiaotong University, LanZhou, GanSu, China, 2014.
25. Genesis Microchip. *gm6015 Preliminary Data Sheet*; Genesis Microchip Company: Anaheim, CA, USA, 2001; pp. 33–34.
26. Tong, H. Research of LCD Dynamic Control LED Backlight Algorithm. Mater's Thesis, Hefei University of Technology, Hefei, AnHui, China, 2012.
27. Hore, A.; Ziou, D. Image quality metrics: PSNR vs. SSIM. In Proceedings of the 20th International Conference on Pattern Recognition, IEEE Computer Society, Istanbul, Turkey, 23–26 August 2010.
28. Song, S.J.; Kim, Y.I.; Bae, J. Deep-learning-based pixel compensation algorithm for local dimming liquid crystal displays of quantum-dot backlights. *Opt. Express* **2019**, *27*, 15907–15917. [CrossRef] [PubMed]

© 2020 by the authors. Licensee MDPI, Basel, Switzerland. This article is an open access article distributed under the terms and conditions of the Creative Commons Attribution (CC BY) license (http://creativecommons.org/licenses/by/4.0/).

Article

Comparison of Image Fusion Techniques Using *Satellite Pour l'Observation de la Terre* (SPOT) 6 Satellite Imagery

Paidamwoyo Mhangara [1,2,*], Willard Mapurisa [1] and Naledzani Mudau [1]

1. South African National Space Agency, Innovation Hub, Pretoria 0087, Gauteng, South Africa; wmapurisa@sansa.org.za (W.M.); nmudau@sansa.org.za (N.M.)
2. School of Geography, Archaeology and Environmental Studies, University of the Witwatersrand—Johannesburg, Wits 2050, Johannesburg, South Africa
* Correspondence: paida.mhangara@wits.ac.za

Received: 27 January 2020; Accepted: 18 February 2020; Published: 10 March 2020

Featured Application: High resolution pansharpened images are used for detailed land use and land cover mapping.

Abstract: Preservation of spectral and spatial information is an important requirement for most quantitative remote sensing applications. In this study, we use image quality metrics to evaluate the performance of several image fusion techniques to assess the spectral and spatial quality of pansharpened images. We evaluated twelve pansharpening algorithms in this study; the Local Mean and Variance Matching (IMVM) algorithm was the best in terms of spectral consistency and synthesis followed by the ratio component substitution (RCS) algorithm. Whereas the IMVM and RCS image fusion techniques showed better results compared to other pansharpening methods, it is pertinent to highlight that our study also showed the credibility of other pansharpening algorithms in terms of spatial and spectral consistency as shown by the high correlation coefficients achieved in all methods. We noted that the algorithms that ranked higher in terms of spectral consistency and synthesis were outperformed by other competing algorithms in terms of spatial consistency. The study, therefore, concludes that the selection of image fusion techniques is driven by the requirements of remote sensing application and a careful trade-off is necessary to account for the impact of scene radiometry, image sharpness, spatial and spectral consistency, and computational overhead.

Keywords: pansharpening; image fusion; image quality; *Satellite Pour l'Observation de la Terre* (SPOT) 6; spectral consistency; spatial consistency; synthesis

1. Introduction

High spatial resolution satellite imagery is increasingly adopted globally to support spatial planning and monitoring of the built-up environment as evidenced by the proliferation of high-resolution commercial satellite sensors such as Pleiades, Worldview 1–4, *Satellite Pour l'Observation de la Terre* (SPOT) 6 and 7, Superview, and a wide range of high-resolution services and products derived from these sensors. Most modern satellite sensors carry onboard spectral bands of different spatial resolutions and spectral frequencies. In most instances, satellite sensors have narrow multispectral bands of relatively courser spatial resolution and a wide panchromatic band with higher spatial resolution. To facilitate better image visualization, interpretation, feature extraction, and land cover classification, an image fusion technique called pansharpening is used to merge the visible multispectral bands (red, blue, and green bands) and the panchromatic band to produce color images with higher spatial resolution [1–7]. The panchromatic band has wide spectral coverage in the visible and near-infrared wavelength regions. Pansharpening is aimed at producing a synthesized multispectral image with an enhanced spatial resolution equivalent to that of a panchromatic band [8–13].

Remote sensing using high-resolution satellites is now accepted as a dispensable tool that has the potential to support decision making in a wide range of social benefit areas, such as infrastructure and transportation management, sustainable urban development, disaster resilience, sustainable precision agriculture, and energy and water resources management. The demand for services and products that require users to discern features at high spatial and spectral precision has led most Earth observation service providers to develop geospatial products that use pansharpened satellite imagery that emerges from the fusion of the high spatial resolution panchromatic band and lower resolution multispectral bands [14–16].

Many studies have proved the value of pansharpened imagery in discerning geometric features from satellite imagery, cartography, geometric rectification, change detection, and in improving land cover classification accuracies [17–20]. Many pansharpening techniques have been developed over time to enable users to fully exploit the spatial and spectral characteristics available on most satellite systems. Pansharpening techniques aim to simultaneously increase spatial resolution while preserving the spectral content of the multispectral bands [11,20–22].

Pansharpening methods are classified into three broad categories: component substitution (CS)-based methods; multiresolution analysis (MRA)-based methods; and variational optimization (VO)-based methods. A new generation of pansharpening methods based on deep learning has been evolving in recent years. Component substitution methods rely on the application of a color decorrelation transform to convert unsampled lower-resolution multispectral bands into a new color system that differentiates the spatial and spectral details; fusion occurs by partially or wholly substituting the component that contains the spatial geometry by the panchromatic band and reversing the transformation [23]. Most studies report that while component substitution methods produce pansharpened products of good spatial quality the products suffer spectral distortions. Component substitution is considered more computationally efficient and robust in dealing with mismatches between the multispectral and panchromatic bands [10,23,24]. Typical examples of component substitution methods include principal component analysis (PCA) transform, Brovey's band-dependent spatial detail (BDSD), partial replacement adaptive CS (PRACS), Gram–Schmidt (GS) orthonormalization, and intensity-hue-saturation (IHS) transform. Multiresolution analysis-based methods fuse the high frequencies inherent in the panchromatic band into the unsampled multispectral components through a multiresolution decomposition [23]. In contrast to component substitution methods, pansharpened products generated from multiresolution analysis are considered to produce superior spectral quality but are prone to spatial distortions, particularly when multispectral bands are misaligned with the panchromatic band [9,10]. This is especially the case in multiresolution analysis techniques that apply transformations that are not shift-invariant to engender multiresolution analysis. Examples of multiresolution methods include high-pass modulation (HPM), Laplacian pyramid, discrete wavelet transform, and contourlet transform [23]. Such a transformation converts unsampled lower-resolution multispectral bands into a new color system that differentiates the spatial and spectral details and fusion occurs by partially or wholly substituting the component that contains the spatial geometry by the panchromatic band and reversing the transformation [23]. In recent years, a plethora of novel pansharpening methods have been developed to address the deficiencies of traditional image fusion algorithms. Most of the new pansharpening techniques are broadly clustered into generic categories such as component substitution (CS), multiresolution analysis (MRA), Bayesian, model-based optimization (MBO), sparse reconstruction (SR), and variational optimization (VO)-based methods [8,9,23,25].

The spectral, radiometric, and spatial integrity of pansharpened imagery is critical for several quantitative remote sensing applications. To ascertain the spectral and spatial quality of pansharpened images, many quality metrics were developed. Preservation of spectral content is measured by statistical indicators such as correlation coefficient (CC), root means square error (RMSE), relative-shift means (RM), the universal image quality index, structure similarity index (SSIM), and spectral angle mapper (SAM). A few quantitative measures were also developed to assess the spatial consistency of pansharpened imagery and these include the spatial correlation coefficient (SCC) and the spatial RMSE [10].

Pansharpened SPOT 6/7 and SPOT 5 imagery distributed by South Africa National Space Agency(SANSA) is extensively used by government departments, municipalities, and public entities in South Africa to support spatial planning, crop, and natural resource monitoring. SANSA has distributed pansharpened orthobundles and an annual wall-to-wall national 2.5 m mosaic for SPOT 5 from 2005 to 2012 and a biannual 1.5 m SPOT 6/7 mosaic from 2013 up to 2018. While these pansharpened products were successfully exploited by users, quality assessment of the pansharpened products was limited to visual inspections of the products. In most cases, users of pansharpened imagery require pansharpened products that retain the spectral content of the multispectral image and enhance their spatial detail. The objectives of this study are therefore to compare different pansharpening techniques by using quantitative image quality metrics and recommend the most ideal method with minimum spectral and spatial distortions for the operational production of the SPOT 6 mosaic.

2. Materials and Methods

The SPOT 6/7 multispectral and panchromatic dataset over Pretoria, South Africa was used for the study. SPOT 6 and SPOT 7 are identical sun-synchronous optical satellites launched on 12 September 2012 and 30 June 2014, respectively that co-orbit in the constellation at an altitude of 694 km and are phased at 180 degrees (Airbus, Toulouse, France, 2018). The spectral configuration of the satellites consists of blue (450–520 nm), green (530–590 nm), red (625–695 nm) and near-infrared (760–890 nm) multispectral bands with a spatial resolution of 6 m and a panchromatic (450–745 nm) band with a spatial resolution of 1.5 m and dynamic range of 12 bits per pixel. SPOT 6/7 are capable of contiguous image segments of more than 120 km × 120 km or 60 km × 180 km from a single pass along one orbit.

To meet the operational needs of generating a national wall-to-wall mosaic of South Africa, we selected established pansharpening methods for quantitative quality assessment. The Bayesian (BAY), Brovey transform (BRO), color normalized spectral (CNS) sharpening, Ehlers fusion technique (EHLERS), Gram–Schmidt (GRS), local mean and variance matching (LMVM), modified intensity hue saturation (MIHS), Pansharp algorithm (PANSHARP), principal component analysis (PCA), ratio component substitution (RCS), and wavelet resolution merge (WAVELET) techniques were evaluated in the study.

The PANSHARP algorithm available in the PCI Geomatica software is a statistics-based fusion technique aimed at maximizing spatial detail while minimizing color distortions [26]. It attempts to preserve the spectral characteristics of the data. Developed by Zhang [27], the algorithm uses the least-squares method to approximate the grey value relationship between the original multispectral, panchromatic, and fused images to achieve the best color representation. The modified intensity hue saturation (MIHS) fusion technique merges high-resolution panchromatic data with lower resolution multispectral data to produce a pansharpened image that retains sharp spatial detail and a realistic resemblance of the original multispectral scene colors. This approach assesses the spectral overlap between each multispectral band and the high-resolution panchromatic band and weighs the merge based on these relative wavelengths. The MIHS method was developed to address a shortcoming of the intensity-hue-saturation (IHS) transformation where color distortions occurred due to discrepancies in spectral characteristics between panchromatic and multispectral bands. The IHS fusion transforms the RGB (red, green, and blue) space into the IHS color space and subsequently replaces the intensity band with a high-resolution pan image in the fusion before performing a reverse IHS transformation. The Ehlers (EHLERS) fusion technique uses an IHS transform coupled with Fourier domain filtering and aims to maintain the spectral characteristics of the fused image [22]. This is achieved by using the high-resolution panchromatic image to sharpen the multispectral image while avoiding adding new grey level information to its spectral components by first separating the color and spatial information.

The spatial information content is then embedded as an adaptive enhancement to the images using a combination of color and Fourier transforms [22]. The Brovey transform (BRO) algorithm applies a ratio algorithm to combine the images. This is done by first multiplying each multispectral band by a high-resolution pan band and subsequently dividing each product by the sum of the multispectral bands. It is known to preserve the relative spectral contributions of each pixel but substitutes scene brightness with the high-resolution panchromatic (PAN) image [28]. The principal component analysis (PCA) transform converts intercorrelated Multispectral (MS) bands into a new set of uncorrelated components. The first component that resembles a high-frequency band is replaced by a high-resolution panchromatic band for the fusion. The panchromatic band is fused into low-resolution multispectral channels by performing a reverse PCA transform. A high-resolution fused image is generated after the reverse PCA transformation [29]. The color normalized spectral sharpening (CNS) algorithm implemented in Environment for Visualizing Images (ENVI) software is employed to simultaneously sharpen any defined number of bands and retain the characteristics of the original bands in terms of data type and dynamic range. In this case, the higher resolution bands are used to sharpen the lower resolution bands and in the ENVI implementation, the lower resolution multispectral bands are expected to fall in the same spectral range with the high-resolution panchromatic channel [30,31]. The multispectral bands are clustered into spectral segments defined by the spectral range of the high-resolution panchromatic sharpening band. The pansharpened image is generated by multiplying the high-resolution panchromatic with each lower resolution multispectral band before normalizing the computation by dividing the sum of the input spectral channels in each segment.

The wavelet resolution merge (WAVELET) fusion approach sharpens low-resolution multispectral bands using a matching high-resolution panchromatic band by first decomposing the high-resolution panchromatic band into a set of low-resolution multispectral bands with corresponding wavelet coefficients (spatial details) for each level. This is done by infusing the high-resolution spatial into each of the multispectral bands by performing a reverse wavelet transform on each MS band together with the corresponding wavelet coefficients. In a sense, wavelet-based processing is akin to Fourier transform analysis, except fast Fourier transform analysis uses long continuous (sine and cosine) waves, whereas wavelet transform analysis applies short and discrete wavelets [32–35]. The Gram–Schmidt (GRS) pansharpening algorithm available in the ENVI fuses the high-resolution panchromatic band to the lower resolution multispectral bands by simulating the panchromatic band from the multispectral band by averaging the multispectral bands. A Gram–Schmidt transformation is computed from the simulated panchromatic band and the multispectral band, whereby the simulated panchromatic band is used as the first band. Further, the high spatial resolution panchromatic band is substituted with the first Gram–Schmidt band before applying an inverse Gram–Schmidt transformation to generate the pansharpened multispectral bands [36,37]. The ratio component substitution (RCS) pansharpening algorithm implemented in Orfeo ToolBox [38] fuses orthorectified panchromatic (PAN) and multispectral (XS) images using a low pass sharpening filter as shown in the computation below (OTB, 2019).

$$\frac{XS}{\text{Filtered (PAN)}} \text{PAN E} \qquad (1)$$

where E is a vector of random errors that is considered to be stochastically independent of Z.

The Bayesian fusion (BAY) applies elementary calculus in the fusion of the panchromatic and multispectral images to generate a pansharpened image [38]. This fusion approach uses the statistical relationships amongst the spectral bands and the panchromatic band. Bayesian pansharpening techniques use three images that include a panchromatic band and a multispectral image resampled to the same spatial resolution as the panchromatic band. The panchromatic band is weighted in comparison to the multispectral bands. A thorough mathematical description of the Bayesian pansharpening algorithm implemented in Orfeo ToolBox is provided by [39]. This pansharpening technique is dependent on the notion that the variables of interest, expressed as vector Z, are not directly observable and related to observable variable Y through an error-like equation.

$$Y = g(Z) + E \quad (2)$$

where g(Z) is considered a set of functionals.

The LMVM pansharpening algorithm implemented in OTB software uses an LMVM filter that applies a normalization function at a local scale within the images to equate the local mean and variance values of the high spatial resolution panchromatic band with those of the lower resolution multispectral image [38,40]. The resulting small residual differences are then considered to arise from the high-resolution panchromatic band [40]. Rubiey [40] further notes that this form of filtering improves the correlation between the pansharpened image and the original multispectral image. The LMVM algorithm is highlighted below.

$$F_{i,j} = \frac{\left(H_{i,j} - \overline{H}_{i,j}\right) \cdot s(L)_{i,j(w,h)}}{s(H)_{i,j(w,h)}} E \quad (3)$$

where $F_{i,j}$ refers to the fused image, $H_{i,j}$ and $L_{i,j}$ denote high and low spatial resolution images respectively at pixel coordinates i,j. $(H)_{i,j(w,h)}$ and $(L)_{i,j(w,h)}$ are local means calculated inside the window of size (w, h). s denotes the local standard deviation.

Spectral and Spatial Quality Evaluation of Pansharpened Images

Using Ward's three property criteria, we tested the spectral synthesis and consistency properties of the pansharpened images using image quality indices. According to Wald [41], the first property stipulates that the pansharpened image, once degraded from its original resolution, should be as identical as possible to the original image. Secondly, the pansharpened image should be as identical as possible to the image that a matching sensor would detect with the highest resolution. Last, the multispectral pansharpened image should be as identical as possible to the multispectral set of images that the matching sensor would detect with the highest resolution. For assessment purposes, these three properties are further condensed into two properties: consistency and synthesis. The Ward protocol for the quality assessment of pansharpened imagery stipulates that consistency can be tested by downsampling the merged image from the higher spatial resolution to its original spatial resolution. The nearest neighbor resampling method was used in the downsampling process to ensure minimum transformation of the pixel values. To validate the synthesis property, the original high spatial resolution panchromatic band and the lower spatial resolution multispectral bands were downsampled to their lower resolutions.

To validate the synthesis property, we first degraded both the multispectral images and the panchromatic band by a factor of 4. This downsampling procedure meant the spatial resolution of the multispectral images changed from 6 m to 24 m while the panchromatic band changed from 1.5 m to 6 m. The degraded multispectral and pansharpened images were then fused and the pansharpened image was then subsequently compared to the original multispectral images for quality assessment. To verify the consistency property, we first pansharpened the native multispectral and panchromatic images to create a fused image that we further downsampled by a factor of 4, thus changing its spatial resolution of the pansharpened image from 1.5 m to 6 m. We subsequently compared the downsampled pansharpened image to the original 6 m multispectral image. The process was applied for all eight pansharpening techniques assessed in this paper.

To quantitatively assess the spectral consistency of the pansharpened results the following statistical measures were used: correlation coefficient (CC), Erreur Relative Global Adimensionnelle de Synthese (ERGAS), difference in variance (DIV), bias, root mean square error (RMSE), relative average spectral error (RASE), and universal image quality index (UIQI). The quality of the synthesis in an important property in pansharpening and we used the ERGAS indices using the original multispectral and panchromatic band as a reference to assess the quality of the synthesis. The ERGAS index, when used in the spatial and spectral dimension, is indicative of the amount of spatial and spectral distortions, respectively. The spatial consistency of the pansharpened results was assessed using a spatial metric that computes the spatial correlation coefficient (SCC) between the high-frequency components of the fusion product and the original PAN. In this case, we used a 3 × 3 Laplacian edge detection convolution filter to filter the bands of the pansharpened images and the original panchromatic band before computing the correlation coefficients between them.

The CC is one of the most widely used statistical measures of the strength and direction of the linear relationship between two images [37]. It is used to determine the amount of preservation of spectral content in two images. The CC between each band of the reference and the pansharpened image indicates the spectral integrity of the pansharpened image. The best fusion will have a higher value close to +1. RMSE measures the similarity between each band of the original and fused image. It measures the changes in the radiance of the pixel values for each band of the input multispectral image and pansharpened image. It is a very good indicator of the spectral quality when considered along homogeneous regions in the image. The best fusion will have a lower value close to zero [42]. RASE characterizes the average performance of a method in the considered spectral bands. The value is expressed in percentage and tends to decrease as the quality increases. UIQI measures the difference in spectral information between each band of the merged and reference image to estimate the global spectral quality of the merged images. It models distortion using three parameters: loss of correlation, luminance distortion, and contrast. The best fusion will have a higher value close to +1. ERGAS is indicative of the synthesizing quality of the pansharpened image. It is a global quality index that is sensitive to mean shifting and dynamic range change. ERGAS measures the amount of spectral distortion in the image. The best fusion will have a lower value, mostly when less than the number of bands [43]. Bias reveals the error and spectral accuracy of the pansharpened image. Ideal values are considered to be close to zero. The difference in variance (DIV) measures the quality of the image fusion by calculating the mean difference in variances between the pansharpened image and the original multispectral image. The quality of the pansharpening is considered ideal if the values are closer to zero.

3. Results and Discussion

The results of this study are presented and discussed in this section. Spatial consistency, spectral consistency, and spectral synthesis are presented in Tables 1–9.

3.1. Spatial Consistency Quality Assessment

The spatial consistency results are highlighted in Table 1 below.

Table 1. Spatial consistency: correlation coefficient (CC) Laplacian filtering. Abbreviations: Bayesian fusion (BAY); Brovey transform(BRO); Color Normalized Spectral sharpening (CNS); Ehlers fusion technique (EHLERS); Gram–Schmidt (GRS); Local Mean and Variance Matching (IMVM), Modified Intensity Hue Saturation (MIHS), Pansharp algorithm (PANSHARP), Principal component analysis (PCA); Ratio Component Substitution (RCS); WAVELET, Wavelet Resolution merge fusion (WAVELET).

BAND #	BAY	BRO	CNS	EHLERS	GRS	IMVM	MIHS	PANSHARP	PCA	RCS	WAVELET
1	0.854	0.761	0.853	0.801	0.853	0.785	0.826	0.845	0.846	0.844	0.542
2	0.854	0.834	0.852	0.801	0.853	0.784	0.825	0.845	0.845	0.845	0.542
3	0.854	0.847	0.851	0.801	0.853	0.783	0.824	0.845	0.837	0.845	0.543
AVERAGE	0.854	0.814	0.852	0.801	0.853	0.784	0.825	0.845	0.843	0.844	0.542

Results are reflective of the correlation between the Laplacian filtered bands of the pan sharpened image and the Laplacian filtered panchromatic band. The domain value range from −1 to +1 and ideal values should be close to 1. The ideal value is 1. The results show the best spatial consistency results were produced by the Baysian pansharpening method with Gram–Schmidt in second place and CNS in third place. The wavelet pansharpening technique produced the worst spatial consistency results.

3.2. Spectral Consistency

The results for the spectral consistency evaluation are outlined in Tables 2–8 below.

Table 2. Spectral consistency: correlation coefficient (CC).

BAND #	BAY	BRO	CNS	EHLERS	GRS	IMVM	MIHS	PANSHARP	PCA	RCS	WAVELET
1	0.655	0.499	0.690	0.714	0.586	0.970	0.721	0.620	0.579	0.913	0.645
2	0.587	0.407	0.560	0.584	0.498	0.969	0.585	0.556	0.533	0.866	0.870
3	0.540	0.546	0.452	0.410	0.509	0.968	0.415	0.512	0.543	0.786	0.907
AVERAGE	0.594	0.484	0.567	0.570	0.531	**0.969**	0.574	0.562	0.552	0.855	0.808

The CC results are indicative of spectral similarity between the fused image and original multispectral image. The values range from −1 to +1 and the ideal value is considered to be close to 1. While this metric is quite popular, one of its disadvantages is that it is insensitive to a constant gain and bias between two images and is not able to distinguish subtle fusion artifacts. The results indicate that the IMVM method produced the best results followed by the RCS method. The worst results were produced by the Brovey method.

Table 3. Spectral consistency: Erreur Relative Global Adimensionnelle de Synthese (ERGAS).

BAND #	BAY	BRO	CNS	EHLERS	GRS	IMVM	MIHS	PANSHARP	PCA	RCS	WAVELET
1	7.788	27.518	25.830	6.591	7.322	1.332	5.638	6.808	41.299	2.361	12.158
2	6.737	26.775	24.689	10.511	6.204	1.025	5.448	5.744	34.792	2.288	3.406
3	5.089	25.571	23.650	9.370	4.454	0.736	5.239	4.328	24.757	2.220	2.614
AVERAGE	6.647	26.699	24.801	8.993	6.122	**1.062**	5.457	5.730	34.374	2.296	7.450

The ERGAS results are indicative of the spectral distortions in the fused image. This gives an indication of the general quality of the fused image at a global level. Lower values are considered more ideal and the domain values range from zero to infinity. The best results were produced by the IMVM pansharpening method while RCS was second. The Brovey method performed poorly.

Table 4. Spectral consistency: universal image quality index (UIQI).

BAND #	BAY	BRO	CNS	EHLERS	GRS	IMVM	MIHS	PANSHARP	PCA	RCS	WAVELET
1	0.610	0.008	0.049	0.719	0.569	0.973	0.721	0.614	0.307	0.921	0.548
2	0.524	0.004	0.046	0.532	0.472	0.972	0.569	0.539	0.278	0.869	0.786
3	0.473	0.009	0.046	0.345	0.475	0.972	0.375	0.491	0.308	0.776	0.866
AVERAGE	0.536	0.007	0.047	0.532	0.505	**0.972**	0.555	0.548	0.298	0.856	0.733

The UIQI results show the spectral and spatial distortions in the fused image. Results of this similarity index point to correlation losses as well as distortions in luminance and contrast. The domain values range from −1 to 1 and values close to 1 are considered ideal. The ideal value for UIQI is 1. The IMVM pansharpening algorithm produced the best results while the RCS method took second place. The worst results were produced by the Brovey method.

Table 5. Spectral consistency: relative average spectral error (RASE).

BAND #	BAY	BRO	CNS	EHLERS	GRS	IMVM	MIHS	PANSHARP	PCA	RCS	WAVELET
1	28.002	96.989	91.462	22.001	26.309	4.681	19.458	24.632	156.307	8.240	52.354
2	24.484	97.909	90.393	38.481	22.539	3.587	19.456	20.789	132.507	8.229	11.533
3	18.752	96.851	89.575	34.914	16.500	2.599	19.432	15.842	94.849	8.214	9.395
AVERAGE	23.918	97.573	90.696	32.745	22.025	**3.741**	19.515	20.606	129.356	8.239	31.080

RASE results show the average performance of the fusion algorithm in spectral bands and ideal values should be as small as possible. The results show that the IMVM fusion method produced the best results followed by the RCS method. The PCA method produced the worst results.

Table 6. Spectral consistency: root square mean error (RMSE).

BAND #	BAY	BRO	CNS	EHLERS	GRS	IMVM	MIHS	PANSHARP	PCA	RCS	WAVELET
1	86.162	304.456	285.781	72.925	81.012	14.740	62.375	75.319	456.934	26.118	134.517
2	77.854	309.398	285.298	121.456	71.688	11.840	62.955	66.371	402.044	26.444	39.359
3	58.370	293.318	271.289	107.487	51.095	8.442	60.092	49.640	283.980	25.465	29.982
AVERAGE	74.129	302.390	280.789	100.623	67.932	**11.674**	61.807	63.776	380.986	26.009	67.953

The RMSE results are reflective of the average spectral distortion arising from the image fusion and the results are indicative of spectral quality in homogeneous zones in the image. The domain for RMSE value ranges from zero to infinity and lower values close to zero are considered ideal and reflective of high quality. The best results were produced by the IMVM method followed by the RCS method. The worst results were produced by PCA and the Brovey method.

Table 7. Spectral consistency: difference in variance (DIV).

BAND #	BAY	BRO	CNS	EHLERS	GRS	IMVM	MIHS	PANSHARP	PCA	RCS	WAVELET
1	7.538	1.286	1.475	2.983	6.768	0.676	4.921	5.468	13.377	1.053	7.142
2	6.743	1.120	1.342	2.892	5.500	0.660	4.737	4.612	10.110	1.439	2.243
3	5.604	1.114	1.479	3.438	5.125	0.506	5.371	4.037	9.236	1.319	2.494
AVERAGE	6.629	1.173	1.432	3.104	5.798	**0.614**	5.010	4.706	10.908	1.270	3.959

The results indicate the fusion quality over the whole image by showing difference in variances relative to the original one. The metric reveals a decrease or increase of information content as a result of the pansharpening process. The results are considered ideal positive when the information content decreases and undesirable when the information content increases. The ideal value should be close to 0. The IMVM pansharpening method produced the best results. The Brovey transform method ranked second and PCA had the worst performance.

Table 8. Spectral consistency: bias.

BAND #	BAY	BRO	CNS	EHLERS	GRS	IMVM	MIHS	PANSHARP	PCA	RCS	WAVELET
1	0.108	0.937	0.885	0.131	0.116	0.005	0.086	0.115	1.485	0.006	0.459
2	0.093	0.958	0.884	0.340	0.099	0.004	0.086	0.096	1.259	0.007	0.069
3	0.072	0.956	0.884	0.299	0.073	0.003	0.086	0.072	0.900	0.007	0.058
AVERAGE	0.091	0.950	0.884	0.257	0.096	**0.004**	0.086	0.094	1.215	0.007	0.195

The results are reflective of difference between the original image and fused image and the ideal value should be as small as possible. The IMVM method showed the best results followed by the RCS method. The Brovey transform method showed the worst performance.

3.3. Spectral Synthesis

The spectral synthesis results are shown in Table 9 below.

Table 9. Spectral synthesis: ERGAS.

BAND #	BAY	BRO	CNS	EHLERS	GRS	IMVM	MIHS	PANSHARP	PCA	RCS	WAVELET
1	7.654	28.079	26.385	7.049	8.553	4.988	8.951	8.655	23.266	6.617	13.176
2	6.432	26.975	24.875	6.819	7.092	3.726	5.808	7.139	19.217	6.113	4.341
3	4.793	25.658	23.720	6.576	5.034	2.649	6.354	5.317	13.579	5.698	4.257
AVERAGE	6.426	27.034	25.122	6.846	7.069	**3.921**	7.202	7.196	19.177	6.180	8.398

The best result is indicated by the smallest value. The results indicate that IMVM pansharpening method produced the best spectral synthesis followed by the RCS method. The Brovey method produced the worst synthesis.

The best spectral synthesis in IMVM was reflected by ERGAS 3.921, RCS 6.180, BAY 6.426, EHLERS 6.846, and GRS 7.069.

The IMVM algorithm produced the best pansharpening results in terms of spectral consistency and synthesis as revealed by the CC, bias, DIV, ERGAS, UIQI, RASE, and RMSE results. In terms of spectral consistency, one of the properties tested under Ward's criteria, the results of this study also show that the IMVM pansharpening technique had an average high correlation coefficient of 0.969 in the visible bands, the highest among the fusion algorithms tested in the study. The performance of the IMVM algorithm is further shown by the fact that it had the lowest bias and DIV values of 0.004 and 0.616, respectively. The superiority of the IMVM algorithm is further attested to by a very high UIQI value of 0.972. Such a high UIQI value demonstrates high spectral consistency as it considers factors such as loss of correlation, luminance, and contrast distortion. The IMVM algorithm had the best RMSE, RASE, and ERGAS values of 11.674, 3.741, and 1.062, respectively, the lowest amongst the tested pansharpened methods. The pansharpened image maintains almost the same natural color as the original multispectral images and the same level of spatial detail as the original panchromatic images. Results of the assessment also revealed that the IMVM algorithm had the best synthesis as shown by an ERGAS of 3.921, the lowest in the analysis, indicating that the fused image had minimum distortions and is quite similar to the reference image.

The RCS algorithm ranked second in the assessment and showed good results in terms of spectral consistency and synthesis. The ability of the algorithm to retain spectral information is shown by a correlation coefficient of 0.855, bias of 0.007, DIV of 1.270, ERGAS of 2.296, UIQI of 0.856, RASE of 8.239, and RMSE of 26.009. The other pansharpening methods that performed comparatively well in terms of spectral consistency were the wavelet principal components, MIHS, and PANSHARP methods. The PCA and Brovey methods produced consistently poor results in terms of spectral consistency as shown by the CC, bias, DIV, ERGAS, UIQI, RASE, and RMSE results.

Spectral synthesis is one of the properties that needs to be analyzed under Ward's three property criteria. As pointed out earlier, our results indicate that the IMVM algorithm produces the best spectral synthesis as shown by a very low ERGAS value of 3.921. Once again, the RCS algorithm ranked second with an ERGAS value of 6.180. Good spectral synthesis results were also obtained by the BAY, EHLERS, GRS, PANSHARP, and MIHS fusion techniques. The spectral synthesis results also revealed the poor performance of the Brovey, CNS, and PCA methods as shown by ERGAS values of 27.034, 25.122, and 19.177, respectively.

The third property evaluated in this study in terms of Ward's three property criteria related to spatial consistency. The correlation coefficient results ranked BAY, GRS, CNS, PANSHARP, RCS, PCA, and MIHS algorithms among the top-performing fusion techniques in terms of spatial consistency. While the Bayer algorithm was considered the best in terms of spectral consistency, most of the algorithms showed high spatial correlation with a correlation coefficient above 0.8 and the wavelet principal component method having the lowest value of 0.542. In contrast to the spectral consistency and synthesis results, the IMVM algorithm did not feature among the top-performing algorithms although it still had a high correlation coefficient of 0.784. This result seems to suggest there is a trade-off between spectral consistency and synthesis with spatial consistency.

While the IMVM and RCS pansharpening methods showed superior performance compared to the other fusion methods such as the PANSHARP, MIHS, GRS, wavelet transform, Bayesian, and EHLERS pansharpening techniques, the results of this study clearly show the credibility of these methods in terms of preservation of spectral and spatial information. When selecting the most ideal pansharpening method to use for practical applications, a trade-off is required in terms of factors such as the need for retention of scene radiometry, image sharpness, spatial and spectral consistency, and computational overhead.

Color distortion due to pansharpening could be attributed to the broadening of the panchromatic band into the near-infrared wavelength region in some modern sensors [26]. In the case of SPOT 6/7, the panchromatic bands have a spectral range of 450 nm to 745 nm, clearly overshooting the bands in the visible spectrum and encroaching into the near-infrared region that starts from the nominal red edge at 700 nm. This spectral coverage essentially spans over the visible spectrum that contains the blue (450–450 nm), green (530–590 nm), and red (625–695 nm) spectral channels. The extension of the panchromatic band affects the grey values of the panchromatic channel rendering some traditional pansharpening techniques less effective. The PANSHARP algorithm, for instance, is resilient to this challenge in that it is a statistics-based technique that uses the least-squares method to determine the best fit between the grey level values of the spectral bands being merged and adjusts the contribution of each band to the pansharpening result to minimize color distortions. Zhang [26,27] also highlights that the statistics-based approach utilized in the PANSHARP algorithm lessens the influence of dataset discrepancy and automates the pansharpening process. This assertion is supported in this study as shown by the superior performance of the IMVM, RCS, and Bayer's fusion techniques. The high performance of the IMVM image fusion algorithm was confirmed in similar studies. Witharana [44] reported that the IMVM algorithm produced some of the best fusion results when compared to a range of pansharpening algorithms when evaluated using CC, RMSE, Deviation Index (DI), SD, and DIV metrics. Nikolakopoulos and Oikonomidis [43] compared fusion techniques and confirmed that the LMVM algorithm produced the best spectral consistency and synthesis when applied to Worldview-2 data. As in our case, other techniques that produced favorable spectral consistency and synthesis results included PANSHARP, MIHS, EHLERS, GRM, and wavelet principal components techniques [44,45].

The shortcomings of traditional fusion techniques such as PCA, Brovey transform, and wavelet fusion are well described by Zhang [26]. To improve the quality of pansharpening results of traditional pansharpening methods some propositions recommended include stretching the principal components in PCA pansharpening to give them a spherical distribution. Alternatively, the first principal component could be cast-off. Modifications of traditional pansharpening techniques are necessary to deal with some of the limitations confronted in dealing with new satellite sensors. In a general sense, the quality of image geometric and radiometric rectifications done before the pansharpening directly impacts on the quality of all pansharpening results for all the image fusion techniques.

Lastly, the spectral integrity of pansharpened images is an important requirement for most quantitative remote sensing applications. While this study used an array of reference-based metrics to assess the image quality of various pansharpened images in terms of spectral consistency, spatial consistency, and image synthesis, the information content within the images was not quantified. The use of image information metrics such as Shannon entropy and Boltzmann entropy [46–50] enables the quantification of the average amount of information in the fused images and could be used to effectively assess the efficacy of various pansharpening methods in terms of the ability to retain or enhance both spectral and spatial information.

4. Conclusions

Pansharpening in increasingly becoming an important procedure critical in meeting the ever-increasing demands for high-resolution satellite imagery. Preservation of spectral and spatial information is an important requirement for most quantitative remote sensing applications. In this study, image quality metrics were used to evaluate the performance of twelve image fusion techniques. Twelve pansharpening algorithms were presented in this study and the IMVM algorithm was the best in terms of spectral consistency and synthesis followed by the RCS algorithm. Although the IMVM and RCS image fusion techniques showed better results compared to the other pansharpening methods, it is pertinent to highlight that our study also showed the credibility of the other pansharpening algorithms in terms of spatial and spectral consistency as shown by the high correlation coefficients achieved in all methods. The spatial and spectral quality of the pansharpening could, therefore, be improved by implementing some modifications to the traditional pansharpening techniques to deal with the discrepancy that arises due to the broadened panchromatic band that extends to the near-red region. The use of statistics-based techniques such as the IMVM, PANSHARP, and Bayers algorithms used in this study could address this shortcoming. In terms of spatial consistency, BAY, GRS, CNS, PANSHARP, RCS, PCA, and MIHS algorithms showed very good spatial consistency as shown by the high spatial correlation coefficients. The study noted that the algorithms that ranked higher in terms of spectral consistency were outperformed by other competing algorithms in terms of spatial consistency. We, therefore, conclude that the selection of image fusion techniques is driven by the requirements of remote sensing application and a careful trade-off is necessary to account for the impact of scene radiometry, image sharpness, spatial and spectral consistency, and computational overhead.

Author Contributions: Conceptualization, P.M.; methodology, P.M.; validation, P.M., W.M., and N.M.; formal analysis, P.M.; investigation, P.M., W.M., and N.M.; resources, P.M.; writing—original draft preparation, P.M.; writing—review and editing, P.M., W.M., and N.M.; project administration, P.M. All authors have read and agreed to the published version of the manuscript.

Funding: This research received no external funding.

Conflicts of Interest: The authors declare no conflicts of interest.

References

1. Pohl, C.; Van Genderen, J.L. Review Article Multisensor Image Fusion in Remote Sensing: Concepts, Methods and Applications. *Int. J. Remote Sens.* **1998**, *19*, 823–854. [CrossRef]
2. Ranchin, T.; Wald, L. Fusion of high spatial and spectral resolution images: The ARSIS concept and its implementation. *Photogramm. Eng. Remote Sens.* **2000**, *66*, 49–61.
3. Siddiqui, Y. The modified IHS method for fusing satellite imagery. In Proceedings of the ASPRS 2003 Annual Conference Proceedings, Anchorage, Alaska, 5–9 May 2003; pp. 5–9.
4. Thomas, C.; Wald, L. Comparing distances for quality assessment of fused images. *EARSEL Symp.* **2007**, 101–111.
5. Thomas, C.; Wald, L.; Thomas, C.; Wald, L.; Mtf-based, A.; Thomas, C.; Paris, M.D.; Wald, L.; Paris, M.D. A MTF-Based Distance for the Assessment of Geometrical Quality of Fused Products. In Proceedings of the 9th IEEE International Conference on Information Fusion, Florence, Italy, 10–13 July 2006; pp. 1–7.
6. Wang, Z.; Bovik, A.C.; Sheikh, H.R.; Simoncelli, E.P. Image quality assessment: From error visibility to structural similarity. *IEEE Trans. Image Process.* **2004**, *13*, 600–612. [CrossRef]
7. Yuhendra; Alimuddin, I.; Sumantyo, J.T.S.; Kuze, H. Assessment of pan-sharpening methods applied to image fusion of remotely sensed multi-band data. *Int. J. Appl. Earth Obs. Geoinf.* **2012**, *18*, 165–175. [CrossRef]
8. Alparone, L.; Wald, L.; Chanussot, J.; Thomas, C.; Gamba, P.; Bruce, L.M. Comparison of pansharpening algorithms: Outcome of the 2006 GRS-S data-fusion contest. *IEEE Trans. Geosci. Remote Sens.* **2007**, *45*, 3012–3021. [CrossRef]
9. Amro, I.; Mateos, J.; Vega, M.; Molina, R.; Katsaggelos, A.K. A survey of classical methods and new trends in pansharpening of multispectral images. *Eurasip J. Adv. Signal Process.* **2011**, *2011*, 1–22. [CrossRef]
10. Xu, Q.; Zhang, Y.; Li, B. Recent advances in pansharpening and key problems in applications. *Int. J. Image Data Fusion* **2014**, *3*, 175–195. [CrossRef]
11. De Béthune, S.; Muller, F.; Donnay, J.-P. Fusion of multispectral and panchromatic images by local mean and variance matching filtering techniques. In Proceedings of the Second International Conference en Fusion of Earth Data, Sophia Antipolis, France, 28–30 January 1998; pp. 31–36.
12. Chen, Y.; Zhang, G. A Pan-Sharpening Method Based on Evolutionary Optimization and IHS Transformation. *Math. Probl. Eng.* **2017**, *2017*. [CrossRef]
13. Ehlersa, M.; Klonusa, S.; Åstrandb, P.J.; Rossoa, P. Multi-sensor image fusion for pansharpening in remote sensing. *Int. J. Image Data Fusion* **2010**, *1*, 25–45. [CrossRef]
14. Ghassemian, H. A review of remote sensing image fusion methods. *Inf. Fusion* **2016**, *32*, 75–89. [CrossRef]
15. Strait, M.; Rahmani, S.; Markurjev, D.; Advisor, F.; Wittman, T. Evaluation of Pan-Sharpening Methods. 2008. Available online: https://pdfs.semanticscholar.org/a67f/0678c147df99c275f2064ea4b0d78d290528.pdf (accessed on 10 March 2020).

16. Wald, L.; Ranchin, T.; Mangolini, M. Fusion of satellite images of different spatial resolutions: Assessing the quality of resulting images. *Photogramm. Eng. Remote Sens.* **1997**, *63*, 691–699.
17. Blaschke, T. Object based image analysis: A new paradigm in remote sensing? In Proceedings of the American Society for Photogrammetry and Remote Sensing Annual Conference, ASPRS 2013, Baltimore, MD, USA, 26–28 March 2013; Volume 24, pp. 36–43.
18. Cheng, Y.; Pedersen, M.; Chen, G. Evaluation of image quality metrics for sharpness enhancement. *Int. Symp. Image Signal Process. Anal. ISPA* **2017**, *18*, 115–120.
19. DrÇŽguÅ£, L.; Csillik, O.; Eisank, C.; Tiede, D. Automated parameterisation for multi-scale image segmentation on multiple layers. *Isprs J. Photogramm. Remote Sens.* **2014**, *88*, 119–127.
20. Ghosh, A.; Joshi, P.K. Assessment of pan-sharpened very high-resolution WorldView-2 images. *Int. J. Remote Sens.* **2013**, *34*, 8336–8359. [CrossRef]
21. Cakir, H.I.; Khorram, S. Pixel level fusion of panchromatic and multispectral images based on correspondence analysis. *Photogramm. Eng. Remote Sens.* **2008**, *74*, 183–192. [CrossRef]
22. Ehlers, M. Multisensor image fusion techniques in remote sensing. *ISPRS J. Photogramm. Remote Sens.* **1991**, *46*, 19–30. [CrossRef]
23. Duran, J.; Buades, A.; Coll, B.; Sbert, C.; Blanchet, G. A survey of pansharpening methods with a new band-decoupled variational model. *Isprs J. Photogramm. Remote Sens.* **2017**, *125*, 78–105. [CrossRef]
24. Li, H.; Jing, L.; Tang, Y. Assessment of pansharpening methods applied to worldview-2 imagery fusion. *Sensors* **2017**, *17*, 89. [CrossRef]
25. Meng, X.; Shen, H.; Li, H.; Zhang, L.; Fu, R. Review of the pansharpening methods for remote sensing images based on the idea of meta-analysis: Practical discussion and challenges. *Inf. Fusion* **2019**, *46*, 102–113. [CrossRef]
26. Zhang, Y. Understanding image fusion. *Photogramm. Eng. Remote Sens.* **2004**, *70*, 657–661.
27. Zhang, Y. Problems in the fusion of commercial high-resolution satelitte as well as Landsat 7 images and initial solutions. *Int. Arch. Photogramm. Remote Sens. Spat. Inf. Sci.* **2002**, *34*, 587–592.
28. Kalpoma, K.A.; Kudoh, J. Image fusion processing for IKONOS 1-m color imagery. *IEEE Trans. Geosci. Remote Sens.* **2007**, *45*, 3075–3086. [CrossRef]
29. Zhang, Y.; He, B.; Li, X. A Pan-sharpening method appropriate to vegetation applications. *Chin. Opt. Lett.* **2009**, *7*, 781–783. [CrossRef]
30. Vrabel, J.; Doraiswamy, P.; Stern, A. Application of hyperspectral imagery resolution improvement for site-specific farming. In Proceedings of the ASPRS 2002 Conference Proceedings, Washington, DC, USA, 19–26 April 2002.
31. Vrabel, J.C.; Doraiswamy, P.; McMurtrey, J.E., III; Stern, A. Demonstration of the accuracy of improved-resolution hyperspectral imagery. In Proceedings of the Algorithms and Technologies for Multispectral, Hyperspectral, and Ultraspectral Imagery VIII, Anaheim, CA, USA, 11–13 April 2017; International Society for Optics and Photonics: Washington, DC, USA, 2002; Volume 4725, pp. 556–567.
32. King, R.L.; Wang, J. A wavelet based algorithm for pan sharpening Landsat 7 imagery. In Proceedings of the IGARSS 2001. Scanning the Present and Resolving the Future. Proceedings. IEEE 2001 International Geoscience and Remote Sensing Symposium (Cat. No. 01CH37217), Sydney, Australia, 9–13 July 2001; Volume 2, pp. 849–851.
33. Lemeshewsky, G.P. Multispectral image sharpening using a shift-invariant wavelet transform and adaptive processing of multiresolution edges. In *Proceedings of the Visual Information Processing XI*; International Society for Optics and Photonics: Washington, DC, USA, 2002; Volume 4736, pp. 189–200.
34. Lemeshewsky, G.P. Multispectral multisensor image fusion using wavelet transforms. In *Proceedings of the Visual Information Processing VIII*; International Society for Optics and Photonics: Washington, DC, USA, 1999; Volume 3716, pp. 214–222.
35. Strang, G.; Nguyen, T. *Wavelets and Filter Banks*; SIAM; Wellesley-Cambridge Press: Cambridge, MA, USA, 1996.
36. Laben, C.A.; Brower, B.V. Process for Enhancing the Spatial Resolution of Multispectral Imagery Using Pan-Sharpening. U.S. Patent No. 6,011,875, 4 January 2000.
37. Sarp, G. Spectral and spatial quality analysis of pan-sharpening algorithms: A case study in Istanbul. *Eur. J. Remote Sens.* **2014**, *47*, 19–28. [CrossRef]

38. CNES OTB CookBook. 2018. Available online: https://www.orfeo-toolbox.org/tag/cookbook/ (accessed on 14 January 2020).
39. Fasbender, D.; Radoux, J.; Bogaert, P. Bayesian data fusion for adaptable image pansharpening. *Ieee Trans. Geosci. Remote Sens.* **2008**, *46*, 1847–1857. [CrossRef]
40. Al-Rubiey, I.J. Increase the Intelligibility of Multispectral Image Using Pan-Sharpening Techniques for Many Remotely Sensed Images. *IBN Al-Haitham J. Pure Appl. Sci.* **2017**, *28*, 29–41.
41. Wald, L. *Data Fusion: Definitions and Architectures: Fusion of Images of Different Spatial Resolutions*; Presses des MINES: Paris, France, 2002.
42. Zoran, L.F. Quality evaluation of multiresolution remote sensing images fusion. *UPB Sci. Bull. Ser. C* **2009**, *71*, 38–52.
43. Du, V.Q.; Younan, N.H.; King, R. Shah n the performance evaluation of pan-sharpening techniques. *IEEE Geosci. Remote Sens. Lett.* **2007**, *4*, 518–522. [CrossRef]
44. Nikolakopoulos, K.; Oikonomidis, D. Quality assessment of ten fusion techniques applied on worldview-2. *Eur. J. Remote Sens.* **2015**, *48*, 141–167. [CrossRef]
45. Witharana, C.; Civco, D.L.; Meyer, T.H. Evaluation of pansharpening algorithms in support of earth observation based rapid-mapping workflows. *Appl. Geogr.* **2013**, *37*, 63–87. [CrossRef]
46. Jagalingam, P.; Hegde, A.V. A Review of Quality Metrics for Fused Image. In Proceedings of the Aquatic Procedia, Mangaluru, India, 1 January 2015; pp. 133–142.
47. Price, J.C. Comparison of the Information Content of Data from the LANDSAT-4 Thematic Mapper and the Multispectral Scanner. *IEEE Trans. Geosci. Remote Sens.* **1984**, *22*, 272–281. [CrossRef]
48. Shannon, C.E. A mathematical theory of communication. *Bell Syst. Tech. J.* **1948**, *27*, 379–423. [CrossRef]
49. Verde, C.N.; Mallinis, G.; Tsakiri-Strati, M.; Georgiadis, C.; Patias, P. Assessment of radiometric resolution impact on remote sensing data classification accuracy. *Remote Sens.* **2018**, *10*, 1267. [CrossRef]
50. Roberts, J.W.; van Aardt, J.A.; Ahmed, F.B. Assessment of image fusion procedures using entropy, image quality, and multispectral classification. *J. Appl. Remote Sens.* **2008**, *2*, 023522.

© 2020 by the authors. Licensee MDPI, Basel, Switzerland. This article is an open access article distributed under the terms and conditions of the Creative Commons Attribution (CC BY) license (http://creativecommons.org/licenses/by/4.0/).

Article

Data-Driven Redundant Transform Based on Parseval Frames

Min Zhang [1], Yunhui Shi [1,*], Na Qi [1] and Baocai Yin [1,2]

[1] Beijing Key Laboratory of Multimedia and Intelligent Software Technology, Faculty of Information Technology, Beijing University of Technology, Beijing 100124, China; lengyuewuyan@yeah.net (M.Z.); qina@bjut.edu.cn (N.Q.); ybc@bjut.edu.cn (B.Y.)
[2] Computer Science and Technology, Dalian University of Technology, Dalian 116023, China;
* Correspondence: syhzm@bjut.edu.cn

Received: 18 January 2020; Accepted: 17 April 2020; Published: 22 April 2020

Abstract: The sparsity of images in a certain transform domain or dictionary has been exploited in many image processing applications. Both classic transforms and sparsifying transforms reconstruct images by a linear combination of a small basis of the transform. Both kinds of transform are non-redundant. However, natural images admit complicated textures and structures, which can hardly be sparsely represented by square transforms. To solve this issue, we propose a data-driven redundant transform based on Parseval frames (DRTPF) by applying the frame and its dual frame as the backward and forward transform operators, respectively. Benefitting from this pairwise use of frames, the proposed model combines a synthesis sparse system and an analysis sparse system. By enforcing the frame pair to be Parseval frames, the singular values and condition number of the learnt redundant frames, which are efficient values for measuring the quality of the learnt sparsifying transforms, are forced to achieve an optimal state. We formulate a transform pair (i.e., frame pair) learning model and a two-phase iterative algorithm, analyze the robustness of the proposed DRTPF and the convergence of the corresponding algorithm, and demonstrate the effectiveness of our proposed DRTPF by analyzing its robustness against noise and sparsification errors. Extensive experimental results on image denoising show that our proposed model achieves superior denoising performance, in terms of subjective and objective quality, compared to traditional sparse models.

Keywords: parseval frame; transform; sparse representation

1. Introduction

A transform is a classical technique in signal processing, such as compression, classification, and recognition [1–5]. Traditional transforms, based on analytic orthogonal bases such as DCT, DFT, and Wavelets [1,6], suffer from two shortcomings: they do not depend on the data, and they reconstruct each image by approximation in the same subspace spanned by a non-redundant basis of the transforms, which limits the compact representation of natural signals.

Various models for sparse approximation have appeared in recent decades and play a fundamental role in modeling natural signals, with applications of denoising [7–10], super-resolution [11–13], and compression [1]. Such techniques exploit the sparsity of natural signals in analytic transform domains such as DCT, DFT, and various learning-based dictionaries [14–16].

There are two typical models for sparse representation: synthesis [10,14,15] and analysis [16–19] models. So far, most sparse models rely on the concept of synthesis, which represents the underlying signal as a sparse combination of atoms from a given dictionary. Specifically, $\mathbf{x} = \mathbf{D}\boldsymbol{\alpha}$, where $\mathbf{x} \in \mathbb{R}^N$ is the original signal, $\mathbf{D} \in \mathbb{R}^{N \times M}$ is the given dictionary whose columns are the atoms, and $\boldsymbol{\alpha} \in \mathbb{R}^M$ is the sparse coefficient, which is usually measured by the ℓ_0-norm $\|\cdot\|_0$. A learning analysis sparse model was proposed by Elad [14,19], formulated as $\|\Omega x\|_0 = r$ with notation similar to that of the synthesis one. Instead of reconstructing the signal using a few atoms in dictionary (like in the synthesis model), an analysis model decomposes a signal in a sparse fashion, based on an assumption that the signal lies in a sparse subset of the dictionary.

An analysis model can be straightforwardly regarded as a forward transform if its corresponding backward transform Ω^* is available. Recent research on transforms [2,4,5,20,21] has demonstrated the advantages of applying sparse constraints in transform learning. Motivated by this idea, many studies have been devoted to image denoising [5,20], classification [3,4], and other signal processing methods [21]. Learning-based transforms with sparse constraints measure the transform error, called sparsificaiton error, in the analysis or frequency domain, rather than in the temporal domain. Given training data $\mathbf{X} \in \mathbb{R}^{N \times L}$ with signal vectors $\mathbf{x}_i \in \mathbb{R}^N, i = 1, \ldots, L$ as its columns, the problem of training a square sparsifying transform $\mathbf{W} \in \mathbb{R}^{N \times N}$ [21] is formulated as

$$\min_{\mathbf{W},\mathbf{Y}} \|\mathbf{W}\mathbf{X} - \mathbf{Y}\|_F^2 + \mu \|\mathbf{W}\|_F^2 - \lambda \log \det(\mathbf{W}) \qquad (1)$$

$$\text{s.t. } \|\mathbf{y}_i\|_0 \leq s,$$

where $\mathbf{y}_i, i = 1, 2, \ldots, L$ are the columns of $\mathbf{Y}$ satisfying a sparse constraint and $\mu \|\mathbf{W}\|_F^2 - \lambda \log \det(\mathbf{W})$ is a regularizer, which keeps $\mathbf{W}$ non-singular.

As we can see, learning-based models effectively reveal the relationship between the transform and the data. The square transform, which consists of a non-redundant basis, cannot express complicated images. In 2014, an overcomplete transform learning model called OCTOBOS [20] was proposed, which consists of a series of square transforms to represent different features of natural images. However, the number of transforms must be pre-defined, which admits limited flexibility in applications.

In recent years, frames, as an overcomplete system, have been applied in image processing such as denoising [22,23], image compressive [24] and high resolution image reconstruction [25]. A frame can be regarded as an extension of an orthogonal basis, as a frame $\Phi \in \mathbb{R}^{N \times M} (N < M)$ also spans an N-dimensional space. Compared to a general frame, a tight frame (e.g., wavelet tight frames [26], ridgelets [27], curvelets [28], shearlets [29], and others) can achieve wider use, as the lower and upper frame bounds are equal. A tight frame inherits the good characteristics of an orthogonal basis in signal processing, as its rows are orthogonal [30]. In a sparse representation, a redundant frame serves as an overcomplete dictionary to represent the signal [23]. With the development of data-driven approaches, learning-based tight frames have recently been researched [31–33]. In [31], redundant tight frames were used in compressed sensing. In [32], tight frames were applied to few-view image reconstruction. In [33], a data-driven method was presented, in which the dictionary atoms associated with a tight frame are generated by filters. In general, these studies model the frame learning problem in the dictionary learning form with tight frame constraints. These methods focus on tight frames, as the singular values of a tight frame are equal, which leads to simple optimization. A tight frame is a Parseval frame if the frame bounds are equal to 1. In fact, a Parseval frame is a redundant extension of the concept of a standard orthogonal basis. Due to its super-performance in linear signal representation, it can be well-used in sparse signal representation and optimization.

In this paper, we propose a data-driven redundant transform model based on Parseval frames (DRTPF for short), and present a model for learning DRTPF as well as a corresponding algorithm for solving the model. The algorithm consists of a sparse coding phase and a transform learning phase. The sparse coding phase updates the sparse coefficients and a threshold value using a conventional Batch Orthogonal Matching Pursuit (BtOMP) and pointwise thresholding. The transform learning phase performs the update of the frame using Gradient Descent and a relaxation or contraction singular values mapping, as well as updating the dual frame, in an atom-wise manner, using Least Squares. The advantages of the proposed DRTPF model (as well as the algorithm) are demonstrated with natural image denoising. To summarize, this paper makes the following contributions:

1. We propose the DRTPF method by integrating redundant Parseval frames with sparse constraints. The DRTPF method consists of a forward transform and a backward transform, which correspond to a frame and its dual frame, respectively. In other words, DRTPF bridges synthesis and analysis models by assuming that two models share almost the same sparse coefficients.
2. DRTPF outperforms traditional transforms and frames by learning from data which exploits the features of natural images, whereas traditional transforms and frames admit a uniform representation of various images, which tend to fail to characterize the intrinsic individual-specific features.
3. Traditional transforms are usually orthogonal transforms and the signals remain isometric, yet they suffer from weak robustness due to their strict properties. In contrast, DRTPF preserves the signals in a bounded fashion, which admits higher robustness and flexibility.
4. We propose a model for learning DRTPF and compare DRTPF with traditional transforms and sparse models in robustness analysis and image denoising experiments. Both qualitative and quantitative results demonstrate that DRTPF outperforms traditional transforms and sparse models.

The rest of this paper is organized as follows. Section 2 reviews the related work on frames. Section 3 proposes the framework of DRTPF, including the form of DRTPF (Section 3.1) and the learning model and corresponding algorithm for DRTPF (Section 3.2). In Section 4, we demonstrate the effectiveness of our DRTPF model by analyzing the convergence of the corresponding algorithm and give experimental results on robustness analysis and image denoising, as well as evaluating the effectiveness of DRTPF compared with traditional transforms and sparse models.

2. Related Work

Let $\mathbf{H}$ be an N-dimensional discrete Hilbert space. A sequence $\{\boldsymbol{\phi}_i\}_{i=1}^M \in \mathbf{H}$ is a frame if and only if there exist two positive numbers A and B such that [30]

$$A\|\mathbf{x}\|_2^2 \leq \sum_{i=1}^M |<\mathbf{x}, \boldsymbol{\phi}_i>|^2 \leq B\|\mathbf{x}\|_2^2 \quad \forall \mathbf{x} \in \mathbf{H}^N. \tag{2}$$

A and B are called the bound of the frame and we call formula 2 the frame condition, as it is a termination of frame. Furthermore, $\{\boldsymbol{\phi}_i\}_{i=1}^M$ is tight if $A = B$ is possible [30]. In particular, $\{\boldsymbol{\phi}_i\}_{i=1}^M$ is a Parseval frame if $A = B = 1$ is satisfied. There are two associated operators can be defined between the Hilbert space $\mathbf{H}^N$ and a Square integrable Space $l_2^M(\cdot)$ once a frame is defined: One is the analysis operator, $\mathbf{T}$, defined by

$$(\mathbf{T}\mathbf{x})_i = <\mathbf{x}, \boldsymbol{\phi}_i>, \quad \forall \mathbf{x} \in \mathbf{H}^N, \tag{3}$$

and the other is its adjoint operator, $\mathbf{T}^*$, which is called the synthesis operator:

$$\mathbf{T}^*\mathbf{c} = \sum_{i=1}^M c\boldsymbol{\phi}_i \quad \forall \mathbf{c} = (c_i)_{i \in J} \in l_2^M(\mathbf{T}). \tag{4}$$

Then, the frame operator can be defined by the following canonical expansion

$$\mathbf{F}\mathbf{x} = \mathbf{T}^*\mathbf{T}\mathbf{x} = \sum_{i=1}^M <\mathbf{x}, \boldsymbol{\phi}_i> \boldsymbol{\phi}_i. \tag{5}$$

Let $\mathbf{x} \in \mathbb{R}^N$ be an arbitrary vector in $\mathbf{H}$. A reconstruction function is an expression with the following form

$$\mathbf{x} = \sum_{i=1}^M <\mathbf{x}, \boldsymbol{\psi}_i> \boldsymbol{\phi}_i, \quad \forall \mathbf{x} \in \mathbf{H}, \tag{6}$$

where the sequence $\{\psi_i\}_{i=1}^{M} \in \mathbf{H}$ is called the dual frame of $\{\phi_i\}_{i=1}^{M}$. Obviously, $\{\psi_i\}_{i=1}^{M}$ is not unique, unless $\{\phi_i\}_{i=1}^{M}$ is an orthogonal basis. In fact, for an arbitrary given frame $\{\phi_i\}_{i=1}^{M}$, there is a series of dual frames corresponding to it. The non-uniqueness of the dual frame allows us to achieve a better expression of the signal by optimizing the dual frame.

The frame $\mathbf{\Phi}$ and its dual frame $\mathbf{\Psi}$ can be stacked as the matrices $\mathbf{\Phi} = [\phi_1, \phi_2, \ldots, \phi_M]$ and $\mathbf{\Psi} = [\psi_1, \psi_2, \ldots, \psi_N]$, respectively. The matrices can be regard as sparse representation dictionaries, transform operators and so on. A frame $\mathbf{\Phi}$ with the bounds A and B means that the maximum and minimum singular values of it are equal to A and B respectively. What' more, the singular values of tight frame are all equal, particularly, the singular values of Parseval frame are all equal to 1. Thus, when the frame $\mathbf{\Phi}$ is applied as sparse representation dictionary or transform operator, its condition number are determined by $\frac{B}{A}$. In this way, the model will never provide degenerate dictionary or transform. In fact, frames are matrices with special structure.

3. Data-Driven Redundant Transform Model Based on Tight Frame

In this section, we present our data-driven redundant transform based on Parseval frames (DRTPF, Section 3.1) model along with an efficient redundant transform learning algorithm (Section 3.2) which contains the sparse coding algorithm (Section 3.2.1) and the transform pair update algorithm (Section 3.2.2).

3.1. Data-Driven Redundant Transform

In this subsection, we first propose a threshold-based reconstruction function, with the assumption that the signal is sparse in the dual frame domain. Then, we present the data-driven redundant transform based on Parseval frames model.

Let $\{\phi_i\}_{i=1}^{M}$ be a frame and $\{\psi_i\}_{i=1}^{M}$ be its dual frame. For convenience, we stack them as the matrices $\mathbf{\Phi} = [\phi_1, \phi_2, \ldots, \phi_M]$ and $\mathbf{\Psi} = [\psi_1, \psi_2, \ldots, \psi_N]$, respectively. Let $\mathbf{x} = \hat{\mathbf{x}} + \mathbf{e}$ be a signal vector, where $\hat{\mathbf{x}}$ is the original noiseless signal and $\mathbf{e}$ is a zero-mean white Gaussian noise. The frame reconstruction function (6) can be formulated as $\mathbf{x} = \mathbf{\Phi}\mathbf{\Psi}^T\mathbf{x} = \mathbf{\Phi}\mathbf{\Psi}^T(\hat{\mathbf{x}} + \mathbf{e})$. By assuming the sparse prior of signals over the $\mathbf{\Psi}$ domain, we apply a columnwise hard thresholding operator $\mathcal{S}_\lambda(\cdot)$ (which shall be defined in the next subsection) on $\mathbf{\Psi}^T(\hat{\mathbf{x}} + \mathbf{e})$, such that

$$\hat{\mathbf{x}} = \mathbf{\Phi}\mathcal{S}_\lambda(\mathbf{\Psi}^T\mathbf{x}), \qquad (7)$$

where λ is a vector with elements λ_i corresponding to ψ_i, $i = 1, 2, \ldots, M$. Apparently, $\mathcal{S}_\lambda(\mathbf{\Psi}^T\mathbf{x})$ is the sparse coefficients of $\mathbf{x}$ under $\mathbf{\Psi}$ in the sense of an analysis model, while it also serves as the sparse coefficients under $\mathbf{\Phi}$ in the sense of a synthesis model. In other words, Equation (7) admits that the synthesis and analysis models share almost the same sparse coefficients.

As we all know, the standard orthogonal basis, which is a significant tool in signal representation and transformation, is a special kind of frame with frame bounds $A = B = 1$. In fact, the standard orthogonal basis is a special case of a Parseval frame. In order to exceed the so-called *perfect reconstruction property* of the standard orthogonal basis in signal representation and transform, we refer to the Parseval frame. Therefore, we propose the data-driven redundant transform based on Parseval frame (DRTPF), as follows

$$\mathbf{y} \leftarrow \mathcal{S}_\lambda(\mathbf{\Psi}^T\mathbf{x}), \tag{8}$$

$$\hat{\mathbf{x}} \leftarrow \mathbf{\Phi}\mathbf{y}, \tag{9}$$

$$\text{s.t. } \mathbf{\Psi}\mathbf{\Phi} = \mathbf{I}, \tag{10}$$

$$\|\mathbf{y}\|_0 \leq s,$$

$$\sum_{i=1}^{M} |<\mathbf{x}, \boldsymbol{\phi}_i>|^2 = \|\mathbf{x}\|_2^2, \tag{11}$$

where (8) is the forward transform and (9) is the backward transform. The relationship between $\mathbf{\Phi}$ and $\mathbf{\Psi}$ is formulated as (10), which implies the relationship between the frame and its dual frame. The forward transform operator $\mathbf{\Psi}$ is also a Parseval frame, as it is a dual frame of $\mathbf{\Phi}$. Thus, the projection of the signal $\mathbf{x}$ over the $\mathbf{\Psi}$ domain can be formulated as

$$\sum_{i=1}^{M} |<\mathbf{x}, \boldsymbol{\psi}_i>|^2 = \|\mathbf{x}\|_2^2. \tag{12}$$

Equation (12) indicates that the transform coefficients of the proposed DRTBF are bounded by the original signal $\mathbf{x}$. This constraint leads to a more robust result than traditional sparse models.

To convert DRTPF into an optimization problem, (11) can be written as the more compact expression $\mathbf{\Phi}\mathbf{\Phi}^T = \mathbf{I}$, which characterizes $\mathbf{\Phi}$ in a way that is unrelated to the data. This property indicates that the rows of the frame $\mathbf{\Phi}$ are orthogonal, thus satisfying the so-called *perfect reconstruction property* which ensures that a given signal can be perfectly represented by its canonical expansion (in a manner similar to orthogonal bases).

Assuming $\mathbf{X} \in \mathbb{R}^{N \times L}$ is the training data with signal vectors $\mathbf{x}_i \in \mathbb{R}^N, i = 1, 2, \ldots, L$ as its columns, an optimization model for training DRTPF can be written as

$$\min_{\mathbf{\Phi},\mathbf{\Psi},\lambda,\mathbf{Y}} \|\mathbf{X} - \mathbf{\Phi}\mathbf{Y}\|_F^2 + \eta_1\|\mathbf{Y} - \mathcal{S}_\lambda(\mathbf{\Psi}^T\mathbf{x})\|_F^2 + \eta_2\|\mathbf{Y}\|_0 + \eta_3\|\mathbf{\Phi}\mathbf{\Psi}^T - \mathbf{I}\|_F^2$$

$$\text{s.t. } \mathbf{\Phi}\mathbf{\Phi}^T = \mathbf{I}. \tag{13}$$

The dual frame condition $\mathbf{\Phi}\mathbf{\Psi}^T = \mathbf{I}$ and the Parseval frame condition $\mathbf{\Phi}\mathbf{\Phi}^T = \mathbf{I}$ imply that the difference of $\mathbf{\Phi}$ and $\mathbf{\Psi}$ is in the null space of $\mathbf{\Phi}$. Denote $[\mathbf{a}_1^T, \mathbf{a}_2^T, \cdots, \mathbf{a}_N^T]^T = \mathbf{\Phi} - \mathbf{\Psi}$. The vectors $\mathbf{a}_i, i = 1, 2, \cdots, N$ are orthogonal to $\mathbf{\Phi}$. Thus, it is clear that the dual frame $\mathbf{\Psi}$ contains two subspaces: one spanned by $\mathbf{\Phi}$ and the one spanned by the $\mathbf{a}_i, i = 1, 2, \cdots, N$.

3.2. Transform Learning for the Drtbf Model

As there are no existing algorithm for solving problem (13), we apply the alternative direction method (ADM) and divide (13) into two sub-problems: A sparse coding phase, which updates the sparse coefficients $\mathbf{Y}$ and the threshold value λ, (Section 3.2.1), and the transform operator pair update phase, which computes $\mathbf{\Phi}$ and $\mathbf{\Psi}$, (Section 3.2.2).

3.2.1. Sparse Coding Phase

This subsection presents the sparse coding method for the proposed DRTBF model, in which the sparse coefficients of $\mathbf{Y}$ are obtained by OMP, and the threshold values λ are obtained by a designed elementwise method.

The Y Subproblem

The pursuit of **Y** is equivalent to solving the following problem with fixed $\boldsymbol{\Phi}$, $\boldsymbol{\Psi}$, and λ:

$$\hat{\mathbf{Y}} = \arg\min_{\mathbf{Y}} \|\mathbf{X} - \boldsymbol{\Phi}\mathbf{Y}\|_F^2 + \eta_1 \|\mathbf{Y} - \mathcal{S}_\lambda(\boldsymbol{\Psi}^T \mathbf{x})\|_F^2 + \eta_2 \|\mathbf{Y}\|_0, \tag{14}$$

which can be easily solved by OMP [14,34], as (14) can be easily converted to the classical synthesis sparse expression $\min \|\mathbf{Z} - \mathbf{D}\mathbf{Y}\|_F^2$ such that $\|\mathbf{Y}\|_0$, where $\mathbf{Z} = [\mathbf{X} \ \sqrt{\eta_1}\mathcal{S}_\lambda(\boldsymbol{\Psi}^T\mathbf{x})]$ and $\mathbf{D} = [\boldsymbol{\Phi} \ \sqrt{\eta_1}\mathbf{I}]$.

The λ Subproblem

With fixed $\boldsymbol{\Phi}$, $\boldsymbol{\Psi}$, and **Y**, finding λ is equivalent to solving the following problem

$$\hat{\lambda} = \arg\min_{\lambda} \|\mathbf{Y} - \mathcal{S}_\lambda(\boldsymbol{\Psi}^T \mathbf{x})\|_F^2, \tag{15}$$

which can be decomposed into M individual optimization problems $\arg\min_{\lambda_i} \|\bar{\mathbf{y}}_i - \mathcal{S}_{\lambda_i}(\boldsymbol{\psi}_i^T \mathbf{X})\|_2^2$, $i = 1, \ldots, M$. By denoting $\mathcal{J}_i := \text{supp}(\mathcal{S}_{\lambda_i}(\boldsymbol{\psi}_i^T \mathbf{X}))$ to be the set of indices of non-zero elements of $\mathcal{S}_{\lambda_i}(\boldsymbol{\psi}_i^T \mathbf{X})$, we have

$$\mathcal{S}_{\lambda_i}(\boldsymbol{\Psi}^T \mathbf{x}_j) = \boldsymbol{\Psi}^T \mathbf{x}_j, \ \forall j \in \mathcal{J}_i$$
$$\mathcal{S}_{\lambda_i}(\boldsymbol{\Psi}^T \mathbf{x}_j) = 0, \ \forall j \in \{1, \ldots, L\} \setminus \mathcal{J}_i.$$

As the cardinality of $\mathcal{J}_i$ depends on λ_i, we transform (15) to another optimization problem:

$$\hat{\lambda}_i = \arg\min_{\lambda_i} \underbrace{\sum_{j \in \{1,\ldots,L\} \setminus \mathcal{J}_i} y_{ij}^2}_{f(\lambda_i)} + \underbrace{\sum_{j \in \mathcal{J}_i} (y_{ij} - \boldsymbol{\psi}_i^T \mathbf{x}_j)^2}_{g(\lambda_i)}, \tag{16}$$

where y_{ij} denotes the (i,j)th entry of **Y** and $\mathbf{x}_i$ denotes the ith column of **X**. Denote $l(\lambda_i)$ as

$$l(\lambda_i) = \sum_{j \in 1,2,\cdots,L \setminus \mathcal{J}} (y_{ij} - \boldsymbol{\psi}_i^T \mathbf{x}_j)^2 \tag{17}$$

We observe that the function $f(\lambda_i)$ is a monotonically increasing function and that $g(\lambda_i)$ is monotonically decreasing. We take $\boldsymbol{\psi}_i^T \mathbf{x}_i, i = 1, 2, \ldots, L$ as candidates and compute all the values of $f(\lambda_i) + g(\lambda_i)$. Then, the optimal λ_i should lie in an interval determined by $\boldsymbol{\psi}_i^T \mathbf{x}_k$ and $\boldsymbol{\psi}_i^T \mathbf{x}_l$, which correspond to the smallest and the second smallest values of $f(\lambda_i) + g(\lambda_i)$, respectively. Then, any suitable value for λ_i can be selected. The algorithm for the threshold is summarized as Algorithm 1.

3.2.2. Transform Pair Update Phase

The $\boldsymbol{\Psi}$ Subproblem

With fixed **Y** and λ, the optimization problem to obtain $\boldsymbol{\Psi}$ is given by

$$\hat{\boldsymbol{\Psi}} = \arg\min_{\boldsymbol{\Psi}} \|\mathbf{Y} - \mathcal{S}_\lambda(\boldsymbol{\Psi}^T \mathbf{X})\|_F^2 + \frac{\eta_3}{\eta_1} \|\boldsymbol{\Phi}\boldsymbol{\Psi}^T - \mathbf{I}\|_F^2. \tag{18}$$

Algorithm 1: Sparse coding algorithm.

Input and Initialization:

Training data $X \in \mathcal{R}^{N \times L}$, iteration number r, initial value $\lambda = 0$.

Output:

Sparse coefficients Y, and threshold values λ

Process:

1: Compute the sparse coefficients Y via (14), according to the OMP algorithm [14,34].
2: Sort the columns of X and y in increasing order of $|\psi_i^T X|$.
3: **For** $i = 1:r$

    For $j = 1:L$

    Compute all the possible values for $f(\lambda_i) + g(\lambda_i)$ by $f(\psi_i^T x_j) = f(\psi_i^T x_{j-1}) + (y_{ij})^2$; $l(\psi_i^T x_j) = l(\psi_i^T x_{j-1}) + (y_{ij} - \psi_i^T x_j)^2$; $g(\psi_i^T x_j) = \|\psi_i^T x\|_2^2 - l(\psi_i^T x_j)$.; Denote them as a vector ν.

    End for

4: Sort the elements of $|\psi_i^T X|$ and the columns of X in descending order of ν. Denote the first and second samples as x_{i_1} and x_{i_2}. Set $\lambda_i = \frac{|\psi_i^T x_{i_1}| + |\psi_i^T x_{i_2}|}{2}$.

End for

Such a problem is a highly nonlinear optimization problem, due to the definition of $\mathcal{S}_\lambda$. We (columnwise) solve Ψ by updating each column of Ψ while fixing others. The product $\Phi\Psi^T$ can be written as

$$\Phi\Psi^T = \sum_{p=1}^{N} \psi_p \phi_p^T = \psi_i \phi_i^T - (I - \sum_{p \neq i}^{N} \psi_p \phi_p^T). \tag{19}$$

For each ψ_i, we solve the following subproblem:

$$\min_{\psi_i} \|\bar{y}_i - \mathcal{S}_{\lambda_i}(\psi_i^T X)\|_2^2 + \frac{\eta_3}{\eta_1} \|\psi_i \phi_i - z\|_2^2, \tag{20}$$

where $z = I - \sum_{p \neq i}^{N} \psi_p \phi_p^T$. We denote $\mathcal{J}_i$ to be the indices (as before), and then separate the problem into the two following sub-problems:

$$\hat{\psi}_i^1 = \arg\min_{\psi_i} \sum_{j \in \mathcal{J}_i} (y_{ij} - \psi_i^T x_j)^2 + \frac{\eta_1}{\eta_3} \|\psi_i \phi_i^T - z\|_2^2, \tag{21}$$

$$\hat{\psi}_i^2 = \arg\min_{\|\psi_i\|_2 = 1} \sum_{j \in \{1,\ldots,L\} \setminus \mathcal{J}_i} (\psi_i^T x_j)^2, \tag{22}$$

where y_{ij} denotes the (i, j)th entry of Y and x_i denotes the ith column of X. Equation (21) is a quadratic optimization, while Equation (22) has a closed form solution given by the normalized singular vector corresponding to the smallest singular value of $X^{\mathcal{J}}$. Based on the solutions of the two sub-problems, we give the solution of (20) as the average of the two solutions; that is, $\hat{\psi}_i = \frac{1}{2}(\hat{\psi}_i^1 + \|\hat{\psi}_i^1\|_2 \hat{\psi}_i^2)$. Please note that the second solution is added with the magnitude of the norm of the first solution, as (21) serves as a dominant term for the Ψ subproblem, while the solution of (22) maintains no energy but direction.

The Φ Subproblem

With fixed $\mathbf{Y}$, λ, and $\mathbf{\Psi}$, the model to obtain $\mathbf{\Phi}$ is given by

$$\min_{\mathbf{\Phi}} \|\mathbf{X} - \mathbf{\Phi}\mathbf{Y}\|_F^2 + \eta_3 \|\mathbf{\Phi}\mathbf{\Psi}^T - \mathbf{I}\|_F^2$$

$$\text{s.t. } \mathbf{\Phi}\mathbf{\Phi}^T = \mathbf{I}. \tag{23}$$

We convert (24) to an optimization problem which is formulated as

$$\min_{\mathbf{\Phi}} \|\mathbf{X} - \mathbf{\Phi}\mathbf{Y}\|_F^2 + \eta_3 \|\mathbf{\Phi}(\mathbf{\Phi} - \mathbf{\Psi})^T\|_F^2. \tag{24}$$

We denote the target function (24) by $h(\mathbf{\Phi})$ and apply the gradient descent method to the unconstrained version of (24) and project the solution to the feasible space. The gradient is given by

$$\begin{aligned}\nabla h(\mathbf{\Phi}) &= (\mathbf{\Phi}\mathbf{Y} - \mathbf{X})\mathbf{Y}^T + \eta_3[\mathbf{\Phi}(\mathbf{\Phi} - \mathbf{\Psi})^T(\mathbf{\Phi} - \mathbf{\Psi}) + \mathbf{\Phi}(\mathbf{\Phi} - \mathbf{\Psi})^T\mathbf{\Phi}] \\ &= (\mathbf{\Phi}\mathbf{Y} - \mathbf{X})\mathbf{Y}^T + \eta_3 \mathbf{\Phi}(\mathbf{\Phi} - \mathbf{\Psi})^T(2\mathbf{\Phi} - \mathbf{\Psi}).\end{aligned} \tag{25}$$

We summarize our overall algorithm in Algorithm 2.

Algorithm 2: Transform pair learning algorithm.

Input and Initialization:

Training data $\mathbf{X}$, frame bound (A, B), iteration num.

Build frames $\mathbf{\Phi} \in \mathbb{R}^{M \times N}$ and $\mathbf{\Psi} \in \mathbb{R}^{M \times N}$, either by using random entries or using N randomly chosen data.

Output:

Frames $\mathbf{\Phi}$, $\mathbf{\Psi}$, Sparse coefficients $\mathbf{Y}$, and thresholding values λ

Process: For l=1:num

Sparse Coding Step:

1: Compute the sparse coefficients $\mathbf{Y}$ and the thresholding values λ via **Algorithm**(1).

Frame Update Step:

2: Update $\mathbf{\Psi}$ columnwise. Compute $\mathbf{W} = \mathcal{S}_\lambda(\mathbf{\Psi}^T\mathbf{X})$.

For $i = 1 : M$

Denote $\hat{\mathcal{J}}_i$ as the indices of zeros in the ith column of $\mathbf{W}$. Set $\boldsymbol{\psi}_i^T \mathbf{X}^{\hat{\mathcal{J}}_i} = 0$. Compute $\boldsymbol{\psi}_i$ via (21) and (22).

End For

3: Update $\mathbf{\Phi}$ via Gradient Descent, which is given as (25) and the step length is usually set to 0.01.

End for

---

4. Image Denoising

We introduce a novel problem formulation for signal denoising by applying the data-driven redundant transform DRTPF. Image denoising aims to reconstruct a high-quality image $\mathcal{I}$ from its noise corrupted version $\mathcal{L}$, which is formulated as $\mathcal{L} = \mathcal{I} + \mathbf{n}$ where $\mathbf{n}$ is a noisy signal. For a signal satisfying the DRTPF, the denoising model based on DRTPF is formulated as

$$\{\hat{\mathcal{I}}, \hat{\mathbf{Y}}, \hat{\lambda}\} = \min_{\mathcal{I},\{\mathbf{y}_i\}_{i=1}^N,\lambda} \|\mathcal{L} - \mathcal{I}\|_F^2 + \gamma \sum_i \|\mathbf{R}_i\mathcal{I} - \mathbf{\Phi}\mathbf{y}_i\|_F^2 + \gamma_1 \sum_i \|\mathbf{y}_i - \mathcal{S}_\lambda(\mathbf{\Psi}^T\mathbf{R}_i\mathcal{I})\|_F^2 + \gamma_2 \sum_i \|\mathbf{y}_i\|_0, \quad (26)$$

where $\mathbf{R}_i$ is an operator that extracts the ith patch of the image $\mathcal{I}$, $\mathbf{y}_i$ is the ith column of $\mathbf{Y}$, and λ denotes a vector $[\lambda_1, \lambda_2, \cdots, \lambda_M]$ with λ_j operating on the jth element of $\mathbf{\Psi}^T\mathbf{R}_i\mathcal{I}$. On the right side of Equation (26), the first term is the global force, which demands proximity between the degraded image $\mathcal{L}$ and its high-quality version $\mathcal{I}$. The other terms are the local constraints, which ensure that every patch at location i satisfies the DRTPF. This formulation assumes that the noise image $\mathcal{L}$ can be approximated by a noiseless image $\hat{\mathcal{I}}$ whose patch extracted by $\mathbf{R}_i$ can be sparsely represented by the given transforms $\mathbf{\Phi}$ and $\mathbf{\Psi}$.

To solve Problem (26), we apply Algorithm 1 to obtain the sparse coefficients $\mathbf{Y}$ and the threshold values λ. We mainly state the iterative method to obtain $\mathcal{I}$.

Denote $\mathbf{d}^k = \mathbf{\Psi}^T\mathbf{R}_i\mathcal{I}^{k-1}$. We set $\mathbf{O}^k$ as an index set that satisfies $|\mathbf{d}_l^k| \leq \lambda_l, l \in \mathbf{O}^k$. Set $\mathbf{u}^k \in \mathcal{R}^M$ as a vector with elements $\mathbf{u}_l^k = \begin{cases} 1 & l \in \mathbf{O}^k, \\ 0 & \text{otherwise}. \end{cases}$ Then, the non-convex and non-smooth thresholds can be removed, with the substitution $\mathbf{y}_i - \mathcal{S}_\lambda(\mathbf{\Psi}^T\mathbf{R}_i\mathcal{I}^k) \approx \mathbf{y}_i - \mathbf{\Psi}^T\mathbf{R}_i\mathcal{I}^k \odot \mathbf{u}^k$. Thus, in the kth step, the problem that needs to be solved can be expressed as

$$\{\hat{\mathcal{I}}^k\} = \min_{\mathcal{I}^{k-1}} \|\mathcal{L} - \mathcal{I}^{k-1}\|_F^2 + \gamma \sum_i \|\mathbf{R}_i\mathcal{I}^{k-1} - \mathbf{\Phi}\mathbf{y}_i\|_F^2 + \gamma_1 \sum_i \|\mathbf{y}_i - \mathbf{\Psi}^T\mathbf{R}_i\mathcal{I}^{k-1} \odot \mathbf{u}^k\|_F^2, \quad (27)$$

where $\odot$ is pointwise multiplication. This convex problem can be easily solved by the gradient descent algorithm.

We summarize the restoration algorithm in Algorithm 3.

Algorithm 3: Denoising algorithm.

Input

Training dictionaries $\mathbf{\Phi}$, $\mathbf{\Psi}$, iteration number r, a degraded image $\mathcal{L}$, set $\mathcal{I}_0 = \mathcal{L}$.

Output:

The high-quality image $\hat{\mathcal{I}}$

1: Compute $\mathbf{Y}$ and λ via the method in Algorithm 1.

For k=1:r

2: Compute $\mathbf{d}^k = \mathbf{\Psi}^T\mathbf{R}_i\mathcal{I}^{k-1}$. Set $\mathbf{O}^k$ as an index set that satisfies $|\mathbf{d}_l^k| \leq \lambda_l, l \in \mathbf{O}^k$. Set

$$\mathbf{u}_l^k = \begin{cases} 1 & l \in \mathbf{O}^k, \\ 0 & \text{otherwise}. \end{cases}$$

3: Solve Problem (27) via the gradient descent algorithm.

End for

---

5. Experimental Results

We demonstrate the effectiveness of our proposed data-driven redundant transform based on Parseval frames (DRTPF) by first analyzing the robustness of the model against Gaussian White Noise. Then we discuss the convergence of the proposed transform learning algorithm and the ability of the proposed DRTPF to provide low sparsification errors. Finally, we evaluate the effectiveness of the proposed DRTPF by applying it to nature image denoising. We use a fixed step size in the transform update and denoising steps of our algorithms.

5.1. Robustness Analysis

In this subsection, we illustrate the robustness of DRTPF by training DRTPF using the image 'Barbara' and testing DRTPF for denoising the same image with Gaussian white noise added. The noise level (standard deviation) δ ranged from 20 to 60 with a step size of 2. In the experiment, the frames Φ and Ψ of size 100×200 were initialized as 1D overcomplete DCT (ODCT) and 10×10 overlapping mean-subtracted patches were used. The patch size was set as 8×8 with stripe 1. We set the parameters $\eta_1 = 1.1$ and $\eta_3 = 1e + 7$, and η_2 was replaced by the ℓ_0 thresholding 0.6σ (i.e., $\|\mathbf{Y}\|_0 \leq 0.6\sigma$). For comparison, our proposed algorithm was compared with K-SVD [14]. The size of dictionary learnt from K-SVD is 8×256 at its optimal state, according to the previous work.

We show the denoising result in Figure 1, from which it is apparent that with higher noise, our DRTPF method outperformed K-SVD more and more. In other words, our proposed model has good robustness. In fact, in our model, the sparse coefficients are calculated accurately by the inner product of the signals and the frame Ψ, and are limited to a certain range. Theoretically, it should be more robust. The learnt transforms Φ and Ψ are illustrated in Figure 2. These figures show that our frame learning method can capture the features in both analysis and synthesis ways. Figure 3 shows two exemplified visual results on the images 'Babara' at noise level $\sigma = 30$ and $\sigma = 50$. From Figure 3 we know that our proposed DRTPF can obtain more clearer features than K-SVD [14].

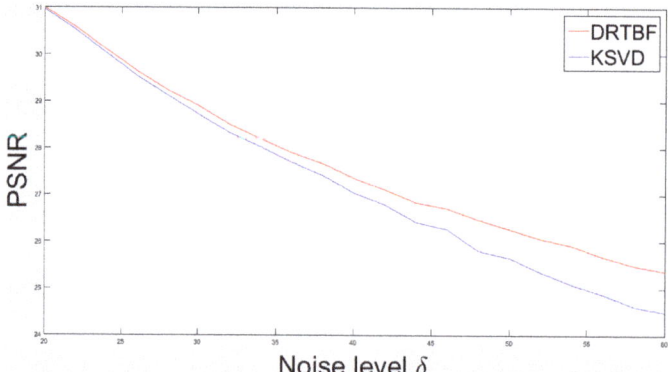

Figure 1. Robustness Analysis. DRTPF is trained and tested using the image 'Barbara'. The X-label is the noise level δ and the Y-label is the PSNR. It can be seen that DRTPF performs more robustly than K-SVD.

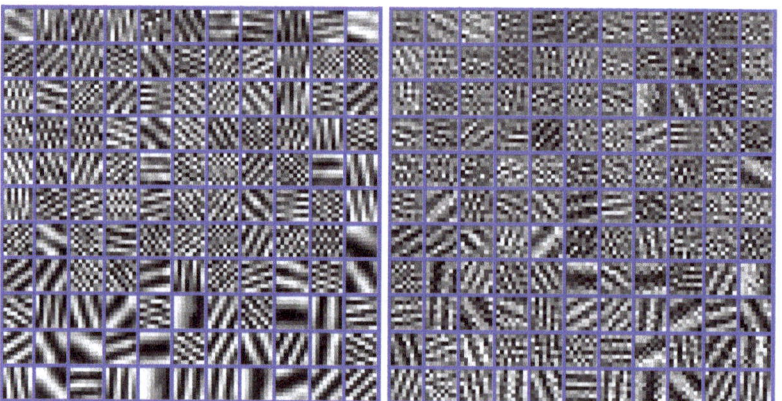

Figure 2. The learnt operators Φ (**left**) and Ψ (**right**) for *barbara*.

Figure 3. Reconstruction of *barbara* using DRTPF (**left**) and K-SVD [14] (**right**). Top: $\sigma = 30$; bottom: $\sigma = 50$.

5.2. Sparsification of Nature Images

A classic sparsifying transform learning model [21] is formulated as

$$\min_{\mathbf{W},\mathbf{Y}} \|\mathbf{W}\mathbf{X} - \mathbf{Y}\|_F^2 - \lambda \log \det \mathbf{W} + \mu \|\mathbf{W}\|_F^2$$

$$\text{s.t. } \|\mathbf{Y}_i\|_0 \leq s \; \forall \, i, \tag{28}$$

where $\mathbf{X}$ is the training data, $\mathbf{Y}$ are the sparse coefficients, and $\mathbf{W}$ is the learnt transform. The quality of the learnt transforms in the experiment [21] was judged based on their condition number and sparsification error. Similar to the experimental setting in [21], we also evaluated the effectiveness of the transforms learnt from our DRTPF by their condition number and sparsification error. The l_2-norm condition number of the transform operator $\mathbf{\Phi}$ is denoted as the ratio of the maximum singular value to the minimum singular value of $\mathbf{\Phi}$; that is,

$$\mathcal{K}_{\mathbf{\Phi}} = \frac{\delta_{max}(\mathbf{\Psi})}{\delta_{min}(\mathbf{\Psi})}. \tag{29}$$

In our case, the condition number $\mathcal{K}_{\mathbf{\Phi}} = 1$, as the maximum and minimum singular values (which are determined by the optimal frame bounds) must be equal to 1. Similarly, we can obtain that $\mathcal{K}_{\mathbf{\Psi}} = 1$. It is the best case when the transform operators have condition number equal to 1. The sparsification error of the model (28) is defined as

$$SE = \|\mathbf{W}\mathbf{X} - \mathbf{Y}\|_F^2. \tag{30}$$

Similarly, we define the 'sparsification error' of the proposed DRTPF, to measure the energy loss due to sparse representation, which is formulated as

$$\widetilde{SE} = \|\mathbf{Y} - \mathcal{S}_\lambda(\mathbf{\Psi}^T \mathbf{X})\|_F^2. \tag{31}$$

The 'sparsification error' indicates the compact ability of the transform $\mathbf{\Psi}$ with reasonable ignorance of the thresholding operator $\mathcal{S}_\lambda(\cdot)$.

Figure 4. The test images 'Barbara', 'Lena', 'Hill', 'Couple', 'Boat', and 'Man'.

To demonstrate that our model and algorithms are insensitive to the initialized transforms, we applied the proposed sparse coding and transform operator pair learning algorithms to train a pair of transforms. The training data are patches of size 10×10 extracted from the image 'Babara' which is shown in Figure 4. The trained transform pair are of size 100×200. We extracted the patches with non-overlap and removed the DC values of every sample. We set the parameters $\eta_1 = 1.1$ and $\eta_3 = 1e + 7$, and η_2 was replaced by the ℓ_0 thresholding 0.6σ, as before. The matrices used for initialization were the 1D DCT matrix, the matrix with random columns sampled from the training data, and the redundant identity matrix. As the transform for DRTPF is redundant, the redundandt identity matrix here is formed as $[\mathbf{I}\ \mathbf{I}]$ where $\mathbf{I}$ is the identity matrix of size 100×100.

The convergence curve of the objective function and the 'sparsification error' are shown in Figure 5. From the left sub-figure of Figure 5 we know that our proposed algorithm for DRTPF is converged, and all the initializations converge to the same result after about 20 iterations which demonstrate that our proposed DRTPF and the corresponding algorithm are insensitive to different initializations. The right sub-figure of Figure 5 shows the 'sparsification error' of the three initialized methods, the 2D DCT transform of and the KLT transform. The 2D DCT is formed by the Kronecker product of two 1D DCT transform, i.e., $\mathbf{D} = \mathbf{D}_0 \otimes \mathbf{D}_0$, where $\mathbf{D}_0$ is the 1D DCT transform of size 8×8 and $\otimes$ denotes the Kronecker product. The KLT transform $\mathbf{K}$ of size 64×64 is obtained by principle component analysis (PCA) method. The 'sparsification error' of 2D DCT and KLT are calculated via the model in [21] at iteration zero. This figure shows that the 'sparsification error' of the proposed DRTPF model is also converged and insensitive to the initialization matrices. In fact, the loss function of the proposed DRTPF mainly contains two partions: $\|\mathbf{X} - \mathbf{\Phi Y}\|_F^2$ and $\|\mathbf{Y} - \mathcal{S}_\lambda(\mathbf{\Psi}^T\mathbf{X})\|_F^2$. The first partion is the recovery loss (i.e., the loss in temporal domain) and the second partion is the 'sparsification error' (i.e., the loss in frequency domain). Our proposed model aims to achieve low error both in temporal domain and frequency domain.

To illustrate the behavior of the proposed DRTPF in image representation, we choose six images shown in Figure 4 to train transforms and recover images. The Figure 6 shows the average sparsity curve and the recovery PSNR values with the increase of the sparsity. From the left sub-figure we know that the images are well sparsified along the iterative process. This figure is generated by setting $\|\mathbf{y}_i\|_0 < 5$ and the recovery PSNR is 32.27 dB. For each sample $\mathbf{x}_i$ vectorized by a 10×10 patch, its correspondinge sparse coefficients $\mathbf{y}_i$ is of length 200. It is easy to know that the sparsity rate is lower than 2.5%. Furthermore, less than 5% of the data need to be stored to recover an image with PSNR larger than 32.27 dB. The right sub-figure of Figure 6 shows the average recovery PSNR values with the increase of the sparsity which is a main measurement for the quality of the learnt transform. From the figure we know that in most of the case, our proposed DRTPF can obtain a better image quality in terms of PSNR with lower sparsity than the compared LST [21] method and the classic DCT transform. The ransform for LST [21] method and the classic DCT transform are of size 64×64. The transform of LST [21]is trained by 4096 8×8 samples extracted from every image shown in Figure 6 with the main of the patches removed. The experiment is set as them illustrated in the paper [21]. When the total sparsity of a 512×512 image is more than 47,000, the recovery results of the proposed DRTPF and the LST [21] are nearly the same. The recovery PSNR at sparsity 47,000 is 37.3 dB.

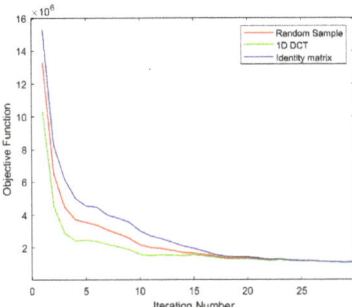
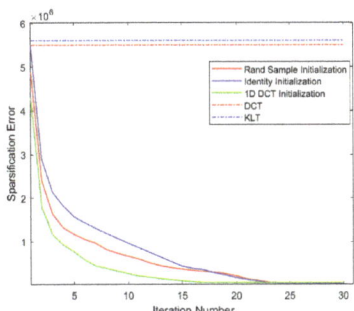

Figure 5. Convergence Curve and Sparsification Error. **Left**: The X-label is the iteration number. **Right**: The Y-label is the objective function and the sparsification error, respectively. It can be seen that our DRTPF learning algorithm is convergent and insensitive to initialization.

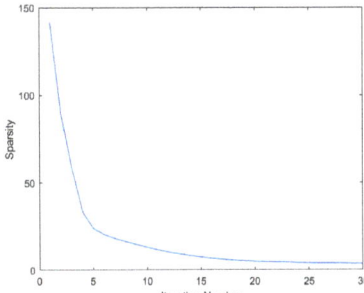
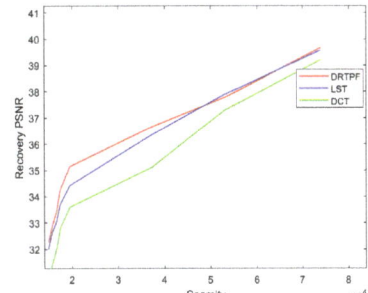

Figure 6. The average Sparsity and Recovery PSNR. **Left**: The X-label is the iteration number and the Y-label is the average sparsity. **Right**: The X-label is the average sparsity and the Y-label is the average Recovery PSNR.

5.3. Image Denoising

In this subsection, we evaluate the performance of our DRTPF model using six natural images of size 512×512, which are shown in Figure 4. We added Gaussian white noise to these images at different noise levels ($\sigma = 20, 30, 40, 50, 60$). We set the parameters $\eta_1 = 1.1$ and $\eta_3 = 1e + 7$, and η_2 was replaced by the ℓ_0 thresholding 0.6σ, as before. We compared DRTPF with the three most related methods of sparse representation: K-SVD [14], the overcomplete transform (T.KSVD) [3], the learning-based frame (DTF [33]), the BM3D [35] and WNNM [36]. The BM3D and WNNM are nonlocal-based methods with the parameters setting as in corresponding paper. We note that DTF works on filters, instead of image patches. In the experiment, our DRTPF method and K-SVD were the same as in Section 5.1. All methods were trained iteratively (25 times). The DTF method was initialized by 64 3-level Harr wavelet filters of size 16×16. The operator size of the T.KSVD method was 128×64 and the patch size it worked on was 8×8 overlapping mean-subtracted patches. The hard thresholding was $s = 30$.

Table 1 shows the comparison results, in terms of average PSNR. As shown in Table 1, our DRTPF method and the DTF method outperformed K-SVD and T.KSVD on most images, i.e., our proposed DRTPF outperforms K-SVD for 0.47 dB and outperforms T.KSVD for 0.76 dB at noise level $\sigma = 60$. This result implies that methods using frames are more robust against noise. Furthermore, the higher the noise level, the better the results of DRTPF method and the DTF method than K-SVD and T.KSVD. We can also see that our DRTPF method outperformed DTF on most of the images, especially when the noise level was very high. In fact, in our model, the sparse coefficients are calculated accurately by the inner product of the signals and the frame Ψ, and are limited to a certain range. Theoretically, it should perform better than the compared method. Figure 7 shows two exemplified visual results on the images 'Boat' and 'Man' at noise level $\sigma = 40$. The PSNR of the K-SVD, T.KSVD, DTF, and the proposed DRTPF are 27.17 dB, 26.14 dB, 26.99 dB, 27.34 dB for 'Man' and 27.23 dB, 26.45 dB, 27.20 dB and 27.39 dB for 'Boat'. Our proposed DRTPF and the DTF method provide more features and higher PSNR values of the two images than K-SVD and T.KSVD. Though the DTF provides higher PSNR values than K-SVD and T.KSVD, and better visual performance, the results of this method suffer from deformation and margin smoothing as it based on filter. The proposed DRTPF shows much clearer and better visual results than the other competing methods without any deformation.

Table 1. Average PSNR results of different noise levels on six images.

σ	Image	Barbara	Boat	Couple	Hill	Lena	Man	Average
20	K-SVD [14]	31.01	30.50	30.15	30.27	32.51	30.26	30.78
	T.KSVD [3]	30.02	29.30	29.25	29.21	31.45	29.01	29.71
	DTF [33]	31.07	30.35	30.20	30.31	32.56	30.07	30.76
	SSM-NTF	31.01	30.47	30.24	30.34	32.50	30.23	30.80
	BM3D [35]	32.01	31.02	30.88	30.85	33.19	30.83	31.47
	WNNM [36]	32.31	31.09	30.92	30.94	33.18	30.84	31.55
30	K-SVD [14]	28.75	28.60	28.07	28.51	30.59	28.43	28.83
	T.KSVD [3]	27.78	27.86	27.46	27.23	29.25	27.13	27.79
	DTF [33]	29.07	28.48	28.22	28.64	30.60	28.26	28.88
	SSM-NTF	29.00	28.63	28.24	28.66	30.73	28.49	28.96
	BM3D [35]	30.12	29.22	28.95	29.23	31.40	29.04	29.66
	WNNM [36]	30.32	29.30	29.02	29.33	31.50	29.10	29.76
40	K-SVD [14]	27.03	27.23	26.54	27.23	29.13	27.17	27.39
	T.KSVD [3]	26.35	26.45	25.98	26.45	28.20	26.14	26.60
	DTF [33]	27.58	27.20	26.87	27.49	29.25	26.99	27.56
	SSM-NTF	27.50	27.39	27.00	27.56	29.35	27.34	27.69
	BM3D [35]	28.68	27.92	27.58	28.08	30.11	27.83	28.37
	WNNM [36]	28.85	27.99	27.64	28.18	30.25	27.90	28.47
50	K-SVD [14]	25.71	26.05	25.42	26.29	27.92	26.18	26.26
	T.KSVD [3]	25.10	25.56	25.03	25.89	27.01	25.40	25.67
	DTF [33]	26.45	26.15	25.84	26.63	28.15	26.09	26.55
	SSM-NTF	26.43	26.32	25.99	26.79	28.40	26.40	26.72
	BM3D [35]	27.48	26.89	26.49	27.20	29.06	26.94	27.34
	WNNM [36]	27.70	26.97	26.60	27.35	29.23	27.01	27.48
60	K-SVD [14]	24.45	25.18	24.57	25.69	27.01	25.40	25.38
	T.KSVD [3]	24.50	24.88	24.36	25.40	26.60	24.78	25.09
	DTF [33]	25.64	25.33	25.04	25.91	27.22	25.38	25.75
	SSM-NTF	25.50	25.45	25.14	26.03	27.33	25.67	25.85
	BM3D [35]	26.36	26.02	25.61	26.44	28.14	26.18	26.46
	WNNM [36]	26.59	26.12	25.74	26.60	28.33	26.26	26.61

All the six methods can be classified to two categories (1) without any extra constraint, e.g., nonlocal similarity, and (2) with additional prior like nonlocal similarity. Our proposed DRTPF belongs to category (1). We would like to point out that our goal was to establish a redundant transform learning method but not focus on image denoising. Our model is plain without applying any extra prior, besides the basic sparsity characteristics of the signals. The experimental results demonstrate that our proposed models can achieve better performance than traditional sparse models in image denoising. However, the methods BM3D and WNNM are based on image nonlocal self-similarity (NSS). The NSS prior refers to the fact that for a given local patch in a natural image, one can find many similar patches to it across the image. Intuitively, by stacking nonlocal similar patch vectors into a matrix, this matrix should be a low-rank matrix and have sparse singular values. The exploitation of NSS has been used to significantly boost image denoising performance. We have not involved this prior into our model.

Figure 7. Visual comparison of reconstruction results by different methods on 'Man' and 'Boat'. From left to right: original, T.KSVD [3], K-SVD [14], DFT [33], and DRTPF.

6. Conclusions

In this paper, we propose a Parseval frame-based data-driven overcomplete transform (DRTPF) to capture features of images. We also propose the corresponding formulations, as well as algorithms for calculating the sparse coefficients and DRTPF model learning. We have proposed a general frame learning method without imposing any structure on the frame. By applying frames to redundant transforms, we combine the ideas of analysis and synthesis sparse models and let them share almost identical sparse coefficients. We conducted robustness analysis, sparsification of nature image and image denoising experiments, which demonstrated that DRTPF can outperform state-of-the-art models, as it exploits the underlying sparsity of natural signals by the integration of frames and sparse models.

In future work, we shall consider more efficient optimization algorithms for DRTPF, which facilitate the representation ability and application of the proposed method.

Author Contributions: M.Z. derived the theory, analyzed the data, performed the performance experiments, and wrote the original draft; Y.S. and N.Q. researched the relevant theory, participated in discussions of the work, and revised the manuscript; B.Y. supervised the project. All authors have read and agreed to the published version of the manuscript.

Funding: This work was supported by NSFC (No.61672066,61976011,U1811463, U19B2039, 61632006, 61906008, 61906009), Beijing municipal science and technology commission (No.Z171100004417023) and Common Program of Beijing Municipal Commission of Education (KM202010005018).

Acknowledgments: This work was supported by Beijing Advanced Innovation Center for Future Internet Technology, Beijing Key Laboratory of Multimedia, and Intelligent Software Technology. We deeply appreciate the organizations mentioned above.

Conflicts of Interest: The authors declare no conflict of interest.

References

1. Marcellin, M.W.; Gormish, M.J.; Bilgin, A.B.; Boliek, M.P. An overview of jpeg-2000. In Proceedings of the DCC 2000. Data Compression Conference, Snowbird, UT, USA, 28–30 March 2000; pp. 523–541.
2. Patel, K.; Kurian, N.; George, V. Time Frequency Analysis: A Sparse S Transform Approach. In Proceedings of the 2016 International Symposium on Intelligent Signal Processing and Communication Systems (ISPACS), Phuket, Thailand, 24–27 October 2016.
3. Eksioglu, M.; Bayir, O. K-SVD Meets Transform Learning: Transform K-SVD. *IEEE Signal Process. Lett.* **2014**, *21*, 347–351. [CrossRef]
4. Ravishankar, S.; Bresler, Y. Learning Sparsifying Transforms For Image Processing. In Proceedings of the 19th IEEE International Conference on Image Processing, Orlando, FL, USA, 30 September–3 October 2012.
5. Ravishankar, S.; Bresler, Y. Learning Doubly Sarse Transforms for Image Representation. In Proceedings of the 19th IEEE International Conference on Image Processing, Orlando, FL, USA, 30 September–3 October 2012.
6. Mallat, S.; Lepennec, E. Sparse geometric image representation with bandelets. *IEEE Trans. Image Process* **2005**, *14*, 423–438.
7. Elad, M.; Aharon, M. Image denoising via sparse and redundant representations over learned dictionaries. *IEEE Trans. Image Process* **2006**, *15*, 3736–3745. [CrossRef]
8. Dong, W.; Zhang, L.; Shi, G.; Li, X. Nonlocally Centralized Sparse Representation for Image Restoration. *IEEE Trans. Image Process* **2013**, *22*, 1620–1630. [CrossRef] [PubMed]
9. Qi, N.; Shi, Y.; Sun, X.; Yin, B. TenSR: Multi-dimensional Tensor Sparse Representation. In Proceedings of the 2016 IEEE Conference on Computer Vision and Pattern Recognition (CVPR), Las Vegas, NV, USA, 26 June–1 July 2016; pp. 5916–5925.
10. Mairal, J.; Bach, F.; Ponce, J.; Sapiro, G.; Zisserman, A. Non-local sparse models for image restoration. In Proceedings of the 2009 IEEE 12th International Conference on Computer Vision, Kyoto, Japan, 29 September–2 October 2009; pp. 2272–2279.
11. Wang, S.; Zhang, D.; Liang, Y.; Pan, Q. Semi-Coupled Dictionary Learning with Applications to Image Super-Resolution and Photo-Sketch Synthesis. In Proceedings of the 2012 IEEE Conference on Computer Vision and Pattern Recognition, Providence, RI, USA, 16–21 June 2012; pp. 2216–2223.
12. Yang, J.; Wang, Z.; Lin, Z.; Cohen, S.; Huang, T. Coupled dictionary training for image super-resolution. *IEEE Trans. Image Process* **2012**, *21*, 3467–3478. [CrossRef] [PubMed]
13. Yang, J.; Wright, J.; Huang, T.; Ma, Y. Image superresolution via sparse representation. *IEEE Trans. Image Process* **2010**, *19*, 2861–2873. [CrossRef] [PubMed]
14. Aharon, M.; Elad, M.; Bruckstein, A. K-SVD: An algorithm for designing overcomplete dictionaries for sparse representation. *IEEE Trans. Signal Process* **2006**, *54*, 4311–4322. [CrossRef]
15. Skretting, K.; Engan, K. Recursive least squares dictionary learning algorithm. *IEEE Trans. Signal Process* **2010**, *58*, 2121–2130. [CrossRef]
16. Yaghoobi, M.; Nam, S.; Gribonval, R.; Davies, M.E. Noise aware analysis operator learning for approximately cosparse signals. In Proceedings of the 2012 IEEE International Conference on Acoustics, Speech and Signal Processing (ICASSP), Kyoto, Japan, 25–30 March 2012; pp. 5409–5412.
17. Ophir, B.; Elad, M.; Bertin, N.; Plumbley, M. Sequential minimal eigenvalues—An approach to analysis dictionary learning. In Proceedings of the 2011 19th European Signal Processing Conference, Barcelona, Spain, 29 August–2 September 2011; pp. 1465–1469.
18. Rubinstein, R.; Peleg, T.; Elad, M. Analysis K-SVD: A Dictionary-Learning Algorithm for the Analysis Sparse Model. *IEEE Trans. Signal Process.* **2012**, *61*, 661–677. [CrossRef]
19. Rubinstein, R.; Faktor, T.; Elad, M. K-SVD dictionary-learning for the analysis sparse model. In Proceedings of the 2012 IEEE International Conference on Acoustics, Speech and Signal Processing (ICASSP), Kyoto, Japan, 25–30 March 2012; pp. 5405–5408.
20. Wen, B.; Ravishankar, S.; Bresler, Y. Learning Overcomplete Sparsifying Transforms With Block Cosparsity. In Proceedings of the ICIP, Paris, France, 27–30 October 2014.
21. Ravishankar, S.; Bresler, Y. Learning Sparsifying Transforms. *IEEE Trans. Signal Process.* **2013**, *61*, 1072–1086. [CrossRef]
22. Parekh, A.; Selesnick, W. Convex Denoising using Non-Convex Tight Frame Regularization. *IEEE Signal Process. Lett.* **2015**, *22*, 1786–1790. [CrossRef]

23. Lin, J.; Li, S. Sparse recovery with coherent tight frames via analysis Dantzig selector and analysis LASSO. *Appl. Comput. Harmon. Anal.* **2014**, *37*, 126–139. [CrossRef]
24. Liu, Y.; Zhan, Z.; Cai, J.; Guo, D.; Chen, Z.; Qu, X. Projected Iterative Soft-Thresholding Algorithm for Tight Frames in Compressed Sensing Magnetic Resonance Imaging. *IEEE Trans. Med. Image* **2016**, *35*, 2130–2140. [CrossRef] [PubMed]
25. Chan, H.; Riemenschneider, D.; Shen, L.; Shen, A.Z. Tight frame: An efficient way for high-resolution image reconstruction. *Appl. Comput. Anal.* **2004**, *17*, 91–115. [CrossRef]
26. Ron, A.; Shen, Z. Affine system in L2(Rd): The analysis of the analysis operator. *J. Funct. Anal.* **2013**, *148*, 408–447. [CrossRef]
27. Candes, E. Ridgelets: Estimating with ridge functions. *Ann. Statist.* **1999**, *31*, 1561–1599. [CrossRef]
28. Candes, E.J.; Donoho, D.L. Recovering edges in ill-posed inverse problems: Optimality of curvelet frames. *Ann. Statist.* **2002**, *30*, 784–842. [CrossRef]
29. Kutyniok, G.; Labate, D. Construction of regular and irregular shearlet frames. *J. Wavelet Theory Appl.* **2007**, *1*, 1–10.
30. Casazza, P.G.; Kutyniok, G.; Philipp, A.F. Introduction to Finite Frame Theory. In *Finite Frames*; Birkhäuser: Boston, MA, USA, 2012.
31. Cao, C.; Gao, X. Compressed sensing image restoration based on data-driven multi-scale tight frame. *J. Comput. Appl. Math.* **2017**, *309*, 622–629. [CrossRef]
32. Li, J.; Zhang, W.; Zhang, H.; Li, L.; Yan, A. Data driven tight frames regularization for few-view image reconstruction. In Proceedings of the 13th International Conference on Natural Computation, Fuzzy Systems and Knowledge Discovery, ICNC-FSKD 2017, Guilin, China, 29–31 July 2017; pp. 815–820.
33. Cai, J.; Ji, H.; Shen, Z.; Ye, G. Data-driven tight frame construction and image denoising. *Appl. Comput. Harmon. Anal.* **2014**, *37*, 89–105. [CrossRef]
34. Rubinstein, R.; Zibulevsky, M.; Elad, M. *Efficient Implementation of the K-SVD Algorithm Using Batch Orthogonal Matching Pursuit*; Technical Report CS-2008-08; Technion-Israel Institute of Technology: Haifa, Israel, 2008.
35. Katkovnik, V.; Foi, A.; Egiazarian, K.; Astola, J. From local kernel to nonlocal multiple-model image denoising. *Int. J. Comput. Vis.* **2010**, *86*, 1–32. [CrossRef]
36. Gu, S.; Zhang, L.; Zuo, W.; Feng, X. Weighted Nuclear Norm Minimization with Application to Image Denoising. In Proceedings of the 2014 IEEE Conference on Computer Vision and Pattern Recognition, Columbus, OH, USA, 23–28 June 2014; pp. 2862–2869.

© 2020 by the authors. Licensee MDPI, Basel, Switzerland. This article is an open access article distributed under the terms and conditions of the Creative Commons Attribution (CC BY) license (http://creativecommons.org/licenses/by/4.0/).

Article

Unconstrained Bilingual Scene Text Reading Using Octave as a Feature Extractor

Direselign Addis Tadesse, Chuan-Ming Liu * and Van-Dai Ta

Department of Computer Science and Information Engineering, National Taipei University of Technology (Taipei Tech), Taipei 106, Taiwan; t106999405@ntut.edu.tw (D.A.T.); t104999002@ntut.edu.tw (V.-D.T.)
* Correspondence: cmliu@csie.ntut.edu.tw; Tel.: +886-2-27712171 (ext. 4251)

Received: 16 February 2020; Accepted: 21 June 2020; Published: 28 June 2020

Featured Application: The potential applications of scene text reading are ordering large pictures and video databases by their literary substance, such as Bing Maps, Apple Maps, and Google Street View, as well as supporting visual impaired people.

Abstract: Reading text and unified text detection and recognition from natural images are the most challenging applications in computer vision and document analysis. Previously proposed end-to-end scene text reading methods do not consider the frequency of input images at feature extraction, which slows down the system, requires more memory, and recognizes text inaccurately. In this paper, we proposed an octave convolution (OctConv) feature extractor and a time-restricted attention encoder-decoder module for end-to-end scene text reading. The OctConv can extract features by factorizing the input image based on their frequency. It is a direct replacement of convolutions, orthogonal and complementary, for reducing redundancies and helps to boost the reading text through low memory requirements at a faster speed. In the text reading process, features are first extracted from the input image using Feature Pyramid Network (FPN) with OctConv Residual Network with depth 50 (ResNet50). Then, a Region Proposal Network (RPN) is applied to predict the location of the text area by using extracted features. Finally, a time-restricted attention encoder-decoder module is applied after the Region of Interest (RoI) pooling is performed. A bilingual real and synthetic scene text dataset is prepared for training and testing the proposed model. Additionally, well-known datasets including ICDAR2013, ICDAR2015, and Total Text are used for fine-tuning and evaluating its performance with previously proposed state-of-the-art methods. The proposed model shows promising results on both regular and irregular or curved text detection and reading tasks.

Keywords: octave convolution; bilingual scene text reading; Ethiopic script; attention

---

1. Introduction

Currently, reading text from a natural image is one of the hottest research issues in computer vision and document processing. It has many applications including ordering large pictures and video databases by their literary substance, such as Bing Maps, Apple Maps, Google Street View, and so on. Moreover, it allows for image mining, office automation, and support for the visually impaired. Thus, scene text is highly important for thoughtful and uniform services throughout the world. However, reading text from natural images poses several challenges, due to the use of different fonts (color, type, and size) and texts being written on more than one script. Moreover, imperfect image condition causes distorted text, and complex and inference backgrounds cause unpredictability. As a result, reading or spotting texts from a natural image becomes a challenging task.

Previously, several considerable research outputs were presented for scene text detection [1–5] and scene text recognition [6,7] independently, which led to a computational complexity and integration problem being used as a text-reading task. To improve these, an end-to-end scene text spotting method was presented in references [8–10], but it still needs improvement in terms of recognition accuracy, memory usage, and speed. For instance, in [11,12] a fully conventional network is applied for scene text detection and recognition by considering the detection and recognition problems independently. For scene text detection, a convolutional neural network (CNN) was applied to extract feature maps from the input image, and then different decoders were used to decode and detect the text region based on the extracted features [5,13,14].

Using the extracted sequences of features at the scene text detection phase, characters/words have been predicted with sequence prediction models [15,16]. These types of approaches led to heavy time cost and ignored the correlation in visual cues for images with a number of text regions, whereas both operations had real integrations. In general, previously proposed scene text detection and recognition approaches were problematic, especially when texts in the image are written in more than one script, different text sizes and text shapes are irregular. Furthermore, most research focused on English language and only a few presented other languages such as Arabic and Chinese. Except our previously presented scene text recognition method [17], there is no research output for scene text reading as well as scene text detection for Ethiopic script-based languages. Ethiopic script is used as a writing system for more than 43 languages, including Amharic, Geez, and Tigrigna.

Amharic is the official language of Ethiopia and the second-largest Semitic language after Arabic [18]. On the other hand, English is used as a teaching medium in secondary schools and higher education. As a result, English and Amharic languages are being used concurrently for different activities in most areas of the country. Thus, designing independent applications of scene text detection and scene text recognition requires multiple networks for solving individual sub-problems, which increases computational complexity and causes accuracy and integrity problems. Additionally, developing detection and recognition as independent sub-problems restrains the recognition of rotated and irregular texts. The characteristics of individual characters for complex languages, for example, Amharic language, in the script, and the availability of bilingual scripts in natural images make the scene text recognition methods to challenging when used independently for detection and recognition. Text detection and text recognition are relevant tasks in most operations and complement each other.

Recently, the proposed multilingual end-to-end scene text spotting system in [9,15,19] had a good result for several languages except for Ethiopic script-based languages. However, in their proposed method, they did not consider the frequency of features (high and low) and the effects of word length in the recognition. In this paper, a bilingual end-to-end trainable scene text reading model is proposed by extracting features from the input image based on their frequency and a time-restricted self-attention encoder-decoder module for recognition. Between the feature-extraction and recognition layers, we use a region proposal network, to detect the text area and predict the bounding boxes.

Figure 1 shows the architecture of the proposed system, which contains feature-extraction, detection, and recognition layers. In the first layer of our proposed network, we use a feature pyramid network (FPN) [20] with ResNet-50 to extract features. Inspired by reference [21], the ResNet-50 vanilla convolutions are replaced by octave convolutions (OctConv), except for the first convolution layer. The OctConv factorizes feature tensors based on their frequencies (high and low) which helps to effectively enlarge the receptive field in the original pixel space and improve recognition performance. Additionally, it optimizes the memory requirement by avoiding redundancy. As stated in [21], OctConv improves object-recognition performance and shows a state-of-the-art result. In the second layer, a region proposal network (RPN) is applied for predicting text/non-text regions and recognizing the bounding boxes of the predicted text region from the input image using the extracted feature at the first layer. Finally, by applying Region of Interest (RoI) pooling based on the predicted bounding boxes to the extracted features, word prediction is performed using a time-restricted self-attention encoder-decoder module. Our proposed bilingual text-reading model is originally presented to read texts from the natural image in an end-to-end manner. The major contributions of the article are summarized as follows:

1. Following [22], we prepare large syntactically generated bilingual (English and Amharic) scene text datasets. Additionally, we collect real datasets that have different shapes and written using the two scripts.
2. Our proposed model extracts feature by factorizing based on their frequencies (low and high), which helps to reduce both storage and computation costs. This also helps each layer gain a larger receptive field to capture more contextual information.
3. The proposed system can detect and read texts from an image that has arbitrary shapes, containing oriented, horizontal, and curved text.
4. The performance of the time-restricted attention encoder-decoder module is examined to predict words based on the extracted and segmented features.
5. Using the prepared dataset and well-known datasets, we perform several experiments and our model shows promising results.

The rest of the paper is organized as follows. Related works are presented in Section 2. In Section 3, we discuss the proposed bilingual end-to-end scene text reading methodology. A short description of the Ethiopic script and datasets that are used for training and evaluating the proposed model is described in Section 4. The experimental set-up and results are discussed in Section 5. Finally, a conclusion is drawn in Section 6.

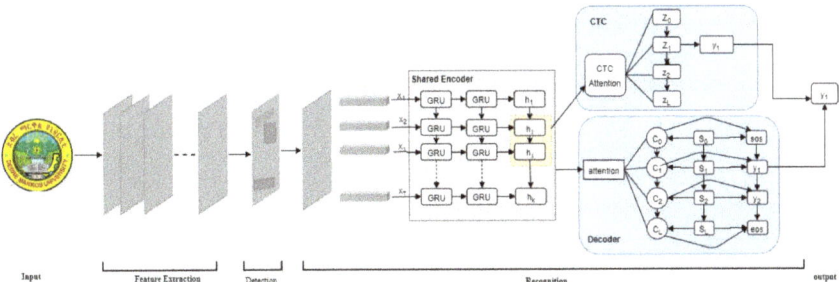

Figure 1. The architecture of the proposed bilingual end-to-end scene text reader model.

2. Related Work

Reading text from a natural image is currently an active field of investigation in computer vision and document analysis. In this section, we introduce related works, including scene text detection, scene text recognition, and text spotting (combining detection and recognition) techniques.

2.1. Scene Text Detection

Traditional and deep-learning machine-learning methods are used to detect texts from a natural image. In [1,3,23–25], scene text detection methods have been presented to detect and bind text areas from a natural image, but this approach has manual computation problems. Lee et al. [25] presented sliding-window-based methods measured by shifting over the image and determining text proximity based on local image highlights. In [26,27], a connected component analysis method was presented to detect scene texts using Stroke Width Transform (SWT) and Maximum Stable Extreme Region (MSER), respectively. However, these approaches are limited when it comes to detecting text regions from distorted images.

Recently, deep-learning techniques improved several machine-learning problems, including scene text detection and recognition problem. Tian et al. [1] presented a Connectionist Text Proposal Network (CTPN), which uses a vertical anchor mechanism that jointly predicts location and text/no-text scores of each fixed width. Shi et al. [14] introduced Segment Linking (SegLink), which is an oriented scene text detection method that segments and then links the text to complete instances using a linkage prediction. Ma et al. [28] presented a novel rotation-based framework to detect arbitrarily oriented texts found in natural images by proposing region proposal network (RPN) and rotation RoI pooling. A deep direct regression-based method for detecting multi-oriented scene text has been presented in [29]. Efficient and accuracy scene Text detector (EAST) [5] has been introduced to effectively detect words or text lines using a single neural network.

2.2. Scene Text Recognition

In the text-reading phases of natural images, text recognition is the second phase after scene text detection. This method can be implemented independently or after scene text detection phases. In the scene text recognition phase, the cropped text regions are fed either from the scene text detection phase or from the prepared input dataset, from which the sequences of labels are decoded. Previous attempts were made by detecting individual characters and refining misclassified characters. Such methods require training a strong character detector for accurately detecting and cropping each character out from the original word. These types of methods are more difficult for Ethiopic scripts due to their complexities. Apart from the character level methods, word recognition [12], sequence to label [30], and sequence to sequence [31] methods have been presented. Liu et al. [32] and Shi et al. [15] presented a spatial attention mechanism to transform a distorted text region from irregular input images into canonical pose suitable recognition. However, both the detection and recognition task performance are determined based on the extracted features. Previously proposed scene text detection and recognition of deep learning-based and conventional machine learning feature extraction methods do not consider the frequency of the input image. Following [21], in this paper, we propose an OctConv with ResNet-50 feature extractor, which extracts features by factorizing based on their frequencies.

2.3. Scene Text Spotting

Recently, several end-to-end scene text spotting methods have been introduced and have shown a remarkable result compared to independent scene text detection and recognition approaches. For instance, Li et al. [10] introduced an end-to-end text spotting technique from natural images using RPN as a text detector and attention Long Short Term Memory (LSTM) as a text recognizer. Liao et al. [8] presented an end-to-end scene text-reading method using Single Shot Detector (SSD) [33] and convolutional recurrent neural network (CRNN) for scene text detection and recognition, respectively. Liu et al. [34] introduced a unified network to detect and recognize multi-oriented scene texts from natural images. Lunadren et al. [35] introduced an octave-based fully convolutional neural network with fewer layers and parameters to precisely detect multilingual scene text. The most recently proposed scene text-reading models are summarized in Table 1.

Table 1. Summary of recently proposed end-to-end scene text recognition models.

Method	Model	Detection	Recognition	Year
Liao et al. [11]	TextBoxes	SSD-based framework	CRNN	2017
Bŭsta et al. [19]	Deep TextSpotter	Yolo v2	CTC	2017
Liu et al. [34]	FOTS	EAST with RoI Rotate	CTC	2018
Liao et al. [8]	TextBoxes++	SSD-based framework	CRNN	2018
Liao et al. [9]	Mask TextSpotter	Mask R-CNN	Character segmentation + Spatial attention module	2019

Improving the feature extraction and recognition network will improve scene text detection, recognition, and text spotting problems. In [21], an OctConv feature extraction method has been proposed for object detection and improves its performance. Octave convolution addresses spatial redundancy, which was not addressed in the previously proposed methods. The OctConv does not change the connectivity between feature maps and it is different from inception multi-path designs [36,37]. In our proposed bilingual text-reading method, we replace the ResNet-50 vanilla convolution with OctConv, which can operate quickly and produce accurate results in the extraction of features. As stated in [38], the limitation of Connectionist Temporal Classification (CTC), attention encoder-decoder, and hybrid (CTC and attention) method is improved using a time-restricted self-attention method for an automatic speech recognition system. In our proposed method, we integrate a time-restricted self-attention encoder-decoder module for recognition with feature extraction and bounding box detection layers.

3. Methodology

In this section, the details of the proposed bilingual scene text-reading model are presented. The architecture of the model, shown in Figure 1, is trained in an end-to-end manner that concurrently detects and recognizes words from a natural image.

3.1. Overall View of the Architecture

Our proposed architecture follows the architecture presented in [9,21]. Our proposed architecture has three functional components, feature-extraction layer, text/non-text detection layer, and recognition layer. In the feature-extraction layer, features are extracted from input natural images and passed to the next layer using an FPN [20] with ResNet-50 [39] by replacing the vanilla convolution with an octave convolution. Then, using the extracted features on the 1st layer as an input, a region proposal network (RPN) [40] predicts text/non-text area and bounding boxes of each text area. Finally, by applying RoI to the outputs of the 2nd layer, text segmentation, and word prediction are done using the time-restricted self-attention encoder-decoder module. Details of each layer are presented below.

3.2. Feature Extraction Layer

Feature extraction is one of the crucial steps in machine learning problems. In the deep learning era, several automatic feature extraction methods have been proposed, including [40–43]. These feature extraction methods were applied to several problem domains and produced good results. Recently, Chen et al. [21], proposed an OctConv method that extracts features based on their frequencies. We use Chen et al.'s feature extraction method to detect text/non-text regions. Naturally, texts found in natural images have different properties (i.e., size, orientation, shapes, and color). These cause a challenge in perfectly detecting the text/non-text region, which directly affects the performance of the recognition task. To overcome this challenge, we build high-level semantic feature maps using FPN with ResNet-50. Different from [9], in our proposed feature extraction layer, we replace vanilla convolutions by OctConv. This factorizes the mixed-feature map tensor into high and low-frequency maps, where the high-frequency feature map tensors encode with fine details, whereas the low-frequency feature map tensors encode with global structures. Compared to vanilla convolution, OctConv reduces spatial redundancy, memory cost, and computation cost.

For given spatial dimensions w and h with the number of feature maps c, the input feature tensor of a convolution layer will be $X \in \mathbb{R}^{c \times h \times w}$. In OctConv, the input vector X factorized along channel dimensions into low feature map (X^L) and high feature map (X^H) frequencies. As stated in [21], the factorization of high feature map and low feature map tensors are computed as follows:

$$X^H = X^{(1-\alpha)c \times h \times w} \tag{1}$$

$$X^L = X^{\alpha c \times \frac{h}{2} \times \frac{w}{2}} \tag{2}$$

where the value of $\alpha \in [0, 1)$.

In the factorization process, fine details are obtained on high-frequency feature maps, whereas differences in speed in spatial dimensions with respect to image location were obtained at low-frequency feature map tensors. This process maps the features that are compacted and replace spatial repetitive feature maps with different resolution maps. On these feature maps, an octave convolution is applied where the vanilla convolution does not work, due to different resolutions of high- and low-frequency feature maps. The octave convolution enables efficient inter-frequency communication and effectively operates on low- and high-frequency tensors. For the factorized high (X^H) and low (X^L) feature tensors, there is a corresponding output feature tensor Y^H and Y^L, respectively. To get each output feature tensor, inter ($Y^{H \to L}$, $Y^{L \to H}$) and intra ($Y^{L \to L}$, $Y^{H \to H}$) frequency convolution update is performed. Each output feature map at location (p, q) is computed using appropriate kernels (W^L and W^H), applying regular convolution for intra-frequency update and removing the need of explicitly computing and sorting on up/down sampling for inter-frequency communication as follows:

$$Y_{p,q}^H = \sum_{i,j \in N_k} \left(W_{i+\frac{k-1}{2}, j+\frac{k-1}{2}}^{H \to H} \right)^T X_{p+i, q+j}^H + \sum_{i,j \in N_k} \left(W_{i+\frac{k-1}{2}, j+\frac{k-1}{2}}^{L \to H} \right)^T X_{(\frac{p}{2}+i),(\frac{q}{2}+j)}^L \quad (3)$$

$$Y_{p,q}^L = \sum_{i,j \in N_k} \left(W_{i+\frac{k-1}{2}, j+\frac{k-1}{2}}^{L \to L} \right)^T X_{p+i, q+j}^L + \sum_{i,j \in N_k} \left(W_{i+\frac{k-1}{2}, j+\frac{k-1}{2}}^{H \to L} \right)^T X_{(2*p+0.5+i),(2*p+0.5+j)}^H \quad (4)$$

The recognition performance of the model is improved because OctConv can extract a larger receptive field for low-frequency feature maps. Most commonly, text found in natural images has low frequencies. Compared to vanilla convolution, OctConv convolves at a factor of 2 receptive fields.

3.3. Text Region Detection Layer

Using RPN and taking the extracted feature maps as an input, text/non-text regions are detected. Following [9] and [20], we assign five anchors at different stages {P2, P3, P4, P5, P6} with the area of anchors {32^2, 64^2, 128^2, 256^2, 512^2}, respectively. Besides, to handle different text sizes {0.5, 1, 2} aspect ratios are implemented at each stage. By doing this, text proposal features are generated. These features are further extracted using RoI align [41], which preserves a more accurate location compared to RoI pooling. Finally, the Fast Region (R)-CNN [41] generates precise bounding boxes for the texts found in the input natural image. Using a soft-Non-maximal suppression (NMS) [42] technique, we select one bounding box for those texts that have more than one bounding box.

3.4. Segmentation and Recognition Layer

After texts are detected at the detection layer, text segmentation and recognition of words are performed. Text instance regions are segmented using four consecutive convolution layers with 3×3 filters and deconvolution layers with 2×2 filters and strides on the outputs of RoI align feature in the previous layer, with predicted bounding boxes. Finally, the outputs of the segmented text instance feature $x = (x_1, x_2, \ldots, x_T)$ are fed for a time-restricted self-attention encoder-decoder module.

In [43], a time-restricted (attention window) self-attention encoder-decoder module is presented for automatic speech recognition, which produces a state-of-the-art result by improving the limitations of CTC (i.e., hard alignment problem and conditional independence constraints) and the attention encoder-decoder module. Unlike [9], we use a time-restricted self-attention module using a bidirectional Gated Recurrent Unit (GRU) as an encoder and a GRU as a decoder. Form the extracted and segmented features, the bidirectional encoder computes the hidden feature vector h_t as follows:

$$z_t = \sigma(W_{xz} x_t + U_{hz} h_{t-1} + b_z) \quad (5)$$

$$r_t = \sigma(W_{xr} x_t + U_{hr} h_{t-1} + b_r) \quad (6)$$

$$h_t' = \tanh(W_{xh} x_t + U_{rh}(r_t \otimes h_{t-1}) + b_h) \quad (7)$$

$$h_t = (1 - z_t) \otimes h_{t-1} + z_t \otimes h_t' \quad (8)$$

where z_t, r_t, h_t', and h_t are update gate, reset gate, current memory, and final memory at the current time step, respectively. W, U, and b are parameter matrices and vector; σ and tanh stand for sigmoid and hyperbolic tangent function, respectively.

Using the embedding matrix W_{emb} the hidden vector h_t is converted to embedding matrix b_t as follows:

$$b_t = W_{emb}h_t, t = u-\tau, \ldots, u+\tau \tag{9}$$

By applying a linear projection on the embedded vector b_t query (q_t), values (v_t), and keys (k_t) vectors are computed as follows:

$$q_t = Qb_t, t = u \tag{10}$$

$$k_t = Kb_t, t = u-\tau, \ldots, u+\tau \tag{11}$$

$$v_t = Vb_t, t = u-\tau, \ldots, u+\tau \tag{12}$$

where Q, K, and V are query, key and value matrices, respectively.

Based on these results, attention weight a_u and attention result c_u are derived as follows:

$$e_{ut} = \frac{q_u^T k_t}{\sqrt{d_k'}} \tag{13}$$

$$a_{ut} = \frac{\exp(e_{ut})}{\sum_{t'=1}^{u+\tau} \exp(e_{ut'})}, \tag{14}$$

$$c_u = \sum_{t=u-\tau}^{u+\tau} a_{ut}h_t \tag{15}$$

To address the conditional independence assumption in CTC, an attention layer is placed before the CTC projection layer ph_u and transforms it to a particular dimension representing the number of CTC output labels. Then, the attention layer output that carries context information is served as the input of CTC projection layer at the current time u.

$$ph_u = W_{proj}c_u + b \tag{16}$$

where W_{proj} and b are the weight matrix and bias of the CTC projection layer, respectively.

Finally, the projected output is optimized as follows:

$$L_{CTC} = -\log \sum_{\pi \in B^{-1}(y)} p(\pi|ph_u) \tag{17}$$

where y denotes the output label sequence. A many-to-one mapping B is defined to determine the correspondence between a set of paths and the output label sequences. The self-attention layer links all positions with a constant number of operations that are performed in sequence.

4. Ethiopic Script and Dataset Collection

4.1. Ethiopic Script

Ethiopic script, which is derived from Geez, is one of the most ancient scripts in the world. It is used as a writing system for more than 43 languages, including Amharic, Geez, and Tigrigna. The script has largely been used by Geez and Amharic, which are the liturgical and official languages of Ethiopia, respectively. Amharic language is the second Semitic language after Arabic. The script is written down in a tabular format in which the first column denotes the base character and the other columns are vowels derived from the base characters, made by slightly deforming or modifying the base characters. The script has a total of 466 characters, out of which 20 are digits, 9 are punctuation marks, and the remaining 437 characters are parts of the alphabet. Developing a scene text recognition system for Ethiopic script is challenging, due to the visually similar characters, especially between base characters and the derived vowels, and the number of characters in the script. Furthermore, the lack of training and testing datasets is another limitation in the development of a scene text reading system for Ethiopic scripts. In this paper, we propose an end-to-end trainable bilingual scene text reading model using FPN, RPN, and time-restricted self-attention CTC.

4.2. Dataset Collection

In any machine learning technique, a dataset plays an important role in training and obtaining a better machine learning model. In particular, deep learning methods are more data-hungry than traditional machine learning algorithms. However, preparing a large dataset was a challenging task specifically for under-resourced languages. In this paper, we use a syntactically generated scene text dataset, and real scene text dataset for training and testing the proposed model, respectively. Following [12], a bilingual scene text dataset is prepared. A detailed description of synthetic dataset generation and real scene text dataset preparation is provided in the following sections.

4.2.1. Synthetic Scene Text Dataset

To train the proposed model, we use a bilingual scene text dataset, which is generated by adding a simple modification to the scene text dataset generation technique presented in [12]. The generated scene text images are like real scene images. This technique is very important to get more training data for those scripts that do not have prepared real scene text datasets. As far as we know, there is no prepared real scene text dataset for Ethiopic script. Moreover, most texts found in natural images are written in two languages (Amharic and English). Due to this, we prepare 500,000 bilingual training datasets from 54,735 words (825,080 characters), which were collected from social, political, and governmental websites that are written in Amharic and English. In the dataset generation process, 72 freely available Ethiopic Unicode fonts, different background images, font size, rotation along the horizontal line, and skew and thickness parameters are tuned. The sample generated scene image and statistics of the generated dataset are presented in Figure 2 and Table 2, respectively.

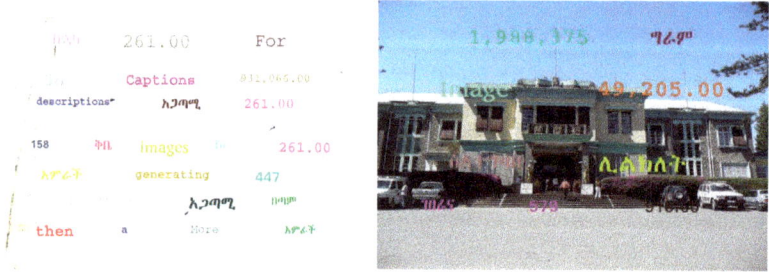

Figure 2. Sample of synthetically generated scene text images.

4.2.2. Real Scene Text Dataset

In addition to the synthetic dataset, we collected 1200 benchmark bilingual real scene text images using photo camera and image search on Google. The images were captured from local markets, navigation and traffic signs, banners, billboards, and governmental offices. We also incorporated several office logos, most of which were written both in Amharic and English with curved shapes. In addition to our prepared dataset, we used the Synthetic [22] dataset to pre-train the proposed model with our synthetic dataset. To refine the pre-trained model and compare its performance with a state-of-the-art model, we used ICDAR2013 [44], ICDAR2015 [40], and Total-Text [45] datasets.

The datasets, we used in the proposed model are summarized in Table 2. Additionally, sample images from the collected datasets are depicted in Figure 3.

Figure 3. Sample of collected real scene text images.

Table 2. Statistics of datasets applied for training and testing the proposed model.

Dataset		Language	Total Images	Training	Testing	Type
Ours	Real	Bilingual	1200	600	600	Irregular
	Synthetic	Bilingual	500,000	500,000	-	Regular
ICDAR2013 [44]		English	462	229	233	Regular
ICDAR2015 [40]		English	1500	1000	500	Regular
Synthetic [22]		English	600,000	-	-	Regular
Total-Text [45]		English	1555	1255	300	Irregular

5. Experiments and Discussions

The effectiveness of the proposed model was evaluated and compared with state-of-the-art methods by pre-training the proposed model using our synthetically generated dataset and a Synthetic dataset. Finally, the pre-trained model was refined by merging the above-mentioned datasets.

5.1. Implementation Details

The proposed model was first pre-trained using our synthetically generated bilingual dataset and Synthetic [22], then fine-tuned using the union of other real-world datasets indicated in Section 4.2.2. Due to the lack of real sample images in the fine-tuning stage, data augmentation and multi-scale training were applied by randomly modifying brightness, hue, contrast, the angle of the image between −30 and 30. Following [9], for multi-scale training, the shorter sides of the input images were randomly resized to five scales (600, 800, 1000, 1200, 1400). We used Adam [46] (base learning rate = 0.0001, $\beta 1 = 0.9$, $\beta 2 = 0.999$, weight decay = 0) as an optimizer. Following the result of [21], we set the value to $\alpha = 0.25$ which denotes the ratio of the low-frequency part.

The experiment of the proposed bilingual scene text reading model is conducted on the Ubuntu machine containing Intel Core i7-7700 (3.60 GHz) CPU with 64 GB RAM and GeForce GTX 1080 Ti 11176 MiB GPU. For the implementation, we use Python 3.7 and PyTorch1.2.

5.2. Experiment Results

Throughout our experimental analysis, we evaluated a single model trained in a multilingual setup as explained in Section 3. To improve the performance of the model, we first pre-trained it using Synthetic dataset [22] and our synthetically generated bilingual dataset which has a total of 430 characters. Then, we fine-tuned the pre-trained model by combining the above-mentioned real scene text datasets. The text recognition results were reported in an unconstrained setup, that is, without using any predefined lexicon (set of words).

The performance of the trained model was verified using our prepared testing dataset and well-known ICDAR detests. As discussed in Section 4.2, the collected images in our dataset contain horizontal, arbitrary, and curved texts. Both the detection and recognition results were promising for horizontal, arbitrary, and curved text. The experiment evaluation for scene text detection on our prepared real scene text dataset showed 88.3% Precision (P), 82.4% Recall (R), and 85.25% F1-score (F). On the other hand, the end-to-end scene text-reading experiment showed 80.88% P, 49.01% R, and 61.04% F. The scene text detection performance of the proposed method for English and Amharic words do not differ much. However, in the end-to-end scene text reading task, 63.4% of errors occurred in the recognition of Amharic words. From incorrectly recognized characters, some of them did not have sufficient samples on the real and Synthetic datasets. Sample detection and recognition results are depicted in Figure 4. Most of the detection errors in our proposed method occurred from false detection of non-text areas of backgrounds.

Figure 4. Sample detection and recognition result for our prepared dataset.

In addition to our testing dataset, we evaluated the performance of our proposed model using ICDAR2013, ICDAR2015, and Total-Text testing datasets, which contain only English texts. The model is fine-tuned for both English and Amharic languages as one model, not for each language. The results of our proposed method and previously proposed methods are shown in Table 3. The experiment showed that our proposed method had a better recognition result on ICDAR2013 and Total-Text datasets. However, the scene text detection result of our proposed method was almost similar to a recently proposed mask text spotter [9] method. We used their architecture and implementation code with a little modification on the feature extraction layer and recognition layer. From the MaskTextSpotter implementation, we modified the ResNet-50 feature extraction by octave based ResNet-50 feature extraction and the text recognition part is modified by self-attention encoder-decoder model. Whereas the preprocessing and RPN implementation is taken from MaskTextSpotter. In Table 4, we compare the scene text detection result of our proposed method with previously proposed methods using ICDAR2013, ICDAR2015, and Total-Text datasets.

Table 3. F1-Score experimental results of the proposed unconstrained scene text reading system compared with previous methods.

Method	ICDAR2013	ICDAR2015	Total-Text
TextProposals+DicNet * [47]	68.54%	47.18%	-
DeepTextSpotter * [19]	77.0%	47.0%	-
FOTS * [34]	84.77%	65.33%	-
TextBoxes * [8]	84.65%	51.9%	-
E2E-MLT ** [48]	-	71.4%	-
Mask Text Spotter ** [9]	86.5%	62.4%	65.3%
Ours	86.8%	62.15%	67.6%

* indicates that the model is trained for English language only; ** indicates that the model is trained for multilingual datasets. Our model is trained for English and Amharic languages, with 430 characters.

Table 4. Scene text detection result of the proposed method compared with previous methods.

Method	ICDAR2013			ICDAR2015			Total-Text		
	P	R	F	P	R	F	P	R	F
PSENet [49]	94%	90%	92%	86.2%	84.5%	85.69%	84%	77.9%	80.9%
TextBoxes++ [8]	92%	86%	89%	87.8%	78.5%	82.9%	-	-	-
Mask Text Spotter [9]	94.8%	89.5%	92.1%	86.8%	81.2%	83.4%	81.8%	75.4%	78.5%
Ours	93.91%	88.96%	91.36%	86.02%	80.97%	83.28%	82.3%	73.8%	77.82%

In the experiment, the proposed bilingual scene text reading method had limitations regarding small font size scene texts and severely distorted images. Furthermore, due to the existence of many characters and their similarities, and the limited number of training samples for certain Ethiopic characters, a recognition error occurred at the time of testing. To improve the recognition performance of the system and the scene text-reading system in general, it is necessary to prepare more training data that contain enough samples for every character.

6. Conclusions

This paper introduced an end-to-end trainable bilingual (English and Ethiopic) scene text reading system using octave convolution and time-restricted attention encoder-decoder module. In the proposed model there were three layers. In the first layer, FPN with ResNet-50 was used as a feature extractor by replacing vanilla convolution with OctConv. Secondly, bounding box prediction and detection of texts were performed using RPN. Finally, recognition of text was performed by segmenting text areas based on the detected bounding boxes on the second layer using a time-restricted attention encoder-decoder network. To measure the effectiveness of the proposed model, we collect and syntactically generate a bilingual dataset. Additionally, we use well-known ICDAR2013, ICDAR2015, and Total Text datasets. Based on the prepared bilingual dataset, the proposed method shows 61.04% and 85.25% F1-measure on scene text reading and scene text detection, respectively. Compared to state-of-the-art recognition performance, our proposed model shows promising results. However, our method shows state-of-the-art results for ICDAR2013 and Total-Text end-to-end text readings. Furthermore, due to the existence of many characters, their similarities, and the limited number of training samples for certain Ethiopic characters, a recognition error occurred at the time of testing. To improve the recognition performance of the system, it is necessary for the future to prepare more training data that contain enough samples for every character. After the publication of the paper, the implementation code and the prepared dataset link will be freely available for the researchers on https://github.com/direselign/amh_eng.

Author Contributions: Conceptualization D.A.T. and experiments, D.A.T. and V.-D.T.; validation, D.A.T. and V.-D.T.; writing – original draft preparation, D.A.T.; writing-review and editing, C.M.L. and V.-D.T.; super vision, C.-M.L.; funding acquisition, C.-M.L.; All authors have read and agreed to the published version of the manuscript.

Funding: This work was supported in part by the Ministry of Science and Technology and National Taipei University of Technology through the Applied Computing Research Laboratory, Taiwan, under Grant MOST 107-2221-E-027-099-MY2 and Grant NTUT-BIT-109-03.

Conflicts of Interest: The authors declare no conflicts of interest.

References

1. Tian, Z.; Huang, W.; He, T.; Qiao, Y. Detecting Text in Natural Image with Connectionist Text Proposal Network. Available online: http://textdet.com/ (accessed on 14 December 2019).
2. Yao, C.; Bai, X.; Sang, N.; Zhou, X.; Zhou, S.; Cao, Z. Scene text detection via holistic, multi-channel prediction. *arXiv* **2016**, arXiv:1606.09002. Available online: http://arxiv.org/abs/1606.09002 (accessed on 31 March 2019).
3. Buta, M.; Neumann, L.; Matas, J. FASText: Efficient unconstrained scene text detector. In Proceedings of the IEEE International Conference on Computer Vision, Santiago, Chile, 7 December 2015; Volume 2015 Inter, pp. 1206–1214.
4. Deng, D.; Liu, H.; Li, X.; Cai, D. PixelLink: Detecting scene text via instance segmentation. *arXiv* **2018**, arXiv:1801.01315. Available online: http://arxiv.org/abs/1801.01315 (accessed on 10 February 2019).
5. Zhou, X.; Yao, C.; Wen, H.; Wang, Y.; Zhou, S.; He, W.; Liang, J. EAST: An efficient and accurate scene text detector. *arXiv* **2017**, arXiv:1704.03155.
6. Jaderberg, M.; Simonyan, K.; Vedaldi, A.; Zisserman, A. Reading text in the wild with convolutional neural networks. *Int. J. Comput. Vis.* **2016**, *116*, 1–20. [CrossRef]
7. He, P.; Huang, W.; Qiao, Y.; Loy, C.C.; Tang, X. Reading scene text in deep convolutional sequences. *arXiv* **2015**, arXiv:1506.04395. Available online: https://arxiv.org/abs/1506.04395 (accessed on 2 April 2019).
8. Liao, M.; Shi, B.; Bai, X. TextBoxes++: A single-shot oriented scene text detector. *arXiv* **2018**, arXiv:1801.02765. [CrossRef] [PubMed]
9. Liao, M.; Lyu, P.; He, M.; Yao, C.; Wu, W.; Bai, X. Mask textspotter: An end-to-end trainable neural network for spotting text with arbitrary shapes. In Proceedings of the 2019 Conference on Computer Vision and Pattern Recognition (CVPR), Long Beach, CA, USA, 16–20 June 2019; LNCS; Volume 11218, pp. 71–88. [CrossRef]
10. Li, H.; Wang, P.; Shen, C. Towards end-to-end text spotting with convolutional recurrent neural networks. *arXiv* **2017**, arXiv:1707.03985. Available online: http://arxiv.org/abs/1707.03985 (accessed on 2 April 2019).
11. Liao, M.; Shi, B.; Bai, X.; Wang, X.; Liu, W. TextBoxes: A Fast text detector with a single deep neural network. *arXiv* **2016**, arXiv:1611.06779. Available online: http://arxiv.org/abs/1611.06779 (accessed on 2 April 2019).
12. Jaderberg, M.; Simonyan, K.; Vedaldi, A.; Zisserman, A. Synthetic data and artificial neural networks for natural scene text recognition. *arXiv* **2014**, arXiv:1406.2227. Available online: http://arxiv.org/abs/1406.2227 (accessed on 2 March 2019).
13. Tian, S.; Bhattacharya, U.; Lu, S.; Su, B.; Wang, Q.; Wei, X.; Lu, Y.; Tan, C.L. Multilingual scene character recognition with co-occurrence of histogram of oriented gradients. *Pattern Recognit.* **2016**, *51*, 125–134. [CrossRef]
14. Shi, B.; Bai, X.; Belongie, S. Detecting oriented text in natural images by linking segments. In Proceedings of the IEEE Conference on Computer Vision and Pattern Recognition 2017, Honolulu, HI, USA, 21–26 July 2017; pp. 2550–2558. Available online: http://openaccess.thecvf.com/content_cvpr_2017/html/Shi_Detecting_Oriented_Text_CVPR_2017_paper.html (accessed on 11 April 2019).
15. Shi, B.; Wang, X.; Lyu, P.; Yao, C.; Bai, X. Robust scene text recognition with automatic rectification. *arXiv* **2016**, arXiv:1603.03915. Available online: http://arxiv.org/abs/1603.03915 (accessed on 21 March 2019).
16. He, K.; Zhang, X.; Ren, S.; Sun, J. Deep residual learning for image recognition. In Proceedings of the 2016 IEEE Conference on Computer Vision and Pattern Recognition (CVPR), Las Vegas, NV, USA, 27–30 June 2016. [CrossRef]
17. Addis, D.; Liu, C.-M.; Ta, V.-D. *Ethiopic Natural Scene Text Recognition Using Deep Learning Approaches*; Springer: Cham, The Netherlands, 2020; pp. 502–511.
18. Simons, G.F.; Fennig, C.D. *Ethnologue: Languages of the World*, 20th ed.; SIL International: Dallas, TX, USA, 2017.

19. Busta, M.; Neumann, L.; Matas, J. Deep Textspotter: An End-to-End Trainable Scene Text Localization and Recognition Framework. In Proceedings of the 2017 IEEE International Conference on Computer Vision, Venice, Italy, 22–29 October 2017; pp. 2204–2212.
20. Lin, T.; Dollár, P.; Girshick, R.; He, K.; Hariharan, B.; Belongie, S. Feature Pyramid Networks for Object Detection. In Proceedings of the IEEE Conference on Computer Vision and Pattern Recognition, Honolulu, HI, USA, 21–26 July 2017; pp. 2117–2125.
21. Chen, Y.; Fan, H.; Xu, B.; Yan, Z.; Kalantidis, Y.; Rohrbach, M.; Yan, S.; Feng, J. Drop an octave: Reducing spatial redundancy in convolutional neural networks with octave convolution. *arXiv* **2019**, arXiv:1904.05049. Available online: http://arxiv.org/abs/1904.05049 (accessed on 20 September 2019).
22. Gupta, A.; Vedaldi, A.; Zisserman, A. Synthetic data for text localisation in natural images. In Proceedings of the IEEE Computer Society Conference on Computer Vision and Pattern Recognition, New York, NY, USA, 17–22 June 2016; Volume 2016-Decem, pp. 2315–2324.
23. Neumann, L.; Matas, J. Scene Text Localization and Recognition with oriented Stroke Detection. In Proceedings of the IEEE International Conference on Computer Vision 2013, Sydney, Australia, 1–8 December 2013; pp. 97–104.
24. Wang, K.; Babenko, B.; Belongie, S. End-to-end scene text recognition. In Proceedings of the IEEE International Conference on Computer Vision, Barcelona, Spain, 6–13 November 2011; pp. 1457–1464.
25. Lee, J.J.; Lee, P.H.; Lee, S.W.; Yuille, A.; Koch, C. AdaBoost for text detection in natural scene. In Proceedings of the IEEE International Conference on Document Analysis and Recognition, Beijing, China, 18–21 September 2011; pp. 429–434.
26. Epshtein, B.; Ofek, E.; Wexler, Y. Detecting text in natural scenes with stroke width transform. In Proceedings of the IEEE Computer Society Conference on Computer Vision and Pattern Recognition, San Francisco, CA, USA, 13–18 June 2010; pp. 2963–2970.
27. Matas, J.; Chum, O.; Urban, M.; Pajdla, T. Robust wide-baseline stereo from maximally stable extremal regions. *Image Vis. Comput.* **2004**, *22*, 761–767. [CrossRef]
28. Ma, J.; Shao, W.; Ye, H.; Wang, L.; Wang, H.; Zheng, Y.; Xue, X. Arbitrary-oriented scene text detection via rotation proposals. *IEEE Trans. Multimed.* **2018**, *20*, 3111–3122. [CrossRef]
29. He, D.; Yang, X.; Liang, C.; Zhou, Z.; Ororbia, A.G.; Kifer, D.; Giles, C.L. Multi-scale FCN with cascaded instance aware segmentation for arbitrary oriented word spotting in the wild. In Proceedings of the 2017 IEEE Conference on Computer Vision and Pattern Recognition (CVPR), Honolulu, HI, USA, 21–26 July 2017; pp. 474–483.
30. Su, B.; Lu, S. Accurate Scene Text Recognition Based on Recurrent Neural Network. In *Computer Vision—ACCV 2014, Lecture Notes in Computer Science*; Cremers, D., Reid, I., Saito, H., Yang, M.H., Eds.; Springer: Cham, The Netherlands, 2014; Volume 9003, pp. 35–48.
31. Lee, C.-Y.; Osindero, S. Recursive recurrent nets with attention modeling for OCR in the wild. Proceeding of the IEEE conference on Computer Vision and Patter Recognition (CVPR 2016), Las Vegas, NV, USA, 26–30 June 2016; pp. 2231–2239.
32. Liu, W.; Chen, C.; Wong, K.-Y.; Su, Z.; Han, J. STAR-Net: A Spatial attention residue network for scene text recognition. *BMVC* **2016**, *2*, 7.
33. Liu, W.; Anguelov, D.; Erhan, D.; Szegedy, C.; Reed, S.; Fu, C.-Y.; Berg, A.C. SSD: Single shot multibox detector. In Proceedings of the European Conference on Computer Vision 2016, Amsterdam, The Netherlands, 8–16 October 2016; pp. 21–37.
34. Liu, X.; Liang, D.; Yan, S.; Chen, D.; Qiao, Y.; Yan, J. Fots: Fast Oriented Text Spotting with a Unified Network. Proceeding of the IEEE conference on Computer Vision and Pattern Recogntiion 2018, Salt Lake City, UT, USA, 18–23 June 2018; pp. 5676–5685.
35. Lundgren, A.; Castro, D.; Lima, E.; Bezerra, B. OctShuffleMLT: A compact octave based neural network for end-to-end multilingual text detection and recognition. In Proceedings of the 2019 International Conference on Document Analysis and Recognition Workshops (ICDARW), Sydney, Aystralia, 22–25 September 2019; pp. 37–42.
36. Szegedy, C.; Ioffe, S.; Vanhoucke, V.; Alemi, A.A. Inception-v4, inception-ResNet and the impact of residual connections on learning. In Proceedings of the 31st AAAI Conference on Artificial Intelligence, San Francisco, CA, USA, 4–9 February 2017; pp. 4278–4284.

37. Szegedy, C.; Liu, W.; Jia, Y.; Sermanet, P.; Reed, S.; Anguelov, D.; Erhan, D.; Vanhoucke, V.; Rabinovich, A. Going deeper with convolutions. In Proceedings of the IEEE Computer Society Conference on Computer Vision and Pattern Recognition, Boston, MA, USA, 7–12 June 2015; Volume 07-12-June, pp. 1–9.
38. Povey, D.; Hadian, H.; Ghahremani, P.; Li, K.; Khudanpur, S. A time-restricted self-attention layer for ASR. Proceedings of 2018 IEEE International Conference on Acoustics, Speech and Signal Processing (ICASSP), Calgary, AB, Canada, 15–20 April 2018; Volume 2018-April, pp. 5874–5878.
39. Zagoruyko, S.; Komodakis, N. Wide residual networks. *arXiv* **2016**, arXiv:1605.07146.
40. Ren, S.; He, K.; Girshick, R.; Sun, J. Faster R-CNN: Towards real-time object detection with region proposal networks. In Proceedings of the Advances in Neural Information Processing System 2015, Montreal, PQ, Canada, 7–12 December 2015; pp. 91–99.
41. He, K.; Gkioxari, G.; Dollar, P.; Girshick, R. Mask R-CNN. In Proceedings of the IEEE International Conference on Compter Vision 2017, Venice, Italy, 22–29 October 2017; pp. 2961–2969.
42. Bodla, N.; Singh, B.; Chellappa, R.; Davis, L.S. Soft-NMS—Improving Object detection with one line of code. In Proceedings of the IEEE International Conference on Computer Vision 2017, Venice, Italy, 22–29 October 2017; pp. 5561–5569.
43. Wu, L.; Li, T.; Wang, L.; Yan, Y. Improving hybrid CTC/attention architecture with time-restricted self-attention CTC for end-to-end speech recognition. *Appl. Sci.* **2019**, *9*, 4639. [CrossRef]
44. Karatzas, D.; Shafait, F.; Uchida, S.; Iwamura, M.; Bigorda, L.G.i.; Mestre, S.R.; Mas, J.; Mota, D.F.; Almazan, J.A.; de Las Heras, L.P. ICDAR 2013 robust reading competition. In Proceedings of the 2013 12th International Conference on Document Analysis and Recognition, Washington, DC, USA, 25–28 August 2013; pp. 1484–1493.
45. Ch'Ng, C.K.; Chan, C.S. Total-Text: A Comprehensive Dataset for Scene Text Detection and Recognition. In Proceedings of the International Conference on Document Analysis and Recognition, Kyoto, Japan, 9–15 November 2017; Volume 1, pp. 935–942.
46. Kingma, D.P.; Ba, J. Adam: A method for stochastic optimization. *arXiv* **2014**, arXiv:1412.6980.
47. Gómez, L.; Karatzas, D. TextProposals: A text-specific selective search algorithm for word spotting in the wild. *Pattern Recognit.* **2017**, *70*, 60–74. [CrossRef]
48. Bušta, M.; Patel, Y.; Matas, J. E2E-MLT—An unconstrained end-to-end method for multi-language scene text. *arXiv* **2018**, arXiv:1801.09919. Available online: http://arxiv.org/abs/1801.09919 (accessed on 11 April 2019).
49. Wang, W.; Xie, E.; Li, X.; Hou, W.; Lu, T.; Yu, G.; Shao, S. Shape robust text detection with progressive scale expansion network. *arXiv* **2019**, arXiv:1903.12473. Available online: http://arxiv.org/abs/1903.12473 (accessed on 6 January 2019).

© 2020 by the authors. Licensee MDPI, Basel, Switzerland. This article is an open access article distributed under the terms and conditions of the Creative Commons Attribution (CC BY) license (http://creativecommons.org/licenses/by/4.0/).

Article

A Smartphone-Based Cell Segmentation to Support Nasal Cytology

Giovanni Dimauro [1,*], Davide Di Pierro [1], Francesca Deperte [2], Lorenzo Simone [3] and Pio Raffaele Fina [2]

1. Department of Computer Science, University of Bari, 70125 Bari, Italy; ddipierro745@gmail.com
2. Department of Computer Science, University of Torino, 10124 Torino, Italy; francesca.deperte@edu.unito.it (F.D.); pio.fina@edu.unito.it (P.R.F.)
3. Department of Computer Science, University of Pisa, 56127 Pisa, Italy; l.simone3@studenti.unipi.it
* Correspondence: giovanni.dimauro@uniba.it; Tel.: +39-805443294

Received: 24 May 2020; Accepted: 29 June 2020; Published: 30 June 2020

Abstract: Rhinology studies the anatomy, physiology, and diseases affecting the nasal region—one of the most modern techniques to diagnose these diseases is nasal cytology, which involves microscopic analysis of the cells contained in the nasal mucosa. The standard clinical protocol regulates the compilation of the rhino-cytogram by observing, for each slide, at least 50 fields under an optical microscope to evaluate the cell population and search for cells important for diagnosis. The time and effort required for the specialist to analyze a slide are significant. In this paper, we present a smartphones-based system to support cell segmentation on images acquired directly from the microscope. Then, the specialist can analyze the cells and the other elements extracted directly or, alternatively, he can send them to Rhino-cyt, a server system recently presented in the literature, that also performs the automatic cell classification, giving back the final rhinocytogram. This way he significantly reduces the time for diagnosing. The system crops cells with sensitivity = 0.96, which is satisfactory because it shows that cells are not overlooked as false negatives are few, and therefore largely sufficient to support the specialist effectively. The use of traditional image processing techniques to preprocess the images also makes the process sustainable from the computational point of view for medium–low end architectures and is battery-efficient on a mobile phone.

Keywords: nasal cytology; automatic cell segmentation; rhinology; image analysis

1. Introduction

Thanks to the numerous studies in the field of computer vision applied to the medical and biomedical field, we now have many additional tools to support specialists in their tasks [1–5]. Modern technologies have improved the acquisition, transmission, and analysis of digital images. A growing benefit is also provided thanks to the spread of fast network connections for smartphones, allowing for the exchange of large amounts of clinical data also useful for remote diagnosis or follow-up [6–8].

Segmentation and contour extraction are important steps towards the analysis of digital images in the medical field, where such images are routinely used in a multitude of different applications [9]. Segmentation algorithms, based on structural analysis, continue to be used, often as an ensemble of segmentation techniques, especially in critical applications, such as lesion localization [10,11]. Other approaches, based on biased normalized cuts or light techniques, are also devised [12,13]. Many studies have also been conducted in the segmentation and classification of cells from digital images. Almost all studies are in the field of hematology. An interesting study into the classification of white blood cells (WBCs) is reported in [14]. In some studies, only segmentation aspects are discussed [15,16], while a neural network-based classifier of cytotypes in the hematological smear of a healthy subject was described in [17]: starting from digital scans of hematological preparations, it showed over 95% accuracy. Many other papers report interesting results about this last theme [18–20].

One of the fields that can benefit from the above technologies is nasal cytology, a branch of otolaryngology, which is gaining increasing importance in the diagnosis of nasal diseases due to the simplicity of the diagnostic examination and its effectiveness. In fact, the global spread of the nasal diseases is significant: allergic rhinitis is estimated to affect 35% of the world's population and the World Health Organization considers it a growing epidemic form as, in a few years, 50% of children may be allergic. Rhinosinusitis affects 4% of the world's population, and nasal polyposis 5%. Non-allergic vasomotor rhinitis affects 15% of people [21].

To the best of our knowledge, to date, there are no public or private laboratories that carry out the examination of the cell population of the nasal mucosa routinely, as instead it is done for hematological tests. This is for different reasons: firstly, because diagnostics based on nasal cytology have grown recently; secondly, because economic interest is still residual; finally, because the spectrum of diagnosable pathologies is not as extensive as in other fields of medicine. Typically, a rhinocytologist who wants to benefit from a cytological study must independently arrange a set of personal instruments, or, more frequently, carry out direct microscopic observation and manual cell counting using a special rhinocytogram.

Methods and techniques designed for hematology cannot be used directly for nasal cytology; for example, the WBC appear in almost all cases as isolated from each other, while nasal mucosa cells often appear amassed in the smear.

The first studies about the automatic extraction and classification of the cells of the nasal mucosa are reported in [22–24] where a diagnostic support system provides cell counting automatically—it uses segmentation algorithms to extract cells and a convolutional neural network to classify them. The sampling process and the diagnosis remain human activities, carried out by the specialist, but the whole time and effort are reduced considerably, letting the accuracy of the diagnoses remain unchanged or even be improved. To the best of our knowledge, there are no further contributions in the literature.

The further request of the stakeholders is to considerably reduce the cost of the analysis and of the instrumentation with the aim of increasing the capillarity of the analysis itself. Therefore, the challenge we have been given is to carry out the entire evaluation of the cell population on a mass device, such as a smartphone, fully automatically (as shown in Appendix A). Devices with limited resources will interact with the surrounding environment and users. Many of these devices will be based on machine learning models to decode meaning and the behavior behind sensors' data, to implement accurate predictions and make decisions [25]. Several research papers have focused on the possibility of bringing artificial intelligence to devices with limited resources and there have been efforts in decreasing the model's inference time on the device. Machine learning developers focus on designing models with a reduced number of parameters in the Deep Neural Network model, thus reducing memory and execution latency, while aiming to preserve accuracy, as far as possible. It is evident that, at the moment, there are several problems to overcome, first among which is the limitation of the computational capacity of mobile architectures [26–34].

In this paper a novel system based on a smartphone is presented to support rhinocytologists during cell observation. It carries out cell extraction from the digital image of the microscopic fields. Once this is done, the specialist can independently evaluate the segmented cells or send them to the Rhino-cyt platform [2], which will also perform the fully automatic classification, giving back the final rhinocytogram. This way he significantly reduces the time for diagnosis.

2. Rhino-Cytology

Nasal cytology is a very useful diagnostic method in rhino-allergology—it allows for the detection of cellular variations of an epithelium exposed to acute/chronic irritations or inflammations of different nature and makes it possible to diagnose some nasal pathologies [35,36]. The strengths of this methodology lie in the simplicity of the diagnostic examination; in fact, it is totally painless, safe, and fast, as it can be conducted in an outpatient clinic. Starting from the assumption that the nasal mucosa of the healthy individual consists normally of only four cytotypes, cytological diagnostics is based on a fundamental axiom that states that, if other cells, such as eosinophils, mastcells, bacteria, spores, and fungal hyphae, are present in the rhinocytogram, then the individual can be affected by a nasal pathology. A quantitative analysis of the pathological cells contained in the nasal mucosa and their state of rest or activation allows for the indication of a targeted therapy to the patient [37].

2.1. A. The Cytodiagnostic Technique

The diagnostic examination is accomplished through the following three main phases:

- Sampling: Consists of collecting a sample of nasal mucosa containing the superficial cells. It is carried out using a disposable plastic curette, called nasal scraping, or a simple nasal swab is preferred for smaller patients;
- Processing: The material collected is placed on a slide and dried in the open air. Then, the slide is stained using the May Grunwald–Giemsa method, which provides the cells with the classic purple staining and highlights all the cytotypes present in the nasal mucosa. Usually, the complete staining procedure takes about 20–30 s with rapid staining techniques;
- Microscopic observation: An optical microscope is used, mainly connected to a special camera to view the cells on a monitor. The diagnostic protocol involves viewing and analyzing 50 digital images for each slide, called fields, usually at 1000X magnification.

The cell count allows a diagnosis to be made simply by counting the cells present in the 50 analyzed fields. This process allows the specialists to draw up a diagnostic report.

2.2. B. Types of Cells Involved

Different types of cells are considered in the diagnosis of nasal diseases. Considering the diversity of the cells present in the nasal mucosa, it is, therefore, appropriate to draw up a classification of the different cytotypes present both in a healthy individual and in an individual with a pathology. The nasal mucosa cells belonging to a cytotype show some elements with high similarity; however, each cytotype appears quite different from all the others. These features allow their automatic classification [23]. A brief description of the appearance of each of the cells located in the nasal mucosa is reported below, and corresponding sample images are shown in Figure 1:

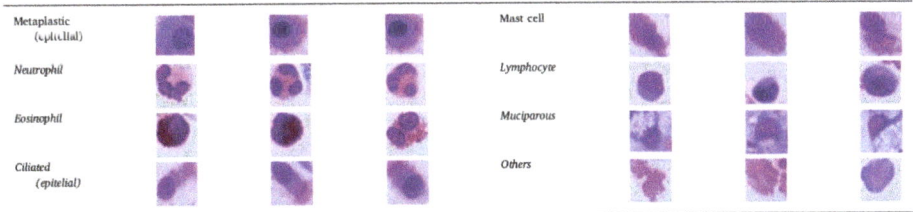

Figure 1. Nasal cells.

Ciliated: Among the most common cytotypes of the nasal mucosa are ciliated cells. They have a polygonal shape and a nucleus situated at various heights from the basement membrane. The apical region, the seat of the ciliary apparatus, is recognized as a well-represented body that includes a large part of the cytoplasm and the nucleus;

Muciparous (goblet cells): The muciparous cell is in the shape of a cup and is a unicellular gland. The nucleus is always situated in the basal position (the strengthener of the nuclear chromatin is typical) while the vacuoles, containing mucinous granules, are located above the nucleus, giving the mature cell its characteristic chalice shape;

Neutrophil: characterized by a polylobate nucleus, whose lobes are joined by very thin strands of nuclear material within the cytoplasm, which contains finely colored granules;

Eosinophil: usually has a bilobed nucleus and acidophilous granules that intensely stain with eosin (hence the name) as an orange-red color;

Mast cell: a granulocyte with an oval nucleus, covered in purple.

The nasal mucosa of a healthy individual normally contains ciliated, mucipara, striated, basal, and sporadic neutrophils cells. In the nasal epithelium, there can also be different types of inflammatory cells, where each of them can be a sign of a nasal pathology. They are known as immunophlogosis cells (eosinophils, mast cell, lymphocyte). Additionally, a significant presence of neutrophils is interesting—knowing the functions they perform helps motivate different therapeutic strategies [37]. Here, metaplastic cells have been merged into one class (epithelial) with ciliated cells because their nuclei are similar and this merging does not influence the diagnostic protocol.

3. Image Acquisition and Processing

Thanks to the large number of contexts in which digital image processing has been successfully in experimentation, its use has also increased in medicine that is becoming highly dependent on it and represents fundamental pillars of modern diagnosis [38–42].

The images of the smears used in this experimentation, supplied by the Policlinico di Bari, have been acquired with a Samsung Galaxy S6 Edge smartphone with a 16 Mpixel digital rear camera, with a photo resolution of 5312 × 2988 pixels and an aperture of F / 1.9. A specific smartphone adapter was also used, as shown in Figure 2. The system proposed here is based on image enhancement, segmentation, and morphological processing [43], which allows for the extraction of the cells present in the photo acquired by the smartphone camera and will be dealt with in this paper shortly.

Figure 2. Image acquisition.

3.1. Image Enhancement

There are several definitions of image enhancement in the literature but the one that best fits the context states that this process allows for the improvement of the quality and information contained in an original image before it is processed [44–46]. The result of this pre-process represents an improved image that highlights some features more relevant than others both for the visual and automated systems, which otherwise would not be visible in the original image; therefore, an image will be easier to interpret in certain contexts.

Image enhancement involves several aspects of an image: those that will be dealt with in this work concern brightness (or luminance), contrast (the difference between the pixel of higher and lower intensity), and saturation.

In Figure 3, the effects of image enhancement techniques on an image of nasal cells with low brightness and contrast are evident. The central image appears sharper and this brings many advantages, as the cells appear more visible and highlighted due to the increased contrast. The image on the right is too bright and needs the so-called gamma correction.

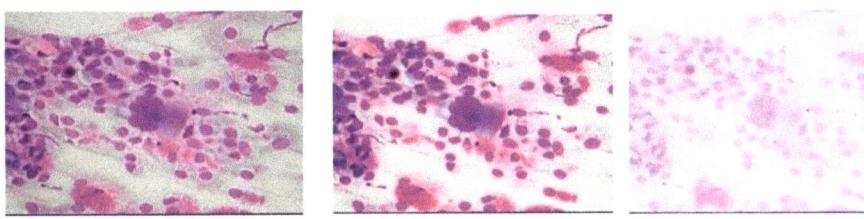

Figure 3. Image Enhancement. Original image (on the left); image with contrast enhancement (in the center); image with brightness enhancement (on the right) that needs gamma-correction.

Gamma correction hides brightness defects in an image using a non-linear function based on the following transformation:

$$o = \left(\frac{I}{255}\right)^Y \cdot 255 \qquad (1)$$

where the γ is called gamma and the I and O values indicate the input value of the pixel and the output value of the non-linear function, respectively. This correction is often used to manipulate contrast in medical images, especially to highlight specific characteristics in an image with low lighting and low contrast.

3.2. Image Segmentation

Image segmentation partitions a digital image into a finite number of different regions, where region means a set of interconnected pixels. A significant number of image segmentation techniques allow the partitioning of a digital image [12,47], some of which have been considered in this project.

Images from the whole smear were taken and analyzed, as explained above, in smaller regions, called fields. In terms of pixels, all fields have the same size. Many attempts were made to choose an optimal dimension of each digital image to speed up processing—ultimately, the fields were resized to 1024 × 768 pixels, which proved to be a fair compromise.

Cell extraction was essentially based on the chromatic characteristics of cells, especially nuclei. For example, neutrophils show a blue-violet core, eosinophils show pink granules, and lymphocytes show a very large nucleus of blue color. Mean Shift filtering makes an image with color gradients and fine-grain texture flattened. In order to set up the system to recognize images of slides prepared with different techniques in the future, experiments were conducted here using grayscale images for the segmentation phase based on the Otsu algorithm. Then, morphological operations and the watershed algorithm were applied, followed by labeling, marking the different "objects" with different shades of color to facilitate subsequent classification. The Canny algorithm was considered as an alternative in rare cases when watershed provides unsatisfying results (e.g., split cells). In these cases, giving the responsibility to the user to manually adjust thresholds, segmentation showed better results than watershed. Of course, this option is considered a marginal one.

3.2.1. Mean Shift

The unsupervised learning Mean Shift algorithm is based on clustering and is also applied to digital images [48–51]. This algorithm, transforms the digital image in Figure 4a, passing through surface construction, as shown in Figure 4b, and cluster detection, in a multidimensional space, as in Figure 4c, where the points represent all pixels assigned to a specific cluster.

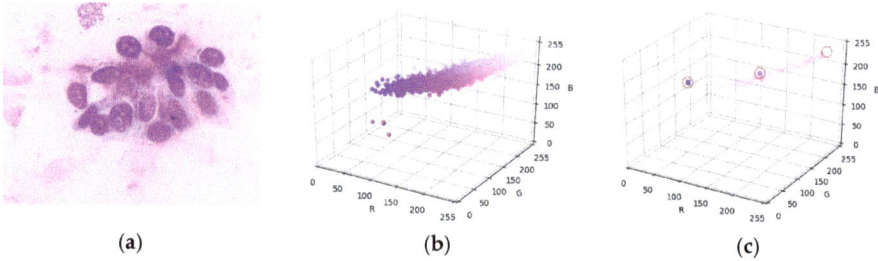

Figure 4. A cell field (**a**), surface construction (**b**), and cluster detection (**c**).

3.2.2. Otsu Segmentation

The Otsu method is a global threshold algorithm. The result obtained represents a binary image. To ensure optimal separation between background pixels and object pixels, and thus effective segmentation, it is necessary to maximize the inter-class variance [52].

3.2.3. Watershed

Watershed performs a digital image partitioning in different regions, especially when there are image elements that are very close to each other or even connected. The resulting image shows higher pixel intensities of each object in the center areas.

3.2.4. Canny Edge Detector

The Canny algorithm finds and recognizes the contours of objects. It takes five steps during which the grayscale input image undergoes several intermediate transformations. The result obtained represents a binary digital image with only the contours highlighted by strongly marked pixels [53,54].

3.3. Morphological Image Processing

Morphological image processing alters the structure and geometric shape of an object and applies morphological operations to that portion of the image at each kernel position [55,56]. The morphological operation used in this work is dilation. It acts mainly near the contours of the cells by adding pixels and making it thicker. Expansion reduces and eliminates possible holes inside the cells, often due to binarization defects.

4. Methods

The software we have designed executes the image processing introduced above, allowing for the identification of cellular elements and their extraction from an RGB digital image, acquired with the smartphone camera. In particular, the following steps are applied.

4.1. Increase in Brightness and Contrast

A preliminary process of image enhancement improves the quality of the original image. In particular, both brightness and contrast are increased so as to reduce or eliminate the light color halos around the cells caused by the staining process of the cytodiagnostic examination, which would otherwise have compromised the detection process in the subsequent stages. The transformation applied to each RGB channel for each pixel (x,y) in the starting image is:

$$g(x,y) = \alpha \cdot f(x,y) + \beta \quad (2)$$

where α and β are the so-called gain and bias, respectively, which are parameters that regulate brightness and contrast, as shown in Figure 5. They were empirically determined: $\alpha = 1.5e$, $\beta = 6$.

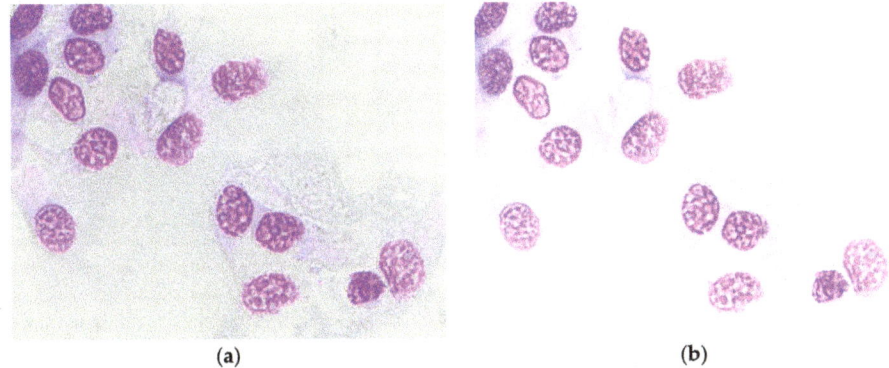

Figure 5. Input image (**a**), output image of brightness enhancement step (**b**).

4.2. Gamma and Mean Shift Correction

Image brightness is "gamma-corrected", further increasing image contrast by making the color shades of the nuclei more saturated; moreover, the Mean Shift algorithm is applied to make the coloring of the cell nuclei more homogeneous, as shown in Figure 6.

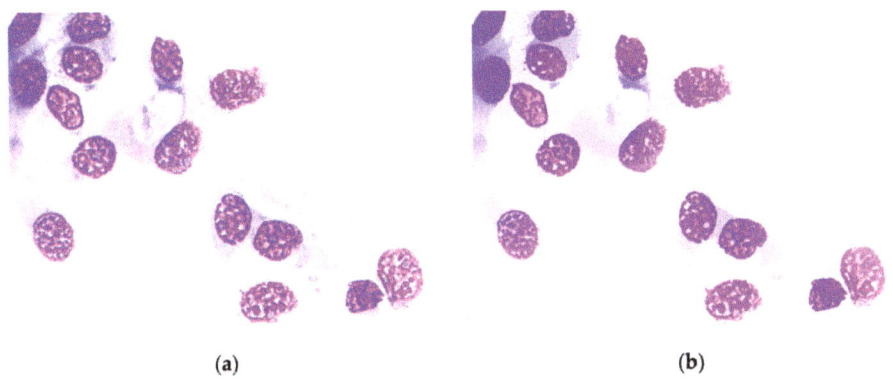

Figure 6. Output images of gamma correction step (**a**) and mean shift (**b**).

4.3. Otsu Binarization

After grayscale conversion, segmentation is made with automatic threshold to separate cells, as shown in Figure 7. To improve image quality and correct any defects due to Otsu's binarization, such as holes in cell nuclei, the process benefits from the use of aperture in combination with dilation.

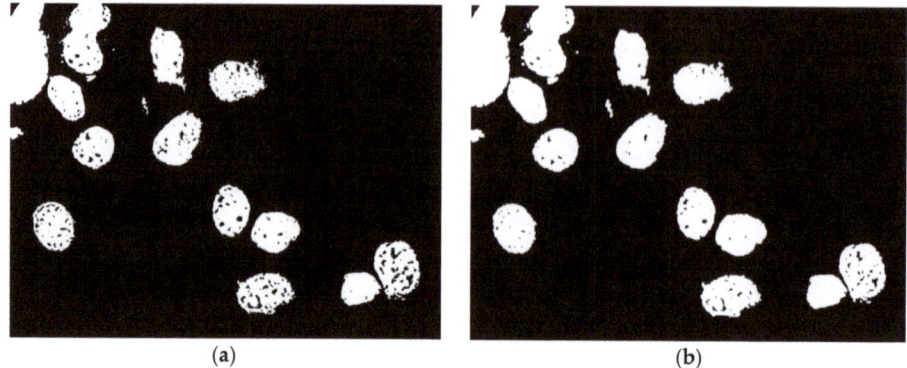

Figure 7. Output images of Otsu's binarization (**a**) and morphological operations (**b**).

4.4. Identification of Markers, Watershed

After marker identification (Euclidean Distance Transform and local maxima detection), the Watershed algorithm is applied, as shown in Figure 8. To improve the performance of the Watershed algorithm, the bandwidth h was defined by studying the range of variation of the cell size by means of a micrometer, a high precision gauge with a typical sensitivity of a hundredth of a millimeter.

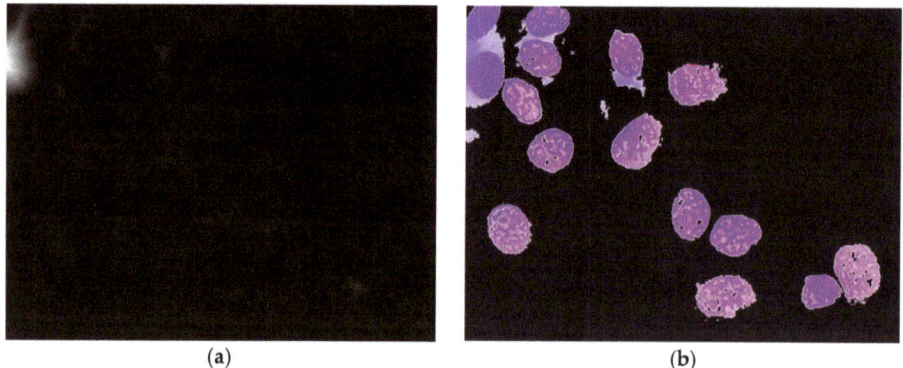

Figure 8. Output images of Euclidean Distance Transform (**a**) and Watershed detected cells (**b**).

4.5. Cropping

The final step of the proposed system carries on ROI detection basing on their area, in order to reduce non-cell regions that can be improperly highlighted. In fact, only regions that have an area included in a specific range (a_1, a_2) are extracted; range values depend on the image resolution. As explained above, we resized the original images to 1024 × 768 pixels and then determined the range experimentally, setting $a_1 = 80$ and $a_2 = 250$. Examples of the cropped cells after applying this operation are given in Figure 9. Figure 10 shows images of the designed app, and in Figure 11 the software pipeline related to cell extraction is reported.

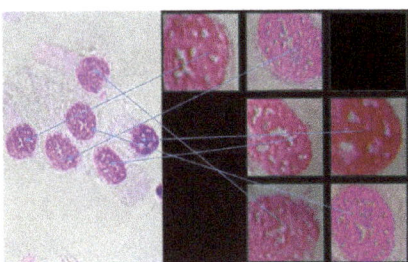

Figure 9. Original image (**left**) and extracted cells (**right**).

(**a**) (**b**)

Figure 10. App home page (**a**), app field gallery (**b**).

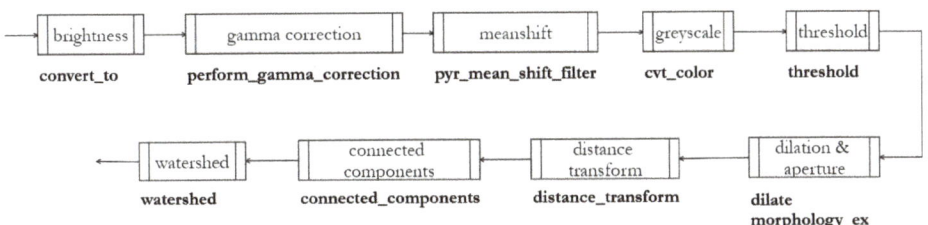

Figure 11. Cell extraction pipeline with methods—see "detect()" in Appendix B.

5. Experimental Results

The cell extractor here described has been tested on 75 digital images representing fields, first performing a standard cell observation and manual counting for each field, and then taking into consideration the cells detected through the system proposed in this paper.

In Figure 12 a qualitative example of the working system for one of the 75 images is reported. The result in terms of the detected cells is shown with a blue bounding box around the segmented objects. The performance of this system is reported in Table 1—all cells and non cells on the 75 slides were also manually labeled by domain experts, to obtain the ground truth.

Table 1. Cell detecting performance.

	Confusion Matrix	
	True Condition	
Predicted	positive	negative
Positive	1224	166
Negative	52	113

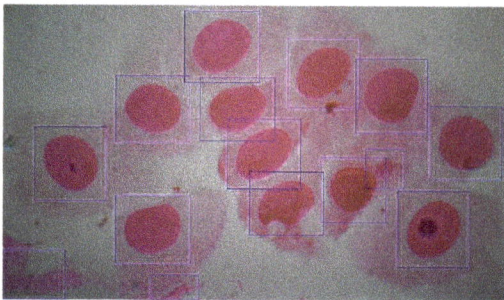

Figure 12. Cell detection.

With reference to Table 1, TP represents cells correctly extracted, FN lost cells, FP non-cells improperly extracted, and TN non-cells discarded.

Starting from these assumptions, the system performances are summarized here:

Accuracy	0.860
Sensitivity (Recall)	0.959
Specificity	0.405
Precision	0.881
F-score	0.918

The measure that must mainly be taken into consideration is certainly sensitivity, which quantifies the avoidance of false negatives. The value 0.96 is satisfactory because it shows that actual positives are not overlooked, as false negatives are few. The FN detected refer, for the vast majority, to heavily-massed cells that the same experts do not consider during the observation. In fact, the manual protocol defined by the experts is tolerant of the typical presence of clusters and specifies that at least 50 fields must be taken into account, increasing them during the observation if they find the excessive presence of clusters or almost empty fields. All of this takes significant effort. In reference to this, and also with the system we have designed, the specialist can increase the number of fields to be acquired and analyzed, proving to be flexible. Even the number of false positives does not worry us because the cells and the other "objects" extracted are classified manually or through the Rhino-cyt platform, which discards the FP with great accuracy.

A final remark should be given about the execution time. Time to process a set of 50 fields manually may exceed half an hour or more. It depends largely on the expertise of the specialist and on the specific field density and cell agglomeration [57].

Time to process a single field automatically may vary depending on how dense the field is. We observed an elapsed time of 4.2 s to process the field in Figure 4, 4.1 s to process the field in Figure 5, and 2.1 s for the field in Figure 9. We estimated the average processing time on 10 slides of differing densities, obtaining 2.9 ± 1.1 s. This result was obtained with a low-end/low-cost smartphone, Xiaomi Redmi Note 7, but of course, it largely depends on the device hardware. In this phase, we really focused on demonstrating the feasibility of the proposed approach in terms of segmentation effectiveness (i.e., the extraction of the cells and getting the approval of specialists about the efficacy and usefulness of this system). Then, it is worthwhile to invest in research and the development of technologies, such as those presented in this paper, while software efficiency can be pursued, but it might not be necessary, given that higher-end smartphones are increasingly more powerful and cheaper.

6. Conclusions

The advancements in the nasal cytology field and the evolution of smartphone technology have allowed for the realization of this project. The aim of designing a system that would support the specialist during the observation phase of the slides has been reached through the development of this system, able to acquire an image from the digital microscope and to extract the cellular elements. The main advantages of this application is that the cell counting activity is faster than the manual process, together with its ease of use and the possibility of sharing images obtained from the observed fields. In fact, the cell images extracted can be sent directly to a specific server, which automatically classifies and counts them, such as the Rhino-Cyt system [23]. A possible use of this system could also be in combination with a microscope, which allows for the automatic sliding of the slide. The specialist could manage the sliding and acquire the photo, as necessary. We are now setting ourselves two main goals. The first is to pursue effective full classification on the board and the second is to integrate other diagnostic tools, such as the one just published in the literature, which aims to diagnose dyskinesia of the hair cells of the nasal mucosa [58].

Author Contributions: Conceptualization, G.D. and P.R.F.; data curation, L.S. and F.D.; formal analysis, F.D. and D.D.P.; methodology, G.D., F.D. and L.S.; project administration, G.D.; resources, G.D.; software, P.R.F. and D.D.P.; validation, S.L.; writing—original draft, G.D. and D.D.P.; writing—review and editing, G.D., P.R.F., D.D.P. All authors have read and agreed to the published version of the manuscript.

Funding: This research received no external funding.

Conflicts of Interest: The authors declare no conflict of interest.

Appendix A

As we have written in the introduction section, to the best of our knowledge, to date, there are no public or private laboratories that carry out the examination of the cell population of the nasal mucosa routinely, as instead it is done for hematological tests. The first studies about the automatic extraction and classification of the cells of the nasal mucosa were published by some of the authors of this paper. Now, specialists would prefer to carry out the entire evaluation of the cell population on a personal device, such as a smartphone, fully automatically, with the aim of increasing the screening and routine monitoring of nasal disease through cytology.

The use of a smartphone-based system also guarantees the preservation of the privacy and security of patient information. On the other hand, it makes it possible to send patient data and images to the Electronic Medical Record [8] to follow-up with the patient or to obtain a "second opinion", an increasingly widespread practice. However, this further possibility is reserved for patients who request it and, for these, a security protocol should be used. When the classification is carried out completely on the smartphone, nothing must be transferred remotely; however, several problems have to be overcome first, among all the limitations of the computational capacity of mobile architectures.

Our system is based on well-known algorithms in the literature—not state-of-the-art, but effective enough for our purpose. These are already sustainable from a computational point of view from medium–low end architectures, such as the Xiaomi, used for this experimentation. The use of traditional image processing techniques to preprocess the image is also battery-efficiently on a mobile phone.

At this stage, the system designed and described in this paper is limited to the extraction of cells from the microscopic field. Once this is done, the specialist can decide to manually evaluate the segmented cells or to send them to the Rhino-cyt platform for a fast classification. So, the system is already very useful.

Appendix B

As can be seen from Figure A1, the system presents a modular architecture, composed of several interacting objects or classes. The structure of the application has been designed to ensure a two-layer division—the presentation layer and the status of the business logic. The first layer includes the Java classes that play the role of activities, having the task to show the screens with the GUI and to define the various behaviors of the application, based on the user interaction with the interfaces. The second layer belongs to the Java classes that implement the algorithm proposed in the previous paragraphs

Appl. Sci. **2020**, *10*, 4567

and accesses the file system of the smartphone, playing the role of operating classes for the back-end. Below are described the main modules and methods.

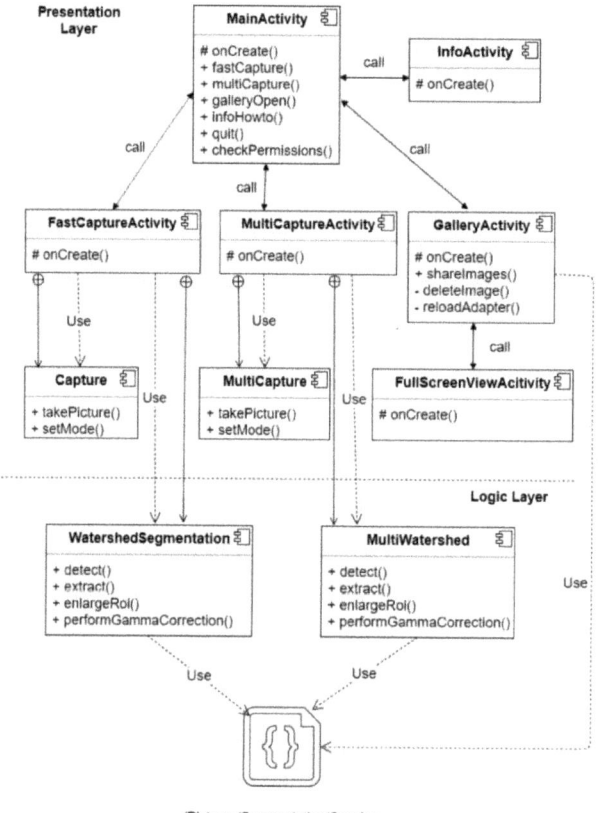

Figure A1. Software architecture.

MainActivity represents the main class, as well as the activity that is activated by the Android operating system, invoking the onCreate method. Other methods of MainActivity are fastCapture, multiCapture, galleryOpen, and infoHowto, invoking other activities that are part of the application, described below. Additionally, quit and checkPermissions methods are invoked, respectively, to close the application and to check if permissions have been granted to allow the app to access the device memory, take pictures, and use the Internet connection.

FastCaptureActivity and Capture are both part of the presentation layer, and represent, respectively, the function that allows you to take a single photo and immediately extract the cellular elements to send, and one of its internal classes. FastCaptureActivity, after its invocation with the onCreate method, uses its inner-class Capture to activate the camera and display the frames captured by the latter, with which it will be possible to capture the digital images to submit to the extraction function. The first of the main methods of the Capture class is takePicture that acquires the photo and, after converting it from Bitmap type to Mat type, it stores it in a variable that will be the input of the algorithm of detection and extraction.

MultiCaptureActivity and MultiCapture, are similar to the previous classes with the only difference being that the MultiCaptureActivity class allows you to take any number of photos, acquired thanks to the MultiCapture class that temporarily saves them in a data structure (ArrayList) and provides them all together with the detection and extraction algorithm.

GalleryActivity and FullScreenActivity deal with the visualization of the cells extracted from the algorithm. In particular, the first deals with the loading of the images extracted, accessing the memory of the device, and their visualization in a gallery, in which all the previews of the extracted cells that will be selectable and shareable will be displayed. In particular, the shareImages and deleteImage methods are used, respectively, to share the selected cells and to delete them from the device memory. The reloadAdapter method is used to update the gallery screen after sharing or deleting images, simply reloading the images from the memory. FullScreenActivity is the activity that is invoked by GalleryActivity every time you press on a preview. This activity allows the full screen display of the selected cell.

InfoActivity displays a screen with instructions on how to use the application correctly.

WatershedSegmentation and MultiWatershed are the internal classes belonging, respectively, to FastCaptureActivity and MultiCaptureActivity activities. They are instantiated every time the process of identification and the extraction of cellular elements from the photo(s) taken are started. Their most important methods are detected, which represents the process related to the identification of the cells, proposed in the algorithm described above, the extract method that extracts the elements identified by the previous method, creating a new image for each of them representing only the region of interest that circumscribes the cell, the enlargeRoi method that allows the user to enlarge the area of the region of interest around the cell, and finally the performGammaCorrection method, invoked by the detect method for the gamma correction. Both classes access the smartphone file system and save the cells in the /Pictures/Segmentation/Session directory. This path will be created automatically the first time you launch the application.

Each of the above activities is associated with a layout defined in XML.

References

1. Dimauro, G.; Caivano, D.; Bevilacqua, V.; Girardi, F.; Napoletano, V. VoxTester, software for digital evaluation of speech changes in Parkinson disease. In Proceedings of the 2016 IEEE International Symposium on Medical Measurements and Applications, MeMeA, Benevento, Italy, 15–18 May 2016; ISBN 9781467391726. [CrossRef]
2. Bevilacqua, V.; Brunetti, A.; Trotta, G.F.; Dimauro, G.; Elez, K.; Alberotanza, V.; Scardapane, A. A Novel Approach for Hepatocellular Carcinoma Detection and Classification Based on Triphasic CT Protocol. In Proceedings of the IEEE Congress on Evolutionary Computation, San Sebastian, Spain, 5–8 June 2017. [CrossRef]
3. Rubaiat, S.Y.; Rahman, M.M.; Hasan, M.K. Important Feature Selection & Accuracy Comparisons of Different Machine Learning Models for Early Diabetes Detection. In Proceedings of the 2018 International Conference on Innovation in Engineering and Technology (ICIET), Dhaka, Bangladesh, 27–28 December 2018; pp. 1–6. [CrossRef]
4. Dimauro, G.; Bevilacqua, V.; Colizzi, L.; Di Pierro, D. TestGraphia, a Software System for the Early Diagnosis of Dysgraphia. *IEEE Access* **2020**, *8*, 19564–19575. [CrossRef]
5. Hasan, M.K.; Aziz, M.H.; Zarif, M.I.I.; Hasan, M.; Hashem, M.M.A.; Guha, S.; Love, R. HeLP ME: Recom-mendations for Non-invasive Hemoglobin Level Prediction in Mobile-phone Environment. *JMIR mHealth uHealth* **2020**, in press. Available online: https://preprints.jmir.org/preprint/16806/accepted (accessed on 20 June 2020).
6. Gigantesco, A.; Giuliani, M. Quality of life in mental health services with a focus on psychiatric rehabilitation practice. *Annali dell'Istituto Superiore di Sanita* **2011**, *47*, 363–372. [CrossRef]
7. Dimauro, G.; Caivano, D.; Girardi, F.; Ciccone, M.M. The Patient Centered Electronic Multimedia Health Fascicle-EMHF. In Proceedings of the 2014 IEEE Workshop on Biometric Measurements and Systems for Security and Medical Applications (BIOMS), Rome, Italy, 17 October 2014; ISBN 9781479951758. [CrossRef]

8. Dimauro, G.; Girardi, F.; Caivano, D.; Colizzi, L. Personal Health E-Record—Toward an enabling Ambient Assisted Living Technology for communication and information sharing between patients and care providers. In *Ambient Assisted Living*; Springer: Cham, Switzerland, 2018; ISBN 9783030059200. [CrossRef]
9. Maglietta, R.; Amoroso, N.; Boccardi, M.; Bruno, S.; Chincarini, A.; Frisoni, G.B.; Inglese, P.; Redolfi, A.; Tangaro, S.; Tateo, A.; et al. Automated hippocampal segmentation in 3D MRI using random undersampling with boosting algorithm. *Pattern Anal. Appl.* **2016**, *19*, 579–591. [CrossRef]
10. Celebi, M.E.; Wen, Q.; Hwang, S.; Iyatomi, H.; Schaefer, G. Lesion border detection in dermoscopy images using ensembles of thresholding methods. *Skin Res. Technol.* **2013**, *19*, e252–e258. [CrossRef]
11. Rasche, C. Melanoma Recognition with an Ensemble of Techniques for Segmentation and a Structural Analysis for Classification. *arXiv* **2018**, arXiv:1807.06905.
12. Dimauro, G.; Simone, L. Novel biased normalized cuts approach for the automatic segmentation of the conjunctiva. *Electronics* **2020**, *9*, 997. [CrossRef]
13. Rasche, C. Fleckmentation: Rapid segmentation using repeated 2-means. *IET Image Process.* **2019**, *13*, 1940–1943. [CrossRef]
14. Piuri, V.; Scotti, F. Morphological classification of blood leucocytes by microscope images. In Proceedings of the 2004 IEEE International Conference on Computational Intelligence for Measurement Systems and Applications, Boston, MA, USA, 14–16 July 2004; pp. 103–108. [CrossRef]
15. Qiao, G.; Zong, G.; Sun, M.; Wang, J. Automatic neutrophil nucleus lobe counting based on graph representation of region skeleton. *Cytom. Part A* **2012**, *81A*, 734–742. [CrossRef]
16. Li, Q.; Wang, Y.; Liu, H.; Wang, J.; Guo, F. A combined spatial-spectral method for auto- mated white blood cells segmentation. *Opt. Laser Technol.* **2013**, *54*, 225–231. [CrossRef]
17. Bevilacqua, V.; Buongiorno, D.; Carlucci, P.; Giglio, F.; Tattoli, G.; Guarini, A.; Sgherza, N.; de Tullio, G.; Minoia, C.; Scattone, A.; et al. A supervised CAD to support telemedicine in hematology. In Proceedings of the 2015 International Joint Conference on Neural Networks, Killarney, Ireland, 12–17 July 2015. [CrossRef]
18. Zheng, Q.; Milthorpe, B.K.; Jones, A.S. Direct neural network application for automated cell recognition. *Cytometry* **2004**, *57A*, 1–9. [CrossRef] [PubMed]
19. Osowski, S.; Siroi, R.; Markiewicz, T.; Siwek, K. Application of support vector machine and genetic algorithm for improved blood cell recognition. *IEEE Trans. Intrum. Meas.* **2009**, *58*, 2159–2168. [CrossRef]
20. Theera-Umpon, N.; Gader, P.D. System-level training of neural networks for counting white blood cells. *IEEE Trans. Syst. Man Cybern. Part C Appl. Rev.* **2002**, *32*, 48–53. [CrossRef]
21. Bousquet, J.; Schünemann, H.J.; Samolinski, B.; Demoly, P.; Baena-Cagnani, C.E.; Bachert, C.; Bonini, S.; Boulet, L.P.; Bousquet, P.J.; Brozek, J.L.; et al. Allergic Rhinitis and its Impact on Asthma (ARIA): Achievements in 10 years and future needs. World Health Organization Collaborating Center for Asthma and Rhinitis. *J. Allergy Clin. Immunol.* **2012**, *130*, 1049–1062. [CrossRef]
22. Dimauro, G.; Girardi, F.; Gelardi, M.; Bevilacqua, V.; Caivano, D. Rhino-Cyt: A System for Supporting the Rhinologist in the Analysis of Nasal Cytology. *Lect. Notes Comput. Sci.* **2018**, 619–630. [CrossRef]
23. Dimauro, G.; Ciprandi, G.; Deperte, F.; Girardi, F.; Ladisa, E.; Latrofa, S.; Gelardi, M. Nasal cytology with deep learning techniques. *Int. J. Med. Inform.* **2019**, *122*, 13–19. [CrossRef]
24. Dimauro, G.; Deperte, F.; Maglietta, R.; Bove, M.; La Gioia, F.; Renò, V.; Simone, L.; Gelardi, M. A Novel Approach for Biofilm Detection Based on a Convolutional Neural Network. *Electronics* **2020**, *9*, 881. [CrossRef]
25. Merenda, M.; Porcaro, C.; Iero, D. Edge Machine Learning for AI-Enabled IoT Devices: A Review. *Sensors* **2020**, *20*, 2533. [CrossRef]
26. Lee, D.D.; Seung, H.S. Learning in intelligent embedded systems. In WOES'99, *Proceedings of the Workshop on Embedded Systems on Workshop on Embedded Systems, Cambridge, MA, USA, 29–31 March 1999*; USENIX Association: Berkeley, CA, USA, 1999; p. 9.
27. Haigh, K.Z.; Mackay, A.M.; Cook, M.R.; Lin, L.G. *Machine Learning for Embedded Systems: A Case Study*; Technical Report; BBN Technologies: Cambridge, MA, USA, 2015.
28. Chen, J.; Ran, X. Deep Learning With Edge Computing: A Review. *Proc. IEEE* **2019**, *107*, 1655–1674. [CrossRef]
29. Sze, V.; Chen, Y.H.; Emer, J.; Suleiman, A.; Zhang, Z. Hardware for machine learning: Challenges and opportunities. In Proceedings of the 2017 IEEE Custom Integrated Circuits Conference (CICC), Austin, TX, USA, 30 April–3 May 2017; pp. 1–8.

30. Howard, A.G.; Zhu, M.; Chen, B.; Kalenichenko, D.; Wang, W.; Weyand, T.; Andreetto, M.; Adam, H. MobileNets: Efficient Convolutional Neural Networks for Mobile Vision Applications. *arXiv* **2017**, arXiv:1704.04861.
31. Iandola, F.N.; Han, S.; Moskewicz, M.W.; Ashraf, K.; Dally, W.J.; Keutzer, K. SqueezeNet: AlexNet-level accuracy with 50x fewer parameters and <0.5MB model size. *arXiv* **2016**, arXiv:1602.07360.
32. Valueva, M.; Valuev, G.; Semyonova, N.; Lyakhov, P.; Chervyakov, N.; Kaplun, D.; Bogaevskiy, D. Construction of Residue Number System Using Hardware Efficient Diagonal Function. *Electronics* **2019**, *8*, 694. [CrossRef]
33. Dimauro, G.; Impedovo, S.; Pirlo, G.; Salzo, A. RNS architectures for the implementation of the 'diagonal function'. *Inf. Process. Lett.* **2000**, *73*, 189–198. [CrossRef]
34. Dimauro, G.; Impedovo, S.; Modugno, R.; Pirlo, G.; Stefanelli, R. Residue-to-binary conversion by the "quotient function". In *IEEE Transactions on Circuits and Systems II: Analog and Digital Signal Processing*; IEEE: Piscataway, NJ, USA, 2003; Volume 50, pp. 488–493. [CrossRef]
35. Gelardi, M. *Atlas of Nasal Cytology for the Differential Diagnosis of Nasal Diseases*; Edi. Ermes: Milano, Italy, 2012; ISBN 9781467530354.
36. Gelardi, M.; Iannuzzi, L.; Quaranta, N.; Landi, M.; Passalacqua, G. Nasal cytology-Pratical aspects and clinical relevance. *Clin. Exp. Allergy* **2016**, *46*, 785–792. [CrossRef]
37. Gelardi, M. Citologia Nasale. Available online: http://www.citologianasale.eu/citologia.htm (accessed on 20 June 2020).
38. Paulista, U.E.; Em, P.D.E.P.; Biológicas, C. *The Electrical Engineering Handbook*; CRC Press: London, UK, 1997; ISBN 978-0133354492.
39. Covington, M.A. Overview of image processing. In *Digital SLR Astrophotography*; Cambridge University Press: Cambridge, UK, 2009; pp. 145–164. ISBN 978-0-511-37853-9.
40. Dimauro, G.; Guarini, A.; Caivano, D.; Girardi, F.; Pasciolla, C.; Iacobazzi, A. Detecting clinical signs of anaemia from digital images of the palpebral conjunctiva. *IEEE Access* **2019**, *7*, 113488–113498. [CrossRef]
41. Dimauro, G.; Baldari, L.; Caivano, D.; Colucci, G.; Girardi, F. Automatic Segmentation of Relevant Sections of the Conjunctiva for Non-Invasive Anemia Detection. In Proceedings of the 2018 3rd International Conference on Smart and Sustainable Technologies (SpliTech), Split, Croatia, 26–29 June 2018; pp. 1–5.
42. Hasan, M.K.; Haque, M.; Sakib, N.; Love, R.; Ahamed, S.I. Smartphone-based Human Hemoglobin Level Measurement Analyzing Pixel Intensity of a Fingertip Video on Different Color Spaces. *Smart Health* **2018**, *5–6*, 26–39. [CrossRef]
43. Shih, F.Y. *Image Processing and Mathematical Morphology: Fundamentals and Applications*; CRC Press: Boca Raton, FL, USA, 2017; ISBN 9781315218557.
44. Bankman, I. *Handbook of Medical Image Processing and Analysis*; Elsevier: Amsterdam, The Netherlands, 2008; p. 1393. ISBN 9780123739049.
45. Dimauro, G. A new image quality metric based on human visual system. In Proceedings of the 2012 IEEE International Conference on Virtual Environments Human-Computer Interfaces and Measurement Systems (VECIMS) Proceedings, Tianjin, China, 2–4 July 2012; pp. 69–73. [CrossRef]
46. Dimauro, G.; Altomare, N.; Scalera, M. PQMET: A digital image quality metric based on human visual system. In Proceedings of the 4th International Conference on Image Processing Theory, Tools and Applications (IPTA), Paris, France, 14–17 October 2014; pp. 1–6. [CrossRef]
47. Kaur, D.; Kaur, Y. Various Image Segmentation Techniques: A Review. *Int. J. Comput. Sci. Mob. Comput.* **2014**, *3*, 809–814.
48. Comaniciu, D.; Meer, P. Mean shift: A robust approach toward feature space analysis. *IEEE Trans. Pattern Anal. Mach. Intell.* **2002**, *24*, 603–619. [CrossRef]
49. Fukunaga, K.; Hostetler, L.D. The Estimation of the Gradient of a Density Function, with Applications in Pattern Recognition. *IEEE Trans. Inf. Theory* **1975**, *21*, 32–40. [CrossRef]
50. Cheng, Y. Mean Shift, Mode Seeking, and Clustering. *IEEE Trans. Pattern Anal. Mach. Intell.* **1995**, *17*, 790–799. [CrossRef]
51. Nedrich, M. Mean Shift Clustering. Available online: https://spin.atomicobject.com/2015/05/26/mean-shift-clustering/ (accessed on 20 June 2020).
52. Otsu, N. A threshold selection method from gray-level histograms. *IEEE Trans. Syst. Man Cybern.* **1996**, *9*, 62–66. [CrossRef]
53. Sahir, S. Canny Edge Detection Step by Step in Python. Available online: https://towardsdatascience.com/canny-edge-detection-step-by-step-in-python-computer-vision-b49c3a2d8123 (accessed on 20 June 2020).

54. Canny, J. A Computational Approach to Edge Detection. *IEEE Trans. Pattern Anal. Mach. Intell.* **1986**, *8*, 679–698. [CrossRef]
55. Dougherty, E.; Lotufo, R.A. *Hands-on Morphological Image Processing*; SPIE Press Book: Bellingham, DC, USA, 2003; ISBN 9780819447203.
56. Efford, N. *Morphological Image Processing, in Digital Image Processing: A Practical Introduction Using Java*; Pearson Education: Harrow, UK, 2000; ISBN 978-0201596236.
57. Dimauro, G.; Bevilacqua, V.; Fina, P.R.; Buongiorno, D.; Brunetti, A.; Latrofa, S.; Cassano, M.; Gelardi, M. Comparative Analysis of Rhino-Cytological Specimens with Image Analysis and Deep Learning Techniques. *Electronics* **2020**, *9*, 952. [CrossRef]
58. Renò, V.; Sciancalepore, M.; Dimauro, G.; Maglietta, R.; Cassano, M.; Gelardi, M. A novel approach for the automatic estimation of Ciliated cells Beating Frequency. *Electronics* **2020**, *9*, 1002. [CrossRef]

© 2020 by the authors. Licensee MDPI, Basel, Switzerland. This article is an open access article distributed under the terms and conditions of the Creative Commons Attribution (CC BY) license (http://creativecommons.org/licenses/by/4.0/).

Article
Leaf Image Recognition Based on Bag of Features

Yaonan Zhang [1,2], Jing Cui [3], Zhaobin Wang [1,2,3,*], Jianfang Kang [1,2] and Yufang Min [1,2]

1. Northwest Institute of Eco-Environment and Resources, Chinese Academy of Sciences, Lanzhou 730000, China; yaonan@lzb.ac.cn (Y.Z.); kangjf@lzb.ac.cn (J.K.); myf@lzb.ac.cn (Y.M.)
2. National Cryosphere Desert Data Center, Lanzhou 730000, China
3. School of Information Science and Engineering, Lanzhou University, Lanzhou 730000, China; cuij18@lzu.edu.cn
* Correspondence: wangzhb@lzu.edu.cn

Received: 3 June 2020; Accepted: 24 July 2020; Published: 28 July 2020

Abstract: Plants are ubiquitous in human life. Recognizing an unknown plant by its leaf image quickly is a very interesting and challenging research. With the development of image processing and pattern recognition, plant recognition based on image processing has become possible. Bag of features (BOF) is one of the most powerful models for classification, which has been used for many projects and studies. Dual-output pulse-coupled neural network (DPCNN) has shown a good ability for texture features in image processing such as image segmentation. In this paper, a method based on BOF and DPCNN (BOF_DP) is proposed for leaf classification. BOF_DP achieved satisfactory results in many leaf image datasets. As it is hard to get a satisfactory effect on the large dataset by a single feature, a method (BOF_SC) improved from bag of contour fragments is used for shape feature extraction. BOF_DP and LDA (linear discriminant analysis) algorithms are, respectively, employed for textual feature extraction and reducing the feature dimensionality. Finally, both features are used for classification by a linear support vector machine (SVM), and the proposed method obtained higher accuracy on several typical leaf datasets than existing methods.

Keywords: feature extraction; shape context; plant recognition; DPCNN; BOF

1. Introduction

The traditional plant classification method is mainly realized by artificial recognition, which has the disadvantages of being time-consuming, susceptible to subjective judgment, and low recognition accuracy, far from meeting the requirements for rapid and accurate plant identification. Therefore, the rapid and accurate identification of plants is very challenging and meaningful. Plant recognition has been a challenging study since early last century, and plants play an irreplaceable role in human life. In the last decades, many researchers have studied image processing and pattern recognition as well as paid extensive attention to plant recognition. They have used images of plant organs (e.g., leaf, flower, fruit, and bark) for plant recognition.

In fact, although the images of flower, fruit, and bark have been employed for plant recognition, they have low recognition rates. In addition, these organ images have some limits; for instance, the flowering period is short and the texture of bark is unstable. Compared with flower, fruit, and bark, leaf images can be collected easily during the year, and its shape and texture are also stable. Therefore, the leaf is used as one of the important features for identifying plants. Most methods for plant recognition based on image processing rely on leaf images. In other words, plant species are recognized by leaf recognition.

In pattern recognition, using shape, texture, and color features for classification has been widely used. Soumyabrata et al. [1] proposed an improved text-based classification method to improve the classification results by integrating color and texture information. In addition, different color components and other parameters were compared and evaluated. Kristin et al. [2] introduced pattern recognition and computer vision as well as the application of texture features and pattern recognition. However, most leaves have small inter-class color differences, and some leaves have large intra-class color differences. As illumination may be uneven under natural conditions, the color features will affect recognition results. Therefore, the proposed method uses shape and texture features, which are more robust.

Both shape and texture features are used for leaf recognition. In 2012, Kumar et al. designed a mobile application Leafsnap, where histograms of curvature over scale (HoCS) [3] as a single (shape) feature was employed for plant identification. Other shape features are also used for leaf recognition, such as centroid-contour distance (CCD) [4], aspect ratio [5], Hu invariant moments [6], polar Fourier transform (PFT) [6], inner distance shape context (IDSC) [7], sinuosity coefficients [8], multiscale region transform (MReT) [9], etc. However, some leaves from different kinds of plants are very similar; the shapes of those leaves even cannot be differentiated by the naked eye. Hence, it is reasonable to use both shape feature and texture feature for leaf recognition. The most commonly used texture features contain entropy sequence (EnS) [10], histogram of gradients (HOG) [11], Zernike moments [12], scale invariant feature transform (SIFT) [13,14], gray-level co-occurrence matrix (GLCM) [15], and local binary patterns (LBP) [15]. Fu et al. [16] proposed a hybrid framework for plant recognition with complicated background. They extracted the block LBP operators as the texture features and calculated the Fourier descriptors as the shape features. Saleem et al. [17] combined 11 shape features, 7 statistical features, and 5 vein features for leaf recognition. Chaki et al. [18] used Gabor filter and GLCM to model texture feature and used a set of curvelet transform coefficients together with invariant moments to capture shape feature. Shao [19] proposed a new manifold learning method, namely supervised global-locality preserving projection (SGLP), for plant leaf recognition. Chaki et al. [20] proposed a novel approach by using the combination of fuzzy-color and edge-texture histogram to recognize fragmented leaf images. Some features based on Gabor filters [21,22], fractal dimension [23], locality projection analysis (SLPA) [24], kernel based principal component analysis (KPCA) [25], bag of word (BOW) [22,26] and convolutional neural networks (CNN) [27] are also used for leaf recognition.

In this paper, a new leaf feature called BOF_DP based on dual-output pulse-coupled neural network (DPCNN) and BOF is proposed, and an improved shape context called BOF_SC is also used in our plant image recognition system. The rest of the paper is organized as follows. Section 2 briefly introduces some related basic theories, including DPCNN and BOF. Section 3 introduces the theories related to feature extraction. Section 4 introduces the details of our proposed recognition method. Section 5 presents some comparative experimental results on several representative leaf image datasets.

2. Theory for Plant Recognition

2.1. Dual-Output Pulse-Coupled Neural Network

DPCNN was proposed by Li for geometry-invariant texture retrieval in 2012 [28]. The structure of DPCNN model is shown in Figure 1.

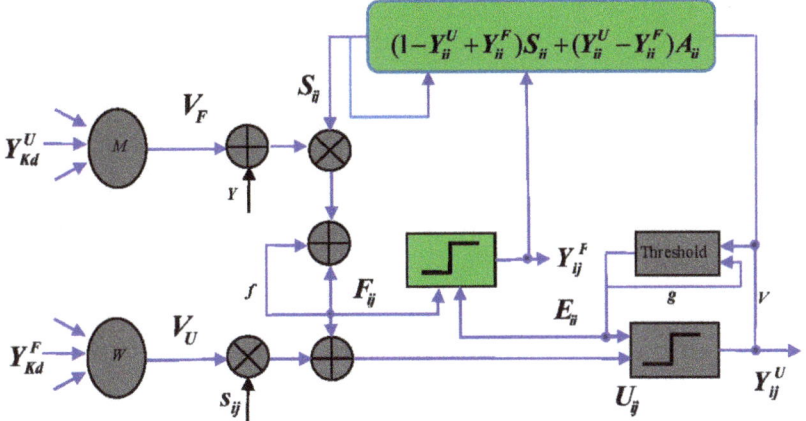

Figure 1. Structure of DPCNN.

The mathematical expressions of DPCNN model are as follows:

$$F_{ij}[n] = fF_{ij}[n-1] + S_{ij}[n](V_F \sum_{k,l} M_{ijkl} Y_{kl}^U[n-1] + \gamma) \qquad (1)$$

$$Y_{ij}^F[n] = \begin{cases} 1, F_{ij}[n] > T_{ij}[n] \\ 0, \text{otherwise} \end{cases} \qquad (2)$$

$$U_{ij}[n] = F_{ij}[n] + V_U S_{ij}[n] \sum_{kd} W_{ijkd} Y_{kd}^F[n] \qquad (3)$$

$$Y_{ij}^U[n] = \begin{cases} 1, U_{ij}[n] > T_{ij}[n] \\ 0, \text{otherwise} \end{cases} \qquad (4)$$

$$T_{ij}[n+1] = gT_{ij}[n] + V_E Y_{ij}^U[n] \qquad (5)$$

$$S_{ij}[n+1] = (1 - Y_{ij}^U[n] + Y_{ij}^F[n])S_{ij}[n] + (Y_{ij}^U[n] - Y_{ij}^F[n])A_{ij} \qquad (6)$$

where S is the external stimulus, and it changes depending on the current outputs Y^F and Y^U. V_E, V_U, V_F, f, and g are fixed constants between 0 and 1. W and M are the connection weights which the current neuron communicates with its neighbors. Y^F is the feeding out and Y^U is the compensating output.

Each neuron of DPCNN is an active neuron, which can be ignited by the feedback input or internal activity of the neuron to generate output pulse. First, the feedback input (F_{ij}) changes due to the influence of external stimuli and external compensation output from neighboring neurons. Once the value of the feedback input (F_{ij}) exceeds the active value, the neuron generates a feedback output pulse. Then, the feedback output, feedback input, and external stimulus from the neighboring neurons work together to change the value of the internal activity (U_{ij}). Once the value of the neuron's internal activity item exceeds its activity threshold, a compensation output pulse is generated. Finally, the activity threshold (E_{ij}) and external excitation (S_{ij}) values are updated.

The pulse sequence generated by pulse-coupled neural network (PCNN) can represent the image edge and texture information; thus, it can extract effective image features. However, there are still some limitations in feature extraction. For example, there is only one pulse generator in the entire neuron model, and the excitation of neurons lacks a compensation mechanism. DPCNN is improved based on the PCNN model. Compared with PCNN, DPCNN has the following advantages: (1) each neuron of DPCNN has two chances to be excited; (2) DPCNN can adaptively change the size of the external excitation of each neuron; and (3) received local stimuli from peripheral neurons are affected by the modulation of the input stimulus. In addition, DPCNN also has translation, rotation, scale invariance, and robustness.

When DPCNN is used for feature extraction, the input image must be a gray image and the intensity of a pixel should be between 0 and 1. In our tests, the parameters were the same as in Ref. [28], except the iterations. The output of each iteration is a binary image, which is called pulse image. The entropy of the pulse image is used as a feature, and, after n times-iteration, the feature EnS, which is a vector with lengths of n, is obtained.

2.2. Bag of Feature

BOF model represents an image as an orderless collection of local features, and it has been widely used in pattern recognition. After the efforts of many researchers, the BOF model, which is used with spatial pyramid matching (SPM) [29] and locality-constrained linear coding (LLC) [30], has good performance in many studies. The flow chart of the BOF classification model is shown in Figure 2.

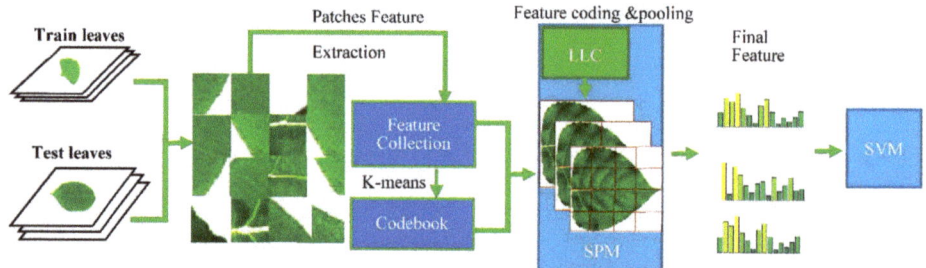

Figure 2. BOF classification system.

LLC is a linear coding scheme with local constraints. Local constraint makes coding results more accurate and acquires spare code, and it improves the speed of training and classification. The mathematical expression of LLC is as follows:

$$\min_c \sum_{i=1}^{M} \|x_i - B_{c_i}\|^2 + \lambda \|d_i \oplus c_i\|^2 \tag{7}$$

$$s.t. \cdot 1^T c_i = 1, \ \forall i$$

where $X = \{x_1, x_2, \ldots, x_N\}$ is the feature descriptor set obtained after the origin image blocking; c_i is the coding result of x_i; $\oplus$ denotes the dot product operation; and d_i is the Euclidean distance between x_i and B.

SPM is an algorithm of image matching, recognition, and classification using spatial pyramid, and it is a method for obtaining the spatial information of the image by statistically distributing image feature points on images of different resolutions. Generally, it has two steps:

(1) Extract features from different scales and combine them together.
(2) Convert features of different lengths into fixed-length features.

When BOF works, each image of the dataset is divided into many blocks, and the size of the block is always 8 × 8. To get a better effect, neighboring blocks are combined as a patch. The collection of patches can be regarded as a bag of components. Generally, the sizes of the patches of the collection are too big, and many patches are similar. Thus, it is reasonable to unify similar patches into a standard component. In fact, the above operation is calculated in feature space such as SIFT space and HOG space. Patches are expressed by feature extracted from themselves; the collection of standard components counted by K-means is called codebook; and the standard component is called code. For each patch, it is described by its neighborhood (the code in codebook) using a histogram which is the function of LLC. Finally, the histogram is pooling by SPM, and the sparse and smooth feature is obtained.

3. Feature Extraction

3.1. Dictionary Learning

As traditional method of learning codebook is based on the unsupervised learning method K-means, which does not take advantage of training label. When K-means works to find the center of clustering, it will calculate the distances between a center and all the points; however, there are only a few parts of points which contribute to the calculation of center. Each cluster center is regarded as a visual vocabulary in the dictionary. When the dataset is large, it will cost a large amount of time and computing resource. The cost of clustering is mainly determined by the size of the feature matrix, and normally the size of the feature matrix is large. The features of the training set are employed to reduce the number of points while finding effective centers. For each species, D centers are counted; its typical value is 8. Combine the cluster centers of each class to get a $D \times n$ dimensional dictionary, where n is the number of species. If the value of the clustering center is too small, the features cannot be accurately clustered, and the error is large. However, if the value of the clustering center is too large, it will increase the calculation amount and time consumption. Therefore, the cluster center value we choose can reduce the learning cost and improve the learning speed.

3.2. Shape Feature Extractions

The shape of leaf is a basic feature of leaf image; when people identify an object, its shape comes to our mind firstly. Similarly, for leaf image recognition, the shape is a simple and fast feature, but the effect of a feature may be not qualified for leaf recognition by itself, as many kinds of leaf images have similar shapes. Thus, in our system, shape feature is a minor feature. As shown in Figure 3, after getting the contour of leaf image, the contour is cut into numerous shape fragments; the middle points of each fragment are shown in Figure 3C.

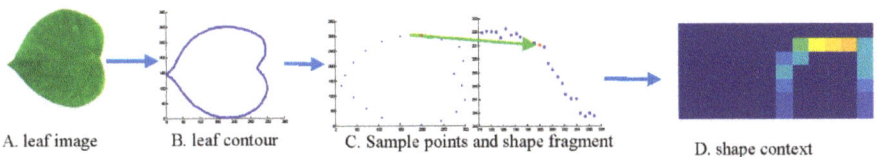

Figure 3. SC acquisition.

Then, shape context is used as a descriptor of each fragment. Finally, the BOF model is used for feature coding and pooling so that we can get a more effective feature. Unlike bag of contour fragments (BCF), in this paper, uniform sampling method and simple fragments are used to improve the speed for feature classification.

3.3. Texture Feature Extractions

When DPCNN works, the parameters must be set firstly; the parameters of DPCNN in this paper are from Ref. [28], except the times of iteration. In our method, the image is divided into many blocks with 8×8 sizes (assuming that the number of patches is N to each kind of leaf images), each block is regarded as a patch. Then, after the iteration of n times, there will be n entropy images, and the entropy of each patch in every entropy image will be counted in order, as shown in Figure 4. If the entropy of one patch is e_i, the entropy vector of the jth patch will be $E_j = [e_1, e_2 \ldots \ldots e_n]$. To a species, the features matrix will be E_{Nn}, and eight codes (center of clustering) will be counted based on this matrix too.

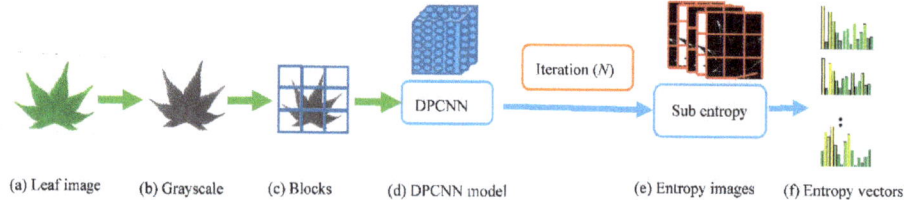

(a) Leaf image (b) Grayscale (c) Blocks (d) DPCNN model (e) Entropy images (f) Entropy vectors

Figure 4. Flow of getting entropy vector.

The process of extracting leaf image features by BOF_DPCNN combining DPCNN and BOF model is mainly divided into four stages: preprocessing, acquisition of DPCNN pulse images, low-level feature extraction, and feature coding. The process of obtaining image features of BOF_DPCNN is shown in Figures 4 and 5. Since the datasets we used are processed, the preprocessing stage can be ignored. As shown in Figure 4, the color image is converted to grayscale image firstly, and then the grayscale image is divided into blocks of the same size. For each small block, the DPCNN model is iterated to obtain the pulse entropy images. Finally, the entropy vectors are calculated from the entropy images to obtain low-level features. The BOF model is used to construct the codebook with low-dimensional features, LLC is used to encode, and SPM is used for pooling, as shown as Figure 5.

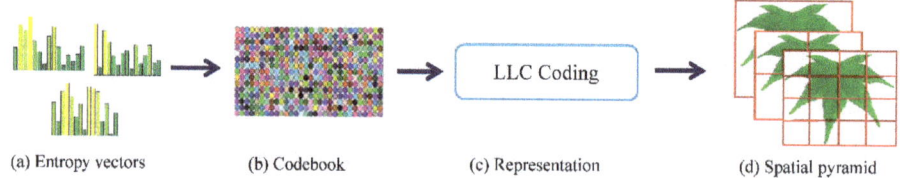

(a) Entropy vectors (b) Codebook (c) Representation (d) Spatial pyramid

Figure 5. Acquisition of image features using BOF_DPCNN: (**a**) entropy vectors obtained by DPCNN model; (**b**) codebook obtained by learning features; (**c**) the LLC coding; and (**d**) SPM for pooling.

4. Proposed Recognition Method

Image recognition has a fixed framework. In general, for plant recognition, object images acquired by special devices (e.g., camera or scanner) are used. In this paper, we select the leaf datasets with clean background for identification. Some key features which can identify the object are extracted from the images through various algorithms. The classifier is employed for classification after feature extraction. Most classifiers need to be trained by samples before classification. Finally, the result is obtained. The proposed method of leaf image recognition also adopts the above framework. The detailed scheme of the proposed method is shown in Figure 6. It can be divided into three steps: leaf image preprocessing, leaf feature extraction, and recognition. These steps are explained in the following.

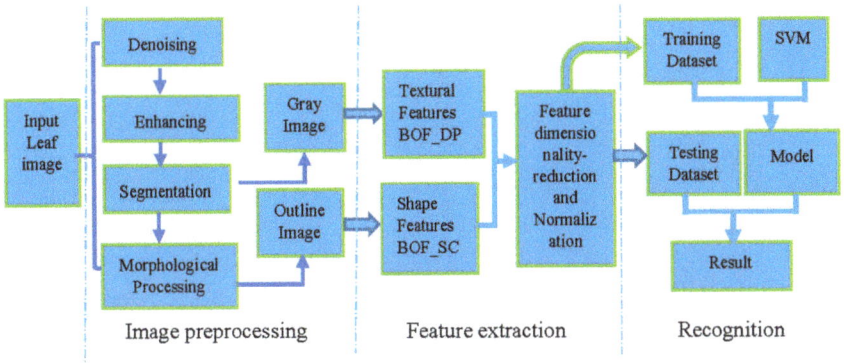

Figure 6. Scheme of the proposed method.

4.1. Image Preprocessing

The leaf image is preprocessed to improve image quality. Image preprocessing contains the following steps.

a. Image denoising: If the leaf image has some background information, the background should be deleted, which will decrease the calculations of features extraction. Because most leaf image datasets are built using optical scanners, the background is simple and easy to be removed by an adaptive threshold segmentation method.

b. Image segmentation: Sometimes the obtained leaf image has a complex background, and it needs to be separated from the background by segmentation. Since most leaf images contain some regions without value, the target region is extracted by a morphology method. Then, a quadrilateral is used to surround the target region. The quadrilateral is obtained from the original image and rotated to horizontal.

c. Image enhancement: Sometimes it is essential to enhance the contrast and texture of the image. Histogram equalization and linear stretching are adopted in this method. Then, high-pass filter is employed to enhance the edge and texture of the leaf image (gray image). Finally, texture feature is extracted from this gray image.

4.2. Feature Fusion

The feature extraction is introduced in Section 3. In this section, the two features are fused to a feature vector. Support F and T are the BOF_SC and BOF_DP features, respectively. Firstly, different weights α and β (support to $\alpha + \beta = 1$) are assigned to F and T, thus the feature vector can be expressed as $FV = [\alpha F, \beta T]$. The larger is the weight, the greater is the role of the feature in the fused feature. Because these weights greatly influence the final recognition result, α and β are usually determined after many experiments. As F and T are sparse matrices, FV is still a sparse matrix; it might be easy for classification, but it requires much memory. Thus, a direct linear discriminant analysis (LDA) algorithm [31] is used for dimensionality reduction. Finally, the final dimensionality of the feature vector is 1000.

4.3. Classification

There are many classifiers for leaf recognition, such as support vector machine (SVM) [10], probabilistic neural network (PNN) [5], K nearest neighbor (KNN) [32], and random forests [33]. The most commonly used is SVM for its high accuracy and easy of use. Liblinear [34] and Libsvm [35] are two popular SVM tools for classification. Although Libsvm and Liblinear can achieve similar results in linear classification, Liblinear is much more efficient than Libsvm in both training and prediction.

When the number of samples is large, Liblinear is significantly faster than Libsvm [36]. Thus, we use Liblinear rather than Libsvm. Given a set of training leaf features $Fv_i, y_i \in [1, \ldots, N]$, where N is the number of leaf species, when Liblinear is used for leaf recognition, the problem can be defined as:

$$r_i = \mathrm{argmax}_{n \in [1,\ldots,N], n \neq y_i} \omega_n^T Fv_i \tag{8}$$

$$\min_{\omega_1,\ldots,\omega_N} \left\{ \sum_{n=1}^{N} \|\omega_n\|^2 + c \sum_i \max(0, 1 + \omega_{r_i}^T Fv_i - \omega_{y_i}^T Fv_i) \right\} \tag{9}$$

$$\hat{y} = \mathrm{argmax}_{n \in [1,\ldots,N]} \omega_n^T Fv_i \tag{10}$$

When Liblinear works, it will learn a multi-class space. r_i represents the ith class learned from training data. In Equation (9), the first part is a linear regularization term or linear kernel. c is the weight of linear kernel. For the testing data, the predicted labels are defined by Equation (10).

5. Experiments and Analysis

5.1. Datasets

As leaf recognition becomes more and more attractive, many open source leaf datasets can be used for studies, such as Flavia [5], ICL [37], Swedish [38,39], MEW2012 [32], and so on.

Flavia dataset (http://flavia.sourceforge.net/) contains 1907 leaf images of 32 kinds, and it is the most used dataset for leaf recognition. Most leaves of Flavia dataset, as shown in Figure 7, are common plants in the Yangtze Delta, China. To each species, there are at least 50 leaves, which is enough for training and testing. These leaves are single leaves with the petiole removed and without complex background.

Figure 7. Standard leaf image of Flavia dataset.

The ICL dataset (http://www.intelengine.cn/English/dataset) is collected by the Intelligent Computing Laboratory of the Chinese Academy of Sciences. The database contains 16,848 leaf images from 220 plants, with a different number of leaf images for each species. Some examples are shown in Figure 8.

Figure 8. Standard leaf image of ICL dataset.

The Swedish leaf dataset (http://www.cvl.isy.liu.se/en/research/datasets/sw) contains leaf images of 15 species each with 75 samples, for a total of 1125 Swedish leaf images. Figure 9 shows some example leaf samples of the Swedish dataset.

Figure 9. Standard leaf image of Swedish dataset.

The MEW (Middle European Woods) dataset is a large dataset containing 153 species of Central European woody plants with a total of 9745 samples. Some examples are shown in Figure 10.

Figure 10. Standard leaf image of MEW dataset.

5.2. Length of DPCNN

When DPCNN works, the iteration is a significant parameter which would influence the effect of features. In Ref. [28], the iteration is set at 47. Generally, for most all PCNN models, e.g., ICM and

SCM, used for feature extraction, iterations are more than 30. To some degree, the iterative process is a process of feature extraction by using a dynamic threshold, which is the most prominent feature of PCNN models.

While the iterative process is also essential for BOF_DP, how much times it costs is the key point of this part. To find the best iteration of DPCNN, the iteration number was changed from 5 to 45 to find a better iteration below 45. In fact, if the iteration were 45 or more, the time for feature extraction would be too long, so the maximum of iteration was set at 45. On the other hand, for an image, the entropy vector is an approximate periodic vector; too many iterations would not be helpful, and, on the contrary, it would lower the feature's productivity. Flavia dataset was selected for testing, where 30 sample images were selected for training for each species, and the remaining images were tested. The average recognition rates are listed in Figure 11. It is clear that the accuracy reaches its peak after a sharp increase. After the peak, when the iteration is 20, the accuracy shows a noticeable steady fall, and it never presents a rising trend. Hence, the best iteration number is around 20.

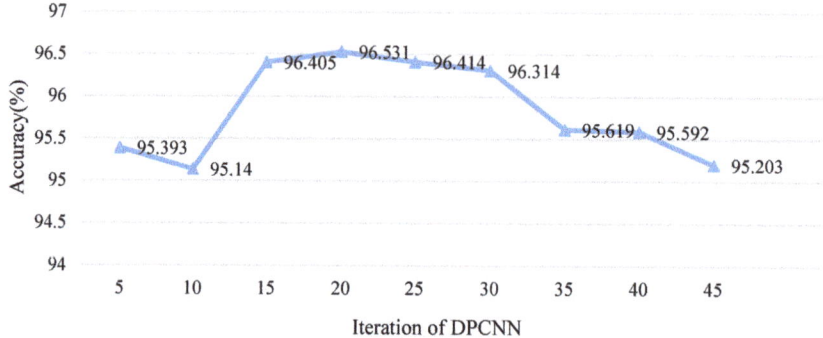

Figure 11. Relationship between Iteration of DPCNN and accuracy.

BOF_DP has the best effect when iteration number is 20 while the traditional DPCNN has the best feature when the iteration number is 47. The iteration process is reduced obviously. To some extent, this may be caused by the method of sub-block processing, when images are divided into smaller pieces. The local feature is more outstanding in each block, but, when the iteration number is oversized, there would be some unnecessary data that can be regarded as noise. Actually, when the iteration number is smaller than 20, the redundancy and noise also exist. Hence, an effective method for feature selection will be helpful for improving the efficiency of the proposed feature.

5.3. Effect and Stability Analysis

The train number of each species (tr_no) was changed from 5 to 30 as shown in Figure 12. To each training set, SIFT with LLC coding was used for comparison, and the training set and testing set were kept the same for each feature. All the accuracies are the average of 10 times.

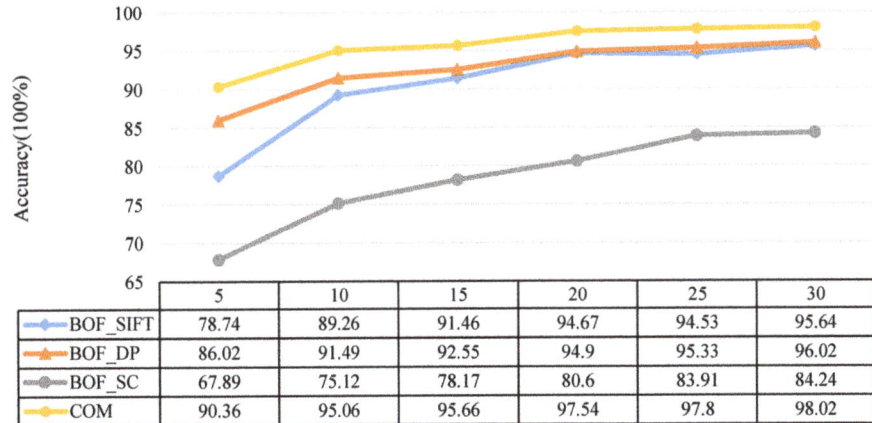

Figure 12. The relationship between the training number of each species and the recognition accuracy.

It is obvious that, for each feature, the accuracy increases with *tr_no*. However, we are most concerned with the proposed feature BOF_DP showing a better effect than BOF_SIFT. Both BOF_SIFT and BOF_DP are better than BOF_SC, and the combined features of BOF_DP and BOF_SC achieved the highest recognition accuracy in the Flavia dataset.

To show the results of recognition clearly, recognition rates for each species are shown in Figure 13. The training number of each class was 30, and the final recognition rate on Flavia dataset was 98.2049%. Except for Species 11 and 25, the recognition accuracies of other species were ideal.

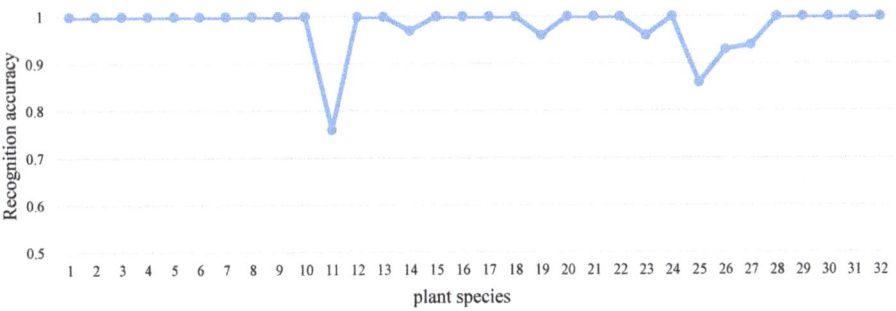

Figure 13. The recognition accuracy of each species in the Flavia dataset.

5.4. Comparison of Features

Some other features were used for comparison, as shown in Table 1. BOF_DP represents the proposed feature, BOW + SIFT represents the features in Ref. [14], BOW + SC is also a proposed method based on SC and BOW in Ref. [14], LLC + SIFT is the original LLC method using SIFT [29], DBCS is a deformation-based representation space for curved shapes, and the authors of [39] proposed an adaptation of k-means clustering for shape analysis in DBCS. 2DPCA [40] is the 2D-based method of principal component analysis (PCA) and uses the bagging classifier with the decision tree as a weak learner. The recognition accuracies of these features are relatively close. 2DPCA has the lowest accuracy among these features. The proposed feature BOF_DP obtains the highest accuracy in the comparison.

Table 1. Comparison of proposed feature with existing features on Flavia dataset.

Method	Species	Total Images	Training/Testing Images	Accuracy (%)
BOW + SC [14]	32	1907	945/962	94.76
BOW + SIFT [14]	32	1907	945/962	94.38
DBCS [39]	32	–	–/–	94.07
MEW [32]	32	1907	945/962	93.66
LLC + SIFT [29]	32	1907	945/962	95.00
2DPCA [40]	33	–	–/–	93.50
BOF_DP	32	1907	945/962	96.34

5.5. Comparison of Different Methods

We also compared the proposed method with other methods on some datasets. To test the effectiveness and extensibility of the proposed feature and system, leaf datasets Flavia, ICL [37], Swedish [38,42], and MEW2012 [32] were used for testing.

As ICL contains so many leaf images, most methods always take a part of ICL dataset for testing. To compare with the MEW method [32], we followed its setting. On each dataset, for each species, half of leaf images were chosen as training sets, and the rest were the testing set. Supposing the number of species is p; if p is an even number, the training leaf images number was $p/2$; otherwise, the training leaf images number was $(p + 1)/2$. Finally, the training set and the testing set were roughly equal (in fact, the testing set was larger than the training set). The detailed data of the four datasets are shown in Table 2. In the following, all tests were repeated 10 times to get a convincing result.

Table 2. Detail information of the four datasets.

Dataset	Swedish	Flavia	MEW2012	ICL
Total number	1125	1907	9745	16848
Training/testing	555/570	945/962	4839/4906	8397/8451
Species	15	32	153	220

First, we compared these methods on the Flavia dataset. The comparison results with other methods are shown in Table 3. ZRM [41] is a method based on Zernike moments. Z&H represents the method of Ref. [11], which is based on Zernike moments and histogram of oriented. VGG16 [42] and VGG19 [42] are the pre-trained models based on CNN architecture with logistic regression. MLAB (Margin, lobes, apex and base) [43] is the phenetic features of leaf. MLBP [44] is the method of extracting texture features based on modified local binary patterns. Muammer Turkoglu and Davut Hanbay [45] proposed the improved descriptors based on LBP, called region mean-LBP (RM-LBP), overall mean-LBP (OM-LBP), and ROM-LBP. RIWD (rotation invariant wavelet descriptor) [46] is a new shape proposed by Ehsan Yousefi et al. GIST [47] is an approach for plant recognition using GIST texture features. Wang et al. [48] proposed a few-shot learning method based on the Siamese network framework (S-Inception) to better classify the small sample size (where n is the number of species used in this experiment and the number of trainings is 20 n). Most of these comparison methods do not introduce the number of training and test samples. Among the comparative methods, the deep learning-based method [42,48] does not obtain the best recognition results, but is slightly lower than other machine learning methods [44–46]. SSV [17] is a fusion feature composed of 11 shape features, 7 statistical features, and 5 vein features. The recognition result of SSV is slightly higher than our proposed method. As shown in Table 3, the training samples of the experiment are far more than the test sample images. It can be seen from the method Z&H [11] in Table 4 that, when the number of training samples increases and the number of test samples decreases, the recognition rate increases. Further, our method uses more total images than SSV. The total images of SSV were 1600, while our total images were 1907. More than 300 images were removed in SSV. The Flavia dataset we used is original and unfiltered. Therefore, it is understandable that the SSV method obtains a slightly better recognition rate under the very superior experimental conditions. Overall, the proposed method is superior to most of other existing methods.

Table 3. Comparison of proposed method with existing methods on Flavia dataset.

Method	Species	Total Images	Training/Testing Images	Accuracy (%)
ZRM [41]	32	1600	1280/320	93.40
Z&H [11]	32	1600	1280/320	97.18
VGG16 [42]	32	1600	-/-	95.00
VGG19 [42]	32	1600	-/-	96.25
MLAB [43]	32	1907	1280/627	94.76
MLBP [44]	33	1907	-/-	97.55
RM-LBP [45]	-	-	-/-	97.94
OM-LBP [45]	-	-	-/-	97.89
RIWD [46]	-	-	-/-	97.50
GIST [47]	32	1907	-/-	95.50
S-Inception [48]	n	-	20n/-	95.32
SSV [17]	32	1600	1280/320	98.75
Proposed Method	32	1907	945/962	98.53

Table 4. Comparison of proposed method with existing methods on Swedish dataset.

Method	Species	Total Images	Training/Testing Images	Accuracy (%)
SMF [49]	15	1125	375/750	95.82
Z&H [11]	15	1125	375/750	95.86
	15	1125	750/375	98.13
MF [50]	15	1125	375/750	97.60
MARCH [51]	15	1125	-/-	96.21
MLBP [44]	15	1125	-/-	96.83
HSCs [52]	15	1125	375/750	96.91
CSD [53]	15	1125	-/-	97.07
MEW [32]	15	1125	555/570	96.53
CBOW [54]	15	1125	-/-	97.23
S-Inception [48]	n	-	20n/-	91.37
Proposed Method	15	1125	555/570	97.93

Table 4 shows the results of different methods on the Swedish dataset. It contains 1125 sample images from 15 species, with 75 images per species. The authors of [49] proposed SMF, which utilizes the area ratio to quantify the convexity/concavity of each contour point at different scales to construct margin feature, and they used a combination of morphological features as shape feature. Yang et al. [50] introduced a novel multiscale Fourier descriptor (MF) based on triangular features, which effectively captures the local and global features of leaf shape. MARCH [51] (multiscale arch height) is a novel multiscale shape description. Wang et al. [52] proposed a hierarchical string cuts (HSCs) method. CSD [53] is a counting-based shape descriptor for leaf recognition, which can capture global and local shape information independently. CBOW is a shape recognition algorithm based on the curvature bag of words (CBOW) model. Generally, the recognition accuracy is improved with the increase of the number of training samples. When the training number of the method Z&H [11] is 750, the recognition result is significantly improved, which is slightly higher than the method we propose. In addition, compared with the other existing methods, the proposed method is superior. S-Inception [48] obtained the lowest recognition accuracy, while MEW [32], MF [50] and CSD [53] were close to the accuracy of the proposed method. The recognition accuracies of the other methods were also very close.

For ICL dataset, some researchers only use part of samples from dataset. Hence, the detailed comparisons are listed in Table 5. GTCLC [55] is a leaf classification method using multiple descriptors. Cem Kalyoncu et al. proposed a new local binary pattern (LBP) descriptor, and they combined it with geometric, shape, texture, and color features for leaf recognition. The authors of [56] used several different descriptors to extract texture and shape features and proposed a pre-training method based on the PID to improve the DBNs. DWSRC (discriminant WSRC) [57] is the method proposed by Zhang et al. for large-scale plant species recognition. The authors of [58] presented the novel relative sub-image sparse coefficient (RSSC) algorithm for mobile devices. DBNs chose 50 species for training and testing and it obtained the highest accuracy with 96%, higher than the proposed method; however, when the number of species in the experiment was 220, the recognition accuracy dropped to 93.90%. When 220 species were selected for training and testing, our proposed method achieved the highest accuracy 94.22%.

Table 5. Comparison of proposed method with existing approaches on ICL dataset.

Method	Species	Total Images	Training/Testing Images	Accuracy (%)
SC [14]	220	16,848	8397/8451	53.93
SIFT [14]	220	16,848	8397/8451	72.26
DPCNN[28]	220	16,848	8397/8451	94.07
MEW[32]	220	16,848	8397/8451	84.62
GTCLC[55]	42	–	–/–	86.80
SMF[49]	50	1500	750/750	84.32
DBNs[56]	50	–	–/–	96.00
	220	–	–/–	93.90
MARCH[51]	220	5720	2860/2860	86.03
ROM-LBP[45]	–	–	–/–	83.71
DWSRC[57]	220	16,846	15,746/1100	91.12
	220	16,846	14,846/2000	90.64
RSSC[58]	220	–	–/–	92.94
Proposed Method	220	16,848	8397/8451	94.22

MEW dataset is also a large dataset. We compared our method with some classic methods, as shown in Table 6. The PCNN proposed by Wang et al. [59], based on pulse-coupled neural network and SVM, is a novel plant recognition method. PCNN and DPCNN have better performance than the others. It is obvious that the method we propose is better than the other methods.

Table 6. Comparison of the proposed method with existing approaches on MEW dataset.

Method	Species	Total Images	Training/Testing Images	Accuracy (%)
SC [14]	153	9745	4839/4906	60.44
SIFT [14]	153	9745	4839/4906	82.52
DPCNN [28]	153	9745	4839/4906	92.81
MEW [32]	153	9745	4839/4906	84.92
PCNN [59]	153	–	–/–	91.20
Proposed Method	153	9745	4839/4906	94.19

6. Conclusions

In this paper, we propose a new feature for plant recognition based on leaf image using DPCNN and BOF and propose a method combining BOF_SC and BOF_DP. In the proposed method, features of leaf are adopted, and SVM is taken as the classifier. Firstly, the proposed features BOF_DP were compared with the existing features on the Flavia dataset. After that, four famous leaf datasets were used to validate the performance of the proposed system. Experimental results show that BOF_DP has a better effect than other features, and our method is superior to other methods in recognition accuracy. However, to the DPCNN model, the parameters may not be optimal. In future work, we will try to find the best way to set the parameters automatically and improve the recognition accuracy.

Author Contributions: Writing—original draft preparation, Z.W. and J.C.; writing—review and editing, Z.W. and J.C.; project administration, Y.Z.; resources, J.K. and Y.M. All authors have read and agreed to the published version of the manuscript.

Funding: This study was jointly funded by China Postdoctoral Science Foundation (Grant No. 2013M532097), National Natural Science Foundation of China (Grant No. 61201421), the Foundation of National Glaciology Geocryology Desert Data Center (Grant No. Y929830201), and the 13th Five-year Informatization Plan of the Chinese Academy of Sciences(Grant No. XXH13506).

Conflicts of Interest: All Authors declare that they have no conflict of interest.

References

1. Dev, S.; Lee, Y.H.; Winkler, S. Categorization of cloud image patches using an improved texton-based approach. In Proceedings of the 2015 IEEE International Conference on Image Processing (ICIP), Quebec City, QC, Canada, 27–30 September 2015; pp. 422–426.
2. Kristin, J.D.; Gerard, M.; Sven, D. Computational Texture and Patterns: From Textons to Deep Learning. *Synth. Lect. Comput. Vis.* **2018**, *8*, 1–113.
3. Kumar, N.; Belhumeur, P.N.; Biswas, A.; Jacobs, D.W.; Kress, W.J.; Lopez, I.C.; Soares, J.V.B. Leafsnap: A computer vision system for automatic plant species identification. In Proceedings of the European Conference on Computer Vision, Florence, Italy, 7 October 2012; pp. 502–516.
4. Hasim, A.; Herdiyeni, Y.; Douady, S. Leaf Shape Recognition using Centroid Contour Distance. *IOP Conf. Ser. Earth Environ. Sci.* **2016**, *31*, 012002. [CrossRef]
5. Wu, S.G.; Bao, F.S.; Xu, E.Y.; Wang, Y.-X.; Chang, Y.-F.; Xiang, Q.-L. A leaf recognition algorithm for plant classification using probabilistic neural network. In Proceedings of the 2007 IEEE International Symposium on Signal Processing and Information Technology, Cairo, Egypt, 15–18 December 2007; pp. 11–16.
6. Singh, K.; Gupta, I.; Gupta, S. SVM-BDT PNN and Fourier moment technique for classification of leaf shape. *Int. J. Signal Process. Image Process. Pattern Recognit.* **2010**, *3*, 67–78.
7. Ling, H.B.; Jacobs, D.W. Shape classification using the inner-distance. *IEEE Trans. Pattern Anal* **2007**, *29*, 286–299. [CrossRef]
8. Kala, J.; Viriri, S. Plant specie classification using sinuosity coefficients of leaves. *Image Anal. Stereol.* **2018**, *37*, 119. [CrossRef]
9. Yu, X.; Gao, Y.; Xiong, S.; Yuan, X. Multiscale Contour Steered Region Integral and Its Application for Cultivar Classification. *IEEE Access* **2019**, *7*, 69087–69100. [CrossRef]
10. Wang, Z.; Sun, X.; Ma, Y.; Zhang, H.; Ma, Y.; Xie, W.; Zhang, Y. Plant recognition based on intersecting cortical model. In Proceedings of the 2014 International Joint Conference on Neural Networks (IJCNN), Beijing, China, 6–11 July 2014; pp. 975–980.
11. Tsolakidis, D.G.; Kosmopoulos, D.I.; Papadourakis, G. Plant leaf recognition using Zernike moments and histogram of oriented gradients. In Proceedings of the Hellenic Conference on Artificial Intelligence, Ioannina, Greece, 15–17 May 2014; pp. 406–417.
12. Kulkarni, A.H.; Rai, H.M.; Jahagirdar, K.A.; Upparamani, P.S. A leaf recognition technique for plant classification using RBPNN and Zernike moments. *Int. J. Adv. Res. Comput. Commun. Eng.* **2013**, *2*, 984–988.
13. Nilsback, M.-E.; Zisserman, A. Automated flower classification over a large number of classes. In Proceedings of the Indian Conference on Computer Vision, Graphics & Image Processing, Bhubaneswar, India, 16–19 December 2008; pp. 722–729.
14. Hsiao, J.-K.; Kang, L.-W.; Chang, C.-L.; Lin, C.-Y. Comparative study of leaf image recognition with a novel learning-based approach. In Proceedings of the IEEE Science and Information Conference, London, UK, 27–29 August 2014; pp. 389–393.
15. Tang, Z.; Su, Y.; Er, M.J.; Qi, F.; Zhang, L.; Zhou, J. A local binary pattern based texture descriptors for classification of tea leaves. *Neurocomputing* **2015**, *168*, 1011–1023. [CrossRef]
16. Fu, B.; Mao, M.; Zhao, X.; Shan, Z.; Yang, Z.; He, L.; Wang, Z. Recognition of Plants with Complicated Background by Leaf Features. *J. Phys. Conf. Ser.* **2019**, *1176*, 032053. [CrossRef]
17. Saleem, G.; Akhtar, M.; Ahmed, N.; Qureshi, W.S. Automated analysis of visual leaf shape features for plant classification. *Comput. Electron. Agric.* **2019**, *157*, 270–280. [CrossRef]
18. Chaki, J.; Parekh, R.; Bhattacharya, S. Plant leaf recognition using texture and shape features with neural classifiers. *Pattern Recognit. Lett.* **2015**, *58*, 61–68. [CrossRef]
19. Shao, Y. Supervised global-locality preserving projection for plant leaf recognition. *Comput. Electron. Agric.* **2019**, *158*, 102–108. [CrossRef]
20. Chaki, J.; Dey, N.; Moraru, L.; Fuqian, S. Fragmented plant leaf recognition: Bag-of-features, fuzzy-color and edge-texture histogram descriptors with multi-layer perceptron. *Opt. Int. J. Light Electron Opt.* **2019**, *181*, 639–650. [CrossRef]
21. Lin, F.-Y.; Zheng, C.-H.; Wang, X.-F.; Man, Q.-K. Multiple classification of plant leaves based on gabor transform and lbp operator. In Proceedings of the International Conference on Intelligent Computing, Shanghai, China, 15–18 September 2008; pp. 432–439.

22. Zheru, C.; Li, H.; Wang, C. Plant species recognition based on bark patterns using novel Gabor filter banks. In Proceedings of the International Conference on Neural Networks and Signal Processing, Nanjing, China, 14–17 December 2003; Volume 1032, pp. 1035–1038.
23. Fuentes, S.; Hernández-Montes, E.; Escalona, J.M.; Bota, J.; Gonzalez Viejo, C.; Poblete-Echeverría, C.; Tongson, E.; Medrano, H. Automated grapevine cultivar classification based on machine learning using leaf morpho-colorimetry, fractal dimension and near-infrared spectroscopy parameters. *Comput. Electron. Agric.* **2018**, *151*, 311–318. [CrossRef]
24. Zhang, S.W.; Lei, Y.K.; Dong, T.B.; Zhang, X.P. Label propagation based supervised locality projection analysis for plant leaf classification. *Pattern Recogn* **2013**, *46*, 1891–1897. [CrossRef]
25. Valliammal, N.; Geethalakshmi, S. An optimal feature subset selection for leaf analysis. *Int. J. Comput. Commun. Eng.* **2012**, *6*, 440–445.
26. Wang, X.G.; Feng, B.; Bai, X.; Liu, W.Y.; Latecki, L.J. Bag of contour fragments for robust shape classification. *Pattern Recogn.* **2014**, *47*, 2116–2125. [CrossRef]
27. Nguyen Thanh, T.K.; Truong, Q.B.; Truong, Q.D.; Huynh Xuan, H. Depth Learning with Convolutional Neural Network for Leaves Classifier Based on Shape of Leaf Vein. In Proceedings of the Intelligent Information and Database Systems, Dong Hoi City, Vietnam, 19–21 March 2018; pp. 565–575.
28. Li, X.J.; Ma, Y.D.; Wang, Z.B.; Yu, W.R. Geometry-Invariant Texture Retrieval Using a Dual-Output Pulse-Coupled Neural Network. *Neural Comput* **2012**, *24*, 194–216. [CrossRef]
29. Lazebnik, S.; Schmid, C.; Ponce, J. Beyond bags of features: Spatial pyramid matching for recognizing natural scene categories. In Proceedings of the IEEE Computer Society Conference on Computer Vision & Pattern Recognition, New York, NY, USA, 17–22 June 2006; pp. 2169–2178.
30. Wang, J.; Yang, J.; Yu, K.; Lv, F.; Huang, T.; Gong, Y. Locality-constrained linear coding for image classification. In Proceedings of the 2010 IEEE Conference on Computer Vision and Pattern Recognition (CVPR), San Francisco, CA, USA, 13–18 June 2010; pp. 3360–3367.
31. Yu, H.; Yang, J. A direct LDA algorithm for high-dimensional data—With application to face recognition. *Pattern Recogn.* **2001**, *34*, 2067–2070. [CrossRef]
32. Novotny, P.; Suk, T. Leaf recognition of woody species in Central Europe. *Biosyst. Eng.* **2013**, *115*, 444–452. [CrossRef]
33. Hall, D.; McCool, C.; Dayoub, F.; Sunderhauf, N.; Upcroft, B. Evaluation of features for leaf classification in challenging conditions. In Proceedings of the IEEE Winter Conference on Applications of Computer Vision, Waikoloa, HI, USA, 5–9 January 2015; pp. 797–804.
34. Fan, R.E.; Chang, K.W.; Hsieh, C.J.; Wang, X.R.; Lin, C.J. LIBLINEAR: A Library for Large Linear Classification. *J. Mach. Learn Res.* **2008**, *9*, 1871–1874.
35. Chang, C.C.; Lin, C.J. LIBSVM: A Library for Support Vector Machines. *Acm Trans. Intel. Syst. Tec.* **2011**, *2*, 1–27. [CrossRef]
36. Alvarsson, J.; Lampa, S.; Schaal, W.; Andersson, C.; Wikberg, J.E.; Spjuth, O. Large-scale ligand-based predictive modelling using support vector machines. *J. Cheminformatics* **2016**, *8*, 39. [CrossRef] [PubMed]
37. Hu, R.X.; Jia, W.; Ling, H.B.; Huang, D.S. Multiscale Distance Matrix for Fast Plant Leaf Recognition. *IEEE Trans. Image Process.* **2012**, *21*, 4667–4672. [PubMed]
38. Söderkvist, O. Computer vision classification of leaves from swedish trees. Master's Thesis, Linkoping University, Linkoping, Sweden, 2001; p. 74.
39. Demisse, G.G.; Aouada, D.; Ottersten, B. Deformation Based Curved Shape Representation. *IEEE Trans. Pattern Anal. Mach. Intell.* **2018**, *40*, 1338–1351. [CrossRef]
40. Tharwat, A.; Gaber, T.; Hassanien, A.E. One-dimensional vs. two-dimensional based features: Plant identification approach. *J. Appl. Log.* **2017**, *24*, 15–31. [CrossRef]
41. Kadir, A.; Nugroho, L.E.; Susanto, A.; Insap Santosa, P. Experiments of zernike moments for leaf identification. *J. Theor. Appl. Inf. Technol.* **2012**, *41*, 82–93.
42. Pearline, A.; Kumar, S.; Harini, S. A study on plant recognition using conventional image processing and deep learning approaches. *J. Intell. Fuzzy Syst.* **2019**, *36*, 1997–2004. [CrossRef]
43. Kolivand, H.; Bong, M.F.; Rahim, M.; Sulong, G.; Baker, T.; Tully, D. An expert botanical feature extraction technique based on phenetic features for identifying plant species. *PLoS ONE* **2018**, *13*, e0191447. [CrossRef]
44. Naresh, Y.G.; Nagendraswamy, H.S. Classification of medicinal plants: An approach using modified LBP with symbolic representation. *Neurocomputing* **2016**, *173*, 1789–1797. [CrossRef]

45. Turkoglu, M.; Hanbay, D. Leaf-based plant species recognition based on improved local binary pattern and extreme learning machine. *Phys. A Statal Mech. Appl.* **2019**, *527*, 121297. [CrossRef]
46. Yousefi, E.; Baleghi, Y.; Sakhaei, S.M. Rotation invariant wavelet descriptors, a new set of features to enhance plant leaves classification. *Comput. Electron. Agric.* **2017**, *140*, 70–76. [CrossRef]
47. Kheirkhah, F.M.; Asghari, H. Plant Leaf Classification Using GIST Texture Features. *IET Comput. Vis.* **2018**, *13*, 369–375. [CrossRef]
48. Wang, B.; Wang, D. Plant Leaves Classification: A Few-Shot Learning Method Based on Siamese Network. *IEEE Access* **2019**, *7*, 151754–151763. [CrossRef]
49. Zhang, X.; Zhao, W.; Luo, H.; Chen, L.; Peng, J.; Fan, J. Plant recognition via leaf shape and margin features. *Multimed. Tools Appl.* **2019**, *78*, 27463–27489. [CrossRef]
50. Yang, C.; Yu, Q. Multiscale Fourier descriptor based on triangular features for shape retrieval. *Signal Process. Image Commun.* **2018**, *71*. [CrossRef]
51. Wang, B.; Brown, D.; Gao, Y.; Salle, J.L. MARCH: Multiscale-arch-height description for mobile retrieval of leaf images. *Inf. Sci.* **2015**, *302*, 132–148. [CrossRef]
52. Wang, B.; Gao, Y. Hierarchical String Cuts: A Translation, Rotation, Scale, and Mirror Invariant Descriptor for Fast Shape Retrieval. *IEEE Trans. Image Process. Publ. IEEE Signal Process. Soc.* **2014**, *23*. [CrossRef]
53. Zhao, C.; Chan, S.S.F.; Cham, W.K.; Chu, L.M. Plant identification using leaf shapes—A pattern counting approach. *Pattern Recognit.* **2015**, *48*, 3203–3215. [CrossRef]
54. Zeng, J.; Liu, M.; Fu, X.; Gu, R.; Leng, L. Curvature Bag of Words Model for Shape Recognition. *IEEE Access* **2019**, *7*, 57163–57171. [CrossRef]
55. Kalyoncu, C.; Toygar, N. GTCLC: Leaf classification method using multiple descriptors. *IET Comput. Vis.* **2017**, *10*, 700–708. [CrossRef]
56. Liu, N.; Kan, J.-M. Improved deep belief networks and multi-feature fusion for leaf identification. *Neurocomputing* **2016**, *216*, 460–467. [CrossRef]
57. Zhang, S.; Zhang, C.; Zhu, Y.; You, Z. Discriminant WSRC for Large-Scale Plant Species Recognition. *Comput. Intell. Neurosci.* **2017**, *2017*. [CrossRef]
58. Prasad, S.; Peddoju, S.K.; Ghosh, D. An adaptive plant leaf mobile informatics using RSSC. *Multimed. Tools Appl.* **2017**, *76*, 21339–21363. [CrossRef]
59. Wang, Z.; Xiaoguang, S.; Zhang, Y.; Ying, Z.; Ma, Y. Leaf recognition based on PCNN. *Neural Comput. Appl.* **2015**. [CrossRef]

© 2020 by the authors. Licensee MDPI, Basel, Switzerland. This article is an open access article distributed under the terms and conditions of the Creative Commons Attribution (CC BY) license (http://creativecommons.org/licenses/by/4.0/).

Article

Automatic CNN-Based Arabic Numeral Spotting and Handwritten Digit Recognition by Using Deep Transfer Learning in Ottoman Population Registers

Yekta Said Can * and M. Erdem Kabadayı

College of Social Sciences and Humanities, Koç University, Rumelifeneri Yolu, 34450 Sarıyer, Istanbul, Turkey; mkabadayi@ku.edu.tr
* Correspondence: ycan@ku.edu.tr

Received: 3 July 2020; Accepted: 3 August 2020; Published: 6 August 2020

Abstract: Historical manuscripts and archival documentation are handwritten texts which are the backbone sources for historical inquiry. Recent developments in the digital humanities field and the need for extracting information from the historical documents have fastened the digitization processes. Cutting edge machine learning methods are applied to extract meaning from these documents. Page segmentation (layout analysis), keyword, number and symbol spotting, handwritten text recognition algorithms are tested on historical documents. For most of the languages, these techniques are widely studied and high performance techniques are developed. However, the properties of Arabic scripts (i.e., diacritics, varying script styles, diacritics, and ligatures) create additional problems for these algorithms and, therefore, the number of research is limited. In this research, we first automatically spotted the Arabic numerals from the very first series of population registers of the Ottoman Empire conducted in the mid-nineteenth century and recognized these numbers. They are important because they held information about the number of households, registered individuals and ages of individuals. We applied a red color filter to separate numerals from the document by taking advantage of the structure of the studied registers (numerals are written in red). We first used a CNN-based segmentation method for spotting these numerals. In the second part, we annotated a local Arabic handwritten digit dataset from the spotted numerals by selecting uni-digit ones and tested the Deep Transfer Learning method from large open Arabic handwritten digit datasets for digit recognition. We achieved promising results for recognizing digits in these historical documents.

Keywords: numeral spotting; historical document analysis; convolutional neural networks; deep transfer learning; handwritten digit recognition

1. Introduction

Historical documents are valuable sources for analyzing historical, social, and economic perspectives of the past. In order to provide immediate access to researchers and to the public, digitization processes of these archives have been carried out in recent decades including non-European handwritten archival collections [1]. Nevertheless, especially during maintenance periods, access to these archives could be restricted. Information retrieval and extraction are only possible through the digitalization processes. Page segmentation, keyword, number and symbol spotting, optical character recognition (OCR) and handwritten text recognition (HTR) are among the most applied techniques for these documents [2].

In page segmentation, the document is analyzed by separating the image into different areas such as graphics, backgrounds, decorations, and texts via page segmentation algorithms [3]. Historical document layout analysis is more difficult when compared to modern document processing since there are more issues to be dealt with: degrading documents, digitization errors, and different layout types, respectively [4]. Consequently, it is challenging to apply page segmentation on historical documents by using rule-based or projection-based methods [3]. Page segmentation can be applied before OCR, HTR and keyword spotting techniques in some cases that is why the page segmentation processes gain importance for the accurate digitization of historical manuscripts. The errors in the page segmentation process affect the output of these processes, which are used the digitalize the handwritten or printed manuscripts [2].

Keyword Spotting (KWS) is another widely used technique for information retrieval from historical documents. There are a lot of different types of keyword spotting. The keyword can be a word, symbol, or a numeral. Another widely known distinction is whether the spotting is done Query-by-Example/Query-by-String [5]. In QbE, the query is provided as a word image example, whereas, in QbS, it is provided as a character string. Other significant distinctions are training-based/training-free; i.e., whether the spotting technique requires or not to be trained on annotated images, and segmentation-based/segmentation-free; i.e., whether the spotting technique is applied to the whole page images or just to segmented images/parts of the whole page [5]. Usually, a training-based method decodes images and spots the most proper keyword position during training. Training-based keyword spotting methods are evaluated as more practical and they overcome multi-writers and multi-fonts issues [6].

Arabic scripts are widely adopted in manuscripts of different countries and cultures, e.g., Ottoman, Arabic, Urdu, Kurdish and Persian [7]. These scripts can be written in different ways, which complicates the page segmentation, keyword spotting, HTR and OCR processes. It is a cursive script in which combined letters form ligatures [7]. Moreover, the Arabic words can consist of dots and diacritics, which makes it even more difficult to extract information [7]. These properties might not cause problems for digit recognition since digits are isolated, but, when keyword spotting and handwritten text recognition algorithms are applied, they will create additional challenges.

Several methods have been proposed, and high identification accuracies are reported for the English handwritten digits [8,9]. Recently, researchers also proposed numeral spotting [10] and handwritten digit recognition systems for Arabic scripts on different datasets ([11–13]). These studies achieved accuracies above 90%. However, the used datasets are created recently, and they do not suffer from the mentioned problems of the historical documents.

In this study, we first automatically spotted the Arabic numerals from the very first series of population registers of the Ottoman Empire conducted in the mid-nineteenth century and recognized these numbers. The household numbers, registered individual ids and ages are written red in the studied documents. We implemented a red color filter to discriminate numerals from the document to take advantage of the structure of the registers. We further trained a CNN-based segmentation scheme for spotting these numerals. Our numeral spotting technique is both training-based and segmentation-based. In the second part, we formed a small Arabic digit dataset from the spotted numerals by selecting uni-digit ones and tested the Deep Transfer Learning (DTL) methods from the models trained in large open datasets for digit recognition. We also compared these results obtained by training and testing a system by using our dataset. We obtained promising results for recognizing Arabic digits in these historical documents.

We organized the rest of the paper as follows. The literature on historical document page segmentation, keyword spotting and Arabic digit recognition will be provided. We described the structure of the formed databases for spotting numerals and digit recognition in Section 3. Our numeral spotting technique and digit recognition method are described in Section 4. In Section 5, the experimental results and discussion are presented. We mention the conclusion and future works of this research in Section 6.

2. Related Works

Arabic document page segmentation has also been studied by using traditional machine learning (ML) techniques. Hesham et al. [7] proposed an automatic layout analysis scheme for Arabic manuscripts. They further appended a line segmentation support. Text and non-text areas were differentiated by using the Support Vector Machine (SVM) algorithm. They also identified words and lines.

Artificial Neural Networks were further tested on Arabic document layout analysis schemes. Bukhari et al. [14] differentiated the central body and the side manuscript by applying the Multilayer Perceptron (MLP) classifier. A dataset is created which includes 38 historical document images and they achieved 95% classification accuracy. Long Short Term Memory (LSTM) and CNN are employed for document page segmentation of scientific manuscripts written in English in [15,16]. Amer et al. developed a CNN-based document page segmentation scheme for Arabic newspapers and Arabic printed manuscripts. They obtained approximately 90% accuracy in detecting text and non-text areas. CNNs have also been employed for historical document layout analysis [2,3,17]. The page segmentation algorithms are important because they could be applied prior to keyword spotting, HTR and OCR techniques in some studies (as in our work) and, therefore, their performance is critical.

There are very few Arabic handwriting keyword spotting studies in the literature [6]. Some QbE studies ([18–20]) are proposed for the historical Arabic documents and used a matching method adjusted to the Arabic script. QbS approaches [21,22] used the HMM technique for keyword spotting in handwritten Arabic manuscripts. They were standard HMM KWS applications without taking the particular properties of the Arabic script into account. A spotting scheme is developed specifically for Arabic handwritten digits/symbols achieved an overall precision of 80% and 83.3% recall [10]. Another prominent keyword spotting research conducted on both historical Arabic dataset VML and George Washington datasets. Barakat et al. [23] applied a convolutional siamese network that uses two identical convolutional networks to rank the similarity between two word images. In this way, they developed a system which is more robust against different writing styles and is able to recognize out of vocabulary words.

After spotting the numerals, Arabic digits should be recognized for information retrieval from the historical manuscripts. Arabic digit recognition is a well-studied topic in the literature [13] (see Table 1). Melhaoui et al. proposed an Arabic digit recognition scheme that used multi-layer perceptron and K-nearest neighbor classifiers [24]. They run tests on the dataset include 600 Arabic digits with 200 testing images and 400 training images. They achieved 99% recognition accuracy on this small database. The HODA dataset was used for testing Persian (which is based on Arabic scripts) handwritten digit recognition systems in the literature [25–27]. Takruri et al. [28] proposed a three-level classifier that uses Support Vector Machine, Fuzzy C Means, and Unique Pixels for the classification of handwritten Arabic digits. They achieved 88% accuracy on the dataset containing 3510 images. Sawy et al. also achieved 88% accuracy by using CNN on the public ADBase dataset [13]. Kateeb et al. used the same dataset (ADBase) and applied the Dynamic Bayesian Network technique for digit recognition. They achieved 85.26% accuracy. Ashiquzzaman et al. achieved 97.3% accuracy by using MLP with appropriate activation and regularization functions on the public CMATERDB 3.3.1 Arabic handwritten digit dataset [29]. They further improved their system accuracy by using data augmentation and dropout to 99.4% [12]. However, as mentioned before, these studies were carried out on modern open datasets, and they did not need to alleviate the low-quality data issues of historical manuscripts. To the best of our knowledge, our study is the first to develop a CNN-based Arabic numeral spotting and handwritten digit recognition system for historical documents by using deep transfer learning methods.

Appl. Sci. **2020**, *10*, 5430

Table 1. The comparison of our study with the Arabic handwritten digit recognition studies on different datasets.

Article	Dataset	Dataset Type	Method	Accuracy (%)
[13] [2017]	ADBase	Modern Arabic	CNN + LeNet50	88
[25] [2018]	HODA	Modern Persian	CNN + LeNet	97.38
[11] [2014]	ADBase	Modern Arabic	Dynamic Bayesian Network	85.26
[26] [2019]	HODA	Modern Persian	CNN + CapsNet	99.87
[27] [2017]	HODA	Modern Persian	CNN + AlexNet	99.44
[30] [2020]	CmaterDb3.3.1	Modern Arabic	CNN	99.76
[31] [2017]	CmaterDb3.3.1	Modern Arabic	Boltzmann Machine + CNN	98.59
[12] [2019]	CmaterDb3.3.1	Modern Arabic	CNN	99.4
Our Study [2020]	HODA	Modern Persian	CNN	99.47
Our Study [2020]	ADBase	Modern Arabic	CNN	99.34
Our Study [2020]	Ottoman Registers 1840s	Historical Arabic Scripts	CNN, Deep Transfer Learning from HODA and ADBase Datasets	80

3. Structure of the Ottoman Registers

In this research, we concentrated on the Nicaea district registers, NFS.d. 1411 and 1452. They are digitally available at the Turkish Presidency State Archives of the Republic of Turkey—Department of Ottoman Archives in jpeg format. We strive to implement an automatic reading method for registers from different precincts of the empire, which are obtained in the mid-nineteenth century. These registers include comprehensive demographic data on the male population in the households, i.e., names, occupations, ages and family relations. Females were neither counted nor recorded in these records. The registers were cataloged and gradually provided for research since 2011. There are approximately 11,000 registers. In this research, we study the generic characteristics of these manuscripts. The size of a digitized page in the recordings was 2210 × 3000 pixels. The first object type is the symbol marking the beginning of a populated place. It is seen in most of the registers and can mark the end of a previous village and start of a new one (see Figure 1). The other objects are individuals or households counted in the register, and they include demographic information about them. If an individual is the first person of a household, in the top of the object, there are two numbers (right and left) showing the number of the household and individual. Otherwise, they put only one number on top of the object showing the number of the individual inside the populated place. In the last line of all objects, the age of individuals is written. These registers sometimes updated by drawing a line on the people when they go to military service or decease. Sometimes the updates mistakenly connect the individual with a neighboring person, which might result in malfunctions in the information retrieval algorithms [4] (see Figure 2).

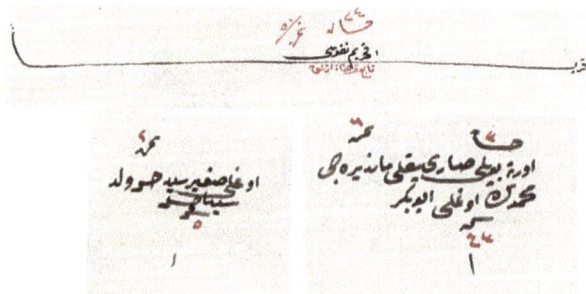

Figure 1. A population start, an individual and a household image samples are demonstrated. In the top, the populated place starting object, in the right bottom, a household and in the left bottom of the image, an individual object is shown.

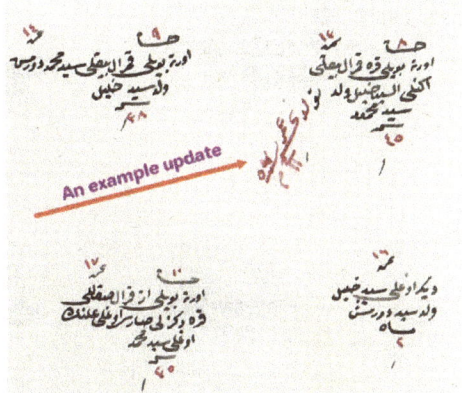

Figure 2. An example update drawn in red color is shown.

4. Methodology

In this section, we will describe our numeral spotting and handwritten digit recognition systems separately.

4.1. Automatic Numeral Spotting in Ottoman Registers

4.1.1. Red Color Filtering

As shown in Figure 1, the numerals are written in red color in the majority of these registers. However, not only the numerals but also the updates are written in red and we have to distinguish them from the numerals. In order to spot them easily, we applied a red color filter on the documents. We converted the image from RGB representation to HSV. The upper and lower limits for the red color used in these historical documents are determined by trial and error. Lower HSV thresholds were selected as (170;70;50), whereas the upper HSV thresholds were determined as (180,255,255). An example original image of the register and the filtered one is shown in Figure 3. The mask background color was chosen as black.

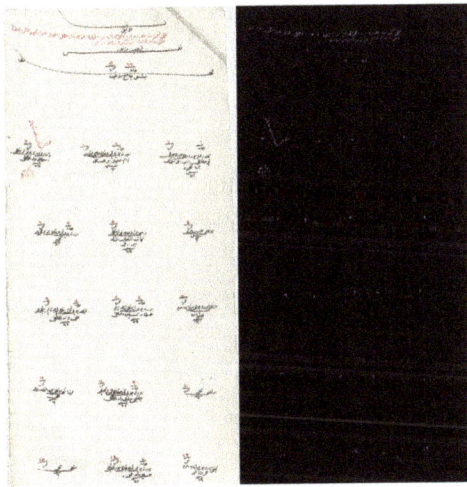

Figure 3. In the left, the original register image is shown. In the right, the resulting image after applying a red color mask is shown.

4.1.2. Creating an Annotated Dataset for Numeral Spotting

In order to employ the dhSegment toolbox [17] for page segmentation, we formed a dataset with annotations. Two classes were created. The first class is the background, which is the area other than numeral regions. We marked this area as black. The second class is the numeral region, and these fields were marked with green. We marked 50 pages of registers that belong to the Nicaea district with the described labels. In those pages, there were approximately 5000 numerals. A sample original image and marked version are presented in Figure 4.

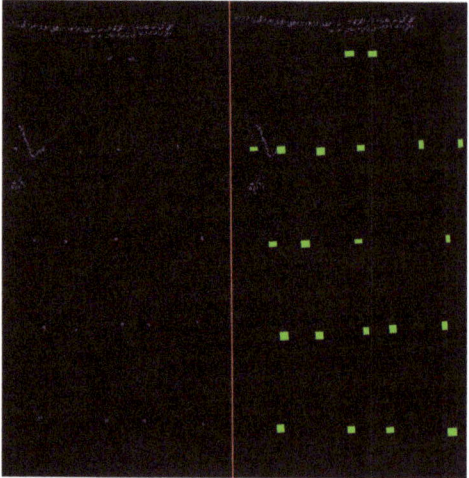

Figure 4. In the left, the red filtered register image is shown. In the right, the numerals marked and annotated for training the CNN model.

4.1.3. Creating a 3-Class Annotated Dataset

We also annotated a 3-class dataset. Numerals, register updates and background are the target classes. We aim to analyze the effect of adding register update class to the numeral spotting performance. Numerals were colored as green; updates were colored as red. The background is black which is the same as the 2-class annotation (see Figure 5).

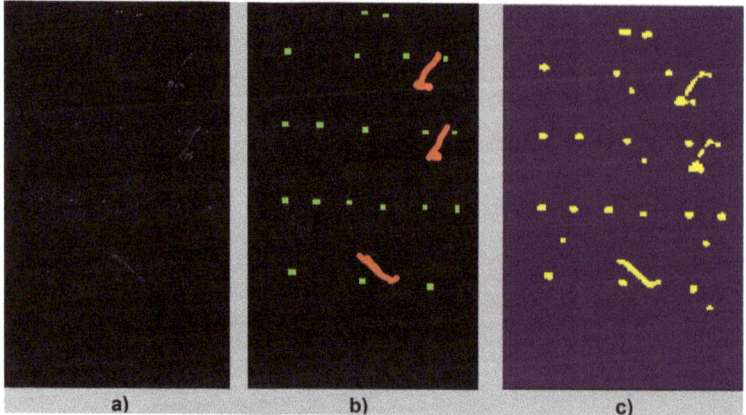

Figure 5. In part (**a**), the masked figure is shown. In part (**b**), the 3-class annotated image and in part (**c**), the prediction of our model (updates and numerals vs. background) are shown.

4.1.4. Training a CNN Model for Numeral Spotting

For training a CNN model for numeral spotting, we used the dhSegment toolbox. It trained a model by using a pretrained Resnet-50 architecture [32]. L2 regularization was employed with 10^{-6} weight decay [17]. Xavier initialization [33] and Adam optimizer [34] were used. Batch renormalization [35] was also applied to prevent a lack of diversity problem. The dhSegment toolbox also downsized pictures and arranged them into 300×300 patches for better fitting into the memory and giving support to batch training. By adding the margins, they prevented the border effects. By using pre-measured weights in the network, they decreased the training time considerably [17]. The training process employs several on-the-fly data augmentation procedures such as scaling (coefficient from 0.8 to 1.2), rotation (from -0.2 to 0.2 rad) and mirroring. Lastly, the toolbox outputs the probabilities of pixels that belong to classified object types. For further details of the toolbox, the paper explaining this toolbox [17] could be examined. For 2-class, a binary matrix comprises of the probabilities that a pixel belongs to the class is created. Pixels could be connected, and components should be created by analyzing this matrix. Connected component analysis tool [17] is applied for forming objects. We can measure the performance of our system after the objects are created for these classes. We presented predicted raw binarized image with the original manuscript and masked image in Figure 6. CPU is used to train the model. It took three hours to train a model for a hundred images. Testing an image, on the other hand, lasted for approximately 10 s.

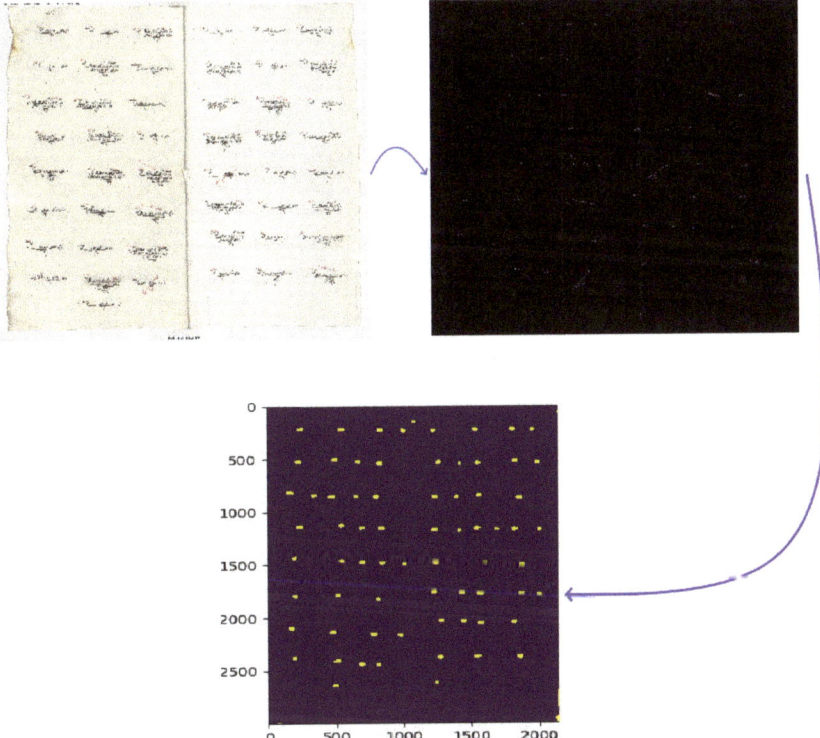

Figure 6. The complete processing of numeral spotting is shown. First, a red mask is applied to the original image. The masked image is shown in the middle. Lastly, a binary prediction image for spotting numerals is created.

4.2. Automatic Digit Recognition Using Deep Transfer Learning

For Arabic digit recognition in the historical registers, we first created a small dataset of 50 digits obtained from the spotted one-digit numerals. The dataset is balanced in terms of digit types. We then used two large datasets for using deep transfer learning. The first one is HODA dataset [36] which includes 70,000 images. The second one is AHDBase [37] which is also composed of 70,000 digits written by 700 participants. Lastly, we presented results obtained by dividing our local dataset (see Figure 7 for samples) into 80% training and 20% test sets.

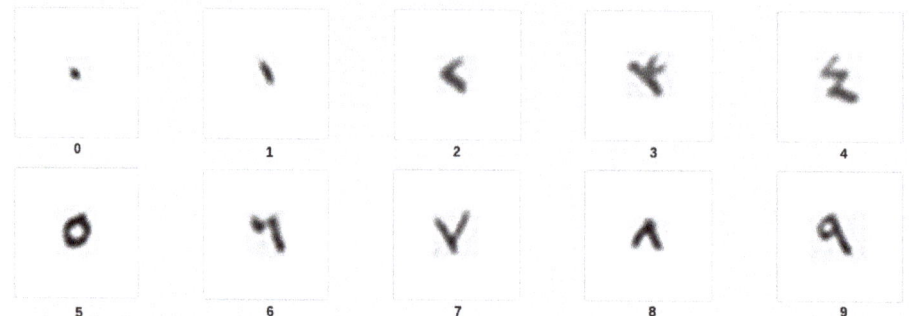

Figure 7. All ten-digit samples from our local data. Fifty digits are selected from the output of the numeral spotting system.

4.2.1. Applying DTL on HODA and AHDBase Datasets

We pretrained two different CNN architectures by using the HODA and AHDBase datasets and tested on our local numeral dataset. These datasets have both 60,000 training samples and 10,000 test samples. By using the training samples as inputs to the CNN architecture (see Figure 8), we obtained 128 features (a vector of 128 numbers) in the final Conv2D layer for both datasets. For each convolutional layer, we applied batch normalization, maxPooling and dropout processes. As the dropout ratio, we used 0.2. MaxPooling layers used pool size as two. To prepare the model for feature extraction, we pretrained the model with all layers by using both HODA and AHDBase datasets and removed the last layers outside the rectangle in Figure 7 which provided the above mentioned 128 features. We then provided our test samples as inputs for this model to predict the 128 features. After extracting these features of our local dataset by using this pretrained "transferred cropped model", we applied different machine learning classifiers (MultiLayer Perceptron (MLP) with one hidden layer (with 100 nodes), kNN with k = 3, Random Forest with 100 trees (RF), Support Vector Machine (SVM) with a radial kernel (cost = 1 and kernel degree = 3) and Linear Discriminant Analysis (LDA)) to them to obtain Arabic handwritten digit recognition results. These classifiers are selected as representatives of the most commonly applied classifier types. The WEKA toolkit [38] was used for applying these classifiers. We used the default parameter settings in the WEKA package.

4.2.2. CNN-Based Handwritten Arabic Digit Recognition on the Local Data

We separated the local data into 80% training and 20% test sets. The local dataset is balanced in terms of digit types. Then, we applied the CNN architecture shown in Figure 8 to train a model for the local data and tested on the remaining separate test set.

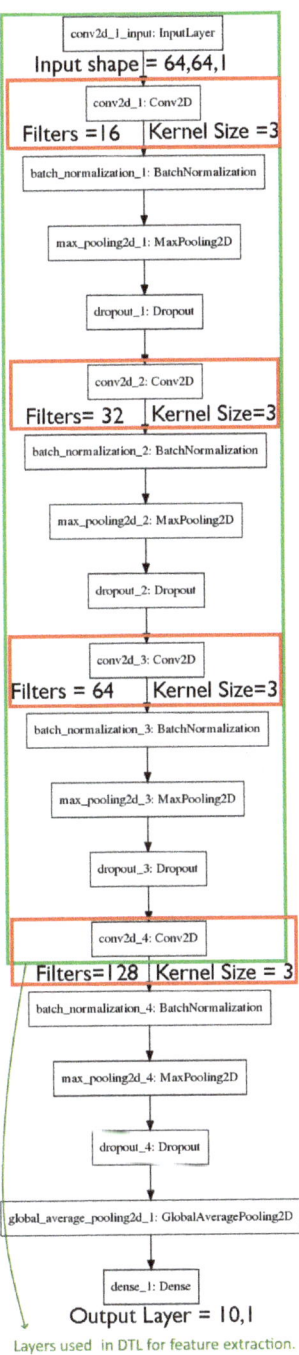

Figure 8. The CNN architecture is shown. The layers in the green rectangle are used for feature extraction in DTL. In order to train a model for local data, all layers are used. Conv2D stands for 2D Convolutional Layer.

5. Experimental Results and Discussion

5.1. Metrics

In order to evaluate our numeral spotting system performance, five metrics were used. Four of them are low-level metrics, and the last metric is a high-level one that we defined for our numeral spotting system. Low-level metrics are pixel-wise precision, recall and f-measure and Intersection over Union. These are widely employed for detecting objects in different image processing applications [39]. We further defined a high-level counting error metric to assess the performance of our numeral spotting method.

5.1.1. Pixel-Wise Precision, Recall and F-Measure

We first used the pixel-wise precision, recall and f-measure metrics. They are computed for each page in the test set and averaged over all pages. They can be calculated as:

$$Precision = \frac{TruePositive}{TruePositive + FalsePositive} \tag{1}$$

$$Recall = \frac{TruePositive}{TruePositive + FalseNegative} \tag{2}$$

$$F_{measure} = \frac{2 \times Precision \times Recall}{Precision + Recall} \tag{3}$$

5.1.2. Intersection over Union

We further computed the Intersection over Union (IoU) metric. The actual area of the segmented objects can be called as the ground truth whereas the connected areas are formed by connecting the adjacent pixel classifications belong to the same class can be called as the prediction area. The IoU can be computed by dividing the intersection of these two areas into the union of these areas.

5.1.3. High-Level Numeral Spotting Error

This last metric is specific to our application for spotting numerals in registers. It could be defined as the percentage of mistakenly classified numerals over the count of numerals from the ground truth. The predicted numeral count is the number of numerals predicted by our model. The ground truth of numeral count is the actual number of numerals in the dataset counted by our team. This metric is named as Numeral Spotting Error (NSE).

$$NSE = || \frac{PredictedNumeralCount - GroundTruthNumeralCount}{GroundTruthNumeralCount} || \tag{4}$$

5.2. Numeral Spotting Results and Discussion

The registers used in the case study are from the Nicaea district. All 50 pages are divided into 80% training and 20% test. The pixel-wise precision, recall, f-measure, IoU, and high-level numeral spotting error results are presented in Table 2. Note that the first four metrics are presented for 2-class classification (background vs. numeral). The last metric is the accuracy of spotting the numerals in the manuscripts. We successfully spotted the numerals in the documents with 96.06% (1 − NSE = %3.94) high-level accuracy. Although the IoU metric is relatively low, the performance of the spotting system shows that the documents are suitable for automatic segmentation processes after the red color mask. We further tested a 3-class classifier (see Table 3). When we added register update class, we obtained lower f-measure classes as expected. The lowest performance is achieved when recognizing the register updates. However, since our main focus is to spot numerals, numeral spotting performance is more important. We obtained 0.61 f-measure score while recognizing only numerals and 0.67 f-measure score while recognizing numerals with updates vs. background which are close to the 2-class f-measure score 0.72.

Table 2. The performance of our numeral spotting model (numerals vs. background) is presented with different metrics.

IoU (%)	NSE (%)	Pixel-Wise Precision	Pixel-Wise Recall (%)	Pixel-Wise F-Measure (%)
49.82	3.94	0.7089	0.7535	0.7247

Table 3. The performance of our 3-class numeral spotting model (numerals and updates vs. background, numerals vs. background, updates vs. backgrounds) is presented with different metrics. PW stands for pixel-wise.

Classification Type	PW Precision	PW Recall (%)	PW F-Measure (%)
Numerals vs. Background	0.4753	0.8704	0.6126
Numerals and Updates vs. Background	0.6164	0.7538	0.6751
Updates vs. Background	0.9009	0.1574	0.2681

5.3. Digit Recognition Results using Deep Transfer Learning

5.3.1. Applying DTL on HODA and AHDBase Datasets

We first trained the CNN model for the training part of the datasets (60,000 images) and tested in the remaining images (10,000 test image) for validating our model. We obtained above 99% accuracy for both datasets (99.47% for HODA Dataset and 99.34% for AHDBase dataset respectively). After that, we applied the DTL method for feature extraction and tested different classifiers with our local dataset. The digit recognition results by applying different classifiers on the features extracted from the local datasets are presented in Table 4. The results of AHDBase are always higher than HODA dataset because their number representation is similar to our dataset. However, since the HODA dataset is created in Iran, the number representation is different from our dataset (see numbers in Figure 9). Zero corresponds to our five, six is similar to two in our historical manuscripts, four and five are totally different in our dataset which is responsible for relatively lower accuracies. A maximum of 72.4% accuracy is achieved by using MLP classifier in AHDBase features. MLP is the most successful classifier on both datasets. We interpreted this results as the neural network structure helps MLP to learn CNN extracted features better. RF and kNN are other successful classifiers on these features for both datasets. We also extracted the same 128 features from our local dataset and tested the accuracies and area under ROC curve results (see Table 5). The accuracies are higher than the DTL results from the modern datasets (AHDBase and HODA) which shows that they could not capture the properties of these historical manuscripts successfully via the DTL method.

Figure 9. HODA representations for Arabic digits are demonstrated [40].

Table 4. Results obtained by applying different classifiers to extracted features by using deep transfer learning. DTL from AHDBase and HODA datasets are shown in separate columns.

Method	DTL from AHDBase	DTL from HODA
LDA	58.6	46.2
RF	62.1	58.6
MLP	72.4	65.5
SVM	57.9	49.0
kNN	64.1	62.1

Table 5. Results obtained by applying different classifiers to extracted features by using deep transfer learning. Results obtained with applying DTL from the local CNN architecture are shown.

Method	Accuracy	F-Measure	Area under ROC
kNN	84.61	0.829	0.964
RF	89.74	0.897	0.970
MLP	92.31	0.923	0.977
SVM	89.74	0.897	0.944
LDA	92.31	0.923	0.958

5.3.2. CNN-Based Handwritten Arabic Digit Recognition on the Local Data

We tested the CNN architecture on the local test dataset. We observed the accuracies of training and test set for 100 epochs (see Figures 10 and 11). We obtained 80% accuracy on the separate test set which is promising and outperformed the DTL accuracies. Both datasets (HODA and AHDBase) are recorded recently (after the 2000s). Therefore, their quality is higher than manuscripts recorded in the 1840s. Therefore, when we trained and tested a CNN model in our local dataset, the system also learns the properties of historical documents. However, when the DTL method is applied from these modern datasets, they could not capture the properties of these historical manuscripts. That could explain the relatively lower performance of DTL techniques. These results are also higher than learning CNN directly from the local data (80%), which shows the advantage of using DTL based feature extraction in our dataset.

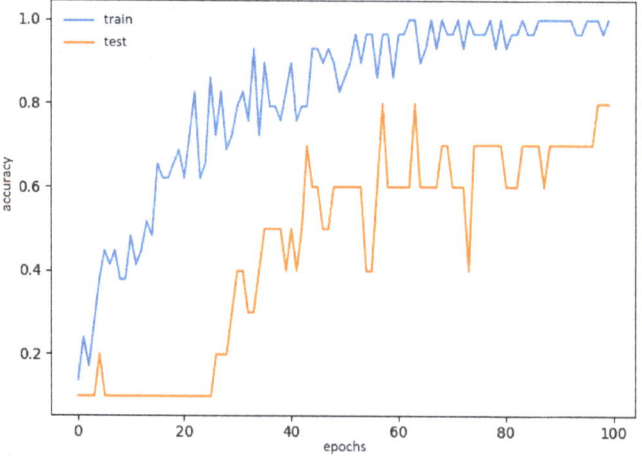

Figure 10. Training and test accuracies of CNN-based handwritten Arabic digit recognition system by epochs are shown. The local dataset is separated to 80% training and 20% test sets.

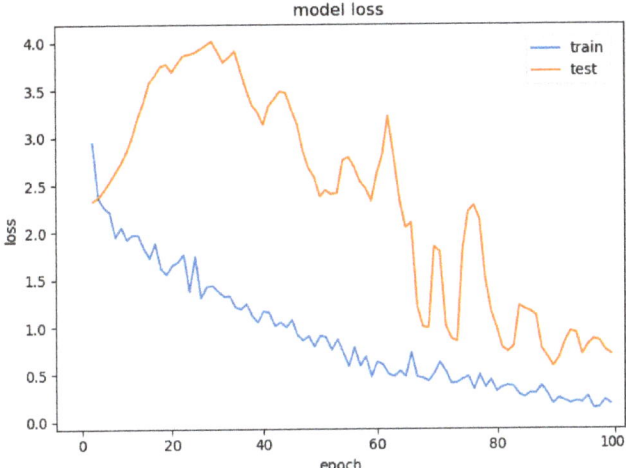

Figure 11. Training and test model loss of CNN-based handwritten Arabic digit recognition system by epochs are shown. The local dataset is separated to 80% training and 20% test sets.

6. Conclusions

In this study, we implemented an automatic Arabic numeral spotting system to a selection of the very first series of population registers of the Ottoman Empire conducted in the mid-nineteenth century. We took advantage of the property of population registers that numerals are written in red color. After applying a red color mask, we developed a CNN-based numeral spotting system. We further formed a small Arabic digit dataset from the detected numerals by selecting uni-digit ones and tested the Deep Transfer Learning (DTL) methods from the models trained in large open datasets for digit recognition. We also compared these results with the CNN architecture trained and tested on the local dataset. For numeral spotting, we obtained 96.06% accuracy which shows that numerals in these historical population registers could be spotted after applying a red filter. After spotting these numerals, we presented the Arabic handwritten digit recognition results by applying DTL from the substantial datasets and a trained CNN architecture on the local dataset. The CNN architecture is trained on the local dataset and tested on the separate test set outperforms DTL methods with the digit recognition accuracy of 80%. This could be explained by the unique properties and the fact that the degradation of historical documents could not be detected when DTL from modern datasets is used. DTL, by using the AHDBase dataset results are always higher than using HODA dataset because its digits are similar to the digits used in the Ottoman population registers. In fact, four digits of the HODA dataset are totally different from the digits of historical Ottoman population registers. The best accuracy obtained by applying DTL with AHDBase is 72% (CNN + MLP) which is lower than CNN alone in the local dataset.

We believe that the contribution of this article will be useful for researchers studying Arabic handwritten digit recognition. From these promising results, we plan to increase the size of the local dataset and carry on further tests. As future works, we plan to develop a keyword spotting system for handwritten text recognition in these population registers in order to detect further personal information belonging to registered individuals such as names, family relations within households, and occupations.

Author Contributions: Y.S.C. is the main writer of the manuscript. He performed the curation and development of the dataset and of the software and conducted the analysis. M.E.K. organized the preparation of the archival sources and initial data gathering. He has provided historical context and information regarding late Ottoman population registers, and contributed to the conceptualization of the case study. All authors have read and agreed to the published version of the manuscript.

Funding: This work was supported by the European Research Council (ERC) project: "Industrialisation and Urban Growth from the mid-nineteenth century Ottoman Empire to Contemporary Turkey in a Comparative Perspective, 1850–2000" under the European Union's Horizon 2020 research and innovation program Grant Agreement No. 679097, acronym UrbanOccupationsOETR. M. Erdem Kabadayı is the principal investigator of UrbanOccupationsOETR.

Conflicts of Interest: The authors declare no conflict of interest.

References

1. Kim, M.S.; Cho, K.T.; Kwag, H.K.; Kim, J.H. Segmentation of handwritten characters for digitalizing Korean historical documents. In *Document Analysis Systems VI*; Marinai, S., Dengel, A.R., Eds.; Springer: Berlin/Heidelberg, Germany, 2004; pp. 114–124.
2. Wick, C.; Puppe, F. Fully convolutional neural networks for page segmentation of historical document images. In Proceedings of the IEEE 2018 13th IAPR International Workshop on Document Analysis Systems (DAS), Vienna, Austria, 24–27 April 2018; pp. 287–292.
3. Xu, Y.; He, W.; Yin, F.; Liu, C.L. Page segmentation for historical handwritten documents using fully convolutional networks. In Proceedings of the IEEE 2017 14th IAPR International Conference on Document Analysis and Recognition (ICDAR), Kyoto, Japan, 9–15 November 2017; Volume 1, pp. 541–546.
4. Can, Y.S.; Kabadayı, M.E. CNN-based page segmentation and object classification for counting population in Ottoman archival documentation. *J. Imaging* **2020**, *6*, 32. [CrossRef]
5. Puigcerver, J.; Toselli, A.H.; Vidal, E. ICDAR2015 competition on keyword spotting for handwritten documents. In Proceedings of the 2015 13th International Conference on Document Analysis and Recognition (ICDAR), Tunis, Tunisia, 23–26 August 2015; pp. 1176–1180.
6. Rouhou, A.C.; Kessentini, Y.; Kanoun, S. Hybrid HMM/DNN system for Arabic handwriting keyword spotting. In *International Conference on Image Analysis and Recognition*; Springer: Berlin/Heidelberg, Germany, 2019; pp. 216–227.
7. Hesham, A.M.; Rashwan, M.A.; Al-Barhamtoshy, H.M.; Abdou, S.M.; Badr, A.A.; Farag, I. Arabic document layout analysis. *Pattern Anal. Appl.* **2017**, *20*, 1275–1287. [CrossRef]
8. Niu, X.X.; Suen, C.Y. A novel hybrid CNN–SVM classifier for recognizing handwritten digits. *Pattern Recognit.* **2012**, *45*, 1318–1325. [CrossRef]
9. Tissera, M.D.; McDonnell, M.D. Deep extreme learning machines: supervised autoencoding architecture for classification. *Neurocomputing* **2016**, *174*, 42–49. [CrossRef]
10. Nobile, N.; He, C.L.; Sagheer, M.W.; Lam, L.; Suen, C.Y. Digit/symbol pruning and verification for Arabic handwritten digit/symbol spotting. In Proceedings of the 2011 International Conference on Document Analysis and Recognition, Beijing, China, 18–21 September 2011; pp. 648–652.
11. AlKhateeb, J.H.; Alseid, M. DBN—Based learning for Arabic handwritten digit recognition using DCT features. In Proceedings of the 2014 6th International Conference on Computer Science and Information Technology (CSIT), Amman, Jordan, 27–28 November 2014; pp. 222–226. [CrossRef]
12. Ashiquzzaman, A.; Tushar, A.K.; Rahman, A.; Mohsin, F. An efficient recognition method for handwritten Arabic numerals using CNN with data augmentation and dropout. In *Data Management, Analytics and Innovation*; Balas, V.E., Sharma, N., Chakrabarti, A., Eds.; Springer: Singapore, 2019; pp. 299–309.
13. El-Sawy, A.; EL-Bakry, H.; Loey, M. CNN for handwritten Arabic digits recognition based on LeNet-5. In *Proceedings of the International Conference on Advanced Intelligent Systems and Informatics 2016*; Hassanien, A.E., Shaalan, K., Gaber, T., Azar, A.T., Tolba, M.F., Eds.; Springer: Cham, Switzerland, 2017; pp. 566–575.
14. Bukhari, S.S.; Breuel, T.M.; Asi, A.; El-Sana, J. Layout analysis for arabic historical document images using machine learning. In Proceedings of the IEEE 2012 International Conference on Frontiers in Handwriting Recognition, Bari, Italy, 18–20 September 2012; pp. 639–644.
15. Breuel, T.M. Robust, simple page segmentation using hybrid convolutional MDLSTM networks. In Proceedings of the 2017 14th IAPR International Conference on Document Analysis and Recognition (ICDAR), Kyoto, Japan, 9–15 November 2017; Volume 1, pp. 733–740. [CrossRef]

16. Augusto Borges Oliveira, D.; Palhares Viana, M. Fast CNN-based document layout analysis. In Proceedings of the IEEE International Conference on Computer Vision, Venice, Italy, 22–29 October 2017; pp. 1173–1180.
17. Ares Oliveira, S.; Seguin, B.; Kaplan, F. dhSegment: A generic deep-learning approach for document segmentation. In Proceedings of the 2018 16th International Conference on Frontiers in Handwriting Recognition (ICFHR), Niagara Falls, NY, USA, 5–8 August 2018; pp. 7–12. [CrossRef]
18. Brik, Y.; Chibani, Y.; Hadjadji, B.; Zemouri, E.T. Keyword-guided Arabic word spotting in ancient document images using Curvelet descriptors. In Proceedings of the IEEE 2014 International Conference on Multimedia Computing and Systems (ICMCS), Marrakesh, Morocco, 14–16 April 2014; pp. 57–61.
19. Kassis, M.; El-Sana, J. Automatic synthesis of historical arabic text for word-spotting. In Proceedings of the IEEE 2016 12th IAPR Workshop on Document Analysis Systems (DAS), Santorini, Greece, 11–14 April 2016; pp. 239–244.
20. Zirari, F.; Ennaji, A.; Nicolas, S.; Mammass, D. A methodology to spot words in historical arabic documents. In Proceedings of the IEEE 2013 ACS International Conference on Computer Systems and Applications (AICCSA), Ifrane, Morocco, 27–30 May 2013; pp. 1–4.
21. Wshah, S.; Kumar, G.; Govindaraju, V. Multilingual word spotting in offline handwritten documents. In Proceedings of the IEEE 21st International Conference on Pattern Recognition (ICPR2012), Istanbul, Turkey, 23–26 August 2012; pp. 310–313.
22. Khayyat, M.; Lam, L.; Suen, C.Y. Arabic handwritten word spotting using language models. In Proceedings of the IEEE 2012 International Conference on Frontiers in Handwriting Recognition, Bari, Italy, 18–20 September 2012; pp. 43–48.
23. Barakat, B.K.; Alasam, R.; El-Sana, J. Word spotting using convolutional siamese network. In Proceedings of the 2018 13th IAPR International Workshop on Document Analysis Systems (DAS), Vienna, Austria, 24–27 April 2018; pp. 229–234.
24. Lekhal, F.; El Hitmy, M.; Melhaoui, O.E. Arabic numerals recognition based on an improved version of the loci characteristic. *Int. J. Comput. Appl.* **2011**, *24*, 36–41.
25. Dehghanian, A.; Ghods, V. Farsi handwriting digit recognition based on convolutional neural networks. In Proceedings of the 2018 6th International Symposium on Computational and Business Intelligence (ISCBI), Basel, Switzerland, 27–29 August 2018; pp. 65–68.
26. Ghofrani, A.; Toroghi, R.M. Capsule-based Persian/Arabic robust handwritten digit recognition using EM routing. In Proceedings of the 2019 4th International Conference on Pattern Recognition and Image Analysis (IPRIA), Tehran, Iran, 6–7 March 2019; pp. 168–172.
27. Farahbakhsh, E.; Kozegar, E.; Soryani, M. Improving persian digit recognition by combining data augmentation and AlexNet. In Proceedings of the 2017 10th Iranian Conference on Machine Vision and Image Processing (MVIP), Isfahan, Iran, 22–23 November 2017; pp. 265–270.
28. Takruri, M.; Al-Hmouz, R.; Al-Hmouz, A. A three-level classifier: Fuzzy C Means, Support Vector Machine and unique pixels for Arabic handwritten digits. In Proceedings of the 2014 World Symposium on Computer Applications Research (WSCAR), Sousse, Tunisia, 18–20 January 2014; pp. 1–5.
29. Ashiquzzaman, A.; Tushar, A.K. Handwritten Arabic numeral recognition using deep learning neural networks. In Proceedings of the 2017 IEEE International Conference on Imaging, Vision Pattern Recognition (icIVPR), Dhaka, Bangladesh, 13–14 February 2017; pp. 1–4. [CrossRef]
30. Ahamed, P.; Kundu, S.; Khan, T.; Bhateja, V.; Sarkar, R.; Mollah, A.F. Handwritten Arabic numerals recognition using convolutional neural network. *J. Ambient Intell. Humaniz. Comput.* **2020**. [CrossRef]
31. Alani, A.A. Arabic handwritten digit recognition based on restricted Boltzmann machine and convolutional neural networks. *Information* **2017**, *8*, 142. [CrossRef]
32. He, K.; Zhang, X.; Ren, S.; Sun, J. Deep residual learning for image recognition. In Proceedings of the IEEE conference on computer vision and pattern recognition, Las Vegas, NV, USA, 27–30 June 2016; pp. 770–778.
33. Glorot, X.; Bengio, Y. Understanding the difficulty of training deep feedforward neural networks. In Proceedings of the Thirteenth International Conference on Artificial Intelligence and Statistics, Sardinia, Italy, 13–15 May 2010; pp. 249–256.
34. Kingma, D.P.; Ba, J. Adam: A method for stochastic optimization. *arXiv* **2014**, arXiv:1412.6980.
35. Ioffe, S. Batch renormalization: Towards reducing minibatch dependence in batch-normalized models. In Proceedings of the Advances in Neural Information Processing Systems, Long Beach, CA, USA, 4–9 December 2017; pp. 1945–1953.

36. Hoda Dataset. Available online: http://farsiocr.ir (accessed on 30 June 2020).
37. AHDBase Dataset. Available online: http://datacenter.aucegypt.edu/shazeem/ (accessed on 30 June 2020).
38. Holmes, G.; Donkin, A.; Witten, I.H. WEKA: A machine learning workbench. In Proceedings of the ANZIIS '94—Australian New Zealand Intelligent Information Systems Conference, Brisbane, Australia, 29 November–2 December 1994; pp. 357–361.
39. Jobin, K.V.; Jawahar, C.V. Document image segmentation using deep features. In *Computer Vision, Pattern Recognition, Image Processing, and Graphics*; Rameshan, R., Arora, C., Dutta Roy, S., Eds.; Springer: Singapore, 2018; pp. 372–382.
40. Hoda Dataset Persian Digits Demonstration [Online]. Available online: https://github.manzik.com/Persian-Handwritten-Digit-Recognizer/JS%20Interactive/ (accessed on 30 June 2020).

© 2020 by the authors. Licensee MDPI, Basel, Switzerland. This article is an open access article distributed under the terms and conditions of the Creative Commons Attribution (CC BY) license (http://creativecommons.org/licenses/by/4.0/).

Article

Pansharpening by Complementing Compressed Sensing with Spectral Correction

Naoko Tsukamoto *, Yoshihiro Sugaya and Shinichiro Omachi

Graduate School of Engineering, Tohoku University, Sendai, Miyagi 980-8579, Japan; sugaya@iic.ecei.tohoku.ac.jp (Y.S.); machi@ecei.tohoku.ac.jp (S.O.)
* Correspondence: natsuka@iic.ecei.tohoku.ac.jp

Received: 30 June 2020; Accepted: 18 August 2020; Published: 21 August 2020

Featured Application: Satellite image processing for change detection, target recognition, classification, map application, visual image analysis, etc.

Abstract: Pansharpening (PS) is a process used to generate high-resolution multispectral (MS) images from high-spatial-resolution panchromatic (PAN) and high-spectral-resolution multispectral images. In this paper, we propose a method for pansharpening by focusing on a compressed sensing (CS) technique. The spectral reproducibility of the CS technique is high due to its image reproducibility, but the reproduced image is blurry. Although methods of complementing this incomplete reproduction have been proposed, it is known that the existing method may cause ringing artifacts. On the other hand, component substitution is another technique used for pansharpening. It is expected that the spatial resolution of the images generated by this technique will be as high as that of the high-resolution PAN image, because the technique uses the corrected intensity calculated from the PAN image. Based on these facts, the proposed method fuses the intensity obtained by the component substitution method and the intensity obtained by the CS technique to move the spatial resolution of the reproduced image close to that of the PAN image while reducing the spectral distortion. Experimental results showed that the proposed method can reduce spectral distortion and maintain spatial resolution better than the existing methods.

Keywords: pansharpening; spectrum correction; intensity correction; compressed sensing; tradeoff process; IKONOS

---

1. Introduction

The optical sensors installed in satellites acquire panchromatic (PAN) and multispectral (MS) region images. PAN sensors observe a wide range of visible and near-infrared (NIR) regions as one band with a high spatial resolution, and the MS sensor observes multiple bands. Pansharpening (PS) is a method used to generate a high-resolution MS images from these two types of data. Due to physical constraints [1], MS sensors are not designed to acquire high-resolution images. In general, high-resolution MS images are obtained via the pansharpening process. PS techniques are used for change detection, target recognition, classification, backgrounds for map application, visual image analysis, etc.

PS has been studied for decades [2,3], and its methodologies can roughly be classified into four types. The first is methods used to generate a pansharpened image by substituting the intensity component of the MS images for that of the PAN image via component substitution. The intensity–hue–saturation (IHS) transform [4], generalized IHS method (GIHS) [5], Brovey transform [6], principal component analysis [6], and Gram–Schmidt transform [7] belong to this group. The second group contains methods used to extract high-frequency components of PAN images via multiresolution analysis (MRA) and then add them to the MS images. To extract high-frequency components, high-pass filter, decimated wavelet transforms [8], a "trous" wavelet transform [9], Laplacian pyramid [10,11], and non-subsampled contourlet transform [12] methods are used. The third group contains methods that use machine-learning techniques such as compressed sensing [13] and deep learning [14,15]. The fourth group is the hybrid methods that combine multiple methods described above. The methods proposed by Vivone et al. [16], Fei et al. [17], and Yin [18] are the ones that combined the component substitution method and the MRA. The combination of the MRA, convolutional neural network (CNN), and sparse modeling was proposed by Wang et al. [19], and the combination of the MRA and CNN was proposed by He et al. [20].

Recently, proposals for hybrid methods using machine-learning techniques have been increasing. Many methods based on compressed sensing (CS) have been proposed based on the 2006 theory [21]. Since Yang et al. [13] proposed a method for super-resolution, it has been frequently applied to PS. Li et al. proposed a method using a learning-free dictionary and CS [22], followed by the proposal of a method using dictionary learning and CS [23]. Although they showed the possibility of using a dictionary without learning, the feasibility of these methods was low because high-resolution MS images that were not realistically available were necessary for dictionary construction. Jiang et al. proposed a method using a high-resolution dictionary generated using a set of pairs of low-resolution MS images and high-resolution PAN images [24]. They then proposed a method for reconstruction by calculating sparse representations in two stages using a learning-free dictionary [25]. Zhu et al. constructed a pair of high-resolution and low-resolution learning-free dictionaries from PAN images [26,27]. Guo et al. proposed a method called online coupled dictionary learning (OCDL) [28], which iteratively performs dictionary learning and reconstruction processes until the reconstructed image becomes stable, based on the sparse representation (SR) theory described by Elad [29]. SR theory shows that better reconstruction results are obtained when the dictionary's atoms are highly related to the reconstructed image. Vicinanze et al. proposed the generation of a learning-free dictionary using the high-resolution and low-resolution dictionaries as the detailed image information [30]. Ghahremani et al. proposed a learning-free dictionary with low-resolution PAN images and high-resolution detailed information extracted from by the ripplet transform of the edges and textures of high-resolution PAN images [31]. Zhang et al. introduced non-negative matrix factorization and proposed estimation of a high-resolution matrix by solving an optimization problem of decomposing the matrix into basis and coefficient matrices [32]. Ayas et al. created a dictionary of high-resolution MS image features by incorporating the tradeoff parameter [24,26] and back-projection [13,33]. It was shown that the spectral distortion was reduced by incorporating back-projection. Yin proposed the cross-resolution projection and the offset [18]. The cross-resolution projection generates high-resolution MS images by assuming that the position estimated by CS is the same for high-resolution and low-resolution images. The offset is used to adjust the reconstructed image.

In these studies, the results of PS depended on the model selection and dictionary selection. Various studies on the structure and construction of dictionaries, model construction, and optimization processes have been conducted. In addition, it was pointed out that CS-based reconstruction does not guarantee the reproduction of the original image [13,29,34], which means that the spatial characteristics may not be incorporated accurately. The fact that it is not an exact reconstruction should be considered when the method is used for spectral analysis. The process of back-projection was introduced by Yang et al. [13] to improve the reconstructed image. This process was also incorporated by Ayas et al. [34] to reduce the spectral distortion. On the other hand, it is also known that ringing artefacts occur when back-projection is performed. In the PS process, low spectral distortion is important as well as high resolution. It is important to consider how to achieve the fidelity of the reproduced image to the ideal image in terms of the spectral and spatial resolution.

In this paper, we focused on reducing the spectral distortion more effectively than the back-projection for resolution enhancement of a visible light image. To this end, we propose a method for pansharpening by combining the CS technique and a component substitution method that calculates the intensity with high spatial resolution and low spectral distortion to enhance the reproducibility. As the component substitution, spectrum correction using modeled panchromatic image (SCMP) [35] is introduced. The observation band of the PAN sensor of IKONOS, an earth observation satellite, was 526–929 nm. The red, green, blue, and NIR bands of the MS sensor of IKONOS were 632–698 nm, 505–595 nm, 445–516 nm, and 757–853 nm, respectively. Therefore, the PAN sensor covered the observation band of the MS sensor including NIR. The NIR information needs to be included when generating PS images using component substitution in order to avoid spectral distortion. The SCMP is a model that can correct this distortion. On the other hand, processing using the CS is expected to have high data reproducibility and it reflects the characteristics of the input image, while the resolution is lower than that generated by the SCMP. In order to improve the fidelity of the reproduced image to the original image, a tradeoff process was applied on the high-resolution intensity images obtained by the CS and the SCMP. It was found that a spatial resolution equivalent to that of PAN image was obtained and spectral distortion was reduced by the proposed method.

2. Materials and Methods

2.1. Image Datasets

Table 1 shows the two image datasets used for the experiments. The first was collected in May 2008 and covers the city of Nihonmatsu, Japan. The second was collected in May 2006 and covers the city of Yokohama, Japan. The two IKONOS images datasets were provided by the Japan Space Imaging Corporation, Japan. The spatial resolutions of the PAN and the MS images in these datasets were 1 m and 4 m, respectively. The original dataset contained PAN images with 1024 × 1024 pixels and MS images with 256 × 256 pixels for Nihonmatsu, and PAN images with 1792 × 1792 pixels and MS images with 448 × 448 pixels for Yokohama.

Table 1. Characteristics of the original, training, and test images of the image datasets. MS: multispectral, PAN: panchromatic.

	Image	Nihonmatsu	Yokohama
Original image	PAN image	1024 × 1024	1792 × 1792
	MS image	256 × 256	448 × 448
Training image	PAN image (for high-resolution dictionary)	256 × 256	448 × 448
Test image	PAN image	256 × 256	448 × 448
	MS image	64 × 64	112 × 112

The training image datasets had high-resolution PAN images with 256 × 256 pixels for Nihonmatsu, and high-resolution PAN images with 448 × 448 pixels for the Yokohama.

To evaluate the quality of the PS images, we experimented with the test images and original images according to the Wald protocol [36]. The test images were used to evaluate the numerical image quality, and the original images were used as reference images for numerical and visual evaluation. We regarded the original images as ground truth images. The spatial resolution of the test PAN images was reduced from 1 to 4 m and that of the test MS images was reduced from 4 to 16 m. Hence, the test image datasets had PAN images with 256 × 256 pixels and MS images with 64 × 64 pixels for the Nihonmatsu, and PAN images with 448 × 448 pixels and MS images with 112 × 112 pixels for the Yokohama. The training and test images were downsampled images of the original image with bicubic spline interpolation.

2.2. Compressed Sensing

Compressed sensing (CS) is a technique used to reconstruct unknown data from a small number of observed data. In theory, the original data can be estimated when the data is sparse [28]. We considered the problem of reconstructing an image $z^h \in \mathbb{R}^{n_0}$ with a higher resolution than the observed low-resolution image $z^l \in \mathbb{R}^{m_0}$ ($m_0 < n_0$). The relationship between the high-resolution image and the low-resolution image can be expressed by Equation (1).

$$z^l = SHz^h = Lz^h,$$
$$L = SH, \tag{1}$$

where S is a downsampling operator and H is a filter that lowers the resolution. At this time, since the dimensionality of z^l is smaller than that of z^h, the solution cannot be uniquely determined.

Based on the compressed sensing theory, the high-resolution image z^h is estimated by Equation (2) from the image element D_h and sparse representation a. The element for reproducing the image is called atom $d_i \in \mathbb{R}^{n_0}$, and the set of atoms is called the dictionary $D_h \in \mathbb{R}^{n_0 \times N_d}$.

$$z^h = D_h a \ s.t. \|a\|_0 \leq m_0, \tag{2}$$

Using Equation (2), Equation (1) can be expressed as

$$z^l = Lz^h = D_l a,$$
$$D_l = LD_h. \tag{3}$$

z^h can be reproduced by z^l using the sparse representation a obtained from Equation (4), in which the sparsity constraint is added to Equation (3).

$$\min_a \|a\|_0 \ s.t. \ \|z^l - LD_h a\|_2^2 \leq \varepsilon. \tag{4}$$

Equation (4) can be solved using optimization methods.

2.3. Proposed Method

Our proposed method combines the advantages of super-resolution based on the theory of compressed sensing and component substitution. In this method, the high-resolution intensity obtained by the SCMP and the high-resolution intensity obtained by the CS-based method are linearly combined using the tradeoff process, and the obtained high-resolution intensity images are fused via the GIHS method to generate PS images. The flow of the proposed method is shown in Figure 1.

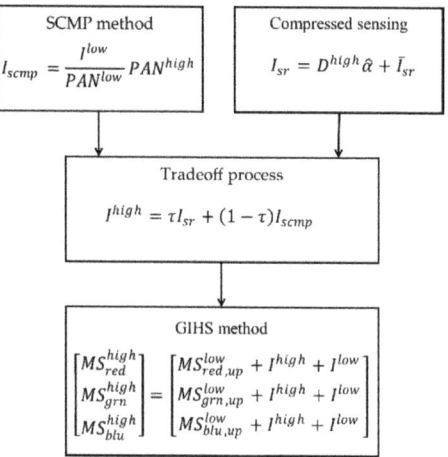

Figure 1. Flow of the proposed method.

2.4. Notation

In the proposed method, four features are extracted from low-resolution images, and the set of features is called the feature map. We used the gradient map proposed by Yang et al. [13] as the feature map. Let $x_i^{high} \in \mathbb{R}^{p^2 \times 1}$ be a patch of size $p \times p$ extracted from a high-resolution image, and $x_i^{low} \in \mathbb{R}^{4p^2 \times 1}$ be a set of four patches of size $p \times p$ extracted from the feature map. The ith training data patch $x_i \in \mathbb{R}^{5p^2 \times 1}$ is defined as $x_i = \begin{bmatrix} x_i^{high} \\ x_i^{low} \end{bmatrix}$. $X = \{x_1, \cdots, x_{N_t}\} \in \mathbb{R}^{5p^2 \times N_t}$, $X^{high} = \{x_1^{high}, \cdots, x_{N_t}^{high}\} \in \mathbb{R}^{p^2 \times N_t}$, and $X^{low} = \{x_1^{low}, \cdots, x_{N_t}^{low}\} \in \mathbb{R}^{4p^2 \times N_t}$ represent the set of patches of the training data, high-resolution training data, and low-resolution training data, respectively, where N_t is the number of training data. $\bar{x}_i^{high}$ indicates the mean value of the intensity values of the ith training data patch x_i^{high}. $D = \begin{bmatrix} D^{high} \\ D^{low} \end{bmatrix} = \{d_1, \cdots, d_{N_d}\}, D \in \mathbb{R}^{5p^2 \times N_d}$ is called a dictionary and $d_i = \begin{bmatrix} d_i^{high} \\ d_i^{low} \end{bmatrix}$ is the ith atom of the dictionary where N_d is the number of atoms. $d_i^{high} \in \mathbb{R}^{p^2 \times 1}$ is a high-resolution dictionary atom of size $p \times p$, and $d_i^{low} \in \mathbb{R}^{4p^2 \times 1}$ is a low-resolution dictionary atom of size $p \times p$. All the atoms are arranged in raster scan order. The high-resolution dictionary $D^{high} \in \mathbb{R}^{p^2 \times N_d}$ and the low-resolution dictionary $D^{low} \in \mathbb{R}^{4p^2 \times N_d}$ are defined as $D^{high} = \{d_1^{high}, \cdots, d_{N_t}^{high}\}$ and $D^{low} = \{d_1^{low}, \cdots, d_{N_t}^{low}\}$, respectively. $Y^{low} \in \mathbb{R}^{4p^2 \times N_{patch}}$ indicates the feature map of the low-resolution input image to be reconstructed, where N_{patch} is the number of patches of the input image. $I_{sr} \in \mathbb{R}^{p^2 \times N_{patch}}$ represents the reconstructed high-resolution image. $\bar{I}_{sr} \in \mathbb{R}^{p^2 \times N_{patch}}$ represents the mean value of the intensity values of the reconstructed high-resolution image patch. The sparse representations are denoted as $\alpha \in \mathbb{R}^{N_t \times N_{patch}}$ and $\beta \in \mathbb{R}^{N_d \times N_t}$, and λ represents the sparsity regularization parameter.

2.5. Estimation of Coefficients for Intensity Correction

The coefficient estimated by SCMP is used for the intensity correction in the proposed method. It is possible to obtain an intensity correction value with little spectral distortion with SCMP. This coefficient is calculated by

$$\underset{c}{\operatorname{argmin}} \|Ac - d\|_2^2 \ \text{s.t.} \ c \geq 0, \tag{5}$$

where

$$A = \begin{bmatrix} -MS_{nir}^{low}(1) & MS_{blu}^{low}(1) & MS_{grn}^{low}(1) & MS_{red}^{low}(1) \\ \vdots & \vdots & \vdots & \vdots \\ -MS_{nir}^{low}(k) & MS_{blu}^{low}(k) & MS_{grn}^{low}(k) & MS_{red}^{low}(k) \\ \vdots & \vdots & \vdots & \vdots \\ -MS_{nir}^{low}(N) & MS_{blu}^{low}(N) & MS_{grn}^{low}(N) & MS_{red}^{low}(N) \end{bmatrix} \in \mathbb{R}^{N \times 4},$$

$$c = \begin{bmatrix} c_1 \\ c_2 \\ c_3 \\ c_4 \end{bmatrix} \in \mathbb{R}^{4 \times 1},$$

$$d = \begin{bmatrix} I^{low}(1) - PAN^{high}(1) \\ \vdots \\ I^{low}(k) - PAN^{high}(k) \\ \vdots \\ I^{low}(N) - PAN^{high}(N) \end{bmatrix} \in \mathbb{R}^{N \times 1},$$

where k indicates the pixel position. N is the number of pixels and $PAN^{high} \in \mathbb{R}^N$ is the downsampled PAN test image, of which the size is the same as that of I^{low} obtained via the bicubic interpolation.

The suffixes *nir*, *blu*, *grn*, and *red* represent the NIR, blue, green, and red color components of the MS image, respectively. For MS^{low}_{nir}, MS^{low}_{blu}, MS^{low}_{grn}, and MS^{low}_{red}, test MS images are used. I^{low} is calculated by

$$I^{low} = \frac{MS^{low}_{red} + MS^{low}_{grn} + MS^{low}_{blu}}{3} \qquad (6)$$

Note that Equation (6) does not include NIR because it is the intensity of the RGB image.

2.6. Dictionary Learning

The high-resolution dictionary and the low-resolution dictionary were constructed via Equation (7) using the corresponding pair of training images. These are shown as Equation (8).

$$\begin{aligned} X^{high} &= D^{high}\beta, \\ X^{low} &= D^{low}\beta \end{aligned} \qquad (7)$$

$$X = D\beta, \qquad (8)$$

where $\beta \in \mathbb{R}^{N_d \times N_t}$ represents the sparse representation and $X = \begin{bmatrix} X^{high} \\ X^{low} \end{bmatrix}$, $D = \begin{bmatrix} D^{high} \\ D^{low} \end{bmatrix}$. The dictionary was obtained by solving the optimization problem of Equation (9), where the regularization conditions and constraints are added to Equation (8).

$$\underset{D,\beta}{\mathrm{argmin}} \frac{1}{2}\|X - D\beta\|_2^2 + \lambda\|\beta\|_1 \ s.t. \ \|d_i\|_2 \le 1, \ i = 1, 2, \cdots, N_t, \qquad (9)$$

where λ is the normalization parameter.

The training data used for dictionary learning were training PAN images for the high-resolution dictionary and the feature map obtained from its corresponding low-resolution training PAN image for the low-resolution dictionary as shown in Table 1. X^{high} and X^{low} were obtained from a high-resolution training PAN image and its corresponding low-resolution training PAN image. Given a high-resolution training PAN image, it was divided into regions of size $p \times p$. The high-resolution patch x_i^{high} was then obtained for each region by $x_i^{high} = x_{raw,i}^{high} - \bar{x}_{raw,i}^{high}$, where $x_{raw,i}^{high}$ is the $p \times p$ image and $\bar{x}_{raw,i}^{high}$ is the mean intensity value of $x_{raw,i}^{high}$, and $X^{high} = \{x_1^{high}, \cdots, x_{N_t}^{high}\}$ is obtained. Given the low-resolution training PAN image, the feature map was calculated with four filters of the first derivative and the second derivative defined by

$$F_1 = [-1, 0, 1], \ F_2 = F_1^T, \ F_3 = [1, 0, -2, 0, 1], \ F_4 = F_3^T,$$

where T indicates transposition. The feature map was divided into patches of $p \times p$, and each patch was normalized. Since the feature map was calculated from the entire image, each patch contained the information of its adjacent patch. By arranging the normalized feature map in the raster scan order for each patch, $X^{low} = \{x_1^{low}, \cdots, x_{N_t}^{low}\}$, $x_i^{low} = \begin{bmatrix} F_1(i) \\ F_2(i) \\ F_3(i) \\ F_4(i) \end{bmatrix}$, $i = 1, 2, \cdots, N_t$ was obtained.

The algorithm of the dictionary learning is described as follows.

(1) Obtain X^{high} and X^{low} from the training data. Each column of $X = \begin{bmatrix} X^{high} \\ X^{low} \end{bmatrix}$ is then normalized.

(2) Set the initial value of the dictionary D. Random numbers that follow the Gaussian distribution with mean 0 and variance 1 are normalized for each patch region.

(3) Estimate the sparse representation β by solving the optimization problem of Equation (10) by fixing the dictionary D.

$$\beta = \underset{\beta}{\mathrm{argmin}} \frac{1}{2}\|X - D\beta\|_2^2 + \lambda\|\beta\|_1 \quad (10)$$

(4) Estimate the dictionary D by solving the optimization problem of Equation (11) by fixing the sparse representation β.

$$D = \underset{D}{\mathrm{argmin}} \|X - D\beta\|_2^2 \; s.t. \; \|d_i\|_2 \leq 1, \; i = 1, 2, \cdots, N_t \quad (11)$$

(5) Steps (3) and (4) are repeated. (In the experiment, we repeated 40 times.)
(6) The obtained dictionary D is normalized for each patch and used as the final trained dictionary D.

2.7. Reconstruction Process

Assuming that the low-resolution image and the high-resolution image have the same sparse representation, the sparse representation of the low-resolution image can be obtained. The sparse representation α was estimated by solving the optimization problem of Equation (12).

$$\underset{\alpha}{\mathrm{argmin}} \frac{1}{2}\|D^{low}\alpha - Y^{low}\|_2^2 + \lambda\|\alpha\|_1 \quad (12)$$

The reconstruction process is performed as follows. In this study, the resolution of RGB image was increased.

(1) The low-resolution RGB images are upsampled via bicubic interpolation to the size of the PAN image. The upsampled low-resolution intensity I_{up}^{low} is calculated using Equation (6) with the upsampled RGB image.
(2) The feature map Y^{low} is obtained from the upsampled low-resolution intensity I_{up}^{low}. After applying the four filters shown in Section 2.6 to I_{up}^{low}, the feature map $Y^{low} \in \mathbb{R}^{4p^2 \times N_{patch}}$ is obtained, where the overlap of adjacent patches are $p \times 1$ and $1 \times p$ for horizontal and vertical directions. $I_{patch}^{low} \in \mathbb{R}^{p^2 \times N_{patch}}$ is then obtained from I_{up}^{low} where the overlap of adjacent patches are $p \times 1$ and $1 \times p$ for horizontal and vertical directions.
(3) The sparse representation $\hat{\alpha}$ is calculated using Equation (12).
(4) The high-resolution intensity image I_{sr} is obtained from the sparse representation $\hat{\alpha}$ and the high-resolution dictionary D^{high} by Equation (13), and it is normalized for each patch. The average value of the jth patch, $\bar{I}_{sr}(j)$, is calculated with the upsampled low-resolution intensity $I_{patch}^{low}(j)$, and it is added to the patch of the high-resolution intensity $I_{sr}(j)$ using Equation (14).

$$I_{sr}(j) = D^{high}\hat{\alpha}(j), \\ \hat{\alpha} \in \mathbb{R}^{Nd \times N_{patch}} \quad (13)$$

$$\hat{I}_{sr}(j) = I_{sr}(j) + \bar{I}_{sr}(j) \quad (14)$$

(5) Using the patches of the obtained high-resolution intensity $\hat{I}_{sr}(j)$, the image is reconstructed. The mean value of the overlapped pixels is used as the value of the pixel in the adjacent overlapping patches.

2.8. Tradeoff Process

The intensity of SCMP is calculated using Equation (15) after obtaining the intensity I_{up}^{low} via Equation (6).

$$I_{scmp}(k) = \frac{I_{up}^{low}(k)}{PAN^{low}(k)} PAN^{high}(k),\tag{15}$$

where k indicates the pixel position. The low-resolution PAN image, PAN^{low}, is obtained using Equation (16).

$$PAN^{low} = I_{up}^{low} + c_1 MS_{up,nir}^{low} - c_2 MS_{up,blu}^{low} - c_3 MS_{up,grn}^{low} - c_4 MS_{up,red}^{low},\tag{16}$$

where I_{up}^{low}, $MS_{up,nir}^{low}$, $MS_{up,blu}^{low}$, $MS_{up,grn}^{low}$, and $MS_{up,red}^{low}$ are the intensities of the low-resolution RGB image, NIR, blue, green, and red, respectively, and these are upsampled to the same sizes as those of the PAN image.

If the PAN image is corrected using the intensity I_{scmp} obtained via SCMP, there will be little loss of spatial information. Since the intensity correction is performed appropriately on the image, the spectral distortion when using SCMP is smaller than that of the other component substitution methods. Figure 2 shows the intensity of the original RGB image, the intensity image generated by SCMP, and the intensity image obtained by CS of Nihonmatsu and Yokohama images. From this figure, it can be seen that the intensity obtained by CS had less spatial information than SCMP. In order to increase the quality of the intensity reproduced by CS using SCMP, the intensities obtained by the CS and the SCMP were combined linearly using the tradeoff parameter τ. In the tradeoff process, the high-resolution intensity images were obtained by SCMP and CS, and these were linearly combined by Equation (17).

$$I^{high} = \tau I_{sr} + (1-\tau)I_{scmp}\ s.t.\ |\tau| \leq 1\tag{17}$$

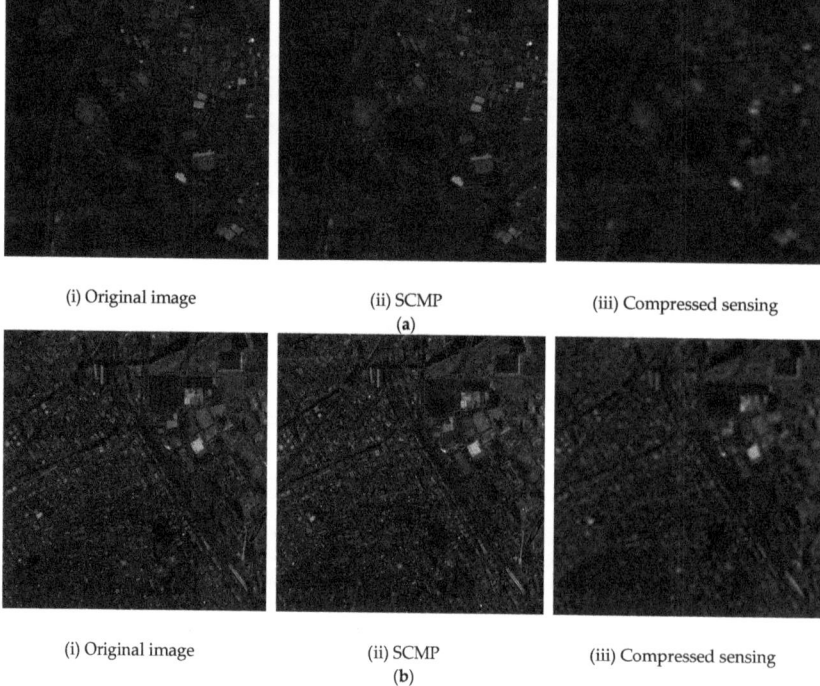

Figure 2. Intensity of RGB images of (**a**) Nihonmatsu, (**b**) Yokohama. (i) Intensity of the original image, (ii) intensity of SCMP, (iii) intensity obtained via compressed sensing.

2.9. Generalized IHS Method

For the fusion process, the generalized IHS method (GIHS) [5] proposed by Tu et al. was used. The intensity was calculated using Equation (6), and Equation (18) was applied to red-, green-, and blue-band RGB images.

$$\begin{bmatrix} MS_{red}^{high} \\ MS_{grn}^{high} \\ MS_{blu}^{high} \end{bmatrix} = \begin{bmatrix} MS_{red}^{low} + I^{high} - I^{low} \\ MS_{grn}^{low} + I^{high} - I^{low} \\ MS_{blu}^{low} + I^{high} - I^{low} \end{bmatrix}, \tag{18}$$

where $MS_{red}^{high}, MS_{grn}^{high}, MS_{blu}^{high}, MS_{red}^{low}, MS_{grn}^{low}$, and MS_{blu}^{low} are the intensities of the high-resolution and low-resolution RGB images.

3. Results

3.1. Experimental Setup

3.1.1. Quality Evaluation

Visual and numerical evaluations were performed according to the Wald protocol [36]. The original MS image was used as the reference image. Correlation coefficient (CC), universal image quality index (UIQI) [37], erreur relative global adimensionnelle de synthese (ERGAS) [38], and spectral angle mapper (SAM) [39] were used for numerical evaluation. These are major evaluation criteria and used in almost all PS-related research [2]. The CC is given by

$$CC = \frac{1}{|B|} \times \sum_{b \in B} CC_b,$$

$$CC_b = \frac{\sum_{i=1}^{N}(O_b(i) - \overline{O_b}) \times (PS_b(i) - \overline{PS_b})}{\sqrt{\sum_{i=1}^{N}(O_b(i) - \overline{O_b})^2} \times \sqrt{\sum_{i=1}^{N}(PS_b(i) - \overline{PS_b})^2}}, \tag{19}$$

where a value closer to 1.0 implies a smaller loss of the intensity correlation and a better result. N and $|B|$ are the total number of pixels in the entire image for each band and the number of bands in the PS image, respectively. $O_b(i)$ and $\overline{O_b}$ denote the ith pixel value of the b-band reference image and its mean value, respectively, and $PS_b(i)$ and $\overline{PS_b}$ denote the ith pixel value of the b-band PS image and its mean value, respectively. UIQI is an index for measuring the loss of intensity correlation, intensity distortion, and contrast distortion and is given by

$$UIQI = \frac{1}{|B|} \times \sum_{b \in B} UIQI_b,$$

$$UIQI_b = \frac{\sigma_{O_b, PS_b}}{\sigma_{O_b} \cdot \sigma_{PS_b}} \times \frac{2 \cdot \overline{O_b} \cdot \overline{PS_b}}{\left(\overline{O_b}\right)^2 + \left(\overline{PS_b}\right)^2} \times \frac{2 \cdot \sigma_{O_b} \cdot \sigma_{PS_b}}{\sigma_{O_b}^2 + \sigma_{PS_b}^2}, \tag{20}$$

where σ_{O_b} and σ_{PS_b} are the standard deviation of the reference and PS images in the b-band, respectively, and σ_{O_b, PS_b} denotes the covariance of the reference and PS images in the b-band. A value closer to 1.0 implies that these losses are small. The size of the UIQI sliding window was 8×8.

The ERGAS is given by

$$ERGAS = 100 \times \frac{h}{l} \times \sqrt{\frac{1}{|B|} \times \sum_{b \in B} \left(\frac{(RMSE_b)^2}{(\overline{PS_b})^2}\right)}, \tag{21}$$

$$RMSE_b = \sqrt{\frac{1}{N} \times \sum_{i=1}^{N} (O_b(i) - PS_b(i))^2},$$

where h and l denote the spatial resolution of the PAN and MS images, respectively. The smaller the ERGAS value, the better the image quality. The SAM is an index for measuring spectral distortion and is given by

$$\text{SAM} = \frac{1}{N}\sum_{i=1}^{N} SAM(i),$$
$$\text{SAM}(i) = \cos^{-1}\left(\frac{\sum_{b\in B} O_b(i) \times PS_b(i)}{\sqrt{\sum_{b\in B}(O_b(i))^2} \times \sqrt{\sum_{b\in B}(PS_b(i))^2}}\right). \quad (22)$$

If the value is closer to 0.0, the spectrum ratio of each band is closer to the reference image.

3.1.2. Dictionary Learning

We used PAN images from the Nihonmatsu and Yokohama datasets as training images for dictionary learning. For training image X and dictionary, the number of training times was 40, the number of atoms of the dictionary D was 1024, and the size of each atom was $p = 4$. The number of patches was 6433 (Nihonmatsu) and 10,000 (Yokohama). The training dataset was a set of 1000 patches randomly selected from these patches. As the training image X, a training PAN image for the high-resolution dictionary was used as the high-resolution data X^{high}, and a training PAN image for the low-resolution dictionary was used as the low-resolution data X^{low}. The low-resolution image was generated by downsampling and upsampling via bicubic interpolation. The sparsity regularization parameter was $\lambda = 0.1$. The sparse representation β was calculated using Equation (10) by solving the L1 norm regularized least-squares problem, and the dictionary D was obtained using Equation (11) by solving the least-squares problem with quadratic constraints. We used the code provided by Lee et al. [40]. The learned high-resolution dictionaries are shown in Figure 3. For Nihonmatsu images, the dictionary created using Nihonmatsu images was used. For Yokohama images, the dictionary created using Yokohama images was used.

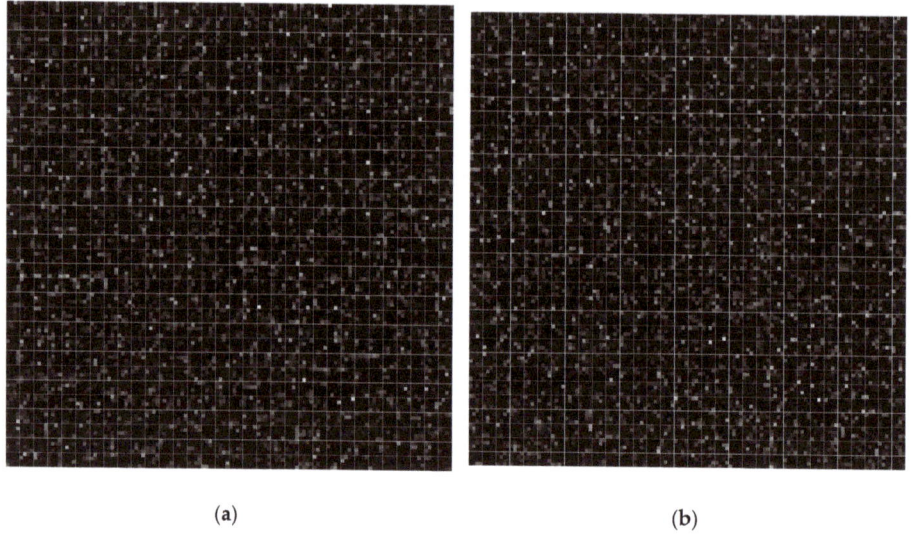

Figure 3. Trained high-resolution dictionaries: (**a**) Nihonmatsu, (**b**) Yokohama.

3.1.3. Reconstruction Process

The bicubic interpolation was used to upsample the intensity I^{low} of the low-resolution RGB image. The size of the patch of the input low-resolution data Y^{low} was $p = 4$, and the overlapping region of adjacent patches was $p \times 1$ for the horizontal direction and $1 \times p$ for the vertical direction. The filter size used for the back-projection process was 5 × 5. The sparse representation a was calculated using Equation (12) by solving the L1 norm regularized least-squares problem. We used the code provided by Lee et al. [40].

3.1.4. Coefficients for Intensity Correction

The correction coefficients estimated by SCMP are shown in Table 2. These values were used for the fusion process.

Table 2. The correction coefficient estimated by SCMP.

Coefficient	Nihonmatsu	Yokohama
c_1 (NIR)	0.3857	0.3789
c_2 (Blue)	0.2199	0.2549
c_3 (Green)	0.1980	0.1123
c_4 (Red)	0.0486	0.1099

3.1.5. Tradeoff Parameter

In the tradeoff process, the intensity images obtained by SCMP and CS were combined by Equation (17) using the tradeoff parameter τ ($0 \leq \tau \leq 1$). The tradeoff parameter is a hyperparameter that should be determined in advance. In general, experimental validation is carried out via cross-validation when there are hyperparameters. Since we used two kinds of satellite images (Nihonmatsu and Yokohama), the value of τ was determined using one of these datasets, and the other dataset was processed using the determined value. In our experiment, the tradeoff parameter was determined using the correlation coefficient (CC) and ERGAS [38]. The results of applying the tradeoff parameter with a step size of 0.1 for image quality evaluation are shown in Table 3. From this result, it was found that the resolution and numerical evaluation were improved when the sum of squares of 1-CC and ERGAS was the smallest. This relationship is shown in Equations (23) and (24).

$$\mathop{\mathrm{argmin}}_{\tau} S(\tau) \; s.t. \; 0 \leq S(\tau) \leq 2 \tag{23}$$

$$S(\tau) = \left(\frac{1 - CC(\tau)}{\max(1 - CC)}\right)^2 + \left(\frac{ERGAS(\tau)}{\max ERGAS}\right)^2 \tag{24}$$

The tradeoff parameter was determined as the value that minimizes Equation (24). Figure 4 displays the results of evaluation of the intensity of RGB images with various tradeoff parameters. The red line shows Nihonmatsu, the blue line shows Yokohama, the solid line is the result of CC, and the dotted line is the result of ERGAS. Figure 5 shows three images with some tradeoff parameter values. The lower the evaluation index S, the better the visual appearance. From these results, the value that minimized $S(\tau)$ was $\tau = 0.4$ for Nihonmatsu and $\tau = 0.3$ for Yokohama. Therefore, in the following experimetns, $\tau = 0.3$ was used for Nihonmatsu and $\tau = 0.4$ was used for Yokohama.

Table 3. CC, ERGAS, and the evaluation index S that determines the tradeoff parameter. The best values are given in bold.

Tradeoff Parameter	Nihonmatsu			Yokohama		
	CC	ERGAS	S	CC	ERGAS	S
0.0	0.899	2.415	1.186	0.944	2.393	0.405
0.1	0.908	2.250	1.016	0.949	2.148	0.327
0.2	0.915	2.123	0.892	0.952	1.996	0.283
0.3	0.920	2.041	0.815	**0.953**	**1.961**	**0.274**
0.4	**0.922**	**2.008**	**0.783**	0.949	2.050	0.302
0.5	0.921	2.027	0.800	0.941	2.248	0.371
0.6	0.916	2.097	0.873	0.926	2.529	0.491
0.7	0.906	2.213	1.011	0.903	2.870	0.679
0.8	0.891	2.369	1.228	0.871	3.251	0.963
0.9	0.871	2.557	1.550	0.828	3.660	1.385
1.0	0.846	2.769	2.000	0.775	4.088	2.000

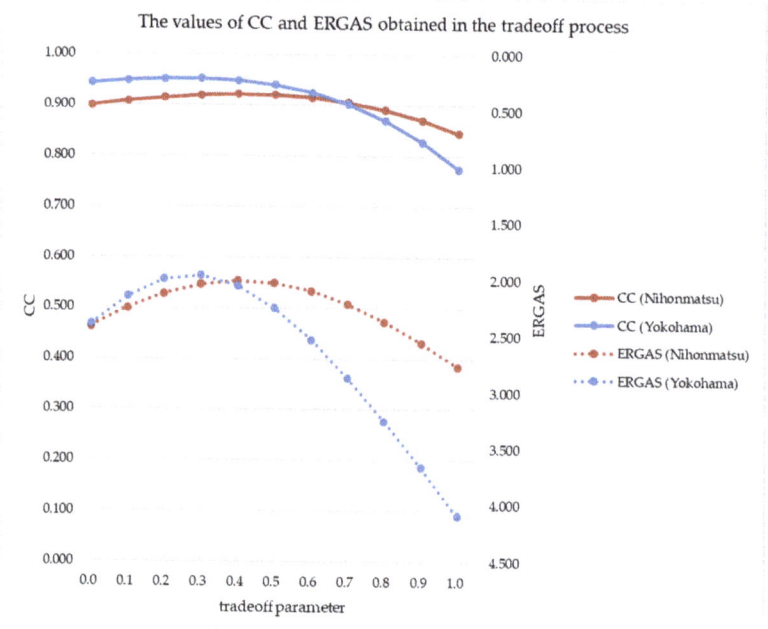

Figure 4. The values of CC and ERGAS obtained in the tradeoff process. CC: solid line, ERGAS: dotted line; Nihonmatsu: blue line, Yokohama: red line.

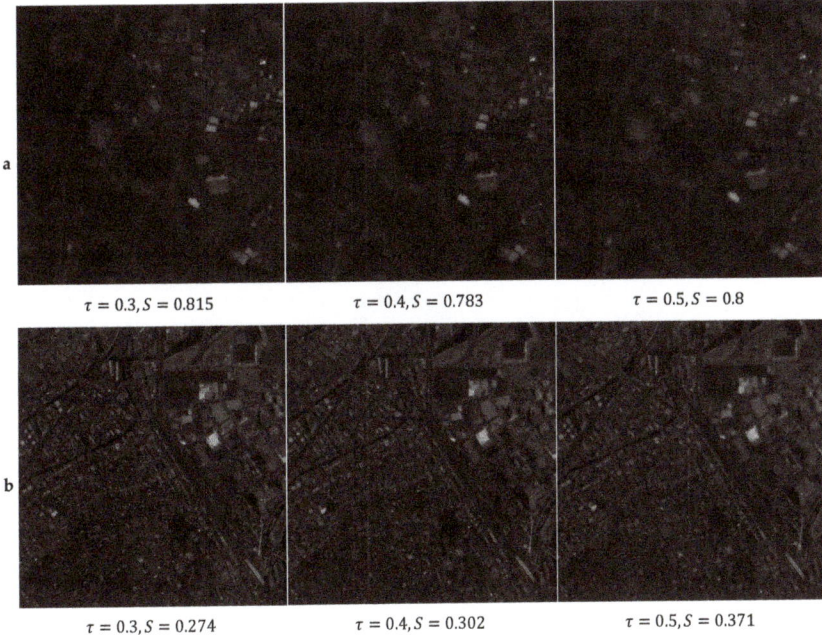

Figure 5. Comparison of intensity of RGB images against the tradeoff parameter. S represents the index that determines the tradeoff parameter. (**a**) Nihonmatsu, (**b**) Yokohama.

3.2. Experimental Results

Table 4 shows the effect of the back-projection (BP). The results of the intensity I_{sr} obtained using the sparse representation (SR) and the intensity obtained by repeating BP ten times with a size 5 filter are shown. These were compared by CC, UIQI, and ERGAS, and applying BP was better in all cases. Table 5 shows the effect of the tradeoff process (TP). The intensity images generated by SCMP, SR, and TP are shown. TP was the best in all evaluations. Table 6 shows the comparison of BP and TP. TP was better in every case.

Tables 7 and 8 show numerical evaluations of the existing methods and the proposed method. The existing methods include fast IHS [5], Gram–Schmidt method (GS) [7], band-dependent spatial detail (BDSD) [41], weighted least-squares (WLS)-filter-based method (WLS) [42], multiband images with adaptive spectral-intensity modulation (MDSIm) [43], spectrum correction using modeled panchromatic image (SCMP) [35], image super-resolution via sparse representation (ISSR) [13] using natural images (Dict natural) and corresponding images (Dict-self), the sparse representation of injected details (SR-D) [30], and the method of sparse representation described by Ayas et al. (SRayas) [34].

Table 4. Numerical evaluation of image intensities with or without the back-projection process of the intensity obtained via sparse representation. The best values are given in bold.

Method	CC		UIQI		ERGAS	
	Nihonmatsu	Yokohama	Nihonmatsu	Yokohama	Nihonmatsu	Yokohama
Ideal	1.0		1.0		0.0	
SR	0.846	0.775	0.807	0.709	2.769	4.088
SR+BP	**0.853**	**0.785**	**0.822**	**0.742**	**2.709**	**4.009**

Table 5. Numerical evaluation of image intensities obtained by SCMP, SR, and the tradeoff process. The best values are given in bold.

Method	CC		UIQI		ERGAS	
	Nihonmatsu	Yokohama	Nihonmatsu	Yokohama	Nihonmatsu	Yokohama
Ideal	1.0		1.0		0.0	
SCMP	0.899	0.944	0.779	0.915	2.415	2.393
SR	0.846	0.775	0.807	0.709	2.769	4.088
TP	**0.920**	**0.949**	**0.825**	**0.926**	**2.041**	**2.050**

Table 6. Comparison of the back-projection and the tradeoff process. The best values are given in bold.

Method	CC		UIQI		ERGAS	
	Nihonmatsu	Yokohama	Nihonmatsu	Yokohama	Nihonmatsu	Yokohama
Ideal	1.0		1.0		0.0	
BP	0.853	0.785	0.822	0.742	2.709	4.009
TP	**0.920**	**0.949**	**0.825**	**0.926**	**2.041**	**2.050**

Table 7. Numerical evaluation of the existing methods and the proposed method by CC and UIQI. The highest scores are printed in bold, and the second highest scores are underlined.

Method	CC		UIQI	
	Nihonmatsu	Yokohama	Nihonmatsu	Yokohama
ideal	1.0		1.0	
fast IHS [5]	0.783	0.914	0.717	0.901
GS [7]	0.508	0.860	0.373	0.838
BDSD [41]	0.860	0.887	0.864	0.851
WLS [42]	0.866	0.884	0.870	0.759
MDSIm [43]	0.791	0.865	0.736	0.823
SCMP [35]	<u>0.883</u>	<u>0.928</u>	0.864	<u>0.910</u>
ISSR (Dict-natural) [13]	0.831	0.765	**0.918**	0.704
ISSR (Dict-self) [13]	0.831	0.759	<u>0.917</u>	0.701
SR-D	0.845	0.786	0.914	0.710
SRayas [34]	0.787	0.758	0.851	0.703
Proposed	**0.906**	**0.937**	0.903	**0.918**

The size of the local estimation of the distinct block of BDSD was 256×256 for Nihonmatsu and 448×448 for Yokohama. For the ISSR settings, the training images for the dictionary included training PAN images and natural images, the number of training times was 40, the number of atoms in the dictionary was 1024, the atom size of the dictionary was $4 \times 4 \times 5$, the sparsity regularization parameter was 0.1, randomly selected 1000 training image patches were used, the upscale was 4 (ratio of resolution of PAN images and MS images of IKONOS), overlap pixel of patches in the reconstruction process was $\mathbb{R}^{1 \times p}$ in horizontal direction and $\mathbb{R}^{p \times 1}$ in vertical direction, the size of the back-projection filter was 5×5, and the number of iterations was 10. For SR-D, high-resolution and low-resolution dictionaries were constructed from the original PAN images without training. The atom size of the high-resolution dictionary was $\mathbb{R}^{28 \times 28 \times 4}$ and the overlapping areas of the adjacent atoms were $\mathbb{R}^{16 \times p}, \mathbb{R}^{p \times 16}$; the atom size of the low-resolution dictionary was $\mathbb{R}^{7 \times 7 \times 4}$ and and the overlapping area of the adjacent atoms were $\mathbb{R}^{4 \times p}, \mathbb{R}^{p \times 4}$. For the SRayas setting, the original IKONOS MS images were used as the training images for the dictionary, the number of training times was 20, the number of atoms in the dictionary was 4096, the size of the dictionary atom was $8 \times 8 \times 4$, the sparsity regularization parameter was $\lambda = 0.15$, the number of training image patches was 2000, the upscale was 4 (ratio of resolution of PAN images and MS images of IKONOS), $\beta = 0.25$, the weight of each spectral band of IKONOS was $w = [0.1071, 0.2646, 0.2696, 0.3587]$, the overlap pixel in the patch of reconstruction process was 0, the back-projection filter size was 3×3, and the number of repetitions was 20. These settings of the existing methods followed those described in the original papers except the distinct block size of BDSD. The code of Vivone et al. [2] was used for GS and BDSD, and the code of Yang et al. [13] was used for ISSR.

Table 8. Numerical evaluation of the existing methods and the proposed method by ERGAS and SAM. The highest scores are printed in bold, and the second highest scores are underlined.

Method	ERGAS		SAM	
	Nihonmatsu	Yokohama	Nihonmatsu	Yokohama
ideal	0.0		0.0	
fast IHS [5]	3.471	3.716	1.898	2.367
GS [7]	5.046	3.563	2.748	**1.950**
BDSD [41]	3.026	3.361	1.925	2.326
WLS [42]	2.815	3.816	1.699	<u>2.123</u>
MDSIm [43]	3.321	3.515	**1.658**	2.189
SCMP [35]	<u>2.673</u>	<u>2.697</u>	1.753	2.176
ISSR (Dict-natural) [13]	3.118	4.419	1.749	2.324
ISSR (Dict-self) [13]	3.124	4.474	1.750	2.331
SR-D	3.007	4.226	1.897	2.649
SRayas [34]	3.497	4.476	1.765	2.299
Proposed	**2.336**	**2.424**	<u>1.688</u>	2.159

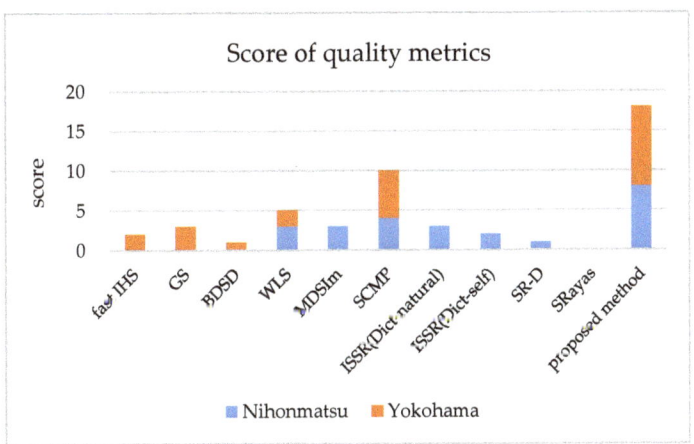

Figure 6. Scores of quality metrics.

In Tables 7 and 8, the highest scores are printed in bold, and the second highest scores are underlined. GS was generally not good except for the SAM of Yokohama. The results of BDSD were unremarkable but stable. SCMP was stable and gave good results. In ISSR, differences in training images had little effect on results. SRayas did not perform as well overall as ISSR and SRayas. Although some results, such as the CC of SR-D of Table 7, MDSIm of Table 8, and SAM of GS were better in part than the proposed method, in many other cases they were less accurate than the proposed method. The results of the proposed method were generally good, although there are some differences due to the tradeoff parameter.

Figure 6 shows the ranking of the quality metric of the numerical evaluations of Tables 7 and 8, except for the proposed method. For each test, the best result was worth three points, the second-best result was worth two points, and the third-best result was worth one point. The highest score was 24 points. This figure shows that only three methods, WLS, SCMP, and the proposed method, were good for both of the images, and the proposed method got the highest score.

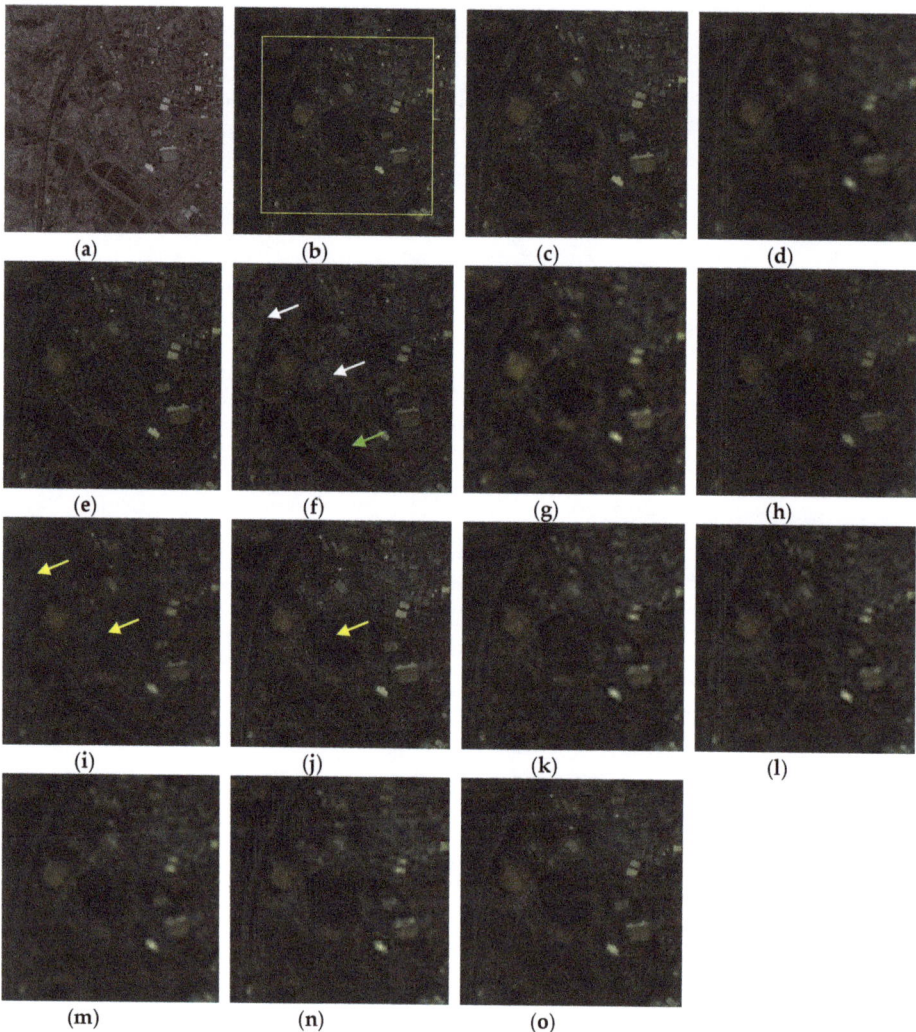

Figure 7. Reference and pansharpened Nihonmatsu images: (**a**) original PAN image (reference image), (**b**) original RGB image, (**c**) ground truth RGB image, (**d**) RGB image upsampled by bicubic interpolation, (**e**) fast IHS, (**f**) GS, (**g**) BDSD, (**h**) WLS, (**i**) MDSIm, (**j**) SCMP, (**k**) ISSR (natural images were used for training), (**l**) ISSR (Nihonmatsu images were used for training), (**m**) SR-D, (**n**) SRayas method, (**o**) proposed method ($\tau = 0.3$).

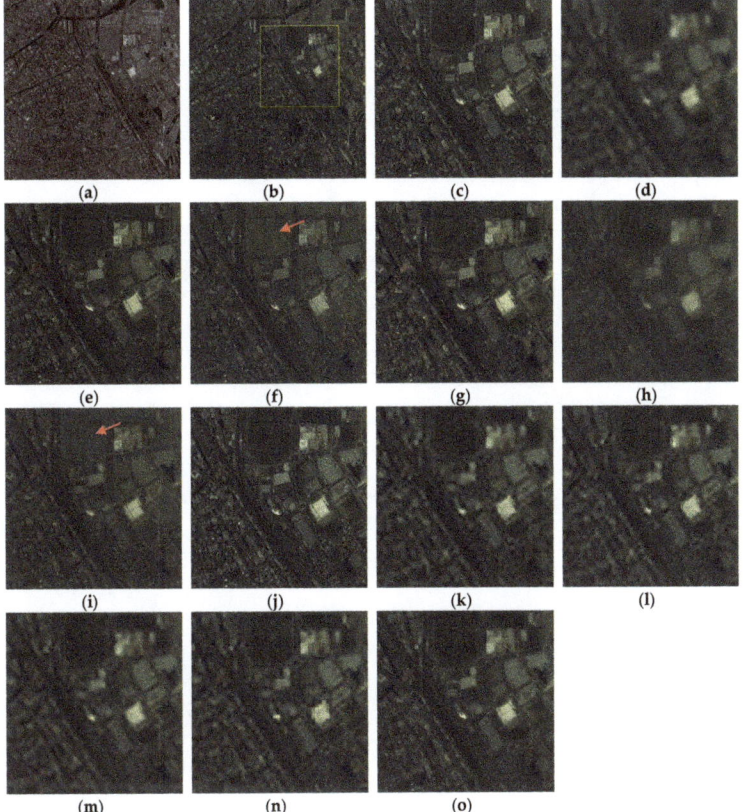

Figure 8. Reference and pansharpened Yokohama images: (**a**) original PAN image (reference image), (**b**) original RGB image, (**c**) ground truth RGB image, (**d**) RGB image upsampled by bicubic interpolation, (**e**) fast IHS, (**f**) GS, (**g**) BDSD, (**h**) WLS, (**i**) MDSIm, (**j**) SCMP, (**k**) ISSR (natural images were used for training), (**l**) ISSR (Yokohama images were used for training), (**m**) SR-D, (**n**) SRayas method, (**o**) proposed method ($\tau = 0.4$).

Figures 7 and 8 show the reference and PS images from the Nihonmatsu and Yokohama datasets, respectively. Since the images were small, the enlarged image surrounded by the yellow frame of the original RGB image (b) is shown in (c)–(o). In Figure 7, in GS (f), the color of green was darker in the rice field area (indicated by the green arrow), while the forest area was whitish. BDSD (g) was more blurred than other images. In MDSIm (i), the color of the forest area was also whitish (indicated by the yellow arrow). In Figure 8, the vegetation area was whitish in GS (f) and MDSIm (i) (indicated by the red arrow). WLS (h) looked hazy. SR-D (m) had lower resolution than the other methods using sparse representation with back-projection. In both Figures 7 and 8, the results of ISSR (k) (l) and SRayas (n) had ringing artefacts. Other images appeared to be reproduced without problems.

4. Discussion

From the results in Table 4, it was found that the back-projection (BP) was effective from the viewpoint of improving spectral distortion. From the results in Table 5, it was found that the tradeoff process (TP) is effective in improving spectral distortion. Furthermore, since the TP was better than the individual methods of sparse representation (SR) and SCMP, it was clarified that these methods complementarily improve the spectral distortion. From the results in Table 6, it was found that the

TP improved spectral distortion more than BP. In the results shown in Tables 7 and 8, the method using GIHS (WLS and SCMP) was better than the existing methods using SR. In addition, it was found that the proposed method, the linear combination of SR and SCMP, gave better results than SCMP alone. One of the problems to be solved in PS processing is the independence of the processed image. In other words, it is important to obtain stable and good results rather than obtaining good results only on a specific image. Although there are some methods shown in Tables 7 and 8 that gave better results than the proposed method, comparing the other evaluation results shows that the results were inconsistent. The reason why the evaluation results were so different could be that these processing methods depend on the processed image.

As shown in Figures 7 and 8, it was found that the reproduction of vegetation area by the GS was unstable. Since the image quality differs depending on the size of the local estimation on the distinct blocks used in BDSD, we evaluated the visibly good images with good numerical values, but the resolution of the image was low. The WLS gave good numerical results with two images, but the images were blurred. Both ISSR and SRayas using BP generated ringing artifacts. Other images seemed to be reproduced without problems in resolution and color. Among them, the proposed method gave the best results in the numerical evaluation.

In this method, resolution enhancement was achieved by using the visible and NIR regions. On the other hand, it can be applied only to the resolution enhancement of RGB images, and not NIR images.

5. Conclusions

In this paper, we proposed a method for pansharpening based on CS theory. In the proposed method, the intensity obtained from the component substitution method and the intensity obtained via the method based on CS theory are fused to reproduce the intensity close to the original. We introduced SCMP as the intensity substitution method and used the tradeoff process for image fusion. Experimental results showed that the proposed method outperformed existing methods in terms of numerical and visual evaluation. The proposed method was also effective for satellites with panchromatic sensors (observed areas are visible and NIR regions) and multispectral sensors (observed areas are red, blue, green, and NIR bands) like IKONOS.

Generally, the intensity image generated by a CS-based method is blurrier than the intensity image generated by the component substitution method, because component substitution captures the intensity of the PAN image. On the other hand, it is expected that the spectral distortion of the intensity image generated by the CS-based method will be lower than that of the image generated by the component substitution method. Since complete restoration is not guaranteed, in order to get the image close to a complete reproduction, back-projection methods can be used. However, they may cause ringing artifacts. Based on these considerations, our proposed method combines the intensities generated by the CS-based method and the component-substitution-based method via the tradeoff process instead of the back-projection to achieve both an improvement of spatial resolution and a reduction of spectral distortion. Experimental results show that the tradeoff process was more effective than the back-projection in generating a pansharpened image of which the spatial resolution was equivalent to that of the PAN image and reducing spectral distortion. Improvement of the accuracy by parameter tuning is important future work.

Author Contributions: Methodology, N.T. and Y.S.; Software, N.T.; Validation, Y.S.; Writing—Original Draft Preparation, N.T.; Writing—Review and Editing, Y.S. and S.O.; Supervision, S.O.; Project Administration, S.O.; Funding Acquisition, S.O. All authors have read and agreed to the published version of the manuscript.

Funding: This work was partially supported by the JSPS KAKENHI Grant Number 18K19772 and the Yotta Informatics Project by MEXT, Japan.

Acknowledgments: The authors thank the Japan Space Imaging Corporation and Space Imaging, LLC for providing the images.

Conflicts of Interest: The authors declare no conflict of interest.

References

1. Amro, I.; Mateos, J.; Vega, M.; Molina, R.; Katsaggelos, A.K. A survey of classical methods and new trends in pansharpening of multispectral images. *EURASIP J. Adv. Signal Process.* **2011**, *2011*, 79. [CrossRef]
2. Vivone, G.; Alparone, L.; Chanussot, J.; Dalla Mura, M.; Garzelli, A.; Licciardi, G.A.; Restaino, R.; Wald, L. A critical comparison among pansharpening algorithms. *IEEE Trans. Geosci. Remote Sens.* **2015**, *53*, 2565–2586. [CrossRef]
3. Ghamisi, P.; Rasti, B.; Yokoya, N.; Wang, Q.; Hofle, B.; Bruzzone, L.; Bovolo, F.; Chi, M.; Anders, K.; Gloaguen, R.; et al. Multisource and multitemporal data fusion in remote sensing: A comprehensive review of the state of the art. *IEEE Geosci. Remote Sens. Mag.* **2019**, *7*, 6–39. [CrossRef]
4. Pohl, C.; Van Genderen, J.L. Review article Multisensor image fusion in remote sensing: Concepts, methods and applications. *Int. J. Remote Sens.* **1998**, *19*, 823–854. [CrossRef]
5. Tu, T.M.; Su, S.C.; Shyu, H.C.; Huang, P.S. A new look at IHS-like image fusion methods. *Inf. Fusion* **2001**, *2*, 177–186. [CrossRef]
6. Zhou, J.; Civco, D.L.; Silander, J.A. A wavelet transform method to merge Landsat TM and SPOT panchromatic data. *Int. J. Remote Sens.* **1998**, *19*, 743–757. [CrossRef]
7. Laben, C.A.; Brower, B.V. Process for Enhancing the Spatial Resolution of Multispectral Imagery Using Pan-Sharpening. U.S. Patent 6,011,875, 4 January 2000.
8. Mallat, S.G. A theory for multiresolution signal decomposition: The wavelet representation. *IEEE Trans. Pattern Anal. Mach. Intell.* **1989**, *17*, 674–693. [CrossRef]
9. Shensa, M.J. The Discrete Wavelet Transform: Wedding the À Trous and Mallat Algorithms. *IEEE Trans. Signal Process.* **1992**, *40*, 2464–2482. [CrossRef]
10. Burt, P.J.; Adelson, E.H. The Laplacian Pyramid as a Compact Image Code. *IEEE Trans. Commun.* **1983**, *31*, 532–540. [CrossRef]
11. Aiazzi, B.; Alparone, L.; Baronti, S.; Garzelli, A. Context-driven fusion of high spatial and spectral resolution images based on oversampled multiresolution analysis. *IEEE Trans. Geosci. Remote Sens.* **2002**, *40*, 2300–2312. [CrossRef]
12. Zhang, Q.; Guo, B. Multifocus image fusion using the nonsubsampled contourlet transform. *Signal Process.* **2009**, *89*, 1334–1346. [CrossRef]
13. Yang, J.; Wright, J.; Huang, T.S.; Ma, Y. Image super-resolution via sparse representation. *IEEE Trans. Image Process.* **2010**, *19*, 2861–2873. [CrossRef] [PubMed]
14. Dong, C.; Loy, C.C.; He, K.; Tang, X. Image Super—Resolution Using Deep Convolutional Networks. *IEEE Trans. Pattern Anal. Mach. Intell.* **2016**, *38*, 295–307. [CrossRef] [PubMed]
15. Masi, G.; Cozzolino, D.; Verdoliva, L.; Scarpa, G. Pansharpening by convolutional neural networks. *Remote Sens.* **2016**, *8*, 594. [CrossRef]
16. Vivone, G.; Addesso, P.; Restaino, R.; Dalla Mura, M.; Chanussot, J. Pansharpening Based on Deconvolution for Multiband Filter Estimation. *IEEE Trans. Geosci. Remote Sens.* **2019**, *57*, 540–553. [CrossRef]
17. Fei, R.; Zhang, J.; Liu, J.; Du, F.; Chang, P.; Hu, J. Convolutional Sparse Representation of Injected Details for Pansharpening. *IEEE Geosci. Remote Sens. Lett.* **2019**, *16*, 1595–1599. [CrossRef]
18. Yin, H. PAN-Guided Cross-Resolution Projection for Local Adaptive Sparse Representation-Based Pansharpening. *IEEE Trans. Geosci. Remote Sens.* **2019**, *57*, 4938–4950. [CrossRef]
19. Wang, X.; Bai, S.; Li, Z.; Song, R.; Tao, J. The PAN and ms image pansharpening algorithm based on adaptive neural network and sparse representation in the NSST domain. *IEEE Access* **2019**, *7*, 52508–52521. [CrossRef]
20. He, L.; Rao, Y.; Li, J.; Chanussot, J.; Plaza, A.; Zhu, J.; Li, B. Pansharpening via Detail Injection Based Convolutional Neural Networks. *IEEE J. Sel. Top. Appl. Earth Obs. Remote Sens.* **2019**, *12*, 1188–1204. [CrossRef]
21. Donoho, D.L. Compressed Sensing. *IEEE Trans. Inf. Theory* **2006**, *52*, 1289–1306. [CrossRef]
22. Li, S.; Yang, B. A new pan-sharpening method using a compressed sensing technique. *IEEE Trans. Geosci. Remote Sens.* **2011**, *49*, 738–746. [CrossRef]
23. Li, S.; Yin, H.; Fang, L. Remote sensing image fusion via sparse representations over learned dictionaries. *IEEE Trans. Geosci. Remote Sens.* **2013**, *51*, 4779–4789. [CrossRef]
24. Jiang, C.; Zhang, H.; Shen, H.; Zhang, L. A practical compressed sensing-based pan-sharpening method. *IEEE Geosci. Remote Sens. Lett.* **2012**, *9*, 629–633. [CrossRef]

25. Jiang, C.; Zhang, H.; Shen, H.; Zhang, L. Two-step sparse coding for the pan-sharpening of remote sensing images. *IEEE J. Sel. Top. Appl. Earth Obs. Remote Sens.* **2014**, *7*, 1792–1805. [CrossRef]
26. Zhu, X.X.; Bamler, R. A sparse image fusion algorithm with application to pan-sharpening. *IEEE Trans. Geosci. Remote Sens.* **2013**, *51*, 2827–2836. [CrossRef]
27. Zhu, X.X.; Grohnfeldt, C.; Bamler, R. Exploiting Joint Sparsity for Pansharpening: The J-SparseFI Algorithm. *IEEE Trans. Geosci. Remote Sens.* **2016**, *54*, 2664–2681. [CrossRef]
28. Guo, M.; Zhang, H.; Li, J.; Zhang, L.; Shen, H. An online coupled dictionary learning approach for remote sensing image fusion. *IEEE J. Sel. Top. Appl. Earth Obs. Remote Sens.* **2014**, *7*, 1284–1294. [CrossRef]
29. Elad, M. *Sparse and Redundant Representations: From Theory to Applications in Signal and Image Processing*; Springer: New York, NY, USA, 2010; ISBN 978-1441970107.
30. Vicinanza, M.R.; Restaino, R.; Vivone, G.; Dalla Mura, M.; Chanussot, J. A pansharpening method based on the sparse representation of injected details. *IEEE Geosci. Remote Sens. Lett.* **2015**, *12*, 180–184. [CrossRef]
31. Ghahremani, M.; Ghassemian, H. Remote Sensing Image Fusion Using Ripplet Transform and Compressed Sensing. *IEEE Geosci. Remote Sens. Lett.* **2015**, *12*, 502–506. [CrossRef]
32. Zhang, K.; Wang, M.; Yang, S.; Xing, Y.; Qu, R. Fusion of Panchromatic and Multispectral Images via Coupled Sparse Non-Negative Matrix Factorization. *IEEE J. Sel. Top. Appl. Earth Obs. Remote Sens.* **2016**, *9*, 5740–5747. [CrossRef]
33. Irani, M.; Peleg, S. Motion analysis for image enhancement: Resolution, occlusion, and transparency. *J. Vis. Commun. Image Represent.* **1993**, *4*, 324–335. [CrossRef]
34. Ayas, S.; Gormus, E.T.; Ekinci, M. An efficient pan sharpening via texture based dictionary learning and sparse representation. *IEEE J. Sel. Top. Appl. Earth Obs. Remote Sens.* **2018**, *11*, 2448–2460. [CrossRef]
35. Tsukamoto, N.; Sugaya, Y.; Omachi, S. Spectrum Correction Using Modeled Panchromatic Image for Pansharpening. *J. Imaging* **2020**, *6*, 20. [CrossRef]
36. Wald, L.; Ranchin, T.; Mangolini, M. Fusion of satellite images of different spatial resolutions: Assessing the quality of resulting images. *Photogramm. Eng. Remote Sens.* **1997**, *63*, 691–699.
37. Wang, Z.; Bovik, A.C. A Universal Image Quality Index. *IEEE Signal Process. Lett.* **2002**, *9*, 81–84. [CrossRef]
38. Wald, L. Quality of high resolution synthesised images: Is there a simple criterion? In *Proceedings of the Third Conference Fusion of Earth Data: Merging Point Measurements, Raster Maps and Remotely Sensed Images*; Ranchin, T., Wald, L., Eds.; SEE/URISCA: Nice, France, 2000; pp. 99–103.
39. Kruse, F.A.; Lefkoff, A.B.; Boardman, J.W.; Heidebrecht, K.B.; Shapiro, A.T.; Barloon, P.J.; Goetz, A.F.H. The spectral image processing system (SIPS)—Interactive visualization and analysis of imaging spectrometer data. *Remote Sens. Environ.* **1993**, *44*, 145–163. [CrossRef]
40. Lee, H.; Battle, A.; Raina, R.; Ng, A.Y. Efficient sparse coding algorithms. In *Proceedings of the 19th International Conference on Neural Information Processing Systems*; Schölkopf, B., Platt, J.C., Hoffman, T., Eds.; MIT Press: Cambridge, MA, USA, 2006; pp. 801–808.
41. Garzelli, A.; Nencini, F.; Capobianco, L. Optimal MMSE pan sharpening of very high resolution multispectral images. *IEEE Trans. Geosci. Remote Sens.* **2008**, *46*, 228–236. [CrossRef]
42. Song, Y.; Wu, W.; Liu, Z.; Yang, X.; Liu, K.; Lu, W. An adaptive pansharpening method by using weighted least squares filter. *IEEE Geosci. Remote Sens. Lett.* **2016**, *13*, 18–22. [CrossRef]
43. Yang, Y.; Wu, L.; Huang, S.; Tang, Y.; Wan, W. Pansharpening for Multiband Images with Adaptive Spectral-Intensity Modulation. *IEEE J. Sel. Top. Appl. Earth Obs. Remote Sens.* **2018**, *11*, 3196–3208. [CrossRef]

© 2020 by the authors. Licensee MDPI, Basel, Switzerland. This article is an open access article distributed under the terms and conditions of the Creative Commons Attribution (CC BY) license (http://creativecommons.org/licenses/by/4.0/).

Article

Aerial Scene Classification through Fine-Tuning with Adaptive Learning Rates and Label Smoothing

Biserka Petrovska [1,*], Tatjana Atanasova-Pacemska [2], Roberto Corizzo [3], Paolo Mignone [4], Petre Lameski [5] and Eftim Zdravevski [5,*]

1. Ministry of Defence, 1000 Skopje, North Macedonia
2. Faculty of Computer Science, University Goce Delcev, 2000 Stip, North Macedonia; tatjana.pacemska@ugd.edu.mk
3. Department of Computer Science, American University, 4400 Massachusetts Ave NW, Washington, DC 20016, USA; rcorizzo@american.edu
4. Department of Computer Science, University of Bari Aldo Moro, Via E. Orabona, 4, 70125 Bari, Italy; paolo.mignone@uniba.it
5. Faculty of Computer Science and Engineering, Ss. Cyril and Methodius University in Skopje, Rugjer Boshkovik 16, 1000 Skopje, North Macedonia; lameski@finki.ukim.mk
* Correspondence: biserka.petrovska@morm.gov.mk (B.P.); eftim@finki.ukim.mk (E.Z.)

Received: 28 July 2020; Accepted: 19 August 2020; Published: 21 August 2020

Abstract: Remote Sensing (RS) image classification has recently attracted great attention for its application in different tasks, including environmental monitoring, battlefield surveillance, and geospatial object detection. The best practices for these tasks often involve transfer learning from pre-trained Convolutional Neural Networks (CNNs). A common approach in the literature is employing CNNs for feature extraction, and subsequently train classifiers exploiting such features. In this paper, we propose the adoption of transfer learning by fine-tuning pre-trained CNNs for end-to-end aerial image classification. Our approach performs feature extraction from the fine-tuned neural networks and remote sensing image classification with a Support Vector Machine (SVM) model with linear and Radial Basis Function (RBF) kernels. To tune the learning rate hyperparameter, we employ a linear decay learning rate scheduler as well as cyclical learning rates. Moreover, in order to mitigate the overfitting problem of pre-trained models, we apply label smoothing regularization. For the fine-tuning and feature extraction process, we adopt the Inception-v3 and Xception inception-based CNNs, as well the residual-based networks ResNet50 and DenseNet121. We present extensive experiments on two real-world remote sensing image datasets: AID and NWPU-RESISC45. The results show that the proposed method exhibits classification accuracy of up to 98%, outperforming other state-of-the-art methods.

Keywords: remote sensing; convolutional neural network; fine-tuning; learning rate scheduler; cyclical learning rates; label smoothing; classification accuracy

1. Introduction

One task of computer vision is image classification and it has been thoroughly studied in the literature. There are many existing algorithms to solve this task. Remote sensing image classification is a more challenging problem due to the fact that objects are randomly rotated within a scene and the background texture is complex. The purpose of aerial scene classification techniques is to classify an image in one of the semantic classes, which are determined upon human interpretation. This problem has been of wide interest in resent research, due to its importance in a wide range of applications, including the surveillance of airports and aviation protection, flora monitoring in agriculture, and recognition of earth cover changes in environmental engineering [1].

RS image classification is possible thanks to the availability of RS images datasets that were collected from earth observation platforms, such as satellites, aerial systems, and unmanned aerial vehicles. The problem is complex and relies on the representation of salient image characteristics by means of high-level features. The latest techniques that include deep learning methods based on Convolutional Neural Networks (CNNs) have shown remarkable improvement in classification accuracy as compared to older ones based on handcrafted features [2,3]. The effectiveness of solutions based on CNNs lies in the possibility to perform knowledge transfer from pre-trained CNNs [4]. The knowledge transfer for image classification can be conducted in different ways, including feature extraction and fine-tuning [5,6].

There are numerous research studies that show that CNNs trained on one classification problem (such as ImageNet) can be successfully exploited to extract features from images in different tasks [7]. Excellent classification results were also achieved in aerial scene classification [8–10]. The first case of adoption of pre-trained CNN schemes for remote sensing image classification was performed by [8], where the pre-trained CNNs AlexNet and Overfeat [11] were employed for feature extraction, and the activations from the first fully connected layer of the CNN architectures were used as image representations. Excellent results with two remote sensing datasets are reported in [8], outperforming several handcrafted visual descriptors. The most popular approach for feature extraction using CNNs is to employ the extracted features from the upper convolutional layers, or the last fully connected layer that precedes the classification layers. However, when the target task of interest significantly differs from the original task, features extracted from lower convolutional layers appear to be more suitable [6].

The most widely used CNN models for aerial scene classification are CaffeNet, GoogleNet, and VGGNet [10,12–15]. These neural networks consist of approximately 30 layers and present a huge number of parameters. The study conducted in [16] evaluated deep features for the classification of traditional images, whether alone or combined with other features. Authors of [9] utilized extracted features from two pre-trained CNNs and, in that way, performed classification of high-resolution aerial scene images. They proposed features that were obtained by fusion of the activations from the mid-level layers and the last fully connected layers of the CNN schemes. Before feature fusion is performed, feature coding algorithms are applied to activations from convolutional layers. VGGNet is used for extracting features from different network layers, and then features are transformed by Discriminant Correlation Analysis (DCA) [13]. The transformed features are concatenated and, after that, a SVM classifier is applied for image classification [17]. The rationale of this process is to use convolution as an efficient way to extract a new compact and effective feature representation from raw data, simplifying the subsequent classification task. This capability of neural networks has also been fruitfully exploited in order to extract feature vector representations for predictive tasks also in the context of graph data [18,19] and time series data [20,21]. Feature fusion can also be found in other articles [22,23].

Two schemes are proposed in the literature. The former uses the original network for feature extraction from RGB images, while the mapped Local Binary Pattern (LBP) coded network is used for feature extraction from LBP feature maps. After this step, feature fusion is performed by the concatenation layer: features go through fully connected layers and they are classified at the end. The latter uses a saliency coded network instead of a mapped LBP coded network. The study [14] used Recurrent Neural Networks (RNNs) for remote sensing image classification. RNNs are employed to build the attention mechanism. In [12] is presented a new loss function, with enforcing metric learning to CNNs features. A metric learning loss was combined with a standard optimization loss (cross-entropy loss). This approach resulted in features that belong to images from the same image class to be very close, while features extracted from images from different classes to be very distant. The approach presented in [24] extracted features from different layers of pre-trained CNNs and concatenated them with prior dimensionality reduction through Principal Component Analysis (PCA). Logistic Regression Classifier (LRC) and SVMs were applied to the compound features. The classification accuracy of a pre-trained CNNs can be further improved through fine-tuning of the weights.

Fine-tuning is a transfer learning method that adjusts the parameters of a pre-trained CNN by resuming the training of the network with a new dataset, that possibly addresses a new task with a different number of classes than the initial output layer of the initial CNN architecture. Fine tuning trains the network with small initial learning rate and a reduced number of training epochs, compared to a complete training process from scratch. During this process, the cost function achieves a better minimum compared to a case with random weight initialization. Several articles [25,26] in the remote sensing community have also studied the advantages of fine-tuning pre-trained CNNs. Authors of [26] assessed a fully-trained CNN in comparison with a fine-tuned one, to discover utility in the context of aerial scene data. The approach presented in [25] employed the fine-tuning technique to classify hyperspectral images. Authors of [27] suggested to fine-tune the weights of the convolutional layers of the pre-trained CNN to extract better image features. The experimental results presented in [9,10] showed that fine tuning CNNs that are pre-trained on ImageNet gives good classification accuracy on aerial scene datasets.

In order to assess different techniques that exploit deep neural networks, authors of [28] evaluated the best scheme and training method, both for supervised and unsupervised networks. The study [29] tried to determine the optimal way to train neural networks, including greedy layer-wise and unsupervised training.

In this paper, we evaluate four different CNN architectures to solve the problem of high-resolution aerial scene classification. We adopt CNNs that are pre-trained on the ImageNet dataset with the purpose of determining their effectiveness in remote sensing image classification tasks. First, we explore the fine-tuning of the weights on the aerial image dataset. In the process of fine-tuning, we remove the final layers of each of the pre-trained networks after the average pooling layer (so called "network surgery") and construct a new network head. The new network head consists of: a fully connected layer, dropout, and a softmax layer. Network training is performed on the modified deep neural network. Subsequently, we exploit fine-tuned CNNs for feature extraction and utilize the extracted features for the training of SVM classifiers, which have been successfully applied in other image classification and transfer learning problems [20,24,30]. In this paper, SVMs are implemented in two versions: with linear kernel and with Radial Basis Function (RBF) kernel. We use a linear decay learning rate schedule and cyclical learning rates and evaluate their suitability for fine-tuning of pre-trained CNNs for remote sensing image classification. Moreover, we apply label smoothing [31] as a regularization technique and assess its impact on the classification accuracy compared with state-of-the-art methods. Figure 1 shows a flowchart of the proposed method.

The main contributions of this paper are (1) evaluation of modern CNNs models on two remote sensing image datasets, (2) analysis of the impact of linear learning rate decay schedule and cyclical learning rates from the aspect of classification accuracy, (3) evaluation of label smoothing on model generalization compared to state-of-the-art techniques, and (4) assessment of the transferability of the features obtained from fine-tuned CNNs and their classification with linear and RBF SVMs classifiers. To the best of our knowledge, the combination of adaptive learning rate and label smoothing was never studied before in the context of aerial scene classification.

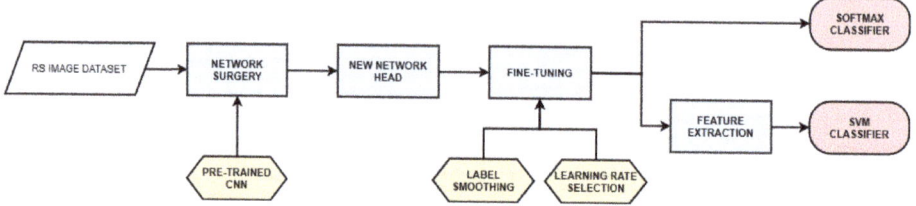

Figure 1. Flowchart of the proposed method.

The remainder of this article is organized, as follows. In Section 2, the methodologies used for fine-tuning of CNNs are presented, and it is described how they were empirically evaluated. The experimental results obtained from the examined remote sensing image classification method are presented in Section 3. Discussion of our method results is given in Section 4. A summary of the results and conclusion of the paper, as well as directions for future research are presented in Section 5.

2. Methods

2.1. Convolutional Neural Networks (Cnns)

CNNs are suitable for many image-related problems, like image segmentation, classification, and object detection. CNN models are structures built from various layers concatenated one on top of the other. Layers consist of neurons that can learn through different optimization algorithms. In our experiments, we used four different CNN architectures: ResNet50, InceptionV3, Xception, and DenseNet121.

The main idea behind ResNet [32] was the introduction of residual learning block. Its purpose is not to learn a non-linear function, but the residual of a function, namely, the difference $F(x)$ between the output $F(x) + x$ and input x of the block, as shown in Figure 2. There are two versions of a residual block: basic version and "bottleneck" version. The basic residual block consists of two 3×3 convolutional layers. The "bottleneck" version of the residual learning block additionally contains two 1×1 convolutional layers, and their aim is to reduce the data dimensionality. Dimensionality reduction leads to a decreased number of network weights, which reduces the computational complexity during network training, thus allowing very deep architectures, as ResNet-152 [32].

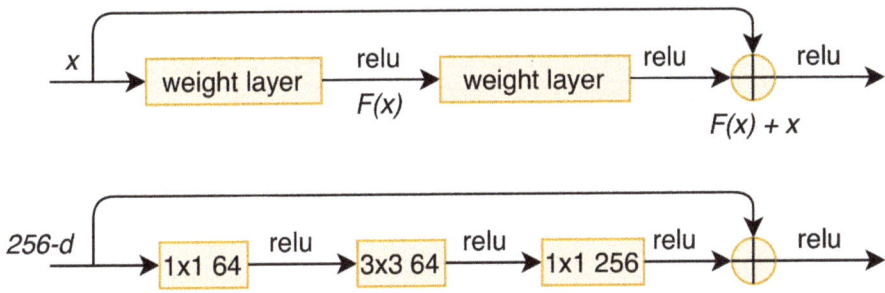

Figure 2. Residual block (top) and "bottleneck" block (bottom) of ResNet [32].

The intuition behind the inception based networks relies on the fact that the correlation within image pixels is local. Taking into consideration local correlations allows for decreasing the number of learning parameters. The first Inception deep CNN was named Inception-v1 [33] and it was introduced as GoogleNet. GoogleNet solves the issue of decreasing the number of learning parameters by including the inception modules in the design of CNN architecture, as shown in Figure 3. The inception module consists of a pooling layer and three convolutional layers with dimensions 1×1, 3×3, and 5×5. Filters with different dimensions are utilized to cover the larger receptive field of each cluster. Outputs from these layers are then concatenated and it represents the module output. Bringing up the batch normalization into the Inception architecture [33,34] resulted in the Inception-v2 model. The third iteration, which was named as Inception-v3 [35], was obtained by additional factorization procedures. This process resulted in three different inception modules: Inception module type 1, obtained by factorization into smaller convolutions; Inception module type 2, reached by factorization into asymmetric convolutions; and, Inception module type 3, which was also introduced to enhance representations with high dimensions.

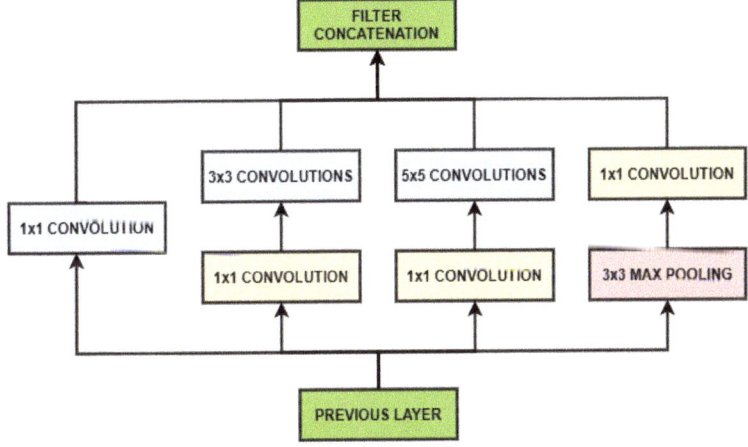

Figure 3. The architecture of a basic inception module [33].

A CNN architecture based on depthwise separable convolution layers is proposed in [36], presuming that it is a good operation to separate the mapping of cross-channel correlations and spatial correlations in the feature maps of CNN construction. This thesis is a stronger version of the thesis beneath the Inception CNN. For this reason, [36] named the CNN architecture Xception, which means "Extreme Inception". He proposed improving Inception-based CNNs with the replacement of Inception modules with depthwise separable convolutions. The idea was to construct models by stacking several depthwise separable convolutions. A depthwise separable convolution, which is also known as "separable convolution", is performed in two steps. The first step is a depthwise convolution, or a spatial convolution implemented separately on every channel of input. The second step is the pointwise convolution. It is a 1×1 convolution that conveys to a new channel space the output of the channels obtained with depth-wise convolution.

In order to provide the highest data flow between network layers, the approach [37] connects all CNN layers, with corresponding dimensions of feature maps, straight with each other. The so-called Dense Convolutional Network (DenseNet), attaches each layer to every other layer in a feed-forward manner. For every layer, its inputs are the feature maps of all previous layers. Each layer's feature maps are conveyed into all succeeding layers, as their input. Figure 4 shows this connectivity pattern schematically. The arrow lines with different colors have the following meaning: they display the input and output of the particular network layer. For example for the second network layer (its feature maps are colored in blue), its inputs are the feature maps of all previous layers and its feature maps are conveyed into all succeeding layers. In Figure 4, BN-RELU-CONV denotes the process of Batch Normalization - Rectified Linear Activation—Convolution. As it can be seen from Figure 4, all of the feature maps go through these operations, and they are concatenated at the end.

When compared to ResNets, the [37] approach does not perform the summation operation on features to lead them afterward into a subsequent layer. On the contrary, it merges features with concatenation.

As can be seen from the schematic layout, the connectivity pattern is dense, so it resulted in the name of CNN Dense Convolutional Network (DenseNet). This CNN contains fewer parameters than other convolutional networks, because the utilization of dense connectivity layout implies that there is no demand to relearn redundant feature maps.

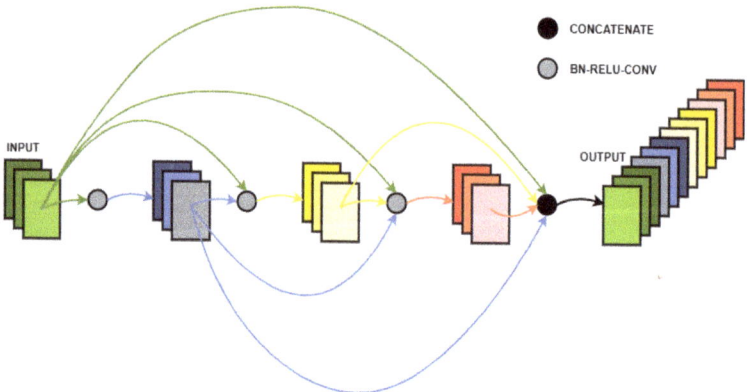

Figure 4. Densely concatenated convolution pattern [37].

2.2. Linear Learning Rate Decay

The most essential hyperparameters when training a convolutional neural network are the initial learning rate, the number of training epochs, the learning rate schedule, and the regularization method (L2, dropout). Most neural networks are trained with the Stochastic Gradient Descent (SGD) algorithm, which updates the network's weights W with:

$$W + = \alpha \cdot gradient \tag{1}$$

where α is the learning rate, which parameter determines the size of the gradient step. Keeping the learning rate constant during network training might be a good choice in some situations, but more often decreasing the learning rate over time is more advantageous.

When training CNNs, we are trying to find global minima, local minima, or just an area of the loss function with sufficiently low values. If we have a constant but large learning rate, it will not be possible to reach the desired loss function values. On the contrary, if we decrease our learning rate, our CNNs will be able to descend into more optimal areas of the loss function [38]. In a part of our experiments, we use a linear learning rate decay schedule, which decays our learning rate to zero at the end of the last training epoch, as shown in Figure 5. The learning rate α in every training epoch is given with:

$$\alpha = \alpha_1 \cdot \left(1 - \frac{E}{E_{max}}\right) \tag{2}$$

where α_1 is the initial learning rate, E is the number of the current epoch, and E_{max} is the maximum number of epochs.

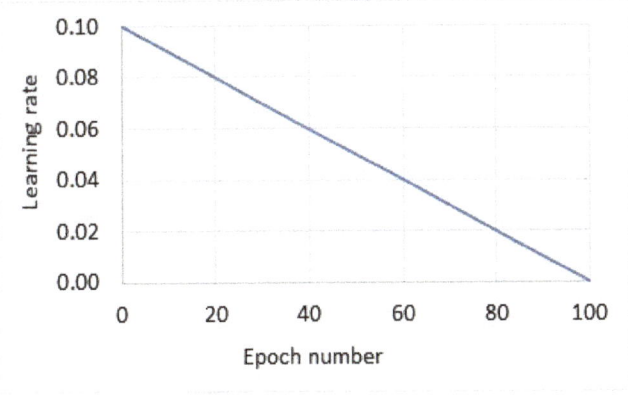

Figure 5. Linear learning rate decay applied to Convolutional Neural Network (CNN) training of 100 epochs.

All of the CNNs used in our experiments for fine-tuning were originally trained on ImageNet with learning rate schedules: ResNet50 and DenseNet121 with step-based learning rate schedule and Inception V3 and Xception with exponential learning rate schedule.

2.3. Cyclical Learning Rates (Clrs)

Cyclical Learning Rates (CLRs) eliminate the need to identify the optimal value of the initial learning rate and learning rate schedule for CNN training [39]. Despite learning rate schedules, where the learning rate is being constantly decreased, this technique allows for the learning rate to oscillate between reasonable limits. CLRs give us the opportunity to have more freedom in the selection of our initial learning rate. CLRs lead to faster neural network training convergence with fewer hyperparameter updates.

Saddle points are points in the loss function where the gradient is zero, but they do not represent minima or maxima. The authors in [40] found out that the efficiency of CLR methods lies in the loss function topology, and showed that saddle points have a worse impact on minimizing the loss function than poor local minima. One cause for getting stuck in saddle points and global minima can be a learning rate that is too small. CLR methods help to fix this issue adapting the learning rate between a minimum value and a maximum value iteratively. Another reason for the efficiency of CLR methods is that the optimal learning rate is somewhere between the lower and upper bound, so the training is performed with near-optimal learning rates.

There are three main CLR policies: *triangular*, as shown in Figure 6, *triangular2*, and *exponential range*. The *triangular* policy is a triangular cycle: the learning rate starts from a lower limit, increases the value to the maximum in half a cycle, and then returns to the base value at the end of a cycle. The difference between *triangular* and *triangular2* policy is that the upper bound of a learning rate is decreased in half after every cycle. Training with a *triangular2* policy provides more stable training. *Exponential range* policy, as its name suggests, includes an exponential decay of a maximum learning rate [39].

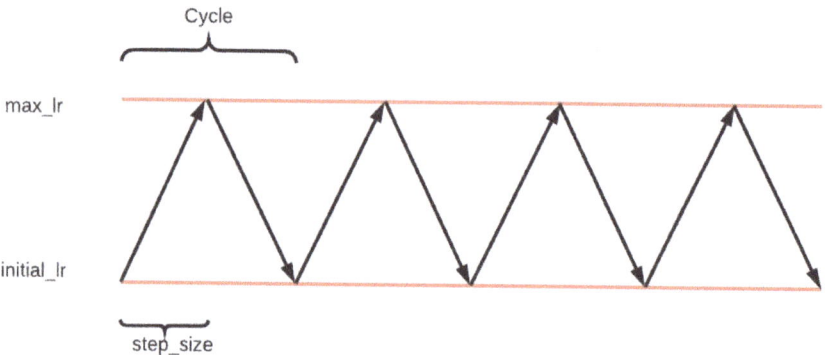

Figure 6. Cyclical learning rate with triangular policy mode.

2.4. Label Smoothing

Label smoothing is a regularization method that allows for a reduction in overfitting and helps CNN architectures to improve their generalization capability. Label smoothing was introduced by [35], and it was shown to boost classification accuracy, adopting a weighted sum of the labels with uniform distribution instead of evaluating the cross-entropy with the "hard" labels from the dataset. "Hard" label assignment corresponds to binary labels: positive for one class and negative for all of the other classes. "Soft" label assignment gives the largest probability to the positive class and very small probability to other classes. Label smoothing is applied to prevent the neural network from being too confident in its prediction. By decreasing the model confidence, we prevent the network training from getting in deep valleys of the loss function [41]. Label smoothing can also be implemented by adding the negative entropy of the softmax output to the negative log-likelihood training objective, weighted by an additional hyperparameter [42–44].

The CNN prediction is a function of the activations in the second to last network layer:

$$p_k = \frac{e^{x^T w_k}}{\sum_{l=1}^{L} e^{x^T w_l}} \qquad (3)$$

where p_k is the probability the network classifies to the k-th class, weights and biases of the final network layer are given with w_k, x is a vector of activations of the second-last network layer fused with '1' to consider the bias. If we train the network with "hard" labels, we intend to minimize the cross-entropy between the real labels y_k and the neural network's predictions p_k, as follows:

$$H(y, p) = \sum_{k=1}^{K} -y_k \log(p_k) \qquad (4)$$

where y_k is '1' for the correct label and '0' for the others. When train network with label smoothing with parameter α, what we minimize is the cross-entropy between the 'smoothed' labels y_k^{LS} and the network predictions p_k, smoothed labels are given with:

$$y_k^{LS} = y_k(1 - \alpha) + \alpha/K \qquad (5)$$

The smoothing technique is used in the proposed method aiming to prevent the neural network from becoming too confident in its predictions and, therefore, increase its robustness and predictive capabilities.

2.5. Datasets

We evaluate our proposed method on two common large-scale remote sensing image datasets, the Aerial Image Dataset (AID) [45] and the NWPU-RESISC45 dataset [46]. A detailed description of the two datasets is given in the following subsections.

AID consists of about 10,000 remote sensing images with dimensions 600 × 600 pixels, assigned to 30 classes [45]. Images are gathered from Google Earth imagery. They are selected from different continents and countries at different times of the year and weather conditions: mostly from China, Japan, Europe (Germany, England, Italy, and France), and the United States. Images from the AID dataset have a pixel resolution of half a meter. Figure 7 presents sample images of each class.

Figure 7. Image classes in the AID dataset: (**a**) airport; (**b**) bare land; (**c**) baseball field; (**d**) beach; (**e**) bridge; (**f**) centre; (**g**) church; (**h**) commercial; (**i**) dense residential; (**j**) desert; (**k**) farmland; (**l**) forest; (**m**) industrial; (**n**) meadow; (**o**) medium residential; (**p**) mountain; (**q**) park; (**r**) parking; (**s**) playground; (**t**) pond; (**u**) port; (**v**) railway station; (**w**) resort; (**x**) river; (**y**) school; (**z**) sparse residential; (**aa**) square; (**ab**) stadium; (**ac**) storage tanks; (**ad**) viaduct.

The NWPU-RESISC45 dataset contains images collected from Google Earth imagery. The name of the dataset comes from its creator Northwestern Polytechnical University (NWPU). It consists of 31,500 aerial images split into 45 classes. Each class has 700 images with dimensions 256 × 256 pixels. Except for four classes (island, lake, mountain, and snowberg), which exhibit a smaller spatial resolution, the other classes have spatial resolutions that vary in the range of 30 m–0.2 m. Figure 8 presents sample images of each class.

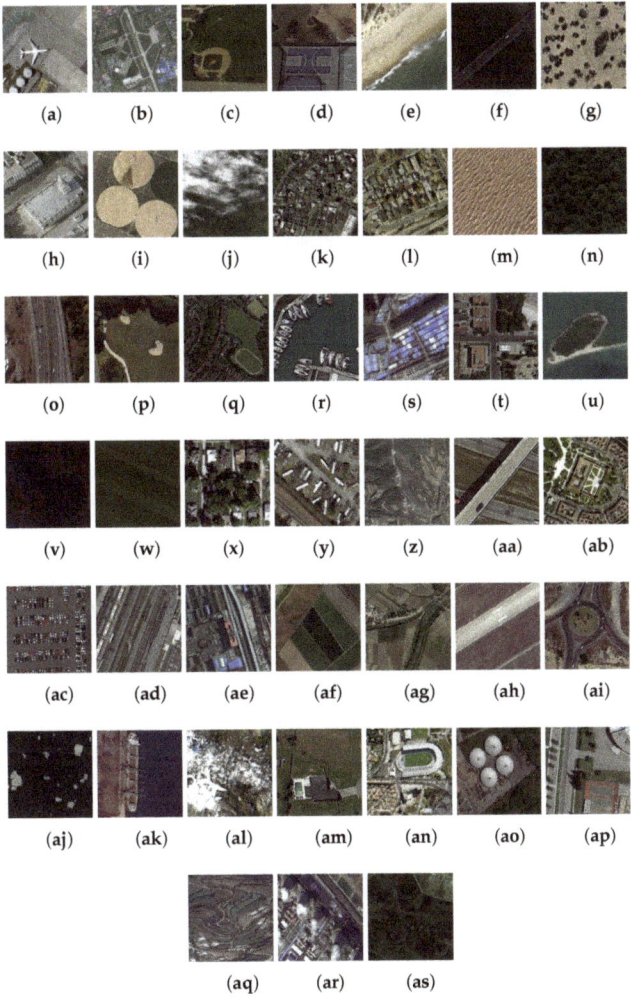

Figure 8. Image classes in the NWPU-RESISC45 dataset: (**a**) airplane; (**b**) airport; (**c**) baseball diamond; (**d**) baseball court (**e**) beach; (**f**) bridge; (**g**) chaparral; (**h**) church; (**i**) circular farmland; (**j**) cloud; (**k**) commercial area; (**l**) dense residential; (**m**) desert; (**n**) forest; (**o**) freeway; (**p**) golf course; (**q**) ground track field; (**r**) harbour; (**s**) industrial area; (**t**) intersection; (**u**) island; (**v**) lake; (**w**) meadow; (**x**) medium residential; (**y**) mobile home park; (**z**) mountain; (**aa**) overpass; (**ab**) palace; (**ac**) parking lot; (**ad**) railway; (**ae**) railway station; (**af**) rectangular farmland; (**ag**) river; (**ah**) roundabout; (**ai**) runway; (**aj**) sea ice; (**ak**) ship; (**al**) snowberg; (**am**) sparse residential; (**an**) stadium; (**ao**) storage tank; (**ap**) tennis court; (**aq**) terrace; (**ar**) thermal power station; (**as**) wetland.

2.6. Experimental Setup

Our proposed method utilizes fine-tuning as a form of transfer learning, performed with linear decay learning rate schedule and cyclical learning rates, as well as label smoothing for aerial scene classification. In the experiments, we used four CNNs that were pre-trained on the ImageNet dataset: ResNet50, InceptionV3, Xception, and DenseNet121. Fine-tuning was performed through "network surgery", i.e., we removed the final layers of each of the pre-trained networks after the average pooling layer. After this, we construct a new network head by adding a fully connected layer, dropout, and softmax layer for classification.

As already mentioned, two large-scale remote sensing image datasets are analyzed in our study: AID and NWPU-RESISC45. Images of the datasets were resized according to the requirements of CNN: 224×224 for ResNet50 and DenseNet121, and 299×299 for InceptionV3 and Xception. The experiments were conducted under the following train/test data split ratios: 50%/50% and 20%/80% for the AID data set and 20%/80% and 10%/90% for NWPU-RESISC45 dataset. The selected split ratios correspond to the ones that were chosen in the related work that we compared our approaches to. The splits were selected randomly and without data stratification.

In-place, data augmentation was used for images from training splits. Data augmentation [47] is a regularization technique that increases the size of the data set, and it almost always results in boosted classification accuracy. Moreover, the label smoothing regularization technique was included in all experiments. Label smoothing was only utilized for the training data splits. It resulted in bigger train loss values compared to the validation loss. On the contrary, label smoothing prevented overfitting and helped our model to generalize better. Overfitting is a common problem when using CNNs with high dimensionality that are pre-trained on datasets of millions of images to solve image classification tasks on datasets that contain a few thousand images.

The first part of the fine-tuning process began with warming-up the new layers of CNN head. New network head layers at the beginning have random initialization of their weights. However, the other network layers after the network surgery have kept their pre-trained weights. Accordingly, it is necessary for the layers of the new network head to start learning the target dataset. During the warming-up process, the only trainable layers were the ones from the new network head; the other network layers were frozen. Warming-up of the new network head was done with a constant learning rate. Fine-tuning of network model continued with Stochastic Gradient Descent (SGD), and, this time, all network layers were "defrosted" for training. Separate experiments were conducted with linear decay of learning rate and for cyclical learning rates with *triangular* policy. The *triangular* policy was chosen, since it is the most widely used in the literature, and it yields the highest classification performance compared to other CLR policies. When the linear decay scheduler was applied, the learning rate was steadily decreasing to zero at the end of the last training epoch. The biggest challenge here was to select the initial learning rate, which was chosen to be 1–2 orders of magnitude smaller than the learning rate the original network was trained with. Regarding CLR, we oscillated the learning rate between the maximum and minimum value, assuming that the optimal one is somewhere in the interval. The choice of the lower and upper limit of CLR is not that sensitive as a selection of initial learning rate at a linear decay scheduler. Here, we used a value for step size four or eight times the number of training iterations in the epoch. The number of training epochs was determined in order to contain an integer number of cycles. This is done to keep the idea behind CLRs satisfied: we start from one minimum value of the learning rate, then we go up to the maximum value and, at the end, we return to the starting learning rate. With this action, we have ended one cycle and started all over again.

The second part of our research was dedicated to the evaluation of the classification methods, namely, a softmax classifier and a SVM classifier with linear and Radial Basis Function (RBF) kernel.

After fine-tuning of each CNN, we calculated the classification accuracy by the softmax layer, which is a part of the new network head, and it was trained together with all of the other network layers. We used fine-tuned CNNs as feature extractors to compare the capability of the softmax classifier with both types of SVM classifiers. We extracted image features of both remote sensing datasets from the fully-connected layer of fine-tuned neural networks. Afterward, the extracted features were exploited to train the linear as well as RBF SVM and classify the images in the datasets. SVM classification was performed for all datasets splits, adopting both linear decay scheduler and CLRs, and label smoothing in every simulation scenario. All of the simulations were performed on OS Ubuntu 18.04 with Keras v2.2.4. Google's library TensorFlow v1.12.0 [48], was backend to Keras. The hardware setup was: CPU i7-8700 3.2 GHz and 64 GB RAM. The graphical processor unit was Nvidia GeForce GTX 1080 Ti, with 11 GB of memory and CUDA v9.0 installed on it.

2.7. Evaluation Metrics

In this article, we use two evaluation metrics: Overall Accuracy (OA) and confusion matrix. These evaluation metrics are commonly used for the analysis and comparison of results with other state-of-the-art techniques in classification tasks. OA is calculated as the ratio between the number of correctly classified test images and the entire number of test images. The value of OA is always less than or equal to 1. The confusion matrix is a graphical presentation (table) of the classification accuracy of each class of the dataset. This table shows partial accuracy in each of the image classes. Columns of the confusion matrix depict the predicted classes and the rows show the actual image classes. The classification model should lead to a diagonal confusion matrix (in the ideal case) or a matrix with high values on the diagonal and very low values in other entries. In our experimental setup, the datasets were split into train and test sets. The split was performed without stratification, randomly, and the train/test ratios were selected according to the scales listed in the previous section.

3. Results

3.1. Classification of Aid Dataset

The experimental results of the proposed method for classification of the AID dataset with SVM classifiers are shown in Tables 1 and 2, for 50%/50% and 20%/80% train/test split ratio, respectively. The above mentioned ratios are common in the literature and they are used in our experiments in order to compare the achieved accuracy with other authors' research. As can be seen from Table 1, when we use ResNet50 and DenseNet121, which architecture is based on shortcut connections, the linear SVM classifier yields better classification accuracy when compared to a softmax classifier. However, when it comes to the inception based pre-trained CNNs InceptionV3 and Xception, the situation is the opposite, and the classification results are better with the softmax classifier when compared to classification with linear SVM of the extracted features from fine-tuned networks. Analysis of Table 2, which depicts the experimental results for 20%/80% train/test split ratio, shows slightly different outcomes: the softmax classifier works better for InceptionV3, Xception, and DenseNet121, but classification with linear SVM classifier is a better option for ResNet50. One possible explanation for this phenomenon is that SVM performs better with vector data of lower dimensionality. On the contrary, higher dimensionality has less impact on softmax classification. In fact, inspecting the neural network architectures mentioned above, we can notice that the ResNet50 architecture presents a fully connected layer of size 512, whereas Inception-based and DenseNet201 architectures present a fully connected layer of 1024 and 1920 units, respectively.

Comparing the softmax and the RBF SVM classification of the AID dataset shows that the RBF SVM classifier outperforms the softmax classifier for 50%/50% train/test split ratio in all simulation scenarios, except for the InceptionV3 and Xception neural network architectures with linear decay scheduler. For the

20%/80% train/test split ratio of the AID dataset, RBF SVM achieves better classification accuracy than softmax, except for ResNet50, InceptionV3, and DenseNet121 with linear decay scheduler.

Table 3 presents a comparison of the proposed method to other state-of-the-art techniques. We achieved the best classification results on the AID dataset with a 50% training set for DenseNet121 with a linear decay scheduler and a RBF SVM classifier, and with a 20% training set for Xception with a linear decay scheduler and a RBF SVM classifier. To the best of our knowledge, our proposed method for 50% training set of AID dataset outperforms all of the other methods in the literature. The standard deviation of achieved classification accuracy of AID dataset is in interval ± (0.1–0.4).

Table 1. Overall accuracy (%) of the proposed method with a 50%/50% train/test ratio of the AID dataset. The bold text highlights the best accuracy per classifier.

Method	Softmax Classifier	Linear SVM Classifier	RBF SVM Classifier
ResNet50			
Linear decay scheduler	95.62	95.88	96.12
Cyclical learning rate	95.52	95.83	96.08
InceptionV3			
Linear decay scheduler	96.41	96.32	95.96
Cyclical learning rate	95.95	95.82	96.18
Xception			
Linear decay scheduler	96.14	96.04	95.96
Cyclical learning rate	96.15	95.97	96.30
DenseNet121			
Linear decay scheduler	96.03	96.10	98.03
Cyclical learning rate	96.21	96.3	96.60

Table 2. Overall accuracy (%) of the proposed method with a 20%/80% train/test ratio of the AID dataset. The bold text highlights the best accuracy per classifier.

Method	Softmax Classifier	Linear SVM Classifier	RBF SVM Classifier
ResNet50			
Linear decay scheduler	93.06	93.09	92.98
Cyclical learning rate	92.91	93.47	93.44
InceptionV3			
Linear decay scheduler	93.7	93.32	93.50
Cyclical learning rate	93.79	93.41	93.93
Xception			
Linear decay scheduler	93.67	93.29	94.14
Cyclical learning rate	93.44	93.36	93.65
DenseNet121			
Linear decay scheduler	93.74	93.26	93.56
Cyclical learning rate	93.54	93.35	93.58

Figures 9 and 10 show the confusion matrices for the AID dataset with a 50%/50% train/test split ratio for ResNet50, linear learning rate decay, and softmax or linear SVM classifier, respectively. Because the classification accuracy achieved with softmax and linear SVM is close, both confusion matrices differ only in the classification outcome for a small number of images.

Fine-tuning of Xception with 20% of the AID dataset as a training set for CLR or linear decay learning rate scheduler and the softmax classifier is depicted in Figures 11 and 12, respectively. Two plots show only the fine-tuning of all network layers with the SGD optimizer, but not the warming-up of network head. From the plots, we can see that training with CLR is more stable with characteristic picks on training and validation loss curves, causing some oscillations that are visible as a waved shape. Additionally, it is noticeable that the training loss is more prominent than validation loss on both Figures, because we have applied label smoothing on training labels only.

Table 3. Overall accuracy (%) of the proposed method compared to reference methods with 50% and 20% of the AID data set as a training set. For our method, we selected the best results obtained for the two training ratios, and report them in bold. Methods are ordered in ascending order by their performance on the 50% training ratio.

Method	50% Training Ratio	20% Training Ratio
GoogleNet+SVM [45]	86.39	83.44
VGG-VD-16 [45]	89.64	86.59
CaffeNet [45]	89.53	86.86
salM^{3}LBP-CLM [49]	89.76	86.92
MCNNs [50]	91.80	/
Fusion by addition [51]	91.87	/
X-Net-LF [52]	92.96	90.87
ARCNet-VGG16 [14]	93.10	88.75
VGG-16 (fine-tuning) [53]	93.60	89.49
VGG-16+MSCP [54]	94.42	91.5
Two-stream fusion [22]	94.58	92.32
Multilevel fusion [55]	95.36	/
GBNet + global Feature [53]	95.48	92.20
Xception with linear decay scheduler and RBF SVM classifier (proposed)	95.96	94.14
InceptionV3-CapsNet [56]	96.32	93.79
EfficientNet-B3-aux [4]	96.56	94.19
GCFs + LOFs [57]	96.85	92.48
D-CNNs with VGGNet-16 [12]	96.89	90.82
Dense-based CNNs + 3D pooling [58]	97.19	95.37
DenseNet121 with linear decay scheduler and RBF SVM classifier (proposed)	98.03	93.56

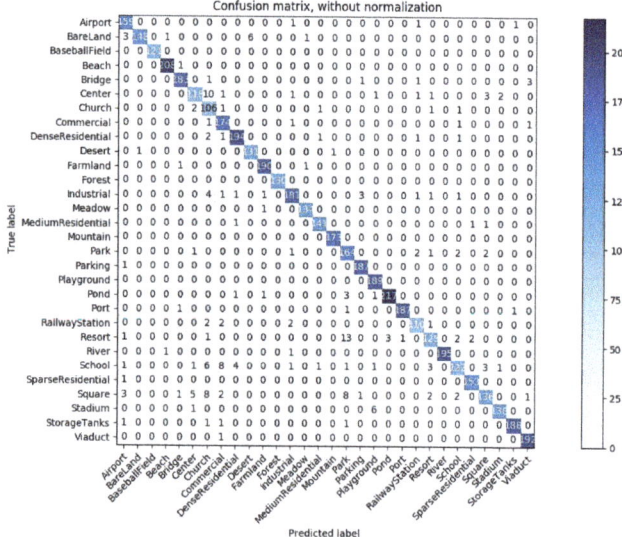

Figure 9. Confusion matrix of the proposed method with a 50%/50% train/test ratio of AID data set for ResNet50, linear learning rate decay, and softmax classifier.

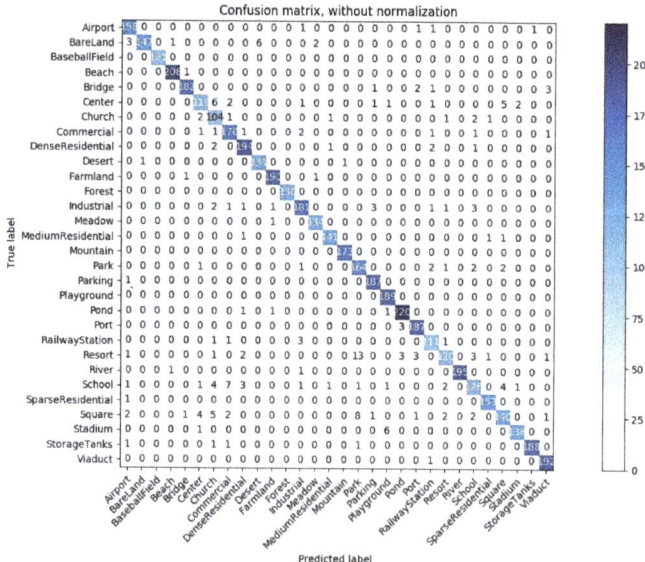

Figure 10. Confusion matrix of the proposed method with a 50%/50% train/test ratio of AID data set for ResNet50, linear learning rate decay, and a linear SVM classifier.

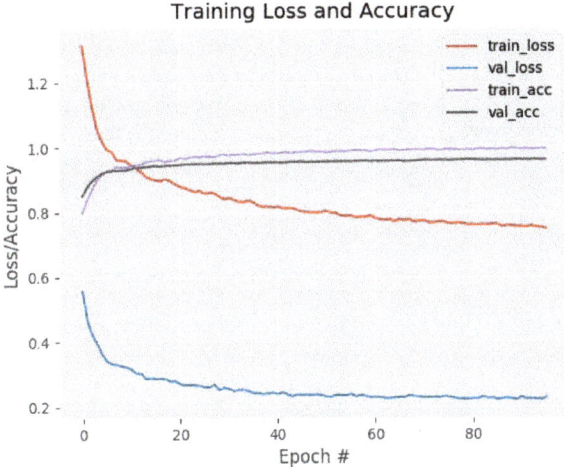

Figure 11. Training plot of the proposed method with 20% of AID dataset as the training set for Xception, cyclical learning rate, and softmax classifier.

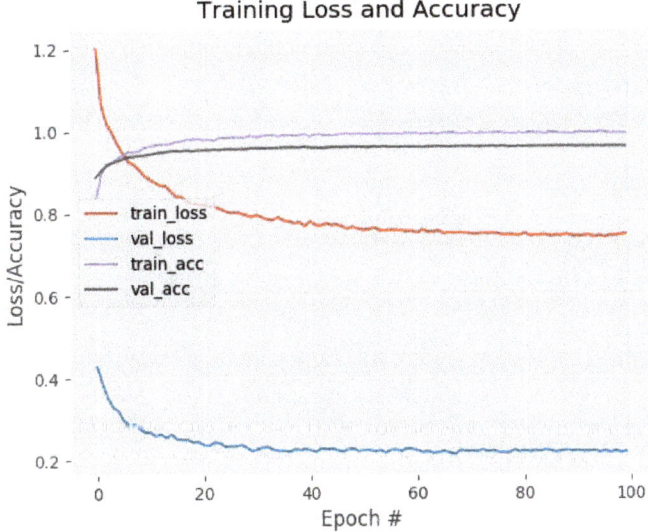

Figure 12. Training plot of the proposed method with 20% of AID data set as the training set for Xception, linear learning rate decay, and softmax classifier.

3.2. Classification of the Nwpu-Resisc45 Data Set

The experimental results of our proposed method with linear and RBF SVM for the NWPU-RESISC45 dataset are displayed in Tables 4 and 5 and Figure 13. Table 4 shows the achieved classification accuracy for a 20%/80% train/test split ratio of the data set. It can be noticed that for linear decay scheduler and as well for CLRs, the linear SVM classifier gives better overall accuracy compared to softmax classifier for all pre-trained CNN. Table 5 shows the obtained classification accuracy for a 10%/90% train/test split ratio for the NWPU-RESISC45 data set. Both train/test split ratios for the analyzed datasets are chosen in order to make experimental comparisons with other studies in the corresponding field of research, which use the same proportions of train/test splits. Here the achieved experimental results are similar to the ones from Table 4. The linear SVM classifier outperforms the softmax classifier in all cases except when we fine-tune the InceptionV3 neural network and Xception with a linear decay scheduler.

Table 4. Overall accuracy (%) of the proposed method with 20%/80% train/test ratio of NWPU-RESISC45 data set. The bold text highlights the best accuracy per classifier.

Method	Softmax Classifier	Linear SVM Classifier	RBF SVM Classifier
ResNet50			
Linear decay scheduler	92.35	92.77	92.89
Cyclical learning rate	92.40	92.85	92.77
InceptionV3			
Linear decay scheduler	93.07	93.18	93.35
Cyclical learning rate	93.04	93.13	92.82
Xception			
Linear decay scheduler	92.63	92.78	92.72
Cyclical learning rate	92.63	92.80	92.87
DenseNet121			
Linear decay scheduler	93.16	93.37	93.60
Cyclical learning rate	92.98	93.26	93.55

Analysing Tables 4 and 5, we notice that classification with RBF SVM classifier yields better experimental results when compared to softmax classification with the NWPU-RESISC45 dataset. For the 20%/80% train/test split ratio RBF SVM outperforms softmax classification in all simulation scenarios, except for InceptionV3 with cyclical learning rates. For the 10%/90% train/test split ratio, softmax yields better classification results only for Xception with linear decay scheduler.

Table 6 compares the examined techniques with other state-of-the-art methods. Our proposed technique obtained the best classification accuracy with DenseNet121 with a linear decay scheduler and linear SVM classifier for the 10%/90% train/test split ratio of the NWPU-RESISC45 dataset. For the 20%/80% train/test split ratio of NWPU-RESISC45 dataset we achieved the best experimental results with DenseNet121 with a linear decay scheduler and RBF SVM classifier. The standard deviation of achieved classification accuracy of NWPU-RESISC45 dataset is in interval ± (0.1–0.3). From Table 6, it can be concluded that there are methods that outperform our proposed method. One of them uses fine-tuning of EfficientNet-B3 with auxiliary classifier [4]. EfficientNet-B3 yields better top-1 and top-5 classification accuracy on ImageNet data set compared to the pre-trained CNNs utilized in this article, and this is probably the main reason for the better overall accuracy. The results reported in [58] are also better than ours. However, they use multiple fusion of features extracted from dataset images or their parts with different dimensions (scale). Instead, we utilized fine-tuning with one image size according to the pre-trained CNNs requirements.

Table 5. Overall accuracy (%) of the proposed method with a 10%/90% train/test ratio of NWPU-RESISC45 data set. The bold text highlights the best accuracy per classifier.

Method	Softmax Classifier	Linear SVM Classifier	RBF SVM Classifier
ResNet50			
Linear decay scheduler	89.42	89.74	90.03
Cyclical learning rate	89.20	89.70	89.99
InceptionV3			
Linear decay scheduler	90.16	90.07	90.36
Cyclical learning rate	90.21	90.18	90.36
Xception			
Linear decay scheduler	89.62	89.59	89.18
Cyclical learning rate	89.40	89.65	89.67
DenseNet121			
Linear decay scheduler	90.25	90.46	90.42
Cyclical learning rate	89.73	89.99	90.11

Table 6. Overall accuracy (%) of the proposed method compared to reference methods with 20% and 10% of NWPU-RESISC45 data set as a training set. For our method, we selected the best results obtained for the two training ratios, and report them in bold. Methods are ordered in ascending order by their performance on the 20% training ratio.

Method	20% Training Ratio	10% Training Ratio
GoogleNet [46]	78.48	76.19
VGG-16 [46]	79.79	76.47
AlexNet [46]	79.85	76.69
Two-stream fusion [15]	83.16	80.22
BoCF [46]	84.32	82.65
Fine-tuning AlexNet [46]	85.16	81.22
Fine-tuning GoogleNet [12]	86.02	82.57
SAL-TS-Net (Yu et Liu 2018a)	87.01	85.02
VGG-16+MSCP [51]	88.93	85.33
Fine tuning VGG-16 [46]	90.36	87.15
D-CNNs with VGGNet-16 [12]	91.89	89.22
Triplet networks [59]	92.33	/
Inception-V3-CapsNet [58]	92.60	89.03
DenseNet121 with linear decay scheduler and linear SVM classifier (proposed)	93.37	90.46
DenseNet121 with linear decay scheduler and RBF SVM classifier (proposed)	93.60	90.42
EfficientNet-B3-aux [4]	93.81	91.08
Dense-based CNNs + 3D pooling [58]	94.95	92.9

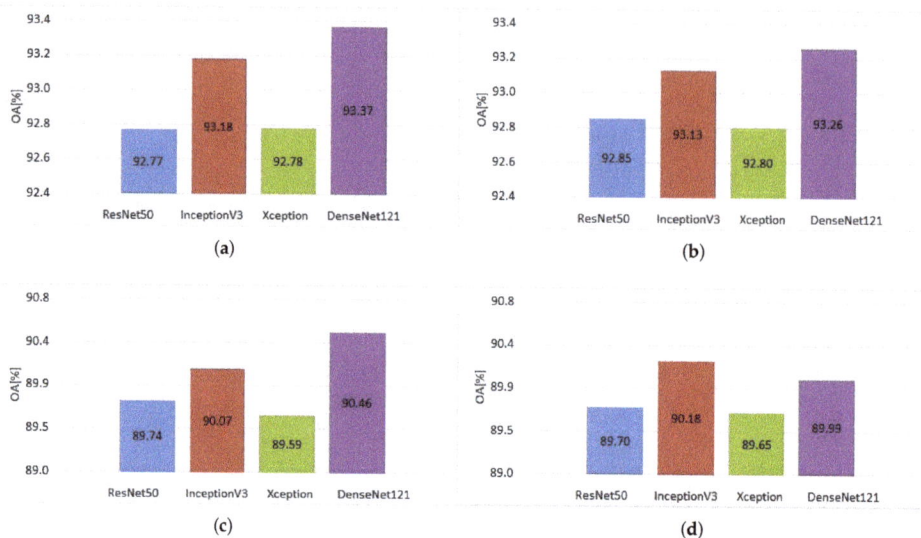

Figure 13. Overall Accuracy over five runs for NWPU-RESISC45 data set with linear SVM classifier and (**a**) 20%/80% train/test split ratio, linear decay scheduler; (**b**) 20%0% train/test split ratio, cyclical learning rates; (**c**) 10%/90% train/test split ratio, linear decay scheduler; (**d**) 10%/90% train/test split ratio, cyclical learning rates.

4. Discussion

We can make several conclusions from our completed simulations and experimental results. All of the presented points, except the last two, refer to research experiments with linear SVM classifier. The last two points refer to cases that include SVM classification with RBF kernel. The main points of this research paper are given, as follows:

- The pre-trained InceptionV3 network yields the highest classification accuracy in transfer learning through fine-tuning for the AID dataset for 50%/50% train/test split ratio and linear SVM classification (Table 1). For the NWPU-RESISC45 dataset, DenseNet121 achieves the best experimental results, but InceptionV3 is the second-best pre-trained CNN. AID dataset images have an original dimension of 600 × 600, and NWPU-RESISC45 dataset images have a dimension of 256 × 256. Each of the pre-trained CNNs requires images with precise dimensions on its input: 299 × 299 for InceptionV3, 224 × 224 for DenseNet121. The achieved sub-optimal results may depend on the cropping of dataset images to the required input dimensions. Taking into consideration the achieved top-one and top-five classification accuracy on the ImageNet dataset, it is somewhat expected that Xception would be the best performing pre-trained CNN, but it is not the case. However, InceptionV3 is right behind Xception according to the achieved results on ImageNet, so it reflects on our research as well.
- Linear learning rate decay scheduler gives better classification accuracy in all experimental scenarios with 50%/50% train/test split for the AID dataset for linear SVM classification. Cyclical Learning Rates (CLRs) are better in cases under 20% training set for the AID data set. Both train/test split ratios of the NWPU-RESISC45 dataset (20%/80% and 10%/90%) have mixed results for linear SVM

classification: half of them in favor of linear decay scheduler, half of them in favor of cyclical learning rates. CLRs might be the right solution for experimental scenarios under a smaller ratio of the training set. Neural network fine-tuning with cyclical learning rates resulted in more stable training and, thus, less prone to overfitting compared to training with linear decay scheduler. In our experiments, we used a *triangular* policy for the CLRs, but it might be an option to use the *triangular2* policy. Whichever policy is implemented, it should provide the right balance between stability and accuracy of training.

- In every simulation scenario, we implemented label smoothing with factor = 0.1 as a form of regularization. We combined it with dropout regularization with factor = 0.5. The dropout layer is part of the new network head, and it was placed just before the softmax layer. Regularization techniques or a combination of them are useful to combat overfitting and to improve generalization of the model. Our goal with the proposed method was to boost the classification accuracy of RS dataset images, so we did not perform experimental scenarios without label smoothing.

- Classification accuracy achieved with linear SVM is higher in more cases than the classification accuracy obtained with the softmax layer. Softmax classifier works better for the AID dataset: it yields better experimental results for InceptionV3 and Xception with 50% of the data set as a training set, and for all CNNs, except for ResNet50 with 20% training data set. Linear SVM classifier is a better option for the NWPU-RESISC45 dataset: it outperforms the softmax layer in all cases, except for fine-tuning InceptionV3 for both types of learning rates and Xception with linear decay scheduler and 10% training/test data ratio. We conclude that feature extraction of fine-tuned CNNs yields better classification results than end-to-end training with the softmax layer for classification. It goes in line with information in Tables 3 and 6, that the best performing method for AID and NWPU-RESISC45 data set classification is based on feature extraction (multiple) and three-dimmensional (3D) pooling of extracted features.

- Performing experimental research into classification of remote sensing datasets with RBF SVM classifiers, shows that it is a superior classification technique compared to softmax classification. For the AID dataset RBF SVM classifier outperforms softmax classification in all cases, except in a few of the simulation scenarios with linear decay scheduler. The situation with NWPU-RESISC45 dataset follows the previous example: from 16 simulation scenarios (for both 20%/80% and 10%/90% train/test split ratios) softmax classifier is better than RBF SVM classifier in only two cases. From Tables 1, 2, 4, and 5 it is noticeable that it yields better classification accuracy for each examined dataset in most of the simulation cases.

- Comparing the linear decay scheduler and cyclical learning rate for RBF SVM classification, leads to similar conclusions as for linear SVM classification. The linear decay scheduler shows better experimental results for bigger training sets (50% training set for AID dataset and 20% training set for NWPU-RESISC45 dataset). Cyclical learning rates appear more suitable for aerial scene classification under smaller training sets.

5. Conclusions

In this paper, we presented a fine-tuning method for image classification of large-scale remote sensing datasets. We showed that the adoption of a linear decay learning rate schedule or Cyclical Learning Rates, combined with regularization techniques, like label smoothing, could produce state-of-the-art results in terms of overall accuracy. Summarizing, SVM with linear or RBF kernel presented more accurate results than softmax when using 10% and 20% training data splits. This behavior is expected, since SVM is known to be more robust in the presence of of small training sets [60]. The above discussion is giving us valuable information for researching more competitive methods to provide progress in remote sensing image classification. After this, we suggest the following directions: (1) assess the method with different types of pre-trained CNNs with different types of neural network architectures, (2) include learning rate finder [39] in order to determine optimal boundaries for cyclical learning rates or initial learning rate for linear decay scheduler, and (3) improve the results by fine-tuning only some layers of pre-trained CNNs, in contrast with unfreezing the whole network architecture for training.

Author Contributions: Conceptualization: B.P., T.A.-P. and E.Z.; Methodology: B.P., T.A.-P., R.C., P.L. and E.Z.; Software: B.P., P.L. and E.Z.; Validation: B.P., R.C., P.L., P.M. and E.Z.; Formal analysis: B.P. and P.M.; Investigation: B.P., R.C., P.L. and E.Z.; Writing—original draft preparation: B.P., R.C., P.L. and E.Z.; Writing—review: B.P., R.C., P.M., P.L. and E.Z.; And editing: R.C., P.M., P.L. and E.Z. All authors have read and agreed to the published version of the manuscript.

Funding: P.M. acknowledges the support of the projects TALIsMAn (ARS01_01116) funded by the Ministry of Education, Universities and Research (MIUR) and MAESTRA (ICT-2013-612944) funded by the European Commission. E.Z. and P.L. acknowledge the support of Faculty of Computer Science and Engineering, Ss. Cyril and Methodius University in Skopje, North Macedonia.

Conflicts of Interest: The authors declare no conflict of interest. The funders had no role in the design of the study; in the collection, analyses, or interpretation of data; in the writing of the manuscript; or in the decision to publish the results.

Abbreviations

The following abbreviations are used in this manuscript:

AID	Aerial Image Dataset
CLR	Cyclical Learning Rate
CNN	Convolutional neural network
DenseNet	CNN Dense Convolutional Network
LBP	Local Binary Pattern
LRC	Logistic Regression Classifier
NWPU	Northwestern Polytechnical University
OA	Overall Accuracy
PCA	Principal Component Analysis
PCA	Principal Component Analysis
RBF	Radial Basis Function
RGB	Red Green Blue
RNN	Recurrent Neural Network
RS	Remote Sensing
SGD	Stochastic Gradient Descent
SVM	Support Vector Machine

References

1. Liang, Y.; Monteiro, S.T.; Saber, E.S. Transfer Learning for High-Resolution Aerial Image Classification. In Proceedings of the IEEE Applied Imagery Pattern Recognition (AIPR) Workshop, Washington, DC, USA, 18–20 October 2016.
2. Cheng, G.; Xie, X.; Han, J.; Guo, L.; Xia, G. Remote Sensing Image Scene Classification Meets Deep Learning: Challenges, Methods, Benchmarks, and Opportunities. *arXiv* **2020**, arXiv:2005.01094.
3. Khelifi, L.; Mignotte, M. Deep Learning for Change Detection in Remote Sensing Images: Comprehensive Review and Meta-Analysis. *IEEE Access* **2020**, *8*, 126385–126400. [CrossRef]

4. Bazi, Y.; Rahhal, M.M.A.; Alhichri, H.; Alajlan, N. Simple Yet Effective Fine-Tuning of Deep CNNs Using an Auxiliary Classification Loss for Remote Sensing Scene Classification. *Remote Sens.* **2019**, *11*, 2908. [CrossRef]
5. Lu, Y.; Luo, L.; Huang, D.; Wang, Y.; Chen, L. Knowledge Transfer in Vision Recognition. *ACM Comput. Surv.* **2020**, *53*, 1–35. [CrossRef]
6. Yosinski, J.; Clune, J.; Bengio, Y.; Lipson, H. How transferable are features in deep neural networks? In Proceedings of the Advances in Neural Information Processing Systems 27: Annual Conference on Neural Information Processing Systems 2014, Montreal, QC, Canada, 8–13 December 2014; pp. 3320–3328.
7. Razavian, A.S.; Azizpour, H.; Sullivan, J.; Carlsson, S. CNN features off-the-shelf: An astounding baseline for recognition. In Proceedings of the IEEE conference on computer vision and pattern recognition workshops, Columbus, OH, USA, 23–28 June 2014; p. 512519.
8. Penatti, O.A.; Nogueira, K.; dos Santos, J.A. Do deep features generalize from everyday objects to remote sensing and aerial scenes domains? In Proceedings of the IEEE Conference on Computer Vision and Pattern Recognition Workshops, Boston, MA, USA, 7–12 June 2015; p. 4451.
9. Hu, F.; Xia, G.S.; Hu, J.; Zhang, L. Transferring deep convolutional neural networks for the scene classification of high-resolution remote sensing imagery. *Remote Sens.* **2015**, *7*, 1468014707. [CrossRef]
10. Nogueira, K.; Penatti, O.A.; Dos Santos, J.A. Towards Better Exploit. Convolutional Neural Networks Remote Sens. Scene Classification. *Pattern Recognit.* **2017**, *61*, 539–556. [CrossRef]
11. Sermanet, P.; Eigen, D.; Zhang, X.; Mathieu, M.; Fergus, R.; LeCun, Y. Overfeat: Integrated recognition, localization, and detection using convolutional networks. *arXiv* **2013**, arXiv:1312.6229.
12. Cheng, G.; Yang, C.; Yao, X.; Guo, L.; Han, J. When deep learning meets metric learning: Remote sensing image scene classification via learning discriminative CNNs. *IEEE Trans. Geosci. Remote Sens.* **2018**, *56*, 2811–2821. [CrossRef]
13. Chaib, S.; Liu, H.; Gu, Y.; Yao, H. Deep feature fusion for VHR remote sensing scene classification. *IEEE Trans. Geosci. Remote Sens.* **2017**, *55*, 4775–4784. [CrossRef]
14. Wang, Q.; Liu, S.; Chanussot, J.; Li, X. Scene classification with recurrent attention of VHR remote sensing images. *IEEE Trans. Geosci. Remote Sens.* **2018**, *99*, 1155–1167. [CrossRef]
15. Yu, Y.L.; Liu, F.X. Dense connectivity based two-stream deep feature fusion framework for aerial scene classification. *Remote Sens.* **2018**, *10*, 1158. [CrossRef]
16. Chatfield, K.; Simonyan, K.; Vedaldi, A.; Zisserman, A. Return Devil Details: Delving Deep Convolutional Nets. *arXiv* **2014**, arXiv:1405.3531.
17. Chen, Y.; Xu, W.; Zuo, J.; Yang, K. The fire recognition algorithm using dynamic feature fusion and IV-SVM classifier. *Clust. Comput.* **2018**, *2*, 7665–7675. [CrossRef]
18. Li, R.; Wang, S. Adaptive Graph Convolutional Neural Networks. In Proceedings of the AAAI Conference on Artificial Intelligence, New Orleans, LA, USA, 2–7 February 2018.
19. Pio, G.; Ceci, M.; Prisciandaro, F.; Malerba, D. Exploiting causality in gene network reconstruction based on graph embedding. *Mach. Learn.* **2020**, *109*, 1231–1279. [CrossRef]
20. Corizzo, R.; Ceci, M.; Japkowicz, N. Anomaly Detection and Repair for Accurate Predictions in Geo-distributed Big Data. *Big Data Res.* **2019**, *16*, 18–35. [CrossRef]
21. Bao, W.; Yue, J.; Rao, Y. A deep learning framework for financial time series using stacked autoencoders and long-short term memory. *PLoS ONE* **2017**, *12*, e0180944. [CrossRef]
22. Yu, Y.; Liu, F. A two-stream deep fusion framework for high-resolution aerial scene classification. *Comput. Intell. Neurosci.* **2018**, *2018*, 13. [CrossRef]
23. Corizzo, R.; Ceci, M.; Zdravevski, E.; Japkowicz, N. Scalable auto-encoders for gravitational waves detection from time series data. *Expert Syst. Appl.* **2020**, *151*, 113378. [CrossRef]
24. Petrovska, B.; Zdravevski, E.; Lameski, P.; Corizzo, R.; Stajduhar, I.; Lerga, J. Deep Learning for Feature Extraction in Remote Sensing: A Case-study of Aerial Scene Classification. *Sensors* **2020**, *14*, 3906. [CrossRef]
25. Yue, J.; Zhao, W.; Mao, S.; Liu, H. Spectral–spatial classification of hyperspectral images using deep convolutional neural networks. *Remote Sens. Lett.* **2015**, *6*, 468–477. [CrossRef]

26. Xie, M.; Jean, N.; Burke, M.; Lobell, D.; Ermon, S. Transfer learning from deep features for remote sensing and poverty mapping. *arXiv* **2015**, arXiv:1510.00098.
27. Castelluccio, M.; Poggi, G.; Sansone, C.; Verdoliva, L. Land use classification in remote sensing images by convolutional neural networks. *arXiv* **2015**, arXiv:1508.00092.
28. Jarrett, K.; Kavukcuoglu, K.; Ranzato, M.; LeCun, Y. What is the best multi-stage architecture for object recognition? In Proceeding of the 2009 IEEE 12th International Conference on Computer Vision, Kyoto, Japan, 27 September–4 October 2009; pp. 2146–2153.
29. Larochelle, H.; Bengio, Y.; Louradour, J.; Lamblin, P. Exploring strategies for training deep neural networks. *J. Mach. Learn. Res.* **2009**, *10*, 1–40.
30. Mignone, P.; Pio, G.; D'Elia, D.; Ceci, M. Exploiting transfer learning for the reconstruction of the human gene regulatory network. *Bioinformatics* **2019**, *36*, 1553–1561. [CrossRef] [PubMed]
31. Müller, R.; Kornblith, S.; Hinton, G.E. When does label smoothing help? In Proceedings of the Advances in Neural Information Processing Systems 32: Annual Conference on Neural Information Processing Systems 2019, NeurIPS 2019, Vancouver, BC, Canada, 8–14 December 2019; pp. 4696–4705.
32. He, K.; Zhang, X.; Ren, S.; Sun, J. Deep residual learning for image recognition. In Proceedings of the IEEE conference on computer vision and pattern recognition, Las Vegas, NV, USA, 27–30 June 2016.
33. Szegedy, C.; Liu, W.; Jia, Y.; Sermanet, P.; Reed, S.; Anguelov, D.; Erhan, D.; Vanhoucke, V.; Rabinovich, A. Going deeper with convolutions. In Proceedings of the IEEE Conference on Computer Vision and Pattern Recognition, Boston, MA, USA, 7–12 June 2015; p. 19.
34. Ioffe, S.; Szegedy, C. Batch Normalization: Accelerating Deep Network Training by Reducing Internal Covariate Shift. *arXiv* **2015**, arXiv:1502.03167.
35. Szegedy, C.; Vanhouck, V.; Ioffe, S.; Shlens, J.; Wojna, Z. Rethinking the Inception Architecture for Computer Vision. In Proceedings of the IEEE Conference on Computer Vision and Pattern Recognition, Las Vegas, NV, USA, 26 June–1 July 2016.
36. Chollet, F. Xception: Deep Learning with Depthwise Separable Convolutions. *arXiv* **2017**, arXiv:1610.02357.
37. Huang, G.; Liu, Z.; van der Maaten, L.; Weinberger, K.Q. Densely Connected Convolutional Networks. In Proceedings of the IEEE Conference on Computer Vision and Pattern Recognition, Salt Lake City, UT, USA, 18–22 June 2018.
38. Bengio, Y. Practical Recommendations for Gradient-Based Training of Deep Architectures. In *Neural Networks: Tricks of the Trade*, 2nd ed.; Springer: Berlin/Heidelberg, Germany, 2012; pp. 437–478.
39. Smith, L.N. Cyclical learning rates for training neural networks. In Proceedings of the 2017 IEEE Winter Conference on Applications of Computer Vision (WACV), Santa Rosa, CA, USA, 24–31 March 2017; IEEE: Piscataway, NJ, USA, 2017; pp. 464–472.
40. Dauphin, Y.N.; de Vries, H.; Chung, J.; Bengio, Y. Rmsprop and equilibrated adaptive learning rates for non-convex optimization. In Proceedings of the Advances in Neural Information Processing Systems, Montreal, QC, Canada, 7–12 December 2015.
41. Müller, R.; Kornblith, S.; Hinton, G. When Does Label Smoothing Help? *arXiv* **2019**, arXiv:1906.02629.
42. Pereyra, G.; Tucker, G.; Chorowski, J.; Kaiser, L.; Hinton, G.E. Regularizing Neural Networks by Penalizing Confident Output Distributions. In Proceedings of the 5th International Conference on Learning Representations (ICLR 2017), Toulon, France, 24–26 April 2017.
43. Guo, C.; Pleiss, G.; Sun, Y.; Weinberger, K.Q. On Calibration of Modern Neural Networks. In Proceedings of the 34th International Conference on Machine Learning (ICML 2017), Sydney, NSW, Australia, 6–11 August 2017; pp. 1321–1330.
44. Goodfellow, I.J.; Bengio, Y.; Courville, A.C. *Deep Learning*; Adaptive computation and machine learning; MIT Press: Cambridge, MA, USA, 2016.
45. Xia, G.; Hu, J.; Hu, F.; Shi, B.; Bai, X.; Zhong, Y.; Zhang, L.; Lu, X. AID: A Benchmark Data Set for Performance Evaluation of Aerial Scene Classification. *IEEE Trans. Geosci. Remote Sens.* **2017**, *55*, 3965–3981. [CrossRef]
46. Cheng, G.; Li, Z.; Yao, X.; Li, K.; Wei, Z. Remote Sensing Image Scene Classification Using Bag of Convolutional Features. *IEEE Geosci. Remote Sens. Lett.* **2017**, *55*, 3965–3981. [CrossRef]

47. Shorten, C.; Khoshgoftaar, T.M. A survey on Image Data Augmentation for Deep Learning. *J. Big Data* **2019**, *6*, 60. [CrossRef]
48. Abadi, M.; Agarwal, A.; Barham, P.; Brevdo, E.; Chen, Z.; Citro, C.; Corrado, G.S.; Davis, A.; Dean, J.; Devin, M. Tensorflow: Large-Scale Machine Learning on Heterogeneous Distributed Systems. *arXiv* **2016**, arXiv:1603.04467.
49. Bian, X.; Chen, C.; Tian, L.; Du, Q. Fusing local and global features for high-resolution scene classification. *IEEE J. Sel. Top. Appl. Earth Obs. Remote Sens.* **2017**, *10*, 2889–2901. [CrossRef]
50. Liu, Y.; Huang, C. Scene classification via triplet networks. *IEEE J. Sel. Top. Appl. Earth Obs. Remote Sens.* **2018**, *11*, 220–237. [CrossRef]
51. Wang, G.; Fan, B.; Xiang, S.; Pan, C. Aggregating Rich Hierarchical Features for Scene Classfication in Remote Sensing Imagery. *IEEE J. Sel. Top. Appl. Earth Obs. Remote Sens.* **2017**, *10*, 4104–4115. [CrossRef]
52. Anwer, R.M.; Khan, F.S.; van de Weijer, J.; Molinier, M.; Laaksonen, J. Binary patterns encoded convolutional neural networks for texture recognition and remote sensing scene classification. *Isprs J. Photogramm. Remote Sens.* **2018**, *138*, 74–85. [CrossRef]
53. Sun, H.; Li, S.; Zheng, X.; Lu, X. Remote Sensing Scene Classification by Gated Bidirectional Network. *IEEE Trans. Geosci. Remote Sens.* **2019**, *58*, 82–96. [CrossRef]
54. He, N.; Fang, L.; Li, S.; Plaza, A.; Plaza, J. Remote Sensing Scene Classification Using Multilayer Stacked Covariance Pooling. *IEEE Trans. Geosci. Remote Sens.* **2018**, *56*, 6899–6910. [CrossRef]
55. Yu, Y.; Liu, F. Aerial Scene Classification via Multilevel Fusion Based on Deep Convolutional Neural Networks. *IEEE Geosci. Remote Sens. Lett.* **2018**, *15*, 287–291. [CrossRef]
56. Zhang, W.; Tang, P.; Zhao, L. Remote Sensing Image Scene Classification Using CNN-CapsNet. *Remote Sens.* **2019**, *11*, 494. [CrossRef]
57. Zeng, D.; Chen, S.; Chen, B.; Li, S. Improving remote sensing scene classification by integrating global-context and local-object features. *Remote Sens.* **2018**, *10*, 734. [CrossRef]
58. Zhang, J.; Lu, C.; Li, X.; Kim, H.J.; Wang, J. A full convolutional network based on DenseNet for remote sensing scene classification. *Math. Biosci. Eng.* **2019**, *16*, 3345–3367. [CrossRef] [PubMed]
59. Liu, Y.; Zhong, Y.; Qin, Q. Scene Classification Based on Multiscale Convolutional Neural Network. *IEEE Trans. Geosci. Remote Sens.* **2018**, *56*, 7109–7121. [CrossRef]
60. Shao, Y.; Lunetta, R.S. Comparison of support vector machine, neural network, and CART algorithms for the land-cover classification using limited training data points. *ISPRS J. Photogramm. Remote Sens.* **2012**, *70*, 78–87. [CrossRef]

 © 2020 by the authors. Licensee MDPI, Basel, Switzerland. This article is an open access article distributed under the terms and conditions of the Creative Commons Attribution (CC BY) license (http://creativecommons.org/licenses/by/4.0/).

Article

Hybrid-Attention Network for RGB-D Salient Object Detection

Yuzhen Chen [1] and Wujie Zhou [1,2,*]

[1] School of Information and Electronic Engineering, Zhejiang University of Science & Technology, Hangzhou 310023, China; 211708802001@zust.edu.cn
[2] College of Information Science and Electronic Engineering, Zhejiang University, Hangzhou 310027, China
* Correspondence: wujiezhou@163.com

Received: 4 July 2020; Accepted: 18 August 2020; Published: 21 August 2020

Abstract: Depth information has been widely used to improve RGB-D salient object detection by extracting attention maps to determine the position information of objects in an image. However, non-salient objects may be close to the depth sensor and present high pixel intensities in the depth maps. This situation in depth maps inevitably leads to erroneously emphasize non-salient areas and may have a negative impact on the saliency results. To mitigate this problem, we propose a hybrid attention neural network that fuses middle- and high-level RGB features with depth features to generate a hybrid attention map to remove background information. The proposed network extracts multilevel features from RGB images using the Res2Net architecture and then integrates high-level features from depth maps using the Inception-v4-ResNet2 architecture. The mixed high-level RGB features and depth features generate the hybrid attention map, which is then multiplied to the low-level RGB features. After decoding by several convolutions and upsampling, we obtain the final saliency prediction, achieving state-of-the-art performance on the NJUD and NLPR datasets. Moreover, the proposed network has good generalization ability compared with other methods. An ablation study demonstrates that the proposed network effectively performs saliency prediction even when non-salient objects interfere detection. In fact, after removing the branch with high-level RGB features, the RGB attention map that guides the network for saliency prediction is lost, and all the performance measures decline. The resulting prediction map from the ablation study shows the effect of non-salient objects close to the depth sensor. This effect is not present when using the complete hybrid attention network. Therefore, RGB information can correct and supplement depth information, and the corresponding hybrid attention map is more robust than using a conventional attention map constructed only with depth information.

Keywords: neural networks; deep learning; salient object detection; RGB-D

1. Introduction

Saliency detection extracts relevant objects with pixel level details from an image. It has been widely used in many fields such as object segmentation [1], region proposal [2], object recognition [3], image quality assessment [4], and video analysis [5]. It has been found that when the background has similar colors to those of a salient object or it is highly complex and salient objects are very large or small, saliency detection solely based on RGB images often fails to provide accurate results. Therefore, depth information is being increasingly used as a supplement to RGB information for saliency detection [6–8]. RGB-D salient object detection based on handcrafted features generally uses depth maps to determine edges, textures, and histogram statistics, and then bottom-up [9] or top-down [10] approaches are used to predict whether a pixel belongs to a salient object. Various methods consider the rarity of pixels in an image at local and global regions [11], while others use prior knowledge to support prediction and obtain accurate detection [12]. However, these methods rely on handcrafted features, empirical parameter setting, and statistical prediction, which limit their performance. In fact, such methods cannot fully extract representative features due to inadequate parameter setting, subjective factors, and redundant or erroneous information. In addition, models of the human visual system may be incomplete and misleading. Alternatively, deep learning methods have emerged in recent years, improving the accuracy of salient object detection [13–16]. By combining the advantages of deep learning and features in depth maps, several stereoscopic saliency detection methods based on neural networks have achieved great leaps in accuracy. For instance, DF combines RGB images and depth maps into a deep learning framework [17]. Then, encoder–decoder networks, such as PDNet [18], provide high accuracy and robustness. Chen et al. further improved the results by proposing hidden structure conversion [19], complementary fusion [20], a dilated convolutional model [21], and modification to loss functions [22] for highly accurate salient object detection. On the other hand, methods based on attention mechanisms can quickly identify the position of objects and then reconstruct the edges for improving salient object detection. Wang et al. proposed a residual network with attention mechanism [23] and then DANet [24] to achieve accurate results by using channel and spatial attention maps.

Current stereoscopic salient object detection based on deep learning usually adopts networks such as VGG [25], ResNet [26], and Inception [27] as its backbone and the U-Net encoding–decoding structure [28] as the framework. However, this is not an ideal solution for saliency detection. As the depth map (disparity map) is an image reflecting the distances to objects, many networks use it to generate an attention map to distinguish objects from the background. However, depth maps have two major limitations. First, the depth map reflects the distance to all objects, and some non-salient objects are the closest to camera and provide the lowest (highest) pixel intensities. Thus, the underlying network may consider such objects as salient, in a phenomenon that we call the depth principle error. Second, data acquisition limitations may degrade the accuracy of edge information in the depth map.

Overall, the neural networks that determine the location of objects using only depth information to construct the attention map may be biased. Using the RGB image to discard the closest non-salient objects in depth maps may improve the detection accuracy. Based on spatial attention maps, we propose stereoscopic salient object detection using a hybrid attention network (HANet). Before processing features for saliency detection, high-level features extracted from the RGB image are encoded into an attention map, which is then mixed with the depth attention map for subsequent joint processing with the saliency features. Experimental results show that this novel method prevents non-salient object interference present in depth maps. In addition, unlike many symmetric neural networks, the proposed asymmetric network has fewer parameters, because the depth map has less information and a large network is unnecessary. Thus, we use a simplified Inception-v4-ResNet2 [29] architecture with fewer parameters to extract the depth attention map and a Res2Net [30] architecture for feature extraction to construct the RGB attention map containing more complex information. The proposed asymmetric HANet can prevent the depth principle error by filtering features with cross-modal attention maps separately obtained from RGB and depth data.

2. Proposed Method

The proposed HANet architecture achieves salient object detection and prevents the depth principle error. The processing pipeline of HANet is shown in Figure 1. HANet can be divided into two main parts. The first part extracts features through eight neural network blocks (shown in blue in Figure 1) for the RGB attention map and through two blocks (shown in green) for the depth attention map. The second part consists of six blocks (shown in orange in Figure 1) that fuse the two types of features to generate a hybrid attention map, and one block (shown in pink) that generates the saliency prediction map according to feature filtering based on the hybrid attention map.

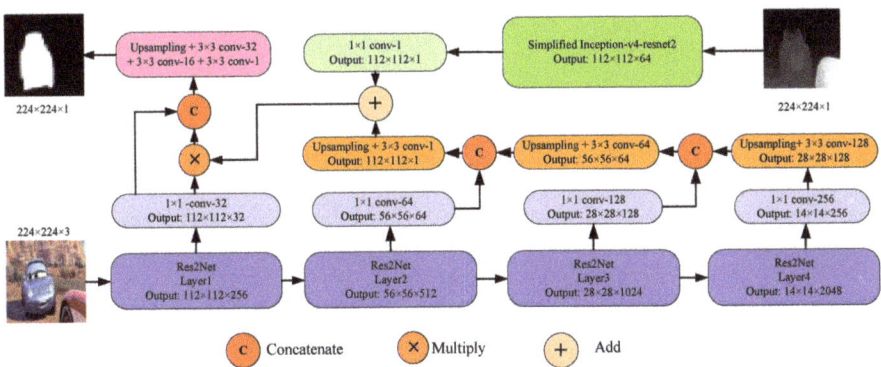

Figure 1. Framework of our HANet. The RGB-D imge is selected form Ref. [31].

2.1. Feature Extraction

We adopt two popular backbone networks for feature extraction. Specifically, Res2Net [30] extracts RGB features, and a simplified Inception-v4-ResNet2 [29] extracts depth features. The latter can handle the relatively less information from depth maps while preventing overfitting and reducing the computation time by omitting unnecessary parameters. Therefore, we establish an asymmetric architecture for this two-steam network.

For RGB images, the Res2Net backbone has been used to extract multilevel features for different tasks, being widely used in semantic segmentation, key-point estimation, and salient object detection. We have conducted comprehensive experiments on many datasets and benchmarks and verified the excellent generalization ability of Res2Net. For salient object detection, we remove all the fully connected layers of Res2Net to ensure that the output is an image. To preserve the feature information, we delete the first max pooling layers of the network and set the stride of the convolution to 1 (instead of 2) to prevent excessive downsampling. This prevents severe information loss and failure to reconstruct object details after saliency detection. As we obtain the features at each downsampling process, Res2Net provides four outputs: low-level features extracted by Layer1, middle-level features extracted by Layer2 and Layer3, and high-level features extracted by Layer4. In [27], 1×1 convolutions have dual purpose: most critically, they are used mainly as dimension reduction modules to remove computational bottlenecks, that would otherwise limit the size of our network. This allows for not just increasing the depth, but also the width of our networks without significant performance penalty. Then, inspired by [27], we use four 1×1 convolutions to reduce the number of channels to one-eighth of the original number, which is high and requires long computation time during both training and inference.

For depth maps, we use a simplified Inception-v4-ResNet2. To reduce the computational complexity, we only adopt its Stem part and five Inception-ResNet-A blocks. In addition, we follow the same procedure for RGB images to ensure that the output is an image. Likewise, we delete the first max pooling layers, set the stride of the convolution to 1, and use 3×3 convolutions to construct the depth attention map.

2.2. Hybrid Attention Predictor

The depth principle error in non-salient objects described above makes the closest objects to the depth sensor to have either the lowest or highest intensities in a disparity map. When a neural network searches for salient objects in depth maps, it can be misled by such objects. Therefore, a single-modal attention map containing only depth information is biased. By leveraging the complementarity between RGB and depth information, we can eliminate the depth principle error by constructing a hybrid attention map. This map combines the RGB and depth modes to obtain a weighted attention map in which each pixels has information on its likelihood to belong to a specific object.

To obtain the hybrid attention map, we devise a decoder network (orange blocks in Figure 1) that consist of a 3 × 3 convolutions and binary interpolation upsampling. After each upsampling, we concatenate the lower-level and current features. The decoder blocks can be represented by the following formula:

$$R^n = \sum_{k=1}^{C} U(F(R_k^{n-1} \oplus r_k^n \cdot W)), \tag{1}$$

where F represents convolution, U represents upsampling, k is the feature channel, R_k^{n-1} is the k-th channel of the $(n-1)$-th RGB attention features extracted by the corresponding block in the decoder network, r_k^{n-1} is the k-th channel of the $(n-1)$-th RGB features extracted by Res2Net, whose number of channels is reduced by the convolutions, $\oplus$ denotes concatenation, and W is the parameter for convolution.

When the RGB attention map is obtained after decoding, we aggregate the depth attention map to generate the hybrid attention map. This cross-modal attention map provides accurate localization of objects in the image. Then, we multiply the map with low-level RGB features, and several convolutions and upsampling operations lead to the prediction map for salient object detection.

2.3. Loss Function

We use the binary cross-entropy as loss function for HANet:

$$L(Y, G) = \sum_h \sum_w [Y(h, w) \log[G(h, w)]] + [1 - Y(h, w)] \log[1 - G(h, w)], \tag{2}$$

where (h, w) represents the pixel values of the image at the corresponding position, Y is the prediction map, and G is the ground truth. Thus, $L(Y, G)$ provides the final loss function values of the prediction and label map.

3. Evaluation Measures and Implementation Details

3.1. Evaluation Measures

To comprehensively evaluate the detection performance of various saliency methods, we adopt five evaluation measures: precision–recall curve, maximum and mean F-measure, mean absolute error, and area under the precision–recall curve [31,32].

The binary saliency map corresponding to a threshold is then compared to the ground truth, and precision P and recall R are computed as

$$P = \frac{\sum_h \sum_w \hat{Y}_b(h, w) - Y(h, w)}{\sum_h \sum_w \hat{Y}_b(h, w)}, \tag{3}$$

$$R = \frac{\sum_h \sum_w \hat{Y}_b(h, w) - Y(h, w)}{\sum_h \sum_w Y(h, w)}. \tag{4}$$

The average precision and recall for images in each dataset are plotted in a precision–recall curve. An adaptive threshold is applied to the grayscale saliency map to obtain the corresponding binary saliency map. For each saliency map, the precision and recall are computed using (3) and (4). Then, F_β is defined as

$$F_\beta = \frac{(1 + \beta^2) PR}{\beta^2 P + R} \tag{5}$$

where β is a positive parameter specifying the relative importance of precision and recall. For consistency while comparing the performance of the proposed network with that of other methods, we set $\beta = 0.3$.

The mean absolute error reflects the average absolute pixelwise difference between the predicted saliency maps and corresponding ground truth. Thus, it is an important measure to evaluate the proposed HANet, and it is given by

$$MAE = \frac{1}{HW} \sum_{w=1}^{W} \sum_{h=1}^{H} \left| \hat{Y}(h,w) - Y(h,w) \right|, \quad (6)$$

where H and W are the numbers of rows and columns in the saliency map, respectively.

3.2. Implementation Details

We implement HANet using the popular PyTorch 1.2.0 library in Python. We apply Adam optimization with learning rate of 0.001, which is reduced by a factor of 2 if no improvement is observed in the validation performance over five consecutive epochs. The NJUD dataset [31] containing more than 2000 images and the NLPR dataset [32] containing 1000 images corresponding pixel-level ground truths are used to evaluate the proposed HANet. We follow the datasets splitting scheme proposed in [18,21], 80% are used for training and the remaining 20% for test. All the images are resized to 224 × 224 pixels. The network is trained over 100 epochs with early stopping, and a minibatch of 2 images is used at every training iteration. In this study, HANet was trained on a computer equipped with an Intel i7- 7750H CPU at 2.21 GHz and an NVIDIA GeForce GTX TITAN Xp GPU.

4. Results and Discussion

4.1. Comparison with State-of-Art Methods

We compared the proposed method with seven state-of-the-art methods: ACSD [31], CDCP [33], DCMC [34], DF [17], MBP [21], PDNet [18], and SFP [35]. Table 1 and Figure 2 show that the proposed HANet outperforms the other evaluated methods. Figure 3 shows various saliency maps obtained from each method in typical scenarios. In the first and second rows, the closest objects are non-salient and have the highest pixel intensities. For the comparison methods, the two images are misjudged due to the depth principle error. In contrast, HANet can correctly detect the salient objects by using the information in the hybrid attention map.

To further demonstrate the effectiveness of HANet, we conducted an ablation study by removing the RGB attention map. The results are shown in the 12th column of Figure 3, where the miscalculation due to the depth principle error appears. On the third and fourth rows, we show the saliency obtained from HANet in scenes with multiple and large salient objects, confirming the effectiveness of the proposed method.

Table 1. Saliency Detection Performance of Different Methods on the Testing set of the NJUD and NLPR Datasets.

Datasets	Criteria	ACSD	CDCP	SFP	DCMC	DF	MBP	PDNet	Ours
NJUD	AUC	0.923	0.822	0.871	0.926	0.928	0.703	0.952	0.964
	MeanF	0.551	0.572	0.482	0.601	0.654	0.479	0.719	0.834
	MaxF	0.733	0.594	0.655	0.740	0.782	0.557	0.796	0.866
	MAE	0.190	0.204	0.202	0.154	0.154	0.207	0.129	0.065
NLPR	AUC	0.837	0.895	0.864	0.931	0.841	0.781	0.957	0.982
	MeanF	0.461	0.600	0.426	0.590	0.660	0.547	0.610	0.827
	MaxF	0.615	0.654	0.562	0.703	0.745	0.598	0.720	0.869
	MAE	0.156	0.126	0.180	0.120	0.112	0.117	0.119	0.055

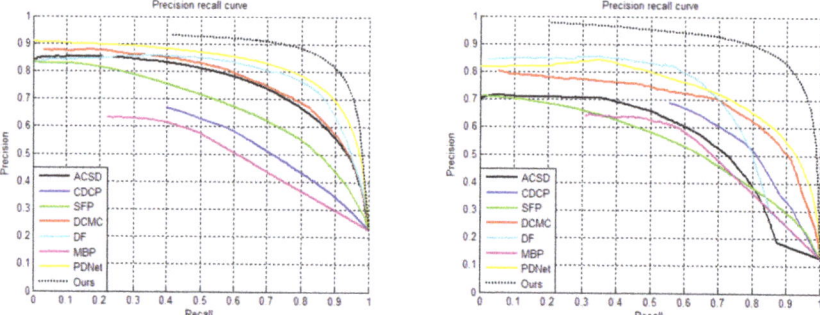

Figure 2. Precision–recall curves of different methods on the testing set of the NJUD and NLPR datasets.

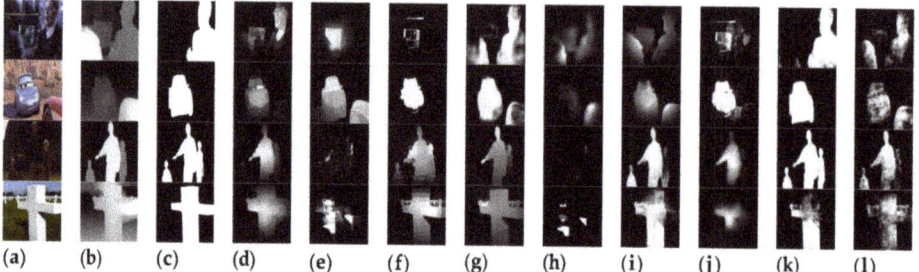

Figure 3. Examples of salient object detection from the testing set. (**a**) Original image, (**b**) depth map, and (**c**) ground truth. Saliency maps obtained from (**d**) ACSD, (**e**) CDCP, (**f**) DCMC, (**g**) DF, (**h**) MBP, (**i**) PDnet, (**j**) SFP, (**k**) proposed HANet, and (**l**) HANet without RGB attention map (ablation study). The RGB-D imges are selected form Ref. [33].

4.2. Ablation Study

To analyze the effectiveness of both the proposed hybrid attention mechanism and RGB attention map to correct mistakes caused by depth principle error, we removed Layer2, Layer3, and Layer4 and their corresponding 1 × 1 convolutions from HANet. In addition, we removed the upsampling and convolution during fusion, and omitted the RGB attention map and thus its combination with the depth attention map. Table 2 and Figure 4 show that the saliency results are substantially deteriorated, as illustrated in the 12th column of Figure 3, where the depth principle error is evident. Therefore, HANet accurately predicts salient objects and eliminates interference caused by the depth principle error.

Table 2. Performance of HANet During Ablation Study on NJUD and NLPR Datasets.

Datasets	Criteria	Single-Attention	Multi-Attention
NJUD	AUC	0.935	0.964
	MeanF	0.670	0.834
	MaxF	0.755	0.866
	MAE	0.150	0.065
NLPR	AUC	0.959	0.982
	MeanF	0.721	0.827
	MaxF	0.783	0.869
	MAE	0.091	0.055

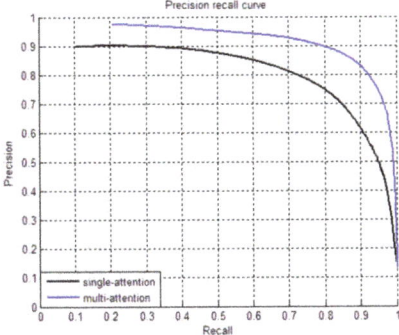 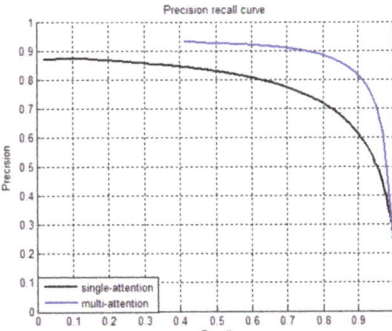

Figure 4. Precision–recall curves obtained from ablation study applied to images from NJUD (left) and NLPR (right) datasets.

4.3. Computational Complexity

The computational complexity of the proposed HANet and the other methods was estimated from tests on the NJUD dataset. It takes approximately 4 h to train HANet using an Intel i5-7500 CPU at 3.4 GHz and an NVIDIA GeForce GTX TITAN Xp GPU. HANet achieves saliency detection at 11.6 fps for images of 224 × 224 pixels. Therefore, our model has low computational complexity and can be applied to real-time image processing systems.

5. Conclusions

We propose HANet, a hybrid network based on an attention mechanism for stereoscopic salient object detection. HANet uses a novel attention method that fuses RGB and depth attention maps to filter the original saliency features. Combined with an encoder–decoder network, HANet provides higher performance on the NJUD and NLPR datasets. Furthermore, an ablation study confirms that the HANet performance decreases when removing the RGB attention map, indicating the effectiveness of the proposed hybrid attention mechanism. The RGB attention map helps solving interference caused by the depth principle error, which occurs when non-salient objects are close to the depth sensor. Moreover, HANet provides high performance in scenes containing multiple objects, large objects, and other complex information.

Author Contributions: Y.C. conceived and designed the experiments, analyzed the data and wrote the paper. W.Z. supervised the work, helped with designing the conceptual framework, and edited the manuscript. All authors have read and agreed to the published version of the manuscript.

Funding: This work was supported by the Natural Science Foundation of China (Grant Nos. 61502429), the Zhejiang Provincial Natural Science Foundation of China (Grant No. LY18F020012), and the China Postdoctoral Science Foundation (Grant No. 2015M581932).

Conflicts of Interest: The authors declare no conflict of interest.

References

1. Zhou, W.; Yuan, J.; Lei, J.; Luo, T. TSNet: Three-stream self-attention network for RGB-D indoor semantic segmentation. *IEEE Intell. Syst.* **2020**. [CrossRef]
2. Bogdan, A.; Thomas, D.; Vittorio, F. Measuring the objectness of image windows. *IEEE Trans. Pattern Anal. Mach. Intell.* **2012**, *34*, 2189–2202.
3. Zhang, H.; Cao, X.; Wang, R. Audio visual attribute discovery for fine-grained object recognition. In Proceedings of the Thirty-Second AAAI Conference on Artificial Intelligence, New Orleans, LA, USA, 2–7 February 2018.
4. Zhou, W.; Lei, J.; Jiang, Q.; Yu, L.; Luo, T. Blind binocular visual quality predictor using deep fusion network. *IEEE Trans. Comput. Imaging* **2020**, *6*, 883–893. [CrossRef]

5. Liu, H.; Jiang, S.; Huang, Q.; Xu, C. A generic virtual content insertion system based on visual attention analysis. In Proceedings of the 16th ACM international conference on Multimedia, Vancouver, BC, Canada, 27–31 October 2008.
6. Zhou, W.; Lv, Y.; Lei, J.; Yu, L. Global and local-contrast guides content-aware fusion for RGB-D saliency prediction. *IEEE Trans. on Syst. Man Cybern. Syst.* **2019**, 1–9. [CrossRef]
7. Desingh, K.; Krishna, K.M.; Rajan, D.; Jawahar, C.V. Depth really matters: Improving visual salient region detection with depth. In Proceedings of the BMVC 2013—British Machine Vision Conference, Bristol, UK, 9–13 September 2013.
8. Lang, C.; Nguyen, T.V.; Katti, H.; Yadati, K.; Kankanhalli, M.; Yan, S. Depth matters: Influence of depth cues on visual saliency. In Proceedings of the 12th European Conference on Computer Vision, Florence, Italy, 7–13 October 2012.
9. Zhou, Q.; Zhang, L.; Zhao, W.; Liu, X.; Chen, Y.; Wang, Z. Salient object detection using coarse-to-fine processing. *J. Opt. Soc. Am. A* **2017**, *34*, 370–383. [CrossRef] [PubMed]
10. Liu, D.; Chang, F.; Liu, C. Salient object detection fusing global and local information based on nonsubsampled contourlet transform. *JOSAA* **2016**, *33*, 1430–1441. [CrossRef] [PubMed]
11. Wang, W.; Lai, Q.; Fu, H.; Shen, J.; Ling, H. Salient object detection in the deep learning era: An in-depth survey. Available online: https://arxiv.org/pdf/1904.09146 (accessed on 18 August 2020).
12. Li, C.Y.; Guo, J.C.; Cong, R.M.; Pang, Y.W.; Wang, B. Underwater image enhancement by dehazing with minimum information loss and histogram distribution prior. *IEEE Trans. Image Process.* **2016**, *25*, 5664–5677. [CrossRef] [PubMed]
13. Keren, F.; Fan, D.P.; Ji, G.P.; Zhao, Q. JL-DCF: Joint learning and densely-cooperative fusion framework for RGB-D salient object detection. In Proceedings of the IEEE/CVF Conference on Computer Vision and Pattern Recognition (CVPR), Seattle, WA, USA, 13–19 June 2020.
14. Zhou, W.; Chen, Y.; Liu, C.; Yu, L. GFNet: Gate fusion network with Res2Net for detecting salient objects in RGB-D images. *IEEE Signal Process. Lett.* **2020**, *27*, 800–804. [CrossRef]
15. Fan, D.P.; Lin, Z.; Zhang, Z.; Zhu, M.; Cheng, M.M. Rethinking RGB-D salient object detection: Models, data sets, and large-scale benchmarks. *IEEE Trans. Neural Netw. Learn. Syst.* **2020**. [CrossRef]
16. Zhang, J.; Fan, D.P.; Dai, Y.; Anwar, S.; Saleh, F.S.; Zhang, T.; Barnes, N. UC-net: Uncertainty inspired rgb-d saliency detection via conditional variational autoencoders. In Proceedings of the IEEE/CVF Conference on Computer Vision and Pattern Recognition (CVPR), Seattle, WA, USA, 13–19 June 2020.
17. Qu, L.; He, S.; Zhang, J.; Tian, J.; Tang, Y.; Yang, Q. RGBD salient object detection via deep fusion. *IEEE Trans. Image Process.* **2017**, *26*, 2274–2285. [CrossRef]
18. Zhu, C.; Cai, X.; Huang, K.; Li, T.H.; Li, G. PDNet: Prior-model guided depth-enhanced network for salient object detection. In Proceedings of the 2019 IEEE International Conference on Multimedia and Expo (ICME), Shanghai, China, 8–12 July 2019; pp. 199–204. [CrossRef]
19. Han, J.; Chen, H.; Liu, N.; Yan, C.; Li, X. CNNs-based RGB-D saliency detection via cross-view transfer and multiview fusion. *IEEE Trans. Cybern.* **2018**, *48*, 3171–3183. [CrossRef] [PubMed]
20. Chen, H.; Li, Y. Progressively complementarity-aware fusion network for RGB-D salient object detection. In Proceedings of the 2018 IEEE/CVF Conference on Computer Vision and Pattern Recognition, Salt Lake City, UT, USA, 18–23 June 2018; pp. 3051–3060. [CrossRef]
21. Zhu, C.; Li, G. A multilayer backpropagation saliency detection algorithm and its applications. *Multimed. Tools Appl.* **2018**, *77*, 25181–25197. [CrossRef]
22. Huang, P.; Shen, C.H.; Hsiao, H.F. RGBD salient object detection using spatially coherent deep learning framework. In Proceedings of the 2018 IEEE 23rd International Conference on Digital Signal Processing (DSP), Pudong, Shanghai, China, 19–21 November 2018.
23. Wang, F.; Jiang, M.; Qian, C.; Yang, S.; Li, C.; Zhang, H.; Wang, X.; Tang, X. Residual attention network for image classification. In Proceedings of the 2017 IEEE Conference on Computer Vision and Pattern Recognition (CVPR), Honolulu, HI, USA, 21–26 July 2017. [CrossRef]
24. Fu, J.; Liu, J.; Tian, H.; Li, Y.; Bao, Y.; Fang, Z.; Lu, H. Dual attention network for scene segmentation. In Proceedings of the 2019 IEEE/CVF Conference on Computer Vision and Pattern Recognition (CVPR), Long Beach, CA, USA, 15–20 June 2019. [CrossRef]
25. Simonyan, K.; Zisserman, A. Very deep convolutional networks for large-scale image recognition. Available online: https://arxiv.org/pdf/1409.1556.pdf (accessed on 18 August 2020).

26. He, K.; Zhang, X.; Ren, S.; Sun, J. Deep Residual Learning for Image Recognition. In Proceedings of the 2016 IEEE Conference on Computer Vision and Pattern Recognition (CVPR), Las Vegas, NV, USA, 27–30 June 2016. [CrossRef]
27. Szengedy, C.; Liu, W.; Jia, Y.; Sermanet, P.; Reed, S.; Anguelov, D.; Erhan, D.; Vanhoucke, V.; Rabinovich, A. Going deeper with convolutions. In Proceedings of the IEEE Conference on Computer Vision and Pattern Recognition (CVPR), Boston, MA, USA, 7–12 June 2015; IEEE: Piscataway, NJ, USA, 2015; pp. 1–9.
28. Ronneberger, O.; Fischer, P.; Brox, T. U-Net: Convolutional networks for biomedical image segmentation. In Proceedings of the International Conference on Medical image computing and computer-assisted intervention, Munich, Germany, 5–9 October 2015.
29. Szegedy, C.; Ioffe, S.; Vanhoucke, V.; Alemi, A. Inception-v4, Inception-ResNet and the impact of residual connections on learning. In Proceedings of the Thirty-first AAAI conference on artificial intelligence, San Francisco, CA, USA, 4–10 February 2017.
30. Gao, S.; Cheng, M.; Zhao, K.; Zhang, X.; Yang, M.; Torr, P.H.S. Res2net: A new multi-scale backbone architecture. *IEEE Trans. Pattern Anal. Mach. Intell.* **2019**, 2938758. [CrossRef] [PubMed]
31. Ju, R.; Ge, L.; Geng, W.; Ren, T.; Wu, G. Depth saliency based on anisotropic center-surround difference. In Proceedings of the 2014 IEEE International Conference on Image Processing (ICIP), Paris, France, 27–30 October 2014; pp. 1115–1119. [CrossRef]
32. Peng, H.; Li, B.; Xiong, W.; Hu, W.; Ji, R. RGBD salient object detection: A benchmark and algorithms. In Proceedings of the 2014 European Conference on Computer Vision, Zurich, Switzerland, 6–12 September 2014.
33. Zhu, C.; Li, G.; Wang, W.; Wang, R. An innovative salient object detection using center-dark channel prior. In Proceedings of the 2017 IEEE International Conference on Computer Vision Workshops (ICCVW), Venice, Italy, 22–29 October 2017; pp. 1509–1515. [CrossRef]
34. Cong, R.; Lei, J.; Zhang, C.; Huang, Q.; Cao, X.; Hou, C. Saliency detection for stereoscopic images based on depth confidence analysis and multiple cues fusion. *IEEE Signal Process. Lett.* **2016**, *23*, 819–824. [CrossRef]
35. Guo, J.; Ren, T.; Bei, J.; Zhu, Y. Salient object detection in RGB-D image based on saliency fusion and propagation. In Proceedings of the 7th International Conference on Internet Multimedia Computing and Service, Zhangjiajie, Hunan, China, 19–21 August 2015. [CrossRef]

© 2020 by the authors. Licensee MDPI, Basel, Switzerland. This article is an open access article distributed under the terms and conditions of the Creative Commons Attribution (CC BY) license (http://creativecommons.org/licenses/by/4.0/).

Article
Object Detection Using Multi-Scale Balanced Sampling

Hang Yu *, Jiulu Gong and Derong Chen

School of Mechatronical Engineering, Beijing Institute of Technology, Beijing 100811, China;
lujiugong@bit.edu.cn (J.G.); cdr@bit.edu.cn (D.C.)
* Correspondence: yuh_0111@bit.edu.cn; Tel.: +86-010-88521997

Received: 16 July 2020; Accepted: 20 August 2020; Published: 1 September 2020

Abstract: Detecting small objects and objects with large scale variants are always challenging for deep learning based object detection approaches. Many efforts have been made to solve these problems such as adopting more effective network structures, image features, loss functions, etc. However, for both small objects detection and detecting objects with various scale in single image, the first thing should be solve is the matching mechanism between anchor boxes and ground-truths. In this paper, an approach based on multi-scale balanced sampling(MB-RPN) is proposed for the difficult matching of small objects and detecting multi-scale objects. According to the scale of the anchor boxes, different positive and negative sample IOU discriminate thresholds are adopted to improve the probability of matching the small object area with the anchor boxes so that more small object samples are included in the training process. Moreover, the balanced sampling method is proposed for the collected samples, the samples are further divided and uniform sampling to ensure the diversity of samples in training process. Several datasets are adopted to evaluate the MB-RPN, the experimental results show that compare with the similar approach, MB-RPN improves detection performances effectively.

Keywords: object detection; small object; multi-scale sampling; balanced sampling

1. Introduction

Object detection is a kind of approaches for objects localization and category classification in digital images, which is one of the most challenging branches in the field of computer vision.

The early approaches are based on handcrafted image features. In [1], a pedestrian detection system is proposed with histogram of oriented gradients(HOG) feature and support vector machine(SVM). In [2], deformable part-based model(DPM) is proposed which enhanced detection accuracy by utilizing HOG features of the whole and part of objects. As the peak of handcraft feature based detection approach, the detection performances of DPM are still not ideal, due to the lack of effective representation of features. Besides, since hand craft feature extractor are always designed for specific object types, hence often result in low robustness in dealing with different category of objects.

In recent years, several object detection approaches based on convolutional neural networks (CNN) are proposed [3–5]. Image features are supervise trained by measuring error between prediction and annotated ground-truth in large-scale object detection datasets. Compare with handcraft features the CNN features' representation ability and robustness against various types of objects are both significantly enhanced. Therefore the detection performances are highly improved. Although deep learning object detection approaches have shown state of the art performance for general object detection, they are still limited in detecting small objects and the performances in detection various scale objects in single input image is also not ideal. The reasons for a low detection performances are as the follow:

1. The proportion of small objects in the image are always relative low, which means they might be excluded from the training process due to improper network hyperparameter settings. However, small objects often have low resolutions and less image information which means the difficulty of training small objects are always higher than general objects, the lack of sampling will further result in a low quality features extraction by the deep neural networks.
2. In natural scenes, the scale of objects are distributed stochastic, which means within a single image there might be objects with large scale variants, it is easy to take the majority of samples and ignore other objects in the process of training.

Overall, in order to further improve detection performances especially in detecting objects mentioned above, the number of small objects and proportion of various scale object in training samples are both important.In this paper an end-to-end object detection approach with multi-scale balanced sampling is proposed to improve the matching mechanism and ensure scale diversity in training samples. The key contribution of the approach is summarized as follow:

1. The samples' matching conditions is adjusted according to the objects' scale so that the the small objects are easier to be matched, which enhance the training samples of small objects.
2. The sample set is divided into multiple intervals according to the samples' scale and their corresponding discrimination difficulty. In addition, each interval is sampled in a balanced fashion to preserve the diversity of sample types during the classification and positioning network training process and to further ensure that the algorithm does not tend to detect a specific type of samples while ignoring the others.
3. Evaluation between proposed approach and others on several benchmarks is proposed, the experiment results show that the detection performances are better than other similar approaches.

The remainder of this paper is organized as follows. In Section 2, background and related works are introduced. In Section 3, framework and implement detail of proposed approach are introduced. Section 4 presents the experiment results and comparisons with other similar approaches. Finally, Section 5 conclude the proposed approach.

2. Related Works

In [6], a deep neural network based object detection approach called RCNN is first introduced. It is composed with three parts: First, by adopting selective search algorithm, RCNN generate a series of candidate region, each of them may responsible for detecting a specific object in the image. Second, extract feature of candidate regions by CNN, the network will be train supervised by measuring the error between prediction and ground-truths. Finally, SVM and bounding box regression is adopted to finetune the predicted results. The framework of RCNN is similar to tradition approaches except CNN is adopt to extract image features instead of handcraft features. In [7], an approach called Fast RCNN is proposed, it take the whole image as inputs, then crop the corresponding features of each candidate region and map them to a uniform size by region of interest(ROI) pooling, finally feed the mapped features into classification and regression network to acquire its category and localization. The fast RNN integrate coarse and finetune process in RCNN which improve both the detection performances and efficiency. In [5], an end-to-end CNN based object detection framework called Faster RCNN is introduced. Instead of generate candidate by selective search, this approach proposed region proposal network(RPN), it first generate a series of anchor boxes with different scale and aspect ratio, each of them is responsible for detecting object or not is depend on the inter section of union(IOU) between its coordinate and annotated ground-truth. As the first end-to-end object detection approach, Faster RCNN laid the foundation of subsequent deep neural network based object detection approaches. In [3], an approach which integrate the function of RPN and classification/regression network in one series convolution layers called SSD is introduced. At present, approaches whose framework are similar to Faster RCNN are summarized as two-stage approaches, in contrast the approaches like SSD are called one-stage approaches.

Based on backbones such as Faster RCNN and SSD, variety of approaches were proposed to enhance the detection performances. For example: Feature Pyramid Networks(FPN) proposed an pyramid architecture image feature extractor, objects in different resolution are arranged to corresponding layers, compare with the origin Faster RCNN, in dealing with a specific object FPN will provide more proper feature [8]. Cascade RCNN proposed training process that discrimination IOU threshold is gradually increased, which makes the classification and regression network training in a easy-to-hard way [9]. RetinaNet proposed focal loss which could enlarge the weight of hard samples, which makes the training process focuses on the hard samples [10]. Libra RCNN proposed a balanced sampling method, feature extraction and loss function in training process [11]. SRetinaNet propose an anchor optimization method which will help detecting small objects with specific parameter setting [12]. GA-RPN propose an anchor optimization method by combining anchor box with semantic features [13].

Regardless approaches being one or two stage, the fundament for object detection is the matching mechanism of anchor and ground-truth, which determines how many samples can be included in the network training. Therefore, it is important to propose a proper matching mechanism for enhancing the detection performances. However, the stochastic of objects scale poses challenges to the matching mechanism [12,13].

3. Proposed Method

3.1. Framework Overview

The overview of proposed approach is shown in Figure 1, where the green cubes denote image feature extracting process, the pink cube denote MB-RPN module and purple cube denote classification/regression networks for finetune. Table 1 shows the details of the network. The specific steps are as follows:

1. Take an digital image as inputs, feed it into ResNet-101 pre-trained network so that the image features are extracted from shallow to deep using Conv1~Conv5 [14].
2. By adopting MB-RPN, samples are dynamically selected according to scale and proportion. MB-RPN can be further decomposed into two parts: multi-scale and balanced sampling.
3. The MB-RPN calculation results are then transformed to the same size through ROI Pooling.
4. The candidate box is then sent to the classification and regression network to obtain the object category and its location.

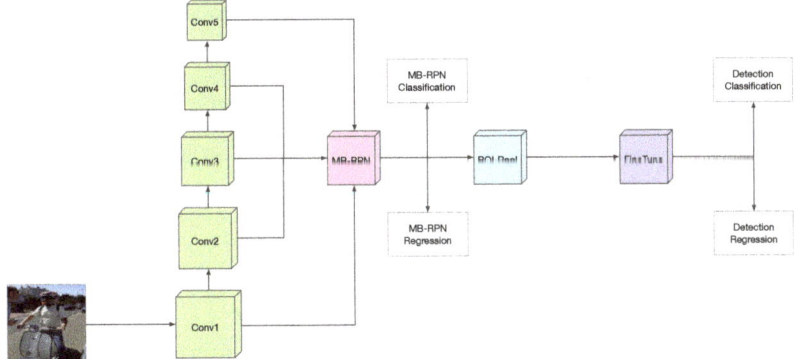

Figure 1. Architecture of Proposed Method.

Table 1. Details of Network.

	Input	Shape	Layer	Output
	Image	$600 \times 600 \times 3$	$conv\_1 * 1, stride2, 64$	Conv1
	Conv1	$300 \times 300 \times 64$	$conv\_3 * 3, maxpool, stride2, 64$	Pool1
	Pool1	$150 \times 150 \times 64$	$\begin{bmatrix} conv\_1 * 1, 64 \\ conv\_3 * 3, 64 \\ conv\_1 * 1, 256 \end{bmatrix} \times 3$	Conv2
ResNet-101	Conv2	$150 \times 150 \times 256$	$\begin{bmatrix} conv\_1 * 1, 128 \\ conv\_3 * 3, 128 \\ conv\_1 * 1, 512 \end{bmatrix} \times 4$	Conv3
	Conv3	$75 \times 75 \times 512$	$\begin{bmatrix} conv\_1 * 1, 256 \\ conv\_3 * 3, 256 \\ conv\_1 * 1, 1024 \end{bmatrix} \times 3$	Conv4
	Conv4	$38 \times 38 \times 1024$	$\begin{bmatrix} conv\_1 * 1, 512 \\ conv\_3 * 3, 512 \\ conv\_1 * 1, 2945 \end{bmatrix} \times 3$	Conv5
MB-RPN	Pool1	$150 \times 150 \times 64$	$conv\_3 * 3, 256$	$MB - RPN_1$
	Conv2	$75 \times 75 \times 256$	$conv\_3 * 3, 256$	$MB - RPN_2$
	Conv3	$38 \times 38 \times 512$	$conv\_3 * 3, 256$	$MB - RPN_3$
	Conv4	$19 \times 19 \times 1024$	$conv\_3 * 3, 256$	$MB - RPN_4$
	Conv5	$10 \times 10 \times 2048$	$conv\_3 * 3, 256$	$MB - RPN_5$
FineTune	Pool1	$14 \times 14 \times 128$	$conv\_3 * 3, 256$	$FineTune_1$
	Conv2	$28 \times 28 \times 256$	$conv\_3 * 3, 256$	$FineTune_2$
	Conv3	$56 \times 56 \times 374$	$conv\_3 * 3, 256$	$FineTune_3$
	Conv4	$112 \times 112 \times 512$	$conv\_3 * 3, 256$	$FineTune_4$
	Conv5	$224 \times 224 \times 640$	$conv\_3 * 3, 256$	$FineTune_5$

3.2. Multi-Scale Sample Discrimination

The main factors affecting the sample matching in training process are the scale of the anchor box and the labelling result IOU discrimination threshold. The large difference between the scale of the small object and the anchor box makes match difficult under the existing discrimination conditions.

For the sampling process of the positive samples, Figure 2a shows the matching results when default shape of FPN anchor boxes is adopted and the discrimination threshold of IOU> 0.7, where the red rectangle indicates the manually marked area containing the object. As it is seen, none of the anchor boxes can be successfully matched with the object area. Therefore, the image is unable to guide the network parameter training because it does not contain any positive sample during the the training process. Figure 2b shows the matching results for the case where the scale of the anchor box is reduced by half. The green rectangle indicates the labeled samples in the training set, and the red rectangle indicates the corresponding matching anchor box, the sample matching results are still far from ideal.

For small objects, the default IOU threshold of FPN is a stringent condition, resulting in a poor matching even in the case where the anchor box scale is reduced. Also, the design of the anchor boxes should fully consider the objects in the image data set with different sizes. Therefore, simple reduction of the anchor box scale might, in return, result in matching failure for the object samples with a normal size. Hence, it is hard to improve the object matching probability solely by reducing the scale of the anchor box for detecting small objects.

(a) default FPN anchor sizes

(b) half of the default FPN anchor sizes

Figure 2. Sampling Results Example on Small objects.

To address the above issue, multi-scale positive sampling approach with dynamic IOU discrimination threshold is proposed. The FPN method has designed five scale-level anchor boxes, namely, A1~A5 according to different scale sizes. According to the scale of anchor boxes, the approach divide three different positive sample intervals from smallest anchor size to the biggest, the criteria for levels of are shown as the follow:

$$\begin{cases} small\_positive & : a_i \in \{A_1\} \\ medium\_positive & : a_i \in \{A_2, A_3\} \\ big\_positive & : a_i \in \{A_4, A_5\} \end{cases} \quad (1)$$

In Equation (1), a_i represents the area of an anchor box, and A1~A5 denote the present area of the anchor boxes in 5 different levels. The IOU discrimination threshold of small and medium anchor boxes are then decreased to 0.5 and 0.6 respectively, to ensure more small and medium boxes will be matched. For large anchor boxes, the default discrimination threshold is kept. By lowering the positive sample discrimination threshold, the anchor box is easier to match with the small object area, and the number of positive samples with the small object area is therefore increased.

Theoretically, lowering the matching threshold for the large-size anchor boxes can also effectively increase the number of matching anchor boxes. However, compared with the small object area, the large object has the following two differences:

1. For the large object it is much easier to meet the discrimination condition of the IOU threshold. As it is seen in Figure 3, the large object located of the image has larger number of matching anchor boxes although for a threshold which has not been decreased. This suggests that further reduction of the threshold has only a limited impact on the increase of the positive samples.
2. Since a large object area contains a rich image feature information, compared to small objects, it is easier to obtain a set of valid discrimination and bounding box regression parameters during

the network training process. Therefore, it is very limited to enhance the effect of detection performances for large objects by reducing the IOU discrimination threshold.

Figure 3. Sampling Results Example on Big Objects.

From the network training perspective, the object detection approaches that are limited by computing resources often need to set an upper limit of samples. Part of the sampling results will be discarded randomly when too much samples are collected. Taking the FPN as an example, the upper limit on the total number of samples is usually 256, and arrange for positive and negative samples are 128 respectively, the redundant samples will be discarded. In this paper, we argue that the sample priority of the small object area should be higher than that of the large objects. In cases where there are a combination of small and large objects in the image, first and most important is to ensure a sufficient number of the small object areas samples for section. Therefore, the same IOU threshold value as the original FPN method is maintained for the large object areas, and the number of positive samples is not increased.

For negative sample sampling, besides considering the match of the anchor box and the object size, it is also necessary to consider the effect of different discrimination difficulty on the accuracy of the algorithm. For the object detection algorithm, the proposed approach divide the negative samples into easy and hard negative samples depending on the IOU threshold. In particular, the easy negative samples help the network to converge quickly. The detection accuracy however is mainly dependent on hard negative samples. Therefore, when collecting negative samples, the ratio of the number of hard to the number of easy negative samples is balanced. Figure 4 shows the example result of negative samples, where blue, green and red rectangles denote small, medium and big negative samples, most of them belong are easy and small samples.

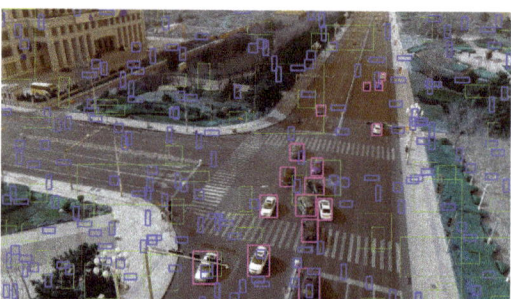

Figure 4. Negative Sample Results of Random Sampling.

To address problem above, the Libra RCNN propose a balance sampling method to ensure the diversity of negative samples: First, according to IOU between anchor boxes and ground-truth the divide negative samples into different intervals. Second, divide the number of negative samples equally according to the intervals and balance sampling in each interval. Within the FPN method, Negative samples are defined as the anchors whose IOU with ground-truth are lower than 0.3, the Libra RCNN further divided it into easy, medium and hard negative intervals which are defined as the follow:

$$\begin{cases} easy\_negative : IOU \in [0, 0.1) \\ medium\_negative : IOU \in [0.1, 0.2) \\ hard\_negative : IOU \in [0.2, 0.3) \end{cases} \quad (2)$$

Based on Libra RCNN, a balance negative sampling method which combining samples' scale and difficulty is proposed. Negative samples were divided into 8 intervals as shown in the Equation3. For medium and big negative samples this approach adopt the similar difficulty dividing approach as Libra RCNN, for instance, the easy_negative_medium negative sample denote the samples whose $IOU \in [0, 0.1)$ and scale $a_i \in \{A_2, A_3\}$. For small negative samples, since the IOU discrimination threshold of positive samples are adjusted to 0.5, the dividing approach of Libra RCNN is easy to cause confusing between positive and negative samples, therefore this approach correspond adjusted the dividing approach that only divide them into two different intervals.

$$\begin{cases} easy\_negative\_small : IOU \in [0, 0.1), a_i \in \{A_1\} \\ hard\_negative\_small : IOU \in [0.1, 0.2), a_i \in \{A_1\} \\ easy\_negative\_medium : IOU \in [0, 0.1), a_i \in \{A_2, A_3\} \\ medium\_negative\_medium : IOU \in [0.1, 0.2), a_i \in \{A_2, A_3\} \\ hard\_negative\_medium : IOU \in [0.2, 0.3), a_i \in \{A_2, A_3\} \\ easy\_negative\_big : IOU \in [0, 0.1), a_i \in \{A_4, A_5\} \\ medium\_negative\_big : IOU \in [0.1, 0.2), a_i \in \{A_4, A_5\} \\ hard\_negative\_big : IOU \in [0.2, 0.3), a_i \in \{A_4, A_5\} \end{cases} \quad (3)$$

3.3. Balanced Sampling

According to the dividing method mentioned above, a balance sampling approach is proposed: the positive samples are balanced according to the scale size to form a positive sample set. For the negative samples determined by the anchor box, the negative sample set is formed by balanced sampling with comprehensive consideration of the difficulty and scale size. For the sample set with an upper limit of N, the sample collection method designed in this paper is demonstrated in Algorithm 1.

Algorithm 1 Balanced Sample Algorithm.

Inputs:
  Positive/Negative Sample Sets;
  2: Number of Select Samples N;
Outputs:
  Sample Set U;
  4: $divide\_num = \frac{N}{set\_num}$
  $U = []$
  6: sort(Sets)
    for set in Sets:
  8:    if $n_{set} > divide\_num$:
        U.append(sample($n_{set}, divide\_num$))
  10:   else:
        U.append(n_{set})
  12:   reshape($divide\_num$)
    return U

Ideally, the total number of positive and negative samples should be equal, therefore this approach initializes $divide\_num$ to the average of the total number of sample sets $\frac{N}{set\_num}$, if number of samples of all the intervals satisfies $n_{set} > divide\_num$, it is only needed to randomly sampling in each interval to generate set U. However, the ideal condition mentioned above is hardly appear in actual situation, therefore balance sampling is a problem that should be considered. If the total number of samples is less than the upper sampling limit N, it is necessary to include all samples in the sample set; Otherwise, the number of uniformly sampled objects in each interval, $divide\_num$, is calculated based on the interval data, set_num. Sampling is then carried out from low to high according to the sample data in each interval. If the number of samples in the current interval, $n_{set} > divide\_num$, then $divide\_num$ samples are randomly selected to be included in the sample collection of the current interval; otherwise, all n_set samples are included in the sample collection, and $divide\_num$ is adjusted for subsequent sampling intervals using the reshape method.

The key point of the balanced sampling method is the reshape method for $n_{set} < divide\_num$. All samples in these kind of interval should be retained since the demand number of samples if more than the actual collected samples. Since the order of sampling approaching is depend on number of samples in each interval, therefore all of the subsequent intervals are redundant, which means the subsequent intervals are satisfy the following condition:

$$\sum_{i=j+1}^{set\_num} > (set\_num - j) * divide\_num + (divide\_num - num_{set}) \quad (4)$$

In Equation (4), j represents the index of the current interval set in all sorted intervals. Since the surplus samples can be collected in the subsequent sampling process, a sufficient number of samples can be still collected. Therefore, as many as possible samples should be collected from the remaining intervals while maintaining the balance. The reshape method for updating $divide\_num$ is designed as the follow:

$$num\_divide = \frac{(N - \sum_{i=1}^{j} n_i)}{set\_num_{left}} \quad (5)$$

In Equation (5), $set\_numleft$ represents the number of remaining intervals. Since samples of each subsequent interval is updated. Take the collection process of the positive samples as an example and suppose that the number of samples in small_positive intervals, nsmall, is the lowest and less than divide_num. Then, $divide\_num$ is updated to $(N - nsmall)/2$ for the sampling process in the subsequent intervals. If the number of samples in the medium_positive and big_positive intervals is greater than the updated value of divide_num, then they are uniformly sampled.hrough the balanced sampling method, factors such as scale and difficulty are fully considered in the process of generating the sample set, which can effectively increase the number of small object samples and ensure sample diversity.

3.4. Loss Function

Similar to other tow-stage methods, the loss function is defined as sum of classification and regression loss:

$$L_{total} = L_{cls}^{RPN} + L_{bbox}^{RPN} + L_{cls}^{Cat} + L_{bbox}^{Reg} \quad (6)$$

In Equation (6), L_{cls} and L_{bbox} denote classification and regression loss of MB-RPN and finetune loss respectively. Cross entropy is adopted for measuring the classification loss:

$$L_{cls}(y_i, y_i^*) = -[y_i^* log(y_i) + (1 - y_i^*) log(1 - y_i)] \quad (7)$$

where y_i and y_i^* denote the predict and annotated category respectively where y_i^* is 1 if the anchor is positive in MB-RPN and y_i^* is 1 at the dimension representing the object's category in label vector. L_{reg} denote the smooth L1 regression loss [7]:

$$L(t_i, t_i^*) = \begin{cases} 0.5(t_i - t_i^*)^2, & |x| < 1 \\ |x| - 0.5, & others \end{cases} \quad (8)$$

where t_i and t_i^* denote predict and annotated coordinate and scale transform:

$$\begin{cases} t_x = (x - x_a)/w_a & t_y = (y - y_a)/h_a \\ t_w = log(w/w_a) & t_h = log(h/h_a) \\ t_x^* = (x^* - x_a)/w_a & t_y^* = (y^* - y_a)/h_a \\ t_w^* = log(w^*/w_a) & t_h^* = log(h^*/h_a) \end{cases} \quad (9)$$

3.5. Discussion

In this section, both the framework and detail of proposed approach are introduced, the overall architecture is similar to FPN except positive/negative candidate sampling method are adjutsted. First, the framework is introduced, including network architecture, pre-trained backbone, object detection pipeline and network detail. Second, this section represents the matching mechanism multi-scale objects, the IOU threshold for small and medium anchors are reduced to ensure more small objects will be matching successfully. Third, a sampling algorithm is introduced to ensure the diversity of sampling results, all the samples are divided into different intervals, the algorithm tries to sample balance amount of samples in each of the interval. Finally, loss function of the proposed approach is introduced, including the cross entropy loss for classification and smooth L1 loss for localization.

4. Experiments

4.1. Benchmarks

The proposed approach are evaluated on two datasets: Object Detection in Aerial Images(DOTA) and e Unmanned Aerial Vehicle Benchmark(UAVB) [15,16], the detail of them are as the follow:

1. DOTA contains over 2000 remote images. All of the images are large size about over 4000 × 4000 pixels. Images are annotated by experts in aerial and remote image interpretation using 15 common object categories, such as plane, ship, harbor, etc. The objects' distribution of each category are shown in Figure 5a, the abbreviation of each category will be shown in Table 2.
2. UAVB contains a unmanned aerial vehicle dataset, each frame is of the size about 560 × 1000 pixels and contains high density small objects. Vehicle category include car, truck and bus. The objects' distribution of each category are shown in Figure 5b.

Table 2. Quantitative performance(AP%) of our model on DOTA benchmark datasets compared with comparison approaches. The best performance on each category is colored in red.

	SSD	RetinaNet	SRetinaNet	FPN	GA-RPN	Libra RCNN	MB-RPN
plane (pl)	81.3	88.7	86.2	88.9	88.4	89.7	90.2
baseball-diamond (bd)	50.6	64.5	57.8	75.8	75.2	73.6	77.0
bridge (bg)	39.1	47.5	21.4	48.6	43.1	49.7	53.0
ground-track-field (gtf)	44.2	49.0	49.5	53.9	53.5	54.8	53.3
small-vechicle (sv)	56.0	58.1	61.1	63.8	67.7	70.3	70.4
large-vehicle (lv)	54.2	57.8	59.0	63.6	66.3	65.0	66.0
ship (sp)	61.1	69.2	74.4	76.7	77.0	77.1	76.8
tennis-court (tc)	84.3	88.2	70.3	90.7	90.1	90.8	90.8
basketball-court (bc)	68.6	73.5	58.1	78.2	78.4	75.0	78.9
storage-tank (st)	61.5	75.6	80.5	81.0	84.1	83.0	83.7
soccer-ball-field (sbf)	21.3	28.4	16.7	36.5	36.8	37.2	41.2
roundabout (ra)	43.6	49.1	55.2	56.8	58.9	60.0	59.4
harbor (hb)	51.6	56.7	35.9	67.3	66.7	67.6	68.3
swimming-pool (st)	47.4	61.1	64.3	71.1	72.0	72.6	70.9
helicopter (hl)	28.0	38.6	57.1	44.7	50.3	62.6	56.5
mAP	56.9	60.6	58.1	65.5	66.8	67.6	68.5

Both the DOTA and UAVB dataset contain all kinds scale and small objects account a large proportion. It means that both the ability of detecting small objects and all the scale of objects are important.

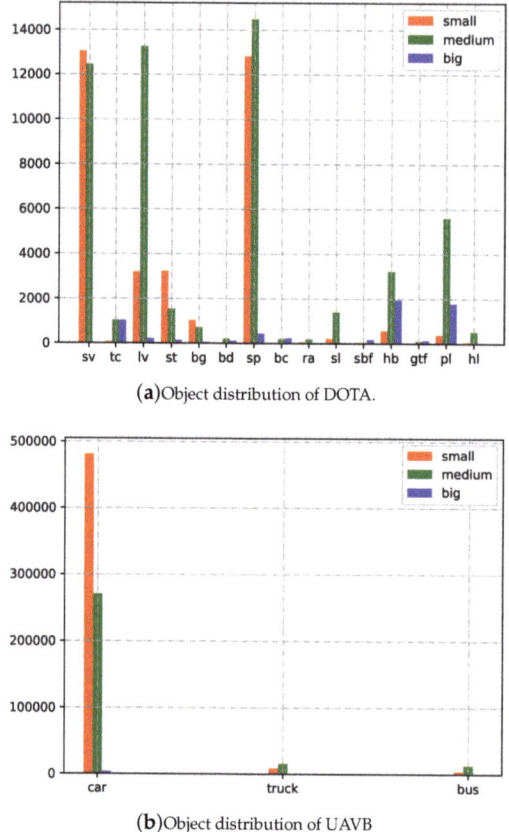

(**a**)Object distribution of DOTA.

(**b**)Object distribution of UAVB

Figure 5. Objects distribution of DOTA and UAVB dataset.

4.2. Implementation Detail

The network is established on Tensorflow and trained end-to-end.MB-RPN loss and detection loss are optimized simultaneous with Nvidia 1080Ti on Ubuntu operation system [17]. ResNet-101 pre-trained network is adopted to extract image features and other convolution layers were initialized randomly [14]. To optimize network parameters, Adam optimizer with lr=10^{-6}, $\beta_1 = 0.9$ and $\beta_2 = 0.999$ is adopted [18].

The input images were set to 600 × 600. For DOTA dataset, since the shape of training and testing images are much larger than input size, to reduce the loss of image resolution the images are cropped into input size with stride of 300 for training and testing and merge test results to original shape. For UAVB dataset, since the shape of training and testing images are similar to input size, it is only needed to resize the images to input size. The size of anchor boxes for layer Conv1~Conv5 are [32,64,128,256,512], which is consistent to the default value of FPN method. For DOTA dataset, aspect ratios of anchor boxes is [$\frac{1}{7}, \frac{1}{5}, \frac{1}{3}, \frac{1}{2}$,1,2,3,5,7] to adapt categories with both normal and slender shape such as bridge. For UAVB dataset, since the shape of all the categories are normal, therefore the aspect ratio is same to default FPN method. Mean average precision(mAP) is adopted to evaluate the proposed approach[19].

4.3. Effectiveness of Multi-Scale Sampling on Positive Sample

To evaluate the effectiveness of Multi-scale sampling for positive samples, the comparison of positive samples distribution on different scales between multi-scale and origin FPN sampling method on DOTA dataset, the result are shown in Figure 6. Since the IOU discrimination thresholds of small and medium objects are reduced, the amount positive samples are highly improved, which means more small anchor boxes are matched. The matching results are also visualized, compare to Figure 7 the matching results has been effectively improved.

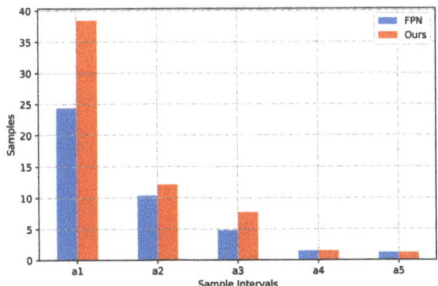

Figure 6. Distribution of multi-scale sampling and origin FPN sampling method.

Figure 7. Example of Multi-scale Sampling Results.

4.4. Effectiveness of Multi-Scale Balanced Sampling on Negative Samples

To evaluate the effectiveness of multi-scale balanced sampling, comparison of negative samples' distribution on different scales and IOU between MB-RPN, FPN and Libra RCNN sampling method on DOTA dataset, the result are shown in Figure 8, where $b_1 \sim b_8$ denote total amount of hard_small to easy_big negative samples. Most of the samples are Easy_small in FPN method, the Libra RCNN alleviate this situation significantly but the majority is still easy samples(b_1, b_3 and b_6), especially the easy_small samples, the multi-scale sampling further improved samples distribution situation. The matching results are also visualized in Figure 9, compare to FPN and Libra RCNN, the matching results has been effectively improved.

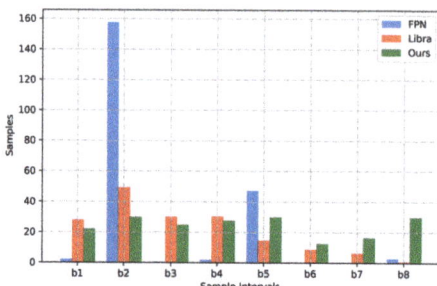

Figure 8. Distribution of multi-scale balanced, FPN and Libra RCNN sampling method.

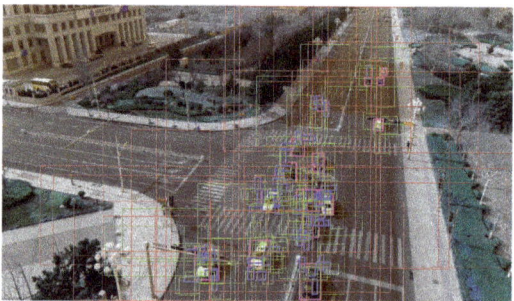

Figure 9. Example of Multi-scale Balanced Sampling Results of FPN, Libra RCNN and Multi-scale Balanced.

4.5. Performance Comparison with Other Method

Several one stage and two stage object detection methods is adopt to evaluate the effectiveness of MB-RPN: SSD [3] RetinaNet [10], FPN [8], Libra RCNN [11], GA-RPN [13] and SRetinaNet [12]. All of these methods except SRetinaNet are implemented with the source code provided by authors. For SRetinaNet method, it is implemented by adjusting hyperparameters of RetinaNet.

Table 2 shows the quantitative results on DOTA, the best performance for each category is colored in red. The mAP of MB-RPN achieves 68.5%, which outperform other methods. Compare with the one-stage approaches, since they are lack of positive/negative discrimination process, the detection accuracy are lower than all of the two-stage approaches obviously. Compare with original FPN, the mAP is 3% higher, moreover the AP of each category is also higher. Compare with GA-RPN and Libra RCNN, the mAP is increased about 1.7and 0.9% respectively, the AP of the most of categories are increased. The visualization comparison between MB-RPN and Libra RCNN is shown in Figure 10, MB-RPN detects more accurate small objects in various challenging cases, e.g., small vehicle objects at bottom left of Figure 10a and middle of Figure 10b. At the same time, the performances of other medium and big objects are not decreased. The above phenomenon proves the effectiveness of MB-RPN in enhancing the detection performances for images with small objects and large scale variants.

Considering the performances gap between one-stage and two-stage approaches, in this paper the performance comparison of UAVB dataset is only carried out between FPN, GA-RPN, Libra RCNN and MB-RPN. Table 3 shows the quantitative evaluation of these approaches, the best performance for each category is colored in red. All of the mAP acquired from the approaches above are not ideal, this may because the imbalance of samples. However, the MB-RPN still largely outperform other approaches on both mAP and AP for each category. Figure 11 provides a visual comparison of our approach and Libra RCNN, since both of the two approaches' performance are not ideal, it only shows the localization results but without categories. It can be seen that MB-RPN detects more small objects such as cars at upper of the input image which is corresponding to sampling results and distribution shown above. The above phenomenon proves the effectiveness of MB-RPN in enhancing the detection performances.

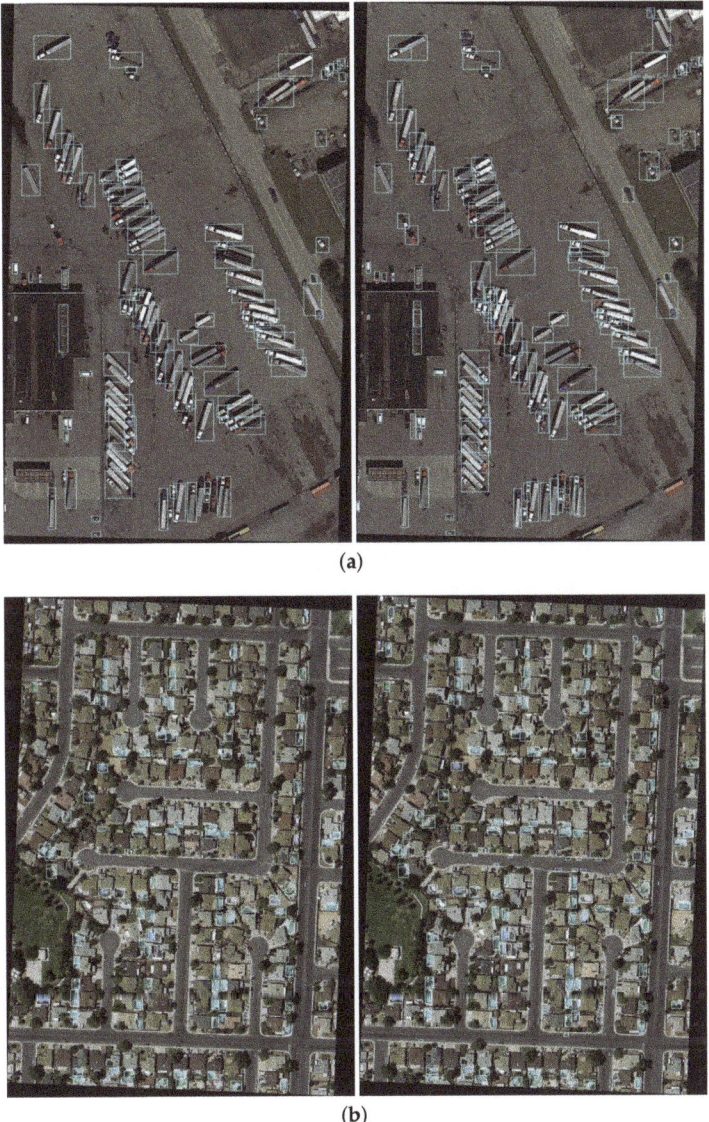

Figure 10. Selected visual comparison of DOTA benchmark dataset. Each subfigure include result of Libra RCNN on the left and MB-RPN on the right. (**a**) small objects (**b**) middle objects.

Table 3. Quantitative performance(AP%) of our model on UAVB benchmark datasets compared with comparison approaches. The best performance on each category is colored in red.

	FPN	GA-RPN	Libra RCNN	MB-RPN
car	45.1	47.2	48.8	51.2
bus	5.3	8.6	7.2	21.7
truck	28.2	31.5	31.1	33.2
mAP	21.1	21.7	23.0	29.4

Figure 11. Selected visual comparison of DOTA benchmark dataset which includes Libra RCNN on the top and MB-RPN on the bottom.

4.6. Disscusion

In this section, the experimental settings and results are introduced. First, the adopted DOTA and UAVB dataset are introduced, including their amounts of training/testing images and the distribution of each category samples. Second, implement details are represented, including the input size, crop mechanism of large images, parameter initialization and optimization method and hardware/software platform. Finally, both quantitative and visualized comparison are represented, the results show that under the equal conditions MB-RPN outperform other similar methods.

5. Conclusions

In this paper, a multi-scale balanced sampling approach for detecting small objects in complex scenes is proposed. With multi-scale positive sampling method, more small objects is able to be included in the network training process. With the balanced negative sampling method, the diversity of negative samples is ensured. Experimental results shows that compare with other similar methods, this approach acquire better performances on the images with small objects and large scale variant objects.

Author Contributions: Conceptualization, H.Y.; methodology, H.Y., J.G.; software, H.Y.; validation, H.Y.; writing—original draft preparation, H.Y.; writing—review and editing, D.C.; supervision, D.C.; funding acquisition, D.C. and J.G. All authors have read and agreed to the published version of the manuscript.

Funding: This research was funded by Beijing Municipal Natural Science Foundation (4182031).

Conflicts of Interest: The authors declare no conflict of interest.

References

1. Pang, Y.; Yuan, Y.; Li, X.; Pan, J. Efficient hog human detection. *Signal Process.* **2011**, *91*, 773–781. [CrossRef]
2. Felzenszwalb, P.F.; Girshick, R.B.; McAllester, D. Cascade object detection with deformable part models. In Proceedings of the 2010 IEEE Computer Society Conference on Computer Vision and Pattern recognition, San Francisco, CA, USA, 13–18 June 2010; pp. 2241–2248.
3. Liu, W.; Anguelov, D.; Erhan, D.; Szegedy, C.; Reed, S.; Fu, C.Y.; Berg, A.C. Ssd: Single shot multibox detector. In *European Conference on Computer Vision*; Springer: Cham, Switzerland, 2016; pp. 21–37.
4. Lin, T.Y.; Maire, M.; Belongie, S.; Hays, J.; Perona, P.; Ramanan, D.; Dollár, P.; Zitnick, C.L. Microsoft coco: Common objects in context. In *European Conference on Computer Vision*; Springer: Cham, Switzerland, 2014; pp. 740–755.
5. Ren, S.; He, K.; Girshick, R.; Sun, J. Faster r-cnn: Towards real-time object detection with region proposal networks. In *Advances in Neural Information Processing Systems*; NeuralIPS: Montreal, QC, Canada, 2015; pp. 91–99.
6. Girshick, R.; Donahue, J.; Darrell, T.; Malik, J. Rich feature hierarchies for accurate object detection and semantic segmentation. In Proceedings of the IEEE Conference on Computer Vision and Pattern Recognition, Columbus, OH, USA, 23–28 June 2014; pp. 580–587.
7. Girshick, R. Fast R-cnn. In Proceedings of the IEEE International Conference on Computer Vision, Santiago, Chile, 11–18 December 2015; pp. 1440–1448.
8. Lin, T.Y.; Dollár, P.; Girshick, R.; He, K.; Hariharan, B.; Belongie, S. Feature pyramid networks for object detection. In Proceedings of the IEEE Conference on Computer Vision and Pattern Recognition, Honolulu, WI, USA, 21–26 July 2017; pp. 2117–2125.
9. Cai, Z.; Vasconcelos, N. Cascade R-CNN: Delving Into High Quality Object Detection. In Proceedings of the IEEE Conference on Computer Vision and Pattern Recognition, Salt Lake City, UT, USA, 18–23 June 2018; pp. 6154–6162
10. Lin, T.Y.; Goyal, P.; Girshick, R.; He, K.; Dollár, P. Focal loss for dense object detection. In Proceedings of the IEEE International Conference on Computer Vision, Venice, Italy, 22–29 October 2017; pp. 2980–2988.
11. Pang, J.; Chen, K.; Shi, J.; Feng, H.; Ouyang, W.; Lin, D. Libra r-cnn: Towards balanced learning for object detection. In Proceedings of the IEEE Conference on Computer Vision and Pattern Recognition, Seoul, Korea, 27 October–2 November 2019; pp. 821–830.
12. Ahmad, M.; Abdullah, M.; Han, D. Small Object Detection in Aerial Imagery using RetinaNet with Anchor Optimization. In Proceedings of the International Conference on Electronics, Information, and Communication, Barcelona, Spain, 19–22 January 2020; pp.1–3.
13. Wang, J.; Chen, K.; Yang, S,.; Loy, C.C.; Lin, D. Region proposal by guided anchoring. In Proceedings of the IEEE Conference on Computer Vision and Pattern Recognition, Long Beach, CA, USA, 16–20 June 2019; pp. 2965–2974.
14. He, K.; Zhang, X.; Ren, S.; Sun, J. Deep residual learning for image recognition. In Proceedings of the IEEE Conference on Computer Vision and Pattern Recognition, Las Vegas, NV, USA, 27–30 June 2016; pp. 770–778.
15. Xia, G.S.; Bai, X.; Ding, J.; Zhu, Z.; Belongie, S.; Luo, J.; Datcu, M.; Pelillo, M.; Zhang, L. DOTA: A large-scale dataset for object detection in aerial images. In Proceedings of the IEEE Conference on Computer Vision and Pattern Recognition, Salt Lake City, UT, USA, 18–23 June 2018; pp. 3974–3983.
16. Du, D.; QI ,Y.; Yu, H.; Yang, Y.; Duan, K.; LI, G.; Zhang, W.; Huang, Q.; Tian, Q. The Unmanned Aerial Vehicle Benchmark: Object Detection, Tracking and Baseline.*Int. J. Comput. Vis.* **2020**, *128*, 1141–1159.
17. Girija, S.S. Tensorflow: Large-scale machine learning on heterogeneous distributed systems. *Softw. Avail. Tensorflow. Org.* **2016**, *39*, 1–9.
18. Kingma D.P.; Ba, J. Adam: A method for stochastic optimization. *arXiv* **2014**, arXiv:1412.6980.
19. Vicente, S.; Carreira, J.; Agapito, L.; Batista, J. Reconstructing pascal voc. In Proceedings of the IEEE Conference on Computer Vision and Pattern Recognition, Columbus, OH, USA, 23–28 June 2014; pp. 41–48.

© 2020 by the authors. Licensee MDPI, Basel, Switzerland. This article is an open access article distributed under the terms and conditions of the Creative Commons Attribution (CC BY) license (http://creativecommons.org/licenses/by/4.0/).

Article

Advances in Optical Image Analysis Textural Segmentation in Ironmaking

Eugene Donskoi * and Andrei Poliakov

CSIRO Mineral Resources, PO Box 883, Kenmore, QLD 4069, Australia; andrei.poliakov@csiro.au
* Correspondence: Eugene.Donskoi@csiro.au; Tel.: +61-422-464-438

Received: 27 July 2020; Accepted: 6 September 2020; Published: 8 September 2020

Featured Application: The algorithms described in the article can be used in any applications of image processing for recognition/segmentation of phases/morphologies, particularly in mineralogical image analysis. Their specific application field is ironmaking and corresponding optical image analysis of iron ore, sinter, and coke.

Abstract: Optical image analysis is commonly used to characterize different feedstock material for ironmaking, such as iron ore, iron ore sinter, coal and coke. Information is often needed for phases which have the same reflectivity and chemical composition, but different morphology. Such information is usually obtained by manual point counting, which is quite expensive and may not provide consistent results between different petrologists. To perform accurate segmentation of such phases using automated optical image analysis, the software must be able to identify specific textures. CSIRO's Carbon Steel Futures group has developed an optical image analysis software package called Mineral4/Recognition4, which incorporates a dedicated textural identification module allowing segmentation of such phases. The article discusses the problems associated with segmentation of similar phases in different ironmaking feedstock material using automated optical image analysis and demonstrates successful algorithms for textural identification. The examples cover segmentation of three different coke phases: two types of Inert Maceral Derived Components (IMDC), non-reacted and partially reacted, and Reacted Maceral Derived Components (RMDC); primary and secondary hematite in iron ore sinter; and minerals difficult to distinguish with traditional thresholding in iron ore.

Keywords: image analysis; texture; structure; optical; coke; iron ore; sinter; image processing; segmentation; identification

1. Introduction

More than 150 years ago Henry Clifton Sorby [1] used optical microscopy for the characterization of rocks and minerals. He developed the basic techniques of petrography, using the polarizing microscope to study the structure of rock thin sections. In the early twentieth century Murdoch [2] started to use measurements of ore mineral reflectance combined with microchemical techniques for mineral identification.

Presently, the mineralogy of commercial raw materials, such as iron ore, can be determined from X-ray diffraction (XRD) analysis, but for subsequent processing purposes it is also important to understand the actual abundance of each mineral, association/liberation characteristics, dimensional characteristics of particles and mineral grains, surface roughness, porosity and density, the presence of different textures, the reciprocal position of mineral grains, and other morphological and morphometric characteristics. For these purposes, imaging techniques such as scanning electron microscopy [3–6], Raman spectroscopy [7] and optical image analysis (OIA) [8–12] are used. Generally, these methods can segment different minerals, but identification of different morphologies of the same mineral requires the further application of textural/structural segmentation.

The standard method for mineral segmentation in OIA is thresholding [13], where minerals are segmented by their color and brightness. An example of hematite thresholding in crushed iron ore sinter is given in Figure 1. Segmentation of hematite, which is the brightest mineral in the digital image, is actually performed using three color channels, but for simplicity, only the red channel reflectivity histogram used to determine the selected phase is shown. The reflectivity range of hematite corresponds to the last peak in the histogram. Figure 1b shows a partially successful attempt to automatically identify hematite. In this example, the hematite areas with relatively lower reflectance are not identified, and from the reflectivity histogram it is evident that the hematite peak is only partially covered by the range between the lower and the upper limits, or thresholds. Only the image pixels with red channel reflectivity within those thresholds are identified as hematite in this example. However when the whole of the last peak in the reflectivity histogram is thresholded, the hematite becomes fully segmented (Figure 1c). The use of multispectral image acquisition systems based on narrow bandwidth (e.g., 10 nm) interference filters show more efficient segmentation of minerals compared to colour imaging using tristimulus (red, green, blue) filters [14–17].

For sinter characterization it is very important to segment the primary, or unreacted, hematite remaining after the sintering process, from the secondary hematite which precipitated from the sinter melt during cooling. The sinter particle at the left hand side of Figure 1a has only secondary hematite present, whereas the particle to the right contains both phases. The large hematite grain indicated by an arrow in the bottom-right corner of the image is a good example of primary hematite. Figure 1b clearly shows that, after partial thresholding, the amounts of both types of hematite were underestimated, which means that thresholding alone is unable to segment one type of hematite from another. The size of hematite grains also cannot be reliably used for segmentation. While primary hematite grains are generally large, it is clear that some of the secondary hematite grains in the particle to the left are larger than some of the primary hematite grains in the particle to the right.

For coke characterization it is important to segment Inert Maceral Derived Components (IMDC) and Reacted Maceral Derived components (RMDC) [18,19]. However, they also cannot be segmented by simple thresholding as discussed in the section on coke characterization.

In order to quantify coke phases that are difficult to segment automatically, as well as certain sinter phases such as primary and secondary hematite discussed above, the traditional approach employs manual point counting by a trained petrographer. The problem with this approach, apart from it being labor intensive and thus expensive, is that it can be very subjective. It is even possible for an individual petrographer to report different results for the same sample if re-analyzed after a significant time.

Automated optical image analysis reduces the subjectivity and makes the characterization more consistent. The approach adopted during OIA to segment phases with similar reflectivity would be analogous to what petrographers employ during manual point counting—i.e., segmentation by structure/texture.

CSIRO's Carbon Steel Futures group developed the optical image analysis software Mineral4/Recognition4 for optical image analysis of major ironmaking feedstock materials such as ores (iron ore in particular) including lump and fine ores, sinters, pellets and briquettes, coal, coke etc. [9,10]. It can comprehensively characterize phase abundances, porosity, liberation/association, texture, and other sample characteristics. The first and the most important step during characterization is the correct identification of phases (see [14]). Even if a multi-thresholding [20] approach is used, it will not necessarily allow for the acceptable segmentation of phases when their reflectivities overlap. To achieve this, a textural identification module was developed for the software, allowing the segmentation of phases which have the same or significantly overlapping reflectivity, but different morphology. To characterize a particular material, an "analysis profile" is developed, which records individual parameter settings and adjustments made during different stages of image analysis. The textural identification unit is a subset of the mineral/phase identification stage. It is engaged when necessary and can perform differently for different materials/phases according to the profile settings.

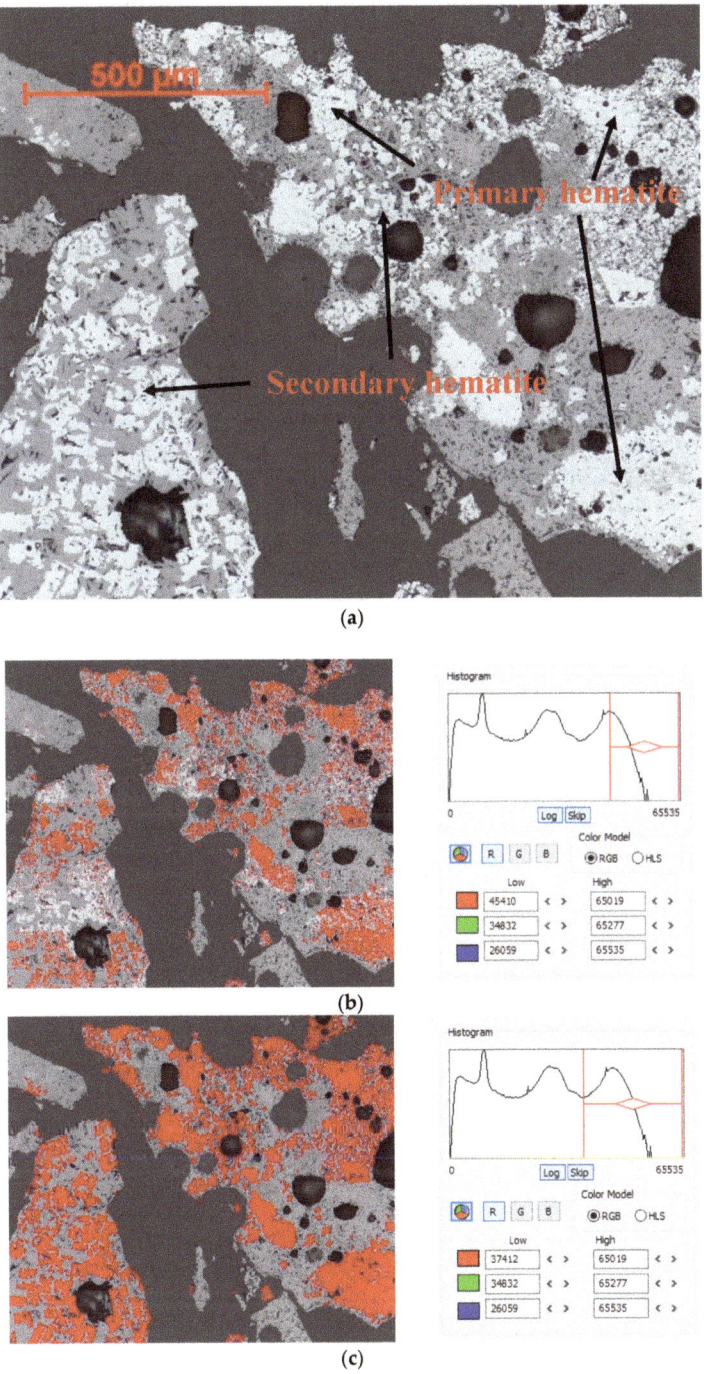

Figure 1. Thresholding of hematite in sinter during image analysis: (**a**) original image; (**b**) partial identification of hematite (segmentation of the brightest part); and (**c**) full identification. Reflectivity histograms show the different red channel low and high threshold values and represent screenshots from Zeiss AxioVision software.

This article demonstrates algorithms developed for textural segmentation of different ironmaking feedstock materials performed by the textural identification module in Mineral4/Recognition4. These algorithms are based on well-established image analysis procedures such as binary Erosion, Dilation, size-based noise reduction (Scrapping) etc. [21]. Similar approaches can also be used for image analysis of any other materials within a very wide range of possible OIA applications.

2. Textural Segmentation in OIA of Coke

Metallurgical coke is one of the major components of the blast furnace load, and its qualities, such as strength, abrasion resistance and reactivity, which are strongly dependent on coke structure/texture, are critical for stable blast furnace operation. OIA enables an improved understanding of the relationships between coke quality, parent coal blend composition and coke structure/texture. This allows for the improvement and optimization of the processes involved in coke production, such as parent coal blending, sizing, coking, etc.

In this section we essentially discuss coke "structure", defining it as the spatial distribution of porosity and the coke matrix, which consists of different coked/reacted macerals. In many disciplines within mineral processing, the term "texture" means approximately the same as "structure". However, when applied to coke characterization, "texture" is understood to mean the spatial distribution of different isotropic and anisotropic carbon types within the coke, typically determined during optical imaging by differences in bi-reflectance [18,19].

During coking of parent coal blends, some macerals, such as different types of vitrinite, are significantly fluidized and thus subject to a stronger reaction. The parts of the coke matrix resulting from such reactions are called Reacted Maceral Derived Components (RMDC). The non-reacted or significantly less reacted types of macerals (inerts) form Inert Maceral Derived Components (IMDC). One of the major tasks during the characterization of coke structure is to determine the relative amounts of carbonaceous materials with different degrees of reaction. The relative abundance and corresponding size distributions of these coke phases show strong significant correlations with different coke strength indices and parent coal blend composition [18]. For example, a study by Donskoi et al. [18] confirmed the earlier findings of Kubota et al. [22] that 1.5 mm is the critical size for IMDC affecting coke strength.

Mineral4 segments and comprehensively characterizes three different phases in coke matrix: unreacted IMDC, partially reacted IMDC and RMDC. Figure 2a shows an image obtained using a narrow bandwidth (±5 nm) green filter (λ = 546 nm) of coke made from medium rank coal. In the image, the unreacted areas (unreacted IMDC), slightly reacted areas (partially reacted IMDC), and the very porous network connecting them together (RMDC) are clearly evident. The results of automated segmentation of these structural components are given in Figure 2b. It is clear that unreacted IMDC grains can have different structures; some are quite dense, showing almost no porosity, whereas others are quite porous. This complicates the task of properly identifying them by structure. Standard segmentation by thresholding is also of limited use here. While the coke matrix as a whole can be reliably thresholded to distinguish it from porosity, there is no critical difference in reflectivity between IMDC and RMDC.

Mineral4 Textural Identification uses three different methods to identify various areas of unreacted IMDC and then combines the results into one unreacted IMDC map. These three methods are bulk identification of IMDC, porous IMDC identification and identification of "washed out" IMDC. Similar methodology is used for identification of the partially reacted IMDC. The remainder of the coke matrix is then considered to be RMDC. It is important to highlight that the understanding of RMDC structure as the one consisting of thin walls and large pores is applied in some IMDC identification methods to exclude areas that are "not IMDC". Generally, for successful structural segmentation, a knowledge of the individual features of all phases is critical.

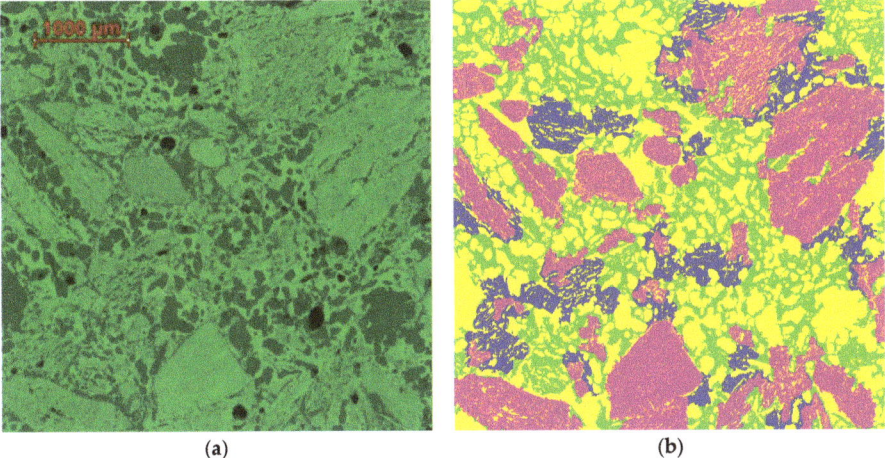

Figure 2. (a) Image of coke made from medium rank coal using a green filter (λ = 546 nm); (b) the structural map corresponding to this image (magenta—unreacted IMDC, blue—partially reacted IMDC, green—RMDC, yellow—porosity).

2.1. Bulk IMDC Textural Identification

"Bulk identification" of IMDC is based on the discrimination of a large nucleus of unreacted, non-porous IMDC surrounded by RMDC or partially reacted IMDC. The algorithm is presented in Figure 3. Initially a binary map of the coke matrix is obtained by thresholding (Figure 3a). Next, this map is dilated to remove the finest porosity (up to 5–7 µm) within different parts of the coke matrix (Figure 3b). In the next step, a strong erosion is applied with the purpose of removing all parts of the coke matrix where porosity is still present (Figure 3c). The majority of the removed matrix is supposed to be porous RMDC or partially reacted IMDC. However, IMDC areas with larger internal pores, as well as IMDC boundaries, may also be affected. Some dilation is applied to re-connect pieces of non-porous IMDC in the following step, in case they were broken apart by erosion because of large internal pores or cracks (Figure 3d). Further down objects smaller than a certain size, which are typically the remnants of coagulated RMDC, are scrapped, after which extra dilation is applied to fully compensate for the previous erosion, thus reconstructing the IMDC grain areas (Figure 3e). When the original coke matrix (Figure 3a) is masked with that map, the result is the full map of non-porous or very finely porous IMDC (Figure 3f). Comparison of IMDC identified in Figure 3f with the unreacted IMDC present in Figure 2b, however, shows that, for instance, the large piece of IMDC in the top-right corner is almost lost. The reason is that this IMDC grain is noticeably more porous compared to those identified by the "bulk identification" method. To identify such IMDC areas the porous IMDC identification method must be used.

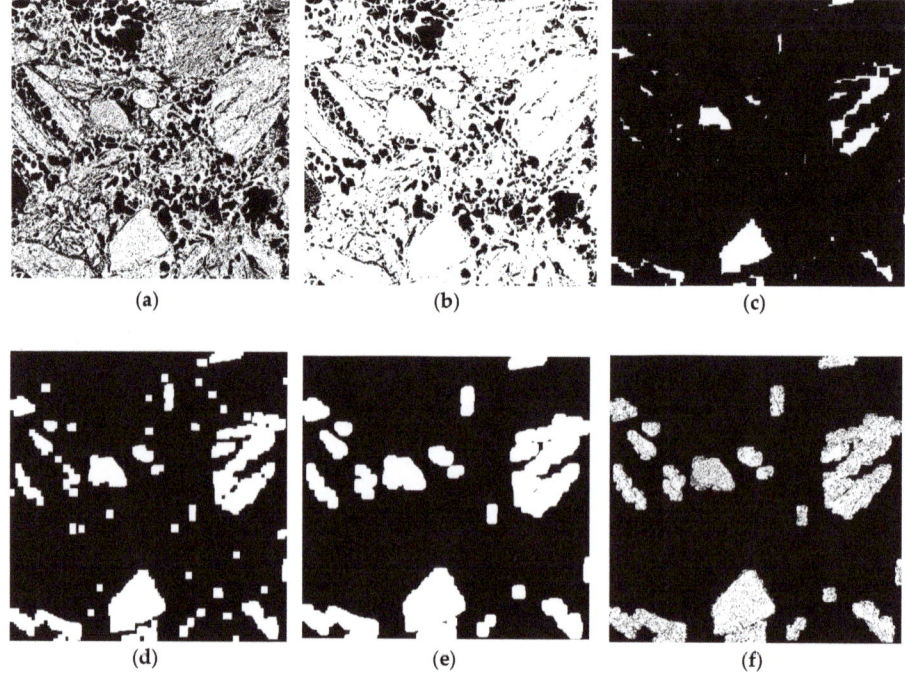

Figure 3. The algorithm of "bulk identification" of unreacted IMDC: (**a**) coke matrix identified as a binary map; (**b**) moderate dilation applied; (**c**) strong erosion applied; (**d**) intermediate dilation; (**e**) scrapping of fine objects and final dilation; (**f**) map of non-porous and very finely porous IMDC.

2.2. Porous IMDC Textural Identification

Even though the method is called "porous IMDC identification", the porosity of such IMDC is still smaller in size than typical porosity present in the reacted or partially reacted part of the coke matrix. To identify porous IMDC, a binary map of coke porosity, which is essentially the inverted map of the coke matrix (Figure 3a), is created (Figure 4a). Further, all fine porosity (less than 10 µm thickness) is scrapped (Figure 4b) and the resulting map is dilated (Figure 4c). In the next step, this map, representing areas where large pores are predominant, is inverted (Figure 4d) and subtracted from the original map of the whole porosity (Figure 4e). These operations allow clusters of fine porosity, which typically represent IMDC areas, to be identified. Such areas can be solidified by strong dilation (Figure 4f). However, this map also contains significant amounts of RMDC, which too can have fine porosity. Strong erosion is then applied to remove possible RMDC areas still associated with large pores (Figure 4g). After subsequent dilation, compensating for such erosion, filling holes and scrapping of small objects with size less than identifiable porous IMDC (Figure 4h) the resulting map is then used to mask the map of the coke matrix (Figure 3a) and obtain a map of porous IMDC (Figure 4i). After a last scrapping of small objects this map is considered final. It is evident that some non-porous IMDC areas are not included in this map, for example, parts of the IMDC grain in the lower central part of the image. It is also clear that porous IMDC identification is capable of segmenting IMDC areas much smaller in size than bulk IMDC identification, even when they are fully surrounded by RMDC (see Figure 2). Small non-porous pieces of IMDC cannot be reliably distinguished from RMDC by analyzing the coke matrix or simple thresholding, but for more precise studies, textural/bi-reflectance characterization can be used [19].

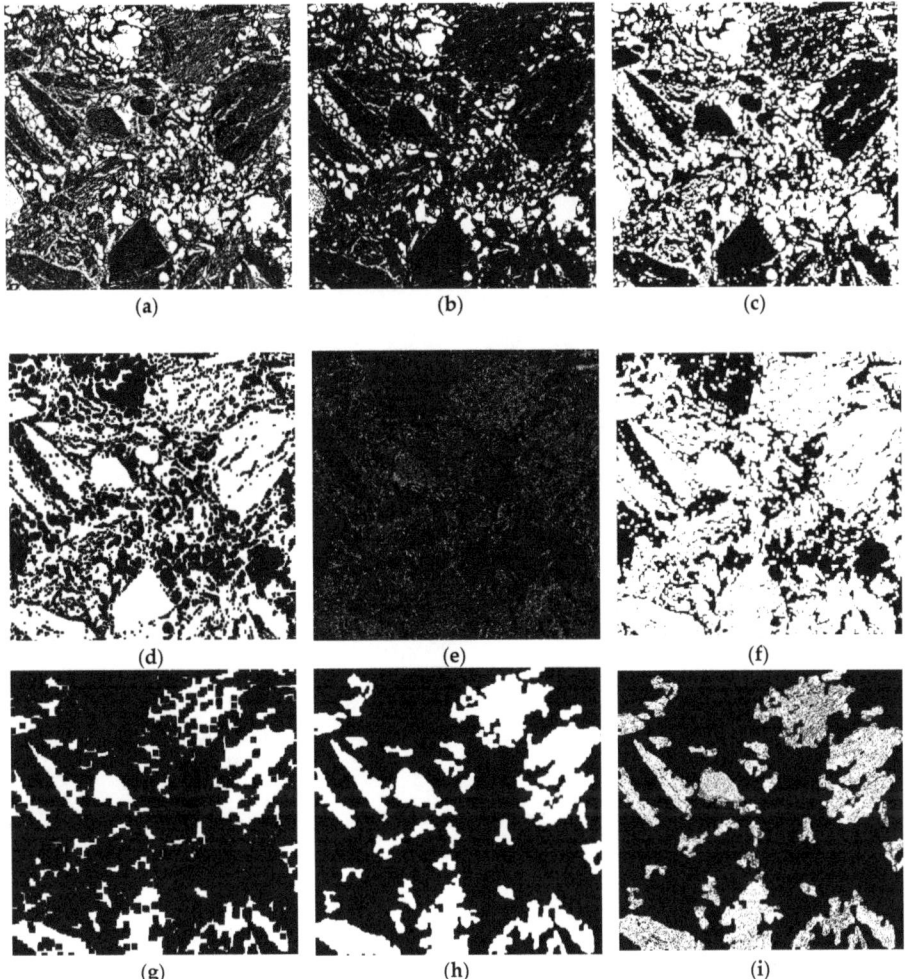

Figure 4. The algorithm of "Porous IMDC Identification" of not reacted IMDC: (**a**) the whole porosity identified as binary map; (**b**) fine porosity removed; (**c**) dilation applied; (**d**) map inverted; (**e**) clusters of fine porosity identified; (**f**) strong dilation (**g**) strong erosion; (**h**) compensating dilation; (**i**) map of porous IMDC.

2.3. "Washed out" IMDC Textural Identification

In the majority of cases, the IMDC identification methods described above work quite well. However, in certain cokes, some IMDC areas are quite dark in appearance, even darker than epoxy, and cannot be thresholded as a part of the coke matrix. In these cases an extra identification method is needed (Figure 5). Several explanations can be offered for such appearance of IMDC. One possibility is that such IMDC may have very fine porosity which is not impregnated by epoxy during block preparation. Alternatively, some of these areas may have a very weak structure and so are destroyed, plucked out and/or "washed out" (the general term used to call these areas) during the polishing of the block surface. The rest of the coke matrix is brighter than epoxy, so these dark areas are not included when coke matrix is segmented.

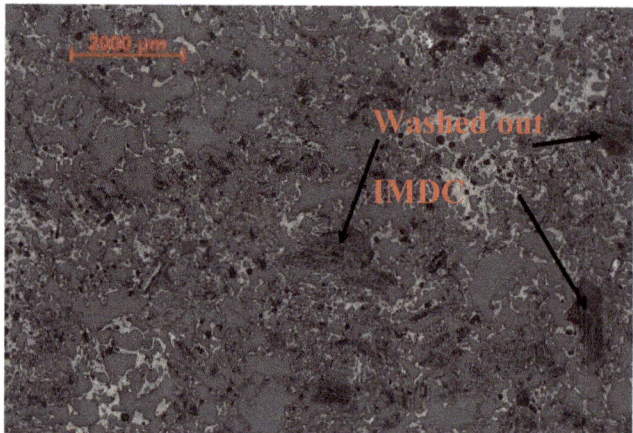

Figure 5. Photomicrograph of coke with the significant presence of dark/"washed out" IMDC.

For segmentation of "washed out" IMDC, thresholding of areas with reflectivity higher than that of porosity but lower than epoxy is performed (Figure 6a,b). Next, moderate dilation is performed (Figure 6c) to preserve the washed out IMDC areas during following strong erosion (Figure 6d). After dilation, compensating for that strong erosion, filling holes and scrapping of undersized objects (Figure 6e), the areas of washed out IMDC are determined. Masking those areas with the combination of the map in Figure 6a and the coke matrix gives the actual map of washed out IMDC (see Figures 2b and 6f).

There exists a possibility that the described method may also identify dark minerals with reflectivity between that of porosity and epoxy. If such minerals are known to be sufficiently present in the sample as relatively large grains, they should be identified texturally prior to IMDC identification in the workflow. If that cannot be achieved, a decision should be made about whether the "washed out" identification method should be included in the whole IMDC identification procedure. For the coke shown in Figure 5, it was in fact critically important to include such identification due to the significant presence of "washed out" areas.

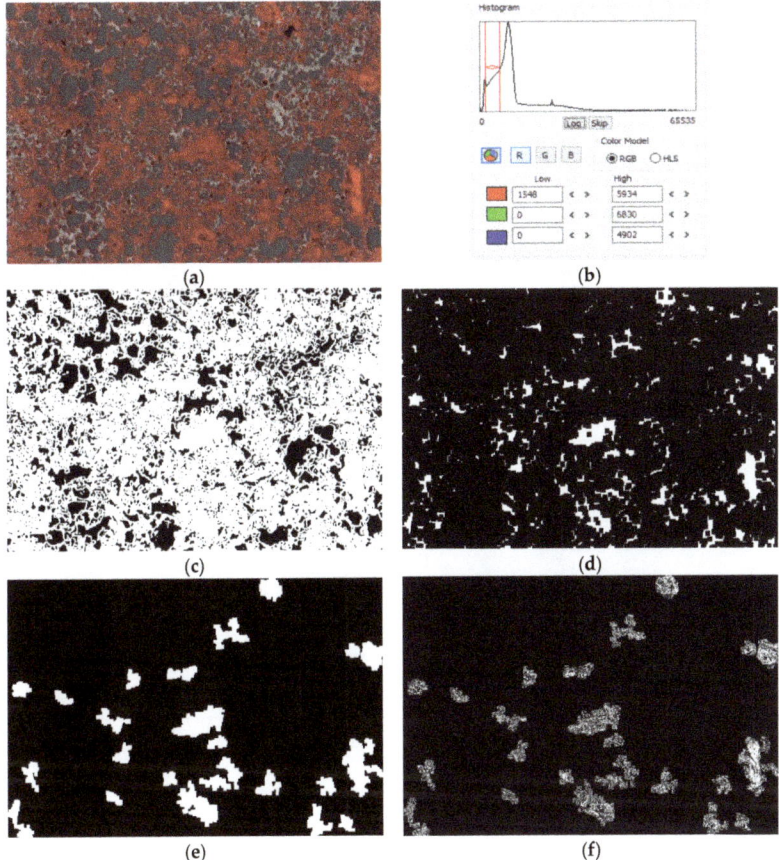

Figure 6. Segmentation of "washed out" IMDC: (**a**) thresholding of areas darker than epoxy but lighter than porosity; (**b**) reflectivity histogram with thresholds corresponding to (**a**); (**c**) dilation of binary map obtained from thresholding; (**d**) strong erosion leaving denser IMCD-like areas; (**e**) areas of washed out IMDC; (**f**) final map of washed out IMDC.

2.4. Textural Segmentation of Partially Reacted IMDC

Partially reacted IMDC (PR IMDC) areas segmented by porous IMDC identification should have porosity smaller in size than that of RMDC, but higher than unreacted IMDC. This is the main criterion used to identify them. The algorithms used for segmentation are the same as for bulk and porous IMDC identification, but the processing parameters are slightly adjusted to segment the correct areas. The result of bulk IMDC identification with increased dilation, erosion and scrap parameters applied for PR IMDC segmentation to the image from Figure 2 is given in Figure 7a. The result of porous IMDC identification with similarly increased parameters is provided in Figure 7b. Figure 7c shows the preliminary PR IMDC area identification obtained by combining the two identifications described above and subsequent removal of areas already identified as non-reacted IMDC. Along with the correct PR IMC identification, Figure 7c also includes some relatively thin and small RMDC areas attached to non-reacted IMDC. These areas can be removed by scrapping, leaving only the valid PR IMDC identified (see Figures 2 and 7d).

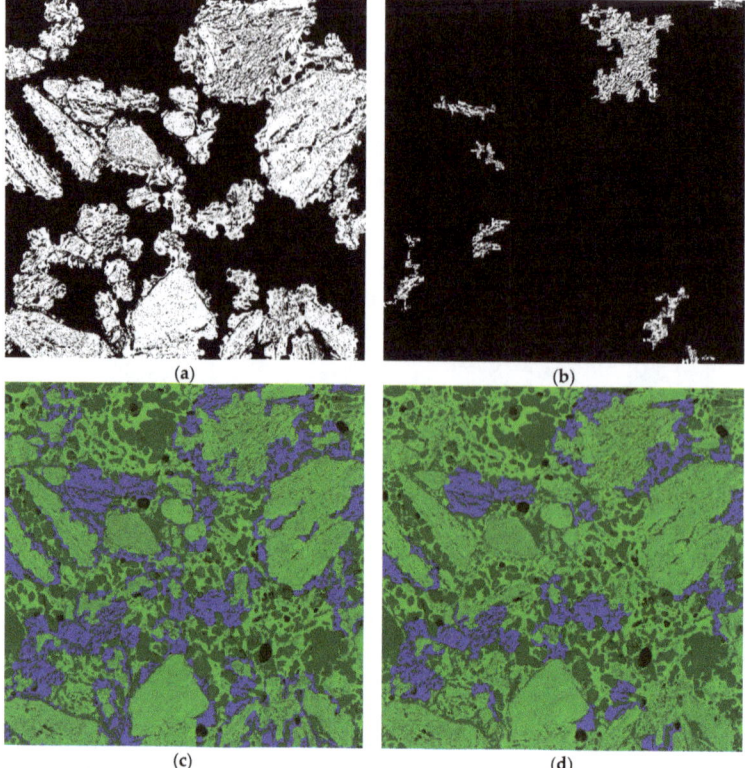

Figure 7. Segmentation of partially reacted IMDC: (**a**) bulk IMDC identification of PR IMDC; (**b**) porous IMDC identification of PR IMDC; (**c**) the combination of (**a**) and (**b**) with not reacted IMDC removed (blue); (**d**) PR IMDC areas (blue).

3. Textural Segmentation in OIA of Iron Ore Sinter

Together with coke, iron ore sinter is the one of the major blast furnace loads. It can constitute up to 70–85% of the total ferrous burden fed to the blast furnace and its quality is also very important for stable blast furnace operation. The quality of sinter (e.g., its strength and reducibility) mainly depends on its petrology and texture, which in turn are determined by the initial ore blend, the fluxes added to the blend, and the sintering conditions. To optimize sinter quality and productivity the relationships between the initial sinter mix, sintering conditions and sinter structure, petrology and porosity must be understood [23–26].

One of the important characteristics of iron ore sinter is the quantity of primary and secondary hematite, which can provide insights into the presence of large grains of hematite in the initial iron ore blend, the degree of reaction and sintering conditions. The two types of hematite have very similar, or the same, mineral chemistry and reflectivity, so they cannot be segmented by standard scanning electron microscopy or optical image analysis methods. However, they have different morphology and phase associations which can be discriminated by OIA. Primary hematite generally does not contain inclusions of melt-precipitated phases and often preserves the morphology of the original ore particle. Secondary hematite, which mostly precipitates during cooling from the sinter melt, has crystals fully surrounded by, and/or including, other melt-precipitated sinter phases, such as Silico-Ferrites of Calcium and Aluminium (SFCA), undifferentiated glass, and larnite (di-calcium silicate). The presence or absence of these spatially associated phases is the key feature used by Mineral4 for textural segmentation of the two types of hematite.

As a starting point for OIA processing, a map of all hematite in the sinter image is obtained by standard thresholding (Figure 1a,c and Figure 8a). A combined map of all phases which are typically associated with secondary hematite, such as SFCA, glass and larnite, is also prepared (Figure 8b). This second map is scrapped of its finest elements (to exclude the effect of imaging artefacts) and then strongly dilated to create a map of areas associated with the melt-precipitated phases (Figure 8c). Next, these areas are removed from the overall map of hematite. After additional scrap, removing undersized regions, only the areas of primary hematite are left in the map (Figure 8d). More dilation follows to compensate for loss during strong dilation of SFCA/glass areas (Figure 8e). Finally the map is masked with the original hematite map (Figure 8f) and fine/undersized objects are removed from it. The resulting identification of primary and, by exclusion, secondary hematite is shown in Figure 9.

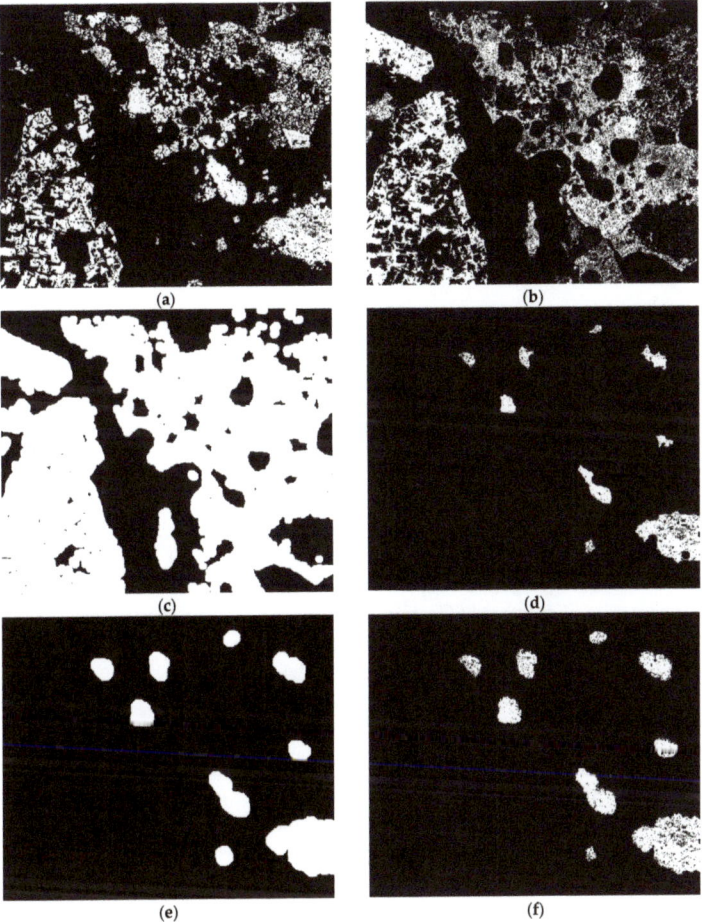

Figure 8. Textural segmentation of primary hematite in iron ore sinter: (**a**) map of all hematite in the image; (**b**) map of SFCA and all phases darker than SFCA; (**c**) map of areas associated with glass and SFCA; (**d**) hematite map without areas associated with melt-precipitated phases; (**e**) map of possible areas for primary hematite; (**f**) identified areas of primary hematite including smaller grains to be removed later based on size.

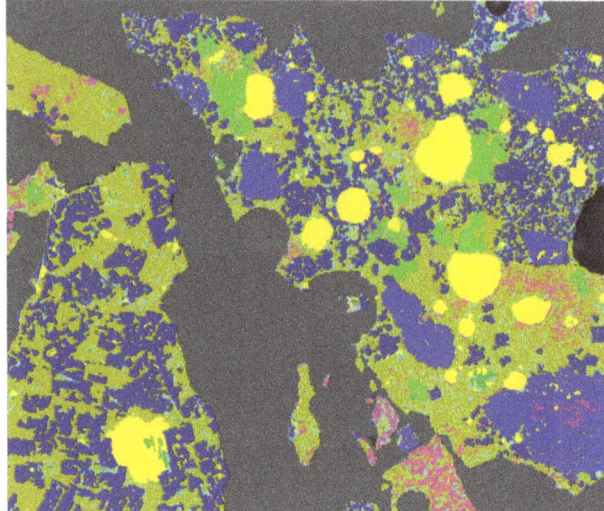

Figure 9. Mineral map for the image in Figure 1a produced by Mineral4 software during automated image analysis: primary hematite—light blue, secondary hematite—dark blue, magnetite—magenta, platy SFCA-I—light green, prismatic/dense SFCA—olive, glass—dark green, larnite—cyan, porosity and epoxy within particles—yellow.

Figure 9 demonstrates the false color map of all sinter phases identified by Mineral4 software during automated image analysis of the crushed sinter shown in Figure 1a. Note that the large grain of primary hematite in the bottom right corner includes some remnant kenomagnetite. Magnetite may still be present in stable ore nuclei remaining after sintering, not just as one of melt-precipitated sinter phases. Therefore, it is not included as part of the melt-precipitated phases in the map (Figure 8b). It is still clear that the majority of magnetite present in Figure 9 is melt-precipitated.

The other pertinent textural segmentation by OIA shown in Figure 9 is that of two types of SFCA: microporous platy SFCA-I (light green) and prismatic/dense SFCA (olive). These two phases have the same reflectivity but different morphology. SFCA-I has slightly higher iron contents which may be determined by SEM methods [27,28]. However, in OIA sinter characterization, textural identification is required for segmentation of different SFCA types. As SFCA-I often has fine porosity evident between adjacent plates, this can be utilized for the textural segmentation. The actual algorithm is very similar to that utilized for porous IMDC identification described above.

4. Textural Segmentation in OIA of Iron Ore

Many authors have demonstrated the importance of iron ore textural characterisation [29–36] for the optimization of downstream processing performance. Donskoi et al. [23,24] showed that the presence of textural information for parent iron ore blend allows a significant improvement in modelling of iron ore sinter quality. It also provides better modelling and deeper understanding of beneficiation processes [34,35,37].

Quantitative mineral characterization, sometimes including identification of different morphologies of the same mineral, is required to correctly texturally classify iron ores. Figure 10a shows an image of iron ore consisting of two hematite types: microplaty hematite (thin, long plates) and martite. To better understand the reactivity of such an ore, its behavior during pelletising, granulation and sintering, it is important to know the abundances of both types of hematite. Textural segmentation in this particular example can be fairly simple, e.g., initial erosion removing the fine structure of microplaty hematite, followed by compensating dilation restoring the martite grains (similar to the steps in bulk IMDC identification shown in Figure 3c,d).

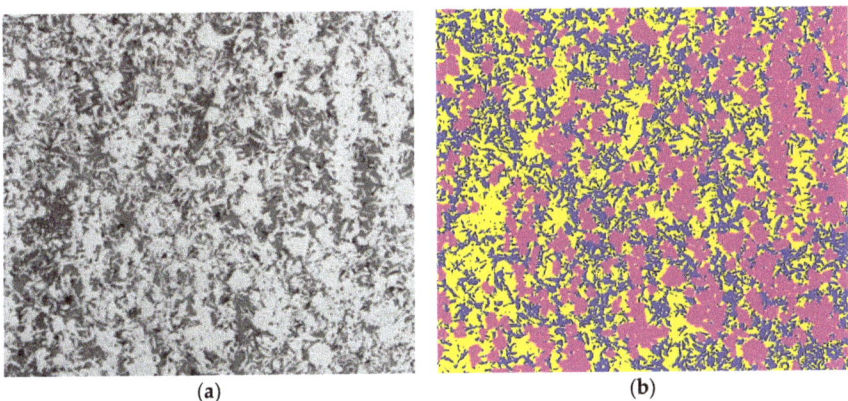

Figure 10. Identification of martite and microplaty hematite by Mineral4: (**a**) original reflected light photomicrograph; (**b**) resulting mineral map (martite—magenta, microplaty hematite—blue; porosity—yellow).

Textural identification may also be of significant help during mineral segmentation in complex cases. Figure 11a shows part of a particle that mainly consists of siliceous goethite with some inclusions of hematite (the brighter grains) and porosity. The area in the top-left corner of the image is epoxy. Segmentation of this siliceous goethite with usual thresholding is problematic because it is rather dark, such that the reflectivity of the epoxy is within the same range as the reflectivity of the goethite. Figure 12a shows an attempted segmentation of the epoxy, which corresponds to the tall narrow peak on the reflectivity histogram (Figure 12b). During this segmentation, significant areas inside the goethite particle were also selected. The reason is that the part of the histogram corresponding to goethite is the relatively wider but lower elevation on which the epoxy peak is based. Obviously, if goethite thresholding is attempted, the whole epoxy area will be selected as well (Figure 12c). To properly segment goethite from epoxy, Mineral4 used multi-thresholding [20] with textural identification. Initially, the area of goethite with reflectivity less than that of epoxy is thresholded (Figure 12d,e). The resulting map is subjected to dilation and erosion (Figure 12f) solidifying the map (this combined image analysis operation is known as Closing), but still some goethite areas remain unselected. Next, the area of goethite with reflectivity higher than epoxy is thresholded (Figure 12g,h) and the same dilation and erosion combination is applied (Figure 12i). The two maps are then combined. After previously identified maps of hematite (corresponding to the small elevation in the right part of the reflectivity histogram), vitreous goethite and porosity are removed, the remaining map gives the final siliceous goethite identification (Figure 11b) which would not be possible to obtain without textural identification.

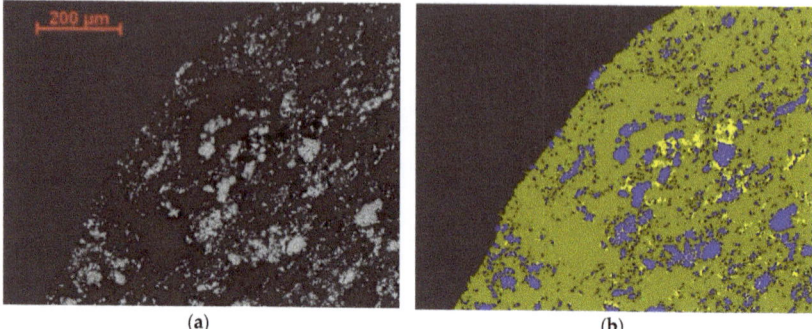

Figure 11. (a) Image of siliceous goethite particle with hematite inclusions; (b) mineral map obtained in Mineral4: siliceous goethite—olive, hematite—blue, vitreous goethite (very fine)—green, porosity—yellow.

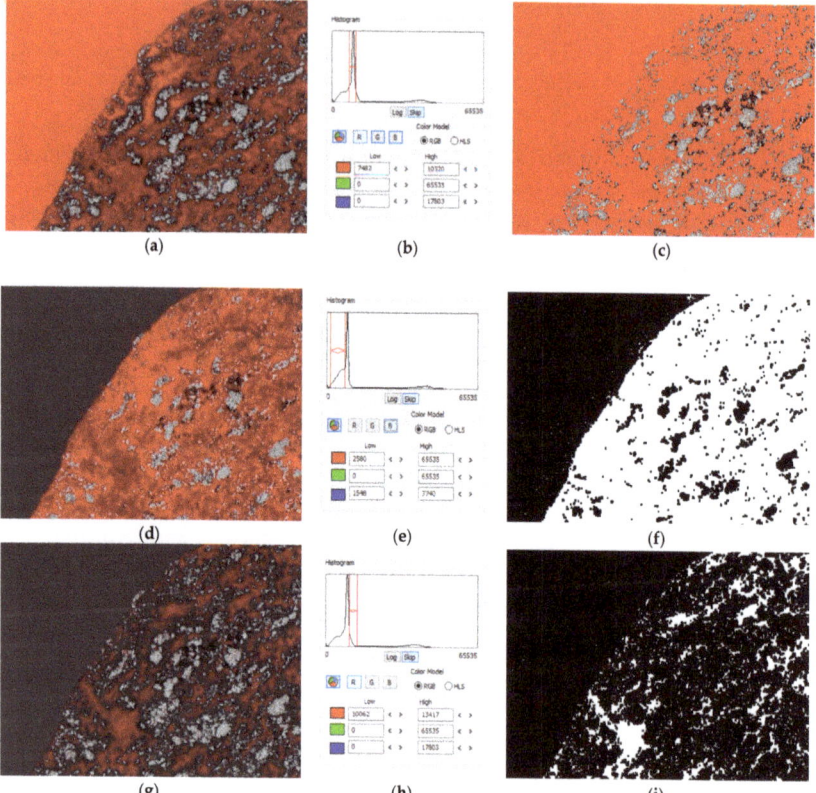

Figure 12. Segmentation of siliceous goethite in Figure 11a: (a) thresholding of epoxy; (b) reflectivity histogram with thresholds corresponding to (a); (c) thresholding of goethite; (d) thresholding of goethite area with reflectivity less than epoxy; (e) reflectivity histogram with thresholds corresponding to (d); (f) the result of thresholding shown in (d) after some dilation and erosion; (g) thresholding of goethite area with reflectivity higher than epoxy; (h) reflectivity histogram with thresholds corresponding to (g); (i) the result of thresholding shown in (g) after dilation and erosion.

5. Conclusions

Optical image analysis characterization for all ironmaking feedstock materials needs to be of the highest quality if it is to be used to better predict downstream processing performance. Mineral and textural characterization of iron ore allows for the improved prediction of downstream processes such as beneficiation and sintering. The complex petrology of iron ore sinter also needs to be accurately characterized for sinter quality optimization. Finally, structural/textural characterization of coke is needed to best understand the connection between coke structure/texture, parent coal blend composition and final coke quality.

CSIRO optical image analysis package Mineral4/Recognition4 allows for the high-quality segmentation of phases in different materials using multi-thresholding and textural identification. In particular, it is capable of segmenting phases with the same reflectivity, but different morphology.

During coke characterization, Mineral4 successfully segments the two types of IMDC, unreacted and partially reacted, and RMDC. Segmentation of unreacted IMDC uses three comprehensive textural identification methods: bulk identification of IMDC, porous IMDC identification and identification of "washed out" IMDC, and finally combines them in one map. A similar approach, based on two methods, is used for partially reacted IMDC segmentation.

For sinter characterization, textural identification in Mineral4 allows for the segmentation of primary and secondary hematite, based on association of secondary hematite with certain other melt-precipitated phases. It also allows for the segmentation of SFCA-I from SFCA, by taking into account the micro-porous structure of the former.

In iron ore characterization, textural identification enables the segmentation of different morphologies of hematite, such as microplaty hematite and martite. Used in combination with multi-thresholding it can reliably segment dark siliceous goethite with reflectivity overlapping with that of epoxy.

This article provides detailed descriptions of textural identification algorithms utilized by Mineral4 for ironmaking-related characterization. These and similar algorithms can also be applied in other image analysis tasks where morphological segmentation is required.

Author Contributions: Conceptualization, E.D.; methodology, E.D. and A.P.; software, A.P. and E.D.; validation, E.D.; formal analysis, E.D. and A.P.; investigation, E.D.; data curation, E.D.; writing—original draft preparation, E.D.; writing—review and editing, E.D. and A.P.; visualization, E.D.; supervision, E.D.; project administration, E.D. All authors have read and agreed to the published version of the manuscript.

Funding: This research was fully funded by CSIRO.

Acknowledgments: The authors wish to thank CSIRO Carbon Steel Futures group staff for valuable suggestions and help during this work. We would like to express our personal acknowledgment to Michael Peterson for his useful corrections, comments and critical revision of this paper, and to Sarath Hapugoda for sharing some images.

Conflicts of Interest: The authors declare no conflict of interest.

References

1. Sorby, H.C. On the microscopical structure of crystals indicating the origin of minerals and rocks. *J. Geol. Soc.* **1858**, *14*, 453–500. [CrossRef]
2. Murdoch, J. *Microscopical Determination of the Opaque Minerals*; John Wiley & Sons: New York, NY, USA, 1916.
3. Gottlieb, P.; Wilkie, G.; Sutherland, D.; Ho-Tun, E.; Suthers, S.; Perera, K.; Jenkins, B.; Spencer, S.; Butcher, A.; Rayner, J. Using quantitative electron microscopy for process mineralogy applications. *J. Min.* **2000**, *52*, 24–25. [CrossRef]
4. Maddren, J.; Ly, C.V.; Suthers, S.P.; Butcher, A.R.; Trudu, A.G.; Botha, P.W.S.K. A new approach to ore characterisation using automated quantitative mineral analysis. In Proceedings of the Iron Ore 2007, Perth, WA, Australia, 20–22 August 2007; pp. 131–132, ISBN 978-192080668-2.
5. Hrstka, T.; Gottlieb, P.; Skala, R.; Breiter, K.; Motl, D. Automated mineralogy and petrology—Applications of TESCAN Integrated Mineral Analyzer (TIMA). *J. Geosci.* **2018**, *63*, 47–63. [CrossRef]

6. Donskoi, E.; Manuel, J.; Austin, P.; Poliakov, A.; Peterson, M.; Hapugoda, S. Comparative study of iron ore characterisation using a scanning electron microscope and optical image analysis. *Appl. Earth Sci. (Trans. Inst. Min. Met. B)* **2014**, *122*, 217–229. [CrossRef]
7. Ramanaidou, E.; Wells, M.; Belton, D.; Verrall, M.; Ryan, C. Mineralogical and Microchemical Methods for the Characterization of High-Grade Banded Iron Formation-Derived Iron Ore, Banded Iron Formation-Related High-Grade Iron Ore. *Rev. Econ. Geol.* **2008**, *15*, 129–156.
8. Pirard, E.; Lebichot, S.; Krier, W. Particle texture analysis using polarized light imaging and grey level intercepts. *Int. J. Miner. Process.* **2007**, *84*, 299–309. [CrossRef]
9. Donskoi, E.; Poliakov, A.; Manuel, J.; Peterson, M.; Hapugoda, S. Novel developments in optical image analysis for iron ore, sinter and coke characterisation. *Appl. Earth Sci. (Trans. Inst. Min. Met. B)* **2015**, *124*, 227–244. [CrossRef]
10. Donskoi, E.; Manuel, J.R.; Hapugoda, S.; Poliakov, A.; Raynlyn, T.; Austin, P.; Peterson, M. Automated optical image analysis of goethitic iron ores. *Miner. Process. Extr. Metall.* **2020**, 1–11. [CrossRef]
11. Gomes, O.D.M.; Paciornik, S. Iron ore quantitative characterization through reflected light-scanning electron co-site microscopy. In Proceedings of the Ninth International Congress on Applied Mineralogy, Brisbane, Australia, 8–10 September 2008; pp. 699–702.
12. Gomes, O.D.M.; Paciornik, S. RLM-SEM co-site microscopy applied to iron ore characterization, Annals of 2nd International Symposium on Iron Ore. São Luís **2008**, *2*, 218–224.
13. Otsu, N. Threshold selection method from gray-level histograms. *IEEE Trans. Syst. Man. Cybern.* **1979**, *9*, 62–66. [CrossRef]
14. Pirard, E. Multispectral imaging of ore minerals in optical microscopy. *Mineral. Mag.* **2004**, *68*, 323–333. [CrossRef]
15. Berrezueta, E.; Ordóñez-Casado, B.; Bonilla, W.; Banda, R.; Castroviejo, R.; Carrión, P.; Puglia, S. Ore Petrography Using Optical Image Analysis: Application to Zaruma-Portovelo Deposit (Ecuador). *Geosciences* **2016**, *6*, 30. [CrossRef]
16. López-Benito, A.; Catalina, J.C.; Alarcón, D.; Grunwald, Ú.; Romero, P.; Castroviejo, R. Automated ore microscopy based on multispectral measurements of specular reflectance. I—A comparative study of some supervised classification techniques. *Miner. Eng.* **2020**, *146*, 106–136. [CrossRef]
17. Leroy, S.; Pirad, E. Mineral recognition of single particles in ore slurry samples by means of multispectral image processing. *Miner. Eng.* **2020**, *132*, 228–237. [CrossRef]
18. Donskoi, E.; Poliakov, A.; Mahoney, M.R.; Scholes, O. Novel Optical Image Analysis Coke Characterisation and its Application to Study of the Relationships between Coke Structure, Coke Strength and Parent Coal Composition. *Fuel* **2017**, *208*, 281–295. [CrossRef]
19. Donskoi, E.; Poliakov, A.; Vining, K. Structural and Textural Characterization of Coke with Optical Image Analysis Software. In Proceedings of the AISTech 2019 Iron and Steel Technology Conference and Exposition, Pittsburgh, PA, USA, 6–9 June 2019; pp. 237–254.
20. Donskoi, E.; Poliakov, A.; Manuel, J.R. Automated Optical Image Analysis of Natural and Sintered Iron Ore. In *Iron Ore: Mineralogy, Processing and Environmental Sustainability*; Lu, L., Ed.; Elsevier Inc.: Cambridge, UK, 2015; pp. 101–159.
21. Seul, M.; O'Gorman, L.; Sammon, M.J. *Practical Algorithms for Image Analysis*; Cambridge University Press: Cambridge, UK, 2000.
22. Kubota, Y.; Nomura, S.; Arima, T.; Kato, K. Effects of coal inertinite size on coke strength. *ISIJ Int.* **2008**, *48*, 563–571. [CrossRef]
23. Donskoi, E.; Manuel, J.R.; Clout, J.M.F.; Zhang, Y. Mathematical modeling and optimization of iron ore sinter properties. *Isr. J. Chem.* **2007**, *47*, 373–379. [CrossRef]
24. Donskoi, E.; Manuel, J.R.; Lu, L.; Holmes, R.J.; Poliakov, A.; Raynlyn, T.D. Importance of textural information in mathematical modelling of iron ore fines sintering performance. *Miner. Process. Extr. Metall. (Trans. Inst. Min. Met. C)* **2017**, *127*, 103–114. [CrossRef]
25. Hapugoda, S.; Lu, L.; Donskoi, E.; Manuel, J. Mineralogical quantification of iron ore sinter. *Miner. Process. Extr. Metall. (Trans. Inst. Min. Met. C)* **2016**, *125*, 156–164. [CrossRef]
26. Sinha, M.; Nistala, S.H.; Chandra, S.; Mankhand, T.R.; Ghose, A.K. Correlating mechanical properties of sinter phases with their chemistry and its effect on sinter quality. *Ironmak. Steelmak.* **2017**, *44*, 100–107. [CrossRef]

27. Honeyands, T.; Manuel, J.; Matthews, L.; O'Dea, D.; Pinson, D.; Leedham, J.; Zhang, G.; Li, H.; Monaghan, B.; Liu, X.; et al. Comparison of the mineralogy of iron ore sinters using a range of techniques. *Minerals* **2019**, *9*, 333. [CrossRef]
28. Honeyands, T.; Manuel, J.; Matthews, L.; O'Dea, D.; Pinson, D.; Leedham, J.; Monaghan, B.; Li, H.; Chen, J.; Hayes, P.; et al. Characterising the mineralogy of iron ore sinters—State-of-the-art in Australia. In Proceedings of the Iron Ore 2017, Perth, Australia, 24–26 July 2017; pp. 49–60.
29. Bonnici, N.; Hunt, J.; Walters, S.; Berry, R.; Collett, D. Relating textural attributes to mineral processing—Developing a more effective approach for the Cadia east Cu–Au porphyry deposit. In Proceedings of the Ninth International Congress for Applied Mineralogy, Brisbane, Australia, 8–10 September 2008; pp. 415–418.
30. Bonnici, N.; Hunt, J.; Berry, R.; Walters, S.; McMahon, C. Quantified mineralogy and texture: Informed sample selection for communication and metallurgical testing. In Proceedings of the Tenth Biennial SGA Meeting, Townsville, Australia, 17–20 August 2009; pp. 679–681.
31. Lamberg, P.; Lund, C. Taking liberation information into a geometallurgical model-case study, Malmberget, Northern Sweden. In Proceedings of the Process Mineralogy'12, Cape Town, South Africa, 7–9 November 2012; pp. 1–13.
32. Lund, C.; Lamberg, P.; Lindberg, T. Practical way to quantify minerals from chemical assays at Malmberget iron ore operations—An important tool for the geometallurgical program. *Miner. Eng.* **2013**, *49*, 7–16. [CrossRef]
33. Lund, C.; Lamberg, P.; Lindberg, T. Development of a geometallurgical framework to quantify mineral textures for process prediction. *Min. Eng.* **2015**, *82*, 61–77. [CrossRef]
34. Donskoi, E.; Holmes, R.J.; Manuel, J.R.; Campbell, J.J.; Poliakov, A.; Suthers, S.P.; Raynlyn, T. Utilization of Iron Ore Texture Information for Prediction of Downstream Process Performance. In Proceedings of the 9th International Congress for Applied Mineralogy, Brisbane, Australia, 8–10 September 2008; pp. 687–693.
35. Donskoi, E.; Poliakov, A.; Holmes, R.; Suthers, S.; Ware, N.; Manuel, J.; Clout, J. Iron ore textural information is the key for prediction of downstream process performance. *Miner. Eng.* **2016**, *86*, 10–23. [CrossRef]
36. Donskoi, E.; Suthers, S.P.; Fradd, S.B.; Young, J.M.; Campbell, J.J.; Raynlyn, T.D.; Clout, J.M.F. Utilization of optical image analysis and automatic texture classification for iron ore particle characterization. *Miner. Eng.* **2007**, *20*, 461–471. [CrossRef]
37. Donskoi, E.; Suthers, S.P.; Campbell, J.J.; Raynlyn, T.; Clout, J.M.F. Prediction of hydrocyclone performance in iron ore beneficiation using texture classification. In Proceedings of the XXIII International Mineral Processing Congress, Istanbul, Turkey, 3–8 September 2006; pp. 1897–1902.

© 2020 by the authors. Licensee MDPI, Basel, Switzerland. This article is an open access article distributed under the terms and conditions of the Creative Commons Attribution (CC BY) license (http://creativecommons.org/licenses/by/4.0/).

Article

The Analysis of Shape Features for the Purpose of Exercise Types Classification Using Silhouette Sequences

Katarzyna Gościewska * and Dariusz Frejlichowski

Faculty of Computer Science and Information Technology, West Pomeranian University of Technology, Szczecin, Zolnierska 52, 71-210 Szczecin, Poland; dfrejlichowski@wi.zut.edu.pl
* Correspondence: kgosciewska@wi.zut.edu.pl

Received: 04 August 2020; Accepted: 23 September 2020; Published: 25 September 2020

Abstract: This paper presents the idea of using simple shape features for action recognition based on binary silhouettes. Shape features are analysed as they change over time within an action sequence. It is shown that basic shape characteristics can discriminate between short, primitive actions performed by a single person. The proposed approach is tested on the Weizmann database using a various number of classes. Binary foreground masks (silhouettes) are replaced with convex hulls, which highlights some shape characteristics. Centroid locations are combined with some other simple shape descriptors. Each action sequence is represented using a vector with shape features and Discrete Fourier Transform. Classification is based on leave-one-sequence-out approach and employs Euclidean distance, correlation coefficient or C1 correlation. A list of processing steps for action recognition is explained and followed by some experiments that yielded accuracy exceeding 90%. The idea behind the presented approach is to develop a solution for action recognition that could be applied in a kind of human activity recognition system associated with the Ambient Assisted Living concept, helping adults increasing their activity levels by monitoring them during exercises.

Keywords: action recognition; silhouette sequences; shape features; ambient assisted living; active ageing

1. Introduction

Human Activity Recognition (HAR) based on the video content analysis approaches is gaining more and more interest thanks to the wide variety of possible applications, such as video surveillance, human-computer interfaces or monitoring of patients and elderly people in their living environments. An exemplary structure of the HAR system may consist of the following general modules: motion segmentation, object classification, human tracking, action recognition and semantic description [1]. If a focus is put to action recognition (exercise classification), it can be assumed that input data type, localised objects and their positions are known. Based on the taxonomy presented in [2] the techniques for action recognition are divided into holistic and local representations. Holistic solutions use global representations of human shape and movement, accumulating several features. The most popular solutions include Motion History Image and Motion Energy Image templates proposed by Bobick and Davis [3] or Space-Time Volume representation introduced by Yilmaz and Shah [4]. Local representations usually are based on interest points which are used to extract a set of local descriptors, e.g., Space-Time Interest Points by Laptev [5]. Instead of aggregating features from all frames, some researchers propose to extract only several foreground silhouettes, so called key poses (e.g., [6,7]). If binary silhouettes are used as input data, various shape features can be extracted and combined, such as shape and contour [8], orientation [9] or skeleton [10]. Apart from traditional approaches, more challenging tasks can benefit from the application of deep learning techniques, such as Convolutional Neural Networks [11]. Ultimately, the choice of methods is dependant, among others, on the application scenario and data complexity.

A task of exercise classification can be related to the Ambient Assisted Living (AAL), which refers to concepts, products and services introducing new technologies for people in all phases of life, allowing them to stay healthy, independent, safe and well-functioning at their living environment. In the era of an ageing society and a significant proportion of older people living alone or unattended, expanding the range of care support options is becoming more and more important. Another major focus of AAL is prolonging the time people can live on their own, being in good health and in good physical shape. This is related to the increasing life expectancy and successful ageing. The World Health Organisation policy in Active Ageing applies to physical, mental and social well-being, and is defined in [12] as "the process of optimizing opportunities for health, participation and security in order to enhance quality of life as people age". Among people aged 45 and over, non-communicable diseases (NCDs) are the most frequent causes of mortality and disability all over the world. The risk of NCDs morbidity is higher in this age group; however, risk factors may originate in younger years. NCDs include, among others, cardiovascular diseases, hypertension, diabetes, chronic obstructive pulmonary disease, musculoskeletal conditions and mental health conditions. One of the risk factors is a sedentary lifestyle [12]. Low level of physical activity and lack of exercises can directly lead to obesity which increases the risk of NCDs as well. The study presented in [13] shows that greater physical fitness is associated with reduced risk of developing many NCDs. The authors of [14] advise promoting positive health behaviour rather than reducing negative ones, such as above-mentioned sedentary lifestyle. It is recommended to focus on the benefits of physical activity, provide motivation and promote self-care. Models based on social-cognitive behavioural theory are indicated as self-regulatory strategies that can contribute to increasing physical activity based on skills such as goal setting and self-monitoring of progress.

This paper follows the idea of active ageing and the use of activity monitoring solutions. However, the approach which is here proposed aims only at recognizing primitive actions that resemble some recommended exercise types [15], such as resistance, aerobic, stretching, balance and flexibility exercises. A specific scenario is assumed in which a person wants to do a workout in front of a laptop where a video with exercises is displayed. The laptop camera captures people's activities and the algorithm analyses them. The classification is performed in order to determine the amount, frequency and duration of a specific exercise. This, in some way, may encourage a person to engage in more physical activity. Due to presented reasoning, Section 2. Related works is focused on the methods and techniques used in action recognition approaches based on video content analysis. In our approach, we use foreground masks extracted from video sequences, each representing single person performing an action. Foreground masks carry information about an object's pose, shape and localisation. Therefore, various features can be retrieved and combined in order to create an action representation—here it is proposed to combine trajectory, simple shape descriptors and Discrete Fourier Transform (DFT).

The rest of the paper is organised as follows: Section 2 presents selected related works, that concern the recognition and classification of similar actions. Section 3 explains consecutive steps of the proposed approach together with applied methods and algorithms. Section 4 describes experimental conditions and presents the results. Section 5 discusses the results and concludes the paper.

2. Related Works

An action can be defined as a single person short activity composed of multiple gestures organised in time that lasts up to several seconds or minutes [1,16], e.g., running, walking or bending. Many actions can be performed for a longer time than several minutes, however due to their periodic characteristic only a short action span is used for recognition. The recognition process is here understood as assigning action labels to sequences of images [17]. Then, action classification can be based on various features, such as colour, grey levels, texture, shape or characteristic points like centroid or contour. Selected features are numerically represented using specific description algorithms in a form of so-called representation or descriptor. According to [2], good representation for action recognition has to be easy to calculate, provide a description for as many classes as possible and reflect similarities between look-alike actions. There is a large body of literature on video-based action recognition and related topics investigating wide variety of methods and algorithms using diverse features. An interest is reflected in the still emerging surveys and reviews (e.g., [2,18–22]). Due to many techniques on action classification reported in the literature, here we refer to several works that correspond to our interests in terms of the methods and data used.

The authors of [23] propose a novel pose descriptor based on the human silhouette, called Histogram of Oriented Rectangles. The human silhouette is represented by a set of oriented rectangular patches, and the distribution of these patches is represented as oriented histograms. Histograms are classified by different techniques, such as nearest neighbour classification, Support Vector Machine (SVM) and Dynamic Time Warping (DTW), among which the last one turned out to be the most accurate. Another silhouette based feature was proposed in [24] which uses Trace transform for a set of silhouettes representing single period of action. The authors introduce two feature extraction methods: History Trace Templates (a sequence representation with spatio-temporal information) and History Triple Features (a set of invariant features calculated for every frame). The classification is performed using Radial Basis Function Kernel SVM and Linear Discriminant Analysis is applied for dimensionality reduction. Action recognition based on silhouettes is presented in [25] as well. All silhouettes in a sequence are represented as time series (using a rotation invariant distance function) and each of them is transformed into so-called Symbolic Aggregate approXimation (SAX). An action is then represented by a set of SAX vectors. The model is trained using the random forest method and various classification methods are tested. The authors of [26] propose a novel feature for action recognition based on silhouette contours only. A contour is divided into radial bins of the same angle using centroid coordinates and a summary value is obtained for each bin. A summary value (variance, max value or range) depends on Euclidean distances from centroid to contour points in every radial bin. The proposed feature is used together with a bag of key poses approach and tested in single- and multi-view scenarios using DTW and leave-one-out procedure.

The authors of [8,9] use accumulated silhouettes (all binary masks of an action sequence are compressed into one image) instead of every silhouette separately. In [8] various contour- and region-based features are combined, such as Cartesian Coordinate Features and Histogram of Oriented Gradients (HOG). SVM and K-nearest neighbour (KNN) classifiers are used (the latter one in two scenarios). In total, seven different features and three classifiers are experimentally tested. The highest accuracy is reported for a combination of HOG and KNN in leave-one-sequence-out scenario. In [9] an average energy silhouette image is calculated for each sequence. Then region of interest is detected and several features are calculated: edge distribution of gradients, directional pixels and rotational information. These feature vectors are combined in action representations which are then classified using SVM classifier. In [10], instead of accumulated silhouettes, the authors propose the cumulative skeletonised image—all foreground objects' skeletons of each action sequence are aligned to the centroid and accumulated into one image. Action features are extracted from these cumulative skeletonised images. In an off-line phase the most discriminant human body regions are selected and classified in an online phase using SVM. The authors of [27] propose a motion descriptor which describes patterns of neighbouring trajectories. Two-level occurrence analysis is performed to discover motion patterns of trajectory points. Actions are classified using SVM with different kernels or random forest algorithm. The approach proposed in [28] employs spectral domain features for action classification, however silhouette features are not involved. Instead, the two-dimensional Discrete Fourier Transform is applied to each video frame and a part of high amplitude coefficients is taken. For a given sequence, selected coefficients of all frames are concatenated into action representation. Larger representations can be reduced using Principal Component Analysis. Action classification is performed using SVM or a simple classifier based on Euclidean distance.

3. Materials and Methods

An action recognition procedure is proposed. It is based on simple features extracted from the entire silhouette and its characteristic points, which are combined into action representation. The proposed approach applies our previous findings and recent research, aiming at improving the results presented in [29]. The dataset and the general processing steps are the same and will be explained in the following subsections. Several changes at the data preprocessing step are introduced, and a new parameter is added for the action representation method that previously yielded the highest accuracy.

3.1. Data Preprocessing

Due to the use of the Weizmann database [30] it is assumed that for each video sequence there is a set of binary images, and these images are foreground masks extracted from video frames. One sequence represents one action type and one image contains one silhouette. Frames in which an object is occluded or too close to the edge of the video frame are removed. The direction of the action is checked and, if necessary, the video frames are flipped so that all objects in the sequence move from left to right. Then, each silhouette is replaced with its convex hull, which reduces the impact of some artefacts (e.g., additional pixels) introduced during background subtraction (see Figure 1 for examples). It is indicated in [29] that the use of convex hulls improves classification accuracy.

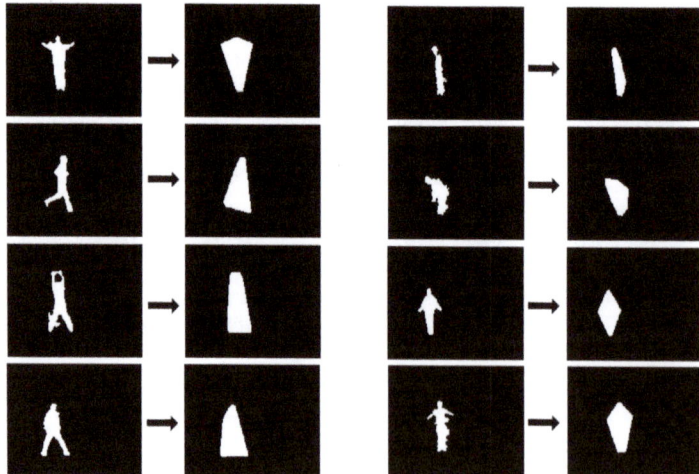

Figure 1. Sample silhouettes from the Weizmann database [30] and the corresponding convex hulls.

Before the actual classification, the dataset is divided into two subsets based on the centroid locations on the consecutive frames. This is related to action characteristics—some of actions are performed by a person standing in place (short trajectory) and the rest contain a person who changes location in every frame (long trajectory). Examples are given in Figure 2. This procedure can be called a coarse classification. It influences subsequent steps of the approach which are performed separately in each subgroup. Therefore, there is a possibility of selecting different features and parameters better suited to the specific action types.

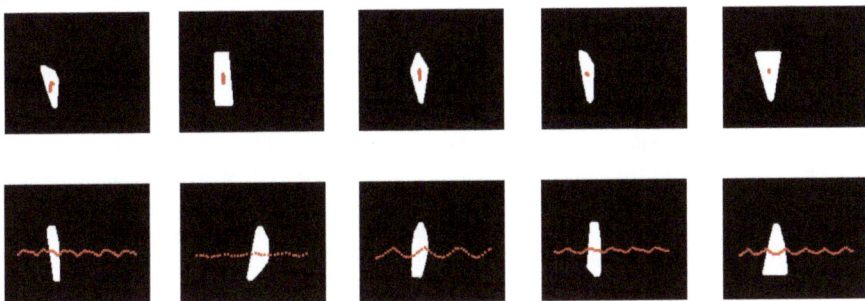

Figure 2. Exemplary trajectories for ten different actions of one actor: actions performed in place are in the top row (bending, jumping-jack, jumping in place, one-hand waving and two-hand waving) and actions with changing location of a silhouette are depicted in the bottom row (jumping forward, running, galloping sideways, skipping and walking). Centroid trajectory is displayed over sample frame from a corresponding video sequence.

3.2. Shape Representation

In this step, each image from the dataset is represented as a single number using a selected shape description algorithm—each number is a simple shape descriptor. The descriptors of all frames from a sequence are combined into one vector and values are normalized to [0, 1] range. This makes it easy to observe how the individual shape features change over time and how they differ between actions. Figure 3 depicts example vectors as line graphs using very simple feature which is an area of a convex hull. Each input action sequence can be denoted as a set of binary masks $BM_i = \{bm_1, bm_2, ..., bm_n\}$, which is represented by a set of normalized descriptors $SD_i = \{sd_1, sd_2, ..., sd_n\}$, and n is the number of frames in a particular sequence.

Simple shape descriptors are basic shape measurements and shape ratios, often used to describe general shape characteristics. A shape measurement is a relative value dependent on the scale of the object. Shape ratio is an absolute value that can be calculated using some shape measurements. Selected simple shape descriptors are listed below (based on [31–34]):

- Area and perimeter, as the number of pixels belonging to the shape's region or contour respectively.
- Feret measures (Feret diameters):
    - X Feret and Y Feret, the distances between the minimal and maximal horizontal and vertical coordinates of a contour respectively;
    - X/Y Feret, the ratio of the X Feret to Y Feret;
    - Max Feret, the maximum distance between any two points of a contour.
- Shape factors:
    - Compactness, the ratio of the square of the shape's perimeter to its area;
    - Roundness, measures shape's sharpness based on area and perimeter;
    - Circularity ratio, defines how a shape is similar to a circle. It can be estimated as the ratio of the shape's area to the shape's perimeter square. It is also called a circle variance and calculated based on the mean and standard deviation obtained using distances from centroid to the contour points;

- Ellipse variance, defines how a shape is similar to an ellipse and can be estimated as a mapping error of a shape fitting an ellipse where both have the same covariance matrix. Similarly to circle variance, mean and standard deviation are used;
  - Width/length ratio, the ratio of the maximal to the minimal distance based on distances between centroid and contour points.
- Minimum bounding rectangle (MBR)—defines a smallest rectangular region that contains all points of a shape. A MBR can be measured in different ways and some ratios can be calculated:
  - MBR measurements, which include area, perimeter, length and width. Length and width can be calculated based on specific pairs of MBR corner points, however in our experiments we always consider the shorter MBR side as its width;
  - Rectangularity, the ratio of the area of a shape to the area of its MBR;
  - Eccentricity, the ratio of width to length of the MBR (length is the longer side of the MBR and width is the shorter one);
  - Elongation, a value of eccentricity subtracted from 1.
- Principal axes method (PAM), which defines two unique line segments that cross each other orthogonally within a shape's centroid. The lengths of the principal axes are used to calculate eccentricity which is the measure of aspect ratio.

3.3. Action Representation

In the next step, all SD vectors are transformed into action representations (AR) using the Discrete Fourier Transform. A SD, in its form, is similar to shape signature and the one-dimensional version of the Discrete Fourier Transform can be applied. The number of elements in each SD is different due to various number of frames in video sequences. Therefore, to prepare action representations equal in size, the N-point Discrete Fourier Transform is calculated, where N is the predefined number of resultant Fourier coefficients. If N is larger than n, then SD vectors are appended with zeros in the time domain (zero-padding) which corresponds to the interpolation in the frequency domain. Otherwise, SD vectors are truncated and then Fourier coefficients are calculated. As a result, each AR contains N absolute values of Fourier coefficients. Usually, it was recommended that the vectors under transformation should have a length equal to a power of 2, due to the computational complexity. However, current implementations of the Discrete Fourier Transform can handle arbitrary size transforms, e.g., Fast Fourier Transform algorithm available in the FFTW library [35].

3.4. Final Classification

For action classification a standard leave-one-out cross-validation procedure is adopted. In each iteration, one sequence is left out and matched with the rest of sequences based on AR vectors. An AR which resulted to be the most similar (or less dissimilar) to the one under processing indicates its class. Indications from all iterations are verified with the original action labels and the percentage of correctly classified objects is taken (classification accuracy). For matching, three different measures are applied, namely Euclidean distance [36], correlation coefficient based on Pearson's correlation [37] and C1 correlation based on L1-norm [38].

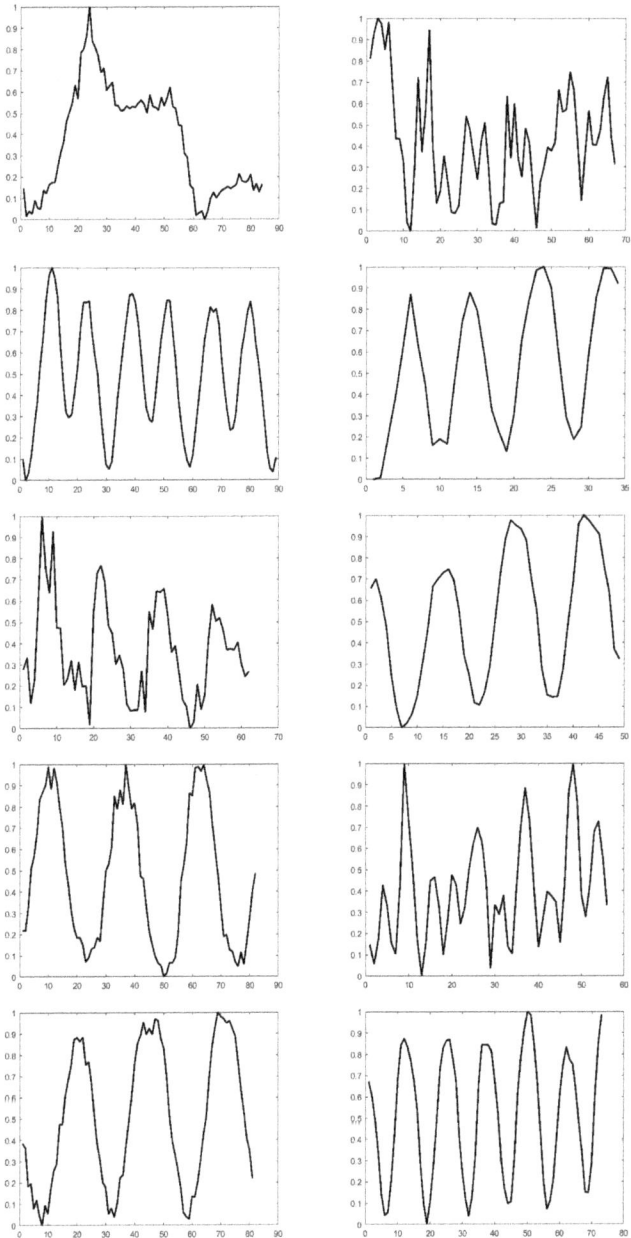

Figure 3. Line graphs showing normalized area values for actions presented in Figure 2. The X axis corresponds to the consecutive frame numbers, while the Y axis corresponds to the normalized area values of the foreground object in each frame. Line graphs in the left column correspond to the actions performed in place (bending, jumping-jack, jumping in place, one-hand waving and two-hand waving), and line graphs for actions with changing location of a silhouette are depicted in the right column (jumping forward, running, galloping sideways, skipping and walking).

4. Experimental Conditions and Results

The experiments were performed with the use of the Weizmann dataset [30], which consists of short video sequences that last up to several seconds (144 × 180 px, 50 fps). Foreground binary masks extracted from the database were made available by its authors and are here used as input data. There are masks for 93 sequences, however three of them are removed—one actor doubled three actions by moving with two different directions. In result, the database has 10 action classes and each action type is performed by nine different actors. During the experiments we follow the data processing steps presented in the previous section. Firstly, each frame is preprocessed individually and then all sequences are divided into two subsets—actions performed in place and actions with changing location of a silhouette. After preprocessing the number of images in a sequence varies from 28 to 146. The group of actions performed in place consists of five action classes: 'bend', 'jump in place', 'jumping jack', 'wave one hand' and 'wave two hands', whereas actions with changing location of a silhouette are: 'jump forward on two legs', 'run', 'skip', 'walk' and 'gallop sideways'. Figure 4 depicts some selected masks after preprocessing step (for two different actions). The next steps, including shape description, action representation and action classification, are performed separately in each subgroup. Ultimately, the classification accuracy values of both subgroups are averaged, which gives the final effectiveness of the approach.

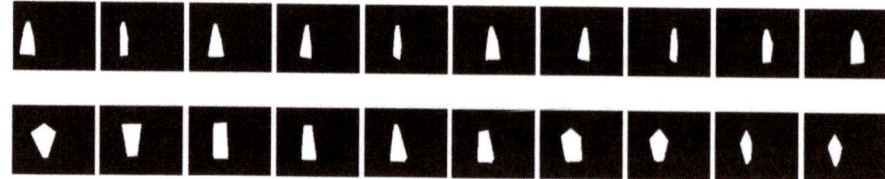

Figure 4. Exemplary preprocessed masks for 'walk' (**top row**) and 'jumping jack' (**bottom row**) actions.

The main part of the experiments refers to the assumed application scenario, which is related to the Ambient Assisted Living and the concept of active ageing. In this scenario, a human activity analysis is performed to identify types of exercises. Physical activity is indicated as one of the methods of preventing the risk of developing non-communicable diseases. Based on the social-cognitive behavioural theory it is advised to promote self-care and incorporate self-monitoring of progress. Nowadays, video content analysis techniques and the popularity of cameras (in laptops, smartphones) facilitate the implementation of exercise monitoring solutions. In order to carry out the experiment concerning the recognition of types of exercises, we composed a database using selected classes from the Weizmann database. Action classes were compared with the recommended exercises presented in [15]. In addition, it was taken into account that exercises are supposed to be performed in a home environment. Due to that, the 'run' class is excluded. Moreover, there are two classes with waving action, therefore the 'wave with one hand' class is excluded as well. The remaining action classes may be associated with the following exercises (based on [15]):

- Aerobic/endurance exercise, in which the body's large muscles move in a rhythmic manner (e.g., walking, skipping, jumping jack);
- Balance training, which includes various activities that increase lower body strength (e.g., galloping sideways, jumping in place, jumping forward on two legs);
- Flexibility exercise, which preserves or extends motion range around joints (e.g., waving, bending).

Several experiments were carried out to investigate the best combination of methods and parameters for the approach. Twenty simple shape descriptors were tested in combination with three matching measures and the use of up to 256 Fast Fourier Transform coefficients. In order to focus only on the highest results and be able to appropriately present them, for each matching measure an experiment is performed with several tests, in which a selected simple shape descriptor and different number of coefficients are used. The results of exercise recognition are provided in Table 1. The best result is considered as the highest accuracy and the smallest action representation. The highest accuracy for actions performed in place is 100% if MBR width is used and the action representation contains 54 elements. It means that each action sequence, regardless of the number of frames, is represented using 54 Fast Fourier Transform coefficients and a representation has a form of a vector with 54 real values. The matching process can be then performed using Euclidean distance or C1 correlation. In total, 100% accuracy is also obtained for X/Y Feret, but more DFT coefficients are required. Actions with changing location of a silhouette are most successfully classified if MBR area is used and action representation contains 32 values—an accuracy of 94.44% is yielded. Again, either Euclidean distance or C1 correlation can be employed. Ultimately, the averaged correct classification rate for exercise types recognition is 97.2% (8 action classes).

Table 1. Experimental results for the recognition of exercise types using 8 classes of the Weizmann dataset. The results are presented separately for actions performed in place and actions with changing location of a silhouette. The highest accuracy values are listed with the indication of the applied simple shape descriptor and the size of an action representation (given in brackets).

8 Classes	Actions Performed in Place	Actions with Changing Location of a Silhouette
Euclidean distance	100.00% MBR width (54)	94.44% MBR area (32)
Correlation Coefficient	97.22% circle variance (48)	83.33% MBR perimeter (35)
C1 Correlation	100.00% MBR width (54)	94.44% MBR area (32)

A second set of experiments concerned the use of the Weizmann database as a benchmark and the comparison of the results for 10 classes with the previous version of our approach, presented in [29]. The results are presented in Table 2. For actions performed in place the highest accuracy is 86.67% (MBR perimeter, 52 DFT coefficients, Euclidean distance) and for actions with changing location of a silhouette the accuracy equals 95.56% (MBR area, 33 DFT coefficients, C1 correlation). If the use of different methods and parameters for each subgroup is assumed, the averaged accuracy for the entire database is 91.12%. This outperforms our previous approach based on simple shape descriptors, that resulted in 83.3% accuracy for actions performed in place (MBR width) and 85.4% (PAM eccentricity) for the other subgroup. The averaged accuracy equalled then 84.35%, which means that the current approach improves the accuracy by nearly 7%.

Table 2. Experimental results for the Weizmann dataset used as a benchmark, presented separately for actions performed in place and actions with changing location of a silhouette. The highest accuracy values are listed with the indication of the applied simple shape descriptor and the size of an action representation (given in brackets).

10 Classes	Actions Performed in Place	Actions with Changing Location of a Silhouette
Euclidean distance	86.67% MBR perimeter (52)	91.11% MBR area (32)
Correlation Coefficient	86.67% width/length ratio (53)	84.44% perimeter and ellipse variance (66)
C1 Correlation	82.22% MBR perimeter (56)	95.56% MBR area (33)

5. Discussion and Conclusions

In the second section of the paper, a description of related works is given. The methods described there, that is [8–10,23–28], were chosen for two main reasons—they concern action recognition and use the Weizmann database. However, the approaches used to represent a frame or a silhouette are diverse. In [23] a set of rectangular patches is used to represent a shape and in [26] only contour points are applied. Some researchers use various transforms, e.g., the authors of [24] apply Trace transform to binarized silhouettes, while in [28] the two-dimensional Fourier transform is applied to the original frames. The opposite approach is the use of cumulative silhouettes [8,9] or cumulative skeletons [10]. Some other techniques are dense trajectories based on salient points [27] and time series [25].

The approach proposed in this paper combines simple shape descriptors with the one-dimensional Fourier transform and standard leave-one-out classification procedure. Each action sequence is firstly described by a set of simple features and represented using a predefined number of Fourier coefficients. Classification is two-stage: firstly, actions are divided into two subgroups based on trajectory length, and secondly, leave-one-sequence-out cross-validation is performed. The proposed approach yields 97.2% accuracy in the assumed application scenario and 91.12% accuracy on the entire Weizmann database. The best results were obtained with the use of features based on a minimum bounding rectangle—its area, width and perimeter. These features are simple; however, if observed over time, they carry much more information about an action. Therefore, the input data can be limited to rectangular objects of interest, representing regions where silhouettes are located. These areas can be tracked over time to extract centroid locations. With these assumptions, the calculation of convex hulls may be omitted.

A comparison of some recognition rates of the proposed approach to other methods tested on the Weizmann dataset is presented in Table 3. Although our approach does not provide a perfect accuracy, it can be compared with some other solutions. It should be mentioned that the presented methods may assume other application scenarios and experimental conditions. Moreover, if we limit the number of classes, it does not always improve the results, which is proven in our experiments. When the classification of actions with changing location of a silhouette is performed for 10 classes, the highest accuracy is 95.56%, while for the limited number of classes it decreases to 94.44%. According to that, we especially refer to the results presented in [8,23,28] that outperformed our results obtained in the experiment concerning the assumed application scenario. The authors of [28] also employ spectral domain features, however these features are extracted from video frames using the two-dimensional Fourier Transform. In our approach the frames are represented using simple shape descriptors, which for each sequence are concatenated into a vector, and the one-dimensional Fourier Transform is applied. Therefore, the initial data dimensionality is lower. The descriptor proposed in [23] requires the extraction of rectangular regions from a human silhouette which may be problematic in case of imperfect silhouettes. The approach proposed in [8] uses accumulated silhouette representation, which requires all foreground masks from an action sequence. In our approach each foreground mask is represented separately, therefore in the case of the real-time scenario the proposed approach can be adjusted to utilise fewer frames.

The proposed approach has some advantages—it can be adapted to different action types by selecting other shape features and matching measures. Action representations are small and easy to calculate because simple algorithms are applied. Moreover, if another distinctive feature is found, instead of centroid or in addition to it, the recognition space could be narrowed in a more efficient manner and eliminate misclassifications. The use of different methods in each subgroup improves overall results. The presented version of the approach is promising; however, an improvement is needed. Our future works include experiments using other databases with larger number of classes corresponding to different exercises. Moreover, recently popular solutions based on deep learning will be tested as well.

Table 3. Comparison of recognition rates obtained on the Weizmann database (cited methods are explained in Section 2. Related works).

Reference	Number of Actions	Accuracy
[28]	10	100%
[23]	9 (without skip)	100%
[8]	10 (93 videos)	98.24%
Proposed	8	97.20%
[9]	10	96.64%
[24]	10	95.42%
[26]	10	93.50%
Proposed	10	91.12%
[25]	10	89.00%
[10]	10	87.52%
[27]	10	78.88%

Author Contributions: Conceptualization, K.G. and D.F.; methodology, K.G.; software, K.G., validation, K.G. and D.F.; investigation, K.G.; writing—original draft preparation, K.G.; writing—review and editing, K.G. and D.F.; visualization, K.G.; supervision, D.F. All authors have read and agreed to the published version of the manuscript.

Funding: This research received no external funding.

Conflicts of Interest: The authors declare no conflict of interest.

References

1. Vishwakarma, S.; Agrawal, A. A survey on activity recognition and behavior understanding in video surveillance. *Vis. Comput.* **2013**, *29*, 983–1009. [CrossRef]
2. Herath, S.; Harandi, M.; Porikli, F. Going deeper into action recognition: A survey. *Image Vis. Comput.* **2017**, *60*, 4–21. [CrossRef]
3. Bobick, A.; Davis, J. The recognition of human movement using temporal templates. *IEEE Trans. Pattern Anal. Mach. Intell.* **2001**, *23*, 257–267. [CrossRef]
4. Yilmaz, A.; Shah, M. Actions sketch: A novel action representation. In Proceedings of the 2005 IEEE Computer Society Conference on Computer Vision and Pattern Recognition (CVPR'05), San Diego, CA, USA, 20–25 June 2005; Volume 1, pp. 984–989.
5. Laptev, I. On Space-Time Interest Points. *Int. J. Comput. Vis.* **2005**, *64*, 107–123. [CrossRef]
6. Baysal, S.; Kurt, M.C.; Duygulu, P. Recognizing Human Actions Using Key Poses. In Proceedings of the 2010 20th International Conference on Pattern Recognition, Istanbul, Turkey, 23–26 August 2010; pp. 1727–1730.
7. Chaaraoui, A.A.; Climent-Pérez, P.; Flórez-Revuelta, F. Silhouette-based human action recognition using sequences of key poses. *Pattern Recognit. Lett.* **2013**, *34*, 1799–1807. [CrossRef]
8. Al-Ali, S.; Milanova, M.; Al-Rizzo, H.; Fox, V.L. Human Action Recognition: Contour-Based and Silhouette-Based Approaches. In *Computer Vision in Control Systems-2: Innovations in Practice*; Favorskaya, M.N., Jain, L.C., Eds.; Springer International Publishing: Cham, Switzerland, 2015; pp. 11–47. [CrossRef]
9. Vishwakarma, D.; Dhiman, A.; Maheshwari, R.; Kapoor, R. Human Motion Analysis by Fusion of Silhouette Orientation and Shape Features. *Procedia Comput. Sci.* **2015**, *57*, 438–447. [CrossRef]
10. Mliki, H.; Rabàa, Z.; Mohamed, H. Human action recognition based on discriminant body regions selection. *Signal Image Video Process.* **2018**, *12*, 845–852. [CrossRef]
11. Yao, G.; Lei, T.; Zhong, J. A review of Convolutional-Neural-Network-based action recognition. *Pattern Recognit. Lett.* **2019**, *118*, 14–22. [CrossRef]
12. World Health Organization. Active Ageing: A Policy Frame-Work. 2002. Available online: http://www.who.int/ageing/publications/active_ageing/en/ (accessed on 15 July 2020).
13. Ross, R.; Blair, S.; Arena, R.; Church, T.; Després, J.P.; Franklin, B.; Kaminsky, L.; Levine, B.; Lavie, C.; Myers, J.; et al. Importance of Assessing Cardiorespiratory Fitness in Clinical Practice: A Case for Fitness as a Clinical Vital Sign: A Scientific Statement From the American Heart Association. *Circulation* **2016**, *134*, e653–e699. [CrossRef]
14. Lachman, M.; Lipsitz, L.; Lubben, J.E.; Castaneda-Sceppa, C.; Jette, A.M. When Adults Don't Exercise: Behavioral Strategies to Increase Physical Activity in Sedentary Middle-Aged and Older Adults. *Innov. Aging* **2018**, *2*, igy007. [CrossRef]

15. Thaxter-Nesbeth, K.; Facey, A. Exercise for Healthy, Active Ageing: A Physiological Perspective and Review of International Recommendations. *West Indian Med. J.* **2018**, *67*, 351–356. [CrossRef]
16. Chaaraoui, A.A.; Climent-Pérez, P.; Flórez-Revuelta, F. A review on vision techniques applied to Human Behaviour Analysis for Ambient-Assisted Living. *Expert Syst. Appl.* **2012**, *39*, 10873–10888. [CrossRef]
17. Poppe, R. A survey on vision-based human action recognition. *Image Vis. Comput.* **2010**, *28*, 976–990. [CrossRef]
18. Aggarwal, J.; Ryoo, M. Human Activity Analysis: A Review. *ACM Comput. Surv.* **2011**, *43*, 16. [CrossRef]
19. Borges, P.V.K.; Conci, N.; Cavallaro, A. Video-Based Human Behavior Understanding: A Survey. *IEEE Trans. Circuits Syst. Video Technol.* **2013**, *23*, 1993–2008. [CrossRef]
20. Cheng, G.; Wan, Y.; Saudagar, A.N.; Namuduri, K.; Buckles, B.P. Advances in Human Action Recognition: A Survey. *arXiv* **2015**, arXiv:1501.05964.
21. Zhang, H.B.; Zhang, Y.X.; Zhong, B.; Lei, Q.; Yang, L.; Du, J.X.; Chen, D.S. A Comprehensive Survey of Vision-Based Human Action Recognition Methods. *Sensors* **2019**, *19*, 1005. [CrossRef]
22. Rodríguez-Moreno, I.; Martinez-Otzeta, J.M.; Sierra, B.; Rodriguez Rodriguez, I.; Jauregi Iztueta, E. Video Activity Recognition: State-of-the-Art. *Sensors* **2019**, *19*, 3160. [CrossRef]
23. Ikizler, N.; Duygulu, P. Histogram of oriented rectangles: A new pose descriptor for human action recognition. *Image Vis. Comput.* **2009**, *27*, 1515–1526. [CrossRef]
24. Goudelis, G.; Karpouzis, K.; Kollias, S. Exploring trace transform for robust human action recognition. *Pattern Recognit.* **2013**, *46*, 3238–3248. [CrossRef]
25. Junejo, I.N.; Junejo, K.N.; Aghbari, Z.A. Silhouette-based human action recognition using SAX-Shapes. *Vis. Comput.* **2014**, *30*, 259–269. [CrossRef]
26. Chaaraoui, A.; Flórez-Revuelta, F. A Low-Dimensional Radial Silhouette-Based Feature for Fast Human Action Recognition Fusing Multiple Views. *Int. Sch. Res. Not.* **2014**, *2014*, 1–11. [CrossRef] [PubMed]
27. Garzon Villamizar, G.; Martinez, F. A Fast Action Recognition Strategy Based on Motion Trajectory Occurrences. *Pattern Recognit. Image Anal.* **2019**, *3*, 447–456. [CrossRef]
28. Imtiaz, H.; Mahbub, U.; Schaefer, G.; Zhu, S.Y.; Ahad, M.A.R. Human Action Recognition based on Spectral Domain Features. *Procedia Comput. Sci.* **2015**, *60*, 430–437. [CrossRef]
29. Gościewska, K.; Frejlichowski, D. Silhouette-Based Action Recognition Using Simple Shape Descriptors. In Proceedings of the International Conference, ICCVG 2018, Warsaw, Poland, 17–19 September 2018; pp. 413–424. [CrossRef]
30. Blank, M.; Gorelick, L.; Shechtman, E.; Irani, M.; Basri, R. Actions As Space-Time Shapes. In Proceedings of the Tenth IEEE International Conference on Computer Vision—Volume 2, ICCV '05, Beijing, China, 17–21 October 2005; IEEE Computer Society: Washington, DC, USA, 2005; pp. 1395–1402. [CrossRef]
31. Yang, L.; Albregtsen, F.; Lønnestad, T.; Grøttum, P. Methods to estimate areas and perimeters of blob-like objects: A comparison. In Proceedings of the IAPR Workshop on Machine Vision Applications, Kawasaki, Japan, 13–15 December 1994; pp. 272–276.
32. Rosin, P. Computing global shape measures. In *Handbook of Pattern Recognition and Computer Vision*; World Scientific Publishing Co. Pte. Ltd.: Singapore, 2005; pp. 177–196. [CrossRef]
33. Zhang, D.; Lu, G. Review of shape representation and description techniques. *Pattern Recognit.* **2004**, *37*, 1–15. [CrossRef]
34. Yang, M.; Kpalma, K.; Ronsin, J. A Survey of Shape Feature Extraction Techniques. *Pattern Recognit.* **2008**, *15*, 43–90.
35. Frigo, M.; Johnson, S.G. The Design and Implementation of FFTW3. *Proc. IEEE* **2005**, *93*, 216–231. [CrossRef]
36. Kpalma, K.; Ronsin, J. An Overview of Advances of Pattern Recognition Systems in Computer Vision. In *Vision Systems*; Obinata, G., Dutta, A., Eds.; IntechOpen: Rijeka, Croatia, 2007; Chapter 10. [CrossRef]
37. Chwastek, T.; Mikrut, S. The problem of automatic measurement of fiducial mark on air images (in polish). *Arch. Photogramm. Cartogr. Remote Sens.* **2006**, *16*, 125–133.
38. Brunelli, R.; Messelodi, S. Robust estimation of correlation with applications to computer vision. *Pattern Recognit.* **1995**, *28*, 833–841. [CrossRef]

© 2020 by the authors. Licensee MDPI, Basel, Switzerland. This article is an open access article distributed under the terms and conditions of the Creative Commons Attribution (CC BY) license (http://creativecommons.org/licenses/by/4.0/).

MDPI
St. Alban-Anlage 66
4052 Basel
Switzerland
Tel. +41 61 683 77 34
Fax +41 61 302 89 18
www.mdpi.com

Applied Sciences Editorial Office
E-mail: applsci@mdpi.com
www.mdpi.com/journal/applsci